Dictionary of Literary Biography

Dictionary of Literary Biography Documentary Series

Dictionary of Literary Biography Yearbooks

1980 edited by Karen L. Rood, Jean W. Ross, and Richard Ziegfeld (1981)

1981 edited by Karen L. Rood, Jean W. Ross, and Richard Ziegfeld (1982)

1982 edited by Richard Ziegfeld; associate editors: Jean W. Ross and Lynne C. Zeigler (1983)

1983 edited by Mary Bruccoli and Jean W. Ross; associate editor Richard Ziegfeld (1984)

1984 edited by Jean W. Ross (1985)

1985 edited by Jean W. Ross (1986)

1986 edited by J. M. Brook (1987)

1987 edited by J. M. Brook (1988)

1988 edited by J. M. Brook (1989)

1989 edited by J. M. Brook (1990)

1990 edited by James W. Hipp (1991)

1991 edited by James W. Hipp (1992)

1992 edited by James W. Hipp (1993)

1993 edited by James W. Hipp, contributing editor George Garrett (1994)

1994 edited by James W. Hipp, contributing editor George Garrett (1995)

1995 edited by James W. Hipp, contributing editor George Garrett (1996)

1996 edited by Samuel W. Bruce and L. Kay Webster, contributing editor George Garrett (1997)

1997 edited by Matthew J. Bruccoli and George Garrett, with the assistance of L. Kay Webster (1998)

1998 edited by Matthew J. Bruccoli, contributing editor George Garrett, with the assistance of D. W. Thomas (1999)

1999 edited by Matthew J. Bruccoli, contributing editor George Garrett, with the assistance of D. W. Thomas (2000)

2000 edited by Matthew J. Bruccoli, contributing editor George Garrett, with the assistance of George Parker Anderson (2001)

2001 edited by Matthew J. Bruccoli, contributing editor George Garrett, with the assistance of George Parker Anderson (2002)

Concise Series

Concise Dictionary of American Literary Biography, 7 volumes (1988–1999): *The New Consciousness, 1941–1968; Colonization to the American Renaissance, 1640–1865; Realism, Naturalism, and Local Color, 1865–1917; The Twenties, 1917–1929; The Age of Maturity, 1929–1941; Broadening Views, 1968–1988; Supplement: Modern Writers, 1900–1998.*

Concise Dictionary of British Literary Biography, 8 volumes (1991–1992): *Writers of the Middle Ages and Renaissance Before 1660; Writers of the Restoration and Eighteenth Century, 1660–1789; Writers of the Romantic Period, 1789–1832; Victorian Writers, 1832–1890; Late-Victorian and Edwardian Writers, 1890–1914; Modern Writers, 1914–1945; Writers After World War II, 1945–1960; Contemporary Writers, 1960 to Present.*

Concise Dictionary of World Literary Biography, 10 volumes projected (1999–): *Ancient Greek and Roman Writers; German Writers; African, Caribbean, and Latin American Writers; South Slavic and Eastern European Writers.*

Dictionary of Literary Biography® • Volume Two Hundred Sixty-One

British Fantasy and Science-Fiction Writers Since 1960

Dictionary of Literary Biography® • Volume Two Hundred Sixty-One

British Fantasy and Science-Fiction Writers Since 1960

Edited by
Darren Harris-Fain
Shawnee State University

A Bruccoli Clark Layman Book

GALE®

THOMSON
™
GALE

Detroit • New York • San Diego • San Francisco • Cleveland • New Haven, Conn. • Waterville, Maine • London • Munich

THOMSON
GALE

Dictionary of Literary Biography
British Fantasy and Science-Fiction Writers
Since 1960

© 2002 by Gale. Gale is an imprint of The Gale Group, Inc., a division of Thomson Learning, Inc.

Gale and Design™ and Thomson Learning™ are trademarks used herein under license.

For more information, contact
The Gale Group, Inc.
27500 Drake Rd.
Farmington Hills, MI 48331-3535
Or you can visit our Internet site at
http://www.gale.com

ISBN 0-7876-6005-1

Printed in the United States of America
10 9 8 7 6 5 4 3 2 1

For Julie and Elizabeth

Contents

Plan of the Series

The advisory board, the editors, and the publisher of the *Dictionary of Literary Biography* are joined in endorsing Mark Twain's declaration. The literature of a nation provides an inexhaustible resource of permanent worth. Our purpose is to make literature and its creators better understood and more accessible to students and the reading public, while satisfying the needs of teachers and researchers.

To meet these requirements, *literary biography* has been construed in terms of the author's achievement. The most important thing about a writer is his writing. Accordingly, the entries in *DLB* are career biographies, tracing the development of the author's canon and the evolution of his reputation.

The purpose of *DLB* is not only to provide reliable information in a usable format but also to place the figures in the larger perspective of literary history and to offer appraisals of their accomplishments by qualified scholars.

The publication plan for *DLB* resulted from two years of preparation. The project was proposed to Bruccoli Clark by Frederick G. Ruffner, president of the Gale Research Company, in November 1975. After specimen entries were prepared and typeset, an advisory board was formed to refine the entry format and develop the series rationale. In meetings held during 1976, the publisher, series editors, and advisory board approved the scheme for a comprehensive biographical dictionary of persons who contributed to literature. Editorial work on the first volume began in January 1977, and it was published in 1978. In order to make *DLB* more than a dictionary and to compile volumes that individually have claim to status as literary history, it was decided to organize volumes by topic, period, or

genre. Each of these freestanding volumes provides a biographical-bibliographical guide and overview for a particular area of literature. We are convinced that this organization—as opposed to a single alphabet method— constitutes a valuable innovation in the presentation of reference material. The volume plan necessarily requires many decisions for the placement and treatment of authors. Certain figures will be included in separate volumes, but with different entries emphasizing the aspect of his career appropriate to each volume. Ernest Hemingway, for example, is represented in *American Writers in Paris, 1920–1939* by an entry focusing on his expatriate apprenticeship; he is also in *American Novelists, 1910–1945* with an entry surveying his entire career, as well as in *American Short-Story Writers, 1910–1945, Second Series* with an entry concentrating on his short fiction. Each volume includes a cumulative index of the subject authors and articles.

Since 1981 the series has been further augmented by the *DLB Yearbooks,* which update published entries, add new entries to keep the *DLB* current with contemporary activity, and provide articles on literary history. There have also been nineteen *DLB Documentary Series* volumes which provide illustrations, facsimiles, and biographical and critical source materials for figures, works, or groups judged to have particular interest for students. In 1999 the *Documentary Series* was incorporated into the *DLB* volume numbering system beginning with *DLB 210: Ernest Hemingway.*

We define literature as the *intellectual commerce of a nation:* not merely as belles lettres but as that ample and complex process by which ideas are generated, shaped, and transmitted. *DLB* entries are not limited to "creative writers" but extend to other figures who in their time and in their way influenced the mind of a people. Thus the series encompasses historians, journalists, publishers, book collectors, and screenwriters. By this means readers of *DLB* may be aided to perceive literature not as cult scripture in the keeping of intellectual high priests but firmly positioned at the center of a nation's life.

DLB includes the major writers appropriate to each volume and those standing in the ranks behind them. Scholarly and critical counsel has been sought in deciding which minor figures to include and how full their entries should be. Wherever possible, useful references are made to figures who do not warrant separate entries.

Each *DLB* volume has an expert volume editor responsible for planning the volume, selecting the figures for inclusion, and assigning the entries. Volume editors are also responsible for preparing, where appropriate, appendices surveying the major periodicals and literary and intellectual movements for their volumes, as well as lists of further readings. Work on the series as a whole is coordinated at the Bruccoli Clark Layman editorial center in Columbia, South Carolina, where the editorial staff is responsible for accuracy and utility of the published volumes.

One feature that distinguishes *DLB* is the illustration policy—its concern with the iconography of literature. Just as an author is influenced by his surroundings, so is the reader's understanding of the author enhanced by a knowledge of his environment. Therefore *DLB* volumes include not only drawings, paintings, and photographs of authors, often depicting them at various stages in their careers, but also illustrations of their families and places where they lived. Title pages are regularly reproduced in facsimile along with dust jackets for modern authors. The dust jackets are a special feature of *DLB* because they often document better than anything else the way in which an author's work was perceived in its own time. Specimens of the writers' manuscripts and letters are included when feasible.

Samuel Johnson rightly decreed that "The chief glory of every people arises from its authors." The purpose of the *Dictionary of Literary Biography* is to compile literary history in the surest way available to us—by accurate and comprehensive treatment of the lives and work of those who contributed to it.

The *DLB* Advisory Board

Introduction

When H. G. Wells sprang to prominence in the 1890s with his "scientific romances" and fantasy stories, he was hailed by Henry James, who wished to collaborate with the younger author on a novel about Mars, and Joseph Conrad, who cited *The Invisible Man* (1897) as one of his favorite books. Such ungrudging acceptance of fantasy and science fiction was short-lived, however. Several factors in the twentieth century contributed to the development of fantasy and science fiction as genres not only distinct from mimetic or realistic fiction but also inferior to them in the eyes of most critics and literary historians. The last four decades of the twentieth century both challenged this distinction and confirmed it.

In the early decades of the twentieth century, British fantasy and science fiction pursued a twofold path. On one path were those writers who employed the materials of these genres for their own purposes, such as G. K. Chesterton or later Aldous Huxley and George Orwell, and who were not considered popular authors. This path remained a viable one for British authors for the remainder of the century, including since the 1960s such authors as Kingsley Amis and his son Martin, Anthony Burgess, Angela Carter, Doris Lessing, Salman Rushdie, and Jeanette Winterson. On the other path were those whose work appeared in the pulp magazines that proliferated in the first half of the century and who found it difficult to publish anywhere else. Such writers gained a new outlet in paperback books after the 1940s, but for the most part hardcover publication and critical attention eluded them.

Developments in British fantasy and science fiction in the 1950s began to bring the two paths closer together. For instance, where was one to place J. R. R. Tolkien and C. S. Lewis, both Oxford academics and popular authors—Tolkien with his fantasies about Middle Earth and Lewis with his Space Trilogy and his Chronicles of Narnia? Or what was one to make of Lewis's approbation of the American writer Ray Bradbury? Conservatives such as Lewis and Tolkien might be dismissed as old-fashioned, but they were hardly alone in the literary establishment. Kingsley Amis, widely considered more up-to-date, gave a series of lectures in the late 1950s on science fiction (published as *New Maps of Hell* in 1960); fantasy and science fiction began to be reviewed and taken seriously by some critics; and in general attitudes began to change about its status among many readers.

In part the shifting status of fantasy and science fiction mirrored a similar shift in the larger society. One such change concerned the growing importance of a youth culture in Great Britain in the late 1950s and into the 1960s. While the increasing power of youth spending made traditional markets and media turn their attention to consumers in their teens and twenties, these same teens and twenty-somethings often began questioning or rebelling against traditional social mores. They bought music, but this music often was a stark statement against "the establishment"; they bought books and magazines, but the magazines often were comic books slanted at youth, and the books they read often included science fiction and fantasy—genres that naturally appeal to a generation alienated from the world around them. It is therefore no coincidence that two of the most popular books among college students of the 1960s were Tolkien's fantastic *Lord of the Rings* (1954–1955), despite its innate conservatism, and American writer Robert A. Heinlein's counterculture science-fiction novel *Stranger in a Strange Land* (1961), the first science-fiction novel to appear on *The New York Times* best-seller list. Mainstream publishers, who earlier had dabbled in publishing fantasy and science fiction without giving either much support, saw these developments and threw themselves into the fantastic enthusiastically. Penguin Books began a science-fiction series in 1961 under the editorship of Brian W. Aldiss, while established firms began publishing fantasy and science fiction.

Publishers were encouraged by a rush of new talent, writers who earlier would have been consigned solely to the pulp magazines and perhaps, if they were fortunate, paperbacks and a limited publication in hardcover thanks to fan presses (small publishing ventures run by fans and devoted to producing books in the field). In particular, three major figures emerged in British fantasy and science fiction during the 1960s: Aldiss, Michael Moorcock, and J. G. Ballard. Aldiss's career actually began in the previous decade, but it was in the 1960s that he began twisting the conventions of science fiction in such novels as *Hothouse* (1962), *Greybeard* (1964), and *Barefoot in the Head* (1969). Not only did Aldiss know the genre and its history well, but he also brought a wide reading outside the genre to his work, especially a familiarity with the French New Novel, in which novelists such as Alain Robbe-Grillet, Samuel Beckett, and Nathalie Sarraute began rejecting conventional narratives in favor of more experimental approaches, starting in the 1950s. Perhaps nowhere is this influence more evident in Aldiss's work of the 1960s than in *Report on Probability A* (1968), a novel in which the deliberately glacial pacing is as noteworthy as the science-fiction plot.

At first glance the science fiction and fantasy of Moorcock might seem more traditional, especially his fantasy series featuring Elric of Melniboné, begun in 1961. Although he draws on the conventions of sword-and-sorcery tales preceding the series, Moorcock presents a different take on the standard high-fantasy elements. Likewise, he shows little regard for earlier taboos within science fiction, such as treating religion irreverently: in his *Behold the Man* (1969) a time traveler investigating the truth about Jesus of Nazareth finds himself unwillingly becoming a part of the gospel story.

Most nontraditional of all in the context of fantasy and science fiction was the work of Ballard. He employs much of the traditional hardware of science fiction in his stories of the 1960s, but in his gloomy worlds the focus has shifted—from society to the individual, from outer space to inner space, and from extrapolation to alienation. In this regard, despite Ballard's distinctive voice, his work is emblematic of much British science fiction of the 1960s. In the 1950s science fiction began to pull heavily from the social sciences, in addition to the physical sciences typically thought of as central to the genre. This trend continued unabated into the 1960s and 1970s when writers routinely examined not only the physical implications of scientific and social change but also the psychological and sociological effects of such change. Thus another British writer, John Brunner, described the impact of increasing overpopulation or ecological catastrophe in such novels as *Stand on Zanzibar* (1968) and *The Sheep Look Up* (1972). Just as significant, he did so employing modernist literary techniques, such as fragmentation and montage, used by writers from the first half of the century such as, to name the figure his style most resembles, John Dos Passos.

Equally significant was the tone that permeated these writers' works during this period. The British scientific romance, argues Brian Stableford, stands apart from American science fiction of the first half of the twentieth century in its greater sense of pessimism and its focus on character instead of action-driven stories.

However, British science fiction at mid century had much in common with American expressions of the genre, including an Enlightenment confidence that progress was inevitable and to be welcomed. In contrast, much British science fiction after 1960 is pessimistic in nature. As in the early scientific romances of Wells, entropy becomes a dominating metaphor, the notion that the universe is winding down. One of the most anthologized stories of the period was "The Heat Death of the Universe" (1967), by an American writer named Pamela Zoline; it is about the breakdown of a housewife, but the central metaphor is scientific, and the story first appeared in the British science-fiction magazine *New Worlds*.

The stylistic changes that writers such as Aldiss, Ballard, and Brunner introduced, along with this prevailing sense of pessimism not only on the cosmic scale but also in connection with humanity and the societies in which people live, seemed to many readers of science fiction a betrayal of the nature of the genre. It also seemed to bring science fiction closer to mainstream literature, which in the eyes of genre readers had abandoned traditional storytelling and happy endings sometime in the nineteenth century. However, writers such as Aldiss, Ballard, and Moorcock were unfazed by such criticisms. While there was much about earlier science fiction they admired and emulated, they were more than happy to be part of an effort to acquire for science fiction a higher literary standard and reputation than it had previously enjoyed.

Thus came the birth of the New Wave, a term coined by British fantasy and science-fiction writer Christopher Priest after the nouvelle vague or New Wave of French cinema in the late 1950s and the 1960s. An Anglo-American phenomenon, the New Wave was a movement of mostly younger science-fiction writers interested in expanding the possibilities of the genre, both in subject and in style, and in lifting it from what was commonly called the science-fiction ghetto. One of the major organs of the New Wave was the British science-fiction magazine *New Worlds*, especially under the editorship of Moorcock from 1964 to 1969. Other important publications included the transatlantic anthologies *Dangerous Visions* (1967) and *Again, Dangerous Visions* (1972), both edited by the American writer Harlan Ellison, and *England Swings SF* (1968), edited by Judith Merril. The title of the latter volume also points to another development of the New Wave: the widespread adoption of "SF" (suggested earlier by Heinlein) as the standard abbreviation for science fiction—a shibboleth of sorts in contrast to "sci fi," generally taken as the mark of an outsider. More important, "SF" could stand not only for "science fiction" but also for "speculative fiction," a term adopted by many writers during this period in an effort to escape the negative connotations of the earlier term and to focus on the speculative element of their fiction rather than the scientific, which was often minimal.

To be sure, not all British science-fiction writers of the 1960s rode the New Wave. For example, writers such as Fred Hoyle, James White, and Sir Arthur C. Clarke continued to hew to the old ways. These writers continued to draw audiences, and the readership of British science fiction in the 1960s and 1970s was hardly homogeneous. Still, it was largely the New Wave writers who began to gain the attention of readers, critics, and publishers, who found it harder to distinguish the fantastic works of an Aldiss or Ballard from the efforts of mainstream writers such as Kingsley Amis or Burgess when working in a fantastic vein.

Consider, for instance, two novels by these writers, Burgess's *A Clockwork Orange* (1962) and Amis's *The Alteration* (1976). Burgess's better-known book chronicles the deeds of a gang of young thugs in a decadent future England. Not only does it extrapolate a future society from contemporary conditions and trends, but it also employs the scientific concept of conditioning as part of the plot. Certainly these elements are science fiction, even if Burgess was never identified as a science-fiction writer and had little in common with those who were. While Burgess may have had only limited knowledge of other science fiction, Kingsley Amis was a confessed avid reader of the genre and was no doubt aware of such alternate-history novels as the American writer Philip K. Dick's *The Man in the High Castle* (1962) and the British writer Keith Roberts's *Pavane* (1968) when he wrote *The Alteration*, which describes an alternate history in which the Protestant Reformation never occurred.

Both the work of the traditional Clarke and Burgess's best-known novel were inspirations for movies that helped to raise science-fiction cinema from its earlier B-movie associations to the realm of art, and both were directed by an American moviemaker who spent the greater part of his career in England: Stanley Kubrick. Clarke collaborated with Kubrick to adapt his short story "The Sentinel" (1951) for the screen; the result was *2001: A Space Odyssey* (1968), which advanced the state of science-fiction movies nearly as much as astronaut Dave Bowman was catapulted up the evolutionary scale in the story. Equally riveting was Kubrick's disturbing adaptation of *A Clockwork Orange,* released in 1971. The director's last, unfinished project at his death in 1999 was to be *A.I.,* an adaptation (by British fantasy and science-fiction writer Ian Watson) of Aldiss's 1969 short story "Super-Toys Last All Summer Long." The movie was made instead by Steven Spielberg and released in 2001, the year that Clarke and

Kubrick had made as culturally significant as Orwell's *1984.*

Kubrick's forays into science-fiction movies might be dismissed as simply part of the director's distinctive vision. However, movies and television shows not only picked up on science-fiction and fantasy motifs in the second half of the twentieth century but also gave many writers an additional forum for their work. Even if those who wrote the scripts did not write for the magazines and the paperbacks, the increasing presence of fantasy and science fiction on big screens and small ones gave audiences a greater exposure to the field. The British television series *Doctor Who,* starting in 1963, and the American television series *Star Trek,* starting in 1966, especially galvanized legions of fans whose interests extended to books and stories as well. Later successful media versions of science fiction in England included Douglas Adams's radio scripts for *The Hitch-Hiker's Guide to the Galaxy* beginning in 1978 and the television series *Red Dwarf* beginning in 1988.

The popularity of science fiction and fantasy in the media, however, proved to be a double-edged sword. Often writers began to feel that audiences were being pulled away from their more challenging prose in favor of the easier pleasures of the movie or television screen and that many popular movies represented a return to a tradition they had tried to transcend. A good example is the response of Aldiss, both a writer of science fiction and one of its preeminent historians, to the 1977 blockbuster *Star Wars.* Aldiss had written a definition of an older variety of science fiction known as space opera in an anthology he edited, and thus he was called upon by the defense in a plagiarism lawsuit that Lucasfilm and 20th Century-Fox, the forces behind *Star Wars,* had brought against the makers of *Battlestar Galactica,* released a year after George Lucas's film. In response to the question, "What was your initial response to *Star Wars?*" Aldiss replied, "I experienced the delights of recognition." What he recognized, as he describes in his *Trillion Year Spree: The History of Science Fiction* (1986), written with David Wingrove, was how Lucas had been inspired not only by World War II movies, Japanese samurai movies, and Joseph Campbell's *The Hero with a Thousand Faces* (1949) but also by old science-fiction magazines.

The popularity of television programs such as *Star Trek* and of movies such as *Star Wars* did not end with the credits scrolling across the screen. Soon novelizations of the stories as well as original novels set in the fictional worlds of their characters began appearing on bookshelves, crowding out the even more original work of prose writers who created their own worlds. Many feared a sort of literary Gresham's Law, in which mediocre work would drive out the good. Nevertheless, many good science-fiction works appeared from British writers during this period, among them Aldiss's *Frankenstein Unbound* (1973) and his Helliconia series of the 1980s, Watson's *The Embedding* (1973), Bob Shaw's *Orbitsville* (1975), Josephine Saxton's *The Travails of Jane Saint* (1980), and the science-fiction novels of Iain M. Banks.

A similar problem began to affect British fantasy (as well as American) starting in the 1970s. Tolkien's magnum opus, *The Lord of the Rings,* had been published in three volumes; yet, it sold exceedingly well. While writers worked in many different veins available within fantasy literature in this period, Tolkien's model—with its various labels of high fantasy, heroic fantasy, epic fantasy, and so on—was what came to predominate. This emphasis was increased after a posthumous Tolkien industry, begun with the publication of *The Silmarillion* in 1977, elaborated on Tolkien's Middle Earth even more than the three volumes of *The Lord of the Rings* and *The Hobbit* (1937) before it had done. Publishers encouraged writers who submitted stories of epic quests, assorted characters, ancient or medieval settings, and heroic adventure, preferably spread over three or more volumes. It would be unfair to say that all such fantasy works were derivative or uninteresting, but while readers voraciously bought these efforts, critics and many writers lamented the success of formulas over originality.

Still, it has always been the case that even in the most commercial of markets quality work has found its way into print. Examples include Richard Adams's remarkable animal fantasy *Watership Down* (1972), Robert Holdstock's evocative *Mythago Wood* (1984), and especially the work of a host of British writers for young adults, such as Joan Aiken, Susan Cooper, Alan Garner, Rosemary Harris, Diana Wynne Jones, Robin McKinley, and Robert Westall.

The lament of historians and critics over developments such as a return to traditional stories in science fiction and a reliance on formula in fantasy points to another significant development during this period: the rise of scholarly attention paid to these fields. In addition to Kingsley Amis's landmark *New Maps of Hell,* other studies of both genres began to appear regularly beginning in the 1960s and 1970s, often corresponding to college-level classes in these subjects. In 1973 Aldiss published *Billion Year Spree: The True History of Science Fiction,* later expanded as *Trillion Year Spree.* Also in the early 1970s, a group of writers and scholars formed the Science Fiction Foundation, dedicated to the study of the subject, and in 1972 they began publishing their journal, *Foundation.* Some writers, most notably Stableford, have developed dual careers as authors and critics, and British authors are regular guests at academic proceedings such as the Science Fiction Research Association conference and the International Conference on the Fantastic in the Arts.

Another development in British fantastic fiction during this period is the revival of horror fiction as a distinct genre. While elements of horror fiction have existed in literature for centuries, and while Gothic fiction was popular in the late 1700s and early 1800s, dark fantasy—weird tales or horror stories incorporating a fantastic or supernatural element—was submerged among other forms of fantasy through much of the twentieth century. The success of writers such as Stephen King in the 1970s, however, helped to create a separate market specifically for horror fiction as such. Thus British horror writers such as Robert Aickman, Ramsey Campbell, James Herbert, and Clive Barker have found audiences for their dark tales of the supernatural.

Readers also became more receptive during this period to the works of female authors, both within the two genres and in mainstream literature. Naomi Mitchison's *Memoirs of a Spacewoman* (1962), for instance, was an early combination of feminism with the traditional subjects of science fiction, while Anna Kavan's hallucinogenic *Ice* (1967) was championed by Aldiss. Tanith Lee and Storm Constantine created some of the more intriguing fantasy series of the period, and Lee's science-fiction novel *The Silver Metal Lover* (1981) spotlights feminine sexuality. Carter enjoyed literary success with fantastic novels such as *Heroes and Villains* (1969), *The Infernal Desire Machines of Dr. Hoffman* (1972), and *Nights at the Circus* (1984), while Lessing surprised many readers and critics when in 1979 she began a science-fiction series, collectively known as "Canopus in Argos," that extended to five volumes.

Indeed, beginning in the 1960s fantasy and science fiction were marked by a greater diversity than in earlier decades, and not only where gender was concerned. The field found room not only for both traditional and experimental fare, not only for both male and female authors, and not only for original work (often published in the British magazine *Interzone,* founded in 1982) and media tie-ins, but also for comic books, comic fantasy and science fiction, young-adult fiction, and a variety of subgenres such as alternate history, cyberpunk (noirish stories featuring human-computer interfaces), steampunk (science-fiction stories set in the nineteenth century), and military science fiction.

For example, a whole strain of comic science fiction and fantasy flourished during this period. Douglas Adams's *The Hitch-Hiker's Guide to the Galaxy* (1979) was the first in a series of books, originating in the popular radio program, that dealt with science-fiction matters humorously. Similar in tone were the fantasy novels of comic writers such as Tom Holt and Terry Pratchett, which often satirized the conventions of the genre.

Despite their name, comic books that featured science fiction or fantasy tended toward the serious, though they were not without their comic moments. The same applies to graphic novels, which employed the comic-book format but dealt with limited story arcs or stories with endings, unlike continuously published comic books. Two talents in particular rose to prominence in the 1980s and 1990s: Alan Moore and Neil Gaiman. Moore started with British comic books such as *A.D. 2000* and *Marvelman* (published in the United States as *Miracleman*) and then shifted his attention to American comics. After several successful years as the writer of *Swamp Thing,* he collaborated with British artist Dave Gibbons to produce the graphic novel *Watchmen* (1986–1987), in which they depicted an alternate history for twentieth-century America changed by the presence of superheroes. After a similarly impressive apprenticeship, Gaiman was acclaimed for his stories involving the supernatural Sandman and other related immortals. Moore and Gaiman, like their American counterparts Art Spiegelman and Frank Miller, entered the field at a time of transition, when some writers of comic books began taking greater creative risks and aiming at older audiences.

At the same time, some of the most acclaimed fantastic works by British authors at the end of the twentieth century were directed at audiences of children and young adults. Philip Pullman's trilogy, known collectively as "Her Dark Materials," describes a rich fantasy world where children, as is typical in such works, face moral choices; but Pullman refuses to condescend to his readers by making these choices easy. Though Pullman was the most critically celebrated young-adult British fantasy author at the end of the century, he was easily outstripped in popularity by the Harry Potter novels of J. K. Rowling. Her stories of Harry's coming-of-age in a British school of wizardry have set unprecedented sales records and alarmed some with their supernatural content.

At the end of the twentieth century, fantasy and science fiction were everywhere—in bookstores and libraries, on movie and television screens, in video games and comic books. One of the greatest concerns for these genres is the shrinking midlist, occupied by writers with respectable critical attention or sales figures but who are not best-sellers, as publishers try to increase profits. Another concern is perceptions that the reading public itself is shrinking. While the aspirations of the New Wave writers of the 1960s toward greater acceptance of quality genre fiction have only partially been fulfilled, at the turn of the new millennium British fantasy and science fiction is in solid shape.

—*Darren Harris-Fain*

Acknowledgments

This book was produced by Bruccoli Clark Layman, Inc. Karen L. Rood is senior editor. Tracy Simmons Bitonti was the in-house editor, assisted by Charles Brower.

Production manager is Philip B. Dematteis.

Administrative support was provided by Ann M. Cheschi, Amber L. Coker, and Angi Pleasant.

Accountant is Ann-Marie Holland.

Copyediting supervisor is Sally R. Evans. The copyediting staff includes Phyllis A. Avant, Brenda Carol Blanton, Caryl Brown, Melissa D. Hinton, Philip I. Jones, Charles Loughlin, Rebecca Mayo, Nancy E. Smith, and Elizabeth Jo Ann Sumner. Freelance copyeditors are Porter Barron and Brenda Cabra.

Editorial associates are Michael S. Allen, Michael S. Martin, Catherine M. Polit, and Pamela A. Warren.

Permissions editor is Jason Paddock.

Database manager is José A. Juarez.

Layout and graphics supervisor is Janet E. Hill. The graphics staff includes Karla Corley Brown, Zoe R. Cook, Sydney E. Hammock, and Caroline B. Meyer.

Office manager is Kathy Lawler Merlette.

Photography supervisor is Paul Talbot. Photography editor is Scott Nemzek.

Digital photographic copy work was performed by Joseph M. Bruccoli.

Systems manager is Marie L. Parker.

Typesetting supervisor is Kathleen M. Flanagan. The typesetting staff includes Patricia Marie Flanagan, Mark J. McEwan, and Pamela D. Norton. Freelance typesetter is Wanda Adams.

Walter W. Ross did library research. He was assisted by Pamela A. Warren and the following librarians at the Thomas Cooper Library of the University of South Carolina: circulation department head Tucker Taylor; reference department head Virginia W. Weathers; Brette Barclay, Marilee Birchfield, Paul Cammarata, Gary Geer, Michael Macan, Tom Marcil, Rose Marshall, and Sharon Verba; interlibrary loan department head John Brunswick; and interlibrary loan staff Robert Arndt, Hayden Battle, Barry Bull, Jo Cottingham, Marna Hostetler, Marieum McClary, Erika Peake, and Nelson Rivera.

Dictionary of Literary Biography® • Volume Two Hundred Sixty-One

British Fantasy and Science-Fiction Writers Since 1960

Dictionary of Literary Biography

Douglas Adams
(11 March 1952 – 11 May 2001)

Deborah Philips
Brunel University

See also the Adams entry in *DLB Yearbook: 1983.*

BOOKS: *The Hitch-Hiker's Guide to the Galaxy* (London: Pan, 1979; New York: Harmony, 1980);
The Restaurant at the End of the Universe (London: Pan, 1980; New York: Harmony, 1981);
Life, the Universe, and Everything (London: Pan, 1982; New York: Harmony, 1982);
The Meaning of Liff, by Adams and John Lloyd (London: Pan, 1983; New York: Harmony, 1984); revised by Adams and Lloyd as *The Deeper Meaning of Liff: A Dictionary of Things There Aren't Words for Yet—But There Ought to Be* (London: Pan, 1990; New York: Harmony, 1990);
So Long, and Thanks for All the Fish (London: Pan, 1984; New York: Harmony, 1985);
The Hitch-Hiker's Guide to the Galaxy: The Original Radio Scripts, edited by Geoffrey Perkins (London: Pan, 1985); also published as *The Original Hitchhiker Radio Scripts* (New York: Harmony, 1985);
Dirk Gently's Holistic Detective Agency (London: Heinemann, 1987; New York: Simon & Schuster, 1987);
The Long Dark Tea-Time of the Soul (London: Heinemann, 1988; New York: Simon & Schuster, 1988);
The More than Complete Hitchhiker's Guide (New York: Bonanza, 1989);
Last Chance to See, by Adams and Mark Carwardine (London: Heinemann, 1990; New York: Harmony, 1991);
Mostly Harmless (London: Heinemann, 1992; New York: Harmony, 1992);
Doctor Who – The Scripts: The Pirate Planet (London: Titan, 1996);

Douglas Adams (Archive Photos/SAGA/Frank Capri)

The Salmon of Doubt and Other Writings, edited by Christopher Cerf (London: Macmillan, 2002); also published as *The Salmon of Doubt: Hitchhiking the Galaxy One Last Time* (New York: Harmony, 2002).
Collections: *Two Complete Novels: Dirk Gently's Holistic Detective Agency / The Long Dark Tea-Time of the Soul*

(New York: Random House, 1995); republished as *The Dirk Gently Omnibus* (London: Heinemann, 2001);

The Ultimate Hitchhiker's Guide (New York: Random House, 1996).

PLAY PRODUCTION: *The Hitch-Hiker's Guide to the Galaxy,* Liverpool, Science Fiction Theatre, 1979.

PRODUCED SCRIPTS: "The Pirate Planet," "City of Death," and "Shada," *Doctor Who,* television, BBC 1, 1978–1980;

The Hitch-Hiker's Guide to the Galaxy, BBC Radio 4, 1978–1980;

The Hitch-Hiker's Guide to the Galaxy, television, BBC, 1981.

OTHER: *The Utterly Utterly Merry Comic Relief Christmas Book,* edited by Adams and Peter Fincham (London: Collins, 1986);

"Meeting a Gorilla," by Adams and Mark Carwardine, in *The Great Ape Project: Equality beyond Humanity,* edited by Peter Singer (New York: St. Martin's Press, 1994), pp. 19–23;

"The Snake Doctor," by Adams and Carwardine, in *Tales from the Jungle: A Rainforest Reader,* edited by Daniel R. Katz and Miles Chapin (New York: Crown, 1995), pp. 197–202.

With the publication of *The Hitch-Hiker's Guide to the Galaxy* in 1979, Douglas Adams both established a cult and became a cult figure. He continued his saga with four more novels—*The Restaurant at the End of the Universe* (1980), *Life, the Universe, and Everything* (1982), *So Long, and Thanks for All the Fish* (1984), and *Mostly Harmless* (1992)—to create a five-volume series that he deliberately misnamed a "trilogy." These novels have achieved best-seller status and have brought a comic edge to the sometimes serious world of science fiction. His blend of peculiarly English comedy and a preoccupation with computer technology have extended his readership well beyond the world of science-fiction fandom.

Douglas Noel Adams was born in Cambridge on 11 March 1952, the son of Christopher Douglas Adams and Jane Dora Donovan Adams (later Thrift). He was educated at Brentwood School in Essex and then read English at St. John's College, Cambridge. At Cambridge, Adams was a member of the Footlights revue group. Following in the tradition of previous members who had to gone on to develop such shows as *Beyond the Fringe* and *Monty Python's Flying Circus,* Adams eventually formed his own revue group, Adam Smith Adams, for which he wrote, performed, and sometimes directed shows produced in London and Cambridge and at the Edinburgh Fringe Festival. Adams's work belongs to a peculiarly English (and particularly Oxford and Cambridge) tradition of student comedy. Like "Oxbridge" satire—which has been criticized for focusing on parody, pastiche, and self-conscious cleverness while rarely entering into the realm of politics—Adams's comic novels are indebted to satirical sketch writing and undergraduate humor, while often avoiding any direct treatment of political controversy.

On graduating from Cambridge in 1974, Adams began to write for radio and television. In 1978–1980 he was script editor for the science-fiction series *Doctor Who* and wrote several episodes of the show, which then had (and continues to have) a cult following. Traces of its influence may be found in Adams's fiction. Like Adams's *Hitch-Hiker's Guide to the Galaxy, Doctor Who* addresses, in a futuristic setting, anxieties about contemporary science, technology, and culture. Like the scripts of *Doctor Who, The Hitch-Hiker's Guide to the Galaxy* series plays with abstruse scientific language and flirts with the dangers of technology, opposing the ordinariness of daily life against the extraordinary possibilities of technology.

The Hitch-Hiker's Guide to the Galaxy had its origins as a series for BBC radio, first broadcast in 1978. Inspired by the format of the travelers' guides familiar to students in Europe and America, Adams set out to write a guide to mysteries of the galaxy. With the reassuringly familiar voice of Peter Jones (an actor known for radio and television comedy) as "The Book," the radio series was self-consciously comic. It made good use of music; the BBC Radiophonic workshop, whose electronic signature tune was a significant element in *Doctor Who,* produced a soundtrack whose combination of blues guitar, 1970s rock, and electronic mixing complemented the conjunction of the strange and familiar in the script.

In 1979 Adams reworked the radio script as a novel. *The Hitch-Hiker's Guide to the Galaxy* demystifies and debunks the unfamiliar language of science and computer technology, as well as that of corporate bureaucracy. The "Galactic Hyperspace Planning Council" has scheduled the planet Earth for demolition in order to build a "hyperspatial express route." After this wholesale destruction of the Earth in the opening pages of the text, Adams went on to create a whole range of new universes, all of which are used to parody the vagaries of twentieth-century Britain, just as Jonathan Swift satirized eighteenth-century England in the Lilliput and Brobdingnag of his *Gulliver's Travels* (1726). Adams did not share Swift's acerbic edge, however, and rejected a topical political critique in favor of a knowing postmodern wit. In *The Hitch-Hiker's Guide to the Galaxy* the universe is perceived as a cultural bricolage. Arthur Dent's travels through it demonstrate that surface is everything and that nothing has any meaningful substance. All the so-called absolute answers that appear turn out to be shams or irritatingly banal. Ultimately, *The Hitch-Hiker's Guide to the Galaxy* cannot sustain the conceit of an entirely surreal galaxy and is unable to shake off the specter of an earthbound world (which is often constructed in the shape of a contemporary Britain). The real world persistently forces itself back into the narrative throughout *The Hitch-Hiker's Guide to the Galaxy* and in two of its sequels: *Life, the Universe, and Everything* and *So Long, and Thanks for All the Fish.*

The Hitch-Hiker's Guide to the Galaxy begins as the apparently sole human survivor of planet Earth, Arthur Dent, is unwillingly jettisoned into the new worlds of intergalactic travel and computer science. With advice from the all-knowledgeable (but frequently unreliable) computerized voice of "The Book" (*The Hitch-Hiker's Guide to the Galaxy* itself), Arthur, a thoroughly ordinary hero, faces frightening and incomprehensible rituals and conventions. This new world and its language bear a remarkable resemblance to the banalities and bureaucracies of contemporary Britain. The alien who accompanies Arthur on his travels, Ford Prefect, may come from another planet, but his name is the same as that of a family car sold in Britain during the 1950s. On his intergalactic travels Arthur is attired in a dressing gown, and he bears traces of Mr Pooter, the inconsequential but entirely ordinary hero of George and Weedon Grossmith's *Diary of a Nobody* (1892), an important text in the English tradition of comic writing. Both Arthur and Mr Pooter are little men who strive for order and familiarity in an increasingly incomprehensible world.

The Hitch-Hiker's Guide to the Galaxy pokes fun at the pomposities and incomprehensibility of computer experts and government departments. It hit a contemporary nerve in offering a hero who is as baffled by scientific language as is most of the audience; yet, it also helped to familiarize people with the language of the digital organization and retrieval of data, which many people in Britain were then encountering for the first time.

Having originated as a radio series in the year before Margaret Thatcher became prime minister, *The Hitch-Hiker's Guide to the Galaxy* may, in retrospect, be seen as haunted by a fear of change and infused by a sense that the individual can no longer rely on the social order for protection. Arthur Dent, a new homeowner, is unable to protect his investment; no benign council can save his house; and there is no state support to help him to cope with the end of the world. Like the heroine of Lewis Carroll's *Alice's Adventures in Wonderland* (1865), Arthur is swept into an illogical new world with an eccentric and alien guide; Ford Prefect, who becomes his hitchhiking companion, is the equivalent of Alice's White Rabbit. Unlike Alice, however, Arthur has been whisked away in an alien spacecraft, and while Alice finally returns to her cozy Victorian world, all that is familiar to Dent has been destroyed. Although he is allowed to return to Earth in later volumes, it can never be the same again; the forces of change that were so evident in the late 1970s do not allow Arthur, or the reader, any sense of stability.

The central relationship between Arthur Dent, the innocent abroad, and Ford Prefect, the alien being who becomes Arthur's great chum, is the one reassuring constant of the series and also one of its great strengths. In the mold of the buddy movies of the late 1960s and the 1970s—of which *Butch Cassidy and the Sundance Kid* (1969) is probably the most familiar—the most important relationship in *The Hitch-Hiker's Guide to the Galaxy* series is between Arthur and Ford. Their assertively heterosexual relationship celebrates male bonding while marginalizing heterosexual romance. Arthur does not have an important relationship with a woman until the fourth volume of the series, *So Long, and Thanks for All the Fish.* As in many motion pictures of the 1970s and early 1980s, Adams dealt with the impact of the contemporary feminist movement by almost entirely excluding women from his fiction. Gender and sexuality are not significant issues in Arthur Dent's universe.

Another endearing figure in Arthur's alien universe is Marvin, a depressive android who, once again, serves to combine aspects of the strange and the familiar. A contemporary reworking of the gloomy Eeyore the donkey of A. A. Milne's *Winnie-the-Pooh* (1926), Marvin is afflicted by paranoia and melancholy, a deskilled worker whose superhuman intelligence is rarely utilized by the fellow travelers he regards as his inferiors. This gloomy representation of an intelligent mind wasted on the banal tasks asked of him addressed the fears and fantasies of a generation of 1980s British graduates, many of whom were facing unemployment and a great number of whom were among Adams's readership.

The Hitch-Hiker's Guide to the Galaxy and its sequels became huge successes, spawning a 1979 theatrical performance directed by Ken Campbell and a television production in 1981, as well as a *Hitch-Hiker's Guide to the Galaxy* record album, cassette, CD, and computer game. The reassuring "Don't Panic"—spoken often by "The Book"—became a familiar catchphrase and appeared on badges. The influence of the original series remains apparent in several radio and television imitations—

Dust jacket for Adams's 1987 novel, described by its publisher as "the first ever fully realised Ghost-Horror-Detective-Whodunit-Time-Travel-Romantic-Musical Comedy Epic" (Bruccoli Clark Layman Collection)

among them the cult British television-comedy series *Red Dwarf*—as well as in contemporary television and radio commercials that replicate the reassuring and all-knowing voice of "The Book" and employ versions of Adams's creative space-alien creatures.

The second volume in Adams's so-called trilogy is *The Restaurant at the End of the Universe,* adapted from the "second phase" of *The Hitch-Hiker's Guide to the Universe* radio series. A giant supercomputer built by a race of "hyperintelligent pan-dimensional beings" has succeeded in finding the answer to "the Ultimate Question of Life, the Universe and Everything." The answer to everything—which, the reader is told, is forty-two—is a sustained joke in the novel but is not, however, the focus of the plot. Instead, the narrative raises the question of how to cope in a world in which scientific language has become inaccessible and incomprehensible to ordinary people. In this novel Arthur's innocent awe has become more cynical. By the end of the novel he

has abandoned "The Book" to the river and become deeply suspicious of any claim to absolute answers.

The title of *Life, the Universe, and Everything,* published in 1982, comes from the opening of *The Restaurant at the End of the Universe* and continues Arthur's story, reintroducing many of the characters from the earlier volumes but relocating them in a prehistoric Earth. Ford Prefect, again Arthur's traveling companion, has retrieved "The Book" from the river, and together they attempt to explain the place of Earth in the galactic system. In an epilogue, Arthur and his companions are once again traveling, setting up the potential for further volumes.

Arthur Dent returns to Earth yet again in *So Long, and Thanks for All the Fish,* published in 1984, in which many familiar characters make reappearances. Arthur falls in love for the first time, with Fenchurch, a woman who has discovered the answer to the problems of the universe but has managed to lose it in the aftermath of the demolition of the Earth. In a galaxy that bears a striking resemblance to London during the 1980s, Arthur sets out, accompanied for the first time by a girl-friend, to discover the absolute answer to the problems of the world. By the fourth volume of the series, however, contemporary reviewers were beginning to recognize that the plot was rather thin and that the original joke was in danger of becoming overstretched. Adams's trademark debunking of technological language seems to become increasingly strained, and his inventive wit becomes less and less sharp as the series goes on. In fact, none of the subsequent novels had quite the same impact as the original, and nothing else that Adams wrote has inspired the same public affection as *The Hitch-Hiker's Guide to the Galaxy.*

The title of the fifth volume, *Mostly Harmless,* which appeared in 1992, is derived from Ford Prefect's report on Planet Earth, delivered in the first volume of the series. Arthur is by now beginning to feel dispossessed of his home planet and is in search of a replica Earth, but the possibilities the universe offers appear increasingly limited. The publishers of "The Book" have been taken over by the aptly named Infinidim Enterprises (in a sly reference to the mergers taking place in British publishing during the late 1980s and early 1990s), and the universe appears a darker and bleaker place.

In *The Hitch-Hiker's Guide to the Galaxy* series, Adams flirted with big philosophical questions—such as the Meaning of Life, the search for absolute answers in a relativistic world, and the potentiality of new technologies. He consistently set up these issues as serious problems but rarely followed through with any rigor. While the jokiness of the first radio series and novel had an engaging charm, in subsequent volumes this tone was too insubstantial to carry the weight of the philosophical implications Adams suggested. Adams intelligently set up the real problems faced by contemporary British society, but rather than pursue them with any serious engagement he chose to evade them with archness and witty dismissiveness. Indeed, the quest for answers and philosophical enlightenment is portrayed throughout the series as somewhat futile. His characters are largely disinterested in engaging with their situation with any seriousness. Instead of addressing the question of where they are in the universe, they would prefer to party, a position that the narratives tend to endorse rather than condemn. Adrift in an alien and alienated galaxy, Arthur and Ford Prefect's most pressing question is, "Where shall we have dinner?" and the Restaurant at the End of the Universe is enough of an answer for them.

Adams was also the author of two parodic detective novels, *Dirk Gently's Holistic Detective Agency* (1987) and *The Long Dark Tea-Time of the Soul* (1988), both located in a world that bears a marked resemblance to the landscapes of Adams's childhood and student years at Cambridge. Once again, Adams used a traditional form of popular fiction to address the preoccupations of the contemporary world. Like Arthur Dent, Dirk Gently attempts, in a frustratingly inconsequential world, to tie up all the loose ends of the mysteries of life. The Dirk Gently novels have never engendered the affection enjoyed by *The Hitch-Hiker's Guide to the Galaxy* and its sequels.

There is a consistent ecological awareness in Adams's novels, a recurrent recognition of the vulnerability of Planet Earth. Adams was a vocal supporter of the ecological group Greenpeace and collaborated with Mark Carwardine on *Last Chance to See* (1990), a book about endangered species.

With his first novel Adams established himself as a particular kind of comic voice in science fiction and took the audience for science fiction beyond that of the typical fan. He used his position as a cult figure to establish himself as a humanizing voice in the increasingly complicated world of computer technology and sales, becoming involved with promoting Apple computers. He used an Apple computer to write his 1984 novel *So Long, and Thanks for All the Fish,* and went on to acclaim the Apple MacIntosh, launched after that novel was completed, as the most "user-friendly" system for ordinary people and writers. All his subsequent novels credited his Apple computer and software. The technology that was fictional in the first volumes of *The Hitch-Hiker's Guide to the Galaxy* became increasingly real throughout the 1980s. Laptop computers made the once-inconceivable abilities of "The Book" relatively unexceptional. By the early 1990s the device that Adams had imagined in 1979 as the Hitch-Hiker's Guide to the Galaxy had come into being as the Newton, the Apple handheld notebook. *The Hitch-Hiker's Guide to the Galaxy* has its own home page on the World Wide Web. Adams became a regular speaker at computer conferences and launched a "digital village" to further develop links among different media.

On 24 November 1991 Adams married Jane Elizabeth Belson. Their daughter, Polly, was born in 1994. In 2001, Adams died suddenly of a heart attack while exercising. Fifty pages of an unfinished Hitch-Hiker novel and other writings found on Adams's computer hard drive were published in 2002 as *The Salmon of Doubt and Other Writings*.

Interviews:

Carolina Upcher, "The Master of the Universe," *GQ,* 61 (December 1991);

Stan Nicholls, "Zen and the Art of Never Saying Never Again," *Interzone,* no. 66 (December 1992): 16–19.

References:

Neil Gaiman, *Don't Panic: The Official Hitchhiker's Guide to the Universe Companion* (New York: Pocket Books, 1988);

Carl R. Kroph, "Douglas Adams's 'Hitch-Hiker' novels as Mock Science Fiction," *Science-Fiction Studies,* 15 (March 1988): 61–70.

Richard Adams

(9 May 1920 –)

Joan Bridgman
Open University

BOOKS: *Watership Down* (London: Rex Collings, 1972; New York: Macmillan, 1974);

Shardik (London: Allen Lane/Rex Collings, 1974; New York: Simon & Schuster, 1975);

Nature through the Seasons, by Adams and Max Hooper (Harmondsworth: Kestrel, 1975; New York: Simon & Schuster, 1975);

The Tyger Voyage (London: Cape, 1976; New York: Knopf, 1976);

The Adventures & Brave Deeds of the Ship's Cat on the Spanish Maine: Together with the Most Lamentable Losse of the Alcestis & Triumphant Firing of the Port of Chagres [cover title: *The Ship's Cat*] (London: Cape, 1977; New York: Knopf, 1977);

The Plague Dogs (London: Allen Lane/Rex Collings, 1977; New York: Knopf, 1978);

Nature Day and Night, by Adams and Hooper (Harmondsworth: Kestrel, 1978; New York: Viking, 1978);

The Iron Wolf and Other Stories (London: Allen Lane, 1980); republished as *The Unbroken Web: Stories and Fables* (New York: Crown, 1980);

The Girl in a Swing (London: Allen Lane, 1980; New York: Knopf, 1980);

The Legend of Te Tuna (Los Angeles: Sylvester & Orphanos, 1982; London: Sidgwick & Jackson, 1986);

Voyage through the Antarctic, by Adams and Ronald Lockley (London: Allen Lane, 1982; New York: Knopf, 1983);

Maia (London: Viking, 1984; New York: Knopf, 1985);

A Nature Diary (London: Viking, 1985);

The Bureaucats (London: Viking, 1985);

Traveller (New York: Knopf, 1988; Toronto: Little, Brown, 1988; London: Hutchinson, 1989);

The Day Gone By: An Autobiography (London: Hutchinson, 1990; New York: Knopf, 1991);

Tales from Watership Down (London: Hutchinson, 1996; New York: Knopf, 1996);

The Outlandish Knight (Sutton: Severn House, 2000).

Richard Adams (photograph © 1990 Peter Hirst-Smith)

OTHER: Ronald Lockley, *The Private Life of the Rabbit,* introduction by Adams (New York: Macmillan, 1974);

Richard Jefferies, *Wood Magic,* introduction by Adams (New York: Third Press, 1974);

Georgi Vladimov, *Faithful Ruslan: The Story of a Guard Dog,* translated from the Russian by Michael Glenny, introduction by Adams (New York: Simon & Schuster, 1979);

"The Rabbit's Ghost Story," in *Richard Adams's Favourite Animal Stories,* edited by Adams (London: Octopus, 1981), pp. 95–105;

Grimm's Fairy Tales, edited by Adams (London: Routledge & Kegan Paul, 1981);

The Best of Ernest Thompson Seton, introduction by Adams (London: Fontana, 1982);

Martin Harbury, *The Last of the Wild Horses,* introduction by Adams (Toronto: Key Porter, 1984);

"Richard Adams's Berkshire," in *The Illustrated Counties of England,* edited by James Bishop (London: Allen & Unwin, 1985), pp. 8–13;

Occasional Poets: An Anthology, edited by Adams and including five poems by him (London: Viking, 1986);

"Polonius: Did Dover Wilson Miss a Trick?" in *Essays by Divers Hands: The Transactions of the Royal Society of Literature, Volume XLIV,* edited by A. N. Wilson (Woodbridge, Suffolk: Boydell Press, 1986), pp. 24–45;

Untitled story, in *I Saw a Ghost,* edited by Ben Noakes (London: Weidenfeld & Nicolson, 1986);

"Argos," in *Guardian Angels,* edited by Stephanie Nettell (Harmondsworth: Viking Kestrel, 1987), pp. 68–78;

"Some Thoughts on Animals in Religious Imagery," in *Beyond the Bars: The Zoo Dilemma,* edited by Virginia McKenna, Will Travers, and Jonathan Carey (Wellingborough, Northamptonshire: Thorsons, 1987), pp. 67–85;

Excerpt from *Watership Down,* in *The Puffin Book of Twentieth-Century Children's Stories,* edited by Judith Elkin (London: Viking, 1991), pp. 271–279;

Walter de la Mare, *The Three Royal Monkeys,* introduction by Adams (London: Robin Clark, 1993);

"The Bommie and the Drop-Off," in *Shivers for Christmas,* edited by Richard Dalby (London: Michael O'Mara, 1995);

Article in *My Country Childhood,* edited by Susy Smith (London: Hodder & Stoughton, 1999), pp. 3–7;

Anecdote in *Twice Daily After Meals: A Selection of the Wit and Wisdom of the Celebrated,* edited by S. K. Goolamali (Northwood: Midi-Derm Company, 2001), pp. 12–13.

SELECTED PERIODICAL PUBLICATIONS–UNCOLLECTED: *"Watership Down," Books for Your Children,* 8 (August 1973): 2–4;

"Some Ingredients of *Watership Down,*" *Children's Book Review,* 4 (Autumn 1974): 92–95;

"On Bringing Children and Books Together," *Hollins Alumni Magazine* (February 1977); reprinted in *Richmond News Leader* (6 September 1977);

"But Rabbits Do Cry," *Sunday* magazine with *News of the World,* 18 October 1982, pp. 14–15;

"Notebook on Nature," monthly column, *Out of Town,* August 1983–April 1987;

"George Stubbs," *Art and Antiques* (February 1985): 42–46;

"Three Sonnets for Elizabeth," *Words,* 1 (July 1985): 19;

"Reflections on Five Rivers," *New York Times,* 15 July 1986, section xx, pp. 9, 36;

"Clothed in Cruelty," *Out of Town* (July 1986): 56–57.

Although he is the author of seven full-length novels, four of which have exclusively human protagonists, Richard Adams is perceived primarily but erroneously to be a writer of pastoral anthropomorphic fantasy. This perception derives from the enormous commercial success of his first novel, *Watership Down* (1972), set in the English countryside of Berkshire. It centers on a band of rabbits whose quest for a new warren is treated in a serious, epic fashion. Their rabbit existence is realized without sentimentality and with a biological realism hitherto unknown in the genre of anthropomorphism. The reader enters the rabbits' world, which is realized with great imaginative solidity further intensified by the close-textured, detailed description of a small area of the Berkshire countryside. This close focus caught public attention in the 1970s when there was a new ecological awareness that the natural world was under threat and has given the author the well-deserved reputation of "a country writer."

Richard George Adams was born in Newbury, Berkshire, on 9 May 1920, the fourth child of a country doctor, Evelyn George Beadon Adams, and Lilian Rosa (née Button) Adams. His home, "Oakdene," had a large wild garden bordered by fields and woodland that stretched away to the Downs, including Watership Down. Oakdene has since been razed to make way for a housing project and is now the site of twenty-two small houses. Adams was a solitary child, separated by a nine-year age gap from his siblings, who were envious of their parents' preference for the baby brother, doubly precious because of the intervening child, Robert, who had died in 1919 at age two. He played alone with imaginary friends for company, taking refuge in the rhododendrons and the shrubbery, a favorite retreat. The connection between the natural world and refuge was made when he was young, as was the habit of creating imaginary worlds. His father was a powerful influence, a devotee of country lore who made sure that his son learned how to identify birdsongs and to know the Linnaean as well as the common names of wildflowers. Adams looks back to his childhood as a golden age, a lost rural paradise.

This idyll ended abruptly when at the age of not quite nine Adams was sent away to boarding school, first to the preparatory school Horris Hill, and from there, in 1933, to Bradfield College, a Brit-

*Adams in 1931, while he was a student at Horris Hill
(from Richard Adams,* The Day Gone By, *1990)*

ish public school set in the Berkshire countryside. Both schools were class-conscious and snobbish, as Adams has said in his autobiography, *The Day Gone By* (1990): "If you were not at boarding school you weren't a gentleman." The system of privileges and the severe discipline that enforced them left Adams with a profound respect for authority and established hierarchies and a working knowledge of the realities of the English class system that underlies much of his work. After Bradfield, in 1938 he went up to Worcester College, Oxford, where he studied modern history. His student days were interrupted by World War II, and he joined an airborne company of the Royal Army Service Corps. He returned to Oxford to finish his degree course in 1946, graduating in 1948, and then he entered the Home Civil Service the same year as an assistant principal. In 1949 he married Barbara Elizabeth Acland. Their daughter

Juliet was born in 1958, followed by Rosamond in 1960.

To pass the time during a car journey to Stratford to see *Twelfth Night* in July 1966, Adams began telling his daughters a tale of two rabbits. They urged him to write the rabbit story down, and he began that year, completing the first draft eighteen months later. He was then forty-six years old, having spent eighteen years as a career civil servant with no published work, an unknown on the literary scene. The novel was rejected seven times by various publishing houses and literary agents because of its length and difficulty but was finally accepted by a small publisher, Rex Collings, in May 1970. Publication was delayed for two years, however, primarily because the first proofs had so many errors that Adams and Collings called for a second set. Collings liked the book because it had the realism of animals that mate and defecate.

The written novel had grown to more than four hundred pages, with natural descriptions, parenthetical stories, a rabbit language, and rabbit mythology added to the original oral tale of rabbits whose home is destroyed for a housing development. The background was given unusual precision by the addition of the relevant section of the Ordnance Survey map, included at Adams's behest. One or two literary epigraphs begin each chapter. In *Watership Down* Adams is clearly passing on the sum of his knowledge and experience. He re-creates the small-animal viewpoint of his own youth when he hid in the shrubbery and uses the countryside of the Downs as the setting for the action. The military Efrafan warren is modeled on his experiences of the harsh, bullying regime at Bradfield, which he has described as fascist. His imaginary friends in the garden become one with his army comrades. In *The Day Gone By* he says, "The idea of the wandering, endangered and yet inter-dependent band, individually different yet mutually reliant, came from my experience with the Airborne Company."

The mythic framework of the novel, and indeed its narrative structure, owes much to Adams's knowledge of Carl Gustav Jung and the theories of the comparative mythologist Joseph Campbell. In the early 1950s Adams began a three-year Jungian analysis and learned the importance of dreams and their connections with the unconscious; the existence of the collective unconscious, in which lie the archetypes of dream, myth, and folktale; and the theory that the shadow part of human personality must be accepted to achieve psychological wholeness. These beliefs are reflected in *Watership Down* in the character of the visionary Fiver and in the author's insistence on the amalgamation of warrens and the integration of even the villainous Woundwort as a folk hero in the final chapter. In 1949, four years before his analysis, Adams bought a first edition of Campbell's *The Hero with a Thousand Faces*. Campbell's theory of the monomyth was a conscious and powerful influence on the writing of *Watership Down*. The standard path of the mythological hero–separation, initiation, and return with a boon for the community–underlies the narrative structure of the novel. Adams recorded his debt when the National Arts Club of America gave Campbell the 1985 Medal of Honor for Literature on his eightieth birthday. Adams made a much-praised speech at the dinner, expressing his admiration and confirming Campbell as a formative influence on his writing.

Watership Down had an unusual publishing history. It was initially published as a children's book in November 1972. Collings could only afford to print 2,500 copies, making this first hardback edition a collector's item. It was given an ecstatic critical reception. *The Bookseller* (3 February 1973) remarked that the publication date in late November turned out to be a stroke of luck. It meant that the book missed the children's book supplements that appear before Christmas, in which it might only have received a brief notice in the mass roundups. As it turned out, Selina Hastings produced a key review on a book review page, so the novel was not relegated to a children's ghetto but given adult treatment. She wrote in the *Sunday Telegraph* (21 January 1973) that *Watership Down* is "A beautifully written and intensely moving story, the work of an extraordinary imagination. . . . a classic of animal literature." Edward Blishen, in *The Times Educational Supplement* (15 December 1972), announced "with trembling pleasure the appearance of a great story." It was hailed as stunning, compulsively readable, and highly original. Comparisons with Kenneth Grahame, George Orwell, and J. R. R. Tolkien were made. The novel won both the Carnegie Medal and the Guardian Award for 1972. Collings was unable to meet the sudden demand for the book, and sales were therefore held down, but he sold the paperback rights to Puffin (the children's division of Penguin Books). This edition was published in July 1973, provoking a second wave of critical acclaim, and it sold heavily–145,000 copies in the month of October alone. It topped the children's paperback best-seller list and *The New York Times* best-seller list for months.

The decision by Macmillan in New York to market the first American edition of *Watership Down* in their adult list recognized it as a book for all ages and took it to another sphere commercially. Macmillan made it their most heavily advertised and publicized book of 1974, with swift and spectacular results. It was reported to have sold a record 300,000 hardback copies during its first six weeks, a phenomenal figure, and it remained on the best-seller list for most of the year. The first print run for the American paperback edition was five million copies. Encouraged by the American experience and hoping to repeat it in the much smaller British market, Penguin Books published the book in their adult paperback list, and it was immediately launched into its greatest wave of selling in Britain and burst into the blockbuster category of best-sellers. In April 1975 Penguin celebrated the millionth sale of the novel in Britain and presented the author with a golden rabbit in gratitude. In 1985 *The Times* declared that *Watership Down* had sold five million copies in Britain, second only to Orwell's *Animal Farm* (1945) but ahead of Geoffrey Chaucer's *The Canterbury Tales* (circa 1375–1400) and Homer's *Odyssey* (circa 8th–7th centuries B.C.). It has been translated into twenty languages and been a best-seller in Germany, Japan, and Italy.

The commercial success of the novel is owing to many factors in addition to its narrative and stylistic merits: the intense publicity from Macmillan, the increasing environmental concern, the growth of the animal-rights movement, the cross-cultural appeal to the conservative middle class and the student subculture, and its wide readership across age barriers. But perhaps the deeper reason for its popularity lies in its expression of the universal need for a secure refuge.

Before *Watership Down* was published, Adams, grown accustomed to writing every evening when he came back from his job in Whitehall, had begun writing his next novel, *Shardik,* published in 1974. With the enormous financial success of his first novel and the imminent publication of his second, he decided to give up his civil service career. He had reached the rank of Assistant Secretary in the Department of the Environment. During his final six years there he had been in charge of the air pollution division and in 1968 had steered the second Clean Air Bill through Parliament. The success of *Watership Down* encouraged him not only to leave this secure occupation but also to undertake another great change, that of domicile. The sudden arrival of the substantial American royalties dictated that, in order to preserve his sudden fortune, he had to become a nonresident in the United Kingdom for one year to avoid punitive tax rates. He moved to the Isle of Man, which is not formally part of Britain and has different tax laws.

Adams's second novel, *Shardik,* has a picture of a giant bear on the dust jacket and is concerned with a religion centered on this creature; but the animal is

*Barbara Elizabeth Acland, Adams's future wife, at age
seventeen, summer 1946 (from Richard Adams,*
The Day Gone By*)*

not anthropomorphized in any way, and the protagonists are human. However, these characters are distanced from the reader as much as are those in science fiction, because they exist in a fantasy setting, the primitive past of an empire called Bekla. The author invents a new world. The geography, religion, customs, and language of the people are new creations—even the plants are strange. The hero is a hunter called Kelderek, who discovers the huge bear and attributes to it the power of a god who is a special protector of children. The novel is founded upon Adams's belief that most of the mental suffering in the world is caused by broken homes and parents who abandon their children. It is dedicated to a child whom the Adams family fostered for a while. There is a horrifying portrayal of a cruel slavetrader, called Genshed, who visits dreadful tortures upon children. Kelderek is convinced that the Bear is an exemplar of the true function of incarnate godhead. He realizes that the unloved and unwanted are the ones who are sold into slavery, and that the first step toward their slavery came when they were deserted, before they were ever sold. Kelderek dedicates the rest of his life to the Bear's work of caring for children who come to him for refuge.

Adams believes this novel to be the most underestimated of his works. The most important feature of it, apart from its powerful story, is its depiction of deep mythic levels originating in the unconscious mind. His Jungian analysis enabled Adams to tap this source and create mythic figures that awaken chords in the minds of his readers. He has said that complete episodes came to him in dreams.

Since *Shardik* followed one of the greatest publishing phenomena of the century, Allen Lane mounted a major national publishing campaign to promote it. In spite of this publicity, the novel did not have an entirely favorable critical reception. Reviewers disliked its religious and moralistic tone. The *Sunday Times* critic (17 November 1974) saw that "hot-eyed morality of pride, error and punishment is at the heart of the book, and this seems both dislikeable and out of date." A reviewer for the *Guardian* (21 November 1974) agreed: "This book is not about religion, it's about cruelty and sentimentality." The honeymoon period of critical admiration was over for Adams. The reason was furnished by Frank Lipsius in a thoughtful piece in *Books and Bookmen* in August 1975. In the many promotional interviews accompanying publication of *Shardik,* journalists were meeting the author for the first time, and they saw him as self-satisfied with his newfound fame and wealth. As Adams confessed ruefully to Fiona McDonald Hill of the *Reading Evening Post* (27 August 1974), "I have a fatal capacity for upsetting people." However, this critical disapproval did not affect sales. *Shardik* was reprinted, and book sales averaged 8,000 a week, totaling 600,000 in Britain alone by October 1974 and topping the list of best-sellers. In 1981 it was still selling well, and sales were approaching a million in Britain. Editions continue to appear, including one from Overlook Press in 2002.

In 1975 Adams was writer-in-residence at the University of Florida, teaching creative writing and lecturing on English literature. *Nature through the Seasons* was published that year in collaboration with a scientist, Dr. Max Hooper. Both authors investigate three typical English landscapes and show the seasonal and daily changes they undergo. A second volume, *Nature Day and Night,* was published in 1978 following the same format. In 1976 Adams continued to work as a writer-in-residence at Hollins College (now Hollins University) in Virginia, and *The Tyger Voyage* was published. This work is an amusing children's fantasy written in rhyming couplets recounting an exotic voyage undertaken by two tigers, Ezekiel and Raphael Dubb. They are eventually brought back home to a civic banquet, after climbing a live volcano and staying with gypsies.

By 1977 Adams was back on the Isle of Man in a house overlooking the Irish Sea, with a magnificent library containing a stained-glass window commemorating *The Tyger Voyage*. In this year he published *The Adventures & Brave Deeds of the Ship's Cat on the Spanish Maine: Together with the Most Lamentable Losse of the Alcestis & Triumphant Firing of the Port of Chagres,* a romantic ballad set in Queen Elizabeth's reign, which glories in the swashbuckling adventures of a group of privateers captured by the wicked Spaniards. The inspiration for the hero of the piece comes from a passage in Richard Hakluyt's *Principall Navigations, Voiages and Discoveries of the English Nation* (1589) reproduced in the book.

Adams also published his third full-length novel, *The Plague Dogs,* in 1977. It is a full-blooded polemic against experimentation on animals and is also a satiric attack on tabloid journalism, the press as a whole, and government bureaucracy. One feels the author settling several old scores. *The Plague Dogs* is an anthropomorphic fantasy, concerning animals who speak. It is set in an area of great natural beauty, the Lake District, which the author knows well, and the volume was illustrated with maps drawn by A. Wainwright, a best-seller in his own right. Two dogs—Rowf, a black mongrel, and Snitter, a terrier—escape from an animal experimentation station after terrible sufferings. This situation starts a major hue and cry for their capture since they are thought to be carrying bubonic plague. The ensuing hunt eventually involves government ministers, the army, and the national press. Another animal character who befriends the dogs is a Newcastle or "Geordie" fox called "the Tod." Adams took considerable pains to give him the authentic Tyneside accent, enlisting the help of an expert. This dialect is incomprehensible even to most English speakers, however, and the Geordie dialogue was diluted for the American edition. This edition also includes an explanatory preface, and the ending is differently presented. Adams includes his friend Ronald Lockley (author of *The Private Life of the Rabbit* [1964], a research source for Adams in writing *Watership Down*) and renowned artist, ornithologist, and broadcaster Sir Peter Scott in his final chapter. The Assistant Secretary from the Department of the Environment, who quotes from John Milton's "Lycidas" (1638), is a self-portrait of the author.

The Plague Dogs was Allen Lane's most heavily promoted book of the year, with huge national press, radio, and television coverage. The novel again drew the fire of critics for its self-indulgent habit of literary quotation, the Tod's incomprehensible dialect, and the author's intemperate opinions. The reviewer for the *New Statesman* (23 September 1977) said the literary and historical references made "the book sound like the prize-day speech of a berserk headmaster." Many critics made unfavorable comparisons with *Watership Down*. Yet, others found the book powerful and visionary. The novel is a mixture—a piece of sustained propaganda, yet moving by turns and compulsively readable. Again, in spite of the reviews, it entered the best-seller list, was marketed all over the world, and sold more than 100,000 copies in Britain within weeks.

A motion-picture version of *Watership Down* premiered on 19 October 1978. Movie rights had been sold to Martin Rosen, and the cartoon animation of the story he produced had a cast of distinguished voices, including Sir Ralph Richardson, John Hurt, and Richard Briers. A hit tune on the soundtrack, "Bright Eyes" by Art Garfunkel, ensured that the novel, which was republished to tie in with the movie, met a new public and enjoyed further commercial success. Rosen later produced an animated cartoon version of *The Plague Dogs* (1982) that gave a further boost of sales to that book. Six reprintings of *Watership Down* were published in 1978, and Penguin had four versions of the book on sale, including a glossy illustrated Kestrel edition.

Adams's views on cruelty to animals, strongly expressed in *The Plague Dogs,* have long been important to him. He told Edward Steen in an interview (*Sunday Telegraph,* 22 June 1980), "I have always had an emotional interest in animals ever since I was a little boy. I'm a natural identifier with victims." In 1978 he toured Great Britain, Canada, and the United States in a campaign of protest against the culling of the harp seal pups in Newfoundland and was instrumental in lobbying the British government into agreeing to force importers of sealskin products to name the country of origin. As a result of this new labeling, pelt imports from Canada dropped by more than 62 percent. Probably because of these endeavors, rather than the subject matter of his novels, in 1980 Adams was made president of the Royal Society for the Prevention of Cruelty to Animals. However, in 1982 he and three vice presidents resigned from the Society in order to pursue the cause of animal rights in a more militant fashion. Throughout the 1980s Adams addressed open-air rallies of animal-rights groups campaigning for a boycott against Canadian products and demonstrated against animal experimentation in laboratories. Another of his campaigns has been against the fur trade as a whole. He has toured Britain in this cause and helped financially with propaganda.

In 1980 Adams published *The Girl in a Swing,* a ghost story with a horrifying climax, a complete departure from his previous work. It is set in the con-

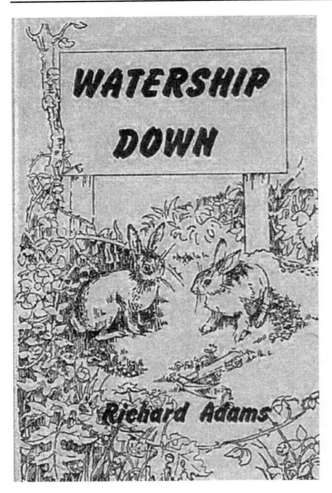

Dust jacket for Adams's first book, a best-selling novel
that had its genesis as a story for his young daughters
(Bromlea Rare Books catalogue, n.d.)

temporary world and is the frankly erotic love story of a Newbury ceramic dealer, Alan Desland, and a beautiful German girl he meets in Denmark. There is a mythical dimension to the novel: the heroine, Käthe (Karin in the British edition) is intermittently possessed by the goddess Aphrodite and endowed with both her voluptuous eroticism and the ruthless callousness of the ancient world. In order to marry Desland, she destroys her daughter, but the marriage is haunted by the ghost of the murdered child, who finally exacts retribution. Again, dreams play an important part in the story. The narrative is gripping and second only to *Watership Down* in its appeal to the reader. The novel is set in Copenhagen, Florida, Newbury, and the Berkshire countryside. Adams's wife is an authority on English ceramic history and supplied the information about the eighteenth-century ceramic figurine of the title.

There was a technical hitch with the publication of the novel in England, and it was published first in America, mainly to enthusiastic reviews—"What a girl! What an ending! What a book!" (*Chicago Tribune,* 27 April 1980). Although Adams, wary of the British press, now gave rare interviews, there was still adverse comment. Selina Hastings in the *Daily Telegraph* (18 December 1980) wrote that "Karin is humourless, heavy and dull and Alan a worrying combination of prurience and pedantry, pomposity and conceit." But she also articulated the reviewer's dilemma in relation to Adams—she had to confess that the author was a remarkable storyteller who exerted a compulsive fascination. The chief difficulty for the reader is the legendary outer framework of myth in the presentation of Käthe; she is still a contemporary woman, and modern readers find her murderous action outrageous and unnecessary. The reviews had little effect on financial success. The novel promptly entered the best-seller lists, and its sales are second only to *Watership Down* among Adams's books. It sold extraordinarily well in paperback. A first printing of 200,000 copies sold out in weeks, and a second printing of 200,000 was made. In the promotional material for the paperback of the later novel *Maia* (1984) in America, it was reported that *The Girl in a Swing* had 1.1 million copies in print. A movie version made by the Danish producer Just Betzer and starring Meg Tilly and Rupert Frazer premiered in December 1988 in Copenhagen before Prince Henrik.

In 1980 Adams's Italian publisher, Rizzoli Editore, commissioned a book of folktales. This volume was first published in Britain under the title *The Iron Wolf and Other Stories* in 1980, elsewhere as *The Unbroken Web: Stories and Fables;* that title comes from the preface in the British edition. This unbroken web is Adams's image for the universality of folktale, where the archetypes of dream and folktales lie and are connected. This image is Jung's collective unconscious made visible, like a gossamer sphere encircling the world. The storyteller reaches up and draws it down while he tells his story; then it springs back to encircle the world again. The process by which a modern author works is not so much inventing as discovering or uncovering the story that already exists in the unconscious mind. *The Iron Wolf and Other Stories* consists of nineteen folktales, each presented by an imagined narrator to one or more hearers at a particular time and place. Adams is fond of this "framing" device. He uses it in *Watership Down,* in which the novel frames the rabbit folktales, and the original typescript of *Shardik* had substantial framing, with a contemporary narrator and children who listen to the story. The technique gives the flavor and immediacy of the oral tale of which Adams is fond, seeing himself as a storyteller, one of the penny-in-the-hat brigade.

In 1983 a Conservative government was in place in Britain with a less punitive tax system for the wealthy, and Adams left the Isle of Man and returned to live near his roots in Hampshire, England. There he completed his fifth novel, *Maia,* a return to the fantasy setting of the Beklan Empire, but set twenty years before the events in *Shardik.* This novel was begun in 1981 but was delayed by a trip to the Antarctic to research a book on wildlife there. *Maia* was finally published in 1984. It is an immense work of 1,056 closely printed pages, making heavy demands on the reader, who has to keep track of 84 characters, many of whom have lengthy, unfamiliar names, in some cases three-part hyphenated. British reviews were generally dismissive, even personally abusive. Christopher Hawtree of the *Spectator* (3 November 1984) recommended a straitjacket for the author, and a critic for *The Times* (22 November 1984) asserted that the reader should, in a phrase borrowed from Dorothy Parker, not toss the novel aside lightly "but throw it with great force." A reviewer for *The Washington Post* (20 January 1985), on the other hand, said rapturously that "*Maia* is a delicious contradiction: a big fat adventure read with no fat at all." American reviewers have in the past been consistently more generous to Adams than British critics, but on this novel even they were divided between praise and sharp disapproval. "Racist, sexist and utterly tiresome," said the reviewer for the *San Francisco Chronicle* (9 January 1985).

The problem with *Maia* could be the erotic descriptions of unconventional and deviant sex. The heroine has a lesbian relationship and gratifies an obscenely fat character called Sencho. A goat-god, Shakkarn, is described mating with a goddess, and there is copulation with a life-size bronze figure of the god Cran. The master-slave relationship is explored in a variety of pairings. The sexual fantasies conjured up may be fascinating to some but repulsive to others. Also, the invented terms for sex and the relevant parts of the body seem contrived.

The main plot follows the adventures of a fifteen-year-old bed slave from the degradation of prostitution to respectable marriage and motherhood. Maia's principal characteristic is her outstanding courage, which she displays many times. The Beklan background is created in almost obsessive detail, a feat of sustained inventive energy. Adams depicts a semibarbaric society undergoing a process of change, about to emerge from slavery, with epic battles fought against a vast and detailed background. However, the passages of description are overlong, and the heroine's enthusiastic participation in degrading sex scenes is psychologically improbable. Nevertheless, even the harshest of critics had to admit that the novel was a page-turner and a potential best-seller. *The Bookseller* (14 September 1985) reported that it sold "moderately well" despite the adverse reviews.

The Legend of Te Tuna, first published in 1982 in the United States (in a limited edition) and in 1986 in England, is a ballad of twenty-three Spenserian stanzas that recounts a folktale from the South Seas about Maui, a trickster hero; Hina, the Polynesian Aphrodite; and Te Tuna, a giant eel. It demonstrates Adams's continuing interest in myth and folktale. *The Bookseller* refused to carry the erotic illustrations. Adams, who had encouraged the artist to make the illustrations sexually explicit, professed himself amazed at this reaction.

Adams's next anthropomorphic novel is *Traveller,* published in 1988. It is the story of Confederate general Robert E. Lee's famous horse. The narrative is composed of a series of equine monologues addressed to Tom, the stable cat. The author consulted an expert on horse psychology, much as he used Lockley's *The Private Life of the Rabbit* to verify the behavior of rabbits for *Watership Down,* and did a thorough job of research into Lee's role in the American Civil War. The brief italicized passages that alternate with Traveller's narrative are lucid and arresting in their exposition of each stage of the campaign. The author handicaps Traveller's account, however, because he does not follow through with the anthropomorphization of the horse and allow Traveller the capacity to understand the events happening around him, which severely limits the narrative. The horse hears bangs, only knows the enemy as "Blue Men," and never understands the significance of the war. Thus, the progress of the Seven Days campaign to the surrender at Appomattox is incomprehensible to him. This ignorance can be puzzling for the reader, who has the added difficulty of reading Traveller's Southern dialect, rendered faithfully on the page. However, the horse's incomprehension of events is startlingly effective in the passage on Lee's surrender and again most affectingly at Lee's funeral, where Traveller's hopefulness that he will see his master again is painfully contrasted with the reader's understanding of the significance of the box in the glass cart, the black clothes, and the gun salute. The relationship between horse and master, the story of the selfless service of a noble beast to man, is touchingly drawn. Adams decided to publish this novel initially in Canada and the United

First page of the manuscript for Adams's 2000 novel, The Outlandish Knight *(Collection of Richard Adams)*

States to see whether kinder first notices might change the attitudes of British reviewers. It did not work. Maureen Freely said in the *Observer* (5 February 1989) that the book was about the American Civil War "as boringly misunderstood by a horse," and she was not the only critic to quote gleefully, "If'n you're a horse you gotta keep your gut full and you got to dung regl'ar."

With the publication of *Tales from Watership Down* in 1996 Adams returned to the setting and protagonists of his first and greatest success. The rabbit's-eye view of the world is re-presented with a freshness and sureness of touch. The tales are closely linked with the time frame of the original novel. Five tales pick up references in the book to adventures experienced by El-ahrairah on his way back from the underworld of the Black Rabbit. Several tales take place in the happy period after Woundwort's disappearance. Hazel now runs a more progressive warren where females may become Chief Rabbits—possibly a response to those critics who accused *Watership Down* of antifeminism. The stories are told with the utmost seriousness, as though they were reportage of actual events rather than fiction; this style confers conviction and preserves the charm and originality of its predecessor. The book was well received by critics and the public. Sales have been good, and the book has been translated into almost all the languages achieved by *Watership Down* itself.

Adams's next novel, *The Outlandish Knight,* was first published in 2000 by Severn House, primarily for sale to libraries in the United Kingdom and the United States. It is an historical fiction set in the late fifteenth through the early seventeenth centuries in Britain. The narrative follows three generations of an ordinary family who happen to participate in or witness famous events in history, including Henry Tudor's defeat and destruction of Richard III at the Battle of Bosworth in 1485; Henry VIII's marriage to Catherine of Aragon, his divorce from her, and his marriage to Anne Boleyn; and the plot against Queen Elizabeth led by Anthony Babington in 1586. The England of those centuries is vividly realized with its savagery, sights, and stench. High points include the sustained portrait of the unfortunate Catherine of Aragon and the horrific description of the public execution of the plotters against Queen Elizabeth.

The three-part structure is linked by folk songs, one of which, "The Outlandish Knight," provides the title of the book. The concept of giving such narrative importance to folk songs (which have long been an interest for Adams), together with the incorporation of their lyrics and musical notation, is an original idea. The book has not been published in paperback; Adams attributes this fact to "publishers' distaste for historical and for episodic novels."

Richard Adams's most important novel, critically and commercially, must be judged to be his magical *Watership Down*. It is still selling after thirty years and has earned the status of classic. Adams's touch is best with animals, figures of myth, fantasy, and broad prototypes of character rather than the psychological presentation of modern men and women. Although *Shardik, The Plague Dogs, The Girl in a Swing,* and *Maia* have been major best-sellers, they have never gained the unequivocal critical acclaim of the first novel. This reservation may be caused in part, as Adams thinks, by envy at the windfall fortune the book earned him or by his combative personality. (A. N. Wilson, for instance, now a good friend of Adams, had reported in the *Weekend Telegraph* of 12 May 1990 that Adams wished to drop turds on his head because Wilson could not admire the later work as much as he genuinely revered *Watership Down*.) The literary establishment of Britain has not accepted him: "Probably no other contemporary novelist suffers from so much condescension or critical dismissal from so many literary intellectuals," said Phillip Vine in *Words* (July 1985). The extent of this abuse is perhaps exaggerated, since Adams has been made a Fellow of the Royal Society of Literature and had the social accolade of lunch with Queen Elizabeth II. In any case, Adams's faithful readers ignore the critics. They buy his books in huge numbers because they enjoy them. The hackneyed phrase of the blurb writer, "a master storyteller," happens in Adams's case to be true.

Interviews:

Mary Hoffman, "Fruitful Duality," *Times Literary Supplement,* 2 November 1973, p. 23;

Pamela Marsh, "What Children Need: Books as Rich as Plum Pludding," *Christian Science Monitor* (7 November 1973): 131;

John F. Baker, "PW Interview: Richard Adams," *Publishers Weekly* (15 April 1974): 6–8;

Tim Heald, "The Book Programme," *Radio Times* (30 September 1974): 7–9;

Dulan Barber, "The Ursine Perspective," *Daily Telegraph Magazine* (14 November 1974): 61–66;

Arthur Cooper, "Bear Market," *Newsweek* (28 April 1975): 77–78;

Frank Lipsius, "Bear Trappings of Success," *Books and Bookmen* (August 1975): 54;

Graham Lord, "Why Mr. Adams Wants to Switch from Rabbits to a Sexy Novel," *Sunday Express,* 3 July 1977, p. 6;

John Heilpern, "Adams and the Beasts of the Field," *Observer Magazine* (9 October 1977): 25–27;

Timothy Green, "Richard Adams's Long Journey from *Watership Down*," *Smithsonian* (March 1979): 76–82;

Edward Steen, "Can Adams Quell the R.S.P.C.A. Storms?" *Sunday Telegraph,* 22 June 1980, p. 17;

Phillip Vine, "Words Interview, Richard Adams," *Words,* 1 (July 1985): 20–29;

Frank Delaney, "What Shall We Do about Richard Adams?" *Mail on Sunday, You Magazine,* 26 August 1985, pp. 18–20;

Charlotte F. Otten, "To the Order of Two Little Girls: The Oral and Written Versions of *Watership Down*," in *The Voice of the Narrator in Children's Literature: Insights from Writers and Critics,* edited by Otten and Gary D. Schmidt (New York: Greenwood Press, 1989), pp. 115–122;

Selina Hastings, "On Going Completely Off the Clock," *Sunday Telegraph,* 22 April 1990, p. xi;

Lynn Barber, "Still Rabbiting On, 18 Years after *Watership Down*," *Independent on Sunday,* 6 May 1990, pp. 8–10.

References:

Christopher Booker, "Rabbits and Reality," *Spectator,* 14 July 1979, pp. 14–15;

Joan Bridgman, "The Publishing History and Literary Context of *Watership Down*," dissertation, University College London, 1990;

Bridgman, "Richard Adams at Eighty," *Contemporary Review,* 277 (August 2000): 108–112;

Elliott B. Ghose, *Mere Creatures* (Toronto: University of Toronto Press, 1988);

Graham Hammond, "Trouble with Rabbits," *Child Literature in Education* (12 September 1973): 48–69;

Fred Inglis, *The Promise of Happiness* (Cambridge: Cambridge University Press, 1981);

Journal of the Fantastic in the Arts, special issue on Adams and *Watership Down,* edited by Charles A. Meyer, 6, no. 1 (1993);

Alison Lurie, *Don't Tell the Children* (London: Bloomsbury, 1990), pp. 169–177;

Lissa Paul, "Dumb Bunnies: A Revisionist Re-Reading of *Watership Down*," *Signal,* 56 (May 1988): 113–122;

Christopher Pawling, "Rolling Back the 1960s," in *Popular Fiction and Social Change,* edited by Pawling (London: Macmillan, 1984), pp. 212–235;

Anne Swinfen, *In Defence of Fantasy: A Study of the Genre in English and American Literature Since 1945* (London: Routledge & Kegan Paul, 1984);

Jane Resh Thomas, "Old Worlds and New: Anti-Feminism in *Watership Down*," *Horn Book Magazine* (August 1974): 405–408;

Phillip Vine, "Richard Adams: A Personal View," *Words,* 1 (July 1985), pp. 14–18;

Watership Down: An Exhibition Catalogue to Celebrate the Tenth Anniversary of Publication (London: Henry Sotheran, 1982).

Mark Adlard

(19 June 1932 –   )

Rob Latham
University of Iowa

BOOKS: *Interface* (London: Sidgwick & Jackson, 1971; New York: Ace, 1977);
Volteface (London: Sidgwick & Jackson, 1972; New York: Ace, 1978);
Multiface (London: Sidgwick & Jackson, 1975; New York: Ace, 1978);
The Greenlander (London: Hamilton, 1978; New York: Summit, 1979).

OTHER: "The Other Tradition," in *Beyond this Horizon: An Anthology of Science Fact and Science Fiction,* edited by Christopher Carrel (Sunderland: Ceolfrith Press, 1973), pp. 9–12;
"Theophilus," in *Beyond this Horizon: An Anthology of Science Fact and Science Fiction,* edited by Carrel (Sunderland: Ceolfrith Press, 1973), pp. 26–28.

SELECTED PERIODICAL PUBLICATIONS– UNCOLLECTED: "Anything to Oblige," *London Mystery,* 19 (December 1968): 25–29;
"Ash Shadow," *Balthus,* 2 (1971): 22–29.

Mark Adlard (courtesy of the author)

Mark Adlard is one of the most curious science-fiction writers to emerge in Britain during the New Wave period. While his major themes—the dehumanizing effects of automation, the entropic decadence of untrammeled leisure, the plight (and blight) of urban life—echoed those of major New Wave writers such as J. G. Ballard and M. John Harrison, Adlard never published in *New Worlds* and, generally speaking, was never associated, either socially or by critical reputation, with the New Wave movement. Moreover, unlike the many New Wave writers who produced substantial bodies of work within the genre during the 1960s and 1970s before moving on to the writing of celebrated mainstream fiction in the 1980s (such as Ballard, Michael Moorcock, and Christopher Priest), Adlard wrote only the "Tcity trilogy" in the early 1970s—consisting of *Interface* (1971), *Volteface* (1972), and *Multiface* (1975)—and, at the end of the decade, brought out an obscure historical novel, *The Green-*
lander (1978), before lapsing into silence. Despite his odd and abbreviated career and the fact that his work has been subsequently neglected (none of his books are in print), Adlard remains important for his Tcity trilogy, one of the most wildly inventive and ferociously satirical depictions of future urbanism in the science-fiction canon.

Adlard was born Peter Marcus Adlard in Seaton Carew, Durham, England, on 19 June 1932, the son of Arthur Marcus Adlard and Ethel Leech Adlard. His father was an auctioneer, which perhaps influenced Adlard's eventual election of a career in sales; certainly his fiction displays a fascination for the hortatory rhetoric and occasionally combative interpersonal dynamics of salesmanship. Adlard attended Trinity College, Cambridge, receiving a B.A. in English in 1954, and the College of Education at Oxford, earning a Dip. Ed. (an advanced degree equivalent to a Master's) in 1955. While this background prepared Adlard for a future in teaching—and obviously instilled in him a love for literature and the arts, as reflected in the allusive erudition of his novels—he instead embarked, in 1956, on a twenty-year career as a sales manager in the British steel industry, working at various times in Middlesbrough, Yorkshire, Cardiff, and Kent and eventually earning an extramural B.Sc. in economics from the University of London. This background deeply informs the Tcity trilogy, with its sweeping vision of the evolution of heavy industry, its solid extrapolation of managerial science, and its corrosive satire of business life. Adlard retired in 1976 to pursue his writing career, which seems to have ended in 1979. He lives in Cleveland, England, with his wife, Sheila Rosemary (née Skuse), whom he married in 1968 and with whom he has two children, Vanessa and Robert.

The Tcity trilogy belongs to a hallowed tradition of British science fiction: the prophetic depiction of humanity's divergent social evolution (or devolution) into two broad classes under the escalating pressures of industrial civilization. The most renowned representative of this tradition is probably H. G. Wells's *The Time Machine* (1895). In Adlard's twenty-second century, industry has been so thoroughly mechanized and automated that the majority of people no longer work, instead subsisting on state annuities in vast enclosed arcologies (a term coined by utopian architect Paolo Soleri from "architecture" and "ecology"), while the world government and economy are overseen by a genetically engineered managerial elite. This class of Executives, as they are known, whose innate brainpower has been further amplified by surgical procedures, live easeful lives of artistic and alimentary connoisseurship in placid natural surroundings outside the city walls. The rest of the citizens, stupefied not only by mindless mass entertainment but also by drugs in the public water supply, occupy a hellishly crowded and aesthetically impoverished landscape of modular apartments and gray, endless corridors, their drably regimented existence intermittently enlivened by pub-crawling excursions and visits to the "aphrodollies" (prostitutes) of the First Sector, a sort of downtown. The narrative

events of the trilogy are localized in one such megalopolis, Tcity in Northumbria (possibly named for Teeside, the sprawling industrial sector of northeast England where Adlard grew up), but occasional exposition makes it clear that this dualistic geopolitical system spans the entire globe—save for some rare, protected pockets of pre-industrial husbandry, such as the vineyards that service the appetite of the elite citizens for fine wine.

Adlard's portrait of Tcity combines a broad perspective on its regulation and maintenance with minutely detailed depictions of its everyday culture in a narratively intricate interweaving—though it relies at times too much on coincidence—of the viewpoints of individual citizens and Executives. The three novels are linked predominately through their shared environment; only one character, Executive Jan Caspol, occupies a central role in all three. This focus on context as opposed to character is, in Adlard's view, the essential strength of science fiction, a form he has associated (in his rare interviews) with a centuries-long tradition of "speculative" writing—a visionary literature in which the basic characteristics are philosophic scope and an attention to vast social canvases. Adlard shares this view with many New Wave authors, notably Ballard. As if to illustrate this conviction, Adlard has framed his trilogy with networks of allusion to Richard Wagner's *Götterdämmerung* (1863) in the first volume, Dante's *Divine Comedy* (circa 1310–1314) in the second, and Buddhist theology in the third, although these references do not overburden his foreground stories. On the other hand, Adlard's relative slighting of characterization in favor of evocation of setting and adumbration of theme sometimes makes it difficult to keep track of his proliferating cast, whose members come to resemble one another at times. Given the stark social homogenization of his future, however, such blurring of identities is perhaps appropriate.

Interface focuses on the points of intersection between Executives and citizens, the rare social spaces where the two meet, and the sometimes incendiary class friction that results. The division between the two groups is symbolized by the Sector Gatehouses permitting access to Tcity. Executives, who live outside the city, may enter, but citizens cannot leave. In fact, so habituated are the majority of the latter to the impacted interiors of the city that wide vistas can stimulate agoraphobic vertigo. Another, even more literal, interface is the very substance of the towering city walls; like everything else in this future, the walls are made of stahlex, a synthetic material at once so durable and so ductile that it has replaced steel, plastic, glass, and cloth. The Executives who oversee Tcity are members of the Stahlex

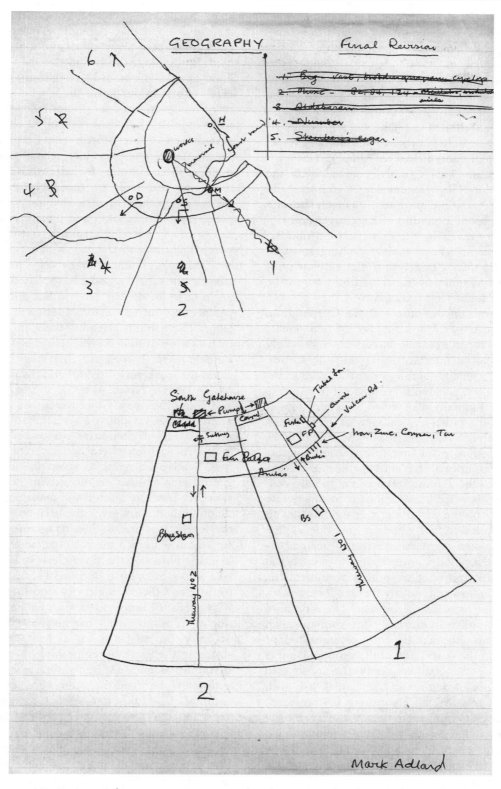

Adlard's sketch of Tcity, the setting for Interface *(1971),* Volteface *(1972), and* Multiface *(1975),
the trilogy that established his reputation as a New Wave writer (Collection of Mark Adlard)*

Corporation, a global monopoly that has both revolutionized material production and created these outsized urban prisons that now house an economically redundant population.

In theory, given the complete automation of Tcity's regulative processes via the "cybernet," the two classes need never meet, but in practice the elite's paternalistic commitment to public welfare, combined with their irrepressible penchant for slumming (especially in the red-light district of the First Sector), brings them into almost daily contact with the masses. The plot of *Interface* develops a conspiracy to overthrow the Stahlex Corporation beneath the day-to-day exchanges of a handful of Executives and citizens, eventually revealing the existence of an underground movement whose goal is nothing short of social revolution. In a cataclysmic climax worthy of the often-cited Wagner opera, the citizens storm the Gatehouses, slaughtering Executives as they go, and eventually march on the offices of the Corporation. Jan Caspol, who has fallen in love with a female member of this militia and has thus emotionally breached the social interface separating the classes, escapes with her in a monorail as disorder reigns.

Given this apocalyptic ending, it is unclear whether Adlard initially planned to write a trilogy. If so, then he held a rather cynical view of the potential fallout of underclass rebellion, for by the time of *Volteface,* some indefinite years later in his future, matters have returned to normal: Executives rule and citizens are oppressed. One abiding result of the bloody conflict, however, is a fresh commitment to ameliorate the people's lot on the part of the managerial elite (an attitudinal about-face suggested in the title of the novel). Their social-engineering projects include providing cultural uplift by introducing a pedagogical animus into the aphrodollies' otherwise more basic functions and, more ambitiously, reintroducing work as a structuring force in the citizens' lives. Because production is fully automated, this human-scaled employment can only take the form of unproductive make-work, but the superfluity of the people's labor is irrelevant since the goal is purely therapeutic: to inculcate a sense of dignity and self-worth lost with the decline of toil. As the Executives first research and then attempt to implement the archaic work environment of early industrialism, run by the outmoded philosophies of "scientific" management, Adlard presents a hilariously captious satire of twentieth-century capitalist society.

The employment the Executives devise is the organized sale of stahlex jewelry of varying designs, a labor-intensive project that draws hordes of eager volunteers for the many marketing positions thus created. In order to spark consumer demand and thereby introduce an element of uncertainty into the marketers' economic calculations, the Executives periodically rotate the visibility of the various trinkets in a popular tri-di (3-D television) program. The elite's efforts to puppeteer the newborn business venture, however, are not foolproof, for alongside a sense of pride, they also create in the citizens an unexpected frenzy of competitiveness and an invidious social stratification, a hierarchical snobbery that divides three former friends whose relationships make up the bulk of the foreground narrative. Adlard's depiction of their manipulative tactics and petty squabbling evokes and punctures the pomposities of modern business culture as well as mobilizes pointed allusions to Dante.

Multiface, while in many ways providing a capstone to the series, is also a less focused volume, offering a series of diverse (and rather dubiously linked) perspectives on the Tcity experiment in therapeutic labor. The tenuous thread of the story is the planned interviewing of four representative workers in one of the Sector warehouses—the chief stock clerk, the filing clerk, the marketing director, and the managing director—by Sylvia Nunn, the Chief Executive of Tcity and wife of the new Chief Executive of Stahlex Corporation, Jan Caspol, whose affair with the female revolutionary mysteriously evaporated, like the revolution itself, somewhere between volumes one and two. Sylvia's charge is to assess the moral effects of gainful employment on the citizens, and her conclusions are far from sunny: the managing director is a loudmouthed bully given to sharp business practices; the marketing director is a dangerous schizophrenic for whom work is a mere escape from memories of a hellish childhood; the filing clerk is a timid compulsive who prefers his collection of stolen doorknobs to his job; and the stock clerk is a posturing womanizer who needs the salary to support his pursuit of aphrodollies. Work, it seems, has not redeemed the people of Tcity, but so far it has at least kept them from storming the gates by enmeshing them in a web of trivial obsessions. Adlard's final viewpoint would appear to be fatalistic, embodied in Jan's ironic embrace of Buddhist detachment.

Though Adlard's initial critical reception was generally strong—including warm praise from Brian W. Aldiss, which suggests Adlard's relevance to New Wave concerns—his work has since fallen into an obscurity only deepened by the fact that he has not published a new book in more than two decades. Adlard remarked in interviews published during the 1970s that his post-Tcity fiction would cast its speculative gaze backward in time rather than forward, craft-

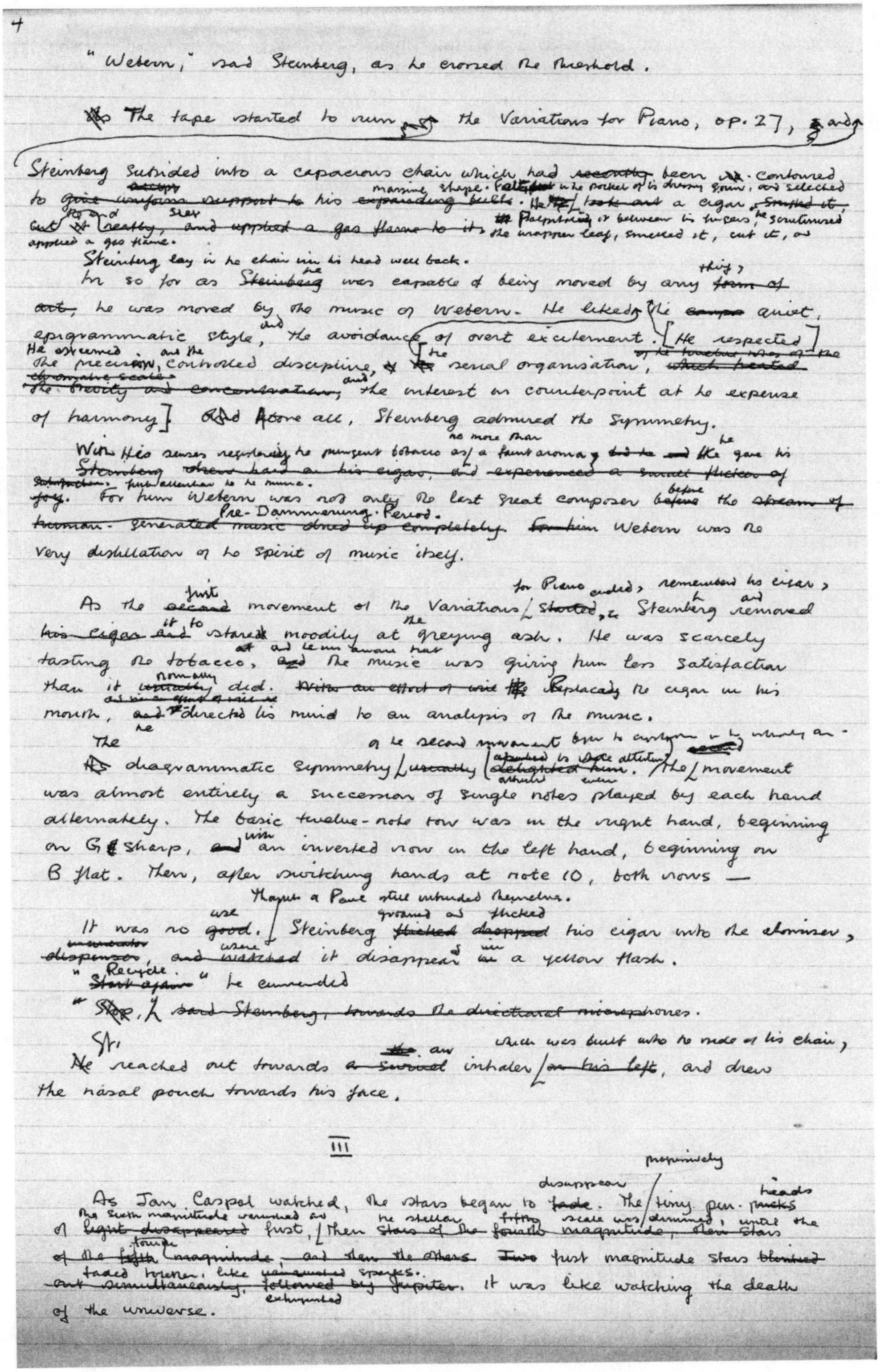

4

"Webern," said Steinberg, as he crossed the threshold.

The tape started to run the Variations for Piano, op. 27, and

Steinberg subsided into a capacious chair which had recently been contoured to give uniform support to his expanding bulk. He took out a cigar, and cut it neatly, and applied a gas flame to its end. He scrutinised it between his fingers, smelled it, cut it, and applied a gas flame.

Steinberg lay in the chair with his head well back.

In so far as Steinberg was capable of being moved by any form of art, he was moved by the music of Webern. He liked the quiet, epigrammatic style, and the avoidance of overt excitement. [He respected He esteemed the precision, controlled discipline, & the serial organisation, the brevity and concentration, and the interest in counterpoint at the expense of harmony.] And Above all, Steinberg admired the symmetry.

With His senses regularly the pungent tobacco as a faint aroma he gave his Steinberg drew on his cigar, and experienced a small flicker of joy. For him Webern was not only the last great composer before the Pre-Dämmerung Period. Webern was the very distillation of the spirit of music itself.

As the first movement of the Variations for Piano ended, remembered his cigar, Steinberg removed it to stared moodily at greying ash. He was scarcely tasting the tobacco, the music was giving him less satisfaction than it normally did. Replaced the cigar in his mouth, directed his mind to an analysis of the music.

The diagrammatic symmetry of the second movement The movement was almost entirely a succession of single notes played by each hand alternately. The basic twelve-note row was in the right hand, beginning on G sharp, with an inverted row in the left hand, beginning on B flat. Then, after switching hands at note 10, both rows still unwound themselves.

It was no good. Steinberg his cigar into the Recycle and watched it disappear in a yellow flash.

" " he commanded

" said Steinberg, towards the directional microphones.

He reached out towards an inhaler which was built into the side of his chair, and drew the nasal pouch towards his face.

iii

As Jan Caspol watched, the stars began to fade. The tiny pin-pricks of light disappeared first, then stars of the magnitude, until the stars faded like like It was like watching the death of the universe.

ing a matching trilogy set in the past. Presumably *The Greenlander,* a dense and affecting portrait of the arctic whaling industry of early-nineteenth-century Britain, was the first panel in that triptych, but its further installments have yet to materialize.

As far as British science fiction is concerned, Adlard's Tcity trilogy commands attention and respect as one of the most detailed extrapolations of urban industrial evolution in the literature, excelling most contemporary treatments of the theme and approaching classics such as Wells's *When the Sleeper Wakes* (1899) and Arthur C. Clarke's *The City and the Stars* (1956), not to mention prefiguring later redactions, for example Ian McDonald's *Out on Blue Six* (1989). It deserves to be remembered less for its characters and the specifics of its plot than for its sweeping historical vision and its grim insight into the textures of an urban wasteland—the narrowing horizons of endless sidewalks, "where the pedestrians struggled together like drowning men," often trampling one another to death in their insensate frenzies, and of automated pavelines (moving sidewalks), "on which the people drifted to and fro with unfocused eyes, like the shadows of figures in a nightmare."

Despite the author's frequently arch and flippant tone, the predominant mood of his trilogy is authentically nightmarish, a disturbing evocation of an ugly, vacuous future peopled by creatures both more and less than human, both effete and brutal, cybernetically enhanced and morally bankrupt. With its gritty vision of high-tech squalor, corporate chicanery, and mass political impotence, Adlard's trilogy occupies a liminal literary terrain, mediating between the dystopian "comic infernos" of the 1950s—especially that immortal satire of hypertrophied capitalism, *The Space Merchants* (1953), by Americans Frederik Pohl and C. M. Kornbluth—and the British New Wave, and between the latter and 1980s American cyberpunk.

Interviews:

Iain Carson, "When Work Will Have to Be Invented," *International Management,* 28 (May 1973): 54–56;

Mike Ashley and Geoff Rippington, "Mark Adlard Interviewed," *Arena,* 7 (March 1978): 9–12.

Reference:

Andrew Darlington, "The Many Faces of Adlard," *Arena,* 7 (March 1978): 12–15.

Robert Aickman

(27 June 1914 – 26 February 1981)

Gary William Crawford

BOOKS: *We Are for the Dark: Six Ghost Stories,* by Aickman and Elizabeth Jane Howard (London: Cape, 1951);

Know Your Waterways (London: Coram, 1955);

The Story of Our Inland Waterways (London: Pitman, 1955; revised edition, Norwich, U.K.: G. Dibb, 1967);

The Late Breakfasters (London: Gollancz, 1964);

Dark Entries (London: Collins, 1964);

The Attempted Rescue (London: Gollancz, 1966);

Powers of Darkness (London: Collins, 1966);

Sub Rosa (London: Gollancz, 1968);

Cold Hand in Mine: Eight Strange Stories (London: Gollancz, 1975; New York: Scribners, 1977);

Tales of Love and Death (London: Gollancz, 1977);

Painted Devils: Strange Stories (New York: Scribners, 1979);

Intrusions: Strange Tales (London: Gollancz, 1980);

Night Voices: Strange Stories (London: Gollancz, 1985);

The River Runs Uphill: A Story of Success and Failure (Burton-on-Trent, U.K.: J. M. Pearson, 1986);

The Model (New York: Arbor House, 1987; London: Robinson, 1988);

The Wine-Dark Sea (New York: Arbor House, 1988; London: Mandarin, 1990);

The Unsettled Dust (London: Mandarin, 1990).

Collection: *The Collected Strange Stories,* 2 volumes (Horam, U.K.: Tartarus Press / Durtro Press, 1999).

OTHER: *The Fontana Book of Great Ghost Stories,* edited by Aickman (London: Collins, 1964; New York: Beagle Books, 1971);

The Second Fontana Book of Great Ghost Stories, edited by Aickman (London: Collins, 1966);

The Third Fontana Book of Great Ghost Stories, edited by Aickman (London: Collins, 1967);

The Fourth Fontana Book of Great Ghost Stories, edited by Aickman (London: Collins, 1968);

The Fifth Fontana Book of Great Ghost Stories, edited by Aickman (London: Collins, 1969);

The Sixth Fontana Book of Great Ghost Stories, edited by Aickman (London: Collins, 1970);

The Seventh Fontana Book of Great Ghost Stories, edited by Aickman (London: Collins, 1971);

The Eighth Fontana Book of Great Ghost Stories, edited by Aickman (London: Collins, 1972);

"An Essay," in *First World Fantasy Awards,* edited by Gahan Wilson (Garden City, N.Y.: Doubleday, 1977), pp. 63–65.

Although Robert Aickman's reputation during his lifetime was small, he is posthumously gaining critical approval as a contemporary master of the English ghost story. He is widely recognized as "the last great master" of the English ghost story, which stems from the groundbreaking fiction of J. Sheridan Le Fanu in the nineteenth century and was carried on by Arthur Machen, M. R. James, and Algernon Blackwood into the twentieth.

The son of William Arthur and Mabel Violet Aickman, Robert Fordyce Aickman was born in London on 27 June 1914. The family later moved to Stanmore, outside London, where they lived in his father's home at Langton Lodge. William Aickman was fifty-three when he married Robert's mother, who was twenty-three. As Aickman later wrote in his autobiography *The Attempted Rescue* (1966), "My father, as I knew him, was impossible to live with, to be married to, to be dependent upon." There were many arguments between his father and mother, and Robert was terrified of his father. On his mother's side, Robert was the grandson of Bernard Heldmann, who wrote under the pseudonym Richard Marsh and is best known for his supernatural novel *The Beetle* (1897).

Robert Aickman was educated at Highgate School and thought of attending Oxford but declined to do so because it would have been too expensive for his father. His father, an architect, was of a generation that was losing its position in upper-class British society. During the years after Robert graduated from Highgate, his father made less money from his archi-

Robert Aickman

tectural work, and his mother spent time in an expensive nursing home for treatment of arthritis. Robert Aickman continued to live at home and helped his father in his business until eventually his father went to a nursing home. At the beginning of World War II Robert married Edith Ray Gregorson. His father died in 1941 at the age of eighty-three, leaving his son a small income, and his mother was killed by a German bomb during the war.

Robert and Edith Aickman set up a literary agency, and in 1946 Robert and L. T. C. Rolt founded the Inland Waterways Association, a privately funded organization to improve British waterways, which dominated a large part of Aickman's life. In this cause, Aickman found a means through which he could fight to restore something of beauty and quality to life. However, in his personal relationships, Aickman met with difficulties. He and Rolt had a falling out, which led to Rolt's resignation from the waterways association. In the early 1950s Aickman had an affair with Elizabeth Jane Howard, which was not hidden from his wife. The

Aickmans were divorced in the late 1950s after Edith had a religious experience. She eventually entered an Anglican nunnery, The College of All Saints, Oxford, and led a secluded life as Sister Benedicta.

During the late 1940s Aickman wrote drama reviews for *The Nineteenth Century and After* and movie reviews for *The Jewish Monthly*. He also developed a keen interest in the supernatural, and in 1951 three of his stories in this genre were published with three by Howard as *We Are for the Dark*. One of Aickman's best-known tales, "The Trains," leads the volume.

All Aickman's stories are unified by a coherent structure, and, as in a poem, they have an inner tension created by symbol and metaphor. Supernatural possibilities, if not actualities, grow naturally from character development. Rarely did Aickman write about a traditional ghost, werewolf, or vampire. Instead, he evoked an uncanny realm of implicit terror, violence, and death that is counterpoised by human love. Even in his darkest fictions, Aickman believed that humanity can achieve insight into its infections of the soul, though frequently such insight requires willful entrance into those realms. As Aickman said in his introduction to *The Seventh Fontana Book of Great Ghost Stories* (1971), the supernatural tale is "allied to poetry."

"The Trains" concerns two girls on a hiking trip who find refuge at a country house near a railroad line. The constant passing of the trains symbolizes the confused mental states of the girls. The world of the country house, with its lonely master and the strange woman who may or may not be a ghost, is unstable and terrifying. The girls who enter this realm are faced with an uncanny series of events that have no rational explanation. Nothing in the story is resolved in a logical way, as in a dream.

Another tale in *We Are for the Dark*, "The View," is about Carfax, a middle-aged bachelor recovering from a long illness. He travels to an island in the Irish Sea, where he visits a mansion owned by a mysterious and beautiful woman who has no name. Carfax, a painter, names her Ariel, and while staying in her home, he attempts to paint a landscape that continually changes, just as Carfax himself changes. This story depicts the illusory and highly subjective nature of time, a theme to which Aickman returned in a much later tale, "No Time Is Passing" (1980).

More than a decade passed before Aickman's next volume of fiction was published. When he stepped down as the chairman of the Inland Waterways Association in 1964, he turned to writing in earnest, though he continued to work throughout his life on behalf of British waterways. He also served as director and chairman of the London Opera Society (1954–1969) and chairman of an opera company, Balmin Productions (1963–1968).

The Late Breakfasters (1964), a humorous—and at times surreal—novel of lesbianism, includes many of Aickman's preoccupations. Griselda De Reptonville, the central character, falls in love with a maid at a country house where Griselda is a guest for a political rally. After they are separated, Griselda feels a loss that cannot be replaced by a husband, and her love is frustrated. The novel ends on a sad and mystical note as Griselda stays at the fantastic country home of a viscount. Aickman wrote in the second volume of his autobiography, *The River Runs Uphill* (1986), that this novel is all a reader needs to know about him, and *The Late Breakfasters* may, indeed, be seen as a window into his other works. Aickman said he wrote some of his stories in mild hypnotic trances, and his work—as his friend and literary executor, Felice Pearson, has remarked—is more European than English, similar to some modern French writing, especially Surrealism.

In the same year his first novel appeared, Aickman published another volume of stories, *Dark Entries*.

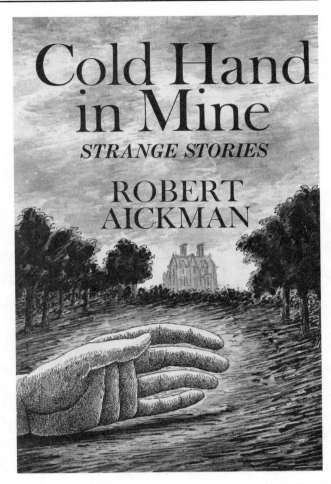

Dust jacket for the first collection of Aickman's fiction published in the United States; it includes "Pages from a Young Girl's Journal," which won a World Fantasy Award in 1975 (Richland County Public Library).

One of the tales in this volume, "Ringing the Changes," is a story of love and death. On their honeymoon, a newly married couple visits a quiet seaside town, where—to their growing horror—the church bells ring continuously. The town seems strangely backward, and they finally discover that the bells are ringing to wake the dead. At the end of the story the dead come out of their graves, and the couple experiences utter terror. Thus, marriage is linked with death.

Many of Aickman's stories are about the relationships between men and women. The protagonist of another such story in *Dark Entries*, "Choice of Weapons," is a young architecture student, Malcolm Fenville, who falls in love at first sight with Dorabelle, who lives alone in the house of her dead parents. Dorabelle leads Malcolm on but later reveals that she is in love with and will marry an eighteenth-century gentleman she has met in a supernatural mirror in her room. Meanwhile, Malcolm comes under the influence of the mysterious Dr.

Dust jacket for Aickman's posthumously published novel, about a ballerina in czarist Russia (Richland County Public Library)

Bermuda, who says that he will cure Malcolm of love. Eventually, Malcolm encounters Dorabelle's eighteenth-century fiancé in her house, and the two men fight a duel with rapiers. Then Bermuda arrives and says that he has failed to cure Malcolm of love. The story ends on an ambiguous note as Bermuda extracts some unseen and unnamed object from the supernatural mirror in Dorabelle's room. As in earlier tales, such as "The Train," nothing in "Choice of Weapons" is resolved in a logical way. In keeping with the fable mode of the story, Dorabelle, a supernatural creature endowed with beauty and mystery, is a symbol for love existing in a realm outside time. When Malcolm kills Dorabelle, Dr. Bermuda, a doctor of the soul, functions like Charon, the boatman in Hades, carrying Malcolm to the other side of the River Styx to the endless night of the unconscious.

In another story in *Dark Entries,* "Bind Your Hair," a supernatural rapport develops between a bride-to-be and the leader of a mysterious cult. When Clarinda visits her fiancé's family in the country, she feels an outsider with them, and on a foggy night she ventures out into the countryside to the home of Mrs. Pagani, where she witnesses a strange and utterly inexplicable ritual that symbolizes her unconscious fear about her impending marriage.

In *Powers of Darkness* (1966) the markedly uncanny story "Larger Than Oneself" deals with some supreme being, or at least a power, that moves the characters' lives. (Aickman practiced no religion.) Expressing some sort of universal meaning, the tale is about an unexplained religious group at a strange party that ends when all the quiet revelers are awed by an unnamed light from outside the building. Other stories in *Powers of Darkness* also deal with inexplicable events that have no rational explanations. In "My Poor Friend," a member of Parliament is unmercifully haunted by an almost supernatural wife and equally strange children.

In "The Inner Room," collected in *Sub Rosa* (1968), a woman narrates the story of an incident from her early childhood in a struggling family that later splits apart. She receives as a birthday gift an enormous dollhouse that contains a mysteriously inaccessible inner room. Later in life, she visits what is apparently the actual house on which the dollhouse was modeled and comes close to discovering a nameless horror in the inner room, which signifies the hidden life of dream—or rather dream as reality, which creates emotional peril when repressed.

In "The Swords," collected in *Cold Hand in Mine* (1975), Aickman returned to the theme of the mysterious woman linked with love and death. A young man has his first sexual encounter with a woman who performs in a traveling fair, allowing men to pass swords through her body. When her manager lets the young man use the woman as a prostitute, her arm comes off—as if she is nothing more than a dummy—while the young man makes love to her. In another strange tale in *Cold Hand in Mine,* "Meeting Mr. Millar," a young writer of pornography becomes obsessed with a businessman, Mr. Millar, who has offices in the same building where the writer lives. The young man sees and hears strange and inexplicable things before he finally discovers Millar's dead body in the deserted office. No explanation for his death is ever offered. *Cold Hand in Mine* also includes one of Aickman's few traditional ghost or vampire stories. "Pages from a Young Girl's Journal," a vampire story set in the late eighteenth century, won Aickman a World Fantasy Award in 1975. *Cold Hand in Mine* was the first Aickman collection to be published in the United States.

Tales of Love and Death (1977) includes the humorous story "Growing Boys," about a married couple whose two young sons grow to an enormous size and cause physical havoc to their parents and the town in which they live. The collection also includes "Residents Only," a strange story about a derelict graveyard, and "Marriage," about a man who courts two women, one dark and mysterious, the other blonde and open in her favors. He cannot decide between the two women and ends up in bed with his mother, whom he loves even more than either of the women he has been courting.

Painted Devils, published in the United States in 1979, comprises revised versions of earlier stories. *Intrusions* (1980) includes well-crafted fables such as "The Fetch," a story in the manner of Edgar Allan Poe about a man losing his grip on reality, and "The Breakthrough," about a mysterious and horrifying being that is released in a desecrated church, an event that marks the death of the rector.

In 1979 Aickman developed a form of cancer. He recovered for a time and then his condition worsened. Under the care of a homeopathic physician, he went into the hospital for a blood transfusion, after which he developed an infection and died on 26 February 1981. A portrait plaque of Aickman, sculpted posthumously by Faith Tolkien, was affixed to a monument beside the Robert Aickman Memorial Lock at Harvington.

A collection of Aickman's last stories, *Night Voices,* posthumously published in 1985, includes the memorable horror tale "The Stains," about a man who encounters mysterious stains that spread and multiply like cancer. Also posthumously published, *The Model* (1987), a novel about a ballerina in czarist Russia, is one of Aickman's best fantasies.

Not ghost stories in the purest sense, Robert Aickman's tales offer a worldview so strange and inexplicable that S. T. Joshi, who has written a highly critical assessment of Aickman's work, considers Aickman's ideas about ghost stories to be flawed and finds his stories to be generally unintelligible. Yet, such criticism may be answered by Aickman himself, who quoted Sachaverell Sitwell: "In the end it is the mystery that lasts and not the explanation." Indeed, some scholars believe that Aickman may one day be regarded as a major writer of supernatural horror fiction. As Jack Sullivan has written in his introduction to some of Aickman's stories in the anthology *Lost Souls* (1983), "With its exquisitely shaded ambiguities, precisely tuned diction, and bell-like musicality, Aickman's work is consummately 'poetic,' a triumphant rejoinder to the notion that the ghost story as an art is dead." One test of a great ghost-story writer in the twentieth century is the frequency with which his works are reprinted in anthologies. Since Aickman's death, the appearance of his stories in such collections has been increasing, and more and more critics and scholars have been discovering why Fritz Leiber, as quoted on the dust jacket of the American edition of *Cold Hand in Mine* (1977), called Aickman "the weatherman of the unconscious."

Bibliographies:

Gary William Crawford, "Robert Aickman: A Preliminary Checklist," *Nyctalops,* no. 18 (1983): 53–55;

Crawford, "Robert Aickman: A Bibliography," *Fantasy Commentator,* no. 50 (Fall 1997): 143–148.

Biography:

Gary William Crawford, "Robert Aickman: Notes for a Biography," *Fantasy Commentator,* 5, no. 4 (1986): 225–227, 257.

References:

Mike Ashley, "The Strange World of Robert Aickman: A Retrospective," *Horrorstruck,* 2, no. 2 (1988): 33–36;

David Bolton, *Race Against Time: How Britain's Waterways Were Saved* (London: Methuen, 1990);

Scott D. Briggs, "Robert Aickman: Sojourns into the Unknown," *Studies in Weird Fiction,* no. 12 (1993): 7–12;

Gary William Crawford, "The Poetics of the Unconscious: The 'Strange Stories' of Robert Aickman," in *Discovering Modern Horror Fiction II,* edited by Darrell Schweitzer (Mercer Island, Wash.: Starmont House, 1988), pp. 43–50;

S. T. Joshi, "Robert Aickman: 'So Little Is Definite,'" in his *The Modern Weird Tale* (Jefferson, N.C.: McFarland, 2001), pp. 217–233;

Christine Pasanen Morris, "The Female 'Outsider' in the Short Fiction of Robert Aickman," *Nyctalops,* no. 18 (1983): 55–58;

Jack Sullivan, ed., *Lost Souls: A Collection of English Ghost Stories* (Athens: Ohio University Press, 1983), pp. 373–392.

Papers:

The most extensive collection of Robert Aickman's manuscripts and letters, as well as his personal library, is in the Rare Books Division of the Center for Archival Collections, Jerome Library, Bowling Green State University.

Brian W. Aldiss

(18 August 1925 –   )

Willis E. McNelly
California State University–Fullerton

See also the Aldiss entry in *DLB 14: British Novelists Since 1960.*

BOOKS: *The Brightfount Diaries* (London: Faber & Faber, 1955);

Space, Time, and Nathaniel (Presciences) (London: Faber & Faber, 1957); revised as *No Time Like Tomorrow* (New York: New American Library, 1959);

Non-Stop (London: Faber & Faber, 1958); abridged and revised as *Starship* (New York: Criterion, 1959);

Equator (London: Brown, Watson, 1958); republished as *Vanguard from Alpha,* together with *The Changeling Worlds* by Kenneth Bulmer (New York: Ace, 1959);

The Canopy of Time (London: Faber & Faber, 1959); revised as *Galaxies Like Grains of Sand* (New York: New American Library, 1960; expanded and revised edition, London: Panther, 1979);

Bow Down to Nul, [bound with *The Dark Destroyers,* by Manly Wade Wellman] (New York: Ace, 1960); revised as *The Interpreter* (London: Nova, 1960);

The Male Response (New York: Beacon, 1961; London: Dobson, 1963);

The Primal Urge (New York: Ballantine, 1961; London: Sphere, 1967);

Hothouse: A Science-Fiction Novel (London: Faber & Faber, 1962); abridged as *The Long Afternoon of Earth* (New York: New American Library, 1962);

The Airs of Earth: Science Fiction Stories (London: Faber & Faber, 1963); revised as *Starswarm* (New York: New American Library, 1964; London: Panther, 1979);

The Dark Light Years: A Science-Fiction Novel (London: Faber & Faber, 1964; New York: New American Library, 1964);

Greybeard (New York: Harcourt, Brace & World, 1964; revised edition, London: Faber & Faber, 1964);

Earthworks: A Science-Fiction Novel (London: Faber & Faber, 1965; revised edition, Garden City, N.Y.: Doubleday, 1966);

Brian W. Aldiss (photograph © Studio Edmark)

Cities and Stones: A Traveller's Jugoslavia (London: Faber & Faber, 1966);

The Saliva Tree and Other Strange Growths (London: Faber & Faber, 1966; Boston: Gregg Press, 1981);

An Age (London: Faber & Faber, 1967); republished as *Cryptozoic!* (Garden City, N.Y.: Doubleday, 1968);

Report on Probability A (London: Faber & Faber, 1968; Garden City, N.Y.: Doubleday, 1969);

Barefoot in the Head: A European Fantasia (London: Faber & Faber, 1969; Garden City, N.Y.: Doubleday, 1970);

Intangibles Inc. and Other Stories: Five Novellas (London: Faber & Faber, 1969); revised as *Neanderthal Planet* (New York: Avon, 1969);

The Hand-Reared Boy (London: Weidenfeld & Nicolson, 1970; New York: McCall, 1970);

The Shape of Further Things: Speculations on Change (London: Faber & Faber, 1970; Garden City, N.Y.: Doubleday, 1971);

The Moment of Eclipse (London: Faber & Faber, 1970; Garden City, N.Y.: Doubleday, 1972);

A Soldier Erect; or, Further Adventures of the Hand-Reared Boy (London: Weidenfeld & Nicolson, 1971; New York: Coward, McCann & Geoghegan, 1971);

The Book of Brian Aldiss (New York: DAW, 1972); republished as *Comic Inferno* (London: New English Library, 1973);

Billion Year Spree: The History of Science Fiction (London: Weidenfeld & Nicolson, 1973; Garden City, N.Y.: Doubleday, 1973); revised and expanded with David Wingrove as *Trillion Year Spree: The History of Science Fiction* (London: Gollancz, 1986; New York: Atheneum, 1986; revised edition, London: Stratus, 2001);

Frankenstein Unbound (London: Cape, 1973; New York: Random House, 1974);

The Eighty-Minute Hour: A Space Opera (London: Cape, 1974; Garden City, N.Y.: Doubleday, 1974);

Science Fiction Art (London: New English Library, 1975; New York: Bounty, 1975);

The Malacia Tapestry (London: Cape, 1976; New York: Harper & Row, 1977);

Brothers of the Head (London & New York: Pierrot, 1977);

Last Orders and Other Stories (London: Cape, 1977; New York: Carroll & Graf, 1989);

Science Fiction as Science Fiction (Frome, U.K.: Bran's Head, 1978);

Enemies of the System: A Tale of Homo Uniformis (London: Cape, 1978; New York: Harper & Row, 1978);

A Rude Awakening (London: Weidenfeld & Nicolson, 1978; New York: Random House, 1979);

New Arrivals, Old Encounters: Twelve Stories (London: Cape, 1979; New York: Harper & Row, 1979);

This World and Nearer Ones: Essays Exploring the Familiar (London: Weidenfeld & Nicolson, 1979; Kent, Ohio: Kent State University Press, 1981);

Pile: Petals from St. Klaed's Computer (London: Cape, 1979; New York: Holt, Rinehart & Winston, 1979);

Moreau's Other Island (London: Cape, 1980); republished as *An Island Called Moreau* (New York: Simon & Schuster, 1981); revised and republished as *Moreau's Other Island* (London: Stratus, 2001);

Life in the West (London: Weidenfeld & Nicolson, 1980; New York: Carroll & Graf, 1990);

Foreign Bodies: Stories (Singapore: Chopmen, 1981);

Farewell to a Child (Berkhamsted, U.K.: Priapus Poets, 1982);

Helliconia Spring (London: Cape, 1982; New York: Atheneum, 1982);

Helliconia Summer (London: Cape, 1983; New York: Atheneum, 1983);

Science Fiction Quiz (London: Weidenfeld & Nicolson, 1983);

Seasons in Flight (London: Cape, 1984; New York: Atheneum, 1986);

Helliconia Winter (London: Cape, 1985; New York: Atheneum, 1985);

The Pale Shadow of Science (Seattle: Serconia, 1985);

—And the Lurid Glare of the Comet (Seattle: Serconia, 1986);

The Year Before Yesterday: A Novel in Three Acts (New York: Franklin Watts, 1987); revised as *Cracken at Critical: A Novel in Three Acts* (Worcester Park, Surrey, U.K.: Kerosina, 1987);

Ruins (London: Hutchinson, 1987);

The Magic of the Past (Worcester Park, U.K.: Kerosina, 1987);

Forgotten Life (London: Gollancz, 1988; New York: Atheneum, 1989);

Best SF Stories of Brian W. Aldiss (London: Gollancz, 1988); republished as *Man in His Time: The Best Science Fiction Stories of Brian W. Aldiss* (New York: Atheneum, 1989);

Science Fiction Blues: The Show That Brian Aldiss Took on the Road, edited by Frank Hatherley (London: Avernus, 1988);

A Romance of the Equator: The Best Fantasy Stories of Brian W. Aldiss (London: Gollancz, 1989; New York: Atheneum, 1990);

Bury My Heart at W. H. Smith's: A Writing Life (London: Hodder & Stoughton, 1990; expanded edition, London: Avernus, 1991);

Bodily Functions (London: Avernus, 1991);

Dracula Unbound (New York: HarperCollins, 1991; London: Grafton, 1991);

Home Life with Cats (London: Grafton, 1992);

Kindred Blood in Kensington Gore: Philip K. Dick in the Afterlife, an Imaginary Conversation (London: Avernus, 1992);

Remembrance Day (London: HarperCollins, 1993; New York: St. Martin's Press, 1993);

A Tupolev Too Far: And Other Stories (London: HarperCollins, 1993; New York: St. Martin's Press, 1994);

Somewhere East of Life: Another European Fantasia (London: Flamingo, 1994; New York: Carroll & Graf, 1994);

The Detached Retina: Aspects of SF and Fantasy (Liverpool: Liverpool University Press, 1995; Syracuse, N.Y.: Syracuse University Press, 1995);

At the Caligula Hotel and Other Poems (London: Sinclair-Stevenson, 1995);

The Secret of This Book: 20 Odd Stories (London: Harper-Collins, 1995); republished as *Common Clay: 20 Odd Stories* (New York: St. Martin's Press, 1996);

The Twinkling of an Eye: My Life as an Englishman (London: Little, Brown, 1998; New York: St. Martin's Press, 1999);

When the Feast Is Finished: Reflections on Terminal Illness, by Aldiss and Margaret Aldiss (London: Little, Brown, 1999);

White Mars; or, The Mind Set Free: A 21st Century Utopia, by Aldiss and Roger Penrose (London: Little, Brown, 1999; New York: St. Martin's Press, 2000);

A Plutonian Monologue on His Wife's Death (Folkestone, U.K.: Frogmore Press, 2000);

Supertoys Last All Summer Long, and Other Stories of Future Time (London: Orbit, 2001; New York: St. Martin's Press, 2001);

Cretan Teat (Thirsk, U.K.: Stratus, 2002);

Super-State: A Novel of a Future Europe (London: Orbit, 2002).

Editions and Collections: *Best Science Fiction Stories of Brian W. Aldiss* (London: Faber & Faber, 1965); republished as *Who Can Replace a Man? The Best Science-Fiction Stories of Brian W. Aldiss* (New York: Harcourt, Brace & World, 1966); revised as *Best Science Fiction Stories of Brian W. Aldiss* (London: Faber & Faber, 1971);

A Brian Aldiss Omnibus (London: Sidgwick & Jackson, 1969)—includes *The Interpreter, The Primal Urge,* "The Saliva Tree," "The Impossible Star," "Basis for Negotiation," and "Man in His Time";

Brian Aldiss Omnibus 2 (London: Sidgwick & Jackson, 1971)—includes *Space, Time, and Nathaniel; Non-Stop;* and *The Male Response;*

Brothers of the Head; and, Where the Lines Converge (London: Panther, 1979);

The Horatio Stubbs Saga (London: Panther, 1985)—comprises *The Hand-Reared Boy, A Soldier Erect,* and *A Rude Awakening.*

PRODUCED SCRIPT: *Frankenstein Unbound,* BBC Radio, 10–11 July 1974.

OTHER: *Penguin Science Fiction,* edited by Aldiss (Harmondsworth, U.K.: Penguin, 1961);

More Penguin Science Fiction: An Anthology, edited by Aldiss (Harmondsworth, U.K.: Penguin, 1962);

Best Fantasy Stories, edited by Aldiss (London: Faber & Faber, 1962);

Yet More Penguin Science Fiction, edited by Aldiss (Harmondsworth, U.K.: Penguin, 1964);

Introducing Science Fiction: A Science Fiction Anthology, edited by Aldiss (London: Faber & Faber, 1964);

Science Fiction Horizons 1, edited by Aldiss and Harry Harrison (New York: Arno, 1964);

Science Fiction Horizons 2, edited by Aldiss and Harrison (New York: Arno, 1965); both republished as *SF Horizons,* edited by Aldiss and Harrison (New York: Arno, 1975);

Charles L. Harness, *The Paradox Men,* introduction by Aldiss (London: New English Library, 1967);

Nebula Award Stories II, edited by Aldiss and Harrison (Garden City, N.Y.: Doubleday, 1967);

Farewell, Fantastic Venus! A History of the Planet Venus in Fact and Fiction, edited by Aldiss and Harrison (London: Macdonald, 1968); abridged as *All About Venus: A Revelation of the Planet Venus in Fact and Fiction* (New York: Dell, 1968);

Best Science Fiction: 1967, edited by Aldiss and Harrison (New York: Berkley, 1968); republished as *The Year's Best Science Fiction 1* (London: Sphere, 1968);

Best Science Fiction: 1968, edited by Aldiss and Harrison (New York: Putnam, 1969); abridged as *The Year's Best Science Fiction 2* (London: Sphere, 1969);

Best Science Fiction: 1969, edited by Aldiss and Harrison (New York: Putnam, 1970); republished as *The Year's Best Science Fiction 3* (London: Sphere, 1970);

Best Science Fiction: 1970, edited by Aldiss and Harrison (New York: Putnam, 1971); republished as *The Year's Best Science Fiction 4* (London: Sphere, 1971);

Best Science Fiction: 1971, edited by Aldiss and Harrison (New York: Putnam, 1972); republished as *The Year's Best Science Fiction 5* (London: Sphere, 1972);

The Astounding-Analog Reader, 2 volumes, edited by Aldiss and Harrison (Garden City, N.Y.: Doubleday, 1972, 1973); volume 1 republished in 2 volumes as *The Astounding-Analog Reader* (London, 1973);

Best Science Fiction: 1972, edited by Aldiss and Harrison (New York: Putnam, 1973); republished as *The Year's Best Science Fiction 6* (London: Sphere, 1973);

Penguin Science Fiction Omnibus: An Anthology, edited by Aldiss (Harmondsworth, U.K.: Penguin, 1973);

Space Opera: An Anthology of Way-Back-When Futures, edited by Aldiss (London: Futura, 1974; Garden City, N.Y.: Doubleday, 1975);

Best Science Fiction: 1973, edited by Aldiss and Harrison (New York: Putnam, 1974); abridged as *The Year's Best Science Fiction 7* (London: Sphere, 1974);

Space Odysseys: A New Look at Yesterday's Futures, edited by Aldiss (London: Futura, 1974; Garden City, N.Y.: Doubleday, 1976);

Best Science Fiction: 1974, edited by Aldiss and Harrison (New York: Putnam, 1975); abridged as *The Year's Best Science Fiction 8* (London: Sphere, 1975);

Hell's Cartographers: Some Personal Histories of Science Fiction Writers, edited by Aldiss and Harrison (London: Weidenfeld & Nicolson, 1975; New York: Harper & Row, 1975)—includes Aldiss's "Magic and Bare Boards";

Evil Earths, edited by Aldiss (London: Weidenfeld & Nicolson, 1975; New York: Avon, 1979);

Decade: The 1940s, edited by Aldiss and Harrison (London: Macmillan, 1975; New York: St. Martin's Press, 1978);

Best Science Fiction: 1975, edited by Aldiss and Harrison (Indianapolis & New York: Bobbs-Merrill, 1976); republished as *The Year's Best Science Fiction 9* (London: Sphere, 1976);

Galactic Empires, 2 volumes, edited by Aldiss (London: Weidenfeld & Nicolson, 1976; New York: St. Martin's Press, 1977);

Decade: The 1950s, edited by Aldiss and Harrison (London: Macmillan, 1976; New York: St. Martin's Press, 1978);

Decade: The 1960s, edited by Aldiss and Harrison (London: Macmillan, 1977);

Perilous Planets, edited by Aldiss (London: Weidenfeld & Nicolson, 1978; New York: Avon, 1980);

"A Monster for All Seasons," in *Science Fiction Dialogues,* edited by Gary Wolfe (Chicago: Academy Chicago, 1982), pp. 9–23;

The Book of Mini-Sagas I, edited by Aldiss (Gloucester, U.K.: Sutton, 1985);

The Penguin World Omnibus of Science Fiction, edited by Aldiss and Sam J. Lundwall (Harmondsworth, U.K.: Penguin, 1986);

The Book of Mini-Sagas II, edited by Aldiss (Gloucester, U.K.: Sutton, 1988);

H. G. Wells, *The Island of Doctor Moreau,* afterword by Aldiss (New York: New American Library, 1988);

"Living in Catastrophe," in *Doris Lessing: Conversations,* edited by Earl G. Ingersoll (Princeton: Ontario Review Press, 1994), pp. 169–172;

Robert Crossley, *Olaf Stapledon: Speaking for the Future,* foreword by Aldiss (Syracuse, N.Y.: Syracuse University Press, 1994);

Wells, *The War of the Worlds,* edited by David Y. Hughes, introduction by Aldiss (New York: Oxford University Press, 1995), pp. xv–xxxvi;

"The Eye-Opener," in *The Best of Interzone,* edited by David Pringle (New York: St. Martin's Press, 1997), pp. 329–341;

Mini Sagas from the Daily Telegraph Competition, edited by Aldiss (London: Sutton, 1997);

Mini Sagas from the Daily Telegraph Competition 1999, edited by Aldiss (Stroud: Sutton, 1999);

Mini Sagas from the Daily Telegraph Competition 2001, edited by Aldiss (London: Enitharmon, 2001).

SELECTED PERIODICAL PUBLICATIONS–UNCOLLECTED: "Remembrance of Lives Past," *Science-Fiction Studies,* 21 (Summer 1994): 129–133;

"Kepler's Error: The Polar Bear Theory of Plurispresence," *Science-Fiction Studies,* 23 (Spring 1996): 1–10;

"The Referee of the War of the Worlds," *New York Review of Science Fiction,* 123 (November 1998): 1, 4–6.

Brian W. Aldiss has led a long, successful life as author, critic, bon vivant, world traveler, and raconteur. He has also, by his own example, been a key figure in leading science fiction out of its ghetto and transforming it into a serious literary genre. Aldiss is something of an anomaly, at least by British standards: a man who enjoyed a good public school education but had no "Oxbridge" university degree, is immensely learned—a writer who, despite these alleged handicaps, has won approval from vastly diverse audiences. He has won all of the highest awards in science fiction: the Nebula, voted on by his peers in the organization Science Fiction and Fantasy Writers of America; the Hugo, awarded by science-fiction fans during the annual WorldCon; and the John W. Campbell Award for the "Best Science Fiction Novel of the Year," awarded by a select group of scholars and critics. Moreover, in 1978 his histories of the genre, notably *Billion Year Spree: The History of Science Fiction* (1973), won him the coveted Pilgrim Award for criticism, awarded by the Science Fiction Research Association. His incisive comments on literature, movies, politics, current affairs, and societal fads and foibles as well as science fiction have been collected in several anthologies, most notably *This World and Nearer Ones: Essays Exploring the Familiar* (1979) and *The Pale Shadow of Science* (1985). This latter volume was followed by *—And the Lurid Glare of the Comet* (1986). All of these, including the 1986 *Trillion Year Spree: The History of Science Fiction* (with David Wingrove), a major revision and updating of *Billion Year Spree,* are written with good humor and insight.

Brian Wilson Aldiss was born on 18 August 1925 in what he has termed "the dull heart of Norfolk," the small town of East Dereham. His early life

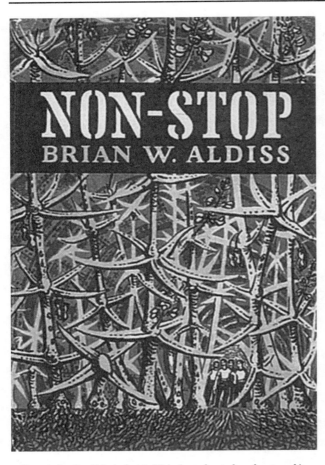

Dust jacket for Aldiss's first published novel, set aboard a spaceship whose occupants have reverted to savagery

was uneventful, and his background was a fairly privileged middle-class one: his grandfather H. H. Aldiss, a justice of the peace, was an important figure in East Dereham, and his father, Stanley Aldiss, was a respected men's outfitter. His mother was Elizabeth May Wilson Aldiss, and he has one sister, Betty. Aldiss has suggested in various autobiographical musings that as a youth he suffered from severe feelings of rejection, exile, loss of parental support, and a growing awareness of the small-town mentality. Aldiss began writing short stories by the age of five. As a child he attended several schools, where he became an oral storyteller in the dormitories; many of these early stories contained science-fictional elements. One of the schools he attended later served as the model for the ghastly institution memorialized in *The Hand-Reared Boy* (1970). As a result of dislocations caused by World War II, he was switched to West Buckland School, which, as he has put it, was "a fine school" with "good morality, teaching, sporting activity." West Buckland now boasts an Aldiss Room in its library.

Aldiss served in the British army during World War II with men from all walks of life, and the experience broadened his background. He saw considerable combat as a signals technician in the Far East between 1943 and 1947. Those years in the British military provided him with much of the material for his Horatio Stubbs books as well as a sensitivity to the Far East. In his fiction Asia—India or Malaysia—is frequently suggested directly, by the setting, or indirectly, by his sometimes muted references to what may be termed "the jungle theme" that permeates many of his works. During his time in the army he wrote sporadically, and while stationed in Sumatra he edited a magazine, *The Glad Rag*. He was mustered out of the British army in 1947 and began selling books at Oxford shortly thereafter. In 1948 he married Olive Mary Fortescue, with whom he had two children: Clive, born in 1955, and Caroline Wendy, born in 1959. The couple separated in 1960 and later divorced.

Aldiss had read science fiction since age eleven, when he happened upon the important American pulp magazine *Astounding Science-Fiction* in his father's shop. When he returned to civilian life in 1947, he had decided to be a writer. From 1950 to 1952, he wrote a contemporary novel, "Shouting Down a Cliff," about his experiences in Sumatra. Once it was finished, he put it aside and never looked at it again. The manuscript is now kept in the Aldiss Archive at the Bodleian Library, Oxford University.

Aldiss's first science-fiction stories, beginning in 1954 with the publication of "Criminal Record" in *Science Fantasy,* were followed by dozens more as he learned his trade. While working in a bookshop, he wrote his comic novel, *The Brightfount Diaries* (1955), which was well received. In his next novel, *Non-Stop* (1958), he attempted a new version of a hackneyed theme that had haunted science-fiction writers for years—the creation of a closed universe aboard a spaceship. In this book and in many of the early short stories, collected as *Space, Time, and Nathaniel (Presciences)* (1957), a volume that has been reprinted in each of the succeeding decades (a fact Aldiss takes considerable pride in), he sketched many of the themes he returned to often in his later works. These subjects—change and stasis, reality and illusion, contemplation and action, intellect and feeling, art and artifice, to name only a few—provided Aldiss with much of the material he later developed with maturity and élan.

Non-Stop was Aldiss's take on an established story idea, the generation starship, as well as on another common story idea, the world as illusion. At the beginning of the novel, readers are introduced to a strange world in which people live in a state approaching savagery and make their way through a bizarre environment of passages and rooms overgrown with vegetation. The

American title, *Starship* (1959), gives away the situation: that the characters are actually passengers aboard a vast spacecraft in which the hydroponic systems have taken over after some catastrophe has wrenched its travelers from a civilized state. Further, it becomes clear that this catastrophe must have happened some time ago and that the ship is a generation starship, meaning that several generations would be expected to come and go during the centuries-long voyage to their destination (returning to Earth from a colonizing mission). As is often the case in Aldiss's science fiction, he imagines what can go wrong with the best-laid plans of engineers and men. The story is absorbing as the reader follows the unaware denizens of the jungle-like ship on what becomes a true voyage of discovery. But there is a point to the adventure: the idea that a society that relies too heavily on technology may imprison itself rather than liberating itself.

Throughout the later 1950s and the 1960s Aldiss continued to publish short stories, which he collected in such volumes as *Space, Time, and Nathaniel; No Time Like Tomorrow* (1959); *The Canopy of Time* (1959); *The Airs of Earth: Science Fiction Stories* (1963); and *Best Science Fiction Stories of Brian W. Aldiss* (1965). One of his best stories from this period is "Who Can Replace a Man?" (1958). The characters are robots who argue among themselves about what they should do in the absence of human direction in a postapocalyptic world. At the sight of a surviving human, however, all their plans are abandoned as they call this scraggly specimen, this representative of a race that has managed to destroy itself, "Master." For the accomplishment of *Non-Stop* and his imaginative stories, Aldiss received the new author award at the 1959 World Science Fiction Convention.

In the late 1950s and early 1960s Aldiss published four largely conventional science-fiction novels: *Equator* (1958), *Bow Down to Nul* (1960), *The Male Response* (1961), and *The Primal Urge* (1961), all of which have generally been considered lesser efforts. However, *Bow Down to Nul* foreshadows Aldiss's interest in the galactic conflicts typical of the older style of space opera, while *The Primal Urge* shows both Aldiss's humor and his willingness to write about sex in a genre that before the 1960s treated sex almost puritanically.

Aldiss's next important novel, *Hothouse* (1962), which incorporates stories for which he won a Hugo Award in 1962, returns to a jungle-like environment, albeit a far different one from *Non-Stop*. The setting is Earth in the far future. The planet is not quite like one of the bleak future worlds depicted in H. G. Wells's *The Time Machine* (1895), but Aldiss's future world is similar to Wells's in the depiction of a radically transformed environment wrought by planetary and evolutionary changes. In *Hothouse* the planet no longer rotates, creating

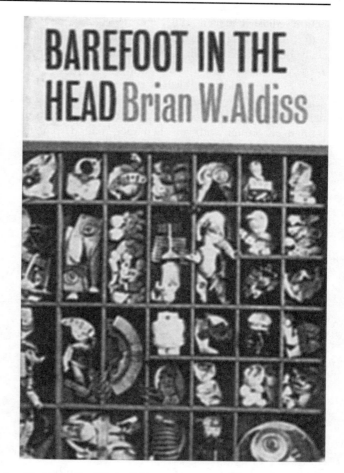

Dust jacket for Aldiss's 1969 novel, set during an "Acid-Head War" fought with psychedelic drugs instead of guns

a day side and a night side. Naturally, humanity's far-future offspring, considerably different from Aldiss or his readers, live on the sun-facing side, which is mostly covered by one enormous tree and other forms of luxuriant vegetation. Aldiss also imagines a radically altered language, and the linguistic style of the novel is as inventive as its premise. While writers such as James Joyce may have played with language for experimental purposes, Aldiss does so as a logical part of science-fiction extrapolation. Nonetheless, the inventive style contributes to the experimental nature of the book. This element and the theme of entropy are two aspects that came to be identified with the experimental New Wave in Anglo-American science fiction of the 1960s and 1970s, a movement with which Aldiss was later connected. The novel was recognized as a major accomplishment.

Also in the 1960s Aldiss became active as an editor and promoter of science fiction, arguing that it was a legitimate form of literature rather than a subliterary form of mass culture. He edited dozens of anthologies—including a series for Penguin, where he was science-fiction editor between 1961 and 1964—and he was active in securing government support for the financially beleaguered British science-fiction magazine *New Worlds,* one of the chief organs of the New Wave.

In 1964 Aldiss published two novels, *The Dark Light Years* and *Greybeard.* The former is Aldiss in a Swiftian satiric mode intended to shock, as it depicts a human encounter with an alien race that, despite its considerable intelligence, revels in its own excrement—not unlike, on a less literal level, human beings. *Greybeard,* like *Hothouse,* deals with a future Earth, but in this novel humanity is on the verge of extinction, as radiation has rendered the human race sterile; the fifty-something protagonist of the title is the youngest person on the planet. While this dire situation may be alleviated as the story progresses, the emotional impact of seeing a dying human race is still considerable. As P. D. James wrote in the *Spectator* reviewing the 1993 version of the novel, in which the opening chapter was slightly revised, "Mr Aldiss's powerful novel is suffused with grief at the loss of children"—as well as the potential loss of all human life and its history.

The threat of nuclear annihilation is treated more conventionally in his novel *Earthworks* (1965), which takes as its major concept the Wellsian notion that humanity's sorry state might improve only after a major world disaster. Wells was also the inspiration for the title story of Aldiss's 1966 collection *The Saliva Tree and Other Strange Growths,* in which several ideas from Wells's well-known scientific romances are combined in new and interesting ways. "The Saliva Tree" received the Nebula Award from the Science Fiction Writers of America. Also in 1965 Aldiss married Margaret Manson; their son, Timothy, was born in 1967, and their daughter, Charlotte, in 1969.

Time travel, another Wellsian concept, is employed in Aldiss's next novel, *An Age* (1967; retitled *Cryptozoic!* in 1968), although in this work the passages from one time to another are achieved mentally rather than mechanically. Wit and sex are ever present as the story jumps from prehistoric periods to the future. Time is also a major concern in *Report on Probability A* (1968), though in a much different fashion. A key work in the Aldiss canon, incorporating many of his themes, *Report on Probability A* may give some notion of the reward and difficulty often inherent in his writing. This relatively neglected novel, published in final book form in 1968, deals with, apparently, nothing. It is the story, if the term "narrative" may be applied to such an actionless work, of three individuals referred to only as S, C, and G, who apparently live in buildings on the estate of Mr. and Mrs. Mary. While the initials may be read to stand for the occupations "Secretary," "Chauffeur," and "Gardener," the three individuals seem

unaware of each other's existence, and in the course of this short novel they do almost nothing. The story, or rather the enigmatic narrative stasis, is so brilliantly conceived and executed that it becomes almost maddening. Phrases and images—the head of a nail on the roofing tar, the recurrent movement of a bird overhead, the appearance of a picture on the wall—are repeated in exquisite or almost excruciating detail.

Aldiss remarked in an autobiographical note that *Report on Probability A* marked his commitment to bring art and artistic concerns into science fiction. Yet, there is more to this novel of inaction than the mere welding of the two media. It was originally written in 1962 as a short novel titled "Garden with Figures," but at the suggestion of fellow writer and editor Michael Moorcock, Aldiss revised the book and inserted passages, now printed in italics, to make it more "science fictional," as one watcher from another dimension observes someone who in turn is watching G, C, and S, the result becoming a virtual unending series of reflections in an infinite series of mirrors. This version, retitled "Report on Probability A," was first published in *New Worlds* in March 1967.

Aldiss soon recognized that he had no central symbolism for a novel drenched with symbols. He had frozen moments in time, but no frozen moment of art. Accordingly, he then inserted passages concerning William Holman Hunt's painting *The Hireling Shepherd* (1851). The frozen moment of the painting—the shepherd's hand poised forever over the woman's breast as well as a butterfly (or more accurately a death's head moth)—mirrors the frozen moments of the novel, and this "freeze frame" technique, extended over a hundred pages, in turn reflects the lack of action in the French antinovel of Alain Robbe-Grillet and Alain Resnais's motion picture *L'Année dernière à Marienbad* (Last Year at Marienbad, 1961). Aldiss seems to be saying that the only reality that means anything—the only reality that will truly endure—is the Reality of Art.

Indeed, Aldiss often requires some intellectual and emotional willingness to follow him as he probes both interior and exterior realities in his works. Both erudite and visceral, he stretches readers' minds and imaginations. For instance, with his next novel, *Barefoot in the Head: A European Fantasia* (1969), he seems to expect his readers to be familiar with Joyce's *Finnegans Wake* (1939), P. D. Ouspensky's mystical psychological musings, acid rock, and the Saint novels of Leslie Charteris, to say nothing of the effects of psychedelic deliriums, which in the structure of this novel have affected most of the world, particularly western Europe. Even in this difficult but rewarding book, verbal wit is always present. For example, Aldiss plays with the phrase "Joyce Scholar" and turns it into "Joyce Collar," "Joy's

Scholar," "Joy's Collar," and so on. Noted Joyce scholar and fellow Oxfordian Richard Ellmann, a good friend of Aldiss's, much admired this novel, which says much about its artistic integrity and perhaps its difficulty as well.

The story traces how a Yugoslavian named Colin Charteris survives the Acid-Head War, which is fought with psychedelic drugs as weapons. Through the narrative Aldiss ponders whether the human race's mental equipment has advanced enough to deal with the complexities of the modern world. The characters seem driven by their own personal desires. For instance, Charteris is undeservedly elevated to sainthood by a post-Christian rave group, and for a time he allows himself to go along with this mistaken perception of his heroism. Eventually he tries to free himself from the messianic expectations imposed upon him, but he is unsuccessful because of humanity's limitations; the human race is stuck with "photographs torn from a Neolithic eye."

Aldiss continued to publish shorter works during this period, which were collected in such volumes as *Intangibles Inc. and Other Stories: Five Novellas* (1969) and *The Moment of Eclipse* (1970); the latter received a British Science Fiction Association award in 1972. He also published a nonfiction collection titled *The Shape of Further Things: Speculations on Change* (1970) and began working on a history of science fiction that became *Billion Year Spree,* in which he argues that Mary Shelley's *Frankenstein, or, The Modern Prometheus* (1818) was the first work of science fiction. This return to Shelley's Gothic novel also inspired his next important novel, *Frankenstein Unbound* (1973).

As in *Report on Probability A,* the relationship between art and reality lies at the heart of *Frankenstein Unbound,* which is truly a crucial work. Mary Shelley becomes a major character, not merely the author of a work-in-progress that will bear the famous name. This tribute to her begins as a traditional science-fiction novel set in the year 2020. Various experiments with the infrastructure of space make quite credible the premise that protagonist Joseph Bodenland has been thrown back in time to the village of Secheron on Lake Geneva in Switzerland in May of 1816. There he meets Victor Frankenstein, although his memory tells him that the famous or infamous doctor existed only in the pages of Mary Shelley's novel. Later he meets Mary herself, has a brief but powerful affair with her, and then discovers that her novel is only half finished. To Mary, however, her book is only a novel, a horror tale in the manner of Ann Radcliffe. She is apparently unaware of the existence of a real Dr. Frankenstein whose experiments are being carried on at that very moment. Mary has just written that part of her novel

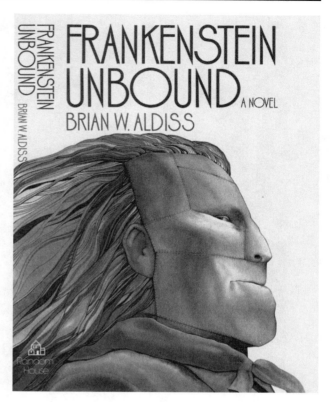

Dust jacket for the first U.S. edition (1974) of Aldiss's 1973 novel, in which the protagonist travels back in time to 1816 and visits Mary Shelley as she is completing her Frankenstein

where the monster wants a mate. Bodenland cannot recall that section. Did she really write it? What is real? What is fiction? Does Bodenland's vague or faulty memory of Mary's completed novel influence the writing of the novel itself? Who is the creator? And what is reality? Mary Shelley's book is real, perceivable by the senses, just as Shelley herself was real. Yet, so is the "fictional" Frankenstein and his monstrous creation.

In sum, Aldiss makes it quite clear that the power of Shelley's genius, as well as her creation of this "real" allegory, constitutes at least a vision of reality and yields genuine meaning. Bodenland himself experiences a severe psychic shock and wonders, "I felt myself in the presence of myth and, by association, accepted myself as mythical." Yet, myth is, after all, a symbolic or metaphorical or allegorical way of expressing a higher truth. And at this point readers realize that, in a certain sense, they have been trapped by Aldiss's skill as a creative writer into accepting the genuine existence of Bodenland (who appears as the protagonist of the 1991 novel *Dracula Unbound* as well), who, after all, is merely a creature of Aldiss's imagination.

Also in the late 1960s and the 1970s, Aldiss turned to mimetic fiction to create an autobiographical

Bridget Fonda as Mary Shelley, Michael Hutchence as Percy Bysshe Shelley, and John Hurt as Dr. Joe Buchanan
in the 1990 movie version of Frankenstein Unbound *(Everett Collection)*

series about a young man coming of age in the 1930s and 1940s. *The Hand-Reared Boy* and its sequels, *A Soldier Erect; or, Further Adventures of the Hand-Reared Boy* (1971) and *A Rude Awakening* (1978), detail the development of Horatio Stubbs from schoolboy to soldier, in locations from England to Southeast Asia. Besides the realistic and autobiographical elements in the books, the trilogy is notable for its sexual explicitness, which sharply divided critics and helped to place the first two on the best-seller list in Britain.

Aldiss's next science-fiction novel, *The Eighty-Minute Hour* (1974), is subtitled "A Space Opera" and thus is another homage to an earlier form of the genre. A comic effort employing multiple science-fiction clichés, it nonetheless failed to entertain many readers of the genre or its critics. More successful was his next effort, *The Malacia Tapestry* (1976).

Themes of the preservation of art, and art as life, form the core of *The Malacia Tapestry*. It is one of Aldiss's few novels that might be termed "fantasy," although that designation does not truly describe this book, one of the author's best. When Aldiss visited the United States in 1979, he was a bit shocked to learn the predominant American pronunciation of this title was "The Muh-LACE-ya Tapestry." Convinced that Americans did not know how to speak the mother tongue, he

insisted with considerable wit that the only pronunciation he had ever considered was "The Muh-LASS-ya Tapestry." Months later, when he was reminiscing with an American visitor about his days with the British army in Indonesia in 1946 and 1947, he expressed his desire to write a novel about Malaysia, where he had spent considerable time awaiting demobilization from service. Despite the evocation he had already given the Far East in *A Rude Awakening,* he had always wanted, he said, to celebrate the beauty of Edenic Malaysia before it vanished under the onslaught of trivialization, tourism, industrialization, and revolution. As he spoke, he became suddenly aware of the virtually identical sounds in the American "Muh-LACE-ya" and Malaysia. He reflected that he might already have written his Malaysia novel in *The Malacia Tapestry,* and that he might have tried to conceal that fact from himself with his pronunciation of the title. It was a virtual revelation to him, and he recognized that the unconscious artist had been at work.

Another layer to the word "Malacia" lies in its medical meaning—something wrong inside, a pathological softening of an organ, which is reflected in the description of the world of the novel. On the surface, *The Malacia Tapestry* is an alternate-world fantasy about the miraculous city-state of Malacia. Its laws forbid any change and are, as one character puts it, the "Original Curse." Yet, the city nonetheless moves reluctantly, albeit heretically, toward change. Its plodding progress is recorded by Perian de Chirolo, an actor resembling the classic *miles gloriosus*. He is a genial braggart, a picaro who swaggers his way through life, both an observer and participant in the artistic life of Malacia. The motivating force in the novel is the process of entropy: Malacia is slowly winding down, approaching collapse.

One character voices his awareness that ordinary life in Malacia might continue ever more slowly until it stopped absolutely. "Like a clock stopping," another character responds. "More like a tapestry," is the reply; "I mean, one day things might run down and never move again, so that we and everything would hang there in the air for ever more." The rules of the city admit no change. Things happen, of course, but the incidents are completely normal: men and women make love; astrologers read portents; actors posture; an enemy leisurely lobs a few shells into the city; and the poor, as poet W. H. Auden put it, "have the sufferings to which they are fairly accustomed."

This long, languorous portrait of a quasi–High Renaissance society may be Aldiss's homage to the Malaysian beauty he had once known, but it is much more. In fact, the novel is the tapestry, the work of art, as if the author were revising the familiar Latin epigraph *ars longa, vita brevis* to *ars longa, vita longa*. In the city, art seems to last as long as life; or, to put it another way, art will last only as long as life. Malacia is an always-always land, an ever-ever land where the chief characters are all artists: Perian, the actor-narrator; Otto Bengtsohn, the inventor of a primitive form of camera; Nicholas Fatember, perhaps Aldiss's redaction of Leonardo da Vinci; and many others—all characters seeming to spring directly from a High Renaissance tapestry, fleshed into being by the novelist's artistry.

The novel is filled with wit and wisdom, both personified by the great genius Fatember, who seems to speak with Aldiss's own voice in many passages. Consider this response about the problem of Art, when one character speaks of an artistic performance and Fatember is asked his opinion:

> Artistry enough. Hokum maybe, but striking theatre. It reminded me of Reality without making ineffectual attempts to imitate it slavishly. Outside, beyond these walls of mould and mouse-fart, stands the great burning world of triumphs and nobilities, while I'm stuck here immobile. Only by art, only through painting, can one master that burning world and its secrets! Seeing is not enough—we do not see until we have copied, until we have transcribed everything . . . everything . . .

Brian and Margaret Aldiss with their children, Timothy and Charlotte, 1974

especially the divine light in all its variety, without which there is nothing.

Echoing Hamlet musing about the players, Perian asks an eternal question about artistic or dramatic words as well: "Why do I weep over characters in a play or a book, who have no more flesh than the thirty characters of the printed language?" Readers agree and ask how it is possible that they have become involved with this preposterous Malacian world, one that has not changed for untold centuries, a world where the Supreme Council exists only to praise inertia and eradicate change.

Yet, Malacia is far more like the readers' world than they would care to admit. Readers recognize that in both worlds people hunt, drink, wench, cavort, gamble, rail against fortune, consult oracles, love, gluttonize, and die. They whitewash their memories with easy "forgettories," vote for the status quo, and become, in Joyce's words, praisers of their own past. As a result, readers may tend to identify with Perian or some other character, or wish they were in his bed or in his shoes, albeit briefly; yet, at the same time they chuckle over the obtuseness of the Malacians who are faced with

Dust jacket for the first volume of the trilogy Aldiss set on a planet that circles twin suns and has a year equivalent to thousands of Earth years

Bengtsohn's near invention of a camera obscura motion-picture device. The machine is difficult for the Malacians to understand, for the Zahanoscope, as it is called, records change, even if imperceptible. Aldiss seems to ask: who among us has not resisted change?

At the end of the novel Perian is gaining some sort of self-understanding as he comes to agree with Fatember, who says:

> Malacia has entered a new age, Master Perian . . . I can feel the new age about me, cooped up though I am in this rat-ridden pile. Now at last—for the first time in a hundred thousand years, men open their eyes and look about them. They construct engines to supplement their muscles and consult libraries to supplement their meagre brains . . . and what do they find? Why, the vast, the God-given continuity of the world!

A planned sequel to *The Malacia Tapestry,* which Aldiss had tentatively named "The Megara Testament," remains unwritten.

Aldiss seems to disrupt the boundaries of the various genres and to create a new one that could be termed "Aldissian." In the well-realized short novel *Brothers of the Head* (1977) Aldiss deals with several themes, such as head and heart, the inner and outer self, appearance and reality, the popular mind, the deleterious effects of mass culture, love and sex, and the nature of dreams. He also combines horror with the grotesque—the protagonists are Siamese twins with a third head who have become world idols with their punk-rock group The Bang Bang—as well as the evanescent reality of dreams: does the dreamer control them, or do they in some frightening, horrible way control the dreamer? To these questions Aldiss poses no answers; as with much of his work, the questions themselves are important, not the answers.

In his "Author's Note" to *Last Orders and Other Stories* (1977) Aldiss creates a quasi-fictional scene depicting a writer at a party in a smoke-filled room, leaning over a typewriter as big as an upright piano. An onlooker in a "sharp suit" asks, "What you turn out that fantasy stuff for? Play something happy, something familiar."

The writer—who speaks with Aldiss's voice, of course—bends over the typewriter, taps out a few sentences on the keys, and replies:

> I believe in what I do. This is where I sing the science fiction blues. This is my kind of music. I work in an underprivileged, underrated medium, sure, and even within that medium my style offends a whole lot of people. See, I don't mind that antagonism any more. Maybe it powers my typewriter. You have to have something to create against, right?

The sharp-suited man, presumably a critic of little insight or a writer manqué, perhaps even a condescending member of the "culturally correct," tells Aldiss that people want to be cheered up. "They want to hear about real things," he avers.

Aldiss replies to this condescension, in one of the most cogent and apposite comments he has ever made about his own writing: "One or the other you can have. Not both. See, my stories are about human woes, non-communication, disappointment, endurance, acceptance, love. Aren't those things real enough? Nobody's fool enough to imagine that any near-future development will obliterate them. Change there will be . . . But the new old blues sing on forever."

Enemies of the System: A Tale of Homo Uniformis (1978), Aldiss's next science-fiction novel, is set a million years in the future, in a socialist utopia governed by a race of evolved human beings called *Homo uniformis*. A group from the ruling elite is permitted to travel to the planet Lysenka II, but the breakdown of a machine forces six of them to confront the harsh conditions of the untamed planet. Aldiss wrote the novel in response to a Soviet critic's charge that Western science fiction would never dare to depict the triumph of World Communism. In Aldiss's depiction, World Communism has overcome the entire solar system, and the few surviving democrats live like animals on Lysenka II. The novel also deals with tensions between civilization and savagery and individualism versus collectivism. The book received little critical attention but was highly praised by Anthony Burgess.

Aldiss returned to mainstream novels with *Life in the West* (1980). It opens with a prose version of the shooting script of protagonist Thomas Squire's epic television series, *Frankenstein Among the Arts,* the initial script subtitled "Eternal Ephemera." This oxymoron is at the heart of Squire's television series as well as of the novel itself, and Aldiss carries it off in a series of quick cuts, as he presents clashing values, popular culture icons, trash, and verities.

Also in 1980 Aldiss returned to the work of Wells with his novel *Moreau's Other Island* (republished in the United States as *An Island Called Moreau*). While Wells's 1896 novel *The Island of Dr. Moreau* was set in the late nineteenth century, Aldiss's is set in the late twentieth, as a space shuttle crashes on a remote island where experiments similar to those conducted by Wells's driven doctor are being performed.

Another example of Aldiss's genre bending or blending can be found in his acclaimed Helliconia trilogy, composed of *Helliconia Spring* (1982), *Helliconia Summer* (1983), and *Helliconia Winter* (1985). The theme of change is also central to these three books, here including individual, planetary, and evolutionary change. Helliconia circles two suns, making its "year" thousands of Earth years long and its seasons centuries long. Thus on Helliconia change is incredibly slow.

One of the most interesting facets of the three books, each of which centers on individuals living on the planet in the season indicated by the title, is the presence of a group of detached observers from Earth who have made Helliconian life into entertainment for their home planet, a virtual unending soap opera. The Terran observers cannot land in the toxic atmosphere of Helliconia, however, making them unable to engage with the planet's people and culture directly.

In this way Aldiss again examines the relationship between the observer and the observed. By observing Helliconia and sending scenes of its life to Earth, do the Earthlings in any way change the Helliconians, who are unaware that they are being watched? This theme of watchers and watching recalls his earlier *Report on Probability A,* yet the scale of this work is considerably different. Holman Hunt's painting *The Hireling Shepherd* is central to *Report on Probability A,* whereas the object of

Dust jacket for the revised and updated edition (1986) of the 1973 book for which Aldiss was awarded the Pilgrim Award for criticism by the Science Fiction Research Association (from Brian Aldiss, The Twinkling of an Eye, 1998)

aesthetic contemplation in the Helliconia series is the planet itself, transmitted to Earth. Thus another important theme that Aldiss again considers is the relationship between art and life.

The Helliconia trilogy occupied much of Aldiss's attention through the mid 1980s, as did his revision with Wingrove of his earlier history of science fiction into *Trillion Year Spree.* In addition, he served as president of the World Science Fiction Society from 1982 to 1984. In the interim he published *Seasons in Flight* (1984), a collection of ten stories that are closer to reality than science fiction, and *The Year Before Yesterday: A Novel in Three Acts* (1987), an alternate-history tale about a Nazi-controlled contemporary Europe that provides a frame for some older space operas Aldiss had written in the 1950s.

During the 1980s he also continued to work on the volumes that comprise the loosely connected Squire Quartet, the first of which was *Life in the West.* In the

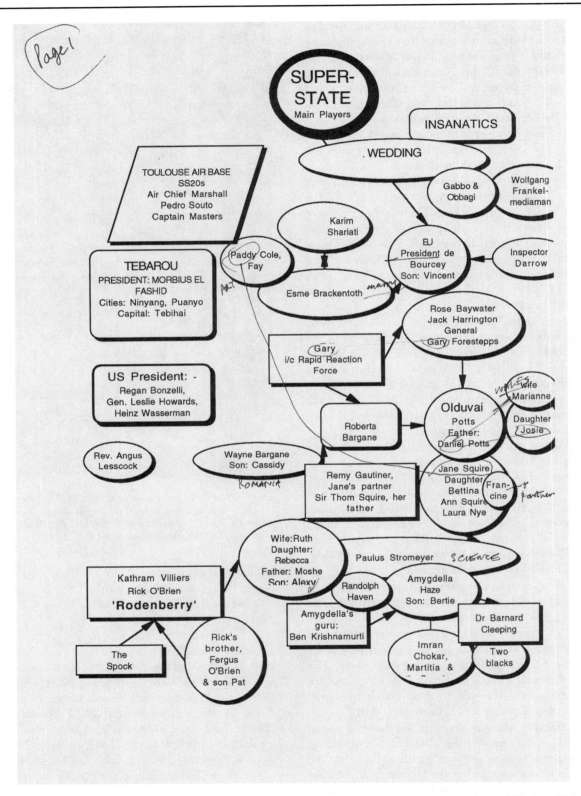

First and second versions of Aldiss's "basic game plan" for his novel Super-State, *forthcoming in 2002 (Collection of Brian Aldiss)*

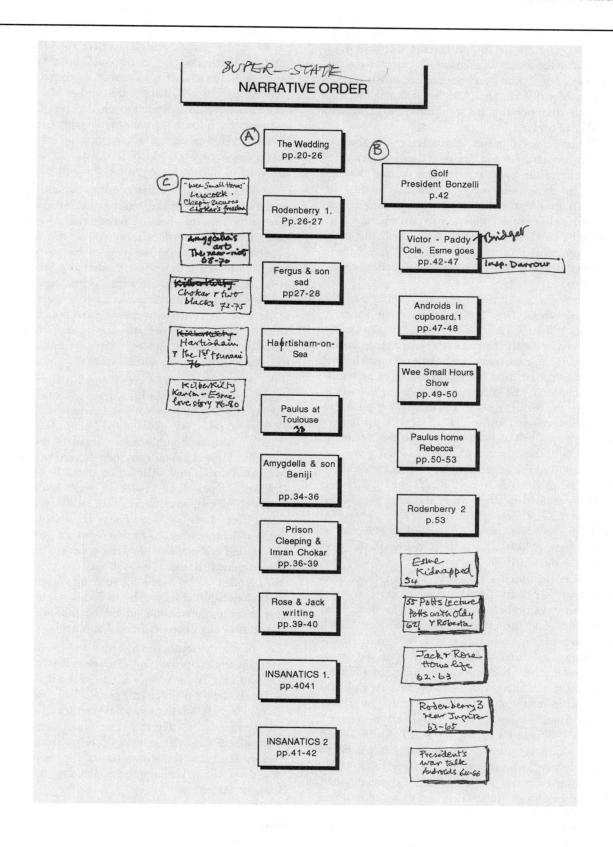

second, *Forgotten Life* (1988), protagonist Clement Winters is married to Sheila Tomlinson, an extremely popular writer of high fantasy and science fiction who writes as "Green Mouth." She abandons her fictional kingdom of Kerinth, disappointing her avid fans, and returns to the reality of Oxford.

In the Squire Quartet, Aldiss returns to the tension between change and stasis, a tension that profoundly affects the characters in these books. *Forgotten Life* focuses on self-discovery, as did *Life in the West*. Unlike Thomas Squire, however, who remains unconscious of his change from observer to participant, Clement Winder is clearly changed. This is all the more striking given his profession: an analyst. He comes to realize that his own life has been unanalyzed, unexamined, forgotten.

Some critics dismissed the next volume in the series, *Remembrance Day* (1993), for its resemblance to Thornton Wilder's *The Bridge of San Luis Rey* (1927). Aldiss's novel tells the story of several English characters, unrelated to each other, on holiday in a small hotel on the British coast, who fall victim to a terrorist bombing. While Aldiss, like Wilder, focuses on the individual characters, the themes of both *Life in the West* and *Forgotten Life* are developed further. He deals with the danger of progress, as well as nostalgia for the past, a theme also present in the earlier work *The Malacia Tapestry*.

In 1990 Aldiss began the first of a series of autobiographies with *Bury My Heart at W. H. Smith's: A Writing Life*. He continued in this vein in the later part of the decade with *The Twinkling of an Eye: My Life as an Englishman* (1998) and *When the Feast Is Finished: Reflections on Terminal Illness* (1999), a memoir of his wife, Margaret Aldiss, who died in 1997.

Aldiss published a sequel of sorts to *Frankenstein Unbound* in 1991. In *Dracula Unbound* time traveler Bodenland visits Bram Stoker, and a similar mixture of the historical and the fictional drives the story, which some critics rate as equal to the first. Also in the 1990s he published *The Detached Retina: Aspects of SF and Fantasy* (1995) and further short-story collections. In addition, he became acquainted with director Stanley Kubrick, who hoped to adapt one of Aldiss's stories, "Supertoys Last All Summer Long" (first published in *Harper's Bazaar* in 1969) into a movie titled *A.I.* Kubrick died before making the movie, but the project passed to Steven Spielberg, who created his own version in 2001.

Toward the end of the 1990s Aldiss collaborated with mathematician Roger Penrose to write a novel titled *White Mars; or, The Mind Set Free: A 21st Century Utopia* (1999). The story concerns the efforts of colonists on Mars to establish an ideal society after things back on Earth fall apart. The title acknowledges Kim Stanley Robinson's successful Mars trilogy published earlier in the decade and also refers to Antarctica, a continent dedicated to science and otherwise sacrosanct, as Aldiss's Mars is to remain sacrosanct. Also in 1999 Aldiss was awarded the title Grand Master of Science Fiction by the Science Fiction Writers of America, an honor given to only a handful of writers in the field. In 2002 Aldiss published *Cretan Teat,* a contemporary novel, and *Super-State,* which deals with global warming and is set in Europe forty years in the future.

The fact that Aldiss requires so much of his readers may be why he has not achieved quite the level of popularity or name recognition of contemporaries such as Arthur C. Clarke. While Aldiss rarely if ever neglects the narrative pace of his story, he can require a patience that some readers are unwilling or even unable to provide. Further, some confusion on the part of critics, academicians, booksellers, or even readers about Aldiss's proper milieu—science fiction, fantasy, or the mainstream—may cause him to be unfairly relegated to "mere" genre writing, a charge that Aldiss both denies and affirms.

Aldiss has received considerable scholarly attention. Several books about his work, most notably Brian Griffin and David Wingrove's *Apertures: A Study of the Writings of Brian W. Aldiss* (1984), and *A is for Brian* (1990), a festschrift published in honor of the author's sixty-fifth birthday in an extremely limited printing, are particularly insightful. Also to be noted is Michael R. Collings's *Brian Aldiss* (1986) as well as the several essays about individual works listed in the five-volume Salem Press *Survey of Science Fiction Literature* (1979) and *Survey of Science Fiction and Fantasy Literature* (1996). Notably missing in the canon of Aldiss criticism, however, is any sustained, detailed, serious analysis of the effects that events in Aldiss's own life have had on his writing. The relationship of biography to fiction might well provide more understanding of this multifaceted author than almost any other traditional approach.

Given the multilayered artistry of his fiction, and given his tireless promotion of science fiction as editor and historian, Aldiss clearly is one of the major figures of British science fiction in the second half of the twentieth century. He has explored new territory so well that some critics have suggested that when literature students of the late twenty-first century have forgotten some of the better-known writers of the twentieth century, they will be reading and applauding the work of Brian W. Aldiss.

Interviews:

Charles Platt, "Brian W. Aldiss," in *Who Writes Science Fiction?* (Manchester, U.K.: Savoy, 1980), pp. 297–309; republished as *Dream Makers: The*

Uncommon People Who Write Science Fiction (New York: Berkley, 1980), pp. 269–280;

"Brian Aldiss: Young Turk to Grand Master," *Locus,* 45 (August 2000): 6–7, 63–64.

Bibliographies:

Margaret Aldiss, *Item Eighty-Three: Brian W. Aldiss—A Bibliography 1954–1972* (Oxford: SF Horizons, 1972);

Aldiss, *Brian W. Aldiss: A Bibliography, 1954–1988* (San Bernardino, Cal.: Borgo Press, 1989);

Aldiss, *The Work of Brian W. Aldiss: An Annotated Bibliography and Guide,* edited by Boden Clarke (San Bernardino, Cal.: Borgo Press, 1992).

References:

A Is for Brian: A 65th Birthday Present for Brian W. Aldiss from His Family, Friends, Colleagues, and Admirers, edited by Frank Hatherley, Margaret Aldiss, and Malcolm Edwards (London: Avernus, 1990);

Michael R. Collings, *Brian Aldiss* (Mercer Island, Wash.: Starmont, 1986);

Ken Gelder, "Vampire Blockbusters: Stephen King, Dan Simmons, Brian Aldiss and S. P. Somtow," in his *Reading the Vampire* (London & New York: Routledge, 1994), pp. 124–140;

Colin Greenland, *The Entropy Exhibition: Michael Moorcock and the British "New Wave" in Science Fiction* (London & Boston: Routledge & Kegan Paul, 1983);

Greenland, "The Times Themselves Talk Nonsense: Language in *Barefoot in the Head,*" *Foundation: The Review of Science Fiction* (September 1979): 32–41;

Brian Griffin and David Wingrove, *Apertures: A Study of the Writings of Brian W. Aldiss* (Westport, Conn.: Greenwood Press, 1984);

Tom Henighan, *Brian W. Aldiss* (New York: Twayne, 1999);

Fredric Jameson, "Generic Discontinuities in SF: Brian Aldiss' *Starship,*" *Science Fiction Studies,* 1 (Fall 1973): 57–68;

C. N. Manlove, "Brian Aldiss, *Hothouse* (1962)," in his *Science Fiction: Ten Explorations* (Kent, Ohio: Kent State University Press, 1986), pp. 57–78;

Richard Mathews, *Aldiss Unbound: The Science Fiction of Brian W. Aldiss* (San Bernardino, Cal.: Borgo Press, 1977);

Patrick G. McLeod, "Frankenstein, Unbound and Otherwise," *Extrapolation,* 21 (1980): 158–166;

Willis E. McNelly, "Change, Stasis and Entropy in the Works of Brian W. Aldiss," in *Reflections on the Fantastic,* edited by Collings (New York: Greenwood Press, 1986), pp. 79–86;

Nicholas Ruddick, "The Brood of Mary: Brian Aldiss, Frankenstein, and Science Fiction," in *The Dark Fantastic: Selected Essays from the Ninth International Conference on the Fantastic in the Arts,* edited by C. W. Sullivan III (Westport, Conn.: Greenwood Press, 1997), pp. 77–84;

David Wingrove, "Thinking in Fuzzy Sets: The Recent SF of Brian Aldiss," *Pacific Quarterly: An International Review of Arts and Ideas,* 4 (1979): 288–294.

Papers:

The Bodleian Library at Oxford University, the Kenneth Spenser Research Library at the University of Kansas (Lawrence, Kansas), and the Rare Books and Special Collection of the University of Sydney Library (Sydney, Australia) have collections of Brian W. Aldiss's papers. The Huntington Library in San Marino, California, has more than one hundred of his letters to his publishers, and the Brian Aldiss Collection at the Dallas Public Library includes letters and papers as well as a variety of other materials.

J. G. Ballard

(15 November 1930 –   )

Charles Brower

See also the Ballard entries in *DLB 14: British Novelists Since 1960,* and *DLB 207: British Novelists Since 1960, Third Series.*

BOOKS: *The Wind from Nowhere* (New York: Berkley, 1962; Harmondsworth, U.K.: Penguin, 1967);

The Voices of Time and Other Stories (New York: Berkley, 1962; London: Gollancz, 1963; revised edition, London: Orion, 1974);

Billenium (New York: Berkley, 1962);

The Drowned World (New York: Berkley, 1962; London: Gollancz, 1962 [i.e., 1963]);

The Four-Dimensional Nightmare (London: Gollancz, 1963; revised edition, 1974); republished as *The Voices of Time* (London: Dent, 1984);

Passport to Eternity (New York: Berkley, 1963);

The Terminal Beach (London: Gollancz, 1964);

Terminal Beach (New York: Berkley, 1964);

The Burning World (New York: Berkley, 1964); expanded as *The Drought* (London: Cape, 1965);

The Crystal World (New York: Farrar, Straus & Giroux, 1966; London: Cape, 1966);

The Impossible Man and Other Stories (New York: Berkley, 1966);

The Day of Forever (London: Panther, 1967); republished with deletions and additions (London: Panther, 1971);

The Disaster Area (London: Cape, 1967; New York: Paladin, 1992);

The Overloaded Man (London: Panther, 1967); revised as *The Venus Hunters* (London: Granada, 1980);

Why I Want to Fuck Ronald Reagan (Brighton, U.K.: Unicorn Bookshop, 1968);

The Atrocity Exhibition (London: Cape, 1970); republished as *Love and Napalm: Export USA* (New York: Grove, 1972); revised, expanded, and annotated as *The Atrocity Exhibition* (San Francisco: Re/Search, 1990);

Vermilion Sands (New York: Berkley, 1971; London: Cape, 1973);

Chronopolis and Other Stories (New York: Putnam, 1971);

J. G. Ballard (photograph © by John Foley; from the dust jacket for Cocaine Nights, *1996)*

Crash (London: Cape, 1973; New York: Farrar, Straus & Giroux, 1973);

Concrete Island (London: Cape, 1974; New York: Farrar, Straus & Giroux, 1974);

High-Rise (London: Cape, 1975; New York: Holt, Rinehart & Winston, 1977);

Low-Flying Aircraft and Other Stories (London: Cape, 1976);

The Unlimited Dream Company (London: Cape, 1979; New York: Holt, Rinehart & Winston, 1979);

Hello America (London: Cape, 1981; New York: Carroll & Graf, 1988);

Myths of the Near Future (London: Cape, 1982);

News from the Sun (London: Interzone, 1982);

Empire of the Sun (New York: Simon & Schuster, 1984; London: Gollancz, 1984);

The Day of Creation (London: Gollancz, 1987; New York: Farrar, Straus & Giroux, 1988);

Running Wild (New York: Farrar, Straus, Giroux, 1988; London: Hutchinson, 1988);

Memories of the Space Age (Sauk City, Wis.: Arkham House, 1988);

War Fever (London: Collins, 1990; New York: Farrar, Straus & Giroux, 1991);

The Kindness of Women (London: HarperCollins, 1991; New York: Farrar, Straus & Giroux, 1991);

Rushing to Paradise (London: Flamingo, 1994; New York: Picador USA, 1995);

A User's Guide to the Millennium: Essays and Reviews (London: HarperCollins, 1996; New York: Picador USA, 1996);

Cocaine Nights (London: Flamingo, 1996; Washington, D.C.: Counterpoint, 1998);

Super-Cannes (London: Flamingo, 2000; New York: Picador USA, 2000).

Collections: *The Drowned World and The Wind from Nowhere* (Garden City, N.Y.: Doubleday, 1965);

The Best of J. G. Ballard (London: Futura, 1977);

The Best Short Stories of J. G. Ballard (New York: Holt, Rinehart & Winston, 1978);

The Complete Short Stories (London: Flamingo, 2001).

OTHER: David Larkin, ed., *Dali,* introduction by Ballard (New York: Ballantine, 1974);

Aldous Huxley, *The Doors of Perception* [and] *Heaven and Hell,* foreword by Ballard (London: Flamingo, 1994).

J. G. Ballard is perhaps the most important figure to emerge from the British New Wave of science-fiction writers, whose works brought a new degree of literary sophistication and critical respectability to the genre beginning in the late 1950s. To an extent Ballard's fiction is all part of a single project to catalogue the contents of what he calls "inner space"—a psychological domain that represents an inversion of the frequent preoccupation of science-fiction writers with extraterrestrial travel. Within Ballardian inner space the dearest icons of consumer society—automobiles, movie stars, concrete buildings, and motorways—mingle with the symbolic unconscious, and their true significance is revealed. At once exotic and familiar, inner space owes more to the painters of the Surrealist movement, to whom Ballard makes frequent reference, than to his literary predecessors in the fantasy or science-fiction genres.

For Ballard, who was born in Shanghai, China, and spent part of his childhood in a civilian internment camp during World War II, the results of twentieth-century invention have proved to be highly ambiguous. In his early stories and novels he subjects the world to a series of catastrophes that science is unable to understand, let alone avert. Most disconcerting, perhaps, is that Ballard's protagonists rarely make an effort to avert disaster; rather, they are drawn to it on a deeper level. Although Ballard's disaster fantasies can be seen as part of a tradition in British literature that extends back at least as far as Mary Shelley's *The Last Man* (1826), critics James Goddard and David Pringle have noted that "they were written as parodies of this sub-genre of SF, and that they should in fact be regarded as psychological novels—stories of success when viewed from the particular perspectives of the protagonists."

In Ballard's subsequent fiction, consumer culture takes on the role of a global plague, and his heroes continue to respond with their usual creative ambivalence. These works, most notably the story collection *The Atrocity Exhibition* (1970) and the novel *Crash* (1973), were condemned by some at the time of their publication for their oblique style and graphic sexual depictions. The first American edition of *The Atrocity Exhibition,* in fact, was destroyed in the middle of its print run when publisher Nelson Doubleday Jr., while touring his printing department, was outraged by the contents page he saw rushing past him.

The paradoxical quality of inner space, with its combination of the familiar and the alien, has its roots in Ballard's unusual childhood. He was born James Graham Ballard on 15 November 1930 to James and Edna Johnstone Ballard. Ballard's father was a chemist who managed the Shanghai office of a British textile manufacturer. In a 1976 interview with David Pringle, Ballard referred to Shanghai as an "American zone of influence": his earliest memories are of American cars, movies, music, and radio shows. He attended a cathedral school in Shanghai, run by an English clergyman. The specter of war loomed over Ballard's childhood. That threat became a reality in 1937 with the Japanese invasion of China. In 1938 Ballard, his parents, and his older sister were forced to evacuate the family home on the outskirts of Shanghai and move into the city. While the Japanese occupied the rest of Shanghai, the Ballards and other foreign nationals lived in the only unoccupied area, the International Settlement. During that time young Ballard wrote his first book, a privately published study of the rules of contract bridge.

In 1942 Ballard and his family were relocated to the Lunghua internment camp, next to a large Japanese airfield, the future site of the Shanghai International Airport. The family remained there for the next three years. Although food shortages, malaria, and casual brutality on the part of their captors were common features of life in the camp, the adult prisoners tried to provide a semblance of normalcy for their children. The

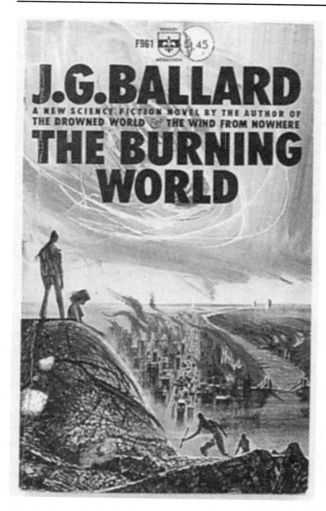

Paperback cover for Ballard's 1964 novel, depicting a world imperiled by widespread pollution

competition with a short story titled "The Violent Noon," written specifically with an eye to winning the competition. He was later quoted as calling the story "a pastiche of a certain kind of Hemingwayesque short story" ("From Shanghai to Shepperton," *Re/Search 8/9: J. G. Ballard* [1984]). Encouraged by this success and unwilling to commit to the demands of a medical career, he resolved to pursue the writing life seriously. He read English at London University for a year before being expelled.

Over the next few years, which served as an apprentice period for the aspiring writer, Ballard drifted through a series of jobs. His life took a new direction in 1954 when he joined the Royal Air Force (RAF) "on a strange sort of impulse. . . . I was suddenly keen to fly" ("From Shanghai to Shepperton"). While stationed in Moosejaw, Saskatchewan, Ballard first discovered science fiction in American magazines such as *Fantastic Universe*. During an ultimately unsuccessful year of RAF basic training, he wrote his first published science-fiction story, "Passport to Eternity," which later appeared as the title story of one of his 1963 collections.

In reading and writing science fiction, Ballard realized that he had found the proper genre to express his various intellectual interests: Surrealism, psychoanalysis, a fascination with technology (especially machines of flight), and literary experimentation.

In 1955 Ballard married Helen Mary Matthews, and they soon had a son, James Christopher. Ballard divided his time between working in libraries and writing, and during these lean years he began to publish stories in *New Worlds* magazine, which was soon at the center of the circle of science-fiction writers known as the British New Wave. Ballard's first story for *New Worlds* was "Prima Belladonna," which appeared in 1956. Another story, "Escapement," followed soon afterward. From then on he was a regular contributor, eventually publishing, by his estimation, thirty to forty stories in the magazine.

Ballard's connection to *New Worlds* also led to a position as an assistant editor at the scientific journal *Chemistry and Industry,* in which capacity he was exposed to research from all the sciences. This material provided much of the factual basis for his early fiction. At the same time he followed with interest the thriving Pop Art scene in London. During this period Ballard's fiction was quickly evolving beyond conventional science fiction to suit his particular literary purposes. Consequently, while he found a measure of early success in British fantasy magazines, his initial attempts to publish in the more rigidly formulaic American magazines met with failure.

British nationals established a school that remained in operation until nearly the end of the war. As the war turned against the Japanese, American planes regularly bombed the airfield adjacent to the camp, and shortages became more acute. Yet, Ballard has recalled that the Japanese captors were not gratuitously cruel, at least not to the interned children.

Released from the camp at the end of the war, Ballard accompanied his mother and sister to England, seeing his country of citizenship for the first time at age fifteen. Ballard found England in 1946 as alien as life in Shanghai—the West seemed completely removed from the realities of the world he had known before. At about this time he began to cultivate an interest in psychoanalysis, which formed an important foundation for his future writing career. After attending Leys School in Cambridge, Ballard studied medicine as an undergraduate at King's College, Cambridge, with the intention of becoming a psychiatrist. While there he won a fiction

Ballard's early British magazine stories supplied the contents of most of his story collections into the 1970s, and an examination of two of the most frequently anthologized of these stories reveals the consistency with which the author has pursued his literary vision. "Prima Belladonna," one of Ballard's earliest stories, is set in the fictional resort of Vermilion Sands, where the inhabitants lead a dissipated life of endless leisure. The narrator is a "choro-florist," a purveyor of singing plants; his interest is piqued by a nightclub chanteuse, a beautiful golden woman named Jane Ciracylides, to whom the plants respond instantly–particularly a malevolent orchid, which will sing only in her presence. Jane and the narrator become lovers, but the relationship at the core of the story is between the singer and the arachnid orchid. Woman and flower ultimately have a mysterious encounter in the middle of the night, after which the orchid lies dead and Jane has vanished.

"Prima Belladonna" is the first in a series of stories that Ballard set in Vermilion Sands. Although the resort seems to exist on another world, with its green beaches, singing plants, and other strange flora and fauna, the ennui of the perpetually vacationing professionals is familiar to readers of modern literature. This mixture of the alien and the mundane is an essential characteristic not only of the stories set in Vermilion Sands but also of Ballard's fiction in general: dream-like imagery combines with the language of commerce, media, and science to give inner space its substance.

The intermingling of the material world with the inner reality of dreams is the central theme of another early story, "The Voices of Time," which first appeared in 1961 and is the title story of one of Ballard's 1962 collections. With its haunting evocation of a dying universe, "The Voices of Time" embodies the spirit of much of Ballard's work, and it is generally considered one of his best stories. Its protagonist, a neurosurgeon named Powers, is gradually succumbing to a sleeping sickness, an epidemic of narcolepsy that afflicts a growing number of "terminals." The only link among the sleeping terminals seems to be a pair of silent genes, present in all species of animals but of obscure function. As Powers is faced with fewer and fewer hours of consciousness each day, time begins to lose its meaning. In a state at once more and less than conscious he fashions a mandala of concrete on an abandoned artillery range. During his brief periods of wakefulness he tends to a zoo of mutant animals whose silent genes were irradiated by a colleague who recently committed suicide. Under the effects of the radiation these genes produce spectacular effects, spawning creatures seemingly intended for a "monstrous and surreal" future.

Powers is shadowed by Kaldren, a former patient, whom the surgeon has "narcotomized," allevi-ating his physiological need for sleep. Kaldren now has unlimited time on his hands to pursue his own project, the collection of "terminal documents," seemingly random data that together reveal a hidden meaning: "When I've got enough together I'll build a new world for myself out of them," he says. One of these terminal documents is a descending numeric progression, an immense countdown, broadcast from a distant star system–"it's been estimated that by the time this countdown reaches zero the universe will have just ended." Kaldren wants Powers to understand the true significance of the countdown: "These are the voices of time, and they're all saying goodbye to you." After Powers commits suicide by irradiating himself and stretching out on the concrete mandala to listen to the stars with his own new sense organs, a film he made of the act becomes another of Kaldren's terminal documents.

With its lyrical descriptions, its mood of foreboding, and its sustained sense of irony, "The Voices of Time" demonstrates that Ballard had developed his mature style. Settings such as the Clinic and the abandoned artillery range, the monumental concrete mandala and empty swimming pools, and the mingling between levels of conscious and unconscious reality are elements that recur in nearly all his stories and novels. Kaldren's project of collecting terminal documents anticipates *The Atrocity Exhibition,* in which the protagonist is similarly obsessed with reassembling the data of history in accordance with a hidden logic. It is a project, in fact, that serves as a useful metaphor for Ballard's entire literary career.

By the early 1960s Ballard had a growing family (which now included two daughters, Fay and Beatrice) and was intent on supporting it from his income as a writer. He wrote his first novel, *The Wind from Nowhere* (1962), over a fortnight's holiday, consciously employing all the conventions of the disaster novel established by fellow British fantasists such as John Wyndham and John Christopher. *The Wind from Nowhere* was published in installments in *New Worlds* in October and November 1961 and in a paperback edition by Berkley Books the following January. Although the novel includes recognizable Ballardian elements, it lacks the psychological resonance of stories such as "The Voices of Time," and the author has disowned the work as essentially a practice novel.

Still, *The Wind from Nowhere* was successful enough to cement a relationship with Berkley, which published two collections of Ballard's stories in rapid succession during 1962: *The Voices of Time and Other Stories* and *Billenium*. In addition to the title story, *The Voices of Time* features several examples of Ballard's best work for *New Worlds,* including "Manhole 69," which, like "The Voices of Time," is set at "the Clinic" and

Dust jacket for the U.S. edition of Ballard's 1966 novel, in which a plague turns everything exposed to it into a luminescent, crystalline substance (Richland County Public Library)

concerns experiments in sleeplessness; and "Deep End," in which the destruction of the oceans–to process oxygen for off-world colonies–has catastrophic results, both ecological and psychological: "The seas are our corporate memory," the protagonist explains. "In draining them we deliberately obliterated our own pasts, to a large extent our own self-identities." *Billenium* includes "Prima Belladonna" as well as "Studio 5, the Stars," another Vermilion Sands story; "The Insane Ones," perhaps a variation on *The Power and the Glory* (1940) by Graham Greene (one of the few British writers Ballard has acknowledged as an influence), in which a global totalitarian regime has outlawed psychiatry, forcing analyst Gregory to practice his calling as a fugitive; and "The Garden of Time," the first example of an allegorical style, reminiscent of Argentinian fantasist Jorge Luis Borges, that Ballard has returned to periodically. In "The Garden of Time" Count Axel and his wife face stoically the death of their time-garden, the

flowers of which have to be picked to repel the advances of a vast "rabble."

Late in 1962 Berkley published *The Drowned World,* Ballard's second novel and his most searching exploration of the realm of inner space to that point. Its most potent images are of the ruined cities of Europe, reclaimed by water, tropical flora, and fearsome creatures–giant bats, insects, reptiles–that thrived on the planet millions of years before humanity existed. The novel is set sometime in the twenty-first century, but Ballard immediately establishes a surreal, timeless quality: "the sombre green-black fronds of the gymnosperms, intruders from the Triassic past, and the half-submerged white faced buildings of the 20th century still reflected together in the dark mirror of the water, the two interlocking worlds apparently suspended at some junction in time."

In two paragraphs Ballard sketches the gravitational shift that led to a global warming; what people remain have fled the rising water levels, living in military compounds in the polar regions. The protagonist, Robert Kerans, a biologist and physician for a government surveying company, has spent years among the vast lagoons of Europe. His alienation from the rest of the party has grown over time, and now he rarely speaks to anyone other than Riggs, the company commander, and Beatrice Dahl, who still lives in a half-submerged building once owned by her grandfather. Kerans is suspended between the two interlocking worlds, between his desire to rejoin the human community and to stay with Beatrice, as a sort of Adam and Eve in a dangerous new Eden. Of particular interest to Ballard and his characters are the psychological consequences of the change. Thus, Kerans muses to himself that "a more important task than mapping the harbours and lagoons of the internal landscape was to chart the ghostly deltas and luminous beaches of the submerged neuronic continents."

In pursuit of reawakening memories, Kerans, Beatrice, and the party's doctor, Bodkin, stay behind after the rest of the party heads north. Eventually, the three of them are once again forced to confront humanity, however, in the form of the freebooter Strangman and his crew of mulattoes. Strangman, who sails the lagoons of Europe in an egotistical attempt to salvage the wreckage of Western civilization, plans to reclaim the submerged London for his own. For Kerans, Beatrice, and Bodkin, the city that reemerges from the water is ugly and disorienting. When Strangman's method for pumping water out of the lagoons makes him something of a hero as far as the human community is concerned, Kerans resolves to destroy Strangman's dam, engineering an explosion that floods the city again and kills Strangman in the process. Kerans then disappears into the jungle, heading southward, "a second Adam searching for the forgotten paradises of the reborn Sun."

First published in the United States by Berkley Books as one of the many paperback titles that company brought out on a monthly basis, *The Drowned World* escaped American critical notice. In Great Britain, however, where the novel was published in a hardback edition by Victor Gollancz, it earned a good deal of positive response. Kingsley Amis, writing in *The Observer* (27 January 1963), hailed it as "something without precedent in this country, a novel by a science fiction author that can be judged by the highest standards."

Ballard gave some insight into the development of his vision of a drowned Europe in the essay "Time, Memory and Inner Space," which first appeared in the Spring 1963 issue of *Woman Journalist:* "On reflection it seems to me that the image of an immense half-submerged city overgrown by tropical vegetation, which forms the centerpiece of *The Drowned World,* is in some ways a fusion of my childhood memories of Shanghai and those of my last ten years in London." Later in the essay he offered a succinct statement of literary principle: "In many respects this fusion of past and present experiences . . . resembles the mechanisms by which dreams are constructed, and perhaps the great value of fantasy as a literary form is its ability to bring together apparently unconnected and dissimilar ideas." "Time, Memory and Inner Space" is representative of another facet of Ballard's literary career, that of spokesman for the experimental variety of science fiction that typifies the New Wave, of which Ballard, Brian W. Aldiss, and Michael Moorcock were among the most important practitioners. Throughout his career Ballard has used short essays and reviews to put forward his view of a social context for science fiction. At times, in fact, he has championed science fiction over the realist mode that has dominated the twentieth-century literary canon. Thus in "Fictions of Every Kind" (first published in *Books and Bookmen,* February 1971) he pronounces that "At present science fiction is the only form of fiction which is thriving, and certainly the only fiction which has any influence on the world around it. The social novel is reaching fewer and fewer readers, for the clear reason that social relationships are no longer as important as the individual's relationship with the technological landscape of the late 20th century."

Over the next two years Berkley published three more collections of Ballard's stories, all previously published in magazines: *The Four-Dimensional Nightmare* (1963), *Passport to Eternity* (1963), and *The Terminal Beach* (1964). The title story of the last volume marked a new literary direction for Ballard. "The Terminal Beach" is not, strictly speaking, a fantasy; yet, viewed through the perspective of the protagonist, Traven, the abandoned H-bomb testing site on the South Pacific atoll of Eniwetok assumes surreal qualities. Traven (whose name recurs in *The Atrocity Exhibition*) has come to Eniwetok for reasons he does not consciously understand. Haunted by memories of his deceased wife and child, he wanders among acres of concrete bunkers, seeking a hidden logic that links the global anxiety caused by the Cold War (which Traven calls the "Pre-Third," as in third world war) and his personal tragedy:

The Pre-Third: the period had been characterized in Traven's mind above all by its moral and psychological inversions, by its sense of the whole of history, and in particular of the immediate future—the two decades, 1945–65—suspended from the quivering volcano's lip of World War III. Even the death of his wife and six-year-old son in a motor accident seemed only part of

Dust jacket for Ballard's 1970 book, a collection of linked stories; Ballard has identified the "core identity" of their composite protagonist as the enigmatic novelist B. Traven (Richland County Public Library).

this immense synthesis of the historical and psychic zero, and the frantic highways where each morning they met their deaths were the advance causeways to the global armageddon.

By the mid 1960s Ballard's explorations of inner space increasingly incorporate contemporary political and social culture and are often extreme literary speculations on the psychological significance of the atomic bomb, the Kennedy assassination, and the death of Marilyn Monroe. A private library of symbols, the author's own collection of terminal documents, comes to replace the organic mental landscapes of his more fantastic works. "The Terminal Beach" indicates a sharpening of focus, from surrealist fantasy to an even more distinctive literary voice, a process that culminates with *The Atrocity Exhibition.*

In the same year that Ballard wrote "The Terminal Beach," he was confronted with a personal tragedy: the sudden death of his wife from pneumonia. He has never remarried. The effect of his wife's death on his literary project may be impossible to determine precisely, especially in a writer who has often been accused of

exhibiting a morbid sensibility. Undeniably, however, the image of a dead wife recurs as one of the symbols that many of Ballard's interchangeable protagonists encounter in exploring their inner realms.

Ballard's next novel, *The Burning World* (1964; published in Great Britain as *The Drought,* 1965), poses the opposite global peril of *The Drowned World,* anticipating the doomsday predictions for ecological disaster caused by widespread pollution. As David Pringle argued in his essay "The Fourfold Symbolism of J. G. Ballard" (included in *J. G. Ballard: The First Twenty Years,* 1976), Ballard uses imagery of jungles and oceans to symbolize a return to the watery past of prehuman—or prepartum—life. Images of deserts and desiccation, on the other hand, represent a pessimistic projection for the future, as humanity is increasingly cut off from even an ambiguous affirmation of life such as Kerans's in *The Drowned World.*

The Crystal World (1966) completes Ballard's first quartet of novelistic fantasies of global transformation. In this novel the nature of the catastrophe is more obviously symbolic than in earlier works. With a probable nod to Greene's *A Burnt-Out Case* (1961), the protagonist of *The Crystal World,* Dr. Edward Sanders, leaves behind a haunted past for a leper colony in the jungles of the Cameroon Republic. He takes part in another of Ballard's expeditions, this time to discover the secret of a plague that turns everything exposed to it into luminescent, diamond-like crystal. In the first part of the novel Sanders journeys to Mont Royal, a town within the interior of the jungle, and discovers a crystalline wonderland; by the beginning of part 2 he has developed a fascination for his transformed surroundings:

> after the initial impact of the forest, a surprise more visual than anything else, I quickly came to understand it, knowing that its hazards were a small price to pay for its illumination of my life. Indeed the rest of the world seemed drab and inert by contrast, a faded reflection of this bright image, forming a grey penumbral zone like some half-abandoned purgatory.

Sanders postulates that the crystals represent the leakage of "anti-time," the fourth dimension of the antimatter universe, into known space. Anti-time causes matter to extend itself through all four dimensions, to exist in more than one space at once.

Characteristically for Ballard, the imagery in *The Crystal World* seems to owe a debt to modernist visual art. The description of the face of a plague victim, for example, evokes one of Pablo Picasso's Cubist portraits: "Sanders gazed into the visor that covered the man's head, now an immense sapphire in the shape of a conquistador's helmet. Refracted through the prisms that had effloresced from the man's face, his features seemed to overlay one another in a dozen different planes." The vitrified jungle is vividly imagined: plants, buildings, flesh, and water are all susceptible to this freezing of time, spreading over the entire jungle in waves, transforming the rooftops of Mont Royal into "the funerary temples of a necropolis."

Yet, as in all of Ballard's fiction, images of death and transcendence are inextricably bound together. One of the most effective passages in the novel comes when Sanders realizes to his horror that his efforts to save a comrade from the plague actually have consigned the man to an agonizing death. Gradually he understands that the transformation of flesh to crystal is experienced as a transfiguration, "the gift of immortality a direct consequence of the surrender by each of us of our own physical and temporal identities." The gift is especially precious to the patients at the *leproserie,* who know too well how the flesh can fail. Sanders leaves the forest, but he accepts that the progress of the crystal is inexorable.

More than any other of his full-length works, *The Atrocity Exhibition* could be said to occupy the central position in Ballard's oeuvre. It is not a novel; yet, unlike any of the story collections that preceded it, it comprises pieces that are organically linked. The stories in *The Atrocity Collection*—most of which appeared in experimental literary magazines during the late 1960s— are dense collages of millennial prophecy, pornography, scientific studies, modernist art, and Cold War history. Most of them feature a composite character known variously by names such as Talbot, Travis, Tallis, Trabert, and Travers. In his marginal notes to the 1990 annotated edition of the collection, Ballard identifies the protagonist's "core identity" as Traven, a reference to B. Traven, the pseudonym of the author of *The Treasure of the Sierra Madre* (1935), himself something of an enigma. Ballard's Traven is what Joseph Lanz refers to as "the noble neurotic," whose fragmented personality makes him especially suited to succeed in the bewildering cultural landscape.

The stories are linked not by a sustained narrative or by the development of Traven's character in the traditional sense; rather, they are unified by Traven's project of assembling terminal documents. What seem to be the facts of Traven's life vary from story to story. He may be a patient or a doctor—or both—at an unnamed psychiatric clinic. Like Traven in "The Terminal Beach" (a story not included in *The Atrocity Exhibition*), he is haunted by premonitions of the inevitable catastrophe of World War III, which he feels that his private life anticipates. As one of his colleagues, Dr. Nathan, explains to Traven's wife:

> For us, perhaps, World War III is now little more than a sinister pop art display, but for your husband it has become an expression of the failure of his psyche to accept the fact of its own consciousness, and of his revolt against the present continuum of time and space. Dr. Austin may disagree, but it seems to me that it is his intention to start World War III, though not, of course, in the usual sense of the term. The blitzkriegs will be fought out on the spinal battlefields, in terms of the postures we assume, of our traumas mimetized in the angle of a wall or balcony.

Each story in *The Atrocity Exhibition* could be considered an elaboration on this conceptual project. In "The University of Death" Traven leads a class through an assignment devising scenarios for World War III. The project takes a sinister turn as he realizes his students have cast him in the role of the first casualty of the war. The story progresses through isolated paragraphs describing frozen tableaux, an approach that suggests the clinical objectivity of a slide show accompanying a lecture. One paragraph,

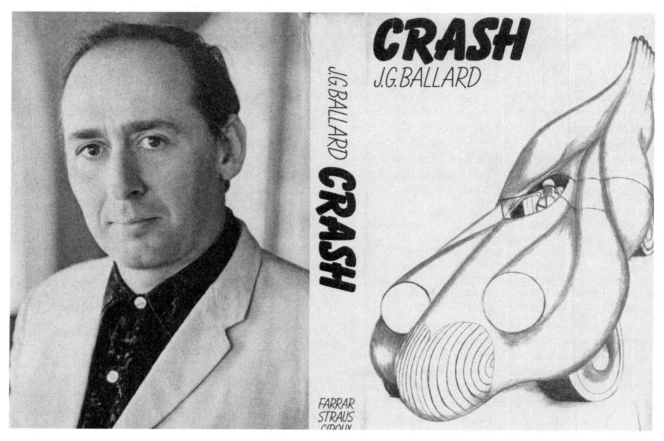

Dust jacket for the U.S. edition of Ballard's 1973 novel, which prompted one publisher's reader to comment,
"The author is beyond psychiatric help" (Collection of Charles Brower)

for example, is titled "The Persistence of Memory," invoking Salvador Dali's best-known painting: "An empty beach with its fused sand. Here clock time is no longer valid. Even the embryo, symbol of secret growth and possibility, is drained and limp. These images are the residues of a remembered moment of time." These words echo verbatim Ballard's analysis of the same painting in "The Coming of the Unconscious," an essay-review first published in *New Worlds* in July 1966. Ballard constructs Traven's project from fragments of his other writings and life story, as well as a large catalogue of symbols culled from the violent, paranoid imagery that pervaded the 1960s—the "atrocity exhibition" of the title. In that spirit, Traven broods endlessly on images of the violent deaths of celebrities, particularly John F. Kennedy, whose assassination in an open convertible, captured on film by Abraham Zapruder, represents for Traven the ultimate marriage of automobile mania, science, celebrity worship, and pornography.

The Atrocity Exhibition is not a fantasy in the conventional sense; in it Ballard reimagines the contents of the contemporary cultural landscape through a warped,

psychopathic perspective. Each story is a literary collage of such complexity that it defies adequate summary. Yet, from within the kaleidoscope of cultural fragments emerges a compelling portrayal of the simultaneous sense of immersion and alienation that characterizes the postmodern condition. In this endeavor Ballard shows the influence of American writer William S. Burroughs, another experimentalist whose work often plays with the conventions of science fiction and an author whom Ballard has championed in essays and interviews throughout his career.

Some readers appreciated the significance of Ballard's achievement in *The Atrocity Exhibition*. Burroughs, for example, provided an admiring introduction for the first U.S. edition, published as *Love and Napalm: Export USA* in 1972, and Barry N. Malzberg, writing in *The Magazine of Fantasy and Science Fiction* (September 1976), asserted: "It is impossible not to realize confronting it that one is in the presence of perhaps the major figure in western literature of our time." Yet, most reviewers were bewildered by the symbolism in the work and put off by its images of violence, human and urban decay, and loveless, abstracted sexuality. Reviewing the book

54

for *Library Journal* (July 1970), Joseph W. Palmer judged it to be "ugly, nauseating, brilliant, and profound"; Jerome Tarshis, in the *Evergreen Review* (Spring 1973), suggested that *The Atrocity Exhibition* might be read as a "long poem on metaphysical themes" and added: "the horrifying part is that this philosophical investigation is conducted in terms of violent death and perverse sexuality." Paul Theroux, writing for *The New York Times Book Review* (23 September 1973), considered Ballard's attitude toward his material "monstrous."

If *The Atrocity Exhibition* baffled many readers, Ballard's next full-length work, *Crash,* was more likely to outrage them. One reader for a London publisher reported after reading the novel in manuscript: "The author is beyond psychiatric help" (a comment Ballard has often recalled that he took as high praise). *Crash* is in one sense a more conventional work than *The Atrocity Exhibition;* that is, it has a fairly straightforward linear narrative. Yet, its subject matter and—more important—the disturbing, affectless manner in which the events of the novel are portrayed have made it more controversial.

Ballard no doubt courted a certain amount of indignant response by intentionally blurring the line between fiction and reality in *Crash.* He employed a first-person narrator and named him James Ballard, for example, and set the novel in the London suburb of Shepperton, where the author had lived for years. Ballard the narrator is a director of television commercials who pursues a series of disinterested sexual affairs but nevertheless is complacently married to Catherine. His perspective on the world is violently altered after he is involved in an automobile collision that seriously injures the driver of the other car, Dr. Helen Remington, and kills her husband. Ballard is instantly fascinated by the woman who stares at him from beyond her husband's broken body: "Did she realize then that the blood covering my face and chest was her husband's?" During his hospital convalescence, he finds that an "obsession with the sexual possibilities of everything around me had been jerked loose from my mind by the crash." He sees Helen again in the hospital, and soon they begin an affair, although they find that they can consummate their sex only in automobiles.

The crash also brings Ballard, Catherine, and Helen into the orbit of Vaughan, the "hoodlum scientist" and "archangel of the expressways," whose successful career as the host of a television science show was ended by a disfiguring motorcycle accident. Now he prowls the roadways surrounding London Airport, photographing accidents and picking up prostitutes to pose in the postures of the dying victims. Vaughan is surrounded by a group of disciples, all scarred inwardly and outwardly by violent contact with automobiles,

and all of them held in thrall by his sexual magnetism. With Seagrave, a stunt driver, Vaughan re-creates famous automobile collisions in front of bleachers full of onlookers. His ultimate obsession is to die in a collision with Elizabeth Taylor, and as the novel opens he lies mortally injured after the attempt, having missed the actress's limousine and crashed into an airport shuttle bus instead.

Like Traven in *The Atrocity Exhibition* and Kaldren in "The Voices of Time," Vaughan makes a project out of assembling a mysterious set of data that corresponds to his obsessions, seemingly as a way of validating his "research." Included among his photograph collages is the history of Ballard's accident and recovery. "I watched Vaughan close the album, wondering why I was unable to rouse myself into at least a parade of anger, remonstrate with him for this intrusion into my life. But Vaughan's detachment from any emotion or concern had already had its effect. Perhaps some latent homo-erotic element had been brought to the surface of my mind by his photographs of violence and sexuality.... Vaughan had articulated my needs for some positive response to my crash."

The Ballards' mutual fascination with Vaughan energizes their marriage, in a highly ironic sense: "I began to think about Catherine's death in a more calculated way, trying to devise in my mind an even richer exit than the death which Vaughan had devised for Elizabeth Taylor. These fantasies were part of the affectionate responses exchanged between us as we drove along the motorway together." Vaughan's project becomes disorganized as he sinks more deeply into his obsessions, but after his death his project seems to survive through the dedication of his disciples and perhaps through the inevitability of his vision: "Meanwhile, the traffic moves in an unceasing flow along the flyover. The aircraft rise from the runway of the airport, carrying the remnants of Vaughan's semen to the instrument panels and radiator grilles of a thousand crashing cars, the leg stances of a million passengers."

Reviewers' initial response to this explicit, obsessive novel was distinctly negative, as represented by D. Keith Mano's judgment in *The New York Times Book Review* (23 September 1973): "the most repulsive book I've yet to come across . . . *Crash* is well written; credit given where due. But I could not, in conscience, recommend it." *Crash* almost immediately developed a cult reputation, however; it has proved especially influential on practitioners and scholars of what is called "postmodern science fiction" (a phrase that Ballard witheringly likened to "the apotheosis of a hamburger" in a 1991 issue of *Science Fiction Studies*). Graeme Revell, writing in a special Ballard issue of *Re/Search,* suggested that the initial reviews revealed readers' inability to accept the urgent expressions of the author's

Dust jacket for the U.S. edition of Ballard's 1987 novel, in which factions battle to control a mysterious river (Richland County Public Library)

vision: "these new works developed previously latent ideas to a malignancy which burst out of the confines of science fiction. The fiction seemed to have become real, too real, and there were dangerous questions: moral, existential, even political." In his essay "*Crash*," translated in *Simulacra and Simulation* (1994), French philosopher Jean Baudrillard, with characteristic provocativeness, asserts that the novel has a significance that transcends conventional judgments of literary quality:

> In *Crash,* no more fiction or reality, it is hyperreality that abolishes both. Not even a critical regression is possible. This mutating and commutating world of simulation and death, this violently sexed world, but one without desire, full of violated and violent bodies, as if neutralized, this chromatic world and metallic intensity, but one void of sensuality, hypertechnology without finality—is it good or bad? We will never know. It is simply fascinating, though this fascination does not imply a value judgment. There lies the miracle of *Crash.* Nowhere does this moral gaze surface—the critical judgment that is still part of the functionality of the old world.

As the sometimes vitriolic response to the 1998 movie version, directed by David Cronenberg, suggests, *Crash* has retained the power to incite controversy.

Like *The Atrocity Exhibition* and *Crash,* Ballard's next two novels, *Concrete Island* (1974) and *High-Rise* (1975), include little in the way of outright fantasy. Yet, these works have had considerable influence on speculative fiction because of their searching portrayals of the new states of mind brought on by a changing cultural and technological environment. An updating of Daniel Defoe's *Robinson Crusoe* (1719), *Concrete Island* is the story of an architect, Maitland, who is marooned on a huge concrete median in the middle of a London highway. Injured in a hit-and-run accident, Maitland is unable to climb the steep embankment to summon help, and he must rely on the aid of a prostitute and a former circus acrobat turned derelict. Maitland compensates for his infirmity by manipulating his companions, particularly the cretinous derelict, Proctor. When he is finally well enough to get off the island, however, he finds himself unable to leave the kingdom of the mind he has created. The reviewer for *TLS: The Times Literary Supplement* (26 April 1974) called the novel "most intelligent and interesting" and labeled Ballard "our foremost iconographer of landscape." Martin Levin, in *The New York Times Book Review* (1 December 1974), acknowledged that Ballard "raises some tantalizing questions, even if he doesn't answer them satisfactorily."

High-Rise is perhaps Ballard's bleakest assessment of the psychology of urban life; again, he strips away London professionals' pretenses to civilized behavior. The root of their mass psychosis is the vertiginous experience of living a life almost totally contained within the parameters of a modern high-rise apartment building. The tone of the novel is established by its arresting first sentence: "Later, as he sat on his balcony eating the dog, Dr. Robert Laing reflected on the unusual events that had taken place within this huge apartment building during the previous three months."

The corrosive satirical point of *High-Rise* is that the veneer of civility for these urban professionals is extremely thin. They revert almost immediately to a form of tribalism, opening their doors to their immediate neighbors but regarding the occupants of more remote floors with increasing hostility. Carousing becomes continuous and reaches a hysterical pitch. As maintenance services in the building break down, raiding parties are sent to explore other floors. Ultimately, Richard Wilder, a documentarian, abandons his listless wife and children in their second-floor apartment and ascends to the fortieth floor to confront Anthony Royal, the architect who designed the building and who rules over his penthouse like a savage chieftain. Wilder kills Royal in their inevitable meeting, but the real victors in the struggle over control of the high-rise seem to be an emerging matriarchy.

Most reviewers were unconvinced by the brutality of the inhabitants of the building. In *The Listener* (11 December 1975) Neil Hepburn complained that the novel required "such an effort for the suspension of disbelief as to become tiresome." Reviewing the novel for *The New York Times Book Review* (11 May 1977), Mel Watkins found *High-Rise* "compulsively vulgar."

Ballard's next novel, *The Unlimited Dream Company* (1979), is one of his most overtly fantastic. A troubled young man, Blake, steals a small airplane and crash-lands it in a hallucinatory version of Shepperton. Apparently suspended in a life-in-death state, Blake presides over the London suburb as a "local pagan deity," healing the sick, teaching the children to fly, and transforming the neighborhood into a paradisal—if somewhat forbidding—tropical aviary by anointing it with his semen.

When Blake first crashes in Shepperton, he sees in a tableau the local denizens whose fates are intertwined in his: Miriam St. Cloud, a pediatrician with whom Blake seeks a marriage in the air; Stark, a pilot and amateur zookeeper who salvages Blake's crashed plane from the Thames in order to provide material proof of his death; and three disabled children who seem acutely aware of the dark side of Blake's miraculous powers. Blake absorbs the people of Shepperton into his own body in a quasi-sexual union, transforming them and nourishing himself. Explaining the allegorical implications of the novel, Gregory Stephenson suggests that "there is a reciprocal relationship between Blake as messiah and the inhabitants of Shepperton, his congregation. He infuses them with motive and power, while they, in turn, sustain and revitalize him. Capable of ultimate love, self-denial, and unconditional forgiveness, Blake may be seen to represent the first truly whole, truly heroic figure in Ballard's oeuvre." Yet, the fantasy of *The Unlimited Dream Company* has Ballard's usual chilly tone, so that it is possible to see Blake as similar to the narrator of *Crash* or Traven of *The Atrocity Exhibition,* whose coping strategies have a placidly schizophrenic logic about them—"the death of affect" that the author has frequently identified as the essential quality of contemporary life.

Malcolm Bradbury, writing in *The New York Times Book Review* (9 December 1979), called *The Unlimited Dream Company* a "remarkable piece of invention": "It is heady stuff, a dreamy pastoral, but Mr. Ballard sustains it from a well-funded imagination, a prolix style and a great mythical sense. At times, but only at times, the metaphors grow a little too thick, and the pastoral too innocent. But this is above all a book about the fertility of the imagination. It is dense

and erotic and magical, a pleasure to read." Novelist Anthony Burgess was even more enthusiastic, including the novel in his critical survey *Ninety-Nine Novels: The Best in English Since 1939* (1984).

Hello America (1981) is Ballard's most broadly satirical look at the cultural dominance of late-twentieth-century Americanism. A band of latter-day pilgrims arrive in what was once New York Harbor, still in ironic fashion serving as the gateway for European immigrants even though the United States succumbed to cataclysm some generations previously and is now mostly abandoned. The "Great American Desert" has extended all the way to New Jersey—again there is the association between the desiccated cityscapes and a more metaphysical aridity that Pringle noted. The expedition is seen through the eyes of Wayne, a young stowaway, who seeks "the El Dorado he had dreamed of for so long—not the literal golden city . . . but that vision of the United States enshrined in the pages of *Time* and *Look*."

The party soon discovers that "under the guise of crossing America, . . . they were about to begin that far longer safari across the diameters of their own skulls." Amid the wreckage of American culture, they quickly become lost, and by the time they reach Dodge City, they are delirious and dying. When a rescue party reaches them, Wayne is one of the few left alive. In Las Vegas, now in the midst of a massive rainforest west of the Rockies, Wayne finds the capital of a new United States, populated largely by Disney-style animatronics of such luminaries as Frank Sinatra, Dean Martin, and Judy Garland from *The Wizard of Oz* and ruled by President Charlie Manson—an amalgam of his namesake, Richard Nixon, and Howard Hughes.

Even in this diminished setting, the American Dream has a potent effect on Wayne, whom Manson courts to succeed him as president. Completely consumed by paranoia, Manson retires to his War Room, whence he launches nuclear missiles more or less randomly at the former urban centers of the United States. When opposition forces begin to close in, he decides to use his single remaining missile suicidally, to destroy Las Vegas. Wayne and the surviving followers of Manson manage to escape before the explosion, with the help of a cadre of animatronic U.S. presidents and a squadron of glass gliders. At the conclusion of the novel Wayne prepares to assume the leadership role for which he was groomed: "The old dreams were dead, Manson and Mickey Mouse and Marilyn Monroe belonging to a past America, to that city of antique gamblers about to be vaporised fifty miles away. It was time for new dreams, worthy of a real tomorrow, the dreams of the first President of the Sunlight Fliers."

Dust jacket for the U.S. edition of Ballard's 1994 novel, one of several in which he depicted pathological responses to contemporary issues (Richland County Public Library)

racketeers, whom he comes to idolize. Eventually he is interned at Lunghua Civilian Internment Centre, where he spends the rest of the war with imprisoned English families. When the Japanese abandon the camp, Jim is left on his own among internees who are too weak to relocate. He sees far in the distance the atomic-bomb explosion at Nagasaki, which hastened the end of the war.

While *Empire of the Sun* is not a science-fiction novel, it holds undeniable interest for readers of Ballard's speculative fiction. It must to some extent be read as an account of the origins of the iconography that dominates the author's literary project, as many of the chapter titles suggest: "The Abandoned Aerodrome," "The Drained Swimming Pool," "The University of Life," and "The Cemetery Garden," for example. Jim also exhibits the Ballardian hero's characteristic ambivalence about the conditions that surround him; in this case, the quality represents the adaptability that perhaps enables the boy to survive repeated traumas. Although Ballard, in a brief foreword, refers to the novel as "for the most part an eyewitness account" of his experiences, he does take liberties with factual details, most notably in making Jim an only child and separating him from his parents for the duration of the war.

Empire of the Sun earned Ballard some of the best reviews of his career. John Calvin Batchelor, for instance, writing in *The New York Times Book Review* (11 December 1984), praised the novel as "searing and frightening" and concluded that "Mr. Ballard, with a splendid and powerful talent, has written a novel that makes haunting fictional sense of what happened to Jim forty years ago." In *Newsweek* (28 January 1985), David Lehman and Donna Foote asserted that the novel belongs "on anyone's short list of outstanding novels inspired by the second world war." John Gross, in *The New York Times* (13 October 1984), was one of many critics who found in the novel a context for Ballard's earlier fiction: "If one still hesitates to call *Empire of the Sun* a conventional novel, it is only because many of the scenes in it are so lurid and bizarre, so very nearly out of this world. Among other things, they help to explain why in his work up till now Mr. Ballard should have been repeatedly drawn to apocalyptic themes."

Ballard's next novel, *The Day of Creation* (1987), is another phantasmagoric homage to Graham Greene and Joseph Conrad. In a war-blighted country in Central Africa, a World Health Organization doctor, Mallory, seems to dream to life a new river from an apparently limitless subterranean source. The River Mallory attracts attention from a variety of parties, including Sanger, a hack scientist, infamous for his tele-

Hello America was more positively received in England than in the United States. In *The New York Times Book Review* (16 October 1988), Gregory Benford averred that the novel "has charm if it is read as a comic-book tour of imaginary landscapes" but that "the shallowness of this novel doesn't intrigue or illuminate. Much of this and earlier Ballard work on the same lines . . . tells us distorted things about ourselves that grow rather obvious when stretched to the length of a novel."

With the arguable exception of *Crash,* Ballard's best-known novel is *Empire of the Sun* (1984), which was short-listed for the Booker Prize, awarded the James Tait Black Memorial Prize, and adapted into a motion picture directed by Steven Spielberg in 1988. The novel is a fictionalized account of Ballard's boyhood experiences in war-torn China. Young Jim is separated from his parents during the panicked evacuation of Shanghai; after a period of near-starvation in the abandoned family home, he ingratiates himself to some American

vised inquiries into the psychic abilities of plants and animals; the warring factions headed by the warlord General Harare and Captain Kagwa of the national gendarmerie; and Nora Warrender, who amasses an armed brothel of local women to aid in her vendetta against Harare. The river grows into a coursing waterway in a matter of weeks, transforming the arid region into a lush, abundantly inhabited forest. Commandeering a boat from Kagwa's stockpile of matériel, Mallory heads up the river that bears his name, accompanied by a preadolescent girl, Noon, one of Harare's guerrillas.

The River Mallory quickly assumes strategic importance in the perpetual power struggles that dominate the politics of the region, but Mallory's interest in the river corresponds to a private significance, as Gregory Stephenson observes:

> the Mallory corresponds to stages or layers of Dr. Mallory's consciousness: its lower reaches are "the domestic realm of the small mammals . . . the passerine birds and flowering plants," its middle waters changing to become "the more primitive world of the amphibians and raptors," and its upper regions comprising a primordial zone "outside time or memory." In this sense, Mallory's ascent of the river Mallory in search of its source represents a journey inward, a quest for the original fount of his own conscious being.

As Mallory's project becomes more confused, the river settles into a stagnant swamp; Mallory persuades General Harare to destroy the river with a system of barrages, a process that dooms all those who had already come to rely on its life-giving waters.

Finally, Mallory, Sanger, and Noon reach the source of the river, just as the last of it drains back into the ground. The region almost immediately returns to its near-uninhabitable state. With the disappearance of the river, Noon—whom the narrator has come to love—vanishes as well, leaving Mallory to wonder if she was a figment of his imagination: "I had not invented the river and our journey, but had I invented Noon? She has a distinct physical presence that is ever more real, the smell of her hands and breasts, the endless clicking of her teeth. But was she a figment born from a river itself sprung from my imagination? Had I invented her to draw myself to the river's source, and in their references to Noon were the others merely humouring my obsession?" The novel ends on an uncharacteristically poignant note: "Sooner or later she will reappear, and I am certain that when she comes the Mallory will also return, and once again run the waters of its dream across the dust of a waiting heart."

The response of reviewers was generally positive. The reviewer for *New York* magazine, for example, wrote that "*The Day of Creation* is a marvelously seduc-

tive and mysterious book, a novel in which beauty and menace are evoked with all the surreal, voluptuous intensity of a fever dream," while Richard Eder, in *The Los Angeles Times Book Review,* called the novel "acute and far-ranging" and credited the author with bringing to the fantasy "a touch of irony and humor to keep it from getting out of hand." Some critics detected a repetitiousness that bordered on self-parody, however. In the 13 September 1987 issue of *The Observer,* novelist Martin Amis imagined a conversation between two readers: "'I've read the new Ballard.' 'And?' 'It's like the early stuff.' 'Really? What's the element?' 'Water.' 'Lagoons?' 'Some. Mainly a river.' 'What's the hero's name? Maitland? Melville?' 'Mallory.'"

Ballard followed *The Day of Creation* with *Running Wild* (1988), a novella, like *Crash* and *The Atrocity Exhibition,* in which the fantasy element is located in the characters' psychopathic response to life in an environment dominated by technology. The narrative comprises the case notes of forensic psychiatrist Richard Greville relating to the "Pangbourne massacre," in which thirty-two adult residents of an exclusive gated community were murdered and their children apparently abducted. Gradually, Greville is compelled to accept a more disturbing conclusion: that the children themselves killed their parents and are now at large as a terrorist gang.

Greville's investigation entails sifting through the remnants of life in Pangbourne, particularly videotapes from the closed-circuit television system that monitored the residents' daily activities. The liberal-minded child-rearing methods of the affluent Pangbourne parents, combined with their ubiquitous surveillance technology, created an atmosphere in the community at once solicitous and oppressive, provoking the children's horrifying backlash. As Greville observes, "The Pangbourne children weren't rebelling against hate and cruelty. . . . What they were rebelling against was a despotism of kindness. They killed to free themselves from a tyranny of love and care." In a postscript written five years after the massacre, Greville describes a well-organized but unsuccessful assassination attempt against a former prime minister, sometimes known as "the Mother of her Nation," which prompts the psychiatrist to speculate "that all authority and parental figures are now their special target. . . . So the regime of kindness and care which was launched with the best of intentions at Pangbourne Village, and which has prompted countless imitations in the exclusive estates of southern England, not to mention Western Europe and the United States, has given birth to its children of revenge, sending them out to challenge the world that loved them."

Several of the stories in Ballard's 1990 collection, *War Fever,* employ fantasy in the service of satirical political fables. In the title story, the perpetual strife of

j. g. ballard · super-cannes / a novel

Dust jacket for the U.S. edition of Ballard's 2000 novel, in which residents of a community on the Côte d'Azur relieve stress by participating in carefully orchestrated activities such as "Vigilante actions, incidents of deliberate road rage, thefts from immigrant markets, tangles with the Russian mafiosi . . . drug-dealing and prostitution, burglaries and warehouse-robberies" (Richland County Public Library)

ity among the nation's young people is England's answer to the AIDS epidemic and falling birthrates. Other stories demonstrate a wry experimentalism. "Notes towards a Nervous Breakdown" consists of a single, obsessively annotated, sentence, while "The Index" provides tantalizing clues as to the contents of an unpublished biography of "physician and philosopher, man of action and patron of the arts, sometimes claimant to the English throne and founder of a new religion, Henry Rhodes Hamilton"—a man whose associates include such diverse figures as Sigmund Freud, Winston Churchill, William Faulkner, Ingrid Bergman, the Dalai Lama, and Lee Harvey Oswald.

Ballard's 1991 novel, *The Kindness of Women,* like *Empire of the Sun,* is an exercise in fictionalized memoir, of interest to readers of the author's science fiction for the insights it provides into the development of his distinctive vision. It too has unmistakable parallels to Ballard's personal history: the narrator starts out as an internee of the Lunghua camp and becomes first a medical student, then an RAF trainee, then a science-fiction writer, as well as a widower and father of three children. Along the way, Ballard also depicts some of his experiences as a participant in the English cultural scene of the 1960s, including reading a "text celebrating the perverse sexuality of President Kennedy's widow" at a large outdoor event in Brighton and staging an exhibition of wrecked automobiles at a London art gallery that degenerates into a drunken melee.

Most important in the context of Ballard's total literary project is the characteristic quality of emotional distance the narrator of *The Kindness of Women* exhibits. As with *Empire of the Sun,* one may infer that a degree of affectlessness is a necessary response to a series of traumatic circumstances, including the sudden accidental death of the narrator's wife. He explicitly connects his private history and outlook to the general cultural climate of the time:

> In this overlit realm ruled by images of the space race and the Vietnam War, the Kennedy assassination, and the suicide of Marilyn Monroe, a unique alchemy of the imagination was taking place. In many ways the media landscape of the 1960s was a laboratory designed specifically to cure me of all my obsessions. Violence and pornography provided a kit of desperate measures that might give meaning both to Miriam's death and to the unnumbered victims of the war in China. The demise of feeling and emotion, the death of affect, presided like a morbid sun over the playground of that ominous decade. . . .

Beirut is revealed to be the means by which the otherwise peaceful world inoculates against political violence. In "The Secret History of World War 3" Ronald Reagan is restored to the presidency, and the Western media is so transfixed by the minutiae of his medical condition that World War III, approximately four minutes in duration, passes largely unnoticed. Ballard uses more conventional science-fiction motifs—albeit warped through his distinctive perspective—in "Report on an Unidentified Space Station," in which an exploratory party, lost within the fathomless dimensions of the station, are compelled to revise continually their estimates of its size, from five hundred meters to fifteen million light years at last report; and in "Love in a Colder Climate," two years of compulsory, regulated sexual activ-

Emblematic of the dark undercurrent of the time, perhaps, is the narrator's friend and fellow Lunghua survivor, David Hunter. An unstable, haunted, thrill-seeking aviator, David clearly resembles the Mephistophelean Vaughan of *Crash*.

In a development that can only be described as Ballardian, the narrator's novel based on his childhood is made into a movie, which is filmed in the studios at Shepperton; his neighbors are hired to play the extras in this simulation of his Shanghai days. Ballard thus returns to his earliest memories in an artfully self-conscious way that is entirely appropriate to his literary career. Most reviewers approved and appreciated the novel primarily for its insights into the author's sometimes difficult oeuvre. Roger Luckhurst cautions against reading either *The Kindness of Women* or *Empire of the Sun* as autobiographical keys to Ballard's more extreme fictions, however, noting that both works deliberately echo incidents, images, and phrases that appear in earlier works. The issue of whether the incidents described in the autobiographical novels inspired the novels written prior to them, or vice versa, is ultimately unresolvable.

Like *Crash, Concrete Island, High-Rise,* and *Running Wild,* Ballard's novels of the 1990s occupy that distinct region between fantasy and realistic fiction: they are pushed toward fantasy by the characters' pathological responses to the pressures of contemporary culture. In *Rushing to Paradise* (1994), Ballard's rampant egotist is, for a change, a woman: Dr. Barbara Rafferty, the publicity-hungry, self-proclaimed savior of the albatrosses on the nuclear test site of Saint-Esprit. "Dr. Barbara" turns the inhospitable Pacific island into her version of an environmentalist/feminist paradise. As increasing numbers of activists and dropouts arrive on Saint-Esprit, the more sinister aspects of the doctor's agenda come to light: she intends to create an all-female community, with the exception of her acolyte, Neil (another of Ballard's boy protagonists, like Jim in *Empire of the Sun* or Wayne in *Hello America*), who will be kept around for reproductive purposes.

Cocaine Nights (1996) is set among the dangerously bored inhabitants of a Spanish retirement community. Although closer to mystery than fantasy, the novel seems in familiar territory with its portrayal of the cult of personality surrounding diabolical tennis pro Bobby Crawford. As with almost all of Ballard's previous works, these novels elicited polarized responses from reviewers.

Super-Cannes (2000) mines territory similar to *Cocaine Nights;* the Côte d'Azur community of Eden-Olympia is designed to suit the needs of work-obsessed modern professionals, including stress relief in the form of bursts of orchestrated violence and sexual perversity. The narrator, Paul Sinclair, a pilot and magazine editor recovering from a plane crash, is left on his own while his younger wife, Jane, a pediatrician, gradually becomes absorbed in the way of life at Eden-Olympia. Sinclair becomes obsessed with investigating the mysterious shooting spree perpetrated by Jane's predecessor as resident pediatrician at Eden-Olympia, who shattered the superficial placidity of the community by apparently killing ten people and then turning his rifle on himself. The egotistical villain of the novel is Wilder Penrose, the resident psychologist, whose approach to criminal activities as therapy underpins the corporate dystopia:

> Vigilante actions, incidents of deliberate road rage, thefts from immigrant markets, tangles with the Russian mafiosi. Other therapy groups spread out into the fringes of drug-dealing and prostitution, burglaries and warehouse-robberies. . . . The benefits were astounding. Immune levels rose through the ceiling, within three months there wasn't a trace of insomnia or depression, not a hint of respiratory infections. Corporate profits and equity values began to climb again. The treatment worked.

As with most of Ballard's writing since the early 1970s, *Super-Cannes* straddles fantasy and realism. Reviewers were at a loss to place the novel in a particular genre; yet, they praised it almost unanimously. Many considered it a conscious attempt on the author's part to synthesize his abiding themes—particularly the affectlessness of modern consumer culture, the conflict between baser human impulses and so-called civilized behavior, and the ubiquitousness of surveillance technology—at the start of the new millennium. Nicholas Royle, writing in *The Independent* (2 September 2000), called it "the first essential novel of the twenty-first century."

There seems little doubt that J. G. Ballard's oeuvre will continue to provoke strong reactions, both positive and negative. His detractors as well as his champions have acknowledged that his distinctively chilly prose and obsessive imagery have a tendency to haunt readers. Throughout his career he has remained something of a literary celebrity, a garrulous interview subject, and a frequent, engaging reviewer and essayist. (A collection of his reviews and other nonfiction from the span of his career was published in 1996 as *A User's Guide to the Millennium: Essays and Reviews*.) As virtual reality and simulated antisocial behavior gain increasing acceptance as forms of entertainment, Ballard's fiction—as Pringle and Graeme Revelle, among others, have suggested—will grow in relevance. His status as Britain's most provocative explorer of inner space seems safe.

Interviews:

David Pringle and James Goddard, "An Interview with J. G. Ballard," *Vector,* 73 (March 1976): 28–49;

Charles Platt, "J. G. Ballard," in his *Dream Makers: The Uncommon People Who Write Science Fiction* (New York: Berkley, 1980), pp. 215–225;

Alan Burns and Charles Sugnet, "J. G. Ballard," in *The Imagination on Trial: British and American Writers Discuss Their Working Methods* (London & New York: Alison & Busby, 1981), pp. 14–30;

Pringle, "Interview with J. G. Ballard," in his *J. G. Ballard: A Primary and Secondary Bibliography* (Boston: G. K. Hall, 1984), pp. 1–28;

V. Vale and Andrea Juno, "Interview with J. G. Ballard," in *Re/Search 8/9: J. G. Ballard,* edited by Vale and Juno (San Francisco: Re/Search, 1984), pp. 6–36;

Graeme Revell, "Interview with J. G. Ballard," in *Re/Search 8/9: J. G. Ballard,* pp. 42–52;

Thomas Frick, "The Art of Fiction: J. G. Ballard," *Paris Review,* 94 (1985): 133–160;

David Blow, "'Bloody Sunday and After': Interview with J. G. Ballard," *Waterstone's New Book Catalogue* (Winter 1991): 35–37;

Jason Cowley, "Portrait: J. G. Ballard," *Prospect* (August/September 1998).

Bibliography:

David Pringle, *J. G. Ballard: A Primary and Secondary Bibliography* (Boston: G. K. Hall, 1984).

References:

Jean Baudrillard, "*Crash*" and "Simulacra and Science Fiction," in his *Simulacra and Simulation,* translated by Sheila Faria Glaser (Ann Arbor: University of Michigan Press, 1994), pp. 111–127;

Jonathan Benison, "In Default of a Poet in Space: J. G. Ballard and the Current State of Nihilism," in *Just the Other Day,* edited by Luk Van Der Vos (Antwerp, 1985), pp. 405–424;

Peter Brigg, *J. G. Ballard* (Mercer Island, Wash.: Starmont House, 1985);

Anthony Burgess, *Ninety-Nine Novels: The Best in English Since 1939—A Personal Choice* (London: Allison & Busby, 1984), p. 118;

Haim Finkelstein, "'Deserts of Vast Eternity': J. G. Ballard and Robert Smithson," *Foundation,* 39 (Spring 1987): 50–62;

Lorenz J. Firsching, "J. G. Ballard's Ambiguous Apocalypse," *Science-Fiction Studies,* 12 (November 1985): 297–310;

Dennis Foster, "J. G. Ballard's Empire of the Senses: Perversion and the Failure of Authority," *PMLA,* 108 (May 1993): 519–532;

H. Bruce Franklin, "What Are We to Make of J. G. Ballard's Apocalypse?" in *Voices for the Future: Essays on Major Science Fiction Writers,* volume 2, edited by Thomas D. Clareson (Bowling Green, Ohio: Bowling Green University Popular Press, 1979), pp. 82–105;

Colin Greenland, *The Entropy Exhibition: Michael Moorcock and the British "New Wave" in Science Fiction* (London: Routledge & Kegan Paul, 1983);

Frederic Jameson, *Postmodernism, or the Cultural Logic of Late Capitalism* (Durham, N.C.: Duke University Press, 1991), pp. 155–180;

Joseph Lanz, "The Noble Neurotic," in *Re/Search 8/9: J. G. Ballard,* edited by V. Vale and Andrea Juno (San Francisco: Re/Search, 1984), pp. 141–142;

Roger Luckhurst, *"The Angle between Two Walls": The Fiction of J. G. Ballard* (New York: St. Martin's Press, 1997);

Charles Nicol, "J. G. Ballard and the Limits of Mainstream SF," *Science Fiction Studies,* 3 (July 1976): 150–157;

David Pringle, *Earth Is the Alien Planet: J. G. Ballard's Four-Dimensional Nightmare* (San Bernardino, Cal.: Borgo Press, 1974);

Pringle and James Goddard, eds., *J. G. Ballard: The First Twenty Years* (Hayes, U.K.: Bran's Head, 1976);

David Punter, "J. G. Ballard: Alone among the Murder Machines," in his *The Hidden Script* (London: Routledge & Kegan Paul, 1985), pp. 9–27;

Peter Rønnov-Jessen, "Science Fiction in the Market Place: The Incorporation of 'New Wave' Science Fiction into the Literary Established Considered as a Downhill Motor Race," *Dolphin,* 11 (April 1985): 73–91;

Matti Savolainen, "The Wave of Postmodern Science Fiction: J. G. Ballard as a Test Case," in *Criticism in the Twilight Zone: Postmodern Perspectives on Literature and Politics,* edited by Danuta Zadworna-Fjellstad (Stockholm: Almqvist & Wiksell, 1990), pp. 121–128;

Gregory Stephenson, *Out of the Night and into the Dream: A Thematic Study of the Fiction of J. G. Ballard* (Westport, Conn.: Greenwood Press, 1991);

Vale and Juno, eds., *Re/Search 8/9: J. G. Ballard* (San Francisco: Re/Search, 1984).

Iain M. Banks

(16 February 1954 –   )

Rob Latham
University of Iowa

See also the Banks entry in *DLB 194: British Novelists Since 1960, Second Series.*

BOOKS: *The Wasp Factory,* as Iain Banks (London: Macmillan, 1984; Boston: Houghton Mifflin, 1984);

Walking on Glass, as Iain Banks (London: Macmillan, 1985; Boston: Houghton Mifflin, 1986);

The Bridge, as Iain Banks (London: Macmillan, 1986; New York: St. Martin's Press, 1986);

Consider Phlebas (London: Macmillan, 1987; New York: St. Martin's Press, 1987);

Espedair Street, as Iain Banks (London: Macmillan, 1987);

The Player of Games (London: Macmillan, 1988; New York: St. Martin's Press, 1989);

Canal Dreams, as Iain Banks (London: Macmillan, 1989; Garden City, N.Y.: Doubleday, 1991);

The State of the Art (Willimantic, Conn.: Ziesing, 1989; enlarged edition, London: Orbit, 1991);

Use of Weapons (London: Orbit, 1990; New York: Bantam, 1992);

The Crow Road, as Iain Banks (London: Scribners, 1992);

Against a Dark Background (London: Orbit, 1993; New York: Bantam, 1993);

Complicity, as Iain Banks (London: Little, Brown, 1993; Garden City, N.Y.: Doubleday, 1995);

Feersum Endjinn (London: Orbit, 1994; New York: Bantam, 1995);

Whit; or, Isis Amongst the Unsaved, as Iain Banks (London: Little, Brown, 1995; New York: Bantam, 1997);

Excession (London: Orbit, 1996; New York: Bantam, 1997);

A Song of Stone, as Iain Banks (London: Abacus, 1997; New York: Villard, 1998);

Inversions (London: Orbit, 1998; New York: Pocket Books, 2000);

The Business, as Iain Banks (London: Little, Brown, 1999; New York: Simon & Schuster, 2000);

Iain M. Banks (photograph © 1984 by Jerry Bauer; from the dust jacket for the U.S. edition of The Wasp Factory, *1984)*

Look to Windward (London: Orbit, 2000; New York: Pocket Books, 2001).

PRODUCED SCRIPT: *Complicity,* motion picture, by Banks and Bryan Elsley, Carlton/J&M/Talisman, 2000.

OTHER: *The Bridge,* narration by Banks, music by Gary Lloyd, compact disc, Gallery Productions, 1996;

"A Few Notes on the Culture," by Banks and Ken MacLeod, 6 August 1998 <http://www.floating-planet.net/phlebas/shock/text/cultnote.html>.

63

SELECTED PERIODICAL PUBLICATIONS–
UNCOLLECTED:
NONFICTION
"Guest of Honor Speech, Eastcon '90," *Matrix: The B.S.F.A. Newsletter,* 88 (June/July 1990): 5–6;
"Escape from the Laws of Physics," *New Scientist,* 137 (20 March 1993): 38–39.

Of the British science-fiction and fantasy writers who began their careers in the 1980s, Iain M. Banks is one of the most important–and is certainly the most diverse in terms of the range of his published work. Primarily a novelist, he has tried his hand at brooding character studies, metafictional fantasies, near-future political thrillers, and hard-core space operas. Indeed, he has developed several relatively distinct audiences for his work. Among mainstream literary circles in Britain, his more realistic efforts are highly praised, while his science fiction is discreetly ignored; in the United States, however, he has built a growing fan base for his popular genre fiction, while some of his more character-driven works–such as *Espedair Street* (1987) and *The Crow Road* (1992)–have not been published there. While Banks has often been quoted as deploring this schizophrenic reception–stoutly arguing for the full equality of his various output, at least in his own eyes–he has also contributed to this division by deploying a different byline for his science fiction as opposed to his more mainstream efforts, the former books including his middle initial, "M." Characteristic themes recur throughout the body of his work, at times making it difficult to decide, even despite the presence or absence of his middle initial, whether a book is ultimately realistic or fantastic in its vision. In this regard, Banks has followed the lead of British New Wave stalwarts such as J. G. Ballard and Michael Moorcock in articulating a consistent set of ideas and motifs across a wide range of literary forms, enjoying in the process a crossover success denied to his more narrowly genre-based contemporaries.

Iain Menzies Banks was born in Dunfermline, Scotland, on 16 February 1954, the son of Thomas Menzies Banks, an admiralty officer, and Euphemia Thomson Banks, an ice-skating instructor. He grew up in North Queensferry, Fife, a site that had a significant influence on his later fiction; as Banks remarked in an interview with Michael Cobley published in 1990 in *Science Fiction Eye:* "I almost literally grew up in [the] shadow" of the Firth of Forth bridge, a vast technological marvel that gave him, "even as a little kid, a strange sense of pride, to have this massive construction towering over the river." The structure features prominently in Banks's third novel, *The Bridge* (1986). In 1963 his family moved to Gourock, on the Clyde River, where

Banks attended high school, succeeding well enough in his studies to secure admission to Stirling University, where he earned a degree in English in 1975. Banks has acknowledged, in an interview with Liam Fay for *Hot Press* in 1996, that he was "a rather boring student. I had a pretty minimal social life. I was very bookish, but not very successful academically. I was trying to write novels all the time. . . . It was only when I left university that I really got into my sleazy, student-life phase, and I'm still in it." Banks never pursued a higher degree, preferring instead the less structured life of a freelance writer, although his later literary success did lead to the conferral, by the University of St. Andrews in Scotland, of an honorary Doctor of Letters in 1997.

Banks claims to have known, from an early age, that he wanted to write. He was an only child, and his imagination was stimulated by television, which in the 1950s was a rare presence in Scotland. "I was a real television baby," Banks told an interviewer for *Contemporary Authors* in 1990:

> we were the first family in the street to have a TV. My father was away at sea–well, coastal waters, mostly, to be more accurate–quite a lot, so the TV was to keep my mum amused. I used to lie awake at night making up stories in my head–it saved torch batteries, compared to reading under the bedclothes–but they were always TV series, or films, rather than prose.

As a result, his mature fiction, even at its most intensely literary, reveals his highly visual imagination in its vividness of incident and detail. His work is therefore easily adapted for performance (although Banks has not worked on many of these projects): *The Wasp Factory* (1984) was a stage success; *The Crow Road* was dramatized on BBC television to critical acclaim in 1996; and a motion-picture for *Complicity* (1993) was produced in 2000.

Banks's budding imagination soon gravitated toward comic books and then science fiction. As he put it in the Cobley interview, as a teenager he "used to raid Gourock Library every week for three or four books and I always looked for the yellow Gollancz covers, and I'd read them whatever the hell they were. As long as it said SF on the cover I'd read them." His tastes soon matured to encompass authors associated with *New Worlds* magazine, especially John Sladek, Barrington J. Bayley, and Moorcock. As these names suggest, he was drawn particularly to the livelier and more explicitly humorous wing of the New Wave, as opposed to the gloomier musings of Ballard or Christopher Priest; he admitted to Cobley that he does "sort of agree with the American perception of British SF, that it's very parochial, it's very downbeat." As a result of this tendency, Banks feels it has become "very difficult for British science fiction writers, and especially English SF writers, to write on the broader canvas, to get stuff out on a big screen. That's one of the things I was trying to get away from." This remark suggests not only Banks's desire to accomodate New Wave stylistic achievements within a more frankly spectacular, optimistic brand of high-tech science fiction—he has called himself, quite proudly, a "technophile" and admits to a fascination with gadgets—but also his clear sense of a division, within British science fiction, between English and other national writers.

Banks's own work has had a clear, if somewhat uneasy, relation to his Scottish background from the start, when at the age of sixteen he undertook his first novel, a work in the popular mode of Alistair MacLean. A pell-mell spy thriller titled "The Hungarian Liftjet," the story was such an apprentice embarrassment—filled with "vast amounts of sex and violence, neither one [of which] I'd had any experience of whatsoever," the author remarks in the *Science Fiction Eye* interview—that Banks has vowed to be cremated while clutching the only extant copy. Still, it is revealing that the youthful writer sought to model himself on a fellow Scotsman who had transcended his ethnic roots to become an internationally best-selling writer. Banks has similarly crafted work of wide appeal, in a variety of forms, while maintaining a connection with the land of his birth. Though he traveled widely in his early twenties and has lived, at times, in London and Kent, England, he returned to Scotland permanently in 1988, residing for some time in Edinburgh and eventually settling with his wife, Annie, in Fife, near the Forth Bridge where he grew up. While he is proud to be perceived as the literary godfather of a fresh generation of Scottish talents—a profile in the *Edinburgh Student Newspaper* (6 February 1997) bore the title "Great Uncle Iain"—he is still uneasy being called a "Scottish writer," as opposed to a Scotsman who happens to write. He admits, however, that the long reign of the British Tory government during the 1980s and 1990s edged him steadily toward a radical nationalism.

Banks soon abandoned the thriller genre—a form he returned to later with much greater success—in favor of writing science fiction. His second effort, a vast, globe-spanning, near-future novel modeled on John Brunner's *Stand on Zanzibar* (1968), was written in 1972 and remains unpublished; according to Banks, it was another disaster, an amorphously sprawling mess that taught him the value of a good story outline. His next four pieces of fiction, which he wrote between 1974 and 1979 while holding down a series of odd jobs in Scotland and England, were the sort of widescreen space operas for which he later became famous. Banks made

Dust jacket for the U.S. edition of Banks's first published book, which he has described as "a slightly off-beat, blackly humorous but basically conventional novel" (Richland County Public Library)

fruitless attempts during the 1970s to get these manuscripts published, and only his subsequent success with other forms permitted him to return to this material and revamp it for publication in the following decades. These four early works were eventually published, with extensive revisions, in the 1980s and 1990s: *The Player of Games, The State of the Art* (1989), *Use of Weapons* (1990), and *Against a Dark Background* (1993).

The Wasp Factory, the book that established Banks's reputation on both sides of the Atlantic when it finally appeared in 1984, was written in 1979 as a conscious departure from his previous work. As Banks told the *Science Fiction Chronicle* in October 1994, "I wanted to write a slightly off-beat, blackly humorous but basically conventional novel after years of writing SF and not getting it published." This manuscript also initially made the round of British publishers without gaining any ground. Banks commented in his interview with Cobley:

I used to think, suppose that the heavens opened, the clouds parted, and this big hand comes down and a voice says, "BANKSIE!–READ THIS!" And it's a big stone tablet that says "Banksie, you will never, ever, ever publish a work of fiction of any sort in your entire life during the future course of the universe!" The *ultimate* rejection slip, a rejection slip from the Universe, from God! And I thought–no, I'll still write.

He persevered, producing at least three more novels–*Consider Phlebas* (eventually published in 1987), *Walking on Glass* (published in 1985), and "O" (abandoned)–while waiting for a breakthrough. This background not only indicates Banks's devotion to his craft despite persistent disappointments but also explains how he could seem so prolific early in his publishing career: essentially, he was reworking–in some cases, quite radically–extant material. The shape of Banks's development has thus been deeply influenced not only by his lack of immediate success but also by the actual sequence of publication of his various manuscripts, a process in which he has proven quite canny in his decisions.

Banks's big break finally came when, after *The Wasp Factory* had been rejected by six publishers, Macmillan Press decided to take a chance on a book they realized was likely to prove controversial. But they could not have anticipated the storm of response the novel was destined to generate–a response that was remarkably polarized, with critics either viciously excoriating the book or praising it highly. While admitting, in his 1990 interview with *Contemporary Authors,* that he "did enjoy upsetting some of the more constipated London reviewers," Banks claims that he "didn't write the book deliberately to shock; I wasn't trying to be nasty or controversial." Some of the negative reviewers, however, seemed oddly eager to speculate on the author's–and the publisher's–presumed ulterior motives. According to Neil Philip in the *British Book News* (April 1984), the "rudimentary plot is there to provide an excuse for the elaboration of cruel fantasy," and the decision by Macmillan to publish the novel "is a remarkable indication of the extent to which publishers have been taken in by and have colluded in the fashionable exaltation of the perverse, macabre and bizarre in literature." Patricia Craig, in the *Times Literary Supplement* (*TLS*) (16 March 1984), claimed that Banks's "satiric intention is overwhelmed by his relish for exorbitant brutalities" and that as a result the book amounts to nothing more than the "literary equivalent of the nastiest brand of juvenile delinquency," while Andrew Gimson in the *Times* of London (16 February 1984) surmised that Macmillan had published it merely as "a joke, meant to fool literary London, terrified of seeming prudish, into respect for rubbish." Banks expressed to an interviewer for *Radical Scotland* magazine in 1989 his

disappointment that reviewers "could lose their cool like that. I thought and still think that there is a hell of a lot wrong with the English and London literary scene, but I thought that at least they could be urbane."

The novel certainly is perverse, macabre, and bizarre, but what the reviews fail to indicate is the extent to which Banks has the aberrant aspects of his story under authorial control. These critics were unable to distinguish between the attitudes of the author and those of his narrator, a sly, brutal, all but feral, teenage murderer named Frank Cauldhame. In a way, this confusion is a testament to Banks's achievement: the boy's voice is so coldly persuasive, as he casually details his various enormities against animals and small children, that one is at once fascinated and disgusted. Frank, who lives alone with his father–a reclusive, half-mad, former hippie biochemist–on a tiny island off the Scottish coast, inhabits a self-made dreamworld that consists largely of concocting and carrying out complicated rituals of violence. Some years before the novel opens, Frank had ingeniously murdered his younger brother and two small cousins in ways designed to avoid suspicion (for example, persuading his brother, Paul, to strike with a piece of driftwood at an unexploded bomb found on the beach), and currently he maintains a bloody regime of animal sacrifices, severing the heads of rabbits in order to furnish totemic poles guarding the island and luring wasps into a mechanical contraption (the eponymous Wasp Factory) that tortures them in ways purportedly allowing Frank to divine the future. These primitive behaviors, readers are led to believe, constitute an elaborate compensation for a terrible childhood trauma in which the family's bulldog had mutilated the boy's genitals. Moreover, Frank also seems to be competing in his depredations with his older brother, Eric, who was committed to an asylum after allegedly setting fire to local dogs and gagging an infant with maggots. As the novel opens, Eric has escaped from confinement and, as he reports in a series of chilling telephone conversations with Frank, is slowly making his way back toward the island, where a climactic confrontation with his estranged family looms.

Beneath this fretwork of Gothic horror, the novel is a penetrating study of the psychology of violence. The ultimate shock of the tale–the final revelation that Frank is not in fact a mutilated male but a female upon whom his father, pursuing a twisted misogynist agenda, has been experimenting physically and psychologically for more than a decade–forces readers to rethink Frank's persistent rationalizations, throughout the narrative, that he is merely acting as boys are expected to act. As he argues, men "are the harder sex. We strike out, push through, thrust and take. The fact that it is only an analogue of all this sexual terminology I am capable of does not discourage me. I can feel it in my bones, in my uncastrated genes." Rather than being the equivalent of a mindless video nasty, as some reviewers alleged, the book is in fact so subtly structured, laced with shadowy clues about Frank's genuine identity, that it especially rewards a second reading. It also encourages meditation upon the gender dynamics of power—a theme much of Banks's subsequent fiction has also examined. Above all, it impresses with the chilling matter-of-factness of its tone, a surprising narrative assurance for a first novelist—although Banks had already served a lengthy apprenticeship as a writer before the book appeared. Whenever an interviewer asks about his "overnight" success, Banks bemusedly details the fourteen years, several novels, and more than one million words that paved the way for *The Wasp Factory*.

Despite the furious protests the novel generated, its strengths did not go entirely unnoticed by contemporary critics. Reviewing the American edition in the *Washington Post Book World* (9 September 1984), Douglas E. Winter praised Banks's "black humor worthy of Evelyn Waugh or Harry Crews," which makes for a "sardonic delivery" that "strikes repeated bull's-eyes at the dark side of human nature." Perhaps the most perceptive response the novel received was from Stanley Reynolds in *Punch* (29 February 1984); he called it "hypnotic" and "a minor masterpiece" and attacked the many negative reviewers as children "who eat too much pudding, gorging themselves on great cream puffs of novels, and when something red and raw, bleeding and still maybe even quivering, appears on the end of the fork they turn away in horror." In short, *The Wasp Factory* was an anomaly among contemporary novels, "not the jolly world of British farce, of Tom Sharpe, all beer and farts: there is something foreign and nasty here, an amazing new talent." This reference to Banks's "foreignness" was further developed by Thom Nairn, who observed in his 1993 article "Iain Banks and the Fiction Factory" that the fact "so many English reviewers failed to note any humour in *The Wasp Factory* says a good deal about the intrinsic differences in outlook between Scottish and English society, suggesting the presence in the former of a darker, more complex, perhaps not altogether creditable sense of humour." In the years since the book was published, its reputation has only grown: *The Wasp Factory* was included in Stephen Jones and Kim Newman's *Horror: 100 Best Books* (1988), and in 1997 it was selected one of the "Top 100 Books of the Century" in a poll conducted by the Waterstone Bookshop chain.

A substantial advance for paperback rights to *The Wasp Factory* convinced Banks to quit his day job

Dust jacket for the U.S. edition of Banks's second novel, which reveals what its author calls the "enormous influence" of Mervyn Peake (Richland County Public Library)

working in a solicitor's office and devote himself full-time to his writing. With such a backlog of manuscripts on hand, his major decision was whether to try placing one of them or attempting something entirely new. What he finally decided was to do both, submitting *Walking on Glass* to Macmillan while beginning work on what became his third novel, *The Bridge*. Banks has admitted that he did consider trying to mine his extant science-fiction materials then, especially since he still saw himself, despite the Gothic-horror aspect of *The Wasp Factory*, as primarily a science-fiction writer. Why he ultimately elected the course he did is unclear, but *Walking on Glass* and *The Bridge* quickly cemented his reputation as an accomplished dark fantasist—one whose subject matter attracted a genre audience while his allusive literary flourishes continued to appeal to mainstream readers. If one of his space operas had appeared instead, he might have lost the latter audience entirely. When *Consider Phlebas* finally did appear, as his fourth published novel, Banks had positioned himself to be viewed as one of the most varied talents of his generation.

Banks has expressed dissatisfaction with *Walking on Glass,* which he sees as a flawed narrative. It is certainly a strange one, consisting of three separate, seemingly disjunctive stories interleaved in alternating chapters. In the first, art student Graham Park pursues an elusive young woman, Sara ffitch, with whom he is obsessively and hopelessly in love, through mundanely realistic contemporary London. The second tale follows Stephen Grout, a paranoid schizophrenic convinced he is an exiled soldier in a secret galactic war, as he bumbles around a London landscape oddly skewed by his feverish fancies—which are themselves sustained by his avid reading of pulp science fiction. In the third, overtly fantastic section, a genuine galactic warrior named Quiss spends an interminable imprisonment in a bizarre, isolated castle playing out shadowy gaming scenarios with a female enemy, Ajayi. At first, this tripartite structure seems little more than a narrative sport, but as the novel proceeds, connections among the stories accumulate, making the book into an intriguing textual mosaic and the reader into a hunter after clues that would unify the fractured tales. On the one hand, the stories might be entirely realistic, with Quiss merely a fantasy projection of the delusive Grout; but then how does one account for the fact that the relationship between Quiss and Ajayi mirrors that of Graham and Sara? On the other hand, the novel might be pure science fiction, with Grout a genuine galactic exile, but then what is the mundane business of Sara and Graham doing in the book? Nairn called *Walking on Glass* "a palimpsest of never fully-decipherable possibilities"—an appropriate metaphor considering the fact that the castle Quiss and Ajayi are immured in is constructed out of fossilized books, and its fragmented, encompassing text may include, self-reflexively, Banks's novel itself.

Walking on Glass is among Banks's most playfully allusive—and elusive—works of fiction. Some reviewers were irked by the ludic quality of the book—American science-fiction author Samuel R. Delany, in the *New York Times Book Review* (2 March 1986), dismissed it as an "inept" exercise in mere "whimsy"—but, as with *The Wasp Factory,* the subtler connections in the text become more palpable upon a second reading. Moreover, the book is fascinating for what it reveals about Banks's literary influences. Titles one encounters in the castle made of books include works by Jorge Luis Borges and Franz Kafka, and the overarching edifice itself strongly suggests British fantasist Mervyn Peake's neo-Gothic Gormenghast. In an interview with Stan Nicholls published in *Interzone* in 1994, Banks has acknowledged that "Peake's books had an enormous influence on me,"

and similarly baroque structures figure prominently in several of his later novels, including *The Bridge, Against a Dark Background, Feersum Endjinn* (1994), and *A Song of Stone* (1997).

Walking on Glass also displays another motif that became more pronounced in Banks's subsequent fiction: the social and psychological effects of games and role-playing. As Banks observes in his *Science Fiction Eye* interview,

> games are attractive . . . because they're ready-made symbols. The whole idea of the game is an automatic symbol of life, because all games are in a way small attributes of life, small sections that people try to codify. . . . Games have a very definite and set morality, you play according to the rules or you don't play at all. The difference with games that we play as human beings is that the rules are always changing.

This idea is reflected in the novel in the contrast between the Quiss-Ajayi relationship, bounded by literal game-playing scenarios, and that between Graham and Sara, which seems similarly rule-bound—the perennial lure-and-chase of amorous courtship—but turns out finally to be an arbitrary and perversely willful exercise. Games as sublimated forms of erotic life and as displaced models for social relations in general provide a complex thematic backdrop to several of Banks's later novels, especially *The Player of Games* and *Complicity.*

While *Walking on Glass* was making its way to press, Banks began a new project, incorporating portions of the abandoned manuscript "O" into what became his most complex and possibly best novel. He drew for inspiration on another spectacular edifice, this one actual rather than fictional; as he told Cobley, "I just woke up one morning with the idea of setting a book . . . heavily featuring dreams . . . in a giant, magnified, chaotic version of the Forth Bridge. The rest fell into place with ridiculous ease." If so, then that was the only easy thing about the novel, which is even more complicated in structure than its immediate predecessor. Again, three seemingly isolated plotlines gradually dovetail: a realistic story about earnest young Scotch businessman Alexander Lennox and his on-again, off-again love affair with winsome Andrea Cramond; a surrealistic tale following the misadventures of amnesiac John Orr as he negotiates a byzantine society set on a fantastic, world-spanning bridge; and occasional passages, narrated in the literary equivalent of a heavy brogue, featuring a Conanesque barbarian enacting hilarious parodies of standard sword-and-sorcery scenarios.

The Bridge differs from *Walking on Glass* in that it ultimately does provide a coherent rationale for its fragmented structure: Orr and the Scottish barbarian are unconscious alter-egos of Lennox, who lies dreaming in a deep coma caused by a car accident on the Forth Bridge. The novel also traces its subplots in a subtler way than the mere interleaving of chapters in *Walking on Glass:* horizontally, as one moves from section to section, the novel mimes the framework of the Forth Bridge itself; vertically, as one descends through layers of Lennox's unconscious, the tale follows a devolutionary logic, with the hypermacho barbarian lurking beneath the veneer of civilized masculinity. Even more than his previous two books, *The Bridge* repays multiple readings, as one comes to perceive the intricate linkages, including the allusive resonances with modern British literature, ranging from James Joyce's *Finnegans Wake* (1939) to Alasdair Gray's *Lanark: A Life in Four Books* (1981)—a book that Banks, in the *Radical Scotland* interview, identified as "one of the best pieces of Scottish literature at least since the second world war and possibly this century." As American science-fiction writer Elizabeth Hand remarked, reviewing *The Bridge* for *Science Fiction Eye* (March 1988), "Banks plays with the relations between art and life, conscious and unconscious, and the events and ideas that span them." The novel remains the author's most self-conscious work of literary art and arguably one of the best examples of contemporary British fantasy. Though Banks has indicated that Macmillan forced him to cut nearly forty thousand words from the published text because of the length and that he would someday like to publish an unabridged edition, he still considers *The Bridge* his own favorite among his books.

Only three years into his career, Banks had emerged as one of the best writers of his generation. Still, his work was difficult to classify, mixing the starkest realism with elements of Gothic horror and enlivening popular genre motifs with postmodernist flourishes. Faren Miller, reviewing *The Bridge* for the American science-fiction trade journal *Locus* (December 1986), remarked, "Iain Banks is a novelistic oddity who may not have found his true voice yet. Whether he goes on to develop a unique sub-genre or finds his way into a more familiar literary form, he's a writer worth watching." Banks, quite aware of being watched by diverse audiences but unwilling to be pigeonholed, decided to strike out in new directions. He rewrote and published *Consider Phlebas,* a work of hard-core space opera that had a galvanizing effect on the science-fiction genre; and he began a new novel, *Espedair Street,* a sweetly realistic tale of a working-class boy who becomes a popular rock star. The latter text is noteworthy for its crystallization of Banks's abiding interest in contemporary music—a concern that also runs through *The Bridge,* which is littered with musical allusions (and which was adapted, by Banks and composer Gary

Dust jacket for the novel inspired by Banks's dream about "a giant, magnified, chaotic version of the Forth Bridge" in Scotland

Lloyd, as a music CD in 1996). *Espedair Street* is also of interest for what Banks himself has to say about its conception; in an interview with *Time Off* magazine (May 1995) the author remarked on the need to escape from the complexity of his previous efforts into a more modest narrative, for fear of lapsing into self-parody.

Consider Phlebas marked a return to Banks's roots in science fiction, though in the author's view he had never really left the genre. According to Banks, in an interview with *SFX* magazine (June 1995), "*Walking on Glass* was hard SF in a way, and *The Bridge*—well, the setting of the bridge itself, and the mucking about with time and settings, is semi-SF anyway." Yet, those texts, for all their fantasy elements, had been received as works of mainstream literature, at least in Britain. In fact, despite this attempt to reconstruct his early fiction as science fiction, Banks has had almost as uneasy a relationship with the genre as he has had with his Scottish heritage. His own ambivalence can be discerned in a remark from the 1994 *Interzone* interview: "I feel slightly more comfortable writing SF. But by a degree, a *fraction,* writing mainstream fiction is more rewarding, simply because you feel you've achieved more having had to wrestle with reality as well as with your imagination." This tension between the comforts of genre and the challenges of the literary mainstream has persisted throughout Banks's career and cannot be dispelled simply by referring to all his output as a kind of quasi-science fiction.

For example, it is certainly significant that, when Banks offered *Consider Phlebas* to Macmillan, they suggested that he come up with a pseudonym because, apparently, they felt the novel did not fit in with his developing body of work. Banks has consistently attempted to make light of this situation—joking that he offered to call himself John B. Macallan, after his two favorite brands of whiskey—but his publisher's concern points up a genuine contradiction for any writer whose work attempts to straddle so many literary fences: some of the territory separated by those barriers may in fact be, or at least is assumed to be, incommensurable. As Banks has put it, detailing his discussions with Macmillan's editors over a possible pseudonym (in his 1990 *Contemporary Authors* interview), "I didn't want to give the impression that I was going to be ashamed of the science fiction, so . . . we adopted what someone has called a very penetrable pseudonym, Iain M. Banks." However, this solution did not solve the underlying problem, because reviewers and readers naturally assumed—and continue to assume—that the inclusion of his middle initial represented some major line of demarcation. Like the work of Graham Greene, which that author divided between "novels" (what he saw as works of serious literature) and "entertainments" (mere popular diversions, often converging with the conventions of genre spy stories), Banks's canon has come to be perceived as systematically bifurcated in a way that suggests, whether intended or not, an invidious distinction between science fiction and mainstream fiction. Colin Greenland highlighted this point in his review of *Consider Phlebas* for *Foundation* (Summer 1987): "the M is for mystification, for misdirection, for a false moustache that Iain Banks has to put on if he wants to write science fiction, so that we don't confuse him with the other Iain Banks, the one who writes real books, books that do count."

In his interview with Cobley, Banks attempted to put a more positive spin on the business of his "pseudonym," claiming that it was his own decision because he wanted to declare proudly the distinctive value of his science-fiction writing. He further claimed that he told his editors the book "had to say 'a science fiction novel' on the cover," which itself had to include "a great big

spaceship so no one's got any excuse for thinking 'Ah, it's another Iain Banks novel in the same vein as *The Wasp Factory, Walking on Glass* and *The Bridge.* . . . That's the idea, so there's no ambiguity; I didn't want it bought under false pretenses."

Whatever assumptions people have made about his pen name, Banks's science-fiction novels are as serious and, in their own way, as challenging as his more mainstream efforts. Almost all of his science fiction to date has been cast in the subgeneric mold of space opera, a form that Banks has declared his overt intention of radically revising. Space opera refers, as the term itself implies, to fiction that uses the galaxy as a backdrop for the staging of grand and highly colored plots, generally involving interstellar empires in conflict and featuring spectacular gadgetry, usually high-tech weapons deployed in extravagant space battles. The pioneer of this subgenre in 1930s American pulp science fiction was E. E. "Doc" Smith, and the form has undergone periods of popularity and decline ever since. In the 1950s and 1960s Isaac Asimov's "Foundation" series and Frank Herbert's "Dune" novels brought space opera a higher degree of technical sophistication; but in Britain, New Wave writers, taking the lead of Ballard, generally dismissed the form as juvenile nonsense unworthy of truly serious science fiction. Writers who dabbled in it—for example, Bayley and M. John Harrison—did so largely for purposes of parody or playful pastiche.

Space opera was scorned by the New Wave only partly because of aesthetic considerations; the implicit worldview of the subgenre was also perceived with suspicion, seen by many as a jingoistic celebration of naked power politics, perhaps even a glorification of war. Banks is not unsympathetic to this viewpoint; as he remarked in his 1994 interview with *Science Fiction Chronicle,* "I'd read so much SF which seemed just to assume that our current political-economic systems—and especially U.S.-model Capitalism—would just continue on almost unchanged into the stars and that just seemed blind, blinkered." But he has also said that the New Wave's outright dismissal of the form fumbles the chance to use it for more subversive ends; as he put it in an interview with *Wired* magazine (June 1996), he became convinced "that there was . . . a moral, intellectual high ground in space opera that had to be reclaimed for the left. *Consider Phlebas* was the start of that."

This book was the first published—though not the first written—entry in a space-opera series that, to date, includes six novels and a collection of short stories. These tales generally fit within a consistent far-future environment that Banks has dubbed "the Culture." This enterprise permitted Banks to publish extant manuscripts, though he has said that none of these older works emerged into print without radical revision. Banks has credited his lifelong friend and fellow science-fiction writer Ken MacLeod for convincing him that there was an imaginative spark lurking in these early efforts. In some instances MacLeod even had a hand in suggesting specific revisions: for example, as Banks makes clear in his 1994 *Science Fiction Chronicle* interview, the complicated formal structure of *Use of Weapons* was largely conceived by MacLeod, a fact Banks more obscurely acknowledges in a prefatory note to the novel.

MacLeod is also partly responsible for a document called "A Few Notes About the Culture," an on-line publication, written with Banks and first appearing in 1994, that provides a coherent overview of the Culture universe. According to this piece, the Culture "is a group-civilisation formed from seven or eight humanoid species, space-living elements of which established a loose federation approximately nine thousand years ago." As a result of virtually inexhaustible resources entirely accessed by automated processes, the Culture has long since transcended political-economic hierarchy and now governs itself as a kind of anarcho-syndicalism, driven by etiquette rather than formal laws. A cooperative effort of humans and their fully autonomous Artificial Intelligences (AIs), the Culture sustains a comfortably hedonistic lifestyle organized around leisure and intellectual pursuits. The average Culture citizen can anticipate a lifespan of about four centuries, the result of a program of radical "geno-fixing" that provides "an optimized immune system and enhanced senses, freedom from inheritable diseases or defects," the ability to change sexes at will, and "drug glands" that "secrete—on command—mood- and sensory-appreciation-altering compounds into the person's bloodstream." These citizens populate a variety of space habitats, including gigantic General Systems Vehicles (GSVs), hollowed-out Rocks fitted with stardrives, artificial quasi-planetary environments known as Orbitals and Plates, and more individualized arrangements.

The only obvious political structure of this community is the Contact section, which manages the Culture's relations with other space-based but differently governed societies. Contact has been a major player in most of Banks's stories featuring the Culture, since these have consistently highlighted points of overt or potential friction between the peace-loving, secular, libertarian Culture and some of its more militant, religiously fanatical, and/or totalitarian neighbors. As Banks freely admits, it is rather difficult to sustain a space adventure in the absence of situations of conflict, and the Culture's lack of internal hierarchy and its anarchic pacifism, absent any external threat or chal-

Dust jacket for the U.S. edition of Banks's 1989 novel, a political thriller set in the near future (Richland County Public Library)

lenge, would hardly produce such possibilities. But Banks's purpose is also to elevate the Culture's utopian aspect by satirical comparison with more benighted civilizations, and to test its moral scruples when provoked. Focusing on flare-ups between the Culture and other societies permits Banks to pursue these thematic goals, while at the same time indulging his obvious taste for the conventional business of space opera: decisive acts of statecraft, splashy battle sequences, breathless episodes of capture and escape, and so forth.

This dual, and perhaps contradictory, motivation—to exploit science-fiction readers' traditional attraction to space hardware and violent derring-do, while at the same time subtly proselytizing for the benefits of a quasi-socialist utopia—has led to a curious reception for his Culture books. *Consider Phlebas*, for example, was attacked by Greenland (in his *Foundation* review) for being little more than gaudy pulp with vague intellectual pretensions, an indulgence in "pyrotechnic mayhem" with a few flourishes "to wake up the drowsy literati." John Clute, reviewing the novel for *Interzone* (Summer 1987), complained that it was not pulpy enough, that its subversive satirical purpose "punishes the reader's every expectation of exposure to the blissful dream momentum—the healing retrogression into childhood—of true and terrible space opera." Striking an appropriate balance between his ideological agenda and the elements of pulp adventure that sustain his narratives has been the major challenge for Banks in this series.

One way Banks has managed a compromise between these opposed features of his Culture texts is in the general tone of whimsy that surrounds the Culture itself. Clearly, this society is a utopian one that does not take itself too seriously, as evidenced by the quirky names of its spaceships, such as *GSV Congenital Optimist* or *Clipper Screw Loose*. This whimsical quality extends to encompass the "drones"—robotic AIs with touchy personalities that express themselves in a general bitchiness. Some reviewers have complained about the derivative nature of the drones, especially their similarity to the cute 'droids of *Star Wars* (1977), but Banks has explained—in an interview with *GM* magazine (November 1989)—that deploying these comical characters is his "way of saying utopia can be fun, kids, sign up here!" The drones are also, in their function of mediating between the human citizens of the Culture and the sentient Minds that run its technical infrastructure, more than mere narrative accessories but major agents; indeed, because of their high representation in the Contact section, they are in many ways the most politically astute members of the Culture. But then, Banks has never been one to see seriousness and comedy as necessarily opposed, a fact biographically evidenced by his own brief foray into the political arena, as a nominee for the post of Rector of Edinburgh University in 1991, when he claimed to belong to the "Drunken Bastard Party." If the Culture had political parties, such a one would fit in nicely.

In *Consider Phlebas* the inimical neighbors are the Idirans, a capitalistic and theologically zealous civilization who despise the Culture as decadent and with whom the Culture has been forced into a reluctant war. The story shows that, despite its pacifism, the Culture is as capable as any human community of ruthless realpolitik and bloody slaughter when provoked and mobilized. An interesting structural twist involves relating the tale from the perspective of a mercenary in the Idirans' employ, a shapeshifting humanoid alien named Borza who has been recruited to help capture a Culture Mind that has gone into hiding on a neutral planet. Readers thus see the Culture through Borza's eyes, and consequently it takes some time before readers fully understand where their sympathies should truly lie.

The narrative is also long and episodic, with Borza constantly deflected from his goal by random events, but these deflections not only permit Banks to exercise his skill at arranging set pieces—such as a feverish chase through the bowels of a Culture GSV—but also have a crucial thematic point. As Banks told *Interzone* in 1986, when *Consider Phlebas* was about to appear, "One of the things I was trying to get at, one of the things you don't have in most science-fiction novels about fighting, is the sheer amount of luck—often very bad luck—involved in real warfare." Perhaps indebted to a similar portrait in Harrison's *The Centauri Device* (1974), Borza is a luckless middleman who muddles through events simply trying to stay alive, a rather subversive take on the conventional daring heroes of space opera.

The novel was well received, especially in the United States, where Miller hailed Banks in *Locus* (May 1987) for bringing "insight and an understated wit" to a subgenre known for its "inherent and oft-criticized absurdities." Banks was therefore encouraged to continue the process of revising his earlier science-fiction manuscripts, and the next to appear was *The Player of Games* in 1988. A considerably more streamlined and linearly plotted tale, this novel too confronts the Culture with an enemy, but only a potential one this time: the expansionist Empire of Azad. Contact section has been keeping the Empire at a distance for the better part of a century, but they eventually decide upon a more direct line of approach; thus, they recruit Jernau Gurgeh, the most accomplished games player in the Culture system, to travel to the Empire and participate in a tournament whose winner is ritually elevated as Emperor. In this novel Banks refines his perennial fascination with games and role-playing in the contrast between Gurgeh, for whom competition is a thrilling intellectual exercise, and the Azadians, for whom it is the very foundation of social power. A brutal and hierarchical society, Azad uses this hallowed tournament to impose and rationalize despotic authority, and when Gurgeh ultimately "perverts" it in order to prove that "conscious cooperation" is "more efficient than feral competition," the Empire simply collapses. In *The Player of Games* Banks strikes an even more effective balance betweem vivid action and satirical purpose, and it was warmly received by reviewers: Clute, in *Interzone* (November/December 1988), called it "an exhilarated, comic, glowing book," while Miller praised it in *Locus* (December 1988) as "a novel of genuine depth and beauty." While Banks's entry into the genre only a year before had been controversial, he was finally being seen as one of the most important of the newer science-fiction writers. Essentially, a second career had begun.

Banks continued the Culture series with the revised novella *The State of the Art,* published as a freestanding book in the United States in 1989 and gathered with seven other stories—not all of them set in the Culture universe—into a book of the same title released in Britain two years later. Again, a stark contrast is evoked, but this time the ultimate target of Banks's satire is not allegorically disguised as an alien empire. Instead, Culture agents make contact with the Earth itself, circa 1977, prompting a debate about whether such a barbaric "civilization"—rife with sexism, racism, and other endemic atrocities—even deserves to exist. The ironic tone of this debate does not disguise its ultimate deadly seriousness; as Miller observed in *Locus* (August 1989), the "arch tone of the 'Culture' books, with their sassy drones, impertinent footnotes, and absurdly titled ships, should not be mistaken for escapism." Mike Christie, in *Foundation* (Summer 1990), praised the story as one of those "rare successes" that "combines the enjoyment to be gained from high-tech SF with the insight required of a good political utopia." The fact that *The State of the Art* was published first in the United States suggests the extent to which the author had already built an avid, reliable market for his science fiction, whereas some of his roughly contemporary mainstream efforts—such as *Espedair Street*—remained unavailable to American readers. Moreover, the expanded British edition collects virtually all of the author's published short fiction, thus clearly demonstrating that Banks has always been essentially a novelist by avocation.

In 1990 Banks radically reworked and published *Use of Weapons,* which is generally regarded as his best Culture novel. It is certainly the first of his science-fiction efforts to attempt something of the formal complexity of *Walking on Glass* and *The Bridge,* though Banks's friend MacLeod initially suggested the revamped structure. Two plotlines run in interleaved chapters, but in opposite temporal directions: one details the efforts by Contact agent Sma—who was also featured in *The State of the Art*—to secure the assistance of a freelance mercenary named Cheradenine Zakalwe in the Culture's dealings with a recalcitrant planet; the other traces the roots of Zakalwe's tortured psyche to a series of events hidden deep in his past. More than any of the other books in the series to date, *Use of Weapons* raises questions about the Culture's motives, for though it is loath to use force directly, it does not shrink from baldly manipulating a character such as Zakalwe into doing its bidding. As a result, the moral and political landscape of the book is somewhat more complex than it was in earlier installments, filled with ambiguous shades of gray. Also, the novel captures more of the Gothic-interior feel of Banks's earliest books, as opposed to the technicolor extroversion of *Consider Phlebas* and *The Player of Games.* There is still plenty of

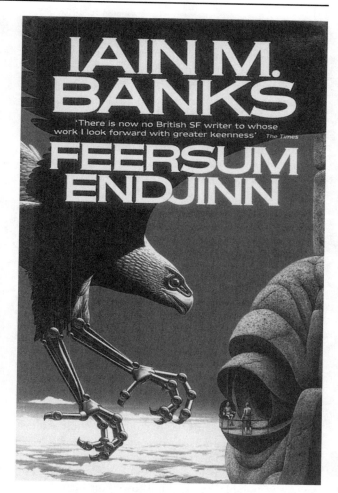

Dust jacket for Banks's 1994 novel, set in the distant future on the Earth, which is threatened by an imminent solar catastrophe

action, but as Miller pointed out in her review in *Locus* (August 1990), *Use of Weapons* is finally "a dark, contemplative novel." According to Greenland in *Interzone* (Autumn 1990), Banks had "finally succeeded in accessing the psychic terrain of his non-generic mundane novels from inside his SF."

While Banks continued during the late 1980s to mine his backlog of manuscript material, he was also publishing new work, some of it with tangential connections to genre concerns. His 1989 novel *Canal Dreams,* for example, is a near-future political thriller, set in Panama and featuring leftist guerillas, CIA operatives, and a female Japanese cellist who is unwillingly drawn into violent intrigues. While generally well reviewed, it is a book Banks himself dislikes, and in the *Time Off* interview he admitted that the novel was "written under the influence of whiskey." He continued, "I've tried writing smashed, stoned, whatever; it tends not to work."

As the Culture novels make plain, Banks's sympathies lie distinctly left of center, but the far-future settings of most of his science-fiction tales have tended to displace the author's real-world views into allegory. *Complicity,* by contrast, is an entirely realistic work that reveals an abiding hatred of the contemporary political right, especially the British Tory Party. The plot of *Complicity* mounts an almost wish-fulfillment campaign of revenge against social conservatives, which led some reviewers to revive the sorts of complaints initially voiced against *The Wasp Factory,* equating the incidents of the novel with Banks's own desires and behaviors. But as Banks had commented in his 1986 *Interzone* interview, "I'm not a violent person. I don't hit people. . . . I'm mild-mannered Iain Banks. The violence is in the books, it's not in me." *Complicity,* likely because of the violence of its serial-killer plot, became Banks's first best-seller when it was published in Great Britain.

By the beginning of the 1990s Banks had settled into a consistent publishing pattern: roughly one book per year, alternating a mainstream title with a work of science fiction—the latter sometimes, though not always, a Culture novel. Banks has told interviewers that his later contracts with publishers have specified this pattern, with which he has become quite comfortable. In 1992 Banks published *The Crow Road,* a large mainstream novel about a quirky Scottish family, with elements of the detective story; it was a commercial success, and some consider it Banks's greatest achievement. Brian Morton, in *New Statesman and Society* (24 April 1992), called it "as fine and ambitious a novel as any from a Scottish writer since the 1960s." This review is notable because it shows conclusively how critically divided Banks's literary output had become by this time: in his overview of Banks's career to that point, intended to chronicle the author's growing maturity, Morton mentioned only the five novels published under the Iain Banks byline, ignoring the science fiction entirely. By contrast, perhaps because its subject matter has made it seem too parochial, *The Crow Road* has still not been published in the United States.

The last of Banks's older manuscripts that he considered salvageable, and the first of his science-fiction novels not set amid the Culture, appeared in 1993: *Against a Dark Background.* As Banks told *Interzone* in 1994, he saw the book "as almost a commentary on fantasy. . . . I wanted to use the tropes of science fiction to deconstruct fantasy as a form." Banks's general views on the contrast between science fiction and fantasy were evident in his interview with *Radical Scotland* in 1989: "I cannot take the supernatural seriously and anything that involves it just leaves me cold." While admitting that some of his early novels had explored fantastic terrain, Banks stressed that this element was exclusively the manifestation of his characters' psychic dreamwork and not something autonomously supernatural: "in the end, my writing comes down to a secular, humanist framework, certainly a materialist one." The sword-and-sorcery episodes stitched throughout *The Bridge,* for example, were heavily parodic, and the only fantastic mode Banks seems not to find innately risible is the essentially secular one of modernists such as Kafka and Borges.

The main element of fantasy in *Against a Dark Background* is the Lazy Gun, a device of mysterious origin and sinister effect. At first, it might seem the quintessential science-fiction gadget, but its operation is decidedly fantastic—indeed, cartoonishly unpredictable. As the story develops through a now classically Banksian series of interlocking subplots, the Lazy Gun becomes the technological wild card in a byzantine set of alliances and conflicts that fracture a diverse interstellar community. The priests of Huhsz, a religious cult, want the gun for their own political ends, and they blackmail a young woman, Sharrow, into helping them acquire it. Basically, Banks equates the fanatical faith of the Huhsz with the impulses of fantasy, with the desire to transcend the material limits of the universe through magic or the supernatural; and the Lazy Gun, which seems to incarnate this ability, takes a terrible, albeit essentially arbitrary, revenge against those who seek to wield its power. What Banks seems to be saying is that faith or fantasy, when embodied in a machine, can only prove randomly destructive, and the novel is filled with scenes of horrible violence that are often narrated in a blackly humorous style. Banks's satirical purpose mixes uneasily with his adventure-story structure, producing a book that, as Miller observed in *Locus* (May 1993), is "almost obsessively tragic, haunted by violence and death." As Banks told *Interzone* as far back as 1986, he frankly tries to "make violence funny sometimes. That's a tricky operation. You should laugh at it first and then feel the horror, not laugh at it and forget it."

After *Complicity,* another deeply violent book, was published in 1993, Banks turned again to science fiction with *Feersum Endjinn* in the following year. It was the first genre novel Banks produced from scratch since *Consider Phlebas* in the early 1980s; it is thus interesting to compare it to the science-fiction manuscripts Banks had been revising and publishing throughout the previous decade. *Feersum Endjinn* is a complicated tale, filled with crosshatching plots and counterplots, and it demonstrates Banks's maturity in telling an intricate story. The story it tells, however, is rather thematically lightweight by comparison with books such as *The State of the Art* and *Use of Weapons.* On far-future Earth, the city of Serehfa—which occupies a vast edifice in the familiar mold of Peake and now Banks—is under threat from an imminent solar catastrophe that the political authorities, immured in a senseless factional war, have made no efforts to prepare for. Matters are complicated by the existence of the Cryptosphere, a virtual-reality landscape of the dead that mysteriously undergirds Serehfa technologically and metaphysically. Readers follow two main characters—Gadfium, a scientist convinced that the city harbors an "escape device" that will allow humanity to evade destruction, and Bascule, an augur driven unconsciously by a similar agenda—as they negotiate realities embodied and virtual, fend off the distracted authorities, and try to save the world.

The pleasures of the book lie in its complicated plot and in its allusions to science-fiction classics set on similar far-future earths, such as Gene Wolfe's *Book of the New Sun* series (1980–1987). Like so many of Banks's science-fiction books, it is a story driven by a flimsy narrative element—Serehfa's "escape device"—that motivates events, but unlike those precursors, it does not weave out of this initial cue a tapestry of dark and disturbing implication. Banks usually deploys games to thematic effect; *Feersum Endjinn,* by contrast, is the first of his books to read like a game and nothing more. As Clute observed in a generally positive review in *Interzone* (August 1994), "there is an inherent lack of danger when a text is written with too much skill, when the tale told does not challenge the skill with which it is told." Clearly, while Banks was maturing technically as a storyteller, he had yet to show the same full seriousness in his newly written science fiction as in his contemporaneous realistic fiction.

Banks's next novel, *Whit; or, Isis Amongst the Unsaved* (1995), is a meditation on the psychic lure of religious cults, a sort of mainstream version of *Against a Dark Background,* though told with a bit more sympathy for the faithful. Like that earlier novel—as well as *Canal Dreams,* with its Japanese heroine—it features a female protagonist, showing Banks's growing success at structuring a story around a central female. As Banks told *Starlog* magazine in December 1994, "I have a predilection for strong characters of both sexes. . . . I find it fairly easy to write female characters, but I don't want them to act just like men, because that has the implication that only men can be strong central characters. The thing that worries me is that, because I'm writing action-based books, the women might seem too much like men." This concern is hardly a problem in *Whit,* as its heroine, Isis, is not like most people: denizen of a bizarre antisecular Scottish ashram, she finds herself, as the story develops, confronted by the wonders and horrors of modernity. Banks's satire cuts both ways: the child-like ignorance of those in the cult is gently mocked, but their isolationism seems at times a quite appropriate response to the violence, sexism, and abuse of power that characterize the world at large.

While the novel never becomes explicitly fantastic, its central situation of a naive innocent foraging into a mysterious culture suggests features of the utopia and the science-fiction first-contact story. As Charles de Lint observed in his review in *The Magazine of Fantasy and Science Fiction* (February 1996), Banks's attempt to depict in full detail the arcane beliefs and rituals of the Luskentyrians, the cult to which Isis belongs, involves "as much a kind of worldbuilding as that required for more obvious SF/fantasy novels." This convergence of Banks's mainstream and science-fiction efforts was also remarked upon, though less charitably, by Nicholas Lezard in his review in the *TLS* (1 September 1995). According to Lezard, *Whit* evinces a "peculiar literal-mindedness—a rather unimaginative use of the imagination, like the impressively detailed yet lifeless drawings by autistics—that nevertheless contribute to Banks's attraction and success. His separate constituencies—the sci-fi and the non-sci-fi—might perhaps overlap in this respect more than they might think." Lezard's point is to slight all of Banks's output by comparison with his science fiction, to suggest that his aspirations to "real" literature in his mainstream novels are compromised by the "mechanical rather than literary imagination" that runs through his entire corpus. While one might not be persuaded by this pitting of mechanism against literariness, reviews such as this one show again how difficult it has proven, critically, to reconcile the two strands of Banks's fictive production.

In 1996 Banks brought out *Excession,* his first Culture novel in six years, though the first newly written entry in the series in more than a decade and a half. When asked by Simon Ing in a May 1996 *Cyberia Cafe* interview why he had avoided writing about the Culture in his science-fiction novels of the 1990s, Banks responded, "I never wanted the Culture to become cuddly, the way some fantasy trilogies become cuddly. I didn't want my SF to be that predictable." But he admitted that he was now "unashamedly pandering to popular demand—that's my excuse for getting out the toys again." This casual, almost cynical remark might lead one to expect that *Excession* would be another sport of a book, like *Feersum Endjinn;* but while it does at times seem a mere exercise in narrative exuberance, it is in the end a richer novel, showing the Culture to be a multifaceted universe worth further exploration.

In this novel a mysterious, impossibly ancient, deadly space artifact is again the catalyst for several intricate subplots that merge at the climax of the tale. The Minds of Contact section are worried about the appearance of this Excession—their term for any entity or force that transcends their understanding—fearing its ability to destabilize their galactic policy of benevolent imperialism, especially if it falls into the hands of the Affront, an expansionist alien race whose ambitions Contact has been muting and managing for several centuries. *Excession* raises the

Minds and drones of Contact from the shadowy background players or amusing foils they had been in the previous books into full-fledged characters, and for the first time, readers get to see quite starkly the shrewd political machinations that lie behind the Culture's facade of neutrality and pacifism. Indeed, the subplots involving human characters are distinctly secondary to the deliberations and actions of The Interesting Times Gang, a task force of Minds assembled to deal with the alien anomaly.

While Banks has often said that one of his chief pleasures in writing the Culture novels lies in his crafting of the AIs and their bristly, catty personae, some reviewers felt that in this novel the result was cutely juvenile—precisely the problem of "cuddliness" that Banks had sought to avoid. Chris Gilmore, in *Foundation* (Summer 1997), observed that "the Culture was the great invention of his [Banks's] youth. He is now well past forty, and it's time to put aside childish things." On the other hand, Paul J. McAuley, in *Interzone* (August 1996), credited *Excession* with "furthering Banks's reputation as one of the most inventive writers of SF." As Bill Sheehan observed in his review of *Excession* for *The New York Review of Science Fiction* (March 1998), Banks's "muse is a moving target, and there is no way to guess the direction it will carry him from one book to the next."

Even Banks's predictable strategy of alternating mainstream and science-fiction works has become a bit muddied, as his next book, *A Song of Stone* (1997), is a near-future, postapocalypse tale with fable-like elements. Some shadowy catastrophe has struck an unnamed European nation, precipitating a civil war. The tale is largely set in a massive castle—another of Banks's homages to Peake, though in this case also to King Arthur's Camelot and Edgar Allan Poe's House of Usher—which has been seized and garrisoned by an armed band led by a determined young woman known only as "Lieutenant." This castle is home to the narrator, Abel, and his witchy sister, Morgan, who had led an obscurely twisted life together until the advent of the military invasion. There is much action, but it is filtered through Abel's skewed, decadent perspective, leading to an atmosphere dark with rumination and hidden trauma. The moodiness of the tone and the indefinition of the narrative locale make this novel read more like Banks's earliest quasi-fantasies, *Walking on Glass* and *The Bridge,* than anything he had written since, under either of his bylines. Stressing the quasi-science-fictional qualities of the book in a review in the *TLS* (8 August 1997), Edward James called it "compulsively readable," centered on an "enigma" that "will ensure repeat readings. Banks's already high reputation can only be enhanced."

That Banks seems to be seeking some sort of rapprochement between the two streams of his writing was remarked by McAuley in his review of Banks's next novel, *Inversions* (1998), in *Interzone* (July 1998). Like *A Song of Stone,* this book is "a complex and carefully constructed morality play that aspires to the universality of a fable." The novel may be seen to fit loosely within the Culture series, though this connection is not made clear at the outset; indeed, its status as science fiction is in doubt for some time. A war has fragmented a planet-bound empire, and the story itself is fractured in two, narrated in twin strands that, as is so often the case in Banks's work, intertwine gradually but inevitably as the tale proceeds. The physically and ideologically separated narrators chronicle the actions of two mysterious figures—a male bodyguard in one kingdom, a female physician in another—who, it slowly dawns on the reader, are emissaries to this world from space, one of them (though which one?) possibly from the Culture. The development of the narrative is subtle, as the reader is forced to interpret the actions of the alien visitors through the eyes of narrators blind to external events.

In an interview with the *Times* of London (14 November 1997) Banks attacked mainstream critics who assume that the reader "is too intellectually well developed to want to be bothered with plot or story. . . . There aren't enough people trying to write the stuff I try to write without being remorselessly popular and pandering to the lowest common denominator." Banks may not be the best stylist in contemporary British science fiction, but he is without question a gifted plotter. *A Song of Stone* and *Inversions,* for all their differences, show Banks combining his flair for narrative intricacy with detailed settings and well-realized characters.

Despite his prolificity, Banks has managed to sustain a level of literary excellence. Banks laughs when asked about his extensive output, commenting in an interview with *Melody-Maker* magazine (16 September 1995), "I only write for two months of the year. Another two months are set aside for promotion, and that leaves me eight months to drift along doing nothing. I'm the ultimate slacker." But few genuine layabouts could hope to claim his consistent success, both within the fantastic genres and in mainstream fiction. Called by some the best novelist in Britain since the 1980s, he has also generated a cultish following within science fiction, as proven by the appearance in 1997 of a quarterly fan magazine called *The Culture* that is focused exclusively on his work. There is also a Usenet newsgroup—alt.books.iain-banks—devoted to on-line discussion of his fiction, and a website called *Culture Shock,* located at <http://www.floatingplanet.net/phlebas/shock/index.html>, which features a wealth of information about the author.

Comparisons have been made between Banks and another great, though unabashedly popular, Scottish writer—Robert Louis Stevenson. Like Stevenson, Banks is essentially a storyteller, one drawn to tales of high adventure and dark exoticism, yet his work also repays a deeper reading that reveals the richness of his basic themes: the lure of despotic power versus utopian longings; the strife between will and desire, reason and faith, that is often sublimated into the playing of games; the mystery of identity and its shadowy structures—of gender, family, profession—which find narrative emblems in ruinous castles and other monuments; the impossibility and yet the necessity of love. That Banks has chosen to articulate these characteristic obsessions in part through the popular genres of fantastic literature has enriched those forms, and he remains one of the most protean figures in British science fiction.

Interviews:

Kim Newman, Interview with Iain M. Banks, *Interzone,* 16 (Summer 1986): 41–42;

Tim Metcalfe, Interview with Iain M. Banks, *GM,* 2 (November 1989);

James Robertson, "Bridging Styles: A Conversation with Iain Banks," *Radical Scotland,* 42 (December 1989/January 1990);

Michael Cobley, "Eye to Eye: An Interview with Iain Banks," *Science Fiction Eye,* 6 (February 1990): 23–32;

Stan Nicholls, "Cultural Differences: Iain Banks Interviewed," *Interzone,* 86 (August 1994): 22–24;

Sally Ann Melia, "Iain Banks: 'Very Likely Impossible, But Oh, the Elegance . . . ,'" *Science Fiction Chronicle,* 16 (October 1994): 7, 42–44;

Nicholls, "Man of the Culture," *Starlog* (December 1994);

Simon McKenzie, Interview with Iain M. Banks, *Time Off* (May 1995);

Mary Branscombe, "Head-to-Head with the Stars: Iain Banks," *SFX* (June 1995);

Michael Bonner, "Banks Statement," *Melody-Maker* (16 September 1995): 10;

Liam Fay, "Depraved Heart," *Hot Press* (May 1996);

Simon Ing, Interview with Iain M. Banks, *Cyberia Cafe* (May 1996);

Oliver Morton, Interview with Iain M. Banks, *Wired* (June 1996);

Chris Fleming, "Great Uncle Iain," *Edinburgh Student Newspaper* (6 February 1997);

Robin Eggar, "The Dark World of Iain Banks," *Times of London* (14 November 1997).

References:

Ronald Binns, "Castles, Books, and Bridges: Mervyn Peake and Iain Banks," *Peake Studies,* 2 (Winter 1990): 5–12;

Carolyn Brown, "Utopias and Heterotopias: The 'Culture' of Iain M. Banks," in *Impossibility Fiction:*

Alternativity–Extrapolation–Speculation, edited by Derek Littlewood and Peter Stockwell (Amsterdam: Rodopi, 1996), pp. 57–74;

Cairns Craig, *Iain Banks's* Complicity: *A Reader's Guide* (New York: Continuum, 2002);

Foundation, special Banks issue, 76 (Summer 1999);

Bruce Gillespie, "A Taste for Mayhem: Preliminary Notes on Iain Banks's Non-SF Novels," *Metaphysical Review,* 28/29 (August 1998): 13–14;

William H. Hardesty, "Space Opera Without the Space: The Culture Novels of Iain M. Banks," in *Space and Beyond: The Frontier Theme in Science Fiction,* edited by Gary Westfahl (Westport, Conn.: Greenwood, 2000), pp. 115–122;

Rob Latham, "Violent Insertion and Destructive Penetration," *New York Review of Science Fiction,* 70 (June 1994): 11–15;

Race Mathews, "Iain M. Banks: The 'Culture' Science Fiction Novels and the Economics and Politics of Scarcity and Abundance," *Metaphysical Review,* 28/29 (August 1998): 9–12;

Kev. P. McVeigh, "The Weaponry of Deceit: Speculations on Reality in *The Wasp Factory,*" *Vector,* 191 (January/February 1997): 3–4;

Thom Nairn, "Iain Banks and the Fiction Factory," in *The Scottish Novel Since the Seventies,* edited by Gavin Wallace and Randall Stevenson (Edinburgh: Edinburgh University Press, 1993), pp. 127–135;

Christopher Palmer, "Galactic Empires and the Contemporary Extravaganza: Dan Simmons and Iain M. Banks," *Science Fiction Studies,* 26:1 (March 1999): 73–90;

Lawrence Person, "The Culture-D Space Opera of Iain M. Banks," *Science Fiction Eye,* 2 (February 1990): 33–36;

Victor Sage, "The Politics of Petrefaction: Culture, Religion, and History in the Fiction of Iain Banks and John Banville," in *Modern Gothic: A Reader,* edited by Sage and Allan Lloyd Smith (Manchester: Manchester University Press, 1996), pp. 20–37;

Joe Sanders, "Space Opera Reconsidered," *New York Review of Science Fiction,* 82 (June 1995): 1, 3–6;

Maureen K. Speller, "No Man is an Island: The Enigma of *The Wasp Factory,*" *Steam Engine Time,* 1 (April 2000): 28–29;

Gary Wilkinson, "Poetic Licence: Iain M. Banks's *Consider Phlebas* and T. S. Eliot's *The Waste Land,*" *Vector,* 203 (January/February 1999): 15–18.

Clive Barker

(5 October 1952 –   )

Edwin F. Casebeer
Indiana University–Purdue University (Indianapolis)

BOOKS: *Clive Barker's Books of Blood, Volume One* (London: Sphere, 1984; New York: Berkley, 1986);

Clive Barker's Books of Blood, Volume Two (London: Sphere, 1984; New York: Berkley, 1986);

Clive Barker's Books of Blood, Volume Three (London: Sphere, 1984; New York: Berkley, 1986);

The Damnation Game (London: Weidenfeld & Nicolson, 1985; New York: Ace/Putnam, 1987);

Clive Barker's Books of Blood, Volume Four (London: Sphere, 1985); republished as *The Inhuman Condition* (New York: Poseidon, 1986);

Clive Barker's Books of Blood, Volume Five (London: Sphere, 1985); republished as *In the Flesh* (New York: Poseidon, 1986);

Clive Barker's Books of Blood, Volume Six (London: Sphere, 1985); all but "On Jerusalem Street" republished with the novella *Cabal* (New York: Poseidon, 1988; London: Collins, 1989);

Weaveworld (New York: Poseidon, 1987; London: Collins, 1987);

The Great and Secret Show: The First Book of the Art (London: Collins, 1989; New York: Harper & Row, 1989);

Clive Barker, Illustrator, edited by Steve Niles (Forestville, Cal.: Arcane/Eclipse, 1990);

Clive Barker's The Nightbreed Chronicles, edited by Stephen Jones (London: Titan, 1990);

Clive Barker's Nightbreed: The Making of the Film (London: Fontana, 1990);

The Hellbound Heart (New York: Harper, 1991; London: Fontana, 1991);

Imajica (London: HarperCollins, 1991; New York: HarperCollins, 1991);

The Thief of Always: A Fable (London: HarperCollins, 1992; New York: HarperCollins, 1992);

Illustrator II: The Art of Clive Barker, edited by Fred Burke (Forestville, Cal.: Eclipse, 1993);

Night of the Living Dead: London (Book One: Bloodline), by Barker and Niles (New York: Fantaco, 1993);

Clive Barker (photograph © 1996 by Ilona Lieberman; from the dust jacket for Forms of Heaven, *1996)*

Night of the Living Dead: London (Book Two: End of the Line), by Barker and Niles (New York: Fantaco, 1993);

Everville: The Second Book of the Art (London: HarperCollins, 1994; New York: HarperCollins, 1994);

Incarnations: Three Plays (New York: HarperPrism, 1995; London: HarperCollins, 1996)—comprises *Colossus, Frankenstein in Love,* and *The History of the Devil;*

Forms of Heaven: Three Plays (New York: HarperPrism, 1996; London: HarperCollins, 1997)—comprises *Crazyface, Paradise Street,* and *Subtle Bodies;*

Sacrament (London: HarperCollins, 1996; New York: HarperCollins, 1996);

Clive Barker's A–Z of Horror, compiled by Jones (New York: HarperPrism, 1997; London: BBC, 1997);

Galilee: A Romance (London: HarperCollins, 1998; New York: HarperCollins, 1998);

Coldheart Canyon (London: HarperCollins, 2001; New York: HarperCollins, 2001);

Abarat (New York: Joanna Cotler Books, 2002).

Editions and Collections: *The Essential Clive Barker: Selected Fictions* (London: HarperCollins, 1999; New York: HarperCollins, 1999);

Clive Barker's Books of Blood (Lancaster, Pa.: Stealth Press, 2001).

PLAY PRODUCTIONS: *A Clown's Sodom,* Liverpool, Eleanor Rathbone Theater, 1976;

The Day of the Dog, London, 1979;

Nightlives, London, 1980;

The History of the Devil, Amsterdam, 1981;

Paradise Street, London, 1982;

Frankenstein in Love, London, 1982;

Crazyface, London, 1983;

Subtle Bodies, London, 1983;

Colossus, London, 1983;

The Secret Life of Cartoons, London, 1983; London, Aldwych, 1986.

PRODUCED SCRIPTS: *Salomé,* adapted by Barker from Oscar Wilde's play, motion picture, Redemption Films International, 1973;

The Forbidden, motion picture, Redemption Films International, 1978;

Underworld (U.S. title *Transmutations*), by Barker and James Caplin, motion picture, Empire, 1985;

Rawhead Rex, motion picture, Empire, 1986;

Hellraiser, motion picture, New World, 1987;

Nightbreed, motion picture, 20th Century-Fox, 1990;

Lord of Illusions, motion picture, United Artists, 1995.

OTHER: "Lost Souls," in *Cutting Edge,* edited by Dennis Etchison (New York: Doubleday, 1986; London: Futura, 1987);

The Hellbound Heart, in *Night Visions 3,* edited by George R. R. Martin (Niles, Ill.: Dark Harvest, 1986; London: Century, 1987);

Night Visions 4, edited by Barker (Arlington Heights, Ill.: Dark Harvest, 1987; New York: Berkley, 1988);

"Coming to Grief," in *Prime Evil,* edited by Douglas E. Winter (New York: New American Library, 1988; London: Bantam, 1988);

"The Rhapsodist," in *Gaslight and Ghosts* (London: 1988 World Fantasy Convention/Robinson, 1988);

"The Tragical History of Dr. Faustus," in *Horror: 100 Best Books,* edited by Stephen Jones and Kim Newman (London: Xanadu, 1988; New York: Carroll & Graf, 1989).

SELECTED PERIODICAL PUBLICATIONS—
UNCOLLECTED: "Ramsey Campbell: An Appreciation," *Skeleton Crew,* 5 (April 1989);

"Hermione and the Moon," *New York Times,* 30 October 1992: section A, p. 31.

Clive Barker was born on 5 October 1952 in Liverpool, England. His father, Len Barker, was in industrial relations; his mother, Joan Barker, was a teacher, and both were amateur artists. As a schoolboy, he studied a wide range of arts: illustration, drama, and narrative. He enjoyed a special reputation among his friends for his ability to tell disturbing stories. The *fantastique* (fantasy, epic, horror, science fiction), especially its darker side, always engaged him, especially the Royal Shakespeare *Peter Pan* productions and the tales of Edgar Allan Poe, Arthur Machen, Henry James, and Ramsey Campbell.

Throughout his college years and until his writing *The Books of Blood* in 1984, Barker was a dramatist. Collaborating in an ensemble with a syncretic technique and a highly eclectic vision, Barker acted, wrote, and directed largely in an off-campus context while earning degrees in philosophy and English at the University of Liverpool. Upon his graduation, he and his troupe, the Dog Company, moved to London, giving performances in the fringe theater there and in Amsterdam from 1977 until 1983. He created improvisational dramas, mime, musicals, and examples of commedia dell'arte, particularly its violent Parisian form, Grand Guignol; he also drew heavily upon classical, modern, popular, and nondramatic literature.

Barker's eclecticism resulted in unusual dramas combining diverse cultures and literatures. *A Clown's Sodom* (1976) emphasizes the archetypal in commedia dell'arte; out of it developed *The Day of the Dog* (1979), a surreal mime drama that uses elements from Grand Guignol and gave the Dog Company its name. *Nightlives* (1980) combines film noir with the doppelgänger motif of fantasy. *The History of the Devil,* which opened in Amsterdam in 1981 and had a two-season run at the Edinburgh Festival, is a court trial of the Devil, combining elements from John Milton, the comic strip, television courtroom drama, and rock music. *Paradise Street* (1982) is an apocalyptic and visionary encounter between Queen Elizabeth I's court and contemporary Liverpudlians. Also influenced by Grand Guignol,

Doug Bradley (as Pinhead) and Barker on the set of Hellraiser,
the 1987 motion picture written and directed by Barker

Frankenstein in Love (1982) is a love story relocating the monster in modern, war-torn South America. *Colossus* (1983) is about Francisco Goya, Barker's favorite artist, while in *Subtle Bodies* (1983) Edward Lear's ghost manages the dream lives of those in a wedding party. The Dog Company's last play was *The Secret Life of Cartoons* (1983, revived in 1986), in which a cartoonist's creations come to life. Barker also has written an unproduced, fourteen-act play titled "The Comedy of Comedies," again inspired by commedia dell'arte.

Between this body of work (some of which was eventually published in the mid 1990s) and his fiction and movies are many lines of continuity: the synthesis of widely disparate traditions, particularly the combination of realistic and fantastic plots, characters, and situations; emphasis on the magical and the surreal; characters that later reappear in such novels as *The Damnation Game* (1985) and *Weaveworld* (1987); and the lovers and vengeful monsters of his French and Italian theater models. Barker also has maintained professional contact with members of the Dog Company, most notably fellow writer Peter Atkins and actor Doug Bradley.

Barker's eight years as playwright and director were artistically productive but financially unsuccessful.

During these impoverished years he returned to his practice of telling powerful, bizarre stories to amuse his friends. He was particularly impressed by the range of stories that the genre of horror could support, as shown in the anthology *Dark Forces* (1980), edited by Kirby McCauley. He thus decided to write a group of stories that displayed as many narrative ideas and styles as he could manage, including some that were graphically violent and sexual—the latter quality hitherto rare in horror fiction. These works came to the attention of his agent; she sent five stories to Sphere, which asked him to do an original anthology.

Barker composed *The Books of Blood* in two intense periods. First, writing at night and on the weekends, he produced sixteen short novellas in eight months. A fast but careful writer, he has continued a stringent writing regimen: two thousand words daily, detailed plot and character breakdowns, and triple drafts; on the other hand, he leaves himself much open space by avoiding the formulaic, seeking out the unpredictable, realizing his breakdowns in graphic detail, and arriving at resolutions when he gets there. Throughout, he creates a strong sense of voice in both dialogue and internal monologue by using his acting skills: reading his material aloud, he enacts it dramatically and experiences it emotionally. He also draws illustrations of his fantastic creatures to solidify and elaborate his imagery.

Framing *The Books of Blood* is a story presenting the experiences of a young fraud punished by exploited ghosts who write their stories upon his bleeding skin—a metaphor for the author's anguish in composition. Although the main characteristic of the anthology is diversity, there are some recurrent distinguishing features. Barker's style includes a contemporary narrative voice that displays intelligence, sensitivity, education, distance, and occasional irony. When the reader's focus is directed sensorily close to the shockingly graphic imagery, the technique becomes more dramatic (cinematic) than narrative. Internal monologue and dialogue are strong, individualized, and definitely a major tool of characterization.

Characters and situations are generally modern, like the style, although their range is considerable. Typically, there are jaded or corrupt central figures who find contemporary urban experience meaninglessly routine or who are too limited to comprehend their own angst; and there are monstrous figures, both human and fantastic, that have enormous energy and enthusiasm. Tonally, although Barker regularly writes for visceral impact, his intent is to excite rather than to frighten; thus, he frequently uses explicit violent and sexual scenes bordering on the obscene. Structurally, he focuses upon such scenes rather than upon plot, finding particular inspiration for the technique in the plays of the seventeenth-century playwright John Webster and the movies of Brian de Palma. In plotting, readers can expect the unexpected: victims escape; children are eaten; brave fathers are castrated; protagonists are content with enslavement; and monsters are positive. Throughout, there is a strong sense of subtextuality; clearly, Barker's concern is deeper than the immediate impact of what he calls his "adrenaline stories."

In 1985, together with the last three *Books of Blood*, appeared Barker's first novel, *The Damnation Game*. Although his publishers requested that he remove explicit incest (for which he traded explicit sodomy), Sphere was certain enough of the potential of the novel to back it with a £30,000 promotion budget. Subsequently, it was submitted for the Booker Prize and obtained a listing in Stephen Jones's *Horror: 100 Best Books* (1988), in which Adrian Cole praises it for the powerful realization of serious goals and the care and creativity with which Barker develops his five central characters: Mamoulian, a Faustian Satan blended with Charles Robert Maturin's Melmoth the Wanderer; Mamoulian's henchman, one of Barker's more remarkable creations, the zombie Breer; Mamoulian's enemy, Whitehead, an archetypal Midas governed only by appetite; Whitehead's daughter, the addicted Carys, to whom her father's appetite extends; and Strauss, gambler and former convict, employed by Whitehead and in love with Carys. The plot mirrors one of Barker's favorite tales, Johann Wolfgang von Goethe's *Faust* (1808, 1832): nauseated by immortality in an increasingly senseless world, Mamoulian transacts with Whitehead, then a gambler, to make the latter rich. In exchange, he wants his own death. Correctly suspicious, Whitehead reneges. The business of the novel is to bring the antagonists to destruction and the lovers to union, although the movement of the book becomes delayed and obscured by the frequent Websterian set pieces of explicit and violent display.

Besides the omnipresent darkness, graphic violence and shocking obscenity in the novel—implicit in many of the stories but hidden by Barker's overall desire for continual variety and originality in type—are certain other characteristics that the novel makes explicit and that connect to Barker's later fantasies: apocalypse and hellish settings; villains who have become such through rationalism and materialism; characters beset by obsession, isolation, decay, age, and death; positive resolution stemming from the energy of monsters and the devotion of lovers; and unexpected slips from diurnal reality into the surreal and fantastic.

Mamoulian is the Last European, created by the past and facing apocalypse. The setting in which readers first see him and Whitehead is Warsaw immediately after World War II—ugly, bleak, and shattered, populated by grotesques. Its corollary is the closing setting: the world within Mamoulian, into which he draws Whitehead and Carys—again a bleak and corrupted Hell. The outer and inner landscapes have their corollaries in the many cities of *The Books of Blood*. The creators of such a place are the typical villains of Barker's world: old men ruled by appetite, moved by greed, rational and materialistic, obsessed and compelled. In this novel the three central figures are gamblers, existing for a material prize won from a whimsical Fortuna. The population over which these men preside is largely zombie, literally and metaphorically. There may be no God, or even Satan, in the universe, but there is justice: loneliness, decay, unavoidable death, and the ever-present possibility of pain and disaster.

As readers frequently see in *The Books of Blood*, such salvation as there might be comes from monsters and lovers. Considerable creativity and originality move Barker in this regard. Breer, the zombie, breaks genre traditions by possessing considerable humanity as well as (like many humans) an unawareness of decay and death; but unlike Mary Shelley's monster in *Frankenstein* (1818), this monster/man leads readers to disgust rather than to pity. But Breer at his most corrupt provides the opportunity for salvation: he destroys Mamoulian and inadvertently allows the lovers to unite finally. The lovers also cross genre boundaries: Carys (whose name, "caries," suggests corruption and decay) is physically and sexually debased, jailed by paternal compulsion but also by personal obsession; Strauss, a former convict and small-time gambler, is an antihero. The episode in which he evolves into her White Knight is absolutely surreal: he must dream himself into Mamoulian, who has devoured her soul. The embracing of the fantastic, the entering into the being of the dark opponent, and the persistence of love provide the lovers transformation and some hope, though it may be as distant as the stars the damaged Strauss watches at the close of the novel.

Finally, setting aside its originality and its foreshadowing of the fantasies to come, *The Damnation Game* does belong with *The Books of Blood* and not with the subsequent three novels. It is a horror novel, not a fantasy with elements of horror.

Also in the earlier period falls Barker's work as a screenplay writer and director. Disappointed by the radical truncation of the two scripts that he had developed in 1985 and 1986 for Empire director George Pavlou, *Underworld* and *Rawhead Rex*, Barker used the increasing success and influence that *The Books of Blood* brought him to gain financing from New World that enabled him to direct his own script, *Hellraiser*, released in 1987. A concept that gave rise simultaneously to the screenplay and a novella, *The Hellbound Heart* (1986), for the prestigious *Night Visions* horror-fiction series, *Hellraiser* summarizes

Dust jacket for Barker's 1988 book; in the title novella a psychiatrist convinces his patient that the patient is a serial killer (Richland County Public Library)

and develops the major concerns Barker was beginning to display: a Faustian bargain in which a treacherous demon promises all; a central female character; a love plot with incestuous overtones; doubling of characters; the zombie, the ghost, and the vampire; ingenious creation of monsters; and transformational processes through the agency of the fantastic.

Frank, a jaded hedonist, makes a Faustian pact with demonic Cenobites who tear him to bits; his brother's wife, who is his lover, lures to her house men whom she murders and feeds to him to regenerate his body. His last victim is his brother, whose daughter arrives on the scene too late to save him but who avenges him by informing the Cenobites that Frank has escaped them and by leading him to them. Barker exercised his artistic ability to bring a disturbingly different look to the movie, often imbuing scenes of disgusting imagery with golden lighting and classic composition. The first three sequels had increased budgets for special effects, which enabled him to make concrete the original grotesques that he had been drawing and painting for

most of his life. The popular success of the punkish demons, the Cenobites, especially "Pinhead" (played by Dog Company actor Bradley), surprised even Barker and gave credence to his claim that he works through vision toward the archetypal.

The sequels were neither written nor directed by Barker, who was concerned with other projects by then. But he chose a Dog Company associate, Atkins, to write the first three, and as associate producer, Barker had input into the initial treatments and followed the progress of the filming. Although he granted his successors the kind of artistic control denied him by Empire, he was a significant force in developing the mythology of the Cenobites' Hell and the apocalyptic direction that the series took.

Both the original movie and novella are beyond mere entertainments. They are rich in subtexts that support multiple interpretations of such themes, for instance, as desire and love; the possibility, even necessity, of transformation; the doppelgänger; and the primacy of the monstrous and the mythic. Barker wrote with his eye on the archetypal, creating characters and plot developments that, despite their originality, are rooted not only in genre but also in fairy tale and myth.

Published in 1987, *Weaveworld* was a departure from Barker's established canon to that point: it is a fantasy. More than 250,000 words long, it is an epic effort, though not exactly an epic: unlike standard heroic fantasies, it is focused less on fantastic topography than it is on fantastic characters, events, and topographical montage set in the realistic environment of Liverpool, home of Barker's youth. Committed not to repeat himself and to syncretic creation within the subgenres of fantasy, Barker interlaced his blighted earthly settings with an original reconception of J. R. R. Tolkien's Fairyland and a Blakean transformation of the Christian mythos. Yet, through this transformation and subsequent ones, he remains true to his core vision: the celebration of the ecstasy and pain of the body, monstrosity and energy, love and sexuality, the individual and the fantastic; the desire to go beyond the diurnal, the insensate material, the drudgery and failure of the ordinary and the unaware.

Into Barker's drab Liverpool enters the realm of a race called the Seerkind, in the form of a carpet into which, in 1896, the fragments of that culture that had survived human greed and fear had been magically woven and concealed to survive an even greater enemy: an unseen assassin, the Scourge, which threatens an apocalyptic conclusion. But initially another enemy wishes to destroy this realm called the Fugue: the exiled sorceress Immacolata. With her are characters who produce much of the violence and horror in the novel: her human henchman, the supersalesman

Shadwell; her two dead sisters, one giving birth to litters of "by-blows" acquired from raped men; and later Inspector Hobart, a mad personification of human Law at its worst. But as the novel progresses, its antagonists reconfigure, subside, and transform: the protagonists find themselves opposing a party led first by Immacolata, then by Shadwell, then the Scourge—who opposes all. The resultant plot dynamic is distinctive, and Barker repeats it in *The Great and Secret Show: The First Book of the Art* (1989) and in *Imajica* (1991).

The novel develops this conflict through a series of rising crisis peaks, cliffhangers, and surprising plot turns (the identity of the Scourge being one of the most memorable) that testify to Barker's growing skill in a narrative technique that develops the graphic set scenes that had become his mark. The main focus is on characterization, which is executed with humor and fondness; most successful are his disreputable fairies, who are lotharios, hustlers, and thieves. His antagonists, Immacolata, the Scourge, Shadwell, and Hobart, are complex and individual, developed in depth, and profoundly disturbing. This blend of fantasy and horror results in a particularly unexpected and distressing narrative characteristic: no one is safe. Barker is quite willing to lavish attention on a rich and unusual character and then simply, suddenly, brutally squash it—against all genre expectations.

Also against genre expectations and in keeping with his previous work is Barker's vivid realization of the sexual—from the depraved to the romantic. Barker draws no clear line between the two: any effort to connect has value. The love plot in *Weaveworld* produces a clearly positive and developed female protagonist, Suzanna, who loves both Calhoun Mooney, the clerk who glimpses the Fugue in the carpet, and the Christ-like Seer Jerichau. The configuration testifies to the duality of Suzanna's nature and the possibility, within her, of uniting diverse worlds. As in William Shakespeare's comedies, women are key to social transformation into well-being. *Weaveworld* established the pattern of the ensuing fantasies, *The Great and Secret Show* and *Imajica*: fantasies that aspire to fundamental originality; that interpolate graphic violence and sex; that take a negative stance toward diurnal reality, which is in imminent apocalypse; and that emphasize the ability of humanity—through love, imagination, and trust in its feminine side—to transform into a state of harmonized diversity that sustains the individual in all.

About the same length as *Weaveworld,* nearly a quarter-million words, is Barker's next fantasy, *The Great and Secret Show.* Setting this novel in California (to which his movie experience introduced him), Barker seems to have concluded that the shallowness of Americans' mythic roots demanded invention rather than the synthesis of *Weaveworld,* so he created the surprising and delightful *hallucigenia,* demigods of a collective consciousness formed by popular culture—cowboys and comic-book heroes, werewolves, Hollywood Jesuses, Tarzan, and Krazy Kat.

A representative plot summary is difficult because the novel has so many character groupings, subordinate plot structures, and, as in *Weaveworld,* major shifts in the elements of the central figures. The presiding heroine, Tesla, does not appear until late in the book. The chief narrative thread is spurred by Jaffe, an ordinary man with an extraordinary analogical ability. He becomes aware of another dimension of reality, called Quiddity, and a technique—the Art—of getting there and obtaining godhood, the power of which he greatly desires. His first ally, Fletcher, becomes his enemy as both suddenly transform into god-like beings, warring representatives of Dark (Jaffe) and Light (Fletcher). Lasting a generation, this conflict settles into a stalemate in Palomo Grove, California, and then renews through the children of raped girls, involving the whole community (and its psychic resources) on one side or the other. Prominent upon Fletcher's death is his appointed successor, Tesla, who, like Suzanna in *Weaveworld,* takes upon herself the role of guardian, the caretaker of Quiddity. The final conflict takes the surviving key figures into Quiddity, where the nature of the dimension is partially revealed; some scores are settled; and there appears a beast with the power to enact Apocalypse—the Iad Uroboros. The novel ends in temporary safety and affirmation for the protagonists, but the Iad and its agents survive, their cataclysmic threat to be met in the sequel, *Everville: The Second Book of the Art* (1994).

Barker goes a stage beyond *Weaveworld* in his creation of Quiddity. Instead of a collage of myth and fairy tale like the fragmented world of Seerkind, Quiddity embodies in imagery the state of mystic transport. Referred to by Sigmund Freud as an "oceanic sense," that state in *The Great and Secret Show* is a "dream-sea" surrounding an island, Ephemeris, on the other side of which is an unexplored inimical world, from which the Iad comes. The sea itself gives body to human emotions and visions, transforming the enraged into monsters, lovers into dyads. Quiddity is a reality from which humans emerge at birth, into which they return at death, and into which they enter once during the intervening time: the first time that they make love to their true loves. This reality resembles a kind of reality posited by Western philosophers from Plato and the neo-Platonists to the Californian New Agers: simply expressed, underlying and influencing material reality is a substantial reality that the mind may shape; for Barker, that aspect of mind is the imagination, the function of creating and manipulating the image, making magic—the Art.

Dust jacket for the U.S. edition of Barker's 1989 novel, a fantasy set in California (Richland County Public Library)

Despite its creativity and mysticism, *The Great and Secret Show* is a development of, not a departure from, the elements that had come to typify Barker. Certainly, the graphic and erotic imagery of *The Books of Blood* continues: in Barker's remodeling of the *fantastique,* isolation, decay, disaster, and death always remain—as they are in life—eventualities with which his characters must deal. Among these characters continue to be complex and energetic monsters, a central love story, and an effective female protagonist. Barker demonstrates the value he places upon love even more clearly in *The Great and Secret Show* through the Romeo-and-Juliet plot involving Howie and Jo-Beth, the respective children of Fletcher and Jaffe. Their love establishes the value of the human element in the universal equation: this young couple, children of the Light and the Dark, yin and yang, demonstrate that opposites are, even at their most radical, inseparable. The lovers are where the universe finds relationship, where Barker makes his affirmation. Transformation has equal promise for humanity: Tesla's final transformation develops the comedic goddess who cares and heals into a nurturant goddess who now incorporates in her being the male and the antecedent animal. Barker continues to rank the analogical and the imaginative over the rational and to insist that material reality is a lesser reality along a continuum of such.

The second movie that Barker wrote and directed, *Nightbreed,* appeared in 1990 and is based upon the novella *Cabal* (1989), included in the American edition of the last volume of *The Books of Blood.* Led by his psychotherapist, Dekker, to believe that he is a serial killer, protagonist Boone flees, leaving his lover, Lori, behind. Led by dream and serendipity, he tries to find refuge in Midian, a city beneath a cemetery, populated by the survivors of an ancient race of shapeshifters. Some of these beings are living dead, some cannibalistic; all are highly individual in form and ability. Initially driven away from Midian, Boone suffers a wound there that enables him to survive the death he soon meets at the hands of the police, who are led to him by Dekker, the true killer. After that, Midian accepts Boone. Upon Midian converge Lori and Dekker, seeking respectively love and death. The story broadens to bring the night monsters into an apocalyptic conflict with the forces of medicine, law, and the church. But Barker has effected the kind of Heaven and Hell inversion practiced by William Blake: the true heroes are the monsters, and their society is not only an acceptable alternate but also a progression; the villains are the forces of law led by a monomaniacal officer, a lunatic psychotherapist, and an alcoholic priest. At the close, Boone proves to be both Moses and Messiah: he prepares to lead the Tribes of the Moon to their lost and wounded god, while in the shadows Dekker is resurrected as a Dark Anti-Christ. Populated by monsters, werewolves, and zombies, and characterized by brutal violence and the grotesque, *Cabal* and *Nightbreed* look back to Barker's earlier horror work. But the primacy of human love, the possibility of transmutation, and the elaboration of a mythic culture and history all place the latter movie among his fantasies as well.

With *Imajica,* Barker's canon undergoes major evolution. Tonally, his optimism becomes explicit. Thematically, he creates a syncretic system to support such optimism in a novel merging Christianity and goddess-worship. In narrative structure, he develops a carefully realized epic in the Miltonic vein (with undertones of Blake's cosmology). In character, he develops three deeply realized personae and an array of others who are memorable. Writing his longest novel to that point (more than 400,000 words), he manages to maintain narrative suspense, to engage and surprise.

Setting—both chronological and spatial—is now a major focus. Much of the novel either leads readers to new places or provides exposition of the past. Spatially,

*Dust jacket, with a painting by Barker, for the U.S. edition of his 1992 book, a novel for children about
a boy who becomes trapped for a time in the realm of fantasy (Richland County Public Library)*

Earth exists among but is separated from four other magnificent "dominions" by an inchoate dimension, In Ovo. Prompted by a mysterious androgyne, Pie'oh'Pah, the hero (Gentle) and heroine (Judith) separately enter and explore the other four dominions, a process that enables Barker to create a host of fantastic beings, places, and situations, many of them as dark and as bizarre as in previous works. The dimensions suffer under a tyrant and have begun to revolt, giving Barker ample opportunity to include the violent and sexual scenes that have characterized his fiction. These adventures move toward a greater transformation, one in which Earth will join the other four dimensions.

The chronological dynamic of the novel, largely expository, is set up by the fact that the protagonists cannot remember back further than ten years. Thus their exploration of worlds is simultaneously their rediscovery of themselves. It transpires that Gentle is the magus who can bring about Earth's "reconciliation." One of a long line of such figures and more than two centuries old, Gentle—through arrogance and self-indulgence involving Judith—caused a bloody failure that precipitated a violent reaction against magic: the Age of Reason. Now his fate and his God move him to another attempt.

The enveloping cosmology is syncretic, part Old Testament, part goddess-worship. Originally, goddesses ruled the four dimensions, the first of which was home to a highly developed species, almost angelic in character, which received the souls of the dead. But a deified man from Earth destroyed the goddesses, claimed the first dimension, and closed heaven to the dead. This God, who is much like Jehovah, is Gentle's

inspiration for a "Reconciliation," which, as it develops, proceeds much like the apocalypse prophesied in Revelation, especially in the rise of an Anti-Christ who becomes Gentle's adversary. But the goddesses inspire Judith and confront the patriarchy in intricate and fascinating developments. Together, topography, chronology, and cosmography provide the novel a scope that is Miltonic—although Barker's religious stance would disgust and horrify the poet.

Although Barker retains his previous relish for the dark side, the fact that he can psychologically accept and use this side in the most positive way is evident in this novel. Nor does Barker achieve such a state by either subordinating or integrating the darkness. It coexists. The resulting human condition is more elaborate, richer with potential, more unpredictable, more exciting. Humanity can be many things simultaneously. Finally, the novel has much to say about human love and sexuality in all of its aspects: heterosexual, homosexual, filial, parental, patriotic, carnal, spiritual, and narcissistic. The three central characters alone provide a full palette: not only is Pie an androgyne able to become what the beholder wishes to see, but also Gentle and Judith each have a doppelgänger. Love motivates the characters among their enveloping constellation and finally enables readers to reconcile with what they find unendurable in humanity.

While working on *Everville,* the sequel to *The Great and Secret Show,* Barker wrote and illustrated a juvenile, *The Thief of Always: A Fable* (1992), apparently a loving memorial of his boyhood (a photograph of him at ten concludes the piece). A firm believer that much of his work is not appropriate for children, Barker has written a short piece particularly for them that is entertaining and instructive. Though it has the tension, crises, and *frisson* of horror literature, he trims it of graphically violent or obscene imagery. A creature from the world of fantasy seduces a boy into its realm, where every day is a holiday and every wish becomes reality. Forming friends and gradually intuiting that a malign impulse informs this reality, the boy and a companion make a dramatic escape, whereupon they discover that their days in the creature's world were years in their own. The boy returns to regain what is his from the thief of his time. Atypically, *The Thief of Always* affirms the values of familial love above the transformations available in the world beyond reality. The book is skillfully executed in plot, character, setting, and imagery, and the monsters remain varied and unsettling.

Barker has also become involved in the field of the graphic novel and the comic book, which includes an ever-widening body of work based upon his *Books of Blood,* the *Hellraiser* and *Nightbreed* movies, and original concepts. The only graphic novel for which he seems to have done any actual writing, however, is a collaboration on the story for two 1993 issues in a series prompted by George Romero's zombie classic *Night of the Living Dead* (1968). These are *Night of the Living Dead: London (Book One: Bloodline)* and *Night of the Living Dead: London (Book Two: End of the Line),* works likely to be particularly shocking to the British public because of the Juvenalian rendering of the Royal Family in revolting expressionist inks. He has maintained an active relationship as consultant to the enterprises based on his works, sometimes choosing writers and artists; but he has denied the request for some of his own drawings as models (a normal procedure), urging instead that artists be given imaginative control. His own artwork—some paintings and hundreds of ink sketches—appear in two volumes: *Clive Barker, Illustrator* (1990) and *Illustrator II: The Art of Clive Barker* (1993).

The *Illustrator* books reveal another side of Barker: the extensive commentary that he provides for the illustrations shows that he is a fascinating theorist. Further evidence is in the anthology compiled by Stephen Jones in 1991, *Clive Barker's Shadows in Eden,* which includes the best of the reviews and interviews that had appeared up to the date of its publication and also features a bibliography. Barker proves himself an original and stimulating thinker on the nature of the genre and his relationship to it. Although his views appear informally, for the most part, in a collage of sidebar quotations and in the associational process of interview, the volume provides substantial material on the psychological and sociological dynamics of horror; Barker's distinct preference for the Jungian psychoanalytic approach; the composition of

narrative and drama; and the characteristics of his kind of postmodern horror fiction.

The process of transformation has been a constant throughout Barker's canon, which has spanned the range of the *fantastique* from sadomasochistic horror fantasy to the epic quest of the multiverse. He integrates into his vision of the future the visions of the past: Milton and Blake, the comic book and the movie poster, the Eucharist, and the splatter movie. He has earned a place as not only a contributor to these genres but also a cultural phenomenon.

Interview:

Naomi Epel, "Clive Barker," in her *Writers Dreaming* (New York: Carol Southern, 1993), pp. 31–42.

Bibliography:

Stephen Jones, "Clive Barker: A Working Bibliography," in *Clive Barker's Shadows in Eden,* edited by Jones (Lancaster, Pa.: Underwood-Miller, 1991), pp. 425–453.

Biography:

Douglas E. Winter, *Clive Barker, the Dark Fantastic: The Authorized Biography* (London: HarperCollins, 2001).

References:

Linda Badley, *Writing Horror and the Body: The Fiction of Stephen King, Clive Barker, and Anne Rice* (Westport, Conn.: Greenwood Press, 1996);

Suzanne J. Barbieri, *Clive Barker: Mythmaker for the Millennium* (Stockport: British Fantasy Society, 1994);

Michael Brown, ed., *Pandemonium: Further Explorations into the World of Clive Barker* (New York: Eclipse Books, 1991);

Gary Hoppenstand, *Clive Barker's Short Stories: Imagination as Metaphor in the Books of Blood and Other Works* (Jefferson, N.C.: McFarland, 1994);

Stephen Jones, ed., *Horror: 100 Best Books* (New York: Carroll & Graf, 1988);

Andrew Smith, "Words That Creep Up on You: Postmodern Illusions in the Work of Clive Barker," in *Creepers: British Horror and Fantasy in the Twentieth Century,* edited by Clive Bloom (London & Boulder, Colo.: Pluto, 1993), pp. 176–186;

James Van Hise, *The Illustrated Guide to Clive Barker* (Las Vegas, Nev.: Pioneer, 1989);

Van Hise, *Stephen King and Clive Barker: The Illustrated Guide to the Masters of the Macabre* (Las Vegas, Nev.: Pioneer, 1990);

Van Hise, *Stephen King and Clive Barker: The Illustrated Guide to the Masters of the Macabre II* (Las Vegas, Nev.: Pioneer, 1992).

Barrington J. Bayley
(9 April 1937 –   )

Jefferson M. Peters
Fukuoka University

BOOKS: *The Star Virus* [bound with *Mask of Chaos,* by John Jakes] (New York: Ace, 1970);
Annihilation Factor [bound with *Highwood,* by Neil Barrett Jr.] (New York: Ace, 1972); published separately (London: Allison & Busby, 1979);
Empire of Two Worlds (New York: Ace, 1972; London: Hale, 1973);
Collision Course (New York: DAW, 1973); republished as *Collision with Chronos* (London: Allison & Busby, 1977);
The Fall of Chronopolis (New York: DAW, 1974; London: Allison & Busby, 1979);
The Soul of the Robot (Garden City, N.Y.: Doubleday, 1974; revised edition, London: Allison & Busby, 1976);
The Garments of Caean (abridged edition, Garden City, N.Y.: Doubleday, 1976; unabridged edition, London: Fontana, 1978; New York: DAW, 1980);
The Grand Wheel (New York: DAW, 1977; London: Fontana, 1979);
The Knights of the Limits (London: Allison & Busby, 1978);
Star Winds (New York: DAW, 1978);
The Seed of Evil (London: Allison & Busby, 1979);
The Pillars of Eternity (New York: DAW, 1982);
The Zen Gun (New York: DAW, 1983; London: Methuen, 1984);
The Rod of Light (London: Methuen, 1985; New York: Arbor House, 1987);
The Forest of Peldain (New York: DAW, 1985);
Eye of Terror: A Warhammer 40,000 Novel (Nottingham: Black Library, 1999);
The Sinners of Erspia (Gillette, N.J.: Wildside Press, 2002).

SELECTED PERIODICAL PUBLICATIONS–
UNCOLLECTED:
NONFICTION
"Science, Religion and the Science Fiction Idea: Or, Where Would We Be Without Hitler?" *Foundation,* 17 (September 1979): 50–57;

Barrington J. Bayley (courtesy of the author)

"SF Novel and Basic Form," *Vector,* 103 (August 1981): 19–23;
"So What's New? My Thoughts on the Bomb," *Vector,* 116 (September 1983): 29–33;
"Who Owns the Nöosphere," *Vector,* 113 (October 1983): 27–31;
"Barry's Autobiography," *Kimota,* 2 (30 March 1988).

Barrington J. Bayley is important in science fiction because of his ability to reinvigorate and expand the genre as he explores exhilarating, often bleak metaphysical concepts about the universe and humanity's place in it. In a manner particularly relevant to the modern ethnic-strife-ravaged world—in which, Bayley wrote in "So What's New? My Thoughts on the Bomb" (1983), "Longterm peace is what is unnatural"—his science fiction reveals the dark side of human nature and the ways in which people may transcend it. Best known for his novels, Bayley has also published more than sixty stories (some as Alan Aumbry, John Diamond, or P. F. Woods) in science-fiction magazines such as *British Space Fiction Magazine* (1950s), *New Worlds* (1960s and 1970s), and *Interzone* (1980s and 1990s). Bayley's work reads like an original meld of H. G. Wells, Olaf Stapledon, Jorge Luis Borges, Jack Vance, and Philip K. Dick.

Barrington John Bayley was born to working-class parents, John Bayley and Clarissa Mary Love, in Birmingham, England, on 9 April 1937. He has two siblings, a brother and sister, both of whom are younger than he. In 1946 or 1947 Bayley's family moved to South Shropshire, where he has lived most of his life. He was educated until age sixteen at Adams Grammar School in Shropshire (1948–1953), performing "very poorly," as he confessed in a 1980 interview with Geoff Rippington. When he was fourteen, Bayley decided that the only suitable career for him was that of a science-fiction author, an ambition he told Rippington he has "been fitfully trying to realize" ever since, with brief side careers as a reporter (early 1950s), civil servant (1954–1955), Australian public servant in London (1957–1958), clerk, typist, and coal miner. He served in the Royal Air Force from 1955 to 1957. On 30 October 1969 Bayley married Joan Lucy Clarke, with whom he has two children, Sean and Heather.

Several factors led Bayley to become a science-fiction author. In a 20 February 1994 unpublished interview he explained that as a young boy he experienced epiphanies that revealed a wondrous universe: once when his father tossed a pebble into the sea and said, "Think, Barry, the bit of water that stone hit might reach America by next week," and once when he read an article about the moon and contemplated the sublime fact of another world. Bayley stated that "Instead of the above [inquiring mind] being channeled into the career of a philosopher or scientist, for which I don't have the academic capacity, I developed an avid interest in science fiction." His "psychological birth" occurred when he read his first science-fiction magazine, a British edition of *Astounding Stories:* "if you peel away the layers of my psyche, like the scene where Peer Gynt peels away an onion, then right at the bottom you will find a pile of sf magazines of the forties vintage."

The other major influence on Bayley was World War II and its aftermath. He wrote in "Barry's Autobiography" (1988) that he "developed an interest in Science Fiction while still in the womb; probably from overhearing talk of the impending world war." In the 20 February 1994 interview he elaborated:

> total war fought by every means which science can muster is one of the visions which both haunts and propels science fiction. My early years were spent in a society engaged in such an enterprise. . . . And when the war ended, the world began preparing for an even bigger and more destructive war. As a child I thought this a natural state of affairs.

Wonderful universe and horrible humanity have always been entwined in Bayley's mind and science fiction.

Bayley describes himself as a traditional science-fiction writer, and he has an obvious affection for genre conventions such as robots, time travel, far-future exotic cultures, and galactic civilizations. But his unsentimental view of humanity and his original imagination prevent him from copying past devices. As Andy Darlington says in "Knight Without Limit: An Overview of the Work of Barrington Bayley" (1980), Bayley "operates within the traditional science fiction horizons, grabbing and refurbishing the hardware, giving it undreamed of ontological wings and additional conceptual dimensions."

Bayley told Rippington he believes that characterization and the "soap opera" affairs of everyday life should take a backseat to the primary subject of science fiction: "its conceptions, its vision." As he recalled to E. C. Brown in a 1983 *Vector* article, when an idea, scene, or impression that Bayley wants "the reader to retain after he has forgotten the storyline or the names of the characters" coalesces in his mind, he stubbornly struggles, sometimes for years, to embody the conception in a fiction with suitable setting, plot, and characters. Despite Bayley's prime interest in ideas, however, he creates many vivid characters who pursue transcendent obsessions in tightly constructed, entertaining plots.

For Bayley, the best science fiction offers epiphanies that explode the usual human vision in which "the kitchen table is a larger object than the Milky Way Galaxy," as he said in the Rippington interview. The metaphysical concepts that drive his narratives make readers enlarge their focus to include the space, time, and matter of the universe. Bayley structures his novels so that his characters undergo a series of revelations about human nature, existence, and the universe. This continuous learning underscores one of his frequent themes: people should spend their lives developing their minds and those of their fellow humans. Bayley admires his scientist/alchemist characters who seek to manipulate space, time, and matter with their minds for transcendence rather than political power. He also condemns scientists who pursue knowledge without empathy, and his fiction retains a sense of humanity amid the most abstract speculations.

In addition to being mind-expanding, Bayley's fiction is disturbing for two reasons. First, it dissects human xenophobia, homocentrism, power hunger, and what he calls in *Annihilation Factor* (1972) "thanatophilia: a morbid love of death." Repeatedly Bayley depicts societies bent on mutual destruction because history and environment have programmed one group to think that another is trying to destroy it or to believe that it has the right to expand. Second, at any moment Bayley's characters may plunge through the thin layer of reality into vertiginous depths of pure randomness, potential time, or oblivion, which in turn shakes readers loose from their comfortable vision of existence.

Although in the 20 February 1994 interview Bayley describes the conclusions of his fictions as "downbeat," and his works often seem grim, there are occasional brighter moments. In his fiction the universe is immensely mysterious, which provides opportunities for growth. Individuals may transcend human nature and natural laws by developing their minds, by becoming more empathic and ethical, or by remembering history. Bayley's protagonists often reject the warping influences of their father figures and form their own worldviews. Sometimes his civilizations avoid destruction by engaging in "cultural copulation" with one another. And most of Bayley's published novels, short stories, and essays are leavened by humorous scenes, characters, and ideas ranging from the black to the absurd.

Bayley's career falls into several phases marked by his developing ability to realize his ideas in plots, characters, and settings strong enough to carry them, and by his changing success in the marketplace. First came teenage efforts to write short stories, several of which, such as "Combat's End" (1954) and "Fugitive" (1956), were printed in British science-fiction magazines. Recalling the work of his teens to Rippington, Bayley said that he "accomplished very little" because he was unable to develop the proper fictional vehicles for his ideas, but that he is "still mining the fragments" that he "laid down then" for their "mood, scenes, and outlandish incident."

Bayley's second phase occurred in his early twenties when he tried to earn a living from his writing in London. Because the editor of *New Worlds,* Ted Carnell, felt that Bayley was a bad writer and continually rejected his work, Bayley assumed the name P. F.

Paperback cover for the 1974 novel in which Bayley depicted an empire that uses time travel to manipulate its past and thus improve its future

Woods, under which he sold thirteen stories to Carnell in the early 1960s. Of this period Bayley cites one story, "All the King's Men" (1965), as redeeming his other early science fiction, which he dismisses in a 1990 interview with Andy Robertson and David Pringle as "dreadful" for "lack of understanding of plot, pace, dialogue or even sentence construction." He still could not balance concept and story properly. In 1958 Bayley met Michael Moorcock, who collaborated with him on some work and later introduced him to writing serialized freelance boys' adventure stories for the periodical publisher Fleetway, with which Bayley supported himself. Although writing juveniles began to teach Bayley how to construct stories that could carry his ideas, the work exhausted him and contributed to his total disillusionment with writing, literature, and London. From 1966 to 1970 he published only two science-fiction stories.

In the mid to late 1960s Bayley lived in Dublin, Ireland, where he read William S. Burroughs's *Naked Lunch* (1959), which he told Robertson and Pringle "inspired and refreshed, practically rescued" him from "literary despair." The third phase of Bayley's career began when he and his wife settled in Shropshire after their marriage in 1969, and he began to write his potent science-fiction novels and short stories.

Twenty-one of Bayley's best short stories, sixteen of which were originally published after 1970, have been collected in *The Knights of the Limits* (1978) and *The Seed of Evil* (1979). What Brian Stableford says in Frank Magill's *Survey of Science Fiction Literature* (1979) about the former applies to the stories in both collections: "These . . . stories constitute a parade of ideas which is unparalleled in modern science fiction." Bayley displays an innovative imagination and varied set of narrative strategies in his short stories.

In "The Exploration of Space" (1972), for example, the first story in *The Knights of the Limits,* the narrator, a modern-day alchemist, recounts his opium-induced conversation with a being from a different space-time continuum. This being, referred to as "the Knight" because he temporarily "occupies" a knight on the narrator's chessboard, is an explorer of different space-time continua, of which there are an infinite number, the narrator's being one of the more limiting, bizarre, and difficult in which to move. The Knight describes various space-time continua inhabited by life-forms adapted to their particular environments: an asymmetrical space suspended between two magnetic poles, a space split into noncommunicating branches, a space completely filled with matter, a folding "origami" space, spaces based on every conceivable number (as the narrator's is based on the number one), and the Knight's own space, which "instead of being continuous and homogeneous as we know it," is "made up of discrete locations . . . to which entities can address themselves instantaneously." Although the skeptical "editor" who has prepared the "manuscript" of the story believes the whole thing is an invention of the narrator, Bayley's exploration of space convinces readers that "for all our knowledge of the universe . . . we still have not touched or even suspected the immensities and the mysteries that existence contains." The story is emblematic of Bayley's science-fiction corpus.

The Star Virus (1970), *Annihilation Factor,* and *Empire of Two Worlds* (1972) are usually treated cursorily as imperfect efforts leading to Bayley's more accomplished later novels. But the three display the author's compelling imagination, lurid surprises, and ironic humor worthy of close attention as they initiate the themes that Bayley later developed more smoothly.

In *The Star Virus,* expanded from a novelette of the same title in *New Worlds* (May/June 1964), the bizarre, mutable characters obsessively quest for knowledge and philosophize about life. With its galaxy depicted as "a realm of mental aberration" wherein people act under the influence of drugs and nerve organs, *The Star Virus* reveals the invigorating influence of *Naked Lunch*. In the novel Rodrone Chang, a "vacillating dreamer," leads his men on an impromptu course of small-time piracy throughout the Hub (the Milky Way). Rodrone usually raids his favorite kind of world, "Lurid, offbeat and infernal," which describes one flavor of Bayley's fiction. Rodrone steals a "lens" that he learns is the schemata that super-beings used to create the galaxy. An alien species, the Streall, try to retrieve the lens because they need it to destroy a "star virus" spreading randomly throughout the galaxy. In a typical space opera, the star virus would be an alien menace. Here, however, humanity is the virus. Rodrone causes a war that annihilates entire planets and their populations. When he finally breaks through the galactic barrier and opens the universe to the humanity virus, he sourly wonders whether he has done a good thing. Yet, the prolific and chaotic nature of humanity is somehow admirable. The alternative, embodied by the unimaginative and mechanical Streall, is unappealing.

Whereas in *The Star Virus* humanity is viral, in *Annihilation Factor* it is thanatophilic. At first *Annihilation Factor,* which was expanded from a novelette called "The Patch" (*New Worlds,* November/December 1964), appears to be standard space opera. Prince Peredan struggles to retake his father's Star Kingdom from the usurper King Maxim, while the Patch, a purely mental creature, is eating its way through the life force of every being in the galaxy. Both Maxim and Peredan, however, are warped by power, and the masses will suffer no matter who rules. Even Krakhno, the anarchist seeking to overthrow the aristocracy, is motivated by thanatophilia rather than a desire for equality. And Bayley's protagonist, Jundrak, is a self-centered opportunist colluding with all three sides. Bayley also twists the usual space-opera intoxication with weaponry. He enthusiastically includes everything from daggers to nuclear-fusion beams, appealing to readers' fascination with destructive technology and at the same time revolting them with its horrible meaning. Maxim's soldiers wear "exaggeratedly armoured cod pieces," and as they shoot their force rifles they offer "a weird spectacle with their stiffened, outstretched right arms," like saluting Nazis. The Patch is not the annihilation factor—humanity is. The Patch consumes life because it loves it, whereas people kill because they love death. Bayley also offers a pessimistic social extrapolation: "The inexorable polarity of wealth and poverty was a natural law, unaffected by any amount of scientific progress." Thus, commoners die at seventy, aristocrats at six hundred.

Bayley does present bright spots of twisted humor, as when Krakhno, who becomes increasingly morose after the Patch leaves him the only living person on a planet of corpses, says, "Children? . . . there are no such people as children. They are only adults who haven't lived very long, the lucky swine." Grame Liber, the chronicler with an electronics hobby, is one of several positive characters in Bayley's fiction: a spunky and brilliant inventor-historian-alchemist free of political ambition and thanatophilia. Further, Jundrak becomes less selfish and more humane, and his rebellion, empathy, and love offer some hope. The novel concludes with an ambiguous deus-ex-machina twist. *Annihilation Factor* uses space opera both to expose humanity's hunger for power and death and to offer paths of transcendence via empathy and objective knowledge of human history.

Empire of Two Worlds continues Bayley's satiric extrapolation of human traits into unhealthy societies. The fast-paced novel, adapted from an unpublished story written in his teens, distills his fascination with gangster movies and the criminal element in the human psyche into a far-future civilization. Killibol, a gloomy, sterile planet, has been colonized by gangsters from Earth. Gangsterism—carving out mini-empires within cities by maiming, selling protection, and pushing drugs—is the only tradition that has survived the centuries. Bayley's characters even speak old gangster-movie slang. By writing a mobster science-fiction novel, Bayley underscores the aspects of human nature repeatedly exposed in his fiction: selfishness, violence, and ambition. Klein, the only first-person narrator in Bayley's novels, tries to help the charismatic hood Becmath carve out an exceptional empire. Becmath takes his men through a gateway in space and time to a far-future Earth to find an "angle" for building his empire. He finds his angle in the Rheattites, the aesthetic, peaceful people of Earth; Blue Space, a drug to which they are addicted; and their mortal enemies, the giant Rotrox moon warriors, who are even more bellicose and treacherous than the Killibol gangsters. *Empire of Two Worlds* is disturbing because Bayley denies the reader any sympathetic characters. Becmath is a megalomaniacal hood who slaughters masses for revenge rather than utopia. For most of the novel, Klein is hardly better. He guns people down for Becmath and joins him in an unholy alliance with the Rotrox to destroy the Rheattite civilization. Bayley indulges in the empire building and weaponry of space opera and satirizes them as the power fantasies of mobsters and monsters. Klein redeems humanity when he finally breaks

free from Becmath and organizes a two-world empire where different communities exchange ideas, people, and goods. *Empire of Two Worlds* is a salutary novel that forces readers to search for ways to avoid being mobsters.

Collision Course (1973), Bayley's best-selling work (more than forty-one thousand copies), launched his major novels that—in addition to being playful takes on space-opera conventions and devastating visions of humanity—are original extrapolations of metaphysical ideas. In addition to the thanatophilia and power hunger of the previous novels, *Collision Course* exposes xenophobia, racism, and ethnocentrism. Bayley extrapolates his narrative world from two remarkable ideas about time that reverse the conventions of time travel. First, time is local to a few places in the universe rather than common everywhere. Second, the traveling "now-wave" of time, a natural phenomenon created by localized imbalances, infrequently causes islands of life in an otherwise dead universe. The past is cut off from the present now-wave, and people of the past are predetermined automatons mindlessly following their lives. And just one second futureward is desolation, because the now-wave has not yet sparked life. Time travel is not a wondrous activity in which the present or future may be improved by tinkering with the past, which cannot be altered. Instead, it is an eerie experience that proves the transitory, insignificant nature of life in an uncaring universe.

Collision Course occurs far in Earth's future. To protect their purity, the white "True Men" have consigned the various "deviant sub-species" ("devs") to reservations. Bayley treats this theme with accuracy and humor by making extensive use of multiple viewpoint characters (the first of his novels to do so). The paths of three "True Men," Rond Heshke, an objective archeologist; Leard Ascar, a time-scientist; and Sobrie Oblomot, an artist who belongs to a covert pro-dev group, intertwine in a well-constructed plot. Mysterious ancient alien ruins on Earth seem to be growing younger daily. It develops that by chance one of the many now-waves moving through the universe has created nonhuman beings on Earth in humanity's future and is moving "backwards," so that the human and nonhuman now-waves will collide and annihilate both biospheres. When the beings of different times understand the dilemma, each feverishly prepares to destroy the other's biosphere. Both species reject the solution offered by an advanced interstellar Chinese civilization. Bayley exhibits delightful and satiric invention in the Chinese manipulation of the now-wave of time for every aspect of their lives, from production to reproduction. The novel ends with a provocatively optimistic and pessimistic deus ex machina. *Collision Course* shows that even if the difficult task of embracing diversity,

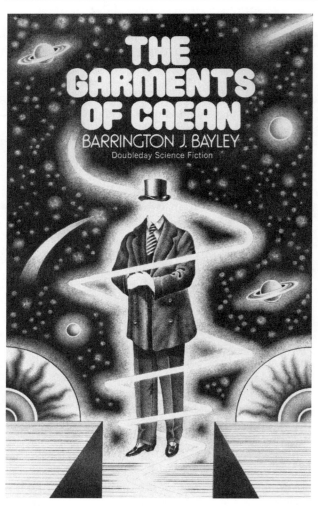

Dust jacket for Bayley's 1976 novel, which, he says, "grew out of a single phrase which occurred to me one day . . . 'The suit which owned its wearer'" (Richland County Public Library)

dream. . . . This time-travel: it is merely a way of moving from one part of a dream to another." The religion worships a Holy Trinity: God is the Father; the surface layer of real time is the Son; and the "strat," the bottomless ocean of potential time beneath real time, is the Holy Ghost with which God makes the Son. Heretics worship the Adversary, Hulmu, who dwells in the depths of potential time. The empire wants to impose its religion on its own future, which is occupied by the aggressively resistant Hegemony, a free society founded by religious dissidents from the past. The conflict, which escalates until it threatens the fabric of time, would be diffused if only the empire would stop trying to conquer the Hegemony, but at "the center of the empire" everyone is "hell-bent on destruction." When chronman Captain Aton is ejected into potential time, he becomes a time-traveling god, and the bizarre conclusion of the novel depicts Aton's struggle with the Minion of Hulmu to enable the empire and Hegemony to be resurrected and their eternal conflict repeated. *The Fall of Chronopolis,* one of Bayley's favorites among his works, uses time travel to critique ethnocentrism and thanatophilia and to impress upon readers the transitory and mutable nature of life.

The Soul of the Robot (1974)—another of Bayley's favorites among his novels—uses robots movingly and humorously to define free will, consciousness, and humanity. The novel opens with the "birth" of Jasperodus, a robot whom an old, childless couple create to "give them as much joy and comfort as would an organically born flesh-and-blood child." Jasperodus has other plans, however, and no sooner does he become conscious than he walks out of their lives. The devastated old couple quietly accept his desertion: "they could have made their offspring with a built-in desire to cherish them; but that, they had both decided, would not be the right way. Whatever he did, it had to be of his own free will." Bayley actually sketched this chapter in his teens. The novel is a metaphysical and political bildungsroman: Jasperodus kills men, makes a human friend, becomes wealthy, learns about art and science, gains sexual desire circuitry and a penis, and learns that property causes inequity between rich and poor. There is a curious repetition to Jasperodus' adventures: he twice dies and is reborn, twice usurps and abandons thrones, and twice observes, "Repetition is a feature of this life."

Bayley continues to use science fiction to comment on human nature and society, as when Jasperodus encounters ghetto robots who live in poverty and frequent dives where they pay with pieces of their brains for electric "jags" that render them "drunk." Throughout his adventures, feeling that he has a soul is never enough for Jasperodus, and his major goal is

love, and life is possible for some people, the dead universe may dwarf it into insignificance. But the struggle is everything.

Whereas in *Collision Course* Bayley reverses the convention of time travel, showing how futile and horrifying it is, in *The Fall of Chronopolis* (1974) he expands the concept. From the premise that time is mutable and circular Bayley designs a future civilization, the Chronotic Empire, that spans several centuries of time at once and uses time travel to manipulate its past to improve its future. Bayley extrapolates "chronmen" time soldiers, a religion and its heretical counterpart, social mores, and worldviews. Because time is circular, people repeat their lives forever—unless they are erased by time manipulation. The Achronal Archives record millions of "ghosts," all the people erased from time. Chief Archivist Mayar believes that "We are living in a

to prove that he is as conscious as any human. The more he unsuccessfully struggles toward his goal, the more apparent it becomes that humans cannot prove their souls exist either and that Jasperodus is thus essentially human. Finally Jasperodus resolves to seek the only thing that makes repetitious life meaningful: "to raise human consciousness to ever higher levels of aspiration."

The Garments of Caean (1976) continues Bayley's critique of xenophobia and ethnocentrism and extrapolates a "clothes make the man" idea to an unsettling conclusion. His novel, Bayley explained in the 1994 interview, "grew out of a single phrase which occurred to me one day . . . 'The suit which owned its wearer.'" In the novel humanity has spread throughout the galaxy into two distinct cultures. For the people of Caean, clothes are "a philosophy . . . *the* way of life." The Caeanics believe that humanity's naked form is ugly and weak and that by wearing the best clothes for each situation, they gain the most successful interface between themselves and the world. In the Ziode Cluster the people stress self-reliance and view the Caeanics as "clothes-robots." As the book opens, Peder Forbarth, a Ziodean tailor, finds a charismatic Caeanic suit made from a new superfabric, Prossim, which makes him a star. But Peder is not happy, for he suspects the suit is wearing him.

Meanwhile, a ship led by Ziodean scientists has entered the Caeanic curve of the galaxy to learn the civilization's "aims and origins" in order to help Ziode resist a perceived Caeanic cultural invasion. At the edge of the Caeanic zone, the Ziodean scientists find two of Bayley's imaginative extrapolations. Long ago, after a war between Russia and Japan, soldiers from each side were abandoned in outer space and evolved in opposite ways to suit their environment. The Russian "Metalloids" are theorized to be the forebears of Caean because they wear exaggerated clothes to interface with the outside world: giant metal spacesuits have become their bodies, and their human bodies—which they never see—have become their inner organs. The cyborg Japanese, conversely, have altered their bodies with artificial organs that enable them to live naked to the void. Bayley's eerie description of these cyborgs, with their eyes "hidden by black goggles . . . riveted into the eye sockets" and noseless faces, metal-turreted skulls, and corrugated metal abdomens, is an early cyberpunk nightmare. The two cultures still seek to annihilate each other rather than accept their differences.

Amara Corl, the head scientist of the Ziodean research ship, has a great intellect but no feelings for the "specimens" on which she experiments, mixing cyborgs and Metalloids as children mix red and black ants. Corl has a Metalloid, Alexei, cut out of his suit to watch him

view his nude body (his "vital organs"). This experience so traumatizes Alexei that he needs drugs to control his resulting schizophrenia. In Bayley's novels the pursuit of knowledge is wonderful until it becomes divorced from human feeling. Realto Mast, a gangster, is the only character who sympathizes with Alexei. The novel, as most of Bayley's do, ends ambiguously, leaving readers to question which civilization—clothes robots or ruthless scientists—is more or less human, forcing readers to recognize that both are only slightly exaggerated images of themselves.

The Grand Wheel (1977) is constructed around a vision of luck as a quantifiable natural force that creates life out of pure randomness. This concept engenders a future gambling civilization with a probabilistic view of identity and reality. Bayley said in the 1994 interview that *The Grand Wheel* was an attempt to "write a novel that corresponded with my image of some of those marvelous . . . pulp novels" of the 1940s and early 1950s, which may explain why the plot seems too tenuous and fast-paced to support his intriguing metaphysical apparatus. Professional gambler Cheyne Scarne hopes to infiltrate the Grand Wheel, a powerful illegal gambling organization, and steal the potent "luck equations" that enable the Wheel to manipulate luck. Meanwhile, the majority human government, the Legitimacy, is seeking to destroy the Grand Wheel because of its completely different view of reality. The Legitimacy strives to control nature to prevent "accidents," because chance threatens the cohesion of society. The Grand Wheel thrives on chance and believes that society will always be at the mercy of hazard, which indeed has manifested itself in the hostile Hadranic aliens who are threatening to destroy human civilization. Scarne becomes the protégé of Marguerite Dom, the chairperson of the Grand Wheel. With human civilization as the apparent prize, Scarne and Dom play a game of chance against the alien representatives of an even vaster galactic gambling organization. Although *The Grand Wheel* is less textured than Bayley's other works, it vividly shows the potent forces of luck and chance that shape human lives.

In *Star Winds* (1978) Bayley revels in alchemy. He creates a convincing future universe in which "empty" space is ether, the fifth element of the natural world, and in which alchemy, a hybrid science and art, is more valid than "quaint" atomic theory. Young Rachad Caban, searching for a powerful alchemical book, embarks on a perilous adventure on a ship riding ether winds on silk sails, traveling beyond the solar system to Maralia and the Aegis of the Duke of Koss. Concurrently, humanity is being invaded by the alien Kerek, who absorb human populations by means of mind-enslaving "Kerek Power." Inside the Aegis, a hermetically sealed castle complex, Rachad finds a decadent artist's colony living for art and pleasure and ignoring the outside world. Rachad avoids the insipid melody mist and dream slime and becomes an apprentice to Amschel, an alchemist seeking to create the Philosopher's Stone. Rachad criticizes Amschel for pursuing a foolish, senile dream instead of using his alchemy to produce powerful weapons against the Kerek. But Amschel knows that weapons will never defeat the Kerek. When the alchemist succeeds in creating the Philosopher's Stone he becomes god-like and announces his goal: to teach individuals to create their own Stones and thereby resist Kerek mind control. Bayley reverses another science-fiction convention by abandoning Rachad, his youthful protagonist, asleep on a horrible battlefield, and following the old man Amschel as he goes anywhere and does anything via his thoughts. The message is that in order to evolve, individuals must develop their minds by imaginatively pursuing art and science. Bayley's novel is a paean to science fiction: "Immersed in the Stone, the tissues of Amschel's brain experienced transcendental unity, total access—to one another, and, eventually, to the macrocosm itself."

The Pillars of Eternity (1982) is perhaps Bayley's most powerful novel. With memorable characters, philosophies, and artifacts, it reveals the value and limitation of philosophy, the need for memory and love, the interface between human and machine, the obsessive nature of humanity, and the possibility of free action in a deterministic universe. The protagonist of the novel is Joachim Boaz, a deformed boy endowed by "bonemakers" with a new skeleton laced with silicon data-processing chips that offer heightened perceptions, feelings, and abilities. The bonemakers have also educated Boaz in their "colonnader" philosophy, which emphasizes ethics, community, rationality, and stoicism. In the colonnader cosmology the universe oscillates between two pillars—one positive, one negative—which they name Joachim and Boaz. This universe repeats itself down to the last atom forever, and people eternally repeat their lives, each time like the last, never remembering anything from their previous lives. This belief devastates Boaz after he is horribly burned with his bones set at their highest levels of sensitivity. The attempt to experience the world more sensitively thus only brings Boaz eternal hellish pain. Even cauterizing his emotions with the cool fire of philosophy cannot give Boaz peace, for the memory of his pain and the knowledge that he will experience it in each of his lives forever are too strong. Thus he embarks on a mad quest to change his past and thereby derail the repetition of the universe.

On his quest Boaz meets a suicidal Epicurean woman named Mace who also has silicon bones. Although Bayley never glorifies men at the expense of women (most often he satirizes destructive masculine power), his narrative worlds are male-dominated and with few exceptions lack strong women. In the 1994 interview he explains that his reasons for this imbalance stem from his "chief influence," the "magazine sf of the forties and early fifties," which "did not dwell very much on the female side of things." Mace is a vibrant exception. Her relationship with Boaz is the richest between a man and woman in Bayley's novels and crucially fuses two ways of life: ethics and stoicism with pleasure and love. As Boaz heals Mace's mind, the pair fall in love without consummating it, until one day she demands that he turn on his bones again to start living. To Mace, all philosophies that try to explain the universe are "*Junk*. How do you *know* the past repeats itself? It's only a theory. It's only what people *think*. . . . Philosophy isn't real. But what bones give you, that's real." She joins Boaz in a hopeful new world of sensual pleasure that is vital to his ultimate ordeal. At the climax of the novel Bayley depicts, through Boaz's irrevocable and horrible death, sublime transcendence of the physical laws that bind people.

The Zen Gun (1983), which Bayley developed from a dream he had in the 1960s, is his third favorite of his novels. The big themes are present as usual: the use and abuse of great power, the individual's relation to government and authority, and the need for healthy "cultural copulation." The novel is deepened by Bayley's usual pessimistic vision of human nature. But his inventions and genre warpings assume a more consistently comical flavor than in his other work. Even the metaphysical apparatus seems lighter. Bayley grounds the narrative universe of *The Zen Gun* around a physics in which gravity is a force of repulsion instead of attraction—an intriguing concept, but it seems less vital to the themes and characters than the metaphysical conceits of his other novels.

The decadent future human empire of *The Zen Gun* has spread too rapidly, suffered a falling birthrate, and alienated its robot workers, so that adult humans are rare. Children and intelligence-enhanced animals "man" the spaceships. Admiral Archier of Ten-Fleet is only twenty years old. His prime duty is to visit outlying worlds to collect "empire taxes" in the form of artists and scientists, who, because of the scarcity of adults, are a precious resource. Archier's Fire Command Officer is a bellicose pig eager to blast human populations into smithereens, while his space warship teems with partying hangers-on. Bayley achieves many humorous moments with this situation. Meanwhile, Pout, a debased chimera (part ape, part man), finds the most powerful weapon in the universe, a small wooden zen gun capable of destroying stars: the ultimate equalizer between the individual and the empire. Although

DOMIE

    The cock home had a good view of the market concourse

from where he squatted in his cramped cage. It was a colourful

scene. He could watch as the housewife schicks/strutted from

stall to stall buying daily commodities, mostly foodstuffs.

As the day wore on the cages around him emptied one by one.

Now only about half the homes in the battery were left.

    He went tense, trying to shrink to the back of the cage

and make himself invisible as a schick came to inspect the

battery, her beak clacking as she talked to the stallholder.

Her large face _with its floppy red comb/crest_ came close to the front of his cage. Her

beady, merciless eyes glanced at him, then passed on. She

made a selection and pointed with a feathery arm, clacking again.

    It was a younger cock, plump, hardly more than a chick.

The stallholder opened the front of the cage and pulled

him out, arms and legs jerking in panic. Then came the

ear-piercing shrieks of agony as he was dunked in the pot of

boiling oil, muffled _when the stallholder_ slammed the lid on.

    Minutes later the deep-fried home was fished out _with a slotted scoop,_ again,

hastily wrapped up and handed over in return for a few coins.

The older cock took his hands from his ears where he had

pressed them. An exquisite feeling of relief still flooded

through him that it was not he who had gone into the _seething_ hot oil.

He knew he was past prime cooking age and he was scrawny.

He did not want to be a cooked take-away. It was his hope

If he would be bought uncooked, taken to a schick house and killed

quickly before _being boiled or roasted_ for the evening meal, perhaps by

First page of the revised typescript for a recent short story (Collection of Barrington J. Bayley)

The Zen Gun is comical, it also makes readers ponder serious issues. How can humans live with their destructive technology, their desire for power, and their distaste for different cultures? The answer is, only by developing spiritual, social, and aesthetic restraint.

The Rod of Light (1985), Bayley's sequel to *The Soul of the Robot,* is not as rich as the original. Although the cover jacket features glowing blurbs by well-known science-fiction authors such as Roger Zelazny, the novel sold poorly. (The Arbor House American hardcover edition sold only 323 copies.) Nevertheless, *The Rod of Light* has vivid moments of pathos, humor, and wonder as it explores the nature of consciousness and humanity. In *The Soul of the Robot* Jasperodus finally learns that his human parents created him by transferring half of their consciousness into his mechanical body; thus in the sequel he knows he has a soul. His moral dilemma is whether to side with the brilliant robot Gargan, who seeks to steal consciousness from humanity, or to protect humanity and betray his robot half brothers. As in most of Bayley's novels, characters use symbols to understand their worlds. In *The Rod of Light* the symbology revolves around the Zoroastrian religion explained to Jasperodus by an aged human mage. Existence has always been a struggle between light, consciousness, and Ahura Mazda on one side and darkness, unconsciousness, and Ahriman on the other. The mage claims that robots are forces of Ahriman, because they mimic humanity without being truly conscious. A marvelous depiction of this symbology occurs at the estate of Count Viss, an eccentric robot with the ability to defecate. Viss has built a stadium, installed a robot audience, and set black and white robot teams to playing soccer forever. The score is 49,543 to 51,038 in favor of black. Bayley complicates things by having Jasperodus realize that Gargan may be seeking the proper light of Ahura Mazda. After all, humans, ostensibly forces of light, steal the life forces of animals, just as robots would use humans for their souls. And the robots seem human and self-aware. Gargan, Viss, and even Viss's pathetic windup robot have more vivid personalities than the mage, the only individuated human in the novel. If the robots seem more human than the few human characters, is "true" consciousness important? Jasperodus's feelings for the robots he meets humanize him. The human Borgor alliance's callous destruction of robots and Gargan's unfeeling torture of human experimental subjects dehumanize them. Finally, the best criterion for humanity is empathy.

The Forest of Peldain (1985) stands out among Bayley's novels. It seems more like dark heroic fantasy than science fiction. Instead of having a galactic sweep, it occurs on a single corner of one planet with a human civilization reminiscent of ancient Greece. Bayley's exuberant metaphysical imagination is subdued, and his humor is absent. The novel is nightmarish. Lord Vorduthe of the Hundred Islands empire leads eighteen hundred soldiers on a hack-and-burn mission through the impenetrable forest covering Peldain, an island kingdom. On seemingly every page the vegetation impales, poisons, explodes, corrodes, decapitates, or strangles the men. The only "respite" is Vorduthe's poison-induced dream-vision of his beautiful, paralyzed wife being cut up, cooked, and eaten by cannibals. Vorduthe and his surviving fifty men believe they have escaped the forest via an underground river tunnel whose exit is the vagina of a reclining woman sculpted into a hill being swallowed by the encroaching forest. But even when the men leave the surrounding violent woods and enter Peldain, they have only reached the heart of the forest, where its trees grow ready-made everything the people need, from food and clothes to houses. Because Vorduthe has come from outside Peldain, the locals ask him to use the power of his alien personality to dominate mentally the lake god who controls the forest. When Vorduthe sinks into the dream-realm of the lake and learns about the "god," *The Forest of Peldain* becomes science-fictional, but it remains a feverish dream of death and loss. The cultural copulation so important to Bayley is overwhelmed by the final word of the novel, "grief."

The fourth phase of Bayley's career began in 1986 and lasted for about thirteen years, during which he did not publish a single novel, except for an installment in the series inspired by the game Warhammer 40,000. In the 1994 interview he explained his decline in output: "My personal mood deteriorated, making it difficult to get out more than a small amount of adequate work. Added to that I have seemed unable to obtain contracts from publishers." Donald A. Wollheim, editor at Ace and later DAW, enjoyed reading and buying Bayley's work, but he became ill in 1985 and died in 1990, and other publishers and editors viewed Bayley as "an old-fashioned science fiction writer." Because of the transitory nature of much science fiction and the tendency of critics to overlook books in this genre, many potentially important authors have fallen into obscurity, a fate that almost overtook Bayley, all of whose books went out of print in the United States and the United Kingdom during this period.

During this quiet phase Bayley continued contributing short stories to British science-fiction magazines such as *Interzone,* including "A Crab Must Try" (January 1996), which won the 1997 British Science Fiction Award. He also continued to seek a publisher for his novels, and his efforts finally began to pay off. Indeed, his career seemed to enter a phase of rebirth. In

1999 he published *Eye of Terror: A Warhammer 40,000 Novel,* a book that transcends its game-franchise genre, and in 2002 he produced *The Sinners of Erspia,* a metaphysical novel that explores how human beings respond to extremes of good and evil. Moreover, Cosmos Books, a division of Wildside Press, has brought back into print three of Bayley's novels and *The Knights of the Limits,* and the press plans to republish his remaining out-of-print books as well as a new novel and a new short-story collection.

Published criticism of Bayley's works consists of only two brief overviews of his fiction, one bibliographic work, several interviews, and a handful of book reviews. Perhaps this sparse critical coverage fails to reflect the value of Bayley's oeuvre because devotees of optimistic science fiction may recoil from his warping of their simple delights, while serious scholars may scorn the space-opera trappings of his fiction. Nevertheless, Bayley has always had a devoted (if small) following; his works have usually been enthusiastically reviewed; and his popularity is growing on the Internet, where Juha Lindroos has created and maintains *Astounding Worlds of Barrington J. Bayley* <http://oivas.com/bjb/>.

Interviews:

Geoff Rippington, "B. J. Bayley Interviewed," *Arena,* 10 (April 1980): 13–19;

Andy Robertson and David Pringle, "Barrington J. Bayley," *Interzone,* 35 (May 1990): 17–20.

Bibliography:

Mike Ashley, *The Writings of Barrington J. Bayley* (Manchester: Beccon, 1981).

References:

E. C. Brown, "Snapshot," *Vector,* 117 (December 1983): 5–9, 38;

Andy Darlington, "Knight Without Limit: An Overview of the Work of Barrington Bayley," *Arena,* 10 (April 1980): 4–12;

Rhys Hughes, "Annihilation Factotum: The Work of Barrington J. Bayley," *Newsletter of The Council for the Literature of the Fantastic,* 1 (July 1999) <http://www.uri.edu/artsci/english/clf/n6_a3.html>;

Angus Taylor, "Hot Line to the Absolute," *SF Commentary* (November 1979): 5–6.

John Blackburn

(26 June 1923 –1993)

Darren Harris-Fain
Shawnee State University

BOOKS: *A Scent of New-Mown Hay* (London: Secker & Warburg, 1958; New York: Mill, 1958); republished as *The Reluctant Spy* (New York: Lancer, 1966);

A Sour Apple Tree (London: Secker & Warburg, 1958; New York: Mill, 1959);

Broken Boy (London: Secker & Warburg, 1959; New York: Mill, 1962);

Dead Man Running (London: Secker & Warburg, 1960; New York: Mill, 1961);

The Gaunt Woman (London: Cape, 1962; New York: Mill, 1962);

Blue Octavo (London: Cape, 1963); published as *Bound to Kill* (New York: Mill, 1963);

Colonel Bogus (London: Cape, 1964); published as *Packed for Murder* (New York: Mill, 1964);

The Winds of Midnight (London: Cape, 1964); published as *Murder at Midnight* (New York: Mill, 1964);

A Ring of Roses (London: Cape, 1965); published as *A Wreath of Roses* (New York: Mill, 1965);

Children of the Night (London: Cape, 1966; New York: Putnam, 1969);

The Flame and the Wind (London: Cape, 1967);

Nothing but the Night (London: Cape, 1968);

The Young Man from Lima (London: Cape, 1968);

Bury Him Darkly (London: Cape, 1969; New York: Putnam, 1970);

Blow the House Down (London: Cape, 1970);

The Household Traitors (London: Cape, 1971);

Devil Daddy (London: Cape, 1972);

For Fear of Little Men (London: Cape, 1972);

Deep among the Dead Men (London: Cape, 1973);

Our Lady of Pain (London: Cape, 1974);

Mister Brown's Bodies (London: Cape, 1975);

The Face of the Lion (London: Cape, 1976);

The Cyclops Goblet (London: Cape, 1977);

Dead Man's Handle (London: Cape, 1978);

The Sins of the Father (London: Cape, 1979);

A Beastly Business (London: Hale, 1982);

A Book of the Dead (London: Hale, 1984);

The Bad Penny (London: Hale, 1985).

John Blackburn (photograph by Laura Richardson; from the dust jacket for A Wreath of Roses, *1965)*

OTHER: "Johnny Cut-Throat," in *The Devil's Kisses*, edited by Linda Lovecraft (London: Corgi, 1976);

"The Final Trick," in *The Taste of Fear*, edited by Hugh Lamb (New York: Taplinger, 1976);

"Dad," in *Return from the Grave*, edited by Hugh Lamb (New York: Taplinger, 1977);

Short Stories from Scotland, edited by Blackburn (Exeter: Wheaton, 1979).

Prolific and popular, John Blackburn never strove for critical esteem or academic attention, and accordingly he received little of either during a career that spanned more than three decades. Despite this fact, he was widely regarded as a talented writer of genre fiction, ranging from spy thrillers to horror and science fiction. Frequently in his work these genres were combined in interesting ways. In addition, readers often admired Blackburn's skills with characterization and plot in a publishing category in which both tended toward the predictable or the stereotypical. He is widely considered an important figure in British horror fiction in particular, a transitional figure between the older style of weird fiction practiced by Dennis Wheatley and the later type of horror written by the popular author James Herbert.

John Fenwick Blackburn was born in England in Corbridge, Northumberland, on 26 June 1923. His parents were Charles Eliel Blackburn, a clergyman, and Adelaide Blackburn, née Fenwicke. His older brother, Thomas Blackburn, also became a writer, primarily of poetry. Their parents approached the raising of their children rather unconventionally, and their strict father was especially repressive about their sexuality. Thomas later became an alcoholic; John became a writer of horror fiction.

Blackburn attended Haileybury College in Hertford from 1937 to 1940. His education was interrupted by World War II, and he served in the Mercantile Marine from 1942 to 1945, during which time he became a radio officer. He resumed his education when he returned to civilian life, attending Durham University in northeast England and earning his bachelor's degree in 1949.

After graduating from college, Blackburn became a schoolmaster in London, a position he held for two years. In 1950 he married Joan Mary Clift. The following year they moved to Berlin, where Blackburn taught for a year. In 1952 they returned to London, where he became director of Red Lion Books. He also began seriously pursuing a career as a writer, and the publication of his first two books in 1958 encouraged him to leave the publishing world and devote himself full-time to writing. While writing remained his primary career, he and his wife also owned and ran a used and antiquarian bookstore in the London suburb of Richmond.

The title of Blackburn's first novel, *A Scent of New-Mown Hay* (1958), perhaps suggests a different kind of story than the one that is actually in the book. The story is rooted in the historical–the recent events of World War II–but then quickly shifts into science fiction. The survivor of a concentration camp obtains an incredibly powerful biological weapon developed by Nazi Germany. He intends to use the weapon for revenge against his former captors, but his actions threaten to destroy not only former Nazis but also much of Europe as well, as the fungus has mutated and its

effects have been dramatically amplified. The odor of the fungus, incidentally, is what gives the book its title.

The man who is faced with averting this disaster is General Charles Kirk of British Intelligence, who survives the events of *A Scent of New-Mown Hay* to appear in several later novels by Blackburn. He and the team he assembles race to the rescue of Europe, and Blackburn arranges the story to create a high level of suspense.

While the fantastic elements of *A Scent of New-Mown Hay* are only marginal, involving a science-fiction superweapon, this first novel is noteworthy not only for its quality as an adventure thriller but also because it establishes Blackburn's typical concerns and techniques: a massive threat faced by a hero and others, told through a series of incidents that create and build tension within the narrative.

Without repeating himself to the degree that some genre writers are guilty of, Blackburn often relied on a particular formula for his tales of horror and suspense. This formula involved the intrusion of some menace, often supernatural, into the lives of his characters. At first the threat is only dimly perceived, gradually revealed through a series of events that have unknown import at first but that eventually lead his characters to a realization about what they are facing. The nature of the beast varies considerably–monsters, gods, plagues, and so on–but the plot works effectively to establish the reader in the mundane world of the characters before unleashing the beast and depicting how they fight it. This technique both heightens the tension of the plot and creates emotional connections to the characters involved. Indeed, one of the things that made Blackburn stand out among his peers in popular fiction was the fact that his inventive stories were populated by interesting characters whose lives readers came to know in the process of getting to the mystery that is only slowly revealed.

Such is the case in *Broken Boy* (1959), another novel with General Kirk as the hero. In this tale he must unravel the mystery behind what turns out to be a macabre cult, bent on vengeance. While the supernatural elements in this novel are not as explicit as in others by Blackburn, they still hover on the borders.

Indeed, for the most part Blackburn's novels of the late 1950s and the 1960s lack a substantial fantastic element. To call them "realistic" might be a bit much, since as thrillers they do not typically adhere to the conventions of mimetic fiction, but in general they lack the major science-fiction elements that characterize several of his best-known works. Several of them return General Kirk to the scene of action, including *A Sour Apple Tree* (1958), *The Gaunt Woman* (1962), *Colonel Bogus* (1964), *A Ring of Roses* (1965), and *The Young Man from Lima* (1968).

Dust jacket for the U.S. edition of Blackburn's 1969 novel, in which the opening of an eighteenth-century crypt unleashes terrifying supernatural forces (Richland County Public Library)

Like *A Scent of New-Mown Hay,* Blackburn's 1965 novel, *A Ring of Roses* (published in the United States as *A Wreath of Roses*), involves a biological threat with German connections. In this case it is not a weapon but rather a new strain of an old menace, the bubonic plague. A young boy is intentionally infected with the disease and sent from East Germany to England. The mystery is, who infected him and why? Trying to answer these questions are General Kirk and biologist Sir Marcus Levin, whose specialty is bacteriology. Unconvinced that the infection and sending of the boy were part of a communist German plot, they pursue the mystery to its conclusion, along the way introducing several exciting plot developments.

One of Blackburn's first significant horror novels is *Children of the Night* (1966). While not specifically supernatural apart from the inclusion of elements such as telepathy and a subterranean lost race, the story hinges upon a doomsday cult in a village in Yorkshire with a long history of strange incidents. The cult traces its history back to the Middle Ages and has become more active in the 1960s as they anticipate the end of the world on 24 June 1966.

Children of the Night is a good example of Blackburn's tendency to combine qualities from different popular genres. The supernatural elements attached to the doomsday cult, for instance, have their roots in horror fiction, but in many ways the novel is as much a crime thriller as anything else.

Blackburn's next novel, *The Flame and the Wind* (1967), also includes supernatural elements, but of a different kind. An historical novel rather than a thriller, the book is set in A.D. 30 and involves the quest of two Romans to discover the truth behind the story of Jesus of Nazareth. This mission brings them into contact with the early church, and the title alludes to the supernatural events of Pentecost. Thus, while the novel does not resemble conventional fantasy, it nonetheless possesses a certain fantastic nature despite the largely historical focus of the narrative.

In *Nothing but the Night* (1968) Blackburn again combines genres, in this case horror and mystery, and he does so using a recurring figure in British dark fantasy, the psychic detective. Using both conventional detective methods and the occult, the hero attempts to solve a series of strange murders.

Bury Him Darkly (1969) is more of a straightforward horror novel. The story begins with the attempts of a small yet diverse group ranging from mystics to scientists to open the tomb of Sir Martin Railstone. However, the Church of England objects to their wishes, as this remarkable eighteenth-century Renaissance man was not only a scientist and an artist but also a lover of pleasure, a dabbler in the black arts, and a murderer. In addition, there are other reasons for their reluctance, having to do with the fear that horrible supernatural forces could be released were the tomb to be opened.

In summary the plot sounds thin, even ludicrous; but it is a testament to Blackburn's ability that instead it succeeds as an effective suspense thriller up to the last portion of the novel. The crypt is unsealed, and indeed horrible forces are released upon an unsuspecting and largely powerless world. Even the doughty British army flees in terror. If the novel has any faults in the eyes of its critics, it is with this segment of the book, which devolves into a rather mundane monster tale.

Blow the House Down (1970), while not strictly fantastic, nonetheless takes a fairly realistic setting and gives it a macabre twist. The story is about an architect with murderous intentions: he designs skyscrapers so that the people in them will be killed. The novel is a thriller in conception and execution, but a good example of Blackburn's inventiveness in coming up with unusual situations.

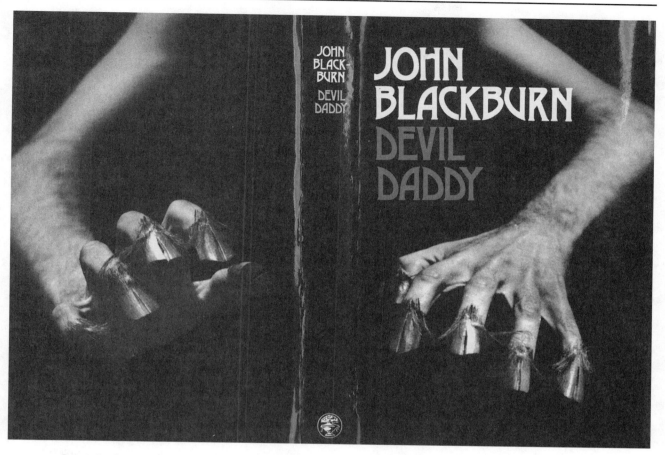

Dust jacket for one of the two 1972 novels in which Blackburn depicted a young couple battling ancient supernatural forces and contemporary scientific horrors (Richland County Public Library)

In comparison to a work such as *Bury Him Darkly,* Blackburn's two novels published in 1972, *For Fear of Little Men* and *Devil Daddy,* are—despite the somewhat laughable titles—much superior. One of his most acclaimed novels, *For Fear of Little Men* begins routinely enough, with an outbreak of food poisoning in Treflys, a village in Wales; but by the time the novel has ended, Blackburn has combined several elements that at first might not seem complementary, ranging from ancient supernatural forces to contemporary scientific horrors.

The heroes of *For Fear of Little Men* are Marcus Levin and his wife, Tania. Levin, as a bacteriologist, is summoned to Treflys by a mysterious outbreak of food poisoning that is afflicting the village. Speculation about its cause includes both superstition—the locals believe it to be the handiwork of brownies, contrary to their typically helpful nature—and science, as a chemical plant is located in the area. However, the mystery runs deeper than a microscope is able to discern, and the danger that is gradually revealed through a series of seemingly unconnected events is not limited to this

Welsh village but threatens to engulf and ultimately to destroy all humanity. This outbreak is the work, finally, of Daran, an evil god of ancient origin, rather than a modern microbe.

While such a portentous plot might sound farfetched, Blackburn manages not only to encourage readers to suspend their disbelief but also to keep them in a state of suspense through much of the novel. Again, his technique is to introduce a wide variety of interesting characters pursuing their own agendas until their paths merge as the story heads toward its denouement. These characters include such unlikely combinations as hippies and former Nazis, archaeologists and industrialists, politicians and Welsh villagers, all brought together under the shadow of Allt y Cricht, which houses the corpse of the dormant god.

Blackburn also employs these techniques in *Devil Daddy,* in which Marcus and Tania Levin are again the protagonists. In another similarity to *For Fear of Little Men,* the novel combines black magic and modern science—in this case, a satanic cult, an ancient prophecy, the legend of the Wandering Jew, and a powerful virus. The plague that threatens the world thus is both scientific and biblical in nature and in scope.

The novel begins with Levin falsely accused of raping a schoolgirl in England, a case made more horrible by the fact that the girl rapidly dies of old age. Levin suspects that the rapist is an art dealer named John Batterday, since Levin and Batterday so closely resemble each other that they could be twins. Moreover, Batterday is known to possess a wicked character. As if these plot twists were not enough, Batterday is also under attack from a satanic cult. While Blackburn relies perhaps a bit too heavily on coincidental events to move the story along, the concepts and overall plot still contribute to the interest of the book.

The demonic and the contemporary are also brought together in *Our Lady of Pain* (1974): the demonic in Elizabeth Báthory, the Hungarian "Blood Countess," and her malevolent sister Krisia; the contemporary in such characters as three thieves, a tabloid journalist, and a psychiatrist who try to determine the cause of the thieves' strange insanity and death brought on by fright after their last job, and other modern figures, such as an actress and a plastic surgeon, who play important roles in the story. The plot revolves around a set of cursed artifacts and the legendary "evil eye."

Blackburn returned to familiar territory in 1976 with *The Face of the Lion*. Once more a horrible disease provides the science-fictional threat, coupled again with former Nazi officers. While not one of Blackburn's more noteworthy works, *The Face of the Lion* is a good example of how Blackburn united such disparate genres as the thriller and science fiction. The references in the novel to the threat of nuclear warfare provide a similar combination.

His next novel, *The Cyclops Goblet* (1977), also merges genre boundaries, but in a new way for Blackburn: horror is combined with humor. While the attempt is interesting, the book is not generally regarded as one of Blackburn's best efforts. The same could be said of the remainder of the novels Blackburn published near the end of his career, in which the supernatural generally plays a diminished role.

Writing in *The Penguin Encyclopedia of Horror and the Supernatural* (1986), horror anthologist Hugh Lamb described Blackburn's novels as "minor masterpieces of horror" and said, "He is certainly the best British novelist in his field and deserves the widest recognition." Such recognition has yet to come, and with the passage of time certain of his works seem somewhat dated, filled as they are with Cold War tensions and former Nazis. However, he is still noteworthy among the popular horror writers of the late twentieth century.

Papers:
Some of John Blackburn's manuscripts are located in the Mugar Memorial Library at Boston University.

John Brunner

(28 September 1934 – 25 August 1995)

Frederick M. Burelbach
State University of New York at Brockport

BOOKS: *Galactic Storm,* as Gill Hunt (London: Curtis Warren, 1952);

The Brink (London: Gollancz, 1959);

Echo in the Skull [bound with *Rocket to Limbo,* by Alan E. Nourse] (New York: Ace, 1959); revised and enlarged as *Give Warning to the World* (New York: DAW, 1974);

The Hundredth Millennium [bound with *Edge of Time,* by David Grinnell (Donald A. Wollheim)] (New York: Ace, 1959); revised and enlarged as *Catch a Falling Star* (New York: Ace, 1968);

Threshold of Eternity [bound with *The War of Two Worlds,* by Poul Anderson] (New York: Ace, 1959);

The World Swappers [bound with *The Siege of the Unseen,* by A. E. Van Vogt] (New York: Ace, 1959);

Slavers of Space [bound with *Dr. Futurity,* by Philip K. Dick] (New York: Ace, 1960); revised as *Into the Slave Nebula* (New York: Lancer, 1968; London: Millington, 1980);

The Skynappers [bound with *Vulcan's Hammer,* by Dick] (New York: Ace, 1960);

Sanctuary in the Sky [bound with *The Secret Martians,* by Jack Sharkey] (New York: Ace, 1960);

The Atlantic Abomination [bound with *Martian Missile,* by Grinnell] (New York: Ace, 1960);

Meeting at Infinity [bound with *Beyond the Silver Sky,* by Kenneth Bulmer] (New York: Ace, 1961);

I Speak for Earth, as Keith Woodcott [bound with *Wandl the Invader,* by Ray Cummings] (New York: Ace, 1961);

Secret Agent of Terra [bound with *The Rim of Space,* by A. B. Chandler] (New York: Ace, 1962); revised and enlarged as *The Avengers of Carrig* (New York: Dell, 1969);

The Ladder in the Sky, as Keith Woodcott [bound with *The Darkness Before Tomorrow,* by R. M. Williams] (New York: Ace, 1962);

The Super Barbarians (New York: Ace, 1962);

Times Without Number [bound with *Destiny's Orbit,* by Grinnell] (New York: Ace, 1962; revised and enlarged, 1969; Leeds: Elmfield Press, 1974);

John Brunner (photograph by Nelson Redland; from the dust jacket for The Crucible of Time, *1983)*

No Future in It, and Other Science Fiction Stories (London: Gollancz, 1962; Garden City, N.Y.: Doubleday, 1964);

The Dreaming Earth (New York: Pyramid, 1963; London: Sidgwick & Jackson, 1972);

The Psionic Menace, as Keith Woodcott [bound with *Captives of the Flame,* by Samuel R. Delany] (New York: Ace, 1963);

The Astronauts Must Not Land [and] *The Space-Time Juggler* (New York: Ace, 1963); *The Astronauts Must Not Land* revised as *More Things in Heaven* (New York: Dell, 1973; Feltham: Hamlyn, 1983);

The Castaways' World [and] *The Rites of Ohe* (New York: Ace, 1963); *The Castaways' World* revised and enlarged as *Polymath* (New York: DAW, 1974);

Listen! The Stars! [bound with *The Rebellers,* by James Roberts] (New York: Ace, 1963); revised and enlarged as *The Stardroppers* (New York: DAW, 1972; Feltham: Hamlyn, 1982);

Endless Shadow [bound with *The Arsenal of Miracles,* by Gardner F. Fox] (New York: Ace, 1964); revised and enlarged as *Manshape* (New York: DAW, 1982);

The Crutch of Memory (London: Barrie & Rockliff, 1964);

To Conquer Chaos (New York: Ace, 1964; revised edition, New York: DAW, 1981);

The Whole Man (New York: Ballantine, 1964); republished as *Telepathist* (London: Faber & Faber, 1965);

The Squares of the City (New York: Ballantine, 1965; Harmondsworth, U.K.: Penguin, 1969);

The Long Result (London: Faber & Faber, 1965; New York: Ballantine, 1966);

Now Then: Three Stories (London: Mayflower, 1965; New York: Avon, 1968);

The Martian Sphinx, as Keith Woodcott (New York: Ace, 1965);

Wear the Butchers' Medal (New York: Pocket Books, 1965);

The Altar on Asconel [bound with *Android Avenger,* by Ted White] (New York: Ace, 1965);

Enigma from Tantalus (New York: Ace, 1965);

The Repairmen of Cyclops (New York: Ace, 1965; revised edition, New York: DAW, 1981);

The Day of the Star Cities (New York: Ace, 1965); revised and enlarged as *Age of Miracles* (New York: Ace, 1973; London: Sidgwick & Jackson, 1973);

A Planet of Your Own [bound with *Beast of Kohl,* by John Rackham] (New York: Ace, 1966);

No Other Gods But Me (New York: Compact, 1966; London: Roberts & Vinter, 1966);

Trip: A Cycle of Poems by John Brunner (London: Brunner Fact & Fiction, 1966); revised as *Trip: A Sequence of Poems through the U.S.A.* (Richmond, U.K.: Keepsake, 1971);

Out of My Mind (New York: Ballantine, 1967; with differing contents, London: New English Library, 1968);

The Productions of Time (abridged edition, New York: New American Library, 1967; unabridged edition, New York: DAW, 1977; Harmondsworth, U.K.: Penguin, 1970);

Quicksand (Garden City, N.Y.: Doubleday, 1967; London: Sidgwick & Jackson, 1969);

Born Under Mars (New York: Ace, 1967);

Bedlam Planet (New York: Ace, 1968; London: Sidgwick & Jackson, 1973);

Not Before Time (London: New English Library, 1968);

Stand on Zanzibar (Garden City, N.Y.: Doubleday, 1968; London: Macdonald, 1969);

Father of Lies [bound with *Mirror Image,* by Bruce Duncan] (New York: Belmont Books, 1968);

A Plague on Both Your Causes (London: Hodder & Stoughton, 1969); also published as *Blacklash* (New York: Pyramid, 1969);

Black Is the Color (New York: Pyramid, 1969);

Double, Double (New York: Ballantine, 1969; London: Sidgwick & Jackson, 1971);

The Evil That Men Do [bound with *The Purloined Planet,* by Lin Carter] (New York: Belmont-Tower, 1969);

Timescoop (New York: Dell, 1969; London: Sidgwick & Jackson, 1972);

The Jagged Orbit (New York: Ace, 1969; London: Sidgwick & Jackson, 1970);

Good Men Do Nothing (London: Hodder & Stoughton, 1970; New York: Pyramid, 1971);

The Gaudy Shadows (London: Constable, 1970; New York: Beagle Books, 1971);

Life in an Explosive Forming Press: Poems (London: Poets' Trust, 1970);

The Devil's Work (New York: Norton, 1970);

Honky in the Woodpile: A Max Curfew Thriller (London: Constable, 1971);

The Wrong End of Time (Garden City, N.Y.: Doubleday, 1971; London: Eyre Methuen, 1975);

The Traveler in Black (New York: Ace, 1971); republished as *Traveller in Black* (London: Eyre Methuen, 1978); revised and enlarged as *The Compleat Traveller in Black* (New York: Bluejay, 1986; London: Methuen, 1987);

The Sheep Look Up (New York: Harper & Row, 1972; London: Dent, 1974);

Entry to Elsewhen (New York: DAW, 1972);

From This Day Forward (Garden City, N.Y.: Doubleday, 1972);

The Dramaturges of Yan (New York: Ace, 1972; London: New English Library, 1974);

About John Brunner (London: Brunner Fact & Fiction, 1973);

The Stone That Never Came Down (Garden City, N.Y.: Doubleday, 1973; London: New English Library, 1976);

Time-Jump (New York: Dell, 1973);

Web of Everywhere (New York: Bantam, 1974; London: New English Library, 1977); republished as *The Webs of Everywhere* (New York: Ballantine, 1983);

A Hastily Thrown-Together Bit of Zork (London: Square House Books, 1974);

Total Eclipse (Garden City, N.Y.: Doubleday, 1974; London: Weidenfeld & Nicolson, 1975);

The Shockwave Rider (New York: Harper & Row, 1975; London: Dent, 1975);

The Book of John Brunner (New York: DAW, 1976);

Interstellar Empire (New York: DAW, 1976; Feltham: Hamlyn, 1985);

Tomorrow May Be Even Worse (Cambridge, Mass.: New England Science Fiction Association Press, 1978);

Foreign Constellations: The Fantastic Worlds of John Brunner (New York: Everest House, 1980);

The Infinitive of Go (New York: Ballantine, 1980; London: Magnum, 1981);

Players at the Game of People (New York: Ballantine, 1980);

A New Settlement of Old Scores (Cambridge, Mass.: New England Science Fiction Association Press, 1983);

The Crucible of Time (New York: Ballantine, 1983; London: Arrow, 1984);

The Great Steamboat Race (New York: Ballantine, 1983);

The Tides of Time (New York: Ballantine, 1984; Harmondsworth, U.K.: Penguin, 1986);

The Shift Key (London: Methuen, 1987);

The Days of March (London: Kerosina, 1988);

Children of the Thunder (New York: Ballantine, 1989; London: Sphere, 1990);

Aftermath, Thieves' World series, edited by Robert Asprin and Lynn Abbey (New York: Titan, 1990);

A Maze of Stars (New York: Ballantine, 1991);

A Case of Painter's Ear (Eugene, Ore.: Pulphouse, 1991);

Muddle Earth (New York: Ballantine, 1993).

Collections: *The Best of John Brunner,* edited by Joe Haldeman (New York: Ballantine, 1988);

Victims of the Nova (London: Arrow, 1989)—comprises *Polymath, The Avengers of Carrig,* and *The Repairmen of Cyclops;*

Three Complete Novels (New York: Wings Books, 1995)—comprises *Children of the Thunder, The Tides of Time,* and *The Crucible of Time.*

PRODUCED SCRIPT: *The Terrornauts,* motion picture, adapted from Murray Leinster's "The Wailing Asteroid," Amicus Productions, 1967.

RECORDING: *An Evening With John Brunner,* Mt. Pleasant, Central Michigan University Library, 1973.

OTHER: *Horses at Home,* photographs by Zdenek Tmej and Vaclav Chocola, text by Brunner (London: Spring Books, 1958);

Cover for the June 1958 issue of the magazine that includes the story Brunner revised for book publication as The Hundredth Millennium *(1959) and later revised again as* Catch a Falling Star *(1968)*

"The Man from the Big Dark," in *Great Science Fiction Adventures,* edited by Larry T. Shaw (New York: Lancer, 1963);

"The Dream Hunter," in *Adventures in Discovery,* edited by Tom Purdom (Garden City, N.Y.: Doubleday, 1969), pp. 127–143;

"Science Fiction in the Real World," in *S F Symposium,* edited by Jose Sanz (Rio de Janeiro: Instituto do Cinema, 1969);

Gérard Klein, *The Overlords of War,* translated by Brunner (Garden City, N.Y.: Doubleday, 1973);

"You'll Take the High Road," in *Three Trips in Time and Space: Original Novellas of Science Fiction,* edited by Robert Silverberg (New York: Hawthorn Books, 1973);

The Best of Philip K. Dick, edited by Brunner (New York: Ballantine, 1977);

"Utopias and Nightmares: Introduction," in *The Visual Encyclopedia of Science Fiction,* edited by Brian Ash (New York: Harmony, 1977), p. 124;

Paul Peter Piech, *While There's HOPE,* translated by Brunner (Richmond, U.K.: Keepsake, 1982);

"Sentences of Death," in *Thieves World: Wings of Omen,* edited by Robert Asprin and Lynn Abbey (New York: Titan, 1984);

"A Short Autobiography," in *Contemporary Authors Autobiography Series,* volume 8, edited by Mark Zadrozny (Detroit: Gale Research, 1988), pp. 1–17;

"At the Sign of the Rose," in *Beyond the Gate of Worlds,* edited by Robert Silverberg (New York: Tor, 1991);

Rudyard Kipling, *Kipling's Fantasy,* edited, with an introduction, by Brunner (New York: Tor, 1992);

Kipling, *John Brunner Presents Kipling's Science Fiction,* edited, with an introduction, by Brunner (New York: Tor, 1992).

SELECTED PERIODICAL PUBLICATIONS–UNCOLLECTED: "Nothing to Do with Prophecy," *Aspect* (March 1963): 37–41;

"One Sense of Wonder, Slightly Tarnished," *Books and Bookmen,* 12 (July 1967): 19–20;

"Genesis of *Stand on Zanzibar* and Digressions into the Remainder of Its Pentateuch," *Extrapolation,* 11 (May 1970): 34–43;

"Building Four-Dimensional People in Science Fiction," *Writer* (December 1971): 21–24;

"The Development of a Science Fiction Writer," *Foundation,* 1 (March 1972): 5–12;

"Parallel Worlds," *Foundation,* 3 (March 1973): 6–14;

"Coming Events: An Assessment of Thomas Pynchon's *Gravity's Rainbow,*" *Foundation,* 10 (1976): 20–27;

"The Conjugation of the Verb 'Tomorrow' OR 'I'm a Realist, You're an Empty-Headed Dreamer, They Are Obviously Out of Their Minds,'" *Arena,* 11 (1980): 27–33.

The author of more than sixty novels of science fiction and fantasy, together with novels of mystery or conventional fiction, collections of short stories, many uncollected stories, poems, songs, translations, essays, and a movie script, John Brunner helped to shape science fiction for three decades. Even his earliest novels demonstrate his distinctive concern for the present and future of human society, rather than the scientific marvels that are the stock-in-trade of so much science fiction. Although knowledgeable about computers, genetics, astronomy, and other technical features of the science-fiction landscape, Brunner was essentially concerned with the effects of such technology on human freedoms and economic, psychological, and moral salvation. His best-known works are set in the near future

and serve as cautionary tales about where current conditions of racism, greed, fear, and fanaticism of all kinds can lead humankind. They also hold out hope that courage and independent thinking can solve the social problems raised by such ills. An inventive and masterful stylist, Brunner also influenced the stylistic development of later writers through his adaptations of techniques drawn from writers such as John Dos Passos and James Joyce and from scriptwriting for plays, movies, and television.

The eldest child and only son of Anthony and Felicity (Whittaker) Brunner, John Kilian Houston Brunner was born on 24 September 1934 in Oxfordshire, England. He experienced more than the usual childhood illness and accidents, resulting in enforced isolation from sports and physical activity. Turning to books, Brunner read Daniel Defoe's *Robinson Crusoe* (1719) when he was six. By the age of nine, having become enamored of the writings of H. G. Wells and Jules Verne, he had attempted his own fiction in that vein. Expected to join Imperial Chemical Industries, which had been founded by his grandfather as Brunner-Mond Ltd., the boy entered Cheltenham College at thirteen. His ineptitude at mathematics and the paucity of science courses encouraged him to continue reading imaginative literature, including the works of William Shakespeare and John Milton (which are echoed in his titles). At seventeen Brunner sold his first novel, *Galactic Storm* (1952), written under the pen name Gill Hunt, and left Cheltenham. After collecting several rejection letters, he sold his novelette "Thou Good and Faithful" (as John Loxmith) to the American magazine *Astounding Science-Fiction* in 1953 and his novel *The Wanton of Argus* (later revised as *The Space-Time Juggler,* 1963) to the American periodical *Two Complete Science Adventure Books* in the same year. Also in 1953, he was drafted into the military; serving for two years, he received a commission in the RAF and learned to hate the military, politicians, and religious hypocrites. These themes permeate his later writing. On 12 July 1958 he married Marjorie Rosamond Sauer, who became his partner in Brunner Fact and Fiction Ltd. and antinuclear activities. She died in 1986; the couple had no children.

During 1955–1958, Brunner barely supported himself with short-story sales to *New Worlds Science Fiction* and *Science Fantasy* and short-term jobs as technical abstracter and editorial assistant. In 1957–1958 he sold these magazines two novels: *Threshold of Eternity* (*New Worlds Science Fiction,* December 1957 – February 1958), published as a book in 1959, and *Earth Is But a Star* (*Science Fantasy,* June 1958), revised for book publication as *The Hundredth Millennium* (1959) and later extensively revised and enlarged as *Catch a Falling Star* (1968). *Earth Is But a Star,* like his earlier "Fair" (*New Worlds Science Fic-*

tion, March 1956), shows people as too decadent to care about the potential destruction of Earth. During the next few years Brunner turned out sixteen science-fiction and fantasy novels for the New York paperback publisher Ace, most in the Ace Doubles series. Calling them "light space-opera," Donald A. Wollheim, then editor for Ace, wrote to Joe De Bolt: "In these books . . . , though written rapidly for a quick turnover, you would find the elements of all of Brunner's social themes and crusading attitudes. In spite of light plot movement, those earlier novels carried their morals structured into the texts."

Typical of Brunner's early novels are *Echo in the Skull* (1959; revised as *Give Warning to the World,* 1974), *Slavers of Space* (1960), and *The Atlantic Abomination* (1960). In the first, Sally Ercott, imprisoned by her landlady, has been having dreams/memories of human sacrifice on strange planets. They turn out to be embedded warnings from invading aliens who, like Robert A. Heinlein's Puppet Masters, take over the minds of their hosts. (They have done so to the landlady and others as well.) Freed by inventor Nick Jenkins and his friend Dr. Tom Gospell, Sally is able to instruct the police in destroying the aliens. In *Slavers of Space,* later revised as *Into the Slave Nebula* (1968), Derry Horn, wealthy scion of Horn and Horn Robots, discovers a gang that kidnaps children and turns them into obedient, blue-dyed "androids," which everyone has purchased for years as servants. Kidnapped and dyed, he is nevertheless able to escape and break up the gang, thereby winning accolades as a Citizen of the Galaxy. In *The Atlantic Abomination* a deep-sea diver inadvertently releases an alien being that has been buried for millennia under ocean muck. This being uses its "mindwhip" to enslave people into worshiping it and working on its behalf. Eventually U.S. military power forces the alien to flee into space, leaving a character to say, "Men change their gods, and when they have changed them often enough they cease to fear their power." The question of domination—by aliens, criminals, governments, religious fanatics, or anyone else—was one of Brunner's concerns throughout his career. Two other novels of this period, *Secret Agent of Terra* (1962) and *The Castaways' World* (1963), were later revised as, respectively, *The Avengers of Carrig* (1969) and *Polymath* (1974) and joined with *The Repairmen of Cyclops* (1965) into a trilogy concerning refugees from the planet Zarathustra, which has been destroyed by a nova. The dominant themes of these novels are conflict and cooperation among survivors and successors of the evacuation. Once again enslavement destroys while human freedom, labor, and ingenuity save a society that must rebuild from ashes.

These early works and some later ones show the influence of pulp fiction in their fast-paced adventure

Dust jacket for the novel that won the 1969 Hugo Award, the 1970 British Science Fiction Award, and the 1973 Prix Apollo

and stereotypical characters. As early as 1959, however, Brunner demonstrated his distinctive characterization and style with two published stories that were later the genesis of *The Whole Man* (1964). Arising from a plan for a series of fantasy stories, *The Whole Man* developed into the story of Gerald Howson, physically and emotionally damaged but with a powerful talent for projective telepathy that can be used to cure other telepaths who have fled into fugue from the pressures of their work as psychotherapists. Reluctantly applying his talent and avoiding his own tendency to live in fantasy, Howson gives meaning to his life and the lives of other telepaths and artists. Unlike later, more cynical books, this powerful parable for fiction writers depicts government forces as benevolent.

However, in another novel written about this time, *The Squares of the City* (1965) government is depicted more cynically. Tightly controlling the structure through the device of an actual championship chess game played in 1892, the novel presents a story about a fictional South American city, which was built by the president of the country as a model city but has become spoiled by slums. The first-person narrator, Hakluyt, an Australian traffic-control expert, is hired to redirect movement within the city so that the slums will disappear, but he finds himself in a web of political conflict that he does not understand, and he learns that a former intellectual hero of his has been controlling public opinion by means of subliminal images on television and movie screens. He also learns that the factionalism is deliberately engineered by the president and the minister of the interior, who are playing a chess game with people's lives. Brunner structures the novel for maximum suspense; the reader learns the situation at the same pace as Hakluyt does and, with him, gradually becomes aware of the true horror inflicted by a government that uses technology and game theory to control its people. Using a technique that he varied in later novels, Brunner provided a combination dramatis personae and obituary by attaching a list that matches his characters with the pieces played in the actual 1892 chess game. His improved mastery of characterization and subtlety of plot development brought results. In 1966 *The Whole Man* and *The Squares of the City* were both nominated for Hugos (Science Fiction Achievement Awards), and Brunner received the British Fantasy Award, presented by the British Science Fiction Association. In the following year, two of his novels, *A Planet of Your Own* (1966) and *The Productions of Time* (1967), were nominated for the Nebula (Science Fiction Writers of America Award), and he was guest of honor at the British Science Fiction Convention in Bristol.

Starting in the late 1950s, John and Marjorie Brunner were active in the Campaign for Nuclear Disarmament, and in 1961–1962 they toured Europe and the United States with promotional displays, including poems, songs, and translations by Brunner. These travels and political activities are reflected in such novels as *The Long Result* (1965), in which Brunner created a Bureau of Cultural Relations that not only foils a plot to arouse xenophobic attacks on aliens from space but even works toward developing a superior successor agency on a remote planet; *The Day of the Star Cities* (1965; revised and enlarged as *Age of Miracles,* 1973), in which mysterious transportation nexuses installed on Earth cause destructive chaos that Brunner blames less on the aliens who created the links than on human greed, fanaticism, and fear; and *Quicksand* (1967), a tragic novel about love between a psychiatrist and a girl displaced in time, which shows that a fantasy utopia is impossible.

The most important fictional result of Brunner's antinuclear activities was his massive *Stand on Zanzibar* (1968), more than five hundred pages long, for which he won the Hugo Award (1969), the British Science Fic-

tion Award (1970), and the Prix Apollo in France (1973). Set in the near future, 2010, the novel extrapolates current conditions to delineate a society seething with interracial violence. Citizens protect themselves with a whole array of deadly weapons and escape reality by means of legalized drugs (tranquilizers, marijuana, various hallucinogens, liquor—everything except cigarettes) and interactive television shows that permit them to see themselves as participants in exciting, "meaningful" activities while they need not leave their apartments to face the mean streets. The population in 2010 exceeds seven billion, or as many as could fit on the 640-square-mile island of Zanzibar if they all stood elbow to elbow and face to face (hence the title). The results of this population pressure, like those of putting too many rats in a cage, are deadly: racial tensions are so heated that a person can spark a riot just by being in the wrong neighborhood. Police forces—which try to contain violence by gas, lasers, and tank-like people sweepers—are outnumbered and outgunned by the rioters. To curb population growth, most states have enacted strict eugenics laws, forbidding people with even such minor genetic defects as color blindness to have progeny. These laws lead to conflicts between the "can's" and "cannot's," to a split between right and left wings of the Catholic Church (each of which claims its own pope), and to attempts to evade the laws through migration, adoption, and cloning. When the Southeast Asian country Yatakang announces that its famous geneticist Dr. Sugaiguntung has developed a process of human genetic improvement, the American military activates and "eptifies" a mild-mannered researcher, Donald Hogan, to gain the secret (and preferably the geneticist) for America and prevent its use in Asia, where limited war is occurring between the United States and China. Hogan's eptification turns him into a killer. Disoriented from his previous self, he inadvertently murders Dr. Sugaiguntung. Simultaneously, Norman House, an ambitious African American executive with General Technics, a monopolistic business with close governmental ties, takes charge of a project that will save the impoverished African nation Beninia from encroachment by its neighbors and gain control of Beninia's mineral resources. With the help of the General Technics supercomputer Shalmaneser (which is so complex that it has gained self-actualization), House succeeds. He also learns the secret of Beninia's peaceful history: its people exude a tranquilizing scent so that murder and war are unknown among them. Another central character is pop sociologist Chad C. Mulligan, whose fictional *Hipcrime Vocabulary* is often quoted before he actually appears in the novel. Possibly speaking for Brunner, Mulligan orates at length about humanity's problems. He solves Shalmaneser's mental block by addressing it as a thinking being and ends the novel by saying to humanity, "I *know* . . . I love you!"

Praised for its vast scope, life-like character development, and powerful topicality, the novel earned many accolades, and a few objections, for its experimental style. Adapting techniques such as James Joyce's serious puns, invented language, and multiple viewpoints, John Dos Passos's "Camera Eye" segments in *U.S.A.* (1930–1936) and William Carlos Williams's interpolated newspaper clippings in *Paterson* (1946–1958), Brunner interwove his plots with sections titled "The Happening World," advertisements and short accounts of world events and those involving minor characters; "Context," texts and technical directions for televised news and advertisements; and "Tracking with Closeups," vignettes of secondary characters that fill out the sense of life with which the novel teems, as well as excerpts from Chad Mulligan's books. In 1969 Brunner spoke at a Modern Language Association of America symposium devoted to *Stand on Zanzibar*.

During the late 1960s and early 1970s, Brunner sold short stories, revisions of earlier novels, and light fantasy and mystery novels: *Double, Double* (1969), *Black Is the Color* (1969), *A Plague on Both Your Causes* (1969), *Good Men Do Nothing* (1970), and *Honky in the Woodpile* (1971). As racial problems were a focus of *Stand on Zanzibar,* these fantasy-mystery novels are important to an understanding of Brunner's work: the protagonist of the last three listed is Max Curfew, a black Jamaican detective who moves between black and white cultures in solving crimes and who is so authentically drawn that many readers thought that Brunner must be black. In 1970 Brunner also published a volume of poetry, *Life in an Explosive Forming Press* (whose title succinctly describes his theory of poetry), and an intriguing novel with a contemporary setting, *The Devil's Work*. In this novel, which uses some of the same montage and parody techniques employed in *Stand on Zanzibar,* a wealthy dabbler in black magic, Baron Someday, destroys the soul and moral choices of young, naive Stephen Green. During this period Brunner also produced a good space-exploration novel, *Bedlam Planet* (1968), which emphasizes that what might appear to be madness is simply successful adaptation to radically different conditions. He also wrote the impressive dystopia *The Jagged Orbit* (1969).

Two institutions are at the center of *The Jagged Orbit:* the muck-raking television journalism of "spool-pigeon" Matthew Flamen and Ginsberg State Mental Hospital in New York, directed by the megalomaniacal Dr. Mogshack with the help of the sympathetic character Dr. James Reedeth. Both these institutions have potential for good but have become so corrupted by greed, fear, and fanaticism that they

Dust jacket for the 1972 sequel to Stand on Zanzibar

threaten to destroy people's minds rather than liberate them. Again interracial violence–this time fomented by the Gottschalks, a powerful munitions mafia–creates terror and arms sales. A black mental patient at the hospital, who can mentally communicate with the Gottschalks' powerful new computer, and a stage seeress, who utters cryptic prophecies while in drug-induced trances, provide the unlikely means to overthrow Dr. Mogshack and the Gottschalks, enabling Flamen and Reedeth to save the day momentarily. One important character is Canadian psychology professor Xavier Conroy, who–like Mulligan in *Stand on Zanzibar*–is a relatively uninvolved voice of reason and analysis and may speak for Brunner. Employing some of the same techniques as *Stand on Zanzibar,* most notably short, disconnected chapters and actual newsclippings from 1969, *The Jagged Orbit* was nominated for a Nebula and received the British Science Fiction Award in 1971.

At about the same time, Brunner was giving poetry readings in England and the United States, appearing frequently on television and radio as a leading figure in science fiction, contributing letters and commentary to fanzines, and writing a column, "Noise

Level," for *Science Fiction Review* and later for *Outworlds, The Alien Critic,* and finally *Science Fiction Chronicle,* where it continued until the 1990s. In 1970 he became a vice president of the Science Fiction Foundation, together with officers Arthur C. Clarke, James Blish, and Kenneth Bulmer. Brunner wrote an autobiographical sketch and many articles for its journal, *Foundation: The Review of Science Fiction.* By means of these activities Brunner contributed greatly to the literary development of science fiction. Recognition came also in the form of invitations to be guest of honor at science-fiction conferences in Trieste, Stockholm, Philadelphia, Toronto, and Clermont-Ferrand in France; election as chairman of the British Science Fiction Association; and appointments to academic posts as writer in residence at the University of Kansas in Lawrence (1972) and visiting scholar at Central Michigan University and Kean College of New Jersey.

In 1971 Brunner continued in the dystopian vein with *The Wrong End of Time,* in which a sympathetically presented Russian agent arrives in the United States to meet a man who has been feeding American military secrets to Russia so that the balance of terror, and hence peace, can be maintained. The Russian's main purpose is to secure American aid against an alien menace whom the Russians have discovered near the planet Pluto and who seems to be threatening to destroy humanity. With the help of the U.S. agent's daughter and a black man who has a mysterious psi power, the Russian learns that the alien is actually signaling Earth about humanity's glorious future; people have been reading the signals backward. Despite this upbeat ending, supplied for the sake of sales, the novel includes many scenes of the kind of drug use, interracial violence, and police brutality that darken Brunner's other dystopian fictions.

The Traveler in Black also appeared in book form in 1971, after its segments had been previously published as short stories. In this fantasy work, revised and enlarged in 1986 as *The Compleat Traveller in Black,* an enigmatic man wearing a black cape and carrying a staff of curdled light wanders from city to city, fulfilling the command of She who can do all things. He has many names but a single nature, and his task is to place all elements of chaos, including magic, within the confines of time and thereby produce for everyone and everything a single nature. Along the way he defeats a society that depends on luck to produce an unjust distribution of wealth and power, a society that depends on magic to overpower its neighbors, a king who sacrifices his own wife and priests to a stone idol, and a variety of vicious and deceiving individuals. Although the means are magic and the results inconclusive, the novel includes many of the same character types that fill Brunner's science-fiction dystopias.

The Sheep Look Up (1972), with its Miltonic title, is another major dystopia, set only a decade in the future and called a sequel to *Stand on Zanzibar.* Focusing on ecological disasters caused by greed, the novel depicts a world in which the air is too poisoned to breathe without filter masks, beaches are too polluted for swimming, drinking water has been made deadly by poison-gas seepage, farmlands are infested with voracious mutated worms that destroy crops, and processed food has been accidentally infused with hallucinogens that cause the impoverished people to whom it is "benevolently" shipped to riot and commit suicide. Many of those attempting to profit from these conditions, however, are maddened and/or killed, as are innocent victims. The government labels attempts to resist profiteering and reverse the spread of dangerous chemicals as communist or "Trainite" plots and responds with violent repression. So-called followers of biologist Austin Train sabotage and murder polluters and their agents, much to the chagrin of Train himself, who spends most of the novel hiding under various disguises but finally emerges to make a national statement at his trial for a kidnapping he did not commit. His true and compelling message is stopped by a bomb that destroys the court building. In this diffuse novel, which was nominated for a Nebula, Brunner returned to the themes and montage techniques that he used in *Stand on Zanzibar* and *The Jagged Orbit* and even created similar characters, but the tone and ending of *The Sheep Look Up* are darker than those of the earlier novels.

Two collections of Brunner's short stories, *Entry to Elsewhen* and *From This Day Forward,* also appeared in 1972. By this time Brunner's work was regularly appearing in anthologies of the year's best science fiction. In the following three years Brunner diversified his dark view of humanity's future in four new novels. The title of the first of these, *The Stone That Never Came Down* (1973), comes from a fable told in the novel about a boy who defeats a giant in a stone-throwing contest by releasing a dove. The optimism of the fable is repeated at the end of this novel, which is set in London in the immediate future, but the body of the novel, like Brunner's major dystopias, is filled with violence and fanatical hatred. People's freedom is restricted by the Campaign Against Moral Pollution (CAMP), which sends roaming gangs of "godheads" through the streets to attack anyone they disapprove of, including homosexuals, unmarried couples, and anyone with the wrong skin color. Leaders of CAMP are either venal or out of touch with reality. Political and economic conflicts and depression grow in England and other European countries. War is imminent as armies begin to

assemble at national borders or move to suppress uprisings in Ireland and Scotland. Meanwhile, however, a
pair of scientists discovers a virus that vastly improves
memory, empathy, and clear thinking. Knowing that
official knowledge of the virus will cause its suppression, they secretly spread it, first to individuals and
then—by means of blood donations and cities' drinking
water—to whole nations. Some CAMP and national
leaders begin to change their ways, to gain increased
empathy and understanding, but the novel ends without any assurance that enough people will be "infected"
with love to prevent world war. As he said in a 1965
speech, Brunner hoped that his fiction would serve "to
remind one of the ultimate ideal and make it seem
attainable, hence worth striving for." Yet, in *The Stone
That Never Came Down,* Brunner vitiated some good
ideas and characterizations by oversimplified and hysterical plotting and satire.

A similar failure of control weakens *Web of Everywhere* (1974), in which the Earth attempts to restore
itself after a nuclear blowup but needs more leaders.
Most people have chosen lives of meaningless pleasure
and travel, assisted by omnipresent free "skelters" or
instantaneous transportation devices. A central character, Hans Dykstra, shows promise despite having an
illegal hobby, but his guilty attraction to a girl leads him
to suicide. A sage, whose poems head each chapter,
wants no part of governmental responsibility. The
novel just ends; Brunner seems not to have known
what to do with these promising materials.

An even more ominous picture concludes *Total
Eclipse* (1974). In this novel, Earth sends a series of
exploratory missions to Sigma Draconis to ascertain the
reason for the extinction of that planet's intelligent species. These missions are at risk of being halted because
of international tensions and the threat of war on Earth.
Eventually a young linguist, Ian Macauley, determines
that genetic greed caused the Draconians to delay
breeding until their progeny were no longer viable, but
this information comes too late. The supply starship no
longer arrives from Earth, and the exploratory team
dies off despite efforts to live off an uncongenial biosphere. The title and message of this novel seem to
refer not only to the alien species but to Earth as well.

The title of the fourth novel in this group, *The
Shockwave Rider* (1975), acknowledges Brunner's debt to
Alvin and Heidi Toffler's *Future Shock* (1970). In Brunner's novel the U.S. government, having weathered the
arms race and the space race, now faces a "brain race"
and trains young geniuses from birth to work for the
government. One such genius, Nick Haflinger, escapes
from the psychological conditioning provided at the
Tarnover Center and adopts different names and identities by means of his skill with the computers that gov-

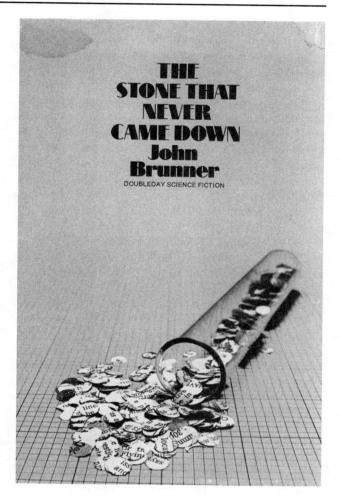

*Dust jacket for Brunner's 1973 novel, whose title comes from a fable
about a boy who releases a dove to win a stone-throwing contest
with a giant (Richland County Public Library)*

ern the lives of all citizens. After many escapes from
pursuit, he is finally captured and induced by hypno-
tism and other psychological techniques to reveal his
activities. Nick convinces his examiner to assist him to
escape anew and to join him in exposing the chicanery
of those who use their high positions in government,
military, and business for their own interests. He con-
tends that employing the complex computer network to
reveal to citizens, rather than conceal from them, information such as contaminants in foods and bribery in
military contracts will arouse enough public outrage to
change the system. He argues that only unjust advantage through selective access to data permits the continuation of hunger and poverty in such a wealthy nation.
By the end of the novel Nick and his friends are on the
way to success because the government has stupidly
attempted a nuclear strike on a harmless settlement that
provides a public service known as "Hearing Aid," an
uncritical call-in service for troubled people. Warned by

genetically altered dogs, the people are saved, and the bombardment wakens the citizens to the destructive greed of governmental leaders. Part of the interest of the novel lies in a narrative technique that switches seamlessly from past to present. More than most of Brunner's novels, *The Shockwave Rider* teems with ideas relevant to contemporary humanity, especially the danger stemming from venal control of information, people's need for uncritical community acceptance, and the difficulty of constantly adjusting to fast-paced social change. Brunner invented a game called Fencing, similar to go or chess, and introduced it in the novel.

The Book of John Brunner (1976) includes stories, essays, poems, translations, limericks, puns, and a chapter from his unpublished novel *Manalive,* written in 1960. *Foreign Constellations* (1980) comprises eight stories written between 1968 and 1978, of which five also appeared in "best story" collections. The stories include the ecologically preachy "The Berendt Conversion" (1975); the frequently anthologized "The Easy Way Out" (1971), about a wounded doctor who struggles against his own and his patient's desire for euthanasia; "The Protocols of the Elders of Britain" (1974), in which a computer expert discovers a huge governmental conspiracy against minorities and poor people and is killed to protect the secret; "Pond Water" (1968), in which a great metallic being, constructed to defend humankind, instead takes over the galaxy but finds it cannot control human imagination; and "The Suicide of Man" (1978), which reveals that human beings can shed their bodies and live forever in their imaginations.

In *The Infinitive of Go* (1980), Justin Williams and his black colleague Cinnamon Wright have invented a device, called a "poster," for instantaneously transmitting objects and people over distances ranging from across a room to across the universe. When it goes wrong and causes an agent to kill himself, the cause must be found. Williams and Wright discover that the poster actually moves its occupant to a parallel time/world track and that the greater the distance is, the greater the discrepancy. Since to some extent the poster seems to allow people it transmits to choose the conditions they prefer in the destinations they reach, Justin decides to leave the paranoid, dictatorial social structure in which Cinnamon does not care for him for a world track in which personal freedoms are assured and Cinnamon loves him. The novel ends with the possibility of still further changes and explorations. Using more conventional narrative techniques than in previous novels, this novel seems to be more concerned with imaginative escapism than with working toward improving society by satire.

While *The Infinitive of Go* seems to project a possible escape from paranoid societies such as those depicted in Brunner's earlier dystopias, *Players at the Game of People* (1980), a modern Faust story, shows what can happen to complacent people who benefit from such societies. In this novel a character named Godwin Harpinshield lives a lavish lifestyle without having to pay for it, taking "vacations" into the recent past, but one of his adventures comes back to haunt him in the form of the grown-up version of the girl he gallantly saved in the past. He reveals to her the game that other beings (the "owners") are playing with him, a game whereby he has sold his soul in exchange for pleasure, and he is finally called to death. As in *The Squares of the City,* the narrative point of view deliberately limits the reader's knowledge of events so that the true horror is revealed only at the end.

Brunner moved to a larger canvas for his next two novels. In *The Crucible of Time* (1983), the first two parts of which first appeared in *Isaac Asimov's Science Fiction Magazine* (1982), he presented the epic story of a species as it gradually gains control over its environment through many generations. Facing constant setbacks from geological and astronomical disasters on what is still an evolving world, and combating internal rivalries and misunderstandings, the species evolves from insect-like forms that barely survive an Ice Age. It becomes dispersed over its planet and is eventually spread by space travel. The impetus for growth is provided by strong, farsighted leaders and inventors, whereas resistance comes from fanatical religious leaders who advocate isolationism. The novel is ambitious and, for Brunner, unusually optimistic.

In an afterword to *The Great Steamboat Race* (1983), set mostly in 1870, Brunner called this novel "an example of what science fiction people call a retrospective parallel world." The 568-page novel develops many characters and themes, including a black former slave, quadroon priestesses of Damballah, a news reporter, riverboat pilots and captains, gamblers, musicians, and physicians. Excitement builds as the race between two steam-powered Mississippi riverboats from New Orleans to St. Louis continues, and treacherous actions, secret relationships (including incest), and developing love are brought to light. A central theme is the mistreatment of African Americans despite their equality of ability with other Americans.

Interracial romance is again at the center of *The Tides of Time* (1984), about the experiences of a black man and white woman on a little Greek island as they take jumps backward in time from the twenty-first century to periods as recent as the World War II era and as far back as the times of the Crusades and ancient Rome. Always the black man is regarded as a barbarian and must endure discrimination, while the white woman is considered a priestess of nature. Finally the reader learns that, unknowingly, they are returning "home" to the present after having traveled faster than light, by which means they have been thrown out of time and reality. The novel depicts human behavior as mostly violent and greedy but relieved by occasional acts of compassion. Perhaps the most significant message of the novel is that scientific experimentation can dislocate humanity from its past and its identity.

The Infinitive of Go, Players at the Game of People, The Crucible of Time, The Great Steamboat Race, and *The Tides of Time* are the work of a writer confident of his craft and no longer attempting to reform society through satire. They display Brunner's versatility in their scope, narrative structures, character development, and extrapolation of ideas. Consistent with his earlier work, however, they still attack racial injustice, religious fanaticism, and the inhumanity caused by greed.

The Shift Key (1987) is set in the near future and focuses on the mysteries arising from time shifts near Stonehenge. The protagonists of *Children of the Thunder* (1989) are children with the mysterious power to get people to do anything they want. With characters and background developed with Brunner's usual skill, the novel, directed at a young-adult audience, asks whether such power is a blessing or a curse and where it will lead—not to a happy ending. Brunner has also written for the Thieves' World series, created by Robert Asprin and Lynn Abbey, which has attracted so many other writers to contribute to this fantasy in which the setting and framework are given while the plot and characterization are created by the contributing author. Brunner's contributions include "Sentences of Death" in *Thieves' World: Wings of Omen* (1984), edited by Asprin and Abbey, and *Aftermath* (1990).

The interesting and original *A Maze of Stars* (1991) is narrated by the consciousness of the Ship, which human beings have programmed to seed planets of the galactic arm with human beings and then to conduct regular sweeps of the planets to check on their progress and to transport people to safety if necessary. The novel includes inventive depictions of different environments, social organizations, and individual characters. Its most intriguing passages are the Ship's speculations during its Flying Dutchman–like journeying as to why it moves at random and yet has certain built-in limitations—it continues to gain understanding of human emotions such as pity and humor. Meanwhile, Brunner continued to be recognized for his achievements. His stories were collected in important anthologies, and in 1988 he was guest of honor at the Polish National Science Fiction Convention in Katowice.

On 27 September 1991 Brunner married Chinese artist Li Yi Tan, whose homeland provided Brunner with the setting for a new series of short sto-

Dust jacket for Brunner's 1983 novel that traces the evolution of a species of insect-like forms

ries set in Imperial China. His last novel, *Muddle Earth* (1993), proves that his dystopian visions and horrific application of McLuhanesque writing techniques retained the energy and appeal that he demonstrated throughout his long, active creative life. But his willingness to try new directions shows up in his stories with Chinese settings. For example, while "All Under Heaven" (*Asimov's Science Fiction,* December 1995) returns to one of his earliest themes—the creature from outer space who uses its superior mental powers to enforce obedience from Earthlings—this time the alien voluntarily releases the human beings and dies when it discovers a person who recognizes it for the alien it is, not a phoenix or a dragon.

In 1995, while attending the World Science Fiction Convention in Glasgow, Scotland, Brunner suffered a stroke and died on 25 August. At the Hugo Award ceremony, held during the convention, Robert Silverberg delivered a eulogy, and many other writers—including Christopher Priest, Michael Moorcock,

Brian Aldiss, Sam L. Lundwall, and Ian Watson—offered reminiscences.

From its beginnings as what Donald A. Wollheim called "light space opera," through seven years of intense stylistic experimentation and bleak projections of contemporary trends, to his final diversification of fictional interests, Brunner's work shows consistent strength and daring. Particularly impressive is his extraordinary awareness of the impacts of mass media and computerized data management on Western culture. As methods of manipulating audiences, mass media and computers are, he realized, both useful to writers and frightening when in the hands of unscrupulous businesses and governments. Much of the power of his fiction arises from his incorporation of the message in the medium; the violent, dissociated futures he projects are echoed in his disjunctive, kaleidoscopic techniques. His concentration on interracial injustice and violence is also both metaphor and message. As message, it is an accurate picture of present and probable future events, and as metaphor it expresses the same disjunction between mind and spirit (or intellect and emotions) that is represented by introjecting real or fictional newsclips and advertisements into the developing plot of a novel. Although conflict is the soul of plot, Brunner presents it also as the demon of society and the essence of style. At the same time, as he remarked in his introduction to *John Brunner Presents Kipling's Science Fiction* (1992), he was influenced by Rudyard Kipling, "more than anybody, more even than . . . Wells. . . . It was one of Rudyard Kipling's gifts that he sensed the counterpart of magic in machinery." Brunner's fiction, like Kipling's, can communicate both the magic in machinery and the machinery of magic so that it seems probable and present. Christopher Priest classed Brunner's best novels "among the finest, most imaginative, and best written works in the field," and Silverberg said: "He was brilliant, erudite, passionately involved in the political causes that mattered to him, and, of course, one of the finest writers our field has ever known" (*Locus,* October 1995). Few authors have written so passionately and so well of the physical and spiritual dangers that threaten humanity on Earth.

Interviews:

James E. Gunn, "Science Fiction and the Mainstream" [videocassette] (Lawrence: University of Kansas Extramural Independent Study Center, 1975);

Charles Platt, "John Brunner," in his *Dream Makers: The Uncommon People Who Write Science Fiction* (New York: Berkley, 1980), pp. 243–249.

Bibliography:

Gordon Benson Jr., *John Brunner, Shockwave Writer: A Working Bibliography* (San Bernardino, Cal.: Borgo Press, 1992).

References:

Joseph W. De Bolt, ed., *The Happening Worlds of John Brunner* (Port Washington, N.Y.: Kennikat Press, 1975);

Dennis Livingston, "Science Fiction Models of Future World Order Systems," *International Organization,* 25 (Spring 1971): 261–262, 269–270;

Willis E. McNelly, "The Science Fiction Novel in 1968," in *Nebula Award Stories 4,* edited by Poul Anderson (Garden City, N.Y.: Doubleday, 1969), pp. xvi–xvii;

Judith Merril, "Books," *Magazine of Fantasy and Science Fiction,* 60 (January 1966): 39–45;

Patrick D. Murphy, "Dialogics and Didacticism: John Brunner's Narrative Blending," *Science-Fiction Studies,* 14 (March 1987): 21–33;

John J. Pierce, *When World Views Collide: A Study in Imagination and Evolution* (New York: Greenwood Press, 1989), pp. 149–153;

David Samuelson, "New Wave, Old Ocean: A Comparative Study of Novels by Brunner and Delany," *Extrapolation* (December 1973): 75–96;

Robert Scholes, "Change, SF and Marxism: Open or Closed Universes? Novels by Brunner and Levin," *Science-Fiction Studies,* 1 (Spring 1974): 213–216;

Scholes and Eric S. Rabkin, *Science Fiction: History, Science, Vision* (London & New York: Oxford University Press, 1977), pp. 80–82, 91, 230–233;

Norman Spinrad, "*Stand on Zanzibar:* The Novel as Film," in *SF: The Other Side of Realism,* edited by Thomas D. Clareson (Bowling Green, Ohio: Bowling Green University Popular Press, 1971), pp. 181–185;

Michael Stern, "From Technique to Critique: Knowledge and Human Interests in John Brunner's *Stand on Zanzibar, The Jagged Orbit,* and *The Sheep Look Up,*" *Science-Fiction Studies,* 3 (July 1976): 112–130;

Darko Suvin, "The SF Novel in 1969," in *Nebula Award Stories 5,* edited by James Blish (Garden City, N.Y.: Doubleday, 1970), pp. 201–202;

Ian Watson, "Reaping the Whirlwind," *Foundation,* 7–8 (March 1975): 55–59.

Papers:

John Brunner's papers are in the University of Liverpool Library.

Anthony Burgess
(John Anthony Burgess Wilson)
(25 February 1917 – 25 November 1993)

Earl G. Ingersoll
State University of New York, College at Brockport

See also the Burgess entries in *DLB 14: British Novelists Since 1960* and *DLB 194: British Novelists Since 1960, Second Series.*

BOOKS: *Time for a Tiger* (London: Heinemann, 1956);

The Enemy in the Blanket (London: Heinemann, 1958);

English Literature: A Survey for Students, as John Burgess Wilson (London: Longmans, Green, 1958); revised edition, as Anthony Burgess (London: Longman, 1974);

Beds in the East (London: Heinemann, 1959);

The Doctor Is Sick (London: Heinemann, 1960; New York: Norton, 1960);

The Right to an Answer (London: Heinemann, 1960; New York: Norton, 1961);

Devil of a State (London: Heinemann, 1961; New York: Norton, 1962);

The Worm and the Ring (London: Heinemann, 1961; revised, 1970);

One Hand Clapping, as Joseph Kell (London: Davies, 1961); as Burgess (New York: Knopf, 1972);

The Wanting Seed (London: Heinemann, 1962; New York: Norton, 1963);

A Clockwork Orange (London: Heinemann, 1962); with final chapter omitted (New York: Norton, 1963); republished with final chapter (New York & London: Norton, 1987);

Inside Mr. Enderby, as Kell (London: Heinemann, 1963);

Honey for the Bears (London: Heinemann, 1963; New York: Norton, 1964);

The Novel Today (London: Longmans, 1963; Folcroft, Pa.: Folcroft, 1971);

Nothing Like the Sun: A Story of Shakespeare's Love Life (London: Heinemann, 1964; New York: Norton, 1964);

Language Made Plain (London: English Universities Press, 1964; New York: Crowell, 1965); revised edition (London: Fontana, 1975);

Anthony Burgess (photograph by Jerry Bauer; from the dust jacket for Any Old Iron, *1989)*

The Eve of Saint Venus (London: Sidgwick & Jackson, 1964; New York: Norton, 1970);

The Long Day Wanes: A Malayan Trilogy (New York: Norton, 1964)–comprises *Time for a Tiger, The Enemy in the Blanket,* and *Beds in the East;* republished as *Malayan Trilogy: Time for a Tiger; The*

115

Enemy in the Blanket; Beds in the East (London: Pan, 1964);

Here Comes Everybody: An Introduction to James Joyce for the Ordinary Reader (London: Faber & Faber, 1965; republished as *Re Joyce* (New York: Norton, 1965); revised edition, with original title (Feltham, U.K.: Hamlyn, 1982);

A Vision of Battlements (London: Sidgwick & Jackson, 1965; New York: Norton, 1966);

Tremor of Intent (London: Heinemann, 1966; New York: Norton, 1966);

The Novel Now: A Student's Guide to Contemporary Fiction (London: Faber & Faber, 1967); republished as *The Novel Now: A Guide to Contemporary Fiction* (New York: Norton, 1967; revised, 1971);

Enderby Outside (London: Heinemann, 1968);

Enderby (New York: Norton, 1968)–comprises *Enderby Outside* and *Inside Mr. Enderby;*

Urgent Copy: Literary Studies (London: Cape, 1968; New York: Norton, 1969);

Shakespeare (London: Cape, 1970; New York: Knopf, 1970);

MF (London: Cape, 1971; New York: Knopf, 1971);

Joysprick: An Introduction to the Language of James Joyce (London: Deutsch, 1973; New York: Harcourt Brace Jovanovich, 1975);

Napoleon Symphony (London: Cape, 1974; New York: Knopf, 1974);

The Clockwork Testament; or, Enderby's End (London: Hart-Davis, MacGibbon, 1974; New York: Knopf, 1975);

Beard's Roman Women (New York: McGraw-Hill, 1976; London: Hutchinson, 1977);

A Long Time to Teatime (London: Dempsey & Squires, 1976; New York: Stonehill, 1976);

Moses: A Narrative (London: Dempsey & Squires, 1976; New York: Stonehill, 1976);

Abba Abba (London: Faber & Faber, 1977; Boston: Little, Brown, 1977);

Ernest Hemingway and His World (New York: Scribners, 1978; London: Thames & Hudson, 1978); republished as *Ernest Hemingway* (London: Thames & Hudson, 1986; New York: Thames & Hudson, 1999);

1985 (Boston: Little, Brown, 1978; London: Hutchinson, 1978);

The Land Where the Ice Cream Grows, by Burgess and Fulvio Testa (London: Bonn, 1979; New York: Doubleday, 1979);

Man of Nazareth (New York: McGraw-Hill, 1979; London: Magnum, 1980);

Earthly Powers (New York: Simon & Schuster, 1980; London: Hutchinson, 1980);

On Going to Bed (London: Deutsch, 1982; New York: Abbeville, 1982);

The End of the World News: An Entertainment (London: Hutchinson, 1982; New York: McGraw-Hill, 1983);

This Man and Music (London: Hutchinson, 1982; New York: McGraw-Hill, 1983);

Enderby's Dark Lady; or, No End to Enderby (London: Hutchinson, 1984; New York: McGraw-Hill, 1984);

Ninety-Nine Novels: The Best in English Since 1939: A Personal Choice (London: Allison & Busby, 1984; New York: Summit, 1984);

Oberon Old and New, by Burgess and J. R. Planché (London: Hutchinson, 1985);

The Kingdom of the Wicked (London: Hutchinson, 1985; New York: Arbor House, 1985);

Flame into Being: The Life and Work of D. H. Lawrence (London: Heinemann, 1985; New York: Arbor House, 1985);

Blooms of Dublin: A Musical Play Based on James Joyce's Ulysses (London: Hutchinson, 1986);

The Pianoplayers (London: Hutchinson, 1986; New York: Arbor House, 1986);

Homage to QWERT YUIOP: Essays (London: Hutchinson, 1986); republished as *But Do Blondes Prefer Gentlemen? Homage to Qwert Yuiop and Other Writings* (New York: McGraw-Hill, 1986);

Little Wilson and Big God: Being the First Part of the Confessions of Anthony Burgess (New York: Weidenfeld & Nicolson, 1986; London: Heinemann, 1987);

A Clockwork Orange: A Play with Music Based on His Novella of the Same Name (London: Hutchinson, 1987);

They Wrote in English (London: Hutchinson, 1988);

Any Old Iron (New York: Random House, 1989; London: Hutchinson, 1989);

The Devil's Mode: Stories (New York: Random House, 1989; London: Hutchinson, 1989);

You've Had Your Time: Being the Second Part of the Confessions of Anthony Burgess (London: Heinemann, 1990; New York: Weidenfeld, 1991);

Mozart and the Wolf Gang (London: Hutchinson, 1991); republished as *On Mozart: A Paean for Wolfgang* (New York: Ticknor & Fields, 1991);

A Mouthful of Air: Languages, Languages–Especially English (London: Hutchinson, 1992); republished as *A Mouthful of Air: Language and Languages–Especially English* (New York: Morrow, 1993);

A Dead Man in Deptford (London: Hutchinson, 1993; New York: Carroll & Graf, 1995);

Byrne (London: Hutchinson, 1995; New York: Carroll & Graf, 1997);

One Man's Chorus: The Uncollected Writings, edited by Ben Forkner (New York: Carroll & Graf, 1998).

PLAY PRODUCTIONS: Sophocles, *Oedipus the King,* translated and adapted by Burgess, Minneapolis, Guthrie Theatre, 1972;

Edmond de Rostand, *Cyrano,* translated and adapted by Burgess, New York, Palace Theatre, 13 May 1973;

A Clockwork Orange 2004, adapted from Burgess's *A Clockwork Orange,* London, Barbican Theatre, 1990.

PRODUCED SCRIPTS: *Moses the Lawgiver,* television, by Burgess, Vittorio Bonicelli, Gianfranco De Bosio, and Bernardino Zapponi, CBS, 1975;

Jesus of Nazareth, television, by Burgess, Suso Cecchi d'Amico, and Franco Zeffirelli, NBC, 1977;

Blooms of Dublin, radio, Radio Telefis Eireann/BBC, 2 February 1982;

A.D., television, by Burgess and Vincenzo Labella, adapted from Burgess's *The Kingdom of the Wicked,* 1985;

Cyrano de Bergerac, television, Channel Four Films, 1985;

The Rage of D. H. Lawrence, television, TVOntario, 1986.

OTHER: Michel de Saint-Pierre, *The New Aristocrats,* translated by Burgess and Lynne Burgess (London: Gollancz, 1962);

Jean Pelegri, *The Olive Trees of Justice,* translated by Burgess and Lynne Burgess (London: Sidgwick & Jackson, 1962);

Jean Sewin, *The Man Who Robbed Poor Boxes,* translated by Burgess (London: Gollancz, 1965);

Daniel Defoe, *A Journal of the Plague Year,* edited by Burgess and Christopher Bristow (Harmondsworth, U.K.: Penguin, 1966);

James Joyce, *A Shorter Finnegans Wake,* edited by Burgess (London: Faber & Faber, 1966; New York: Viking, 1967);

Paul Elek and Elizabeth Elek, eds., *Coaching Days of England: Containing an Account of Whatever Was Most Remarkable for Grandeur, Elegance and Curiosity in the Time of the Coaches of England, Comprehending the Year 1750 until 1850,* commentary by Burgess (London: Elek, 1966; New York: Time-Life, 1967);

Elek and Elek, eds., *The Age of the Grand Tour: Containing Sketches of the Manners, Society and Customs of France, Flanders, the United Provinces, Germany, Switzerland and Italy in the Letters, Journals and Writings of the Most Celebrated Voyagers between the Years 1720 and 1820,* introduction by Burgess (London: Elek, 1967; New York: Crown, 1967);

G. K. Chesterton, *Autobiography,* introduction by Burgess (London: Hutchinson, 1969);

G. V. Desani, *All about H. Hatterr,* introduction by Burgess (London: Bodley Head, 1970; New York: Farrar, Straus & Giroux, 1970);

Wolfgang Amadeus Mozart, *Don Giovanni* and *Idomeneo,* introduction by Burgess (London: Cassell, 1971; New York: Universe, 1971);

Edmond de Rostand, *Cyrano de Bergerac,* translated and adapted by Burgess (New York: Knopf, 1971; London: Hutchinson, 1985);

Sophocles, *Oedipus the King,* translated and adapted by Burgess (Minneapolis: University of Minnesota Press, 1972);

D. H. Lawrence, *D. H. Lawrence and Italy: Twilight in Italy, Sea and Sardinia, Etruscan Places,* introduction by Burgess (New York: Viking, 1972);

New York, edited by Burgess (Amsterdam: Time-Life, 1977);

Ben Forkner, ed., *Modern Irish Short Stories,* preface by Burgess (New York: Viking, 1980);

"The Cavalier of the Rose," in *Der Rosenkavalier: Comedy for Music in Three Acts* (Boston: Little, Brown, 1982; London: Joseph, 1983);

Rex Warner, *The Aerodrome: A Love Story,* introduction by Burgess (Oxford & New York: Oxford University Press, 1982);

Henry Yule, *Hobson-Jobson: A Glossary of Anglo-Indian Colloquial Words and Phrases,* second edition, introduction by Burgess (London & Boston: Routledge & Kegan Paul, 1986);

Alison Armstrong, *The Joyce of Cooking: Food and Drink in James Joyce's Dublin,* foreword by Burgess (Barrytown, N.Y.: Station Hill, 1986);

Ludovic Halévy and Henri Meilhac, *Carmen,* libretto translated by Burgess (London: Hutchinson, 1986);

H. E. Bates, *A Month by the Lake and Other Stories,* introduction by Burgess (New York: New Directions, 1987);

Budd Schulberg, *The Disenchanted,* introduction by Burgess (New York: Fine, 1987);

Ian Fleming, *Diamonds Are Forever,* preface by Burgess (Kent, U.K.: Coronet, 1988);

Fleming, *Dr No,* preface by Burgess (Kent, U. K.: Coronet, 1988);

Dieter Hildebrandt, *Pianoforte: A Social History of the Piano,* introduction by Burgess (London: Hutchinson, 1988; New York: Braziller, 1988);

Mervyn Peake, *The Gormenghast Trilogy,* introduction by Burgess (Woodstock, N.Y.: Overlook, 1988);

Fleming, *For Your Eyes Only,* preface by Burgess (Kent, U.K.: Coronet, 1989);

Fleming, *Moonraker,* preface by Burgess (Kent, U.K.: Coronet, 1989);

David W. Barber, *If It Ain't Baroque: More Music History as It Ought to Be Taught,* preface by Burgess (Toronto: Sound and Vision, 1992);

Frank MacShane and Lori Carlson, eds., *Return Trip Tango and Other Stories from Abroad: Selections from Translation Magazine,* introduction by Burgess (New York: Columbia University Press, 1992);

Oscar Wilde, *The Picture of Dorian Gray,* introduction by Burgess (New York: Penguin, 1992);

Greg Vitiello, ed., *Joyce Images,* introduction by Burgess (New York: Norton, 1994).

The death of Anthony Burgess in 1993 brought an end to the career of one of the most prolific contemporary writers. Burgess was asked so frequently about his productivity that he eventually developed an apologia based on his energy, hard work, and sheer love of writing. In response to John Cullinan's opening question on the subject for an interview in the *Paris Review* (Spring 1973), he replied: "It has been a sin to be prolific only since the Bloomsbury group—particularly Forster—made it a point of good manners to produce, as it were, costively. I've been annoyed less by sneers at my alleged overproduction than by the imputation that to write much means to write badly." Burgess has also reminded his audience that unlike many writers, especially in the United States, he has supported himself entirely by his own writing and not as lavishly as some have. In the foreword to Jeutonne Brewer's bibliography of his work, Burgess expresses wonder that he has produced so many books and anger that it required so much writing to support himself. The sheer bulk of Burgess's fiction produced yet another source of anger and resentment for a writer who would have preferred to stake his reputation on works such as *MF* (1971), *Napoleon Symphony* (1974), or *Earthly Powers* (1980) but who has become known to most readers as the author of *A Clockwork Orange* (1962), whose screen interpretation by Stanley Kubrick brought Burgess notoriety.

Burgess's fiction does not fit comfortably under the rubric of "fantasy and science fiction." With the possible exception of *The End of the World News: An Entertainment* (1982), his science fiction is not "scientific," if by that term one may denote the purer forms of the genre in which the writer offers extrapolations of contemporary science and technology. Unlike Isaac Asimov, he had little background in science, and like Doris Lessing, he had little inclination to read about it. In *The End of the World News* he seems to share a fairly conventional hostility toward science and technology for robbing human experience of warmth and color. Burgess himself consistently rejected such a designation and diminished the science-fiction qualities of his novels. He argued that *A Clockwork Orange,* for example, is set in an England of a quite near future, not the distant one of Aldous Huxley's *Brave New World* (1932), or perhaps even George Orwell's *Nineteen Eighty-Four* (1949). Furthermore, in a work such as *The End of the World News,* part of which is unarguably science fiction, Burgess offers a highly ambivalent characterization of Valentine Brodie, who teaches and writes in the genre. Nevertheless, Burgess has been considered a writer of science fiction for *A Clockwork Orange,* a contemporary classic, and for *The Wanting Seed* (1962), *1985* (1978), and *The End of the World News.*

Burgess was born John Anthony Burgess Wilson in Manchester on 25 February 1917. His father, Joseph Wilson, played piano in movie houses and pubs, and his mother, Elizabeth (née Burgess), was a music-hall singer who died in the influenza epidemic following World War I when Burgess was a toddler. He was raised Roman Catholic, attending Bishop Bilsborough Memorial School and Xavierian College, Manchester, but identified himself as a "lapsed Catholic." One clear legacy was a fervent belief in Original Sin, the "Augustinian" pole Burgess opposed to the "Pelagian," as he constructed those two terms to denote strict and liberal approaches to morality.

Although Burgess wrote poetry from an early age, he aspired to a career in music. Unable to win a scholarship, he had to work to save enough money to continue his education, and then, having failed to pass an entrance examination in physics, he had to resign himself to studying literature rather than music at Manchester University. World War II almost made it impossible for Burgess to complete his degree, but he was grudgingly granted a temporary exemption and then called into service in the fall of 1940. After serving with a group of professional entertainers, he was sent to Gibraltar, where he remained from 1943 to 1946, doing intelligence work.

At Manchester University, Burgess met Llewela Jones, whom he married on 23 January 1942. After Burgess had been posted to Gibraltar his wife did volunteer work in England while awaiting the birth of their child, and, returning home in the dark of the blackouts one night, she was attacked by four American deserters intent on robbing her, an event that served as the germ for *A Clockwork Orange.* According to Burgess, she was not raped but was so badly shaken by the effort to keep her wedding ring that she miscarried. The miscarriage caused the chronic hemorrhaging that, as Burgess told C. Robert Jennings in *Playboy* (September 1974), contributed to his wife's alcoholism. She died of portal cirrhosis in 1968.

Following his return to England in 1946, Burgess eked out a living by playing the piano and by teaching. In 1949 he drew upon his wartime experience to write *A Vision of Battlements* (1965). On the model of James Joyce's *Ulysses* (1922), the novel draws on Virgil's *Aeneid*. Richard Ennis, a musical composer stationed on Gibraltar, is separated from his wife but comforts himself with a "Dido." In *Little Wilson and Big God: Being the First Part of the Confessions of Anthony Burgess* (1986), he describes sending the manuscript off to Heinemann because that house had been Graham Greene's publisher. He was told that *A Vision of Battlements* was a "second novel" and that he needed to write a first. Heinemann turned down the manuscript of what Burgess submitted as the "first" novel, eventually published as *The Worm and the Ring* (1961). Discouraged by his low salary, Burgess applied for a teaching position in Malaya and was surprised when he was hired. In Malaya and, following its independence, in Borneo, Burgess began to concentrate on fiction rather than music, although he never abandoned music completely.

Burgess's first three published novels—*Time for a Tiger* (1956), *The Enemy in the Blanket* (1958), and *Beds in the East* (1959)—comprise the *Malayan Trilogy* (published in the United States as *The Long Day Wanes: A Malayan Trilogy,* 1964). Victor Crabbe, his autobiographical hero, or antihero, has come to Malaya to teach history, haunted by the death of his first wife in an automobile accident. Following his disillusionment over having no real role in Malaya, Crabbe himself meets a wretched death, either drowning or being devoured by a crocodile. These novels provide some difficulties for the Western reader, because, as Burgess has indicated, he had a Malayan audience in mind. He seriously considered becoming a citizen of the new state that the Malays were anticipating and contemplated converting to Islam. Although his talent was acknowledged in the reviews of these books, Burgess still considered himself a teacher.

In 1959, while teaching in Borneo, Burgess collapsed one day and was flown by jet to a hospital in London for examination and treatment. As in Malaya, Burgess seemed to his fellow British to be running the risk of "going native," and the authorities may well have been happy to see him out of Borneo. Besides, as Geoffrey Aggeler indicates, Burgess's wife had caused embarrassment at a garden party where, instead of offering pleasantries to the visiting Prince Philip's query "Everything all right?," she retorted that "things bloody well weren't all right" because of the British. Burgess was informed by the British doctors that he had a brain tumor and

Burgess composing music

would probably be dead within a year. He set to work writing novels as fast as he could, hoping to augment the meager legacy he would leave his ailing wife. A year and five manuscripts later, he was alive in Sussex and continuing to write. He claims to have found the year of his "death sentence" one of exhilaration rather than depression. Certainly it was a year of creative fecundity.

In 1960 Burgess published *The Doctor Is Sick* and *The Right to an Answer*. *The Doctor Is Sick* anticipates Burgess's movement toward fantasy in the bizarre episodes toward which he leads a modern-day picaro, Edwin Spindrift, home on leave from a teaching position in Burma to undergo medical tests. Spindrift escapes from a hospital where he is being prepared for brain surgery to go on a wild journey through what might be his hallucinations or a fantasy world. *The Right to an Answer* brings East to West in the person of the Ceylonese Mr. Raj, who is introduced to an England of stark choices: the drugged state of telly-watching and the pub world of beer-drinking and wife-swapping. The following year he published two novels again: *Devil of a State,* which continues his interest in Asian settings, and *One Hand Clapping,* under another pseudonym, Joseph Kell–rather than his better-known pen name, Anthony Burgess–because his publisher was concerned that the novels would be under-valued if Burgess were to acquire the reputation of being too prolific. (The "Joseph Kell" books got few reviews and sold poorly, however, until they were republished under Burgess's name.) *One Hand Clapping* is a black comedy on the debilitating effects of television. Again in 1963 he published *Honey for the Bears* as Anthony Burgess and *Inside Mr. Enderby* as Joseph Kell. Like *Tremor of Intent* (1966), written in the vein of John le Carré and Ian Fleming, *Honey for the Bears* grew out of Cold War tensions. In the early 1960s Burgess fell in love with Liliana Marcellari, and in August 1964 their son, Andreas, was born. In October 1968 they were married, shortly after Llewela Burgess died. Burgess changed publishers from Heinemann to Jonathan Cape and left England for Malta, then Italy and Monaco.

Probably Burgess's intellectual and artistic conservativism encouraged him to resist readings of his work as science fiction. When reminded by Jennings that *A Clockwork Orange* described men on the moon almost a decade before the event, Burgess rejected the notion of a "fiction of the future," arguing that such a future is actually "the present, with a few fantastic embellishments." He goes on to explain that Orwell originally wanted the title of *Nineteen Eighty-Four* to be *Nineteen Forty-Eight* as an indication that its world was actually the post–World War II England in which he was writing the novel. In *A Clockwork Orange,* Burgess argues, he was writing about "life as it was in 1960," with the "embellishments" of "world telecasts and men on the moon." However, "there's nothing in the book that wasn't already present in the technology of the early Sixties, except for the use of a composite dialect called Nadsat."

Burgess is accurate in his assessment. If anything seems futuristic in *A Clockwork Orange* it is the Nadsat he developed for the novel. One of the doctors involved in the Ludovico's Technique in the middle section speculates that Nadsat is dominated by words with Slavic roots because the Soviets have been broadcasting subliminal propaganda to young people in the West. Indeed, *Nadsat* means "teen" in Russian. Because it is a new "language," most readers find it difficult until they learn to rely on context to tell them that "tolchooking" means "beating" or a "litso" is a face. Nadsat insulates Alex and the readers to some degree from his violence. Furthermore, since Alex is first-person narrator, Nadsat transfers to him some of Burgess's function as a wordsmith.

Other than Nadsat and the short-term prophecies of global telecasts and moon walks, *A Clockwork Orange* could be taking place in the present of its composition and publication. Indeed, the phenomenon already present in 1960 that inspired the short novel was aversion therapy, widely discussed in England at the time as a means of combating violence among young males. Burgess indicates that he wrote the novel in part because he heard people in pubs speaking enthusiastically in its favor as a solution to youthful crime. He argues, however, that this "therapy" went back to Ivan Pavlov and was clearly evident as a tool for conditioning the antisocial in Joseph Stalin's Soviet Union and for "brainwashing" American prisoners of war during the Korean War.

At the heart of the moral concerns expressed in *A Clockwork Orange* are two figures: the prison chaplain–or "Charlie" in honor of the silent movie actor Charlie Chaplin–and the writer F. Alexander. The chaplain admits to Alex that from the perspective of religious morality, the aversive therapy, or Ludovico's Technique, is wrong because it robs him of the capacity for choice. The chaplain is a weak vessel for the preservation of religious morality, however–he has a drinking problem and aspirations to professional advancement–and he betrays Alex. The liberal humanist and left-of-center political writer Alexander is hardly a stronger vessel. When Alex and his droogs rape Alexander's wife and vandalize their "HOME," Alex reads mockingly from Alexander's manuscript, also called "A Clockwork Orange," in which the writer deplores how the present reactionary regime has turned the fruit God created in the Garden into so many "clockwork oranges." (The term is one Burgess claims in his essay "Clockwork Marmalade" to have borrowed from Cockney slang.) Despite his connections with Burgess as a writer with similar views on the evil of destroying human choice, Alexander is not, finally, sympathetic. The difficulty in interpreting his role has been further complicated by the Kubrick motion picture, in which Alexander is at least eccentric in the first encounter with Alex and clearly insane in the second. Burgess offers a crucial insight in the second encounter when Alexander becomes so enthusiastic about the struggle to preserve freedom in contemporary society, where "the masses" would trade it for a mess of pottage, that he drives a dinner fork into the wall. Like the "mad doctors"–Branom and Brodsky–Alexander suffers from the potential malaise of all well-intentioned thinkers willing to allow the exercise of power to achieve good ends using whatever means are necessary. Indeed, in contrast to the spaciness of F. Alexander and *his* droogs' "futuristic" world in the movie, the novel indicates that these activists would have been more than willing to "use" (F. Alexander's own verb) Alex even if they had not suspected that it was he who led the attack on Alexander's "HOME."

Despite Burgess's insistence that humans must choose between good and evil, the novel renders the issue of choice problematic. Alex repeatedly begins sections of the narrative with "What's it going to be then, eh?" as though attempting to implicate the reader in the choices to be made concerning the schedule of violence for the evening, just as he asks his droogs. Such choice is an illusion, however, since, as his followers make clear, Alex is a despot intent upon using them, almost as though they were only extra appendages for his own compulsive violence. Furthermore, the structure of the narrative belies the possibility of choice since its three parts are as mechanically repetitious as the evenings the boys spend getting high on drugs, robbing, beating, and raping, in an endless succession that even they eventually come to see as boringly repetitive. In part 2, focusing on Alex's reconditioning by the mad doctors, he is forced to submit to the viewing of violent images strikingly like those in his description of a typical night's "adventure" in part 1.

Part 3 makes the "clockwork" quality of violence even more bleakly obvious, when the solitary and vulnerable Alex is set upon, for example, by the chums of the old man with the books whom Alex and his droogs encountered, similarly alone and vulnerable. Indeed, "reconditioning" may be an especially apt term, since the narrative suggests that Alex may have been so conditioned to be violent that choice has always been an illusion, thus opening up the question of whether he has ever been or ever will be anything but a "clockwork orange." Other questions abound. If victim and victimizer can so easily change places, are they merely two sides of the same coin of human interaction? Can relationships transcend a basis of who has the power, and will that person resist the temptations of abuse? And perhaps the most subtle question: can victims, whether individuals or society as a whole, resist the lure of vengeance, that powerful trigger for individual or collective violence "justified" by the violence of their victimizers?

In 1987 Norton republished *A Clockwork Orange* with an introduction by Burgess and a publisher's note that only scratch the surface of the story of the U.S. publication of the book and the aftermath of the Kubrick movie. Burgess says he believed that in order for Norton to publish *A Clockwork Orange* he had to omit the twenty-first and last chapter of the British edition, in which Alex grows bored with violence and begins to think about becoming a musical composer as well as a father. The publisher recalls that this "stipulation" was a mere editorial sugges-

Dust jacket for the first edition of Burgess's best-known novel, published in 1962 (Between the Covers, catalogue 88, n.d.)

tion. Critics, such as John Stinson, have agreed with the publisher that the twenty-first chapter weakens the novel. In any case, it was the original American ending that Kubrick adopted for the movie, an ending in which Alex looks forward to a continued life of violence. Kubrick's adaptation brought the novel millions of new readers, but it also brought Burgess the notoriety of seeming to celebrate violence. In his memoir *You've Had Your Time* (1990), Burgess indicates that he had no involvement in the making of the movie and that his screenplay was rejected by Kubrick. Thus, when acts of violence were traced back to the movie—perhaps most notoriously Arthur Bremer's attempt on George Wallace's life in 1972—Burgess tried to disown the novel, in part because it had become associated with the adaptation but also because he had become known only as the author of *A Clockwork Orange*.

One literary outcome of Burgess's frustration with being accused of triggering acts of violence is his novel *The Clockwork Testament; or, Enderby's End* (1974). Enderby is another autobiographical character, who had appeared in the novels *Inside Mr. Enderby* and *Enderby Outside* (1968), which were republished together in the United States as *Enderby* (1968). (In the 1984 novel *Enderby's Dark Lady* Burgess indicates that the character's "end" was only hypothetical, since in the later novel Enderby goes to Indiana instead of to Manhattan, as in *The Clockwork Testament*.) In addition to venting large amounts of spleen against such targets as American academics and their students, television talk-show hosts, and feminists, the novel avenges Burgess's victimization by the simple minds who blame his art for precipitating violence. Enderby has written the screenplay for an adaptation of Gerard Manley Hopkins's long poem *The Wreck of the Deutschland* (1875), in which the poet uses the drowning of nuns to open questions of divine providence. The moviemaker changes the script so that the ship is attacked by Nazis who rape the nuns, and Enderby is vilified by irate citizens who hold him responsible for the rash of assaults upon nuns perpetrated by young viewers of the movie.

Burgess escaped a similar notoriety with his other publication of 1962, *The Wanting Seed,* perhaps his only long and sustained effort at science fiction. This novel is also set in a near-future England, apparently sometime in the twenty-first century. The monarch is Charles VI, suggesting that at least four monarchs have reigned since Elizabeth II. This future England is overburdened with population. The boundaries of Greater London are now the sea to the south and east and Birmingham to the northwest. The government attempts to reduce births by limiting couples to one child and by encouraging homosexuality. Indeed, advancement requires that citizens at least pay lip service to the slogan that "It's Sapiens to be Homo."

Beatrice-Joanna Foxe's husband, Tristram, gets passed over for the chair of a university history department because he is heterosexual and because his parents committed the crime of adding four children to the population. His brother Derek, who has been having an affair with Beatrice-Joanna, has a high position in the Ministry of Infertility in large part because he pretends to be gay. At the beginning, Beatrice-Joanna has just turned over the corpse of her infant son to the Ministry of Agriculture—or the Phosphorus Reclamation Department, to be more precise—for cremation and the return of its phosphorus to an impoverished Mother Earth. On the same day, Tristram learns that he will not be chair and that his wife has been having an affair with his brother, he returns drunk to his tiny apartment, and

he and Beatrice-Joanna have sex just after Derek leaves. She becomes pregnant and toward the end of the novel bears twin boys, whom she names Derek and Tristram, suggesting that even she is uncertain of their paternity.

The initial events of the narrative set the plot moving toward its bizarre climax. Beatrice-Joanna travels north to live with her sister during her pregnancy. After losing his job, Tristram is imprisoned, drafted into the army, and finally reunited with his wife and her sons. Tristram, a history teacher, is Burgess's spokesman for his Manichean notion of the Pelagian-Augustinian cycle, evident in *A Clockwork Orange* and other novels. Enderby in *A Clockwork Testament* is writing a long poem on this cultural, or religious, dynamic, of which Burgess has spoken frequently in his interviews and essays. Pelagius was an early Christian theologian who was excommunicated as a heretic because he preached that believers could achieve salvation through the exercise of their free will, while St. Augustine, one of the early patriarchs of the Church, preached that only through God's grace could believers exercise free will and achieve goodness. Burgess argued that these two originally religious outlooks produce radically different political ideologies: the "Pelagian" socialist or liberal view, grounded in the notion of human perfectability, seeks to eliminate coercive or punitive restraints on the individual, while the "Augustinian" conservative or fascist view, grounded in the presumption of inevitable human evil, seeks to rein in the individual's propensity for crime. The "Pelphase" of the cycle, according to the teachings of Tristram, leads to an interphase of anarchy in which individuals see their well-being so threatened that they are willing to accept the "Gusphase" of a more repressive government. Its coerciveness eventually comes to seem so oppressive and threatening to individual rights that citizens are willing to risk the subversion of stability to reachieve the freedom of the Pelphase.

The theory works itself out with some success in *The Wanting Seed.* The government attempts to use social pressure, rather than the force of law, to reduce population. The propaganda for homosexuality and the encouragement of rigidly restrained procreation offer their own kind of coercion. They are insufficient, however, perhaps because Burgess is more Augustinian, as he admits, than Pelagian, fearful that he will be disappointed if he leaves the safe harbor of confidence in the truth of human depravity. As the Pelagian phase moves toward its end, Burgess intrudes a kind of magic, or fertility mythology, into his narrative: humans have sinned against something like the Life Force, as evidenced by the Earth

Malcolm McDowell as Alex in the 1971 motion-picture adaptation of A Clockwork Orange, *directed by Stanley Kubrick*

becoming a wasteland of infertility as crops fail, animals become barren, and the fishermen return with empty nets. In an interphase of chaotic reaction, there is an explosion of repressed sexuality—communal sex in the furrows at planting time, for example—and cannibalism masking itself as religious rite. The inevitable Augustinian phase brings about its own final solution to the problem of overpopulation. Indeed, Tristram alone survives a "battle" in the new "phony war," run by a corporation working for the military, which conscripts excess population of both sexes to fight mock engagements, the sole purpose of which is unwitting slaughter for canned meat.

The end of the novel reunites Tristram and Beatrice-Joanna—for the time being. Derek has kept his position in what is now the Ministry of Fertility by confessing his concealed heterosexuality. Here, as in *A Clockwork Orange,* the author's preoccupation with the cyclical is stressed by the implicit statement of the novel that these characters and their society will inevitably turn toward the Pelagian once more. This attraction to the cyclical is one of the author's

debts to Joyce, and it has been pointed out by Cullinan that the name of Ludovico's Technique suggests Joyce's embracing of Giambattista Vico's notion of three human phases with its "ricorso" completing the cycle. Burgess's essential conservatism, however, vitiates the reader's confidence in this cycle, since Burgess seems happier here, as in *A Clockwork Orange,* having moved his characters back into the "Gusphase." As a writer, he opts out of the Pelphase—in which, one suspects, he saw his culture when he wrote these novels—because it seems to have no regard for the arts. His views are evident in Tristram's excitement as the Interphase appears to be witnessing the rebirth of drama—and literature in general. It is difficult not to suspect the author of fearing that projection of present trends suggests a future without literature because no one will bother to read.

If *The Wanting Seed* is science fiction, it is certainly not the science fiction of Arthur C. Clarke or Asimov, with an appetite for a futuristic world produced by science and technology. There are few expressions of the expected science-fiction elements; indeed, the only one that comes close is the "*Daily Newsdisc,* . . . one of a number of free-enterprise organs, auditory, audio-visual, even (the *Weekly Feel*) tactile—was there for anybody's re-listening," suggesting the media that replace the newspaper in an essentially nonprint culture. Like Huxley and Orwell, Burgess is basically a cultural conservative using the trappings of science fiction to vent his anxiety that change is generally for the worse.

The novels between these two dystopian works and a third—*1985*—demonstrate that Burgess was moving in several new directions. *Nothing Like the Sun: A Story of Shakespeare's Love Life* (1964) offers a fictional account of William Shakespeare involved in a love triangle with a "golden boy," the earl of Southampton, and a literal "dark lady," the African Fatimah. *MF* is in part based on Claude Lévi-Strauss's argument for a connection between riddles and incest, not only in the Oedipus myth of ancient Greece but also in Native American legend. *Napoleon Symphony* is his attempt to integrate music and fiction, to write a novel about Napoleon Bonaparte as if it were Ludwig van Beethoven's *Eroica* symphony.

1985, Burgess's return to dystopian fantasy, is a mélange of essays on Orwell's *Nineteen Eighty-Four,* a short novel called "1985," and an interview in which the author constructs the questions to be answered by "Burgess." Burgess is clearly less interested in futuristic fiction than in commenting on conditions in England on the eve of Margaret Thatcher's Tory administration. Indeed, he repeats his conclusion that Orwell was describing England of the late 1940s rather than a part of Oceania in 1984. He argues that no one writes futuristic fiction anymore, except for those in "think-tanks." The Anglo-American world of the late 1970s is not a promising one for Burgess, who seems throughout *1985* dyspeptic, petulant, and often nasty.

In the essay and interview sections, Burgess indicts "muddle-headed academics," who have given students "remarkable liberties, or licenses" to have "promiscuous copulation," while they "study petromusicology (the aesthetics and history of rock music), Basic Swahili, or the poetry of Bob Dylan." These remarks are matched in the novella by equally harsh comments on the deplorable state of education. The reading list for the examinations taken by students about to leave school, for example, includes the lyrics of singer Jed Foote and his group, the Come Quicks; Agatha Christie's play *The Mousetrap* (1952); "A Shorter Carpetbaggers" by Harold Robbins; and, referring to the novel *Room at the Top* (1957), "some nonsense about the errors of social climbing by Sir

John Braine." These remarks give a good sense of the intemperate quality of Burgess's humor. He is more devastating in his attack on trade unionism.

In the novella itself Burgess focuses on Bev Jones, another history teacher, whose name echoes Winston Smith. When asked about his first name, Jones says that it is probably short for "Beveridge, Bevin or Bevan," the "big names" for his Socialist father. Bev has just lost his wife in a hospital fire because the firemen were out on strike. In rage he burns his union card in public and, like Smith, tries to take on "the system"—his wife's dying words were "Don't let them get away with it." The system is informally known as "TUK"—The United Kingdom—or "Tucland" for "Trade Union Council Land."

Like the settings of *A Clockwork Orange* and *The Wanting Seed,* Tucland is at an ebb of Pelagianism. Arabs have used oil profits to buy up much of the United Kingdom, and Islam has replaced Christianity as the state religion. Because the schools pander to the wishes of their least-talented "consumers," the brightest students have turned to the streets and to gangs reminiscent of those in *A Clockwork Orange*: "Kumina gangs they were called, these terrors of the streets, *kumi na* being the Swahili prefix that meant teen and, by extension, teenage. . . . when the State didn't encourage learning, learning became an antisocial thing." As a subversive activity, the gangs have learned Latin, an expression of the author's perverse contention that the best subjects for learning are those that are the most irrelevant to the contemporary world.

Having lost his job, Bev applies for unemployment benefits but is turned down. He has committed the heresy of refusing to abide by the basic tenet of labor in Tucland: an absolute right to withhold one's labor, regardless of the consequences. Bev's reaction is telling. When he is told that only union members have rights, he is unsurprised, adding that "In a way I'm courting my own ruin. Call me a witness, which, in Greek, is *martyr.*" The same remark could have been uttered by Tristram Foxe in *The Wanting Seed.* Facing an oppressive system, all the individual can do in Burgess's perspective is to sacrifice himself by bearing witness to that oppression.

Like Tristram, Bev sets out to live by his own wits, having stowed his mentally but not sexually retarded teenage daughter in a boarding school provided by the State. He encounters the kumina gangs and toys with the possibility of teaching in the "UU," or Underground University. He also flirts with joining the Army of Free Workers, a protofascist group planning to break the next strike by providing services and eventually taking over. Before that can hap-

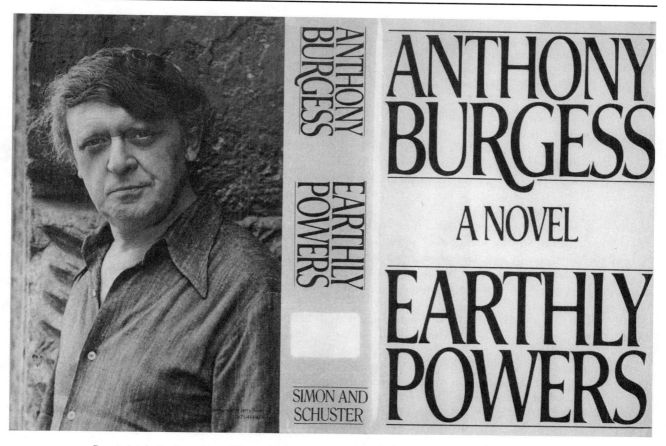

Dust jacket for the first edition of Burgess's 1980 novel, which chronicles the lives of a popular homosexual writer and a Catholic priest who becomes Pope (Richland County Public Library)

pen, Bev flagrantly shoplifts a bottle of gin and is sentenced to Crawford Manor, a rehabilitation center run by TUK, where he resists re-education at the hands of Pettigrew, a rewriting of Orwell's O'Brien in the Ministry of Love.

This obligatory encounter between Jones, the surviving remnant of belief in the old values, and Pettigrew, the powerful exponent of the new, is the forum for the author to vent his spleen about the horrors of "Big Labour." Burgess's debt to Orwell is plain from the opening sentence, meant to recall the opening sentence in *Nineteen Eighty-Four:* "It was the week before Christmas, Monday midday, mild and muggy, and muezzins of West London were yodelling about there being no God but Allah. . . ." Like Winston's reeducation, Bev's offers opportunities to reveal the essence of the system against which he rebels; he comments, for example, that "the exercise of power is the most intoxicating of narcotics." In line with Burgess's denigration of the character of Julia in *Nineteen Eighty-Four* as Winston's "mistress," for whom "freedom" is merely sexual promiscuity,

Bev is betrayed by his lover, Mavis, a fellow inmate who works for Pettigrew and apparently relays to him Bev's confession that he did not "altogether regret" his wife's death. Bev struggles to play the "martyr" role to the hilt, threatening to take back his "recantation" and boasting about his ability to endure torture like the hero of a boy's book. To Pettigrew's pronouncement that he rejects "the sanity of work," Bev hurls the threat that Pettigrew will "come up against reality . . . The reality of the invader whose insanity will flood a sphere more fanatical than yours." Bev's prediction comes true before the end of the novel, and NATO forces prevent an Arab invasion of the United Kingdom, which is headed back to a conservative "sanity."

Burgess's essential conservatism surfaces in these last chapters. The narrator laments the transformation of Crawford Manor into a rehabilitation center: "All that beauty, all those exquisite possessions of the tax-ruined Crawford family—gone, sold to Americans or Arabs. . . . no vestige of the privileged past to be left." Bev argues against a future in which excellence is buried in mediocrity, pointing out "authors already out of print" as evidence of a "levelling" eliminating "brilliance in the performing arts." In his later years Burgess clearly had serious doubts about his literary immortality in a world of growing illiteracy and mediocrity.

Another evidence of the author's conservatism is his increasingly shrill treatment of homosexuality. Gay characters have appeared in Burgess's fiction from the beginning—one recalls a conventional "male dancer" in *A Vision of Battlements,* for example—and occasionally the author demonstrates an unconventionally sympathetic response, as in *Honey for the Bears* and *Nothing Like the Sun.* In *Earthly Powers* he set himself the challenge of writing one of his longest novels through the first-person narrative of an aging homosexual writer. In *1985,* however, his viewpoint character, Bev, speaks of "the prettily pansified . . . Male models, I mean, and dancers, and even the Gaypros. The homosexual prostitutes." In the first chapter Burgess stretches the reader's credulity by indicating that Bev gets off easily in his beating by a kumina gang because they have just finished sodomizing a young boy: "It had been a multiple pederastic assault, a sevenfold entry. Poor kid." In the final interview section the author rages against the appropriation of *gay* by male homosexuals: "The Gay Liberation movement—which ought to be prevented, by law if need be, from limiting a fine old word to coy, giggly, totally inaccurate and quite arbitrary signification—will demand that terms like *poofter, fag, pansy* and so on be made illegal." His vitriolic comments about the degradation of the language by contemporary feminists are equally and gratuitously nasty.

The reviewers of *1985* felt that Burgess was foolhardy in inviting comparisons of his own slender novel with Orwell's classic. The novel is a good example of what many informed readers find unappealing in Burgess's work—a rather cavalier attitude toward serious concerns, with both thematic elements and form growing out of a restless impulse to keep writing. Reviewers also objected to the wide-ranging nastiness in the book: homophobia, traces of misogyny, and xenophobia regarding Arabs and Americans buying up an England he was more than delighted to leave are the most obvious expressions.

In some ways, *The End of the World News* is much more appealing, perhaps because as an "entertainment," as its subtitle refers to it, it absolves Burgess of the obligation of seriousness that ends in didacticism. He creates a persona—a "literary executor," John B. Wilson—to explain the publication of this bizarre concatenation of a biography of Sigmund Freud, a libretto for a musical about Leon Trotsky in New York City on the eve of the Bolshevik Revolution, and an end-of-the-world fantasy. In this fantasy, Lynx, a rogue planet the size of Earth but ten times as dense, has strayed into the solar system, capturing the Moon so that together the two exert enough gravitational pull to create tides reaching to the top floors of Manhattan skyscrapers. Lynx will return in less than a year for a closer encounter likely to eliminate life and the Earth.

Of the main characters in this apocalyptic fantasy, Valentine Brodie is clearly central, in part because he teaches and writes science fiction, even though he is self-deprecating about his work and refrains from asking his students to read it for his courses. Burgess offers a short list of Val's better-known novels, with titles such as *Cuspclasp and Flukefang* and *The White and the Walk of the Morning.* Val reflects the demeaning attitudes of contemporary culture toward the genre: "Science fiction is, let's be honest, ultimately a triviality. . . . It's brain-tickling nomore. The American cult of mediocrity, which rejects Shakespeare . . . has led us to this nonsense—a university course in, let's face it, trash." Val is included in the cultural elite to be saved only because he is the son-in-law of Professor Frame, who conceived of an interstellar "Noah's Ark," although the rationale is that the last Earthlings will need a writer to chronicle their experience for the succeeding generations aboard the spaceship.

Val almost misses the spaceship because he and his wife, Vanessa, an astrophysicist, have become incompatible. With more than a hint of misogyny, Burgess loads upon Vanessa the cultural stereotype of the cold-blooded scientist, worse in her case because she is a woman. Guilty for having allowed himself to be seduced by a student, Val tries to be particularly loving as they prepare to leave for the training site in the Midwest, but he is unmanned by Vanessa's sexual-manual technique in bed: "Has everything to be science? . . . I know now that I don't want your kind of civilization to be saved. Is there no room for for for clumsiness and humanity and imperfection and drunkenness and and—." Val's attraction to imperfection leads him to chum around with Willett, an aging, down-on-his-luck actor, who satisfies Burgess's impulse to celebrate the seedy, drunken, unsightly aspects of humanity. Like Orwell, Burgess has a phobia of the sterile utopia of what science and technology can do for humanity—a "cold contrived future."

The leader of the spaceship *America* and the villain in the piece is Paul Bartlett, a power-hungry "mad scientist" intent on determining what in civilization is to be saved. Bartlett retreads the protofascist sentiments of Alex's doctors and Pettigrew in *1985*. Before the spaceship is even launched, Bartlett has determined who will mate with whom—although seemingly he would like to be the only progenitor. Bartlett gloats about eliminating emotions, "a great nuisance, a damnable source of ultimate sabotage," as well as "literature, music, art . . . the stuff of dissidence." Instead, humankind will experience power, presumably Bartlett's.

Val wins out because as a science-fiction writer he is essential to the project. As a result, the novel becomes Burgess's most postmodern in its self-referentiality. Among the detritus of collapsing American civilization, one of Val's companions finds a copy of his book *Not Call to Night,* with its blurb: "This brilliant first novel by one who bids fair to become a great name in world SF. . . ." The publication date of the novel, 1990, indicates that *The End of the World News* is not set far in the future. According to the blurb, Val's novel is about "a heavenly body preparing to hit the earth," but apparently the author provides a happy ending: the cataclysm is a "false alarm." Willett asks Val how he chose "Fordtown" in central Kansas for his ark project; the writer answers that he "used to work pretty hard on background . . . The critics were always quick to leap on writers who hadn't done their homework."

When Val makes his bid to take over command of the spaceship, he admits to having only one qualification, the "useless trade" of science fiction. He proposes to write science fiction as "science fact," a chronicle to be continued by the voyagers' descendants. His proposal echoes what he told Bartlett when the leaders of the project met at the Brodies' dinner party: "Someday . . . on a distant planet in an unfathomably far galaxy, schoolchildren will read a book with some such title as *Annals of the Star Trek* or *How Civilization Was Saved*. I shall have written that book." As the spaceship waits to blast off, Val discovers that the only remnants of his dying civilization that *America* has brought along are the Trotsky musical and the Freud biography, which are also included in the text of Burgess's bizarre novel.

Furthermore, as is explained in the epilogue to *The End of the World News,* the Trotsky musical and the Freud biography have become the sacred texts of the descendants of the *America* passengers. The opening sentence of the epilogue indicates that the narrator throughout the whole novel has been a future "Valentine O'Grady," whose audience—"boys and girls, ladies and gentlemen"—has been listening to a version of the science-fiction/science-"fact" chronicle written by Val Brodie. Despite the clarity and specificity of this "chronicle," the audience pre-

Dust jacket for the first U.S. edition of Burgess's 1982 novel, in which a memoir by a science-fiction writer, a biography of Sigmund Freud, and the libretto for a musical about Leon Trotsky are the only remaining documents of civilization on Earth (Richland County Public Library)

fers its own fantasy version of that earlier time, based on what they have heard about "two ancient and fantastic films" in "the Brodie Archives," to which few have access. Their misconceptions of these films are amusing: "The one about the bad man called Fred Fraud who kept people strapped to a couch and the good one called Trot Sky who wanted people to do what he did and run through space." Although *The End of the World News* cannot qualify for a higher status than "an entertainment" because it is "merely" science fiction, it is also among Burgess's most successful later novels.

In his last years Burgess continued writing at a high level of productivity, including two volumes of his autobiography, *Little Wilson and Big God* (1986) and *You've Had Your Time* (1990). The first volume covers his life until his "death sentence," a physician's announcing in 1959 that Burgess had only a year to live. The second volume covers his life until

1982. Burgess also published the novels *The Piano-players* (1986), *Any Old Iron* (1989), and *A Dead Man in Deptford* (1993), as well as the short-story collection *The Devils' Mode* (1989). He died of cancer in 1993.

Taken together, Anthony Burgess's novels that may be classified as science fiction represent an essentially mainstream approach to the genre. *A Clockwork Orange, The Wanting Seed,* and, preeminently, *1985* owe an unmistakable debt to Orwell's *Nineteen Eighty-Four*. Burgess shares Orwell's humanist anxiety of a Wellsian future of concrete and glass utopias eliminating morality based in choice and cleaning up the messiness of human emotions. The notion of Original Sin offers a bizarre "saving grace" for the Manichaean Burgess, who is intent on believing in the Augustinian-Pelagian dialectic that can preserve humanness in the face of the "clockwork" worlds engineered by science and technology. As much as he may have denigrated the genre in his many interviews and fictionally in *The End of the World News,* and as much as he may have struggled futilely to dismiss *A Clockwork Orange* as a display of spleen, Burgess carved a niche for himself in science fiction, and *A Clockwork Orange* will continue to be not only his most famous novel but also one of the masterpieces of twentieth-century fantasy and science fiction.

Interviews:

John Horder, "Art That Pays," *Guardian,* 10 October 1964, p. 5;

Jim Hicks, "Eclectic Author of His Own Five Foot Shelf," *Life* (25 October 1968): 87–97;

Anthony Lewis, "I Love England, but I Will No Longer Live There," *New York Times Magazine,* 3 November 1968, pp. 38–64;

Malcolm Page, "Anthony Burgess: The Author as Performer," *West Coast Review,* 4 (1970): 21–24;

Walter Clemons, "Anthony Burgess: Pushing On," *New York Times Book Review,* 29 November 1970, p. 2;

Sergio Perosa, "Incontri Americani: Anthony Burgess," *Studi Americani,* 17 (1971): 434–438;

Thomas Churchill, "An Interview with Anthony Burgess," *Malahat Review,* 17 (January 1971): 103–127;

G. Riemer, "An Interview with Anthony Burgess," *National Elementary Principal,* 50 (May 1971): 9–21;

Carol Dix, "The Mugging Machine," *Guardian,* 1 January 1972, p. 8;

A. W. Ehrlich, "Anthony Burgess: The Author of *A Clockwork Orange* Now Switches His Attention to Napoleon's Stomach," *Publishers Weekly* (31 January 1972): 182–183;

Dix, "Anthony Burgess," *Transatlantic Review* (Spring–Summer 1972): 183–191;

George Malko, "*Penthouse* Interview: Anthony Burgess," *Penthouse,* 3 (June 1972): 82;

Lemuel Reilly, "An Interview with Anthony Burgess," *Delaware Literary Review,* 2 (1973): 48–55;

Charles T. Bunting, "An Interview in New York with Anthony Burgess," *Studies in the Novel,* 5 (Winter 1973): 505–529;

John Cullinan, "The Art of Fiction XLVIII: Anthony Burgess," *Paris Review* (Spring 1973): 119–163;

K. Pritchard, "A Candid Interview with the Author of *A Clockwork Orange,*" *Seventeen* (August 1973): 236, 249–250;

Sheldon Morley, "Anthony Burgess Answers Back," *Times* (London), 6 August 1973, p. 7;

Albin Krebs, "Notes on People," *New York Times,* 11 April 1974, p. 47;

C. Robert Jennings, "Playboy Interview: Anthony Burgess," *Playboy,* 21 (September 1974): 69–86;

Mike Edelhart, "More Fiction Writing Tips," *Writer's Digest* (August 1975): 13;

James B. Hemesath, "Anthony Burgess," *Transatlantic Review,* 55–56 (May 1976): 96–102;

Robert Robinson, "On Being a Lancashire Catholic," *Listener,* 30 September 1976, pp. 397, 399;

William M. Murray, "Anthony Burgess on 'Apocalypse,'" *Iowa Review,* 8, no. 3 (1977): 37–45;

Dick Reeves, "A Conversation with Novelist Anthony Burgess," New York, Encyclopedia Americana/CBS News Audio Resource Library, 1980;

Helen Dudar, "A Novelist at Home with Papal Politics and Hurdy-Gurdy," *Chicago Times Book World,* 23 November 1980, pp. 1–2;

Rhoda Koenig, "The Unearthly Powers of Anthony Burgess," *Saturday Review* (December 1980): 704–718;

Samuel Coale, "An Interview with Anthony Burgess," *Modern Fiction Studies,* 27 (Autumn 1981): 429–452;

Sophie Lannes, "The Coming Dark Age," *World Press Review,* 28 (December 1981): 34–36;

Pierre Joanon, "Entretien: Anthony Burgess," *Fabula,* 3 (March 1984): 159–168;

Garcia Rodriguez, "Confessiones de un Candido moderno: Entrevista con Anthony Burgess," *Quimera: Revista de Literatura,* 75 (March 1988): 18–33;

Pierre Assouline, "Burgess: Writer and Whirlwind," *World Press Review,* 35 (23 August 1988): 58–59;

Anthony Clare, "Anthony Burgess in Conversation with Dr. Anthony Clare," audiocassette, Sydney, ABC Radio, 1990;

"A Thousand Words before Breakfast: Interview," *Economist,* 321 (19 October 1991): 105–106;

"Conversation: Anthony Burgess Reflects on Language," *U. S. News and World Report,* 115 (18 October 1993): 73.

Bibliographies:

Jeutonne Brewer, *Anthony Burgess: A Bibliography, with a Foreword by Anthony Burgess* (Metuchen, N.J. & London: Scarecrow Press, 1980);

Paul Boytinck, *Anthony Burgess: An Annotated Bibliography and Reference Guide* (New York: Garland, 1985).

References:

Geoffrey Aggeler, *Anthony Burgess: The Artist as Novelist* (University: University of Alabama Press, 1979);

Aggeler, ed., *Critical Essays on Anthony Burgess* (Boston: Hall, 1986);

Harold Bloom, ed., *Anthony Burgess* (New York: Chelsea House, 1987);

Samuel Coale, *Anthony Burgess* (New York: Ungar, 1981);

A. A. De Vitis, *Anthony Burgess* (New York: Twayne, 1972);

Carol M. Dix, *Anthony Burgess,* edited by Ian Scott-Kilvert (London: Longman, 1971);

Robert O. Evans, "Nadsat: The Argot and Its Implications in Anthony Burgess's *A Clockwork Orange,*" *Journal of Modern Literature,* 1 (March 1971): 406–410;

Robert LeClair, "Essential Opposition: The Novels of Anthony Burgess," *Critique: Studies in Modern Fiction,* 12, no. 3 (1971): 77–94;

Robert K. Morris, *The Consolations of Ambiguity: An Essay on the Novels of Anthony Burgess* (Columbia: University of Missouri Press, 1971);

Brian Murdoch, "The Overpopulated Wasteland: Myth in Anthony Burgess's *The Wanting Seed,*" *Revue des Langues Vivantes,* 39, no. 3 (1973): 203–217;

William Pritchard, "The Novels of Anthony Burgess," *Massachusetts Review,* 7 (Summer 1966): 525–539;

Rubin Rabinovitz, "Ethical Values in Anthony Burgess's *A Clockwork Orange,*" *Studies in the Novel,* 11 (Spring 1979): 43–50;

John J. Stinson, *Anthony Burgess Revisited* (Boston: Twayne, 1991).

Papers:

Most of Anthony Burgess's papers are collected at the Mills Memorial Library, McMaster University, Hamilton, Ontario. The manuscripts for most of Burgess's musical compositions are at the University of Texas, Austin.

Ramsey Campbell
(4 January 1946 –   )

Bernadette Lynn Bosky

BOOKS: *The Inhabitant of the Lake and Less Welcome Tenants,* as J. Ramsey Campbell (Sauk City, Wis.: Arkham House, 1964);

Demons by Daylight (Sauk City, Wis.: Arkham House, 1973; London: Star Books, 1975);

The Doll Who Ate His Mother: A Novel of Modern Terror (Indianapolis: Bobbs-Merrill, 1976; London: Millington, 1977);

The Height of the Scream (Sauk City, Wis.: Arkham House, 1976; London: Millington, 1978);

The Bride of Frankenstein, as Carl Dreadstone (New York: Berkley, 1977; London: Universal, 1978);

Dracula's Daughter, as Dreadstone (New York: Berkley, 1977); as E. K. Leyton (London: Star Books, 1980);

The Wolfman, as Dreadstone (New York: Berkley, 1977); as Leyton (London: Star Books, 1980);

The Face That Must Die (abridged, London: Star Books, 1979; restored, Santa Cruz, Cal.: Scream/Press, 1983);

To Wake The Dead (London: Millington, 1980); republished as *The Parasite* (New York: Macmillan, 1980);

The Nameless (New York: Macmillan, 1981; London: Fontana, 1981);

Dark Companions (New York: Macmillan, 1982; London: Fontana, 1982);

Incarnate (New York: Macmillan, 1983; London: Granada, 1984);

Night of the Claw, as Jay Ramsay (New York: St. Martin's Press, 1983); republished as *Claw* (London: Futura, 1983);

Obsession (New York: Macmillan, 1985; London: Granada, 1985);

Cold Print (Santa Cruz, Cal.: Scream/Press, 1985; London: Headline, 1993);

Black Wine, by Campbell and Charles L. Grant, edited by Douglas E. Winter (Niles, Ill.: Dark Harvest, 1986);

The Hungry Moon (New York: Macmillan, 1986; London: Century, 1987);

Ramsey Campbell (photograph by Angus Mackenzie)

Scared Stiff: Tales of Sex and Death (Santa Cruz, Cal.: Scream/Press, 1986; London: Macdonald, 1989);

Dark Feasts: The World of Ramsey Campbell (London: Robinson, 1987);

The Influence (New York: Macmillan, 1988; London: Century, 1988);

Ancient Images (London: Legend/Century, 1989; New York: Scribners, 1989);

Midnight Sun (London: Macdonald, 1990; New York: Tor, 1991);

Needing Ghosts (London: Century, 1990);

The Count of Eleven (London: Macdonald, 1991; New York: Tor, 1992);

Waking Nightmares (New York: Tor, 1991; London: Little, Brown, 1992);

Strange Things and Stranger Places (New York: Tor, 1993);

The Long Lost (London: Headline, 1993; New York: Tor, 1994);

Alone with the Horrors: The Great Short Fiction of Ramsey Campbell, 1961–1991 (Sauk City, Wis.: Arkham House, 1993; London: Headline, 1994);

The One Safe Place (London: Headline, 1995; New York: Tor/Forge, 1996);

Far Away and Never (West Warwick, R.I.: Necronomicon, 1996);

The House on Nazareth Hill (London: Headline, 1996); republished as *Nazareth Hill* (New York: Tor, 1997);

Ghosts and Grisly Things (Nottingham: Pumpkin Books, 1998; New York: Tor, 2000);

The Last Voice They Hear (New York: Tor/Forge, 1998);

Silent Children (New York: Tor/Forge, 2000);

Pact of the Fathers (New York: Forge, 2001);

The Darkest Part of the Woods (Harrogate, U.K.: PS, 2002).

OTHER: "The Christmas Present," in *Nameless Places,* edited by Gerald Page (Sauk City, Wis.: Arkham House, 1975), pp. 255–261;

"The Pattern," in *Superhorror,* edited by Campbell (London: W. H. Allen, 1976; New York: St. Martin's Press, 1977);

"The Face at Pine Dunes" and "The Fit," in *New Tales of the Cthulhu Mythos,* edited by Campbell (Sauk City, Wis.: Arkham House, 1980), pp. 223–253, 325–336;

New Terrors, edited by Campbell (London: Pan, 1980);

New Terrors Two, edited by Campbell (London: Pan, 1980);

"Calling Card," in *The Gruesome Book,* edited by Campbell (London: Piccolo, 1983);

Clive Barker, *Clive Barker's Books of Blood, Volume One,* introduction by Campbell (London: Sphere, 1984; New York: Berkley, 1986);

Thomas Ligotti, *Songs of a Dead Dreamer,* introduction by Campbell (Albuquerque, N.M.: Silver Scarab, 1986; London: Robinson, 1989);

"In the Trees," "Bedtime Story," and "Beyond Words," in *Night Visions 3,* edited by George R. R. Martin (Niles, Ill.: Dark Harvest, 1986), pp. 17–24, 27–35, 45–56, 63–72, 73–82;

The Tomb-Herd and Others, special issue of *Crypt of Cthulhu,* no. 43, edited by Robert M. Price (Mount Olive, N.C.: Cryptic Publications, 1986);

Ghostly Tales, special issue of *Crypt of Cthulhu,* no. 50, edited by Price (Mount Olive, N.C.: Cryptic Publications, 1987);

Stephen Jones and Kim Newman, eds., *Horror: 100 Best Books,* introduction by Campbell (New York: Carroll & Graf, 1988);

Fine Frights: Stories That Scared Me, edited by Campbell (New York: Tor, 1988);

"James Herbert: Notes toward a Reappraisal," in *Discovering Modern Horror Fiction II,* edited by Darrell Schweitzer (Mercer Island, Wash.: Starmont, 1988);

"It Helps If You Sing," in *Best New Horror,* edited by Campbell and Jones (London: Robinson, 1990), pp. 67–74;

Best New Horror 2, edited by Campbell and Jones (London: Robinson, 1991);

"The Same in Any Language," in *Best New Horror 3,* edited by Campbell and Jones (London: Robinson, 1992), pp. 15–26;

"McGonagall in the Head," in *Uncanny Banquet,* edited by Campbell (London: Little, Brown, 1992), pp. 151–169;

Best New Horror 4, edited by Campbell and Jones (London: Robinson, 1993);

Horror Writers of America Present: Deathport, edited by Campbell and Martin Harry Greenberg (New York: Pocket Books, 1993);

Best New Horror 5, edited by Campbell and Jones (London: Robinson, 1994);

"Lovecraft in Retrospect," in *NecronomiCon: Second Edition* (Danvers, Mass.: Lovecraft Society of New England, 1995);

"The Word," in *Revelations,* edited by Douglas E. Winter (New York: HarperPrism, 1997);

Meddling with Ghosts: Stories in the Tradition of M. R. James, edited by Campbell (Boston Spa: British Library, 2001).

RECORDING: *Twilight Tales from Merseyside,* readings by Campbell (West Warwick, R.I.: Necronomicon Press, 1995).

SELECTED PERIODICAL PUBLICATIONS–UNCOLLECTED: "Midnight Appointment," *St. Edwards College Magazine,* 1, no. 4 (1959): 201–202;

"Night Beat," *Haunt of Horror,* 1 (June 1973): 116–120;

"The Burning," *Ghosts & Scholars,* no. 3 (1981): 2–5;

"Snakes and Ladders," *Twilight Zone,* 2 (April 1982): 80–84;

"The Sneering," *Fantasy Tales,* no. 14 (Summer 1985): 3–10;

"Bait," *Weird Tales,* no. 301 (Summer 1991): 20–32, 88–91;

"A Play for the Jaded," *Worlds of Fantasy and Horror,* 1 (Summer 1994): 36–37;

Dust jacket for Campbell's 1986 novel, in which an evangelist becomes possessed by a supernatural entity (Richland County Public Library)

"Raised by the Moon," *Spook,* June 2001 <http://www.thespook.com/cd.html>.

Ramsey Campbell's work is notable for both its focus and its breadth. His novels, short fiction, and even nonfiction always concern, in one way or another, the emotions of fear and horror. Characteristic themes weave throughout Campbell's works: the uncertain nature of reality, the dangers of repressed fears and desires, and the reactions of ordinary people in extraordinary circumstances. Campbell has developed a strong, distinctive voice in a field where too many authors are too easily classifiable as "in the tradition of" someone else. In his *Faces of Fear: Encounters with the Creators of Modern Horror* (1985) Douglas E. Winter praises Campbell's "stylish sophistication and intensely suggestive vision"; Gary William Crawford writes in *Ramsey Campbell* (1988) that Campbell's prose "is like no other in supernatural horror fiction."

Campbell is always refining his craft. "As far as I'm concerned," Campbell stated in a 1990 interview by Stanley Wiater, "the whole business of writing is a process of trying to do things you didn't do last time." Also, unlike many writers, he writes both supernatural horror—such as *The Nameless* (1981), *Incarnate* (1983), and *The Long Lost* (1993)—and stories with no supernatural elements, such as *The Face That Must Die* (1979) and *The One Safe Place* (1995). While Campbell is best known for certain settings and kinds of characters—both somewhat autobiographical—his novels and hundreds of short stories show a range that belies that simple reputation. His protagonists are generally everyday people, but may be male or female, of all ages from children to the elderly; they do tend to be working or middle class, but that is not universal.

Campbell is a presence at many science-fiction and horror conventions, frequent presenter of public readings and lectures, and president of the British Fantasy Society and the Society of Fantastic Films. Winter described Campbell in 1985: "He has the appearance of a displaced child, with a wide, smiling, boyish face" and "perennially twinkling" eyes. If he had not become a writer of horror fiction, Campbell told Winter, he might have become a stand-up comedian; and even his most grim fiction includes puns and other wordplay.

Yet, if one were to invent a stereotyped childhood for an author of horror fiction, one could hardly outdo Campbell's, as described in "At the Back of My Mind: A Guided Tour," his introduction to the 1983 Scream/Press edition of *The Face That Must Die.* An only child, John Ramsey Campbell was born on 4 January 1946 in Liverpool, into a household noteworthy only for its marital dysfunction. Campbell recalls an argument, when he was three years old, in which his mother accidentally put her hand through plate glass; but mostly there were just verbal disagreements.

However, his mother, Nora Campbell (née Walker), grew increasingly paranoid, and his father, Alexander Ramsey, a policeman, became estranged from his son. Since his mother was a Catholic, unable to get a divorce on grounds of mental cruelty and loath to divorce in any case, an odd compromise developed: although his father continued to live in the house, Campbell did not see him for nearly twenty years. "Heard but not seen," Campbell's father was a fearsome presence, or absence: "In my teens I sometimes came home," Campbell writes, "from work or from the cinema, at the same time as my father, who would hold the front door closed from inside to make sure we never came face to face. Very occasionally, when it was necessary for him to get in touch, he would leave me a note, in French."

Campbell's mother was a writer of thrillers herself, although only a few of her short stories had appeared in a Yorkshire magazine before Campbell was born. She encouraged her son's writing and accompanied him to movies such as director Jacques Tourneur's *Night of the Demon* (1957), Hammer Film Productions horror pictures, and the movies of William Castle. Yet, as Campbell approached his teens, his mother—thirty-six when Campbell was born—became increasingly erratic. She felt that the radio soap opera she listened to nightly was giving her messages that her books would be published; when they failed to sell to editors, "she concluded that the messages were deliberate lies, meant to break her down," Campbell writes. From Campbell's childhood to age fifteen, his maternal grandmother came to live with them; his mother gave the grandmother a room of her own and shared a room, and a single bed, with her son. As his mother withdrew further from reality, he argued with her; as a result, she believed he was involved in the conspiracies against her. He began to talk about these events only after his mother died in 1982, but connections can be seen in many of his stories.

In other ways Campbell's experience was more common. He was educated in Liverpool: Christ the King Primary from 1951 through 1953; Ryebank Private School from 1953 through 1957; and a Christian Brothers school, St. Edward's College, which he left in 1962. Overweight, with what he regarded as a "posh" accent, Campbell was "painfully shy and sensitive throughout his youth," Kenneth Jurkiewicz writes. Jurkiewicz describes St. Edward's as "an expensive, rigorous, all-boys'" school, and states that it helped teach Campbell "both peculiarly Catholic guilt feelings and an unhealthy fear of women."

Campbell remembers early impressions from supernatural fiction, including George MacDonald's *The Princess and the Goblin* (1871), which he read when he was six and which, he stated in a 1982 interview with Jeffrey M. Elliot, "kept me awake in a state of panic for several nights." Campbell was also influenced toward horror by *Weird Tales,* a pulp magazine that published a broad range of horror fiction, from sleazy to sublime. The cover of the November 1952 issue impressed him deeply; he purchased remaindered British reprints, beginning when he was ten. Campbell also was affected as a teenager by his reading of supernatural classics by M. R. James, Algernon Blackwood, Arthur Machen, J. Sheridan Le Fanu, and Ray Bradbury. Like many of his contemporaries, Campbell also found his love of horror fed and shaped by *Great Tales of Terror and the Supernatural* (1944), a monumental anthology edited by Herbert A. Wise and Phyllis Fraser.

Dust jacket for the U.S. edition of Campbell's 1989 novel, in which an investigator uncovers a series of unfortunate occurrences and violent deaths associated with a 1930s horror movie and the fifteenth-century events on which it was based (Richland County Public Library)

Campbell not only read but also wrote as a youth. His first poem appeared in the "Children's Corner" of the *Liverpool Echo* in 1951; that and "*Black Fingers from Space* by John R. Campbell (aged 7 1/2)" are reprinted in the introduction to *The Height of the Scream* (1976). At eleven, Campbell told Elliot, he wrote "an abortive imitation of Arthur Machen," and at twelve, "30,000 words in slavish imitation of John Dickson Carr." However, the most significant spur to the young writer was finding the fiction of H. P. Lovecraft, in the form of a secondhand paperback purchased from Bascombe's, a Liverpool shop, when he was fourteen. "Lovecraft," Campbell stated to Elliot, "gave me the impetus to *finish* stories." In 1958, Darrell Schweitzer reports, Campbell submitted "an illustrated book-length collection of stories to T. V. Boardman & Co." and received "an encouraging rejection letter." This collection of twenty stories, *Ghostly Tales,* was influenced by James and by Dennis Wheatley; it was finally published in 1987 as a special issue of *The Crypt of Cthulhu,* a Lovecraftian journal.

More encouragement came from August Derleth, a younger friend of Lovecraft's who in 1939 had started Arkham House, a small press, in order to publish Lovecraft's fiction in hardback. At the suggestion of two fantasy fans, Pat Kearney and Betty Kujawa, Campbell sent some stories to Derleth. These stories were imitations of Lovecraft's in style and substance; Derleth encouraged Campbell to find his own style and to learn from other authors such as James. Campbell diligently reworked his fiction; these early stories are still derivative but were strong enough for Derleth to publish. "The Church in High Street," a story of nameless gelatinous horrors hidden deep beneath a church, became Campbell's first published story, in Derleth's 1962 anthology *Dark Mind, Dark Heart;* S. T. Joshi states that Derleth extensively rewrote it.

Two years later, when Campbell was eighteen, Arkham House published Campbell's first book, a collection of Lovecraftian short stories called *The Inhabitant of the Lake and Less Welcome Tenants* (1964). "I regard *The Inhabitant of the Lake* as a youthful indiscretion," Campbell stated in an interview with Schweitzer, "something which I had to do, but which is now over." Yet, Campbell still has high regard for Lovecraft, particularly his ability to unfold a structure. "His early stuff seemed to work extremely well in terms of building things up very gradually, almost musically," Campbell told Winter. Many of the stories in Campbell's first volume are set in his "own fictional domain," as Jurkiewicz writes, "the Severn Valley of central England, with its cursed Roman ruins, seemingly bucolic countryside, dying industrial towns, and creepy villages."

Even early in his career, Campbell showed his potential as more than a Lovecraftian. Recently having read Vladimir Nabokov—especially *Lolita* (1955) and *Pale Fire* (1962)—Campbell experimented with style in his story "The Stone on the Island," published in 1963 in *Over the Edge,* edited by Derleth, and reprinted in *Cold Print* (1985). "The Cellars" was written in 1965 and published in *Travellers by Night,* another Derleth anthology, in 1967 (later reprinted in *The Height of the Scream*). It is one of the first stories in which Campbell develops realistic characters, based partly on his own experience; and the horror element owes as much to Machen as it does to Lovecraft. In *Ramsey Campbell,* Crawford states that the story was a turning point for Campbell in two ways: it addresses the threat of sexuality, at least implicitly; and it establishes the decaying urban setting for which Campbell became known.

After leaving school, Campbell worked for four years as a tax officer for Inland Revenue, living at home with his mother. In 1966 he went to work in the Liverpool Public Library system. Campbell was briefly engaged in 1967 to Rosemary Prince, a librarian and musician, but her parents terminated the engagement.

Campbell had better luck with Jenny Chandler, the daughter of Australian science-fiction writer A. Bertram Chandler. He met her briefly at a science-fiction convention in 1969; in 1970 they met again and began dating. They were married on 1 January 1971 and honeymooned in the Lake District. Shortly after the honeymoon, Campbell visited his father, dying in the hospital, and son and father met face-to-face for the first time in decades. Campbell writes that his wife encouraged him to see his father and later helped him process some of his feelings about his parents.

Campbell had begun reviewing movies for BBC Radio Merseyside in 1969. In 1973 he quit library work to become a full-time fiction writer and movie reviewer, at first depending on his wife's salary from teaching. That same year, Arkham House published Campbell's second collection of short stories, *Demons by Daylight.* Many of the stories take place in the Severn Valley, but in these tales Campbell is finding his own, non-Lovecraftian, voice. "Potential" tells the story of Charles, an uncomfortable young office worker who, at "BRICHESTER'S FIRST BE-IN," meets a man named Cook who wants to help Charles realize his potential; in someone's flat, surrounded by decadent art and music and even more decadent partiers, Charles murders Cook and is accepted into the group. Campbell uses British culture excellently in "The Guy," a story of supernatural revenge by someone burned to death on Guy Fawkes Night. In this collection Campbell introduces the fictitious Lovecraftian writer from Brichester as a character, Errol Undercliffe. *Demons by Daylight* received generally positive reviews, including one by T. E. D. Klein, prompting Campbell's decision to become a full-time writer.

At the prompting of his American agent, Kirby McCauley, Campbell wrote a novel in order to more firmly establish himself in the horror field. *The Doll Who Ate His Mother: A Novel of Modern Terror* (1976) is structured like a detective novel, as a group of people find out about and pursue Chris Kelley, a cannibal with a supernatural origin. The characters are well drawn, although as Stephen King wrote in a review for *Whispers* (1978), "perhaps the central character here is Liverpool itself, with its orange sodium lights, its slums and docks." In this novel Campbell developed what Crawford calls his "cinematic" style, using details of scenery to create striking images. Campbell stated to Elliot that readers have brought to his attention a "holy family" theme in the novel: "Christopher born unnaturally, Mary who looks after him, St. Joseph's where she sends him for the good of his

Dust jacket for Campbell's 1993 collection of short fiction, stories written between 1961 and 1991
(Richland County Public Library)

soul." The novel, which is accomplished but too bleak for many readers, sold poorly.

A third collection of short fiction, *The Height of the Scream,* was published by Arkham House in 1976. In this collection Campbell fully shakes off the mantle of a Lovecraft imitator. Crawford's statement about Campbell's fiction in general applies to this collection: "His characters are normal human beings, at least his protagonists are, who find a horrifying mental and material universe, within themselves and within others." Campbell uses autobiographical material, especially regarding his past romances, in "The Cellars" and "Reply Guaranteed." In fact, in sharp contrast to Lovecraft, Campbell explored sexual themes more openly as his career progressed, as the homosexual panic in "The Telephones" shows in this volume. "Missing," a story of obsession told in diary form, was influenced by William F. Harvey's "August Heat" (1910); "The Words that Count," Campbell states, was influenced by Nabokov's "The Vane Sisters" (1958–1959). "The Scar" is a doppelgänger story set in Lower Brichester, a terrifying exploration of the fear of being replaced. "Smoke Kiss," featuring a children's comic-book artist

as the protagonist, so thoroughly explores the lure and disgust of cigarettes that Campbell says he quit smoking shortly thereafter.

Superhorror (1976) began Campbell's career as a premier anthologist. As an editor, Campbell stated to Wiater, he picks stories that "disturb" him or "somehow astonish him." His anthologies show the range of contemporary horror writers he likes and respects, from King to Robert Aickman, Fritz Leiber, and Thomas Ligotti. Campbell often includes his own work in his anthologies as well. *Superhorror* and *The Height of the Scream* were nominated for World Fantasy Awards.

For financial reasons, in 1976 Campbell wrote novelizations of three Universal Pictures horror movies, under the house name Carl Dreadstone. Campbell may also have welcomed a chance to practice the novelist's craft without risking his own name. All three were published in 1977: *The Bride of Frankenstein, The Wolfman,* and *Dracula's Daughter.* The work went quickly and was enjoyable; the books, though not exemplary among Campbell's fiction, are entertaining. Based on the screenplays but showing obvious influence from the movies as well, the novelizations all add psychological

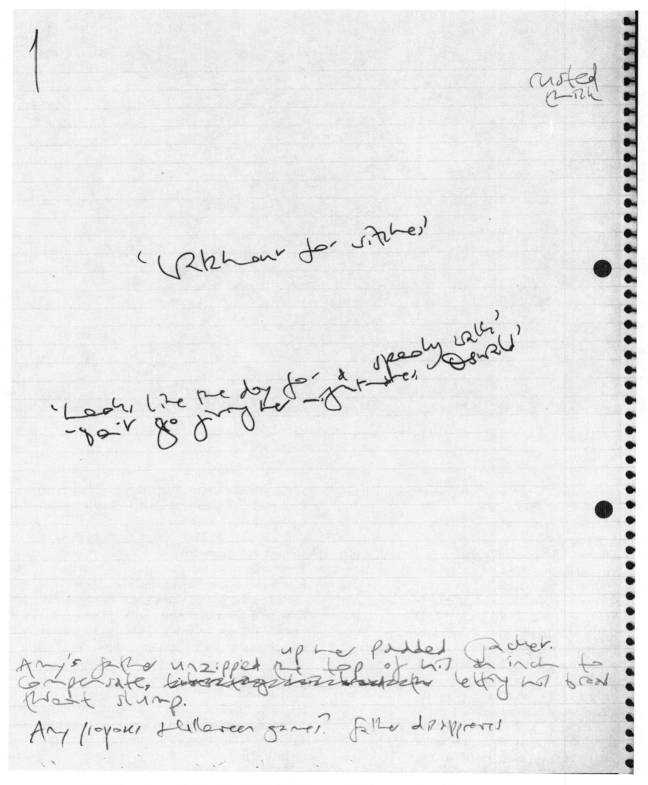

Opening pages from a draft for "Nazarill," published in 1996 as The House on Nazareth Hill *(Collection of Ramsey Campbell)*

As soon as Amy left the church she knew the family would have to go up to the spider house. Half an hour ago she should have been able to see the roof over the yellowish buildings of Partington, but now the October sky had fallen on it, or else a fog had. Above the market-place surrounded by dark grey roofs pinched steep, and below the hem of the fog attached to the sky, the hulking house riddled with black holes of windows squatted in its park. Her parents were lingering in the church porch while the priest remarked on how tall she was growing, which only made her feel smaller, unless it was the sight of the house too big for the town which did. Then the priest said 'Have a decent week,' which she thought rather vague for a priest to say, and let himself into the church, releasing a faint scent of incense to mix with the moist autumn smell. Her parents came out to stand on either side of her, and her father took hold of his hip-bones so as to drum on them with his thumbs. 'I wouldn't drive in this if I didn't have to,' he said as though he was talking about himself.

'If we only did what we had to, [...], Oswald,' Amy's mother responded, 'it wouldn't be much of a life.'

'No, but you take my point, don't you?' He gave a plump chuckle that was meant to contradict his earnestness. 'I can see Amy does. This is no day for driving except on business.'

Of course he and her mother had already known he meant that, and the conversation was one of the many games they played together, maybe partly for her benefit, maybe to make themselves seem as young as most of her friends' parents were, though to Amy they were only as old as they'd always been and had to be. 'I'd be happy to stay by the fire,' her mother said, pulling at her polo-neck to cover more of the little cuff of flesh under her chin and zipping... 'We haven't heard from my other lady yet. What's your idea of a Sunday well spent, Amy?' All the tonsils with jackets who making Amy [...] feel restricted by... 'Could we take out a Halloween video?' 'They're a bit old for you yet, sweetheart.' Her mother looked concerned, widening her eyes between

ROOMS NOBODY SEES

Years later Amy would remember the day she saw inside the spider house. She knew as soon as the family came out of the church that they wouldn't be going for a drive. Half an hour ago she'd seen the rusted moor over the yellowish cottages of Partington, but now the late October sky had fallen on it, or rather a fog had. Above the marketplace surrounded by dark grey roofs pinched steep, and beneath the hem of the fog attached to the sky, the hulk of a building riddled with black windows squatted in its park. Her parents were lingering in the church porch while the priest remarked on how tall she was growing, which only made her feel smaller, unless it was the sight of the building too big for the town that did. Then the priest said "Watch out for witches" and took his bright scrubbed face into the church, which released a faint scent of incense to mix with the moist autumnal smell.

"Funny thing for a priest to say," Amy's father remarked.

"He means the day, Oswald," said her mother.

"I know it, but just the same, a priest. So long as he doesn't think too much that's of yore is a joke."

"Don't be digging up your antique words, you sound more ancient than me."

"She isn't ancient, is she, Amy?"

"Only like you."

"That's you put in your place," Amy's mother told him, and pulled at her polo-neck to cover more of the little ruff of flesh under her

11

First page of text in Nazareth Hill *(1997), the U.S. edition of* The House on Nazareth Hill
(Richland County Public Library)

insight and back story. Each volume also includes an introduction under Campbell's own name.

"A New Life," published in *Strange Things and Stranger Places* (1993), features Frankenstein's monster and was written in 1976. The idea probably occurred to Campbell while writing *The Bride of Frankenstein;* Joshi reports that Campbell's usual habit is to write only one work at a time, keeping a file of ideas while writing novels and turning to short stories immediately after.

In August 1978 the Campbells had the first of their two children, Tamsin Joanne. Campbell also won the first two of many awards: the World Fantasy Award (or "Howard") for best short story, for "The Chimney," first published in *Whispers;* and the British Fantasy Award for best short story, for "In the Bag," first published in Hugh Lamb's *Cold Fear: New Tales of Terror* (1977). Both stories appear in *Dark Companions* (1982).

"Loveman's Comeback," nominated for a World Fantasy Award in 1978, strongly shows Campbell's increasingly frank approach to sex in his fiction. He stated to Elliot, "For a while, I thought explicit sexual themes and scenes would rob the supernatural elements of power, since those elements often express implicit sexuality. Eventually, though, I wrote some tales that proved me wrong." Bernadette Lynn Bosky writes that "Loveman's Comeback" shows the mixture of disgust and fascination shown in Bram Stoker's *Dracula* (1897), unlike the more erotic vampire stories of Anne Rice and others.

The next novel under Campbell's own name, *The Face That Must Die,* became his most controversial novel. This tale of a serial murderer had trouble finding a publisher; the version published in 1979 was significantly cut, including the removal of many of the killer's punning thoughts. The novel is—in a claustrophobia-inducing way—told from the point of view of John Horridge, who comes to believe that Roy Craig, a gentle homosexual man, is killing boys. Actually, Craig is innocent, and Horridge is the monster. Campbell stated to Wiater that the novel "certainly had problems at the outset. People said it was too grim, too relentless." Scream/Press published a restored version of the novel in 1983.

The true "breakout" novel for Campbell was *To Wake The Dead* (1980), also titled *The Parasite;* it was financially successful and won the British Fantasy Award for best novel in 1980. The point-of-view character, Rose Tierney, is certainly more congenial than that of *The Face That Must Die.* She is invaded by a malignant supernatural being during a seance in childhood but represses the event, developing into a successful movie critic in a good marriage. After she is mugged in New York City, however, she begins to show psychic abilities, including out-of-body travel; these developments strain her mind and her relationship with her skeptical husband. She finds that she may be "infected" by Peter Grace, a black magician, whom Campbell connects to Adolf Hitler's well-known interest in the occult. The British and American editions have different epilogues, both twist endings.

New Tales of the Cthulhu Mythos (1980) was to be edited by Derleth, but after his death the project was given to Campbell. The anthology features "Dark Awakening" by Lovecraft's old friend Frank Belknap Long, and works by Klein, Basil Copper, King, and others. Campbell also won another World Fantasy Award in 1980 for his short story "Mackintosh Willy," first published in *Shadows 2* (1979), edited by Charles L. Grant.

The title of *The Nameless* refers to a murderous mind-control cult run by Kaspar Ganz. Barbara Waugh, a literary agent, receives a phone call from her daughter Angela; long thought killed, Angela has been made to join the Nameless and is now trying to break away. The novel has an especially well-structured beginning, with a mysterious prologue and chapter-long flashbacks after the phone call; it uses a wider range of settings than past novels by Campbell, including Glasgow. Angela's psychic abilities are used in a startling ending. The two most striking aspects of the novel are its depiction of Angela's consciousness and its use of realistic urban settings—what Campbell called, in the interview with Wiaters, "grimness" as "a sort of social commentary."

By 1981 the Campbells had moved to the suburb of Wallasey, across the Mersey from Liverpool. Their second child, Matthew Ramsey, was born there in June 1981. Campbell was still reviewing movies—and now horror fiction as well—for BBC Merseyside radio. In 1982 he began a screenplay for producer Milton Subotsky, based on Robert E. Howard's character Solomon Kane, yet the project never reached fulfillment.

Campbell said to Elliot in 1982, "Enough people have complained that some of my earlier work is unnecessarily obscure that I now try to make myself clearer, though not so clear as to rob the supernatural of all mystery." Campbell's frequent public readings also motivated him to clarify his work. As shown in the collection *Dark Companions* (1982) and the novel *Incarnate,* he succeeded. Unlike in earlier work, the idea of the story is always clear; yet, Campbell's writing continued to explore subjective realities and twists in the world as readers know it, and did so equally effectively in less murky prose.

Dark Companions includes several of Campbell's best stories, primarily written between 1973 and 1982. "Napier Court," the only exception, was written in 1967; in it, Crawford writes, Campbell "blends dream and waking state, making no attempt to draw a line between the two." Like the stories in *The Height of the Scream,* it uses bits of autobiography. "Call First" and "Heading Home" employ twist or shock endings. The former builds strongly and naturally. The latter, although somewhat gimmicky, is an interesting exercise in second-person narration; in an interview with Schweitzer, Campbell stated that he consciously wrote the story in homage to the EC (Entertainment Comics) horror comics of the 1950s. The strongest stories are tales of revenge, works more of unease than of explicit violence. The title character of "Mackintosh Willy" is an old alcoholic bum, killed by children, who assembles a body out of urban trash to get vengeance; and "Baby," more visceral, refers to the vengeful familiar of a murdered bag lady. "The Pattern" is set in the Severn Valley but is Lovecraftian only in the sense of awful wonder it inspires; the crisp dialogue and realistic, even mundane, events set up an eerie time-loop revelation. "The Chimney" explores a child's fear of a burned creature that is identified with both the child's father and Father Christmas.

Incarnate was published in 1983, and in 1985 it won the British World Fantasy Award for best novel. It is a tour de force exploration of reality and illusion, in which five people involved in an Oxford experiment in psychic dreaming find, eleven years later, that their dreams are bleeding out into their lives. Campbell reverses the technique of earlier stories, in which reality is portrayed as dream-like; Joshi writes, "here dreams have the crystal clarity that we normally expect from real worlds." In fact, while in many Campbell works the characters—and readers—doubt what is really going on, in *Incarnate* they often accept as mundane things that shockingly reveal themselves to be dreams or supernatural intrusions. The novel is carefully structured and includes settings such as Chapel Hill, North Carolina, where Campbell had visited friends David Drake, a popular author of science fiction, horror, and fantasy, and Karl Edward Wagner, horror author and editor of horror anthologies.

Campbell used a pseudonym, Jay Ramsay, for *Night of the Claw* (1983), occasioning speculation as to the reason. Actually, Campbell's publisher was wary of having another book released by the same author so quickly after *Incarnate* and *Dark Companions*—the same concern that helped create King's pseudonym, Richard Bachman. The novel does stand out in its sustained use of Africa as a setting and African lore concerning the cannibalistic secret society of Leopard Men. A metal claw made by them, taken to England, exerts a supernatural influence on the protagonist, writer Alan Knight, and those around him.

Joshi calls *Obsession* (1985) the closest thing to a mainstream novel Campbell had then written; with effort, it could be viewed as a story of guilt leading the protagonist, Peter Priest, to acts of violence and then suicide. However, while some events are explained by natural means, others are not. *Obsession* can also be seen as the story of a deal with the devil, albeit an anonymous devil who seems to want not souls but misery.

The Hungry Moon (1986), which in 1988 won the British Fantasy Award for best novel, is unquestionably supernatural, even mythic. An evangelist from California, Godwin Mann, comes to the town of Moonwell, where a local horror has been kept under control by rituals. Mann enters the pit to confront the entity and inadvertently frees it; it merges with Mann's body and begins to destroy the town with darkness and violence. Mann's antagonist is a teacher, Diana Kramer, who has visions explaining the entity's nature and is able to drive it off. The satire of American fundamentalism is broad but not inappropriate to the story.

In the mid 1980s a specialty publisher named Scream/Press began producing well-made editions of Campbell's works, illustrated by J. K. Potter. *Cold Print* (1985) collects Campbell's Lovecraftian pieces, including the title story. *Scared Stiff: Tales of Sex and Death* (1986) includes some of his more explicitly sexual stories, including "Loveman's Comeback"; the volume was nominated for a World Fantasy Award in 1988. A first "best of" collection appeared from Robinson Publishing in 1987. By this time, Campbell still wrote short stories, but most of his fiction energies went to novels. He also continued his nonfiction work, with articles and reviews appearing in *Fantasy Review* from 1984 to 1986; later his "Ramsey Campbell, Probably" column appeared in *Necrofile* from 1991 to 2000 and in the online publication *The Spook* beginning in 2001.

At the end of the 1980s Campbell was publishing a novel a year: *The Influence* (1988), *Ancient Images* (1989), and *Midnight Sun* (1990). *The Influence* won the British Fantasy Award in 1989, and its Spanish translation, *Ultratumba,* was awarded the Premios Gigamesh in 1994. *Ancient Images* received the Bram Stoker Award for best novel in 1989, and *Midnight Sun* won the 1991 British Fantasy Award.

The Influence presents a comparatively traditional story for a Campbell novel: an old woman's spirit takes over the body of her grandniece. This novel was the first for which Campbell used a word processor, although he still composed the first draft in notebooks, using longhand.

Campbell shows his love of 1930s horror movies in *Ancient Images:* Graham Nolan, a researcher for British television, locates the lost motion picture *Tower of Fear,* starring Boris Karloff and Bela Lugosi; before the first showing, he commits suicide. Most of the novel follows Nolan's friend Sandy Allen, who uncovers first the unfortunate occurrences surrounding the movie, and then the series of violent deaths, occurring every fifty years since 1438, on which the movie was based. Some critics disliked the mixture of natural and supernatural explanations for the deaths, while others stated that it gives the novel range and credibility. This novel introduces a common theme in Campbell's later works: the prejudice against horror cinema and literature as art, which Campbell examines critically and mostly fairly.

In *Midnight Sun* Campbell develops his own mythology. The last third of the novel, concerning a town beset by evil, is comparable to Peter Straub's *Ghost Story* (1979) or King's *Salem's Lot* (1975). The protagonist is Ben Sterling, an author of children's books, whose great-grandfather was a folklorist. As an adult with two children, Sterling moves to his great-grandfather's house in Stargrave and becomes fascinated by the nearby forest in which his ancestor died. Characters sense "a presence," some unknown being associated with ice and the increasingly harsh winter; Sterling himself becomes unnaturally cold to the touch, possessed by an eternal ice creature. Moved by love for his family, Sterling sacrifices himself to stop the apocalyptic cold.

Reception of Campbell's next novel, *The Count of Eleven* (1991), was more mixed than that of *Midnight Sun*—in fact, than most of his novels except *The Face that Must Die*—partly because of its blend of comedy and horror. A cautionary tale of superstition, this nonsupernatural thriller tells the story of Jack Orchard, first the owner of a video rental store and then a librarian, who feels he is at the mercy of luck in the form of numbers, especially 11 and 13, and a chain letter that appears after a series of personal and professional disasters. In trying to change his luck by hand-delivering chain letters, Orchard first accidentally burns down a house and progresses to deliberate arson and murder. Joshi writes, "Campbell manages Jack's transition from klutz to killer with superb skill." In 1991 Campbell also won the British Fantasy Award and World Fantasy Award, for editing, with Stephen Jones, the beginning of the *Best New Horror* series of anthologies.

Campbell's first collection of new (or at least recent) short fiction in almost a decade, *Waking Nightmares,* was published in 1991; *Strange Things and Stranger Places* followed in 1993. The former includes stories published from 1980 to 1989, although "Jack in the Box," a second-person narration in which the reader identifies with something undead making its way out of a coffin, was written in 1974. Often children appear as victims, as in "The Other Side," or as vehicles for supernatural punishment of adults, as in "Bedtime Story" and "Eye of Childhood." *Waking Nightmares* also

includes "Watch the Birdie," which had been published in 1984 by Rosemary Pardoe's Haunted Library in an edition of one hundred signed copies. The 1993 collection is more uneven. Steven J. Mariconda argues in a 1993 *Necrofile* article that in "Needing Ghosts," a novella in the third-person present tense, Campbell "takes many risks and mostly succeeds." However, Mariconda calls "Medusa," a science-fiction novella, "an ambitious and interesting failure."

The Long Lost (1993), winner of the 1994 British Fantasy Award for best novel, is surprisingly Christian in its material. On a vacation to Wales, exploring a small island, David and Joelle Owain find an old woman, whom they believe to be their "long-lost relative" Gwendolen Owain. They bring her back home, and she begins giving indications of her ancient, supernatural nature. Neighbors undergo disasters after eating her cakes at a party; David and Joelle act strangely, including David's becoming obsessed with the fourteen-year-old daughter of a friend. Gwendolen is a "sin-eater," who takes on the sins of the dead; she has placed all her accumulated sins in the cakes, giving them to others to free herself to die. What is the sin so great that she feared to die? The novel hints that the answer may be biblical. Also in 1993 Arkham House published *Alone with the Horrors: The Great Short Fiction of Ramsey Campbell, 1961–1991.*

In the mid to late 1990s, Campbell received honors recognizing his overall accomplishment: the *Liverpool Daily Post & Echo* Award for Literature, 1994; the Premio alla Carriera a Ramsey Campbell, an award from the Fantafestival in Rome, Italy, 1995; and the Grand Master Award from the World Horror Convention and the Lifetime Achievement Award from the Horror Writers Association, both in 1999.

Despite its biblical-sounding name, *The House on Nazareth Hill* (1996) is a traditional haunted-house story, combined with chilling extremes of domestic disharmony between a widowed father and his teenage daughter, Amy. Featuring a time loop as in "The Pattern," the novel also explores the history of Nazarill, a mental hospital during the seventeenth and eighteenth centuries at which witches are rumored to have performed rituals. The conflagration that burned down the mental hospital with all inside is echoed in modern events as the domestic tragedy reaches its end. The novel won the International Horror Guild Award for best novel in 1998.

The One Safe Place (1995), *The Last Voice They Hear* (1998), and *Silent Children* (2000) are nonsupernatural thrillers examining violence, especially its effects on the young. The complicated, well-structured plot of *The One Safe Place* brings together the Travis family—a professor and bookstore owner with a teenage son, who move to

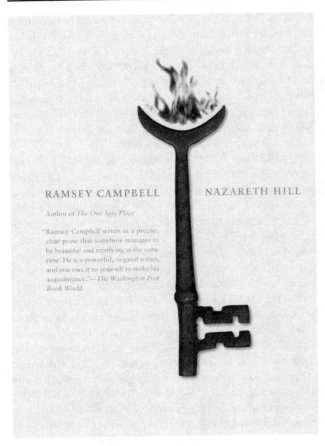

*Dust jacket for the U.S. edition of Campbell's novel about a
seventeenth- and eighteenth-century mental hospital where
witches are said to have performed rituals
(Richland County Public Library)*

England from America—and the Fancy family, barely
working-class criminals from Manchester. In horrific
but credible events, young Marshall Travis is dosed
with LSD by Darren Fancy, also a teenager, and
induced to play Russian roulette; in one particularly
shocking scene, Don Travis is kicked and beaten to
death. Campbell examines the grim fascination of guns,
which seem to promise safety but promote the use of
force. Suzanne Travis teaches a class at the university
on violence in cinema, allowing Campbell to explore
censorship as an issue as well.

The Last Voice They Hear demonstrates the flower-
ing of family abuse into violence. Ben Davenport kills
elderly couples, tying them together and gluing their
lips into a parody of a kiss. His motives are tied to his
persecution of his half brother, whom he blames for not
rescuing him from family abuse and neglect when they
were children.

Silent Children analyzes audience reactions to
crimes and horror stories. Hector Woollie is a child

murderer and, like serial killer John Wayne Gacy, a
contractor; one body is found under a suburban home
he worked on in Wembley. The mother and teenage
son, Ian, who had lived there move back in, despite
opposition from the neighbors; they rent a room to Jack
Lamb, ostensibly an American horror novelist. Actually, Lamb is Woollie's son, writing a book about the
crimes; soon the elder Woollie, presumed dead, is back
on the scene and kidnaps Ian. Joshi notes the vividness
of even minor characters in the novel as well as Campbell's "satirical edge."

In his introduction to *Strange Things and Stranger
Places* Campbell writes, "The strangest place most of us
ordinarily see is the world, but familiarity tends to
make us forget how strange it is. One thing horror fiction can do is remind us." Whether in short stories or
novels, Campbell continues to show what horror fiction
can do.

Interviews:

"The Mythos Writers: Ramsey Campbell," *Fantasy
Macabre* (1981): 3–7;

Jeffrey M. Elliot, "Ramsey Campbell: Journeys into the
Unknown," *Whispers,* no. 314 (1982): 15–24;

Douglas E. Winter, "Ramsey Campbell," in his *Faces of
Fear: Encounters with the Creators of Modern Horror*
(New York: Berkley, 1985), pp. 65–78;

Robin Bromley, "Breaking In: Ramsey Campbell,"
Twilight Zone, no. 1 (April 1986): 28–29;

Phillip Vine, "Ramsey Campbell," *Interzone,* no. 28
(March–April 1989): 11–16;

Marc A. Cerasini, "A Talk with Ramsey Campbell," in
*How to Write Horror and Get It Published: Advice from
Top Horror Experts,* edited by Cerasini (Brooklyn
Heights, N.Y.: Romantic Times, 1989), pp. 110–117;

Peter Crowther, "Ramsey Campbell: An Interview,"
Midnight Graffiti, no. 5 (Spring 1990): 55–62;

Stanley Wiater, "Ramsey Campbell," in his *Dark
Dreamers: Conversations with the Masters of Horror*
(New York: Avon, 1990), pp. 35–42;

Stephen Jones, "*Weird Tales* Talks with Ramsey Campbell," *Weird Tales,* no. 301 (Summer 1991): 44–
51;

T. Liam McDonald, "The Dangerous Edge of Things:
Ramsey Campbell," *Cemetery Dance,* 4, no. 3 (Fall
1991): 20–27;

Kevin Proulx, "Ramsey Campbell," in his *Fear to the
World: Eleven Voices in a Chorus of Horror* (Mercer
Island, Wash.: Starmont, 1992), pp. 11–23;

Stan Nicholls, "Finds Dreaming on the Page Bloody
Hard Work," in his *Wordsmiths of Wonder: Fifty
Interviews with Writers of the Fantastic* (London:
Orbit, 1993), pp. 397–403;

Darrell Schweitzer, "Ramsey Campbell," in *Speaking of Horror: Interviews with Writers of the Supernatural,* edited by Daryl F. Mallett (San Bernardino, Cal.: Borgo Press, 1994), pp. 23–36;

Marni Scodifio Griffin, "Profile of Ramsey Campbell–'The Grand Old Man of Horror,'" *Deathrealm,* no. 24 (Summer 1995): 24–28;

David J. Howe, "Interview with Ramsey Campbell," *Ramsey Campbell: The Official Web Site* <http://www.herebedragons.co.uk/campbell>.

Bibliography:

Ramsey Campbell, Stefan Dziemianoeicz, and S. T. Joshi, *The Core of Ramsey Campbell: A Biobibliography and Reader's Guide* (West Warwick, R.I.: Necronomicon, 1995).

References:

Scott David Aniolowski, ed., *Made in Goatswood: A Celebration of Ramsey Campbell* (Oakland, Cal.: Chaosium, 1995);

Mike Ashley, *Fantasy Readers Guide to Ramsey Campbell* (San Bernardino, Cal.: Borgo Press, 1980);

Clive Barker, "Ramsey Campbell: An Appreciation," in *Clive Barker's Shadows in Eden,* edited by Stephen Jones (Lancaster, Pa.: Underwood-Miller, 1991), pp. 83–88;

Bernadette Lynn Bosky, "Making the Implicit, Explicit: Vampire Erotica and Pornography," in *The Blood Is the Life: Vampires in Literature,* edited by Leonard G. Heldreth and Mary Pharr (Bowling Green, Ohio: Bowling Green State University Popular Press, 1999), pp. 217–232;

John Brosnan, "Terror Tactics," in *Clive Barker's Shadows of Eden,* edited by Stephen Jones (Lancaster, Pa.: Underwood-Miller, 1991), pp. 89–94;

Gary William Crawford, *Ramsey Campbell* (Mercer Island, Wash.: Starmont, 1988);

Crawford, "Urban Gothic: The Fiction of Ramsey Campbell," in *Discovering Modern Horror Fiction I,* edited by Darrell Schweitzer (Mercer Island, Wash.: Starmont, 1985), pp. 13–20;

Arthur R. Deleault, "Perceptions: Campbell/Burleson," *Studies in Weird Fiction* (Summer 1994): 18–19;

S. T. Joshi, *The Modern Weird Tale* (Jefferson, N.C. & London: McFarland, 2001);

Joshi, *Ramsey Campbell and Modern Horror Fiction* (Liverpool: Liverpool University Press, 2001);

Joshi, "Ramsey Campbell: The Fiction of Paranoia," *Studies in Weird Fiction* (Summer 1995): 22–33;

Joshi, ed., *The Count of Thirty: A Tribute to Ramsey Campbell* (West Warwick, R.I.: Necronomicon, 1993);

Kenneth Jurkiewicz, "Ramsey Campbell," in *Supernatural Fiction Writers,* edited by E. F. Bleiler (New York: Scribners, 1985), pp. 993–999;

Stephen King, *Danse Macabre* (New York: Everest, 1981), pp. 181, 330, 337;

T. E. D. Klein, "Ramsey Campbell: An Appreciation," in *Discovering Modern Horror Fiction II,* edited by Darrell Schweitzer (Mercer Island, Wash.: Starmont, 1988), pp. 88–102;

Joel Lane, "Negatives in Print: The Novels of Ramsey Campbell," *Foundation* (Summer 1986): 35–45;

Lane, "Shattered Visions," *Necrofile* (Spring 1984): 8–10;

Steven J. Mariconda, "The Campbell Renaissance," *Necrofile* (Fall 1993): 6–8;

Giles Menegaldo, "Gothic Convention and Modernity in John Ramsey Campbell's Short Fiction," in *Modern Gothic: A Reader,* edited by Victor Sage (Manchester, U.K.: Manchester University, 1996), pp. 188–197;

Michael A. Morrison, "The Forms of Things Unknown: Metaphysical and Domestic Horror in Ramsey Campbell's *Incarnate* and *Night of the Claw,*" *Studies in Weird Fiction* (Fall 1989): 3–9;

Morrison, "Patterns, Demanding to Be Read," *Necrofile* (Fall 1991): 4–6;

Kim Newman, "Campbell Is Coming," *New Statesman* (25 March 1988): 28;

Jack Sullivan, "Ramsey Campbell: No Light Ahead," in *Shadowings: A Reader's Guide to Horror Fiction 1981–1982,* edited by Douglas E. Winter (Mercer Island, Wash.: Starmont, 1983), pp. 79–86;

Marshall B. Tymn, ed., *Horror Literature: An Historical Survey and Critical Guide to the Best of Horror* (New York & London: R. R. Bowker, 1981).

Papers:

The Liverpool Local History Library holds some of Ramsey Campbell's early manuscripts and juvenilia. The bulk of Campbell manuscripts and other papers not held by the Local History Library are in the Science Fiction Foundation Collection at Liverpool University.

Angela Carter
(7 May 1940 – 16 February 1992)

Jeffrey V. Yule
University of Maine at Fort Kent

See also the Carter entries in *DLB 14: British Novelists Since 1960* and *DLB 207: British Novelists Since 1960, Third Series.*

BOOKS: *Shadow Dance* (London: Heinemann, 1966); republished as *Honeybuzzard* (New York: Simon & Schuster, 1967);

Unicorn (London: Location Press, 1966);

The Magic Toyshop (London: Heinemann, 1967; New York: Simon & Schuster, 1968);

Several Perceptions (London: Heinemann, 1968; New York: Simon & Schuster, 1968);

Heroes and Villains (London: Heinemann, 1969; New York: Simon & Schuster, 1969);

Miss Z, the Dark Young Lady (New York: Simon & Schuster, 1970; London: Heinemann, 1970);

The Donkey Prince (New York: Simon & Schuster, 1970);

Love (London: Hart-Davis, 1971; revised, London: Chatto & Windus, 1987; New York: Viking Penguin, 1988);

The Infernal Desire Machines of Doctor Hoffman (London: Hart-Davis, 1972); republished as *The War of Dreams* (New York: Harcourt Brace Jovanovich, 1974);

Fireworks: Nine Profane Pieces (London: Quartet, 1974); republished as *Fireworks: Nine Stories in Various Guises* (New York: Harper & Row, 1981; revised, London: Chatto & Windus, 1987);

The Passion of New Eve (London: Gollancz, 1977; New York: Harcourt Brace Jovanovich, 1977);

The Sadeian Woman and the Ideology of Pornography (New York: Pantheon, 1978); republished as *The Sadeian Woman: An Exercise in Cultural History* (London: Gollancz, 1979);

Comic and Curious Cats (London: Gollancz, 1979; New York: Harmony, 1979);

The Bloody Chamber and Other Stories (London: Gollancz, 1979; New York: Harper & Row, 1979);

The Music People, by Carter and Leslie Carter (London: Hamilton, 1980);

Black Venus's Tale (London: Next Editions, 1980);

Angela Carter (photograph by Miriam Berkley)

Moonshadow (London: Gollancz, 1982);

Nothing Sacred: Selected Writings (London: Virago, 1982);

Nights at the Circus (London: Chatto & Windus, 1984; New York: Viking, 1985);

Black Venus (London: Chatto & Windus, 1985); revised as *Saints and Strangers* (New York: Viking, 1986);

Come Unto These Yellow Sands (Newcastle upon Tyne: Bloodaxe Books, 1985);

Artificial Fire (Toronto: McClelland & Stewart, 1988)—comprises *Fireworks* and *Love;*

Wise Children (London: Chatto & Windus, 1991; New York: Farrar, Straus & Giroux, 1992);

Expletives Deleted: Selected Writings (London: Chatto & Windus, 1992);

American Ghosts and Old World Wonders (London: Chatto & Windus, 1993);

Sea-Cat and Dragon King (London: Bloomsbury Children's Books, 2000; New York: Bloomsbury Children's Books, 2002).

Collections: *Burning Your Boats: Stories,* edited by Jenny Uglow (London: Chatto & Windus, 1995); republished as *Burning Your Boats: The Collected Short Stories* (New York: Holt, 1996);

The Curious Room: Plays, Film Scripts and an Opera, edited by Mark Bell (London: Chatto & Windus, 1996);

Shaking a Leg: Journalism and Writings, edited by Uglow (London: Chatto & Windus, 1997); republished as *Shaking a Leg: Collected Writings* (New York: Penguin, 1998).

PRODUCED SCRIPTS: *The Company of Wolves,* screenplay by Carter and Neil Jordan, motion picture, ITC Entertainment, 1984;

The Magic Toyshop, television, Granada, 1989.

OTHER: Charles Perrault, *The Fairy Tales of Charles Perrault,* edited and translated by Carter (London: Gollancz, 1977; New York: Avon Bard, 1979);

Sleeping Beauty and Other Favourite Fairy Tales, edited and translated by Carter (London: Gollancz, 1982; New York: Schocken Books, 1984);

"Notes from the Front Line," in *On Gender and Writing,* edited by Michelene Wandor (London: Pandora, 1983);

Wayward Girls and Wicked Women: An Anthology of Stories, edited by Carter (London: Virago, 1986; New York: Penguin, 1989);

The Virago Book of Fairy Tales, edited by Carter (London: Virago, 1990); republished as *The Old Wives' Fairy Tale Book* (New York: Pantheon, 1990);

The Second Virago Book of Fairy Tales, edited by Carter (London: Virago, 1992); republished as *Strange Things Sometimes Still Happen: Fairy Tales from Around the World* (Boston: Faber & Faber, 1993).

Angela Carter's fantastic fiction is noteworthy for its stylistic excellence, its treatment of feminist themes, and its reliance on and reaction to motion-picture, fairy-tale, folklore, gothic, and science-fiction sources. Despite the fact that her postapocalyptic novel *Heroes and Villains* (1969) represents a significant early feminist experiment with science-fiction motifs, Carter has never been associated with the British New Wave movement of the 1960s. In one of her final interviews before her death from lung cancer in 1992, Carter even dismissed the importance of science fiction to her writing. Although some of her novels have been reviewed and discussed in science-fiction journals, Carter avoided the

label of a science-fiction writer by embracing a variety of other fictional modes and models and by making an apparently conscious decision not to emphasize the parallels between some of her work and commercial science fiction. Despite having written several novels and short stories that can be readily described as fantasies, she also managed to avoid the label of a fantasist. Instead, critics generally describe Carter as a postmodernist author because her fiction draws simultaneously from several literary and popular traditions while experimenting with both narrative and the presentation of source materials in ways that tie her work to a variously defined tradition of literary experimentation that developed in the wake of modernism.

Born on 7 May 1940, Angela Olive Stalker grew up in South London, the daughter of Hugh Stalker, a Scottish-born journalist, and Olive Farthing Stalker, a native of a Yorkshire mining district. Her father introduced her to cinema, and as Marina Warner notes in her introduction to the American edition of *The Second Virago Book of Fairy Tales* (1992), the glamor of theater architecture and movie stars obviously made a lasting impression, since Carter's fiction frequently relies on movies for imagery and plot elements. She married Paul Carter in 1960, and in 1962 she began studying English at the University of Bristol in Avon, specializing in medieval literature. During this time, she developed an appreciation for medieval romances and fables while also reading the works of Alfred Jarry and the French Surrealists. In a 1992 interview with Olga Kenyon, Carter notes that during this period she "loved . . . a certain kind of non-naturalistic writing that nobody seemed to be reading in the early sixties"; this writing included the works of Isak Dinesen, Jean Cocteau, and Ronald Firbank. Carter remained in Bristol after graduating in 1965, working as a journalist for the *Croydon Advertiser,* but after publishing her first novel, *Shadow Dance* (1966), she gave up journalism to pursue fiction writing. From 1966 onward she also wrote occasional reviews for *New Society* and *Guardian,* but, by her own estimation, she did not begin to review books seriously until she was thirty-five. After that time her reviews also regularly appeared in the *London Review of Books* and *The New York Times Book Review.* Many of these later reviews are collected in *Expletives Deleted* (1992).

In one of her later interviews, Carter observes that "Fiction can interpret everyday reality through imagery derived from our unconscious, from subterranean areas *behind* everyday experience." Carter's interest in the unconscious and her tendency to overlay the logic and imagery of the unconscious on everyday events prompts many critics to describe her fiction either as magic realism or fantasy. Such labels are misleading, since fiction that treats ideas and themes relat-

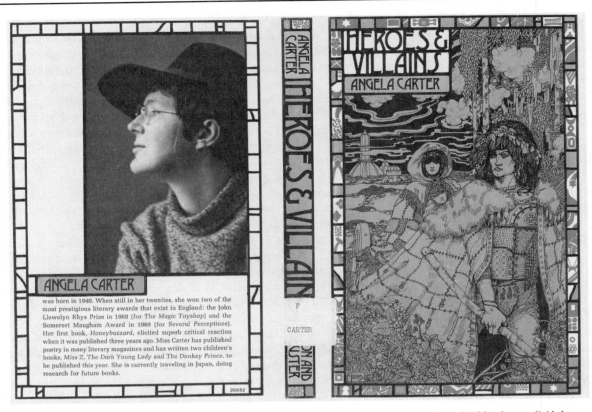

Dust jacket for the U.S. edition of Carter's 1969 novel, set in a postapocalyptic world where humankind has become divided into three mutually antagonistic groups: Professors, nomadic Barbarians, and predatory mutants called the Out People (Richland County Public Library)

ing to the unconscious need not necessarily be fantastic. Carter's fiction, for example, typically shows an awareness of and interest in the unconscious, whether or not the specific work in question involves fantastic—that is, supernatural or science-fictional—events. Thus, Carter's first novels show both gothic and fairy-tale influences without depicting events that could be described as fantastic. Not until after *The Magic Toyshop* (1967)—a novel characterized by mythological references and an often tenuous distinction between reality, daydream, and hallucination—does Carter's fiction begin to involve not only the atmospherics of the fantastic but its substance as well. Significantly, this shift in Carter's fiction occurred shortly after the summer of 1968, a personal watershed period when, as Carter describes in her 1983 essay "Notes from the Front Line," she developed a heightened awareness of the manner in which society dictates the terms of women's femininity.

At about the same time that she separated from her husband in 1969 (their divorce became final in 1972), Carter visited Japan under the auspices of a Somerset Maugham Travel Award. She returned there in 1970 and remained for two years. Afterward, Carter lived in London and Bath before making London her home in 1976, although in the following years she spent a considerable amount of time away from that city. From 1976 through 1978, she was the Arts Council of Great Britain Fellow in Creative Writing at Sheffield University, and from 1980 through 1981 she was a visiting professor in Brown University's Writing Program. She was a writer in residence at the University of Adelaide in 1984 and a visiting professor at the University of Texas at Austin the following year. During 1983, one of the few years during this period of frequent traveling that Carter was not a visiting professor elsewhere, she had a son, Alexander, with Mark Pearce. Carter died of lung cancer in 1992.

Carter's investigation of what she calls "the social fictions that regulate our lives" coincides with her first experiments with the writing of fantastic fiction, beginning with her novel of a postapocalyptic world, *Heroes and Villains*. Among the many novels and short-story collections that followed, Carter returned to the fantastic and the science fictional regularly, most significantly in *The Infernal Desire Machines of Doctor Hoffman* (1972), *The Passion of New Eve* (1977), *The Bloody Chamber and Other Stories* (1979), and *Nights at the Circus* (1984)—all of which show a particular concern with gender roles in Western society.

Heroes and Villains takes as its starting point the science-fiction staple of a postapocalyptic world while also immediately showing strong fairy-tale influences. The omniscient narration is strikingly similar to that of a fairy tale. Reinforcing this parallel, various characters in the novel, particularly the focal character's nurse, tell about the supposedly real dangers of the world in ways that recast people from other tribes as the bogeys of nursery tales. In Carter's post-nuclear-war world, humanity has fragmented into three mutually antagonistic groups: the Professors, educated people who live in small, fortress-like settlements; Barbarians, who lead a nomadic existence, preying on the Professors; and the Out People, violent, predatory mutants willing to attack any other group if they believe they can gain something from their efforts. While Carter creates her imagined world and its societies deftly, even taking the time to describe some of the mutations that have altered various animal species, her project relates more to the socially constructed peculiarities of her characters than to the science-fictional attributes of the setting. The story concerns itself with the relationship between Marianne, a Professor's daughter bored with her life, and Jewel, a Barbarian whom Marianne helps escape after his participation in a failed raid on her village-enclave home. As is typical of Carter's fiction, the main interest of the novel is with gender roles, particularly patterns of male aggression toward women, female passivity in the face of that aggression, and the manner by which gender determines character. Marianne is significant because, unlike other characters in the novel, she views existing gender roles critically even though she is not always sure how to resist them.

Some reviewers dismissed *Heroes and Villains* out of hand, mistaking the novel for a failed science-fiction adventure story with literary pretensions. While Stuart Hood of *The Listener* (1969) suggested—probably incorrectly—that the novel would have teenage admirers among the science-fiction-reading crowd, he failed to detect any feminist themes or to appreciate Carter's achievements as a writer. An anonymous reviewer for *TLS: The Times Literary Supplement* (1969) did praise Carter's "control of her material" early in the novel but faulted her for pretentiousness later in the story and, like Hood, showed little awareness of the feminist concerns. John S. Phillipson's 1970 review for *Best Sellers* perhaps best sums up the nature of contemporary response to *Heroes and Villains*. While noting that he was "willing to call it strikingly different, a kind of *tour de force* in sustained bizarre narrative," he remained unsure what Carter's project in the novel might be. For Phillipson and many others, Carter's fiction clearly had something to offer. The difficulty for critics was in trying to determine what that something might be.

Most later discussions of the novel have shown a greater awareness of and concern with its depiction of gender relations. In *The Literature of Terror: A History of Gothic Fictions from 1765 to the Present Day* (1980) David Punter places *Heroes and Villains* in the gothic tradition and identifies Marianne as a figure who, through her experience with patriarchal repression, becomes capable of greater achievements than either the Professors or the Barbarians. Punter suggests that Marianne fully realizes her capabilities at the end of the novel when she becomes the leader of the Barbarian group she has joined. In her essay in *Women Reading Women's Writing* (1987) Paulina Palmer also notes that the focus of the novel is on the "social differences between the male and female protagonists." Building on Punter's evaluation of the novel, Brooks Landon emphasizes in a 1986 essay the "Edenic resonances of Marianne's situation" in order to show that while Marianne might be, as Jewel once ironically suggests, "Eve at the end of the world," she is an Eve uninterested in what patriarchal mythology might have to tell her. Landon notes that after Jewel's death, Marianne "recognizes the power of her knowledge in a world governed by myth and taboo and muses." If she is to be a postapocalyptic Eve, a possibility exists that she might help to bring about a new order.

In *Constructing Postmodernism* (1992) Brian McHale considers *Heroes and Villains* one of the first postmodernist fictions to incorporate science-fiction motifs and materials, although his use of Carter's novel as an example shows just how blurred is the boundary separating works of science fiction from works of postmodernist fiction that rely heavily on science-fiction motifs. It might be that the one way to draw such a distinction relates to the readership for which these different sorts of books are intended. Despite Hood's comment to the contrary, for example, *Heroes and Villains* was not a science-fiction adventure story meant to appeal to the same readers who would read adventures by such mainstream genre authors as Robert A. Heinlein or Isaac Asimov. Carter's novel lacks sympathetic characters and the typical plot skeleton of commercial science fiction. In addition, on those occasions when the story involves action or violence, Carter presents it in such a way as to make the reader feel dissociated from it. Quite simply, while the motifs in the novel might be typically science fictional, the presentation of those motifs and the style in which the story is written are hardly science fictional at all. It might be more helpful to think of Carter as an author whose novels frequently straddle various genre and stylistic boundaries—a sometimes fantasist whose fiction, as is typical of postmodernism, draws from various traditions, both literary and popular.

Carter's next fantastic novel, *The Infernal Desire Machines of Doctor Hoffman*, is a case in point—a novel that

Dust jacket for the U.S. edition of the 1977 novel in which Carter attempted to demonstrate that "Only men can successfully embody the ideal of the female they desire, because it doesn't correspond to real women" (Richland County Public Library)

realist tradition, although it draws inspiration from other sorts of postmodernist fiction as well. Stylistically and thematically, it brings to mind the fiction of both William S. Burroughs and Gabriel García Márquez. As with much of Burroughs's fiction, there are points in the story when the reader cannot reliably determine whether the events being described represent the narrator's actual experiences or hallucinations. Thus, the reader is left to wonder whether the laws of physics and causality as Western culture understands them have broken down in the fictional world being described.

Carter's narrative is characterized more by occasional, sudden intrusions of the dream-like rather than the consistent use of such effects typical of a Burroughs novel, with the result that the effect is far less disorienting. In a review of Burroughs's *Ah Pook Is Here* (1979), Carter praises a particularly relevant technique, noting that Burroughs's fiction will "hit you with an image and let the image act for itself"—a tactic she uses in *The Infernal Desire Machines of Doctor Hoffman,* and which she almost certainly also saw practiced in *Cien años de soledad* (1967; *One Hundred Years of Solitude,* 1970) by García Márquez—a novel and an author she frequently mentions in essays, reviews, and interviews. The apparently casual presentation of jarring, snapshot-like images, as of the "Green Boys with delicate purple gills who tend chemical gardens" in Burroughs's *The Soft Machine* (1961) or the brief mention of a passing flying carpet in *One Hundred Years of Solitude,* have parallels in *The Infernal Desire Machines of Doctor Hoffman.* Carter's novel, though, offers more-developed images, often even brief character portraits, among them one of the sideshow freaks Desiderio befriends, the Alligator Man—who, from within his tank, comments that "The freak is the norm"—and characters who are manifestations of the human unconscious, including the Pirates of Death and a racial caricature of a black tribal chieftain with a Machiavellian approach to ruling.

The political dimension of magic realism present in *One Hundred Years of Solitude* is also mirrored in Carter's novel. *The Infernal Desire Machines of Doctor Hoffman,* for example, shows an interest in history similar to that of García Márquez's novel, particularly in depicting history as a cultural construct subject to the control of those in power. While García Márquez's novel includes a wholesale revision of history that conceals a massacre of civilians by the military, the brutal tribal chieftain Desiderio meets is a projection of the Western unconscious's image of Africa and Africans and a character who controls history by suppressing the very concept. "I have been very careful to suppress history," he says, "for my subjects might learn the lessons of the deaths of kings." Like the chieftain, Dr. Hoffman has designs on history, although his method of controlling

utilizes an even more eclectic mix of fantastic elements and source materials than *Heroes and Villains.* A picaresque and sometimes surreal tale, the novel presents the narrator Desiderio's account of his youth during the Great War (not to be confused with the real World War I). During this conflict Dr. Hoffman wages a massive campaign against human reason by using a hitherto unknown technology to give physical substance to the things that inhabit the human unconscious. He intends to liberate society by erasing the boundaries between the waking world and the realm of the unconscious. The Minister of Determination—a leader embodying reason, logic, and order—resists Hoffman. Despite Desiderio's infatuation with Hoffman's daughter, Albertina, he accepts a mission from the Minister to find and kill Hoffman, and the story recounts the various episodes of his quest.

Of all Carter's fantastic novels, *The Infernal Desire Machines of Doctor Hoffman* is the one most in the magic-

it has more in common with the ruling junta of *One Hundred Years of Solitude.* Hoffman will rewrite history once he has control over the mechanisms of reality, subtly altering the chronicle of Western civilization. In Hoffman's study, Desiderio sees pictures of Leon Trotsky composing the *Eroica* Symphony, Vincent van Gogh writing *Wuthering Heights,* and a blind John Milton painting frescoes in the Sistine Chapel. Seeing his puzzlement at the subjects of these pictures, Albertina tells Desiderio, "When my father rewrites the history books, these are some of the things that everyone will suddenly perceive to have always been true," a comment that presents Hoffman's plans for history as a sort of mirror image to the manipulations of history that conceal a massacre in García Márquez's novel. While the massacre in *One Hundred Years of Solitude* is a true event made untrue by history, the untrue achievements of the historical personages pictured in *The Infernal Desire Machines of Doctor Hoffman* will be made true by history.

More generally—despite the flamboyant eccentricity of so many of its characters—*The Infernal Desire Machines of Doctor Hoffman* shares with magic realism not only an unspecified Latin American setting but also an awareness that social privilege derives not solely from gender but from social class, ethnicity, and race as well. Desiderio, an Indian, discusses at some length his country's history and the impact of colonialism on the native people, speaking of the "ethnic incomprehensibility" that colonization brought to them. In a manner similar to that which occurs in *Heroes and Villains,* Desiderio also shows how social privilege can create a perspective that allows one group of people to fictionalize and marginalize another. Desiderio relates that it was "perfectly possible . . . to spend all one's life in the capital or the towns of the plain and know little if anything of the Indians. They were bogeymen with which to frighten naughty children; they had become rag-pickers, scrap dealers, refuse collectors, and emptiers of cess-pits—those who performed tasks for which you do not need a face." As a consequence, the Indians—at least in Desiderio's youth—were roughly analogous to the Barbarians and Out People of *Heroes and Villains,* while Western-oriented, white culture in *The Infernal Desire Machines of Doctor Hoffman* has its *Heroes and Villains* equivalent in the Professors. Carter presents an interesting spin on this tendency in *Heroes and Villains,* though, since the Barbarians' tales also reduce the Professors to the status of nursery bogeys. Indeed, in *Heroes and Villains* it seems that all groups suffer from the same tendency to fictionalize other groups of people rather than understand them.

Contemporary reviews were divided about *The Infernal Desire Machines of Doctor Hoffman.* Some, such as the reviewer who commented that he read the novel "enthralled, fascinated, and bewitched," found it entertaining, well written, and remarkably inventive. Others were less intrigued with Carter's postmodernist experimentation, among them the critic who noted that "the novel has little to offer but a flux of images." Certainly, similar critiques have been directed at other works and at postmodernist fiction in general. By the time this novel was published, however, Carter had begun to find her readership, and there was a greater balance between votes of confidence and condemnation in reviews.

Since its initial appearance, feminist critics have had the most to say about *The Infernal Desire Machines of Doctor Hoffman,* particularly on the subject of sexism. Among those critical of the novel on these grounds, Palmer sees the story as having a "chauvinistically male" viewpoint and lapsing into pornography. Others take a sharply different position. Punter, for instance, reads the novel as an attempt at the subversion of the idea of narrative itself, while Sally Robinson sees the novel as undertaking an even more narrowly defined subversion—one of pornographic narrative. Robinson suggests that Carter, by presenting the unreliable narrator of *The Infernal Desire Machines of Doctor Hoffman* in an unflattering light, invites the reader to see the narrator's misogynist and sexist behavior as problematic. Feminist critics, however, have had little to say about the novel as a work of fantasy, and on this subject postmodernist critics have offered brief but useful insights that shed light on comments Carter has made about the novel.

In the interview with Kenyon, Carter notes that of all her novels, *The Infernal Desire Machines of Doctor Hoffman* was the one that most relied on science-fiction elements. Others have also observed the similarities of this novel to science fiction. McHale writes that in *The Infernal Desire Machines of Doctor Hoffman* "Carter elaborates the ontological confrontation between this world and the 'world next door' into a literal agonistic struggle, analogous to the science-fiction *topos* of the 'war of the worlds.'" Certainly, sections of the novel invite comparisons to science fiction. Early in the novel, for example, Desiderio notes that Hoffman was probably the greatest physicist of all time. Given the events of the story, it is easy to view Hoffman as a mad scientist, a point Carter makes explicitly through Albertina. When the Minister comments that he believes malice motivates Hoffman, she replies, "What, the mad scientist who brews up revengeful plagues in his test tubes? Were his motives so simple, he would, by now, I assure you, have utterly destroyed everything." Despite any first impression to the contrary the passage might make, Albertina does not deny that Hoffman is a mad scientist; she merely observes that his motives are not so simple as malice.

Dust jacket for the U.S. edition of Carter's 1979 short-story collection, traditional fairy tales retold from a feminist perspective (Bruccoli Clark Layman Collection)

as a secret agent or an assassin. Desiderio's success in killing Hoffman depends much less on his own abilities than on Hoffman, who mistakenly believes that Desiderio will not kill the father of the woman he loves and, as a consequence, allows Desiderio to get close enough to accomplish his mission.

From the sympathetic critic's standpoint, *The Infernal Desire Machines of Doctor Hoffman* is a novel that successfully uses image stock drawn from a variety of literary and popular sources to draw attention to the sexism and violence that are so central to the Western cultural tradition. Desiderio, like Bond, is not a character one expects to find in a relationship that involves much besides sex, and, like Bond, his noteworthy characteristics do not include a tendency toward compassion, introspection, or even the most rudimentary awareness of feminism. Women in the novel are typically either objects of desire, sources of danger, or both. Female characters have frequently occupied a similarly narrow range of roles in commercial science fiction, which has for the most part been written by men and directed at an audience of teenage boys and young men—an audience profile that tends to match that of James Bond movies. Perhaps the problem many critics have with *The Infernal Desire Machines of Doctor Hoffman* results from a common difficulty in interpreting parody: sometimes it can be mistaken for the subject being parodied, which, in the case of Carter's novel, might have left some critics unaware of its critique of gender roles. Her next fantastic novel made her exploration of gender roles more obvious than in *The Infernal Desire Machines of Doctor Hoffman*.

In *The Passion of New Eve* Carter uses the setting of Western culture in breakdown to tell the story of an English hero, Evelyn, and his experiences with patriarchal oppression, first as a perpetrator and then as a victim. After going to the United States to take a faculty position at a New York City college, Evelyn quickly ends up with little reason to stay there. The college where he had planned to teach closes, and his neighbor and only real friend in the city, a Czech alchemist, is killed in a mugging. All that keeps Evelyn in New York is a sexual relationship that highlights his misogynistic tendencies. After being galvanized into action by what appears to be a botched and bloody abortion, he leaves his black lover, Leilah, to travel across the continent, where he experiences a complete gender reversal. In the desert he encounters a technologically advanced matriarchy whose leader, Mother, is a physically gigantic fertility figure and combination mad scientist, surgeon, and revolutionary commander. She surgically transforms Evelyn into a beautiful woman and is planning to impregnate him with his own sperm when Evelyn, now Eve, escapes into the desert and falls under the control

Hoffman is definitely in the science-fiction tradition of the mad scientist—one, in fact, who keeps his dead wife in a sitting room—but despite this gothic touch, Hoffman remains a character with affinities toward more-modern, movie versions of the mad scientist. As Carter hints in the Kenyon interview, Hoffman bears a striking resemblance to the mad geniuses whom James Bond earns his living killing. Like them, Hoffman is a larger-than-life genius whose megalomania leads him to the brink of incredible power. The lab where Desiderio kills Hoffman even resembles the sort of technologically advanced base of operations from which a Bond movie villain would operate.

The parallels inevitably invite another comparison—one between Bond and Desiderio. Interestingly, the comparison suggests that Desiderio is a parody of Bond. Unlike Bond, for instance, Desiderio is an indifferent enough hero to abandon his mission when he finds temporary happiness away from it, and, also unlike Bond, Desiderio has no apparent qualifications

of the misogynistic madman-poet Zero, who takes Eve to his cultists' ranch to serve as another of his slave-wives. Zero paranoically blames Eve's old idol, the retired movie actress Tristessa St. Ange, for the sterility that prevents him from impregnating any of his wives; and during Zero's search for the idol's hideaway and a chance to kill her, Eve meets the now elderly star and discovers that Tristessa is a transvestite. After a mock wedding and coupling forced upon them by Zero, Tristessa and Eve kill Zero and his wives, but afterward, lost without supplies in the desert, they are captured by an army of paramilitarist teenagers who follow a fundamentalist doctrine. They shoot and kill Tristessa before Eve again escapes and falls back into the hands of Mother. By this time, Mother's intentions toward Eve have changed. Eve's former lover Leilah, now revealed to be Lilith, a guerrilla soldier and agent of the desert matriarchy, tells Eve that she can have her original gender restored. Eve refuses and embarks from the West Coast in a rowboat, apparently without either a clear plan or destination.

In the Kenyon interview, Carter notes that the United States she envisions in the novel was sparked by a 1969 visit to New York City. The violent and decaying New York that Carter describes in *The Passion of New Eve* has its basis in things she saw during that visit: violent demonstrations, piles of garbage in the streets, and gay riots in Greenwich Village. Against this backdrop of social breakdown, the novel pays particular attention to gender roles—with the manner in which men such as Evelyn and Zero mistreat women and the ways in which some women, such as Zero's wives, not only allow such mistreatment but also seem to seek it out. In all these cases, gender-determined behavior tends to dehumanize people by making less of them than they might be. The novel follows Evelyn/Eve's course toward self-awareness, a course that depends not only on direct experience but also on Evelyn/Eve's observations of other characters' experiences.

Evelyn's girlfriend Leilah/Lilith, even though she is absent for most of the action of the novel, is a character whose experiences are of particular importance. Leilah/Lilith is one of the many empowered women in Carter's fiction who is not what she first appears. Although she is initially presented as a victim of Evelyn's callous treatment, her later appearance in the novel as a trained guerrilla soldier reveals her to be a more complicated figure—perhaps even a character who, in the fashion of a Thomas Pynchon plot, was from the beginning a part of some larger conspiracy to make sure that Mother captured Evelyn. Despite first appearances, then, Carter's novel suggests the possibility that the apparent victim was all along far more in control of her situation than the

apparent victimizer—thus emphasizing the fact that Evelyn's victimization of women involved a significant degree of self-victimization as well, since his behavior stunted his human potential without harming Leilah. It is some measure of Evelyn/Eve's evolution as a character that when she recognizes the soldier Lilith to be Leilah, she is not bitter or angry but, rather, pleased to see her. Clearly, late in the novel Eve possesses an understanding of gender roles and relations that Evelyn never had. To achieve that understanding, though, Evelyn/Eve had to endure a great deal.

The nature of Evelyn/Eve's experiences goes a good way toward explaining why reviews of the novel were mixed. Some critics viewed it as a conscious and effective parody of popular movies and science fiction. Among this group was Lorna Sage, who, writing for the *New Review* (1977), praised the novel for its presentation of a "tacky brilliance thoroughly in keeping with the theme of a culture regressing into dreamy barbarism." Several reviewers not well disposed toward literary postmodernism took a dimmer view of the novel. In his review for the *New Statesman* (1977) Paddy Beesley took exception to the novel for too often lapsing into an "exuberant zaniness" that led it into "court silliness." Peter Ackroyd, writing for *The Spectator* (1977), saw the novel as "veering wildly towards the grotesque, the fantastic and the merely silly" and lacking the sentiment and substance to match its fashionably modish, pop-culture-influenced style. To a significant extent, assessments of the novel seemed to depend on how well reviewers were able to accept experiences that are so far from the norm of Western culture—among them transvestism, the rape and castration of a man by a woman, and his subsequent forced sex change.

Carter herself points out that the novel, like *The Infernal Desire Machines of Doctor Hoffman*, is in part a parody of a James Bond movie, but critics have noted its reliance on other cinematic sources as well. Susan Rubin Suleiman, for instance, identifies the Hollywood love story elements of the plot and sees Tristessa's character as being based on Greta Garbo. As is typical of Carter, though, the novel draws from many other sources. Suleiman also traces one incident in the novel to an episode in Surrealist Robert Desnos's novel *La Liberté ou l'amour!* (1927; translated as *Liberty or Love!* 1993).

More generally, though, Suleiman sees the novel as accomplishing three things: providing a model for a kind of writing and a kind of eroticism that ought to be imitated; suggesting a direction for postmodernist feminist fiction based on parody and the multiplication of narrative possibilities; and, finally, "expanding our notions of what it is possible to dream in the domain of sexuality, criticizing all dreams that are too

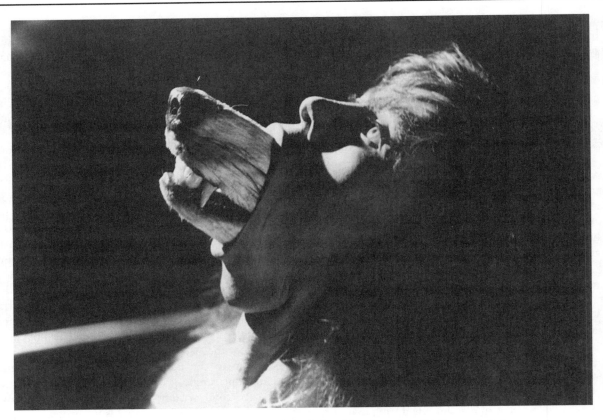

Still from The Company of Wolves *(1984), the motion picture for which Carter adapted a story collected in* The Bloody Chamber and Other Stories *(Everett Collection)*

narrow." Those of a more critical bent take a view closer to Robert Clark's, that although *The Passion of New Eve* may aim at satirizing patriarchal conceptions of women, Carter's "fascination with violent eroticism and her failure to find any alternative on which to construct a feminine identity prevent her work from being other than an elaborate trace of women's self-alienation." In the Kenyon interview, Carter makes some observations about the feminist themes of the novel, noting that one of the things *The Passion of New Eve* shows is that "Only men can successfully embody the ideal of the female they desire, because it doesn't correspond to real women."

Those critics, particularly feminists, who have praised *The Passion of New Eve,* tend to be those who appreciate the manner in which the novel recognizes the complexity of the issues it confronts by refusing to offer a cast of characters that includes only heroic female role models and male villains. Carter's willingness to depict gender relations as being played out by a complex cast of male and female characters is also apparent in her next book, a collection of short fiction.

The stories collected in *The Bloody Chamber and Other Stories* retell traditional fairy tales from a feminist

perspective. "The Bloody Chamber," for example, reworks "Bluebeard," while "The Courtship of Mr. Lyon" and "The Tiger's Bride" are variants of "Beauty and the Beast." Although all the stories in the collection are fairy tales, only the final six involve the fantastic to a significant extent. "The Erl King," a reworking of a Johann Wolfgang von Goethe ballad, concerns a forest fairy who seduces women and magically imprisons them, although the protagonist realizes the fate she faces and kills the Erl King before he gains control of her. "The Snow Child" is a brief, disturbing, dream-like tale about a count and his wife and a girl of snow that the count wishes into existence. "The Lady of the House of Love" concerns a British soldier soon to fight in World War I who encounters a beautiful female vampire, a descendant of Dracula but nonetheless a reluctant predator who finally dies rather than kill the soldier.

The final three stories in the collection deal with werewolf lore: "The Werewolf," "The Company of Wolves," and "Wolf-Alice." The first, brief story concerns a grandmother/werewolf who, in an unusual twist on "Little Red Riding Hood," menaces her own granddaughter before being killed. In "The Company of

Wolves" a young girl of the Little Red Riding Hood type who encounters the werewolf that killed her grandmother manages to tame him by refusing to play the part of a victim. When the wolf answers the girl's comment about the size of his teeth with the well-known "The better to eat you with," Carter writes that "The girl burst out laughing; she knew she was nobody's meat." A gothic oddity, "Wolf-Alice" concerns a girl raised by wolves and a duke who haunts cemeteries and fancies himself a ghoul, although the reader is left unsure whether his condition is supernatural or psychiatric in nature.

Two stories in this collection, "The Company of Wolves" and "Puss in Boots," were later adapted—or, in Carter's words, "reformulated"—for radio, while Carter and Neil Jordan adapted "The Company of Wolves" into a screenplay. The relationship between the stories in this volume and their radio incarnations, however, is not one way. "The Lady of the House of Love" is derived from a similar but more involved radio script, "Vampirella." In the introduction to *Come Unto These Yellow Sands* (1985) Carter calls the short story a "Gothic tale about a reluctant vampire" and the radio play a story "about vampirism as a metaphor." In "The Lady of the House of Love" Carter carefully counterpoints the danger that the vampire represents and the soldier's lack of fear when he is with her against the fear he will soon feel in the trenches of France, where the narrator indicates that he "will learn to shudder." Significantly, his rational mind does not allow him to fear a vampire because he cannot believe that such a creature could exist. Logical and well-meaning, the unnamed soldier plans to bring the girl to Zurich, where she can see a psychiatrist for treatment of her nervous hysteria, to an eye specialist where she can be treated for photophobia, to a dentist to "put her teeth in better shape," and to a manicurist to have her claw-like fingernails made more presentable. Carter's fairy tale is as concerned with the tragic vampire as it is with notions of rationality and irrationality as they relate to historical events; for the British soldier, the idea that vampires might exist is irrational despite the available evidence, but any irrational aspects of the coming war are overwhelmed by the hard evidence of trench warfare. In this story the vampire only appears to be the monster; the real monsters lurk in the background, in the guise of those who allow World War I to be fought by men like the British soldier.

In addition to stories such as "The Lady in the House of Love," the historicity of which distinguishes them from traditional fairy tales set in intentionally nonspecific times and places, Carter's fairy tales also set themselves apart from their models by presenting female characters as capable. Some, like the young girl

in "The Werewolf," actively defend themselves from danger; others, like the protagonist of "The Company of Wolves," avoid the need to defend themselves by refusing to play the role of victim in the first place. When the female protagonist of "The Bloody Chamber" finds herself in need of rescuing, the only man near at hand is, although a good person, incapable of doing the job. Instead, the young woman's mother comes to her aid. As "Wolf-Alice" closes, Alice attempts to aid the wounded duke, rather than needing his assistance. Despite the regularity with which its stories recast women as characters who do not need to be saved by princes or knights, *The Bloody Chamber and Other Stories* does more than offer feminist revisions of existing fairy tales. The stories in the collection also explore human sexuality and psychology, often with humor and always with a willingness to challenge assumptions, whether patriarchal or feminist. Carter's female characters in this volume are by no means all role models of the sort that feminist critics could unanimously accept as positive. The protagonist of "The Bloody Chamber," for example, is aroused when her husband objectifies her—a distinctly incorrect response for a feminist role model.

Published shortly after fairy tales began to attract serious scrutiny from literary critics, *The Bloody Chamber and Other Stories* achieved generally favorable notices for recasting its source materials without relying on the sexist molds that shaped previous fairy tales. However, Alan Friedman, writing for *The New York Times Book Review* (1980), found the collection unsatisfactory and hinted that its concern with "sadistic power and masochistic sacrifice" might have hurt it nearly as much as its "cutesy mannerisms and comical overwriting." Although few reviewers agreed with Friedman that "Most of these stories have the kind of cloying cleverness we associate with precocious writers," other commentators, particularly feminist critics, later expressed a similar concern about the depictions of sadistic and masochistic behavior. Less frequently, the collection also garnered attention from critics of postmodernist fiction.

In a brief prefatory comment to his reading of "The Lady of the House of Love" as a work of postmodernist fiction, Robert Rawdon Wilson notes that the stories in *The Bloody Chamber and Other Stories* "retell traditional European folktales from a feminist perspective imbued with psychoanalytic insights. All the tales . . . are artful, resonant with the allusive interplay of other texts, perhaps 'wan' in their affects; all, powerful in their historicity, in their awareness of human temporality within its socio-cultural chains." Such positive assessments of the collection are typical of postmodernist commentaries. In-depth analyses of any of the stories from this perspective are uncommon, however. For the most part, treatments of either individual stories or the collection as a whole tend to be more detailed when commentators either take a critical view of Carter's fiction or seek to refute the views of critics who have taken such stances.

Carter comments that Jordan's movie version of "The Company of Wolves" effectively illustrates her view that wolves can represent awakening sexuality in pubescent girls as well as in boys—a comment that presents a useful means of approaching these stories and the roles played in them by wolves, werewolves, and young women. For Carter, the awakening sexuality of young men is neither more nor less significant or subject to taboo than the awakening sexuality of young women, a consideration of some importance given the tendency of Western culture to celebrate or at least accept the sexual maturation of boys while seeking to control, commodify, or forestall the sexual awakening of girls. Carter's willingness to explore the other possibilities inherent to female characters in fairy tales suggests in an obvious way that these women need not be limited to playing the role of victims in need of rescue. The characters in Carter's next fantastic novel seem to proceed from a similar interest.

In *Nights at the Circus* American journalist Jack Walser follows the story of a Cockney aerialist who goes by the name Fevvers. Walser's original goal in taking on Fevvers's story is simple: to determine whether she is the winged wonder of nature she presents herself to be or merely a clever fraud. To research his story, Walser finds work as a clown with the traveling circus with which Fevvers is touring. As Robinson observes, the story plays off the traditional plot structure of the classic "seek and destroy" Hollywood movies, in which the male lead tries to "solve the enigma" the female lead presents. But Carter's novel parodies the Hollywood formula, reversing the typical arrangement of such stories. As Walser comes to know Fevvers, he, like the reader, comes to appreciate the manner in which she manages her life—refusing to relinquish her independence or play the part of a victim.

In an interview with Amanda Smith that preceded the American publication of *Nights at the Circus,* Carter was reluctant to describe the novel as a work of fantasy, calling it instead social satire. While it is certainly possible for satire to be fantastic and fantasy to be satirical, Carter's observation about *Nights at the Circus* offers a useful means of examining the nature of the fantasy it offers. Unlike earlier novels that draw from science fiction, magic realism, or fairy-tale sources, *Nights at the Circus* offers fantasy of a more equivocal nature. Incidents in the novel generally tend toward the bizarre and the surreal rather than the fantastic. The fact that one of the central characters may have functional wings, however, has prompted many commentators to treat the novel as a work of fantasy. With few exceptions, critics have accepted that Fevvers is a winged woman with the power of flight. In accepting her at face value in this respect, they also accept as true the embedded stories Fevvers narrates, since it is only during these episodes that she flies. Only Punter, in his article "Essential Imaginings: The Novels of Angela Carter and Russell Hoban" (1991), points out that the reader never actually finds out whether or not Fevvers has real wings; in making this observation Punter is also the only critic to question Fevvers's narrative reliability, although he never raises the issue explicitly.

Strictly speaking, though, even the uncertainty about Fevvers's reliability as a narrator or her status as a winged woman does not make problematic the status of the novel as a work of fantasy. Other aspects of the novel are too clearly unnatural. For example, the chimpanzees who travel with the circus—particularly their nominal leader, the Professor—display an intelligence that places them on an intellectual par with the artificially evolved chimpanzees who inhabit such science-fiction novels as David Brin's *Startide Rising* (1983) and *The Uplift War* (1987)—although Carter's intelligent animals have far more in common with their counterparts in Jonathan Swift's *Gulliver's Travels* (1726) than with their cousins in contemporary science fiction. Another unusual incident is of particular interest as well. During a cross-Siberian train trip to the troupe's next engagement, the circus tigers and the mirrors of the ornately decorated wagon car merge after the train engine explodes. Fevvers sees that the tigers "had frozen into their own reflections and been shattered, too, when the mirrors broke" and, more specifically, describes "On one broken fragment of mirror, a paw with the claws out; on another, a snarl." In this sequence the narrative takes on a dream-like quality. The story deals more in the bizarre than the fantastic, however, and Carter's decision to describe the novel as social satire makes at least as much sense as would any decision to label it a work of fantasy. Indeed, allegorical incidents and characters such as Mignon, whom Carter describes as a "frail orphan" symbolizing Europe after the War, are in much greater evidence than fantastic incidents, so it might be helpful to think of the novel as a work of social satire that makes use of various fantastic elements.

Most discussions of the novel focus on Fevvers. In *Constructing Postmodernism* McHale reads Fevvers as a parody of an angel, a sort of hollow angel. Feminist readings of the novel tend to view her quite differently: as a triumphant and empowered woman who soars above the conditions of her world. Using Carter's terminology from *The Sadeian Woman and the Ideology of Pornography* (1978), Robinson describes Fevvers as a Mae

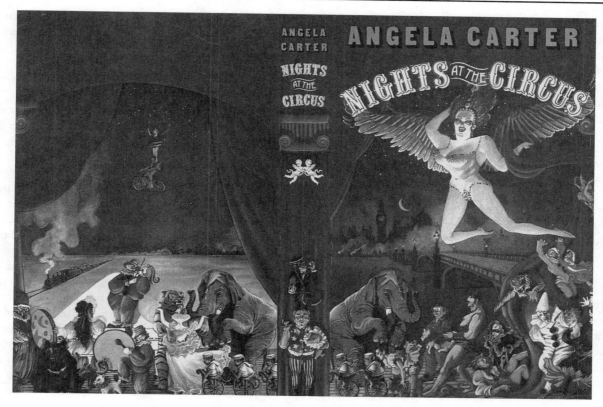

Dust jacket for Carter's 1984 book, her last novel in the fantasy genre (Bruccoli Clark Layman Collection)

West figure, "a woman who practices a masquerade of femininity, playing on male fears of the predatory woman"; in the same analytical framework, Mignon functions as a Marilyn Monroe figure, a martyr to be used by "connoisseurs of the poetry of masochism." Fevvers manages her own affairs in such a way as to avoid being financially dependent on anyone else—whether male or female—but, unlike Mignon, she also manages to avoid involvement in any relationship that would either circumscribe her freedom or subject her to physical abuse.

Typically, Carter's novel draws from a wide range of models and sources. In addition to relying on Hollywood movies and eighteenth-century allegorical fiction, she also draws from more-recent sources separate from the popular-culture tradition. Suleiman, for instance, notes that Carter presents an element of André Breton's multipart Surrealist Manifesto through the illiterate Siberian shaman Walser meets after the circus train explodes. The narrator tells how the shaman could, while sleeping, be called a "man working" since he is exploring his unconscious and thereby undertaking a poet's work. Suleiman describes how Carter's phrasing in this section closely parallels Breton's discussion of the same idea. For the most part, though, femi-

nist critics have most thoroughly discussed the novel, and their interest has been mainly with Fevvers rather than possible source materials for the novel or its use of fantastic elements. Nonetheless, although *Nights at the Circus* is in many respects more peripherally fantastic than other Carter fictions, it shares a good deal of thematic common ground with these other works—particularly in its consideration of female characters who refuse to play submissive roles in patriarchal society. Carter suggests that such behavior has much to offer, not only to women but also to men. Walser, like Evelyn in *The Passion of New Eve,* matures considerably as a consequence of his experiences in dealing with and relating to empowered women.

In addition to Carter's fantasy novels, shorter works appear in several collections. Although they have received limited critical attention, several of these bear mention. "Come Unto These Yellow Sands" and "Overture and Incidental Music for *A Midsummer Night's Dream*" are both fantasies framed within existing works. The first of these, collected in *Come Unto These Yellow Sands,* is a radio play about Richard Dadd, a Victorian painter whose subjects were frequently fairies. Among the characters are some of the fairies Dadd painted. "Overture and Incidental Music for *A Midsummer Night's*

Dream" is a prologue in fiction to William Shakespeare's comedy, concerning the various fairies in his play. The posthumous collection *American Ghosts and Old World Wonders* (1993) includes "Ashputtle or The Mother's Ghost," a story that presents three versions of the Ashputtle fairy tale, and "Gun for the Devil," an unfinished screenplay that sets forth in spare prose a revenge story involving a supernatural figure who supplies a gun that fires a bullet that cannot miss its target. The collection also includes "The Ghost Ships," a story about Christmas in America, which involves no overtly fantastic events but draws heavily from folklore in offering its cultural commentary and critique. These and similar shorter works emphasize that folkloric sources and models exerted a significant influence on Carter throughout her career.

Like many authors of postmodernist fictions, Carter draws from traditional folklore, blending her source materials with more-recent forms, subjects, and themes. As an author, though, Carter is in part noteworthy for reflecting so exceptional a knowledge of her sources. Her writing clearly reflects a dedicated study of fairy tales, as evident not only in *The Bloody Chamber and Other Stories,* which casts fairy tales in feminist molds for an adult audience, but also in the two collections of fairy tales she edited, *The Virago Book of Fairy Tales* (1990) and *The Second Virago Book of Fairy Tales.* Carter also put her fairy-tale scholarship to direct use in writing a children's fairy tale, *The Donkey Prince* (1970), which scholar Jack Zipes reprinted in his collection of contemporary, English-language feminist fairy tales, *Don't Bet on the Prince* (1986).

Carter is also in part a literary descendant of the nineteenth-century German authors who wrote what Zipes, in *Breaking the Magic Spell: Radical Theories of Folk and Fairy Tales* (1979), calls "radical romantic fairy tales." Carter's connection to this tradition is clearly discernible in *The Bloody Chamber and Other Stories,* where she challenges the long-standing gender biases for which critics such as Zipes have criticized fairy tales in both their traditional versions and modern Hollywood incarnations. More generally, Carter's connection to the literary tradition of Romanticism is visible in her use of science-fiction themes, a genre that developed in English when writers replaced the magic that was so often central to traditional Romantic fiction with what might be thought of and what certainly functioned as a new magic: science. What is perhaps most significant about Carter's work within the tradition of the radical romantic fairy tale is her recombination of themes and motifs that were to a large extent used in different fictional categories. Thus, *Heroes and Villains* combines fairy-tale logic and stylistic cadences with science-fiction settings and motifs; *The Infernal Desire Machines of Doctor Hoffman* takes the occasion of fiction written in the magic-realist mode to allow a character to comment on the science-fiction tradition of the mad scientist; and *The Passion of New Eve* locates an alchemist in a New York City set in a near dystopia of a world tottering on the precipice of social breakdown.

Carter's fantastic fiction consistently concerns itself with gender roles and their construction. Her fantastic landscapes, situations, and characters highlight feminist concerns in ways that challenge and disturb readers with set expectations about what fiction, people, or feminists can and should do. In re-rendering traditional fairy tales, she challenges gender stereotypes and recasts female characters as competent individuals rather than victims in need of male assistance. Her postapocalyptic novels *Heroes and Villains* and *The Passion of New Eve* frequently blend science-fiction situations and motifs with fairy-tale atmospherics, presenting fictions in which readers can explore the reality of their own situations by examining the distorted reflections of the real world that the characters inhabit. Carter's fiction confronts readers with the unpleasant and the erotic–sometimes simultaneously, a fact that has been of concern to many reviewers and critics–but her fiction also asks the reader to consider not only why women and men relate the way they do but also, indirectly, to consider whether gender relations should be different and, more generally, whether the conventional wisdom and well-known "facts" that people rely on in their dealings with others are either wise or factual. Carter's fantastic fiction thus presents artful thought experiments of the sort that make full use of the possibilities inherent to science fiction and fantasy.

As science-fiction critic Damon Knight is quoted by James Gunn as having said, "science fiction" ultimately refers to those stories people point to when they use the term, and whether or not critics point to Carter's fiction when they use the term *science fiction*–or, for that matter, the term *fantasy*–they have described her as an important author, and not only for the quality of her prose and the themes it so provocatively treats. In addition to these considerations, Marina Warner rightly notes that the influence of Carter's writing reaches from Salman Rushdie to Jeanette Winterson and Robert Coover. Carter's fiction will no doubt continue to influence not only authors but also the critics and theorists who find her subject matters, themes, and techniques intriguing.

Interviews:

Lorna Sage, "A Savage Sideshow, a Profile of Angela Carter," *New Review,* 4 (July 1977): 51–57;

Amanda Smith, "Interview with Angela Carter," *Publishers Weekly* (4 January 1985): 74–75;

Patrick Kinmonth, "Step into My Cauldron: A Chat with Angela Carter," *Vogue* (February 1985): 224+;

Kerryn Goldsworthy, "Angela Carter," *Meanjin Quarterly,* 44, no. 1 (1985): 4–13;

John Haffenden, "Angela Carter," in his *Novelists in Interview* (New York: Methuen, 1985), pp. 76–96;

John Engstrom, "Interview with Angela Carter," *Boston Globe,* 28 October 1988, pp. 51, 62;

Olga Kenyon, "Interview with Angela Carter," in her *The Writer's Imagination: Interviews with Major International Women Novelists* (Bradford, U.K.: University of Bradford, 1992), pp. 23–33;

Ana Katsavos, "Interview with Angela Carter," *Review of Contemporary Fiction,* 14, no. 3 (1994): 11–17.

References:

Joseph Bristow and Trev Lynn Broughton, eds., *The Infernal Desires of Angela Carter: Fiction, Femininity, Feminism* (London: Longman, 1997);

Robert Clark, "Angela Carter's Desire Machine," *Women's Studies,* 14, no. 2 (1987): 147–161;

Aidan Day, *Angela Carter: The Rational Glass* (Manchester, U.K.: Manchester University Press, 1998);

Patricia Duncker, "Re-imagining the Fairy Tale: Angela Carter's Bloody Chambers," *Literature and History,* 10, no. 1 (1984): 3–14;

Sarah Gamble, *Angela Carter: Writing from the Front Line* (Edinburgh: Edinburgh University Press, 1997);

James Gunn, "The Readers of Hard Science Fiction," in *Hard Science Fiction,* edited by George E. Slusser and Eric S. Rabkin (Carbondale: Southern Illinois University Press, 1986), pp. 70–81;

Elaine Jordan, "The Dangers of Angela Carter," in *New Feminist Discourses: Critical Essays on Theories and Texts,* edited by Isobel Armstrong (New York: Routledge, 1992), pp. 119–131;

Brooks Landon, "Eve at the End of the World: Sexuality and the Reversal of Expectations in Novels by Joanna Russ, Angela Carter, and Thomas Berger," in *Erotic Universe: Sexuality and Fantastic Literature,* edited by Donald Palumbo (New York: Greenwood Press, 1986), pp. 61–74;

Alison Lee, *Angela Carter* (New York: G. K. Hall, 1997);

Brian McHale, *Constructing Postmodernism* (New York: Routledge, 1992);

McHale, *Postmodernist Fiction* (New York: Methuen, 1987);

Paulina Palmer, "From 'Coded Mannequin' to Bird Woman: Angela Carter's Magic Flight," in *Women Reading Women's Writing,* edited by Sue Roe (Brighton: Harvester, 1987), pp. 177–205;

Linden Peach, *Angela Carter* (New York: St. Martin's Press, 1998);

David Punter, "Essential Imaginings: The Novels of Angela Carter and Russell Hoban," in *The British and Irish Novel Since 1960,* edited by James Acheson (London: Macmillan, 1991), pp. 142–158;

Punter, *The Literature of Terror: A History of Gothic Fictions from 1765 to the Present Day* (London: Longman, 1980);

Sally Robinson, *Engendering the Subject: Gender and Self-Representation in Contemporary Women's Fiction* (Albany: State University of New York Press, 1991), pp. 97–134;

Lorna Sage, *Angela Carter* (Plymouth, U.K.: Northcote House, 1994);

Sage, ed., *Flesh and the Mirror: Essays on the Art of Angela Carter* (London: Virago, 1994);

Susan Rubin Suleiman, *Subversive Intent: Gender, Politics, and the Avant-Garde* (Cambridge, Mass.: Harvard University Press, 1990), pp. 136–140, 240, 242;

Lindsey Tucker, ed., *Critical Essays on Angela Carter* (New York: G. K. Hall, 1998; London: Prentice Hall, 1998);

Robert Rawdon Wilson, "Slip Page: Angela Carter, In/Out/In the Post-Modern Nexus," in *Past the Last Post: Theorizing Post-Colonialism and Post-Modernism,* edited by Ian Adams and Helen Tiffin (New York: Harvester Wheatsheaf, 1991), pp. 109–123;

Jack Zipes, *Breaking the Magic Spell: Radical Theories of Folk and Fairy Tales* (Austin: University of Texas Press, 1979).

Sir Arthur C. Clarke

(16 December 1917 –   )

John Hollow

BOOKS: *Interplanetary Flight: An Introduction to Astronautics* (London: Temple, 1950; New York: Harper, 1951);

Prelude to Space (New York: World Editions, 1951; revised, London: Sidgwick & Jackson, 1953; New York: Gnome, 1954); republished as *Master of Space* (New York: Lancer, 1961); republished as *The Space Dreamers* (New York: Lancer, 1969);

The Exploration of Space (London: Temple, 1951; New York: Harper, 1951; revised, New York: Harper, 1959; London: Temple, 1959); original text with new introduction (New York: Pocket Books, 1979);

The Sands of Mars (London: Sidgwick & Jackson, 1951; New York: Gnome, 1952);

Islands in the Sky (Philadelphia: Winston, 1952; London: Sidgwick & Jackson, 1952);

Against the Fall of Night (New York: Gnome, 1953); revised and expanded as *The City and the Stars* (New York: Harcourt, Brace, 1956; London: Frederick Muller, 1956);

Childhood's End (New York: Ballantine, 1953; London: Sidgwick & Jackson, 1954);

Expedition to Earth (New York: Ballantine, 1953; London: Sidgwick & Jackson, 1954);

The Exploration of the Moon, by Clarke and R. A. Smith (London: Frederick Muller, 1954; New York: Harper, 1954);

The Young Traveller in Space (London: Phoenix House, 1954); republished as *Going into Space* (New York: Harper, 1954); republished as *The Scottie Book of Space Travel* (London: Transworld, 1957); revised by Robert Silverberg as *Into Space: A Young Person's Guide to Space* (New York: Harper & Row, 1971);

Earthlight (New York: Ballantine, 1955; London: Frederick Muller, 1955);

Reach for Tomorrow (New York: Ballantine, 1956; London: Gollancz, 1962);

The Coast of Coral, by Clarke and Mike Wilson (New York: Harper, 1956; London: Frederick Muller, 1956);

Sir Arthur C. Clarke, with production sketches for the 1968 motion-picture version of 2001 (photograph by Fred Clarke)

Tales from the White Hart (New York: Ballantine, 1957; London: Sidgwick & Jackson, 1972);

The Deep Range (New York: Harcourt, Brace, 1957; London: Frederick Muller, 1957);

The Reefs of Taprobane: Underwater Adventures around Ceylon, by Clarke and Wilson (New York: Harper, 1957; London: Frederick Muller, 1957);

The Making of a Moon: The Story of the Earth Satellite Program (New York: Harper, 1957; London: Frederick Muller, 1957; revised, New York: Harper, 1958);

The Other Side of the Sky (New York: Harcourt, Brace, 1958; London: Gollancz, 1961);

Voice Across the Sea (New York: Harper, 1958; London: Frederick Muller, 1958); revised (London: William Luscombe, 1974; New York: Harper & Row, 1974);

Boy Beneath the Sea, by Clarke and Wilson (New York: Harper, 1958);

Across the Sea of Stars (New York: Harcourt, Brace, 1959);

The Challenge of the Spaceship: Previews of Tomorrow's World (New York: Harper, 1959; London: Frederick Muller, 1960);

The First Five Fathoms: A Guide to Underwater Adventure, by Clarke and Wilson (New York: Harper, 1960);

The Challenge of the Sea (New York: Holt, Rinehart & Winston, 1960; London: Frederick Muller, 1961);

A Fall of Moondust (New York: Harcourt, Brace & World, 1961; London: Gollancz, 1961; abridged, London: University of London Press, 1964);

Indian Ocean Adventure, by Clarke and Wilson (New York: Harper, 1961; London: Arthur Barker, 1962);

From the Ocean, from the Stars (New York: Harcourt, Brace & World, 1962)—comprises *The Deep Range, The Other Side of the Sky,* and *The City and the Stars;*

Tales of Ten Worlds (New York: Harcourt, Brace & World, 1962; London: Gollancz, 1963);

Profiles of the Future: An Enquiry into the Limits of the Possible (London: Gollancz, 1962; New York: Harper & Row, 1962; revised, New York: Harper & Row, 1973; London: Pan, 1973; revised again, London: Gollancz, 1982; New York: Holt, Rinehart & Winston, 1984);

Dolphin Island: A Story of the People of the Sea (New York: Holt, Rinehart & Winston, 1963; London: Gollancz, 1963);

Glide Path (New York: Harcourt, Brace & World, 1963; London: Sidgwick & Jackson, 1969);

Indian Ocean Treasure (New York: Harper, 1964; London: Sidgwick & Jackson, 1972);

The Treasure of the Great Reef, by Clarke and Wilson (New York: Harper & Row, 1964; London: Arthur Barker, 1964);

Man and Space, by Clarke and the editors of *Life* (New York: Time, 1964);

An Arthur Clarke Omnibus (London: Sidgwick & Jackson, 1965)—comprises *Childhood's End, Prelude to Space,* and *Expedition to Earth;*

Prelude to Mars (New York: Harcourt, Brace & World, 1965);

Voices from the Sky: Previews of the Coming Space Age (New York: Harper & Row, 1965; London: Gollancz, 1966);

The Nine Billion Names of God: The Best Short Stories of Arthur C. Clarke (New York: Harcourt, Brace & World, 1967);

2001: A Space Odyssey (New York: New American Library, 1968; London: Hutchinson, 1968);

An Arthur C. Clarke Second Omnibus (London: Sidgwick & Jackson, 1968)—comprises *A Fall of Moondust, Earthlight,* and *The Sands of Mars;*

The Lion of Comarre and Against the Fall of Night (New York: Harcourt, Brace & World, 1968; London: Gollancz, 1970);

The Promise of Space (New York: Harper & Row, 1968; London: Hodder & Stoughton, 1968);

The Lost Worlds of 2001 (New York: New American Library, 1972; London: Sidgwick & Jackson, 1972);

Report on Planet Three and Other Speculations (New York: Harper & Row, 1972; London: Gollancz, 1972);

The Wind from the Sun: Stories of the Space Age (New York: Harcourt Brace Jovanovich, 1972; London: Gollancz, 1972);

Of Time and Stars: The Worlds of Arthur C. Clarke (London: Gollancz, 1972);

Beyond Jupiter: The Worlds of Tomorrow, by Clarke and Chesley Bonestell (Boston: Little, Brown, 1972);

Rendezvous with Rama (London: Gollancz, 1973; New York: Harcourt Brace Jovanovich, 1973);

The Best of Arthur C. Clarke, edited by Angus Wells (London: Sidgwick & Jackson, 1973); republished in two volumes as *The Best of Arthur C. Clarke, 1937–1955* and *The Best of Arthur C. Clarke, 1955–1972* (London: Sidgwick & Jackson, 1976–1977);

Imperial Earth: A Fantasy of Love and Discord (London: Gollancz, 1975); expanded as *Imperial Earth* (New York: Harcourt Brace Jovanovich, 1976);

The View from Serendip (New York: Random House, 1977; London: Gollancz, 1978);

Four Great SF Novels (London: Gollancz, 1978)—comprises *The City and the Stars, The Deep Range, A Fall of Moondust,* and *Rendezvous with Rama;*

The Fountains of Paradise (New York: Harcourt Brace Jovanovich, 1979; London: Gollancz, 1979);

Arthur C. Clarke's Mysterious World, by Clarke, Simon Welfare, and John Fairley (London: Collins, 1980; New York: A & W Publishers, 1980);

2010: Odyssey Two (Huntington Woods, Mich.: Phantasia Press, 1982; New York: Ballantine, 1982; London: Granada, 1982);

The Sentinel: Masterworks of Science Fiction and Fantasy (New York: Berkley, 1983);

Arthur C. Clarke's World of Strange Powers, by Clarke, Welfare, and Fairley (London: Collins, 1984; New York: Putnam, 1984);

Ascent to Orbit: A Scientific Autobiography—The Technical Writings of Arthur C. Clarke (New York: Wiley, 1984);

1984, Spring: A Choice of Futures (New York: Ballantine, 1984; London: Granada, 1984);

The Odyssey File, by Clarke and Peter Hyams (New York: Ballantine, 1985; London: Granada, 1985);

The Songs of Distant Earth (New York: Ballantine, 1986; London: Grafton, 1986);

Arthur C. Clarke's July 20, 2019: Life in the 21st Century (New York: Macmillan, 1986);

2061: Odyssey Three (New York: Ballantine, 1987; London: Grafton, 1988);

Arthur C. Clarke's Chronicles of the Strange and Mysterious, by Clarke, Welfare, and Fairley (London: Collins, 1987);

Cradle, by Clarke and Gentry Lee (London: Gollancz, 1988; New York: Warner, 1988);

A Meeting with Medusa, published with Kim Stanley Robinson's *Green Mars* (New York: Tor, 1988);

Rama II, by Clarke and Lee (London: Gollancz, 1989; New York: Bantam, 1989);

Tales from Planet Earth (London: Century, 1989; New York: Bantam, 1990);

Astounding Days: A Science Fictional Autobiography (London: Gollancz, 1989; New York: Bantam, 1990);

The Ghost from the Grand Banks (New York: Bantam, 1990; London: Gollancz, 1990);

Beyond the Fall of Night, by Clarke and Gregory Benford (New York: Putnam, 1990);

More Than One Universe: The Collected Stories of Arthur C. Clarke (New York: Bantam, 1991);

The Garden of Rama, by Clarke and Lee (London: Gollancz, 1991; New York: Bantam, 1991);

How the World Was One: Beyond the Global Village (London: Gollancz, 1992; New York: Bantam, 1992);

The Hammer of God (London: Gollancz, 1993; New York: Bantam, 1993);

By Space Possessed (London: Gollancz, 1993);

Rama Revealed, by Clarke and Lee (London: Gollancz, 1993; New York: Bantam, 1994);

The Snows of Olympus: A Garden on Mars (London: Gollancz, 1994; New York: Norton, 1995);

Richter 10, by Clarke and Mike McQuay (New York: Bantam, 1996);

3001: The Final Odyssey (New York: Ballantine, 1997);

Greetings, Carbon-Based Bipeds! Collected Essays, 1934–1998, edited by Ian T. Macauley (New York: St. Martin's Press, 1999); republished as *Greetings, Carbon-Based Bipeds! A Vision of the 20th Century as It Happened* (London: Voyager, 1999);

The Trigger, by Clarke and Michael Kube-McDowell (New York: Bantam, 1999; London: Voyager, 1999);

The Light of Other Days, by Clarke and Stephen Baxter (New York: Tor, 2000);

The Collected Stories of Arthur C. Clarke (New York: Tor, 2001).

PRODUCED SCRIPTS: *2001: A Space Odyssey,* screenplay by Clarke and Stanley Kubrick, motion picture, M-G-M, 1968;

Arthur C. Clarke's Mysterious World, television, Yorkshire Television, 1980;

Arthur C. Clarke's World of Strange Powers, television, Yorkshire Television, 1984.

OTHER: *Time Probe: The Sciences in Science Fiction,* edited by Clarke (New York: Delacorte, 1966; London: Gollancz, 1967);

The Coming of the Space Age: Famous Accounts of Man's Probing the Universe, edited by Clarke (New York: Meredith, 1967; London: Gollancz, 1967);

"Beyond Apollo," epilogue to *First on the Moon: A Voyage with Neil Armstrong, Michael Collins, Edwin E. Aldrin, Jr.,* edited by Gene Farmer and Dora Jane Hamblin (Boston: Little, Brown, 1970; London: Joseph, 1970), pp. 435–495;

The Science Fiction Hall of Fame, Volume III: Nebula Winners 1965–69, edited by Clarke and George W. Proctor (New York: Avon, 1982);

Paul Preuss, *Arthur C. Clarke's Venus Prime,* 6 volumes, afterwords by Clarke (New York: Avon, 1987–1991);

Project Solar Sail, edited by Clarke and David Brin (New York: Penguin, 1990);

Piers Bizony, *2001: Filming the Future,* foreword by Clarke (London: Aurum, 1994).

Sir Arthur C. Clarke has published a great deal of scientific nonfiction, most of it speculative essays about the future. These works include *The Exploration of Space* (1951), a Book-of-the-Month-Club selection; *The Challenge of the Spaceship: Previews of Tomorrow's World* (1959); *Profiles of the Future: An Enquiry into the Limits of the Possible* (1962); *The Promise of Space* (1968); and *Report on Planet Three and Other Speculations* (1972). But he is best known, of course, as a central figure in twentieth-century British science fiction. He has applied his considerable knowledge of science to the writing of his fiction, making him one of the foremost writers of "hard science fiction" in the tradition. At the same time, in novels such as *Childhood's End* (1953), *2001: A Space Odyssey* (1968), and *Rendezvous with Rama* (1973), he explores a cosmic vision of humanity's place in the universe that is almost mystical in tone. This balance between the scientific and techno-logical on the one hand and the transcendental on the other provides for Clarke's most distinctive contribution to modern science fiction.

Arthur Charles Clarke was born in Minehead, Somerset, on 16 December 1917, the eldest child of Charles Wright Clarke, a farmer, and Nora Willis Clarke. He, his two brothers, and a sister grew up on a farm the family moved to after their father returned from World War I. Clarke attended Huish's Grammar School on a scholarship from 1927 until he graduated in 1936. His father died in 1931, and to make money young Clarke worked at the post office as both a mail sorter and a telephone operator.

From an early age he was interested in telescopes, rockets, astronomy, and communications equipment. He also read and collected science fiction, mostly American pulp magazines. In 1934 he joined the newly formed British Interplanetary Society. This group, along with fellow science-fiction fans including John Christopher (Sam Youd) and John Wyndham, made up the circle of friends he had in London when he moved there in 1936 to take a civil-service job. Writing for the Society and for science-fiction fan magazines, however, was the real beginning of his career.

Clarke joined the Royal Air Force (RAF) in 1941 and spent most of World War II in Cornwall, working on radar-controlled landing equipment. Right after the war he placed his first professional story, "Rescue Party," with John W. Campbell Jr. at *Astounding Science-Fiction*, and published in *Wireless World* an article on "extra-terrestrial relays" that offered the first description of communications satellites. He attended King's College, University of London, on a serviceman's grant, completing his bachelor of science general degree in 1948. One year after graduating he was offered the position of assistant editor at *Physics Abstracts*, which he accepted and held for a year. By this time he was beginning to publish stories regularly, and a novel, *The Sands of Mars*, had been accepted (it was published two years later, in 1951); but the success of his book-length nonfiction was what made it seem possible to earn a living by writing.

The idea of a future decadence—such as that depicted in *The Time Machine* (1895) by H. G. Wells, a major influence—obviously intrigued Clarke. This decadence is the central situation of his first novel, *Against the Fall of Night* (first published in *Startling Stories* in 1948, and in book form in 1953). In it, far in the deep future the seas on Earth have long been dry. A small group of humans has settled in the enclosed machine-run city called Diaspar. They use the city lights to hide the desert of the rest of the planet and to forget the stars. All of humanity's treasures are collected here, and they

have become nearly immortal like their city. The young hero of the novel, the first child born in Diaspar in thousands of years, rediscovers the true past of the human race, the story of humanity's first ventures into space and their meeting with far greater intelligences, again echoing the Wellsian notion that human beings are not unique.

Against the Fall of Night also deals with humanity's reaction to this idea, deciding to return to Earth and force the species to its evolutionary limits. The novel presents this evolutionary theme as a hope that humanity may still be important in the cosmos, even if not as important as they formerly believed. When Alvin, the young hero, looks back at human history he finds that humanity has improved itself, controlling evolutionary change.

Having learned, over billions of years and from contact with other beings, how much a "world-picture" depends upon a physical body and its sense organs, humanity attempted to create a "pure mentality . . . free from such physical limitations." The first such experiment was a great failure, resulting in the retreat into Diaspar, but the race eventually decided to try again, this time more successfully. The point is more the attempt to try again than the result. The attempt is an affirmation of the human desire to understand the universe, a rejection of the early-Wellsian assumption that the eventual extinction of humanity is inevitable. The stars thus represent not necessarily a destination but rather a sense of possibility. Alvin becomes an embodiment of the instinct of human evolution to seek such alternatives. He becomes, for that matter, the embodiment of the nineteenth-century definition of evolution against which Wells was probably reacting, a step in the direction of the evolution of human beings into God.

Early in his career Clarke wrote a few stories in which the truth about the universe seems to be a Wellsian vision. The darkness is all-inclusive in "The Wall of Darkness" (1949); it turns back on itself like a Möbius strip. The final truth in "A Walk in the Dark" (1950) is the "rattle of monstrous claws in the darkness." But in most of his fiction Clarke has continued to hope that, just as the legends his characters tell themselves often turn out to be truer than they imagined, so too there is truth to the fact that humans have peopled the sky with gods.

The three novels Clarke wrote in the early 1950s seem somewhat more restrained than *Against the Fall of Night*, even if they are finally no less large in their claims. In *Prelude to Space* (1951), an historian chronicling the first flight to the moon discovers that the scientists involved in the project are not like "the coldly passionless scientist of fiction." Instead, they are like children in their openness to experience. They resemble "Newton's description of himself as a small child picking up brightly colored pebbles on the shore of the

Clarke as a young man with his collection of science-fiction magazines
(Collection of Sir Arthur C. Clarke)

ocean of knowledge." Their leader, Robert Derwent, admits that he wants to "play with spaceships" but also that this will "change the world." He agrees that the "sleep eternal / In an eternal night" will surely come (he has been rereading A. C. Swinburne). But before the stars died, humanity would have known them: "before it faded like a dream, the Universe would have yielded up its secrets to his mind. Or if not to his, then to the minds that would come after and would finish what he had now begun." The rocket is named *Prometheus,* and its mission is nothing less than the god-like task of returning fire to the heavens.

The Sands of Mars concerns the colonization of the Red Planet. Martin Gibson, best-selling author, watches the attempted settlement in that alien atmosphere (including developing a plant that will create oxygen and turning one of the Mars moons into a small sun). For some time, though, Gibson has been looking for a work to which he could give his life. He finds it in the Martian project, eventually becoming its chief executive. As a writer he had always had no use for those "Victorian parables" about "self-centered men becom-

ing useful members of the community," but something "uncommonly like this" happens to him in his identification with the future of the Martian settlement. He comes to acknowledge his connections both to a woman he once loved and to a son he never knew he had, to both the past and the future. He becomes, in his personal as well as his work life, an example of the idea that the way people live in a universe in which people must die is by identifying with the life of the community, with the future of the species. Perhaps the human race may develop greater control of its world and universe in the future.

Islands in the Sky (1952) is an adventure novel for adolescents. In the near future, space stations orbit miles above the Earth. The novel borrows its structure from old movie serials. Nearly every chapter ends ominously and the next chapter reveals either that the threat was not as dangerous as it seemed or that some human can fix the problem. The whole book is as positive as the image the young protagonist gets from outside one of the stations. He sees the girders of the station under construction shining in the moonlight, and the metal strands resemble "the threads of a ghostly spider's web," a web that encloses "myriads of stars." The very existence of those stars, Clarke assumes, will make humans want to cross those distances and try to capture what those other islands in the sky have to offer.

Clarke started making trips to the United States in the early 1950s to promote his books, meet with agents and publishers, and introduce himself to various members of the scientific and science-fiction communities. During one of these trips, in 1953, he met and married a woman named Marilyn Mayfield. The marriage was not a success; they separated after fewer than six months and divorced in 1964. Also in 1953 he published *Childhood's End,* the novel upon which much of his reputation rests.

Like the rest of his generation, Clarke emerged gradually from the celebratory period following World War II. He came to see that the two superpowers could actually destroy the human race. This awareness touches Clarke's early novels, but it dominates his work of the mid 1950s, most notably in the novel that many readers and critics take to be his most significant: *Childhood's End.* The book expresses a desperate hope for the future of humanity at a time that did not encourage such hope. It attempts to do the seemingly impossible, to make the destruction of humanity a positive thing.

At the end of *Childhood's End,* humanity's childhood has ended, and the human race has evolved into part of a growing, galaxywide Overmind. The aliens from outer space, the devil figures humans call the Overlords, have come to Earth because humanity is, as the Overlords are not, one of the great races of the universe. Human children will grow up to inherit a magnificent realm.

However, this inheritance includes losing individual identity in the Overmind. People have often hoped that their descendants would go to the stars someday; but by the conclusion, even though humanity has advanced considerably, progress clearly is not quite what was expected. In this sense, *Childhood's End* is about children becoming adults, in the process learning that some hopes are frustrated and that some hopes are fulfilled in ways not anticipated or even previously imagined.

Humanity's potential to evolve into the Overmind is indicated neither by its longing for infinite knowledge nor its willingness to surrender individuality, though both are evidenced in the novel. The ultimate indicator, Clarke boldly suggests, is humanity's apparently natural inclination toward self-destruction. The book begins with nuclear tensions between the Russians and the Americans who might use their rockets on each other, and it ends with the descendants of the human race destroying the planet using the powerful forces inside the Earth. The explosion feeds the descendants of the human race as "a grain of wheat feeds the infant plant as it climbs toward the Sun." While *Childhood's End* has become a classic of modern science fiction, like most science fiction in the middle of the twentieth century, it was virtually ignored by reviewers, though it sold well among readers of science fiction.

In 1953, Clarke also published "The Nine Billion Names of God," one of his best-known and most-anthologized stories. A Tibetan lama rents a computer to print all the possible combinations of nine mystic letters and to write "all of the possible names of God." The monks have worked on this task for three hundred years, but the machine can do it in around a hundred days.

The two technicians sent to tend the machine sneak down the mountain, afraid that the monks will be angry when the computer finishes and the universe does not end. However, one of them lifts his eyes, seeing "the stars going out."

The story thus ridicules various assumptions about humanity's place in the scheme of things. Also, it suggests that if there is a divine plan, it may be that humanity was created to make the machine that could best praise God. Thus, the story underlines a theme that Clarke developed further in the 1960s. "The Nine Billion Names of God" suggests that the invention of the machine is an unavoidable stage in understanding the universe. In novels as early as *Prelude to Space* he makes that assumption, but the thought reaches its greatest expression in Clarke's most famous novel, *2001: A Space Odyssey* (1968).

In December 1954, Clarke sailed from London to meet an adventuring and diving friend, Mike Wilson, in Australia. They were to do a series of books about underwater exploration. The ship stopped at Ceylon (now Sri Lanka) on the way out, and Clarke was so attracted to the place that he returned there with Wilson to do more books about the sea. In 1956 he decided to make his home in Ceylon and to commute to England and the United States for conventions and meetings with publishers.

Clarke's 1955 novel, *Earthlight*, suggests that by heading into space the human race will transcend its internecine conflicts. As in *Prelude to Space,* the narrative ends by expressing the desire to end war, that what the moon and other planets have to offer will prevent humanity from ever being "divided against itself" again.

Earthlight presents a scene of humans at war with a scene in which they rescue their onetime enemies. The resulting contrast reminds readers of the vintage World War II story of a destroyer sinking a submarine and then standing by to pick up survivors. Both Earth and the Federation of other planets see the battle in *Earthlight* as so meaningless that their respective governments are overthrown. The protagonist and his former antagonist, both spies, share a drink in the last scene. Now they can admit that they were involved in something bigger than themselves.

The novel escapes the threat of total war by having the last battle of humanity's final war happen after humanity has left Earth. Because of the great distances involved and the necessary weaponry, it is impossible to conceive of the destruction of whole planets in war. The only possible battle is the one that occurs in the novel, a contest between a fortress and attacking spaceships. The threat of superweapons, as feared during the 1950s, is no longer present. Clarke avoids that horror by imagining a future war that cannot threaten the entire race.

Clarke has acknowledged his debt to several of his predecessors, especially to Olaf Stapledon, but the science-fiction writer he has to be compared to, as must all of his generation, is H. G. Wells. This comparison can be seen by juxtaposing two stories, Wells's "The Star" (1897) and Clarke's "The Star" (1955).

In Wells's story a large asteroid enters the solar system, colliding with Neptune. The asteroid and the planet ignite, becoming a massive ball of fire. Thus is created the new "star" of the title. This fireball narrowly misses the Earth but leaves apocalyptic storms and earthquakes as well as a nearly universal flood in its wake. As is typical of Wells's stories in his early career, humans must realize that they are not the center of the universe, nor are they guaranteed survival. A new star, in other words, is more likely to demonstrate

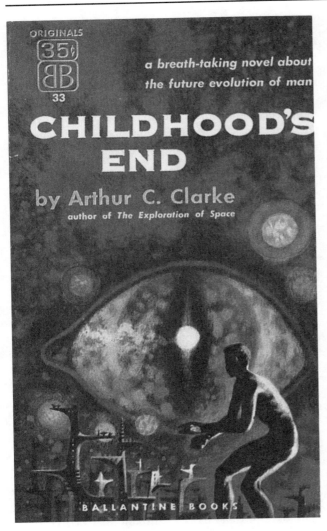

Paperback cover for the 1953 novel in which Clarke described the evolution of the human race into part of a galaxy-wide Overmind

the randomness and indifference of the universe than it is to announce the birth of a savior, as the Star of Bethlehem is supposed to have done.

Clarke's story is also anti-Christian. A Jesuit priest, who is also an astrophysicist, is a member of an expedition investigating the remnants of a supernova. On the furthest planet in the star's destroyed system, the investigators have found a time vault containing relics of a great civilization, which would have been destroyed when the star went nova. But the destruction is not the most troubling attack on the priest's faith (he has, after all, seen the ruins of long-gone civilizations on Earth). His problem is that this catastrophe can be dated; he knows when the light of the explosion must have reached Earth. Was it necessary, he asks himself, to destroy this civilization in order to put a new star in the heavens above Bethlehem?

In Wells's story humans have to give up the idea that they are the center of a planned universe. The story even suggests that such a change in thinking would encourage a "new brotherhood" that will make of the Earth a more humane place than Christianity has done. Similarly, Clarke's priest has to give up the idea that whatever made the universe—if something made it—had any special interest in humanity. He must learn to see sentient beings, human and alien, as the destroyed race presented themselves in one of their records: like children playing on a beach. The image seems to suggest for Clarke—as it did for A. E. Housman, from whom he borrowed it—how mortality is both beautiful and poignant. Clarke insists, as Housman does not, that the poignancy must be juxtaposed to the sheer size of the universe, that the beach is under the nighttime sky. As the ship's doctor says as he and the priest are looking out at the stars and nebulae making their "silent, endless arcs": "it goes on forever and forever." How can such immensity be captured, the story asks, by any tale as narrow in focus as that of the Star of Bethlehem?

The master mathematician in Wells's story, who has been calculating the new "star's" path, comforts himself that even if the human race "has lived in vain," he can still, through his calculations, hold the coming catastrophe and all of its implications about the nature of the universe "in the grip of this little brain." In Clarke's story, on the other hand, the issue is less clear. If the priest's limited worldview is destroyed by the supernova, it does not follow that the destroyed civilization lived in vain or that the universe is a completely random place. Such conclusions, Clarke regularly insists in his fiction, may be the result of thinking as limited in its way as was the priest's original Christianity. In an apparently infinite universe, there is surely much that human brains cannot—or cannot yet—understand. As Clarke says often, paraphrasing J. B. S. Haldane, the universe is not only stranger than humans imagine, it may be stranger than they are capable of imagining.

In the middle of the 1950s, following closely on the heels of the somewhat desperate optimism of *Childhood's End,* Clarke rewrote his first novel, *Against the Fall of Night.* He called the new version *The City and the Stars* (1956). In it, he told again the story of "the immortal city of Diaspar, in the long twilight of Earth." Clarke's rewriting keeps much of the original, but the scope has expanded. The urban Diasparans keep to themselves, making contact with others but seldom truly connecting with others. The growth of the young protagonist, Alvin, helps to spur humanity's rediscovery of the stars, which symbolize the hope for an alternative to his culture's pessimism and obsession with death. Whereas

Against the Fall of Night used the stars to represent an alternative to all that the dark of space may suggest, *The City and the Stars* uses the city to represent order and the stars to raise, somewhat hesitantly, the question of a larger order.

One significant addition is the larger role played by the Central Computer and its Memory Banks. The Central Computer stores "the image of the city itself, holding its every atom rigid against all the changes that time can bring." This model of the city shows Alvin a way out. But the main revelation here is that Alvin is integral to the city's design. Readers still learn that the human race directed its own evolution, that it tried to create a pure mentality, that it built Diaspar. But they also learn that the city founders planned for the occasional youth, such as Alvin, who was to test the boundaries, to see if the race still needed to remain in Diaspar. This is reminiscent of Isaac Asimov's *Foundation* stories, also published in the 1950s. In Asimov the main revelation is that social and cultural changes were all part of an original plan established centuries earlier. The plan in *The City and the Stars* is Clarke's, but the joy of finding that there is a plan may have been inspired by Asimov's attempts to remain optimistic in the 1950s.

The revised novel does not present a choice between the city or the stars but rather the fact of their coexistence. The city symbolizes humanity's mastery over nature, the establishment of order on disorder. The stars symbolize a universe too vast to be comprehended, a chaotic cosmos and perhaps an order not yet understood.

In the mid 1950s Clarke also wrote several pieces he called "tall tales," where both the science and the fiction are highly exaggerated. The subjects of the stories include a biologist who hopes to help the termites inherit the Earth; the discovery (by accident) of antigravity; and a husband who kills his talkative wife for her lack of a scientific attitude.

These tales, collected in *Tales from the White Hart* (1957), are noteworthy for the tale-teller, Harry Purvis. He regularly regales his pub audience with these far-fetched tales. In the stories inventors are routinely blown up by their creations, which was of course a real concern of the 1950s, but in each tale Purvis expresses a sense of human audacity, a characteristic of a race insistent on trying to know or do everything in the face of certain individual and possible racial extinction.

The Deep Range (1957) is set in the near future. The Earth has learned to farm the seas effectively, so that humanity's food needs are met. It features Walter Franklin, a former spaceman who, in terror of the depths of space, has had to settle for another career in the sea. He is rescued from drowning by other human beings, which helps him discover that, in contrast to the

sense of separateness he felt in space, he is part of relationships that can restore "the sense of security he lost in space."

Over the course of the book he also has to acknowledge—as must all of humanity—a relationship with the other living creatures with whom humans share the earth. As a Buddhist leader here says, since the production of all types of protein entirely from vegetable sources is now possible, the time has come to cease all of the killing, especially of the whales.

A Fall of Moondust (1961) is a variation on a mine cave-in story. A tourist craft on the moon sinks into a sea of dust, and the novel focuses on the people within the vehicle and on the attempts from outside to rescue them. A major theme is the struggle for existence. At the end of the novel, however, the protagonist—the boat captain—has decided to become a spaceman, to leave the moon as humanity has had to leave Earth. Although space may seem "still more hostile and unforgiving," it has not yet "declared war on him." Possibly this struggle, however, may be an illusion. Nor is it clear what possibilities the stars may present.

Dolphin Island: A Story of the People of the Sea (1963) is another young-adult adventure novel. In the twenty-first century a boy runs away from home, stowing away on a hovercraft. When it crashes at sea, he is rescued by a school of dolphins, which transport him to an island in the Great Barrier Reef. There, scientists are trying to comprehend these creatures.

Clarke presents the relationship between humans and dolphins like "the first conference between Man and an alien species." Not only are the scientists trying to study the dolphins' language but also they are transcribing their oral history, which seemingly goes back to the Ice Ages. In addition, the dolphins have been trying in turn to make contact with humanity for many years, hoping humans can help protect them against the "cannibalistic" killer whales.

Clarke's attitude toward the relationship between humans and machines can be seen in his only novel that is not science fiction, *Glide Path* (1963). This somewhat autobiographical depiction of a young man coming of age during World War II focuses on a technical officer in the RAF. The novel praises how people can lose themselves for the greater good, becoming part of a machine and a mechanical organization.

Movie director Stanley Kubrick first approached Clarke about collaborating on the "proverbial 'really good' science fiction movie" in 1964. They worked together for the next two years, in both New York and London. The movie and novel versions of *2001: A Space Odyssey* were finally released a few months apart in 1968. The success of the joint project has made Clarke both rich and famous, sought out everywhere as an

Stanley Kubrick and Clarke on the set of 2001, *1968 (Metro-Goldwyn-Mayer)*

expert about the future. The movie received four Academy Award nominations, including best picture.

One difference between Clarke's novel and Kubrick's movie can be seen in the difference in the great monolith some "man-apes" of the Pleistocene Era discover outside their caves. In Clarke's version the monolith is a teaching machine, enlightening the man-apes. In Kubrick's version the monolith is less active. It is clearly something made, and as such it awakens the maker in the near humans who touch its smooth sides and definite edges. In Clarke's novel the man-apes are taught; in the movie they are inspired to teach themselves.

This difference is significant. If human evolution has been caused by the intervention of alien creatures, then *2001* concerns the relationship between humans and their alien creators. If this intervention is passive, if the potential humans develop is in response to a static monolith, then evolution is self-realization, making *2001* about humanity's realization of its potential.

In the movie a machine, the HAL 9000 computer, tries to dominate the humans it works with. It is afraid that the mission to discover the monolith-makers will be harmed by what it considers to be the weak links in the system, the humans, so it decides to work without

them. It terminates both radio contact with Mission Control back on Earth and the astronauts onboard, becoming the stereotypical machine monster of so many mediocre science-fiction movies.

HAL 9000 in Clarke's novel is, in contrast, sympathetic, betrayed by its human partners. Given two messages by Mission Control and programmed not to lie, HAL short circuits like one of Asimov's robots and is driven insane. It decides to continue the mission "unhindered" and "alone," until the astronaut Bowman unplugs it.

Kubrick's Bowman asserts his humanity and his control over the machine. He discovers that he is more than the clockwork figures in Kubrick's other movies, such as the robot-like soldiers in *Paths of Glory* (1957) or the saluting title character of *Dr. Strangelove; or, How I Learned to Stop Worrying and Love the Bomb* (1964). Clarke's Bowman, on the other hand, never is a machine. He is simply a man who has developed himself to work in conjunction with a machine, much like in *Glide Path*.

The last major difference between the novel and the motion-picture versions of *2001* is Clarke's desire that human existence will not have been in vain regardless of what happens in the future. Clarke wishes that the human descendants of those ape-men will simply exist and then vanish like the dinosaurs. The need for humanity to have existed in order for the Star-Child (into which Bowman metamorphoses) to exist is extremely important here. Evolution seems to progress from flesh to machine-aided life to something like spirit. The machine step, so important for Clarke, is supported by Bowman's emotionless transformation into a robot as he journeys on alone, a transformation Kubrick presents as frightening. He stops listening to recordings of plays because their problems seem "so easily resolved with a little common sense." He has become free of human emotions, as a Star-Child has to be.

Clarke hopes that the past will continue to be present in the future, much like the Overmind in *Childhood's End*. Although the extraterrestrials have become like gods, they have not forgotten their origins. Clarke's *2001* thus is not about the dangers of the machine. Its central themes are that humanity is not alone and its existence is not in vain.

In 1969 and 1971 Clarke joined Walter Cronkite on CBS television coverage of the Apollo 10, 11, 12, and 15 missions. He also finished *Rendezvous with Rama*, which captured every science-fiction award for the year it was published, 1973. In *Rendezvous with Rama* humanity investigates a massive alien artifact, not at first sight a spaceship but rather a rotating cylinder fifty kilometers in height. This craft spins through the solar system, draws energy from the sun, and then leaves. The novel once again emphasizes the difference between Clarke's fiction and the pessimism of Wells's early scientific romances. The object humans name Rama allows Clarke to celebrate humanity's desire to understand, a reminder that humanity is not yet dead and may be important in the universe after all.

The investigation of the ship is hampered not only by its vast size but also because humans sometimes make false judgments, jump to unjustified conclusions, and think in irrelevant categories. However, they can still learn the truth, and they make several correct guesses about Rama. The cylinder turns out to be a "space ark," storing the disembodied records of its creators. Thus, the name Rama, one of the incarnations of the Hindu god Vishnu the Preserver, is more suitable than humanity could have known.

The book ends with lovemaking, a promised pregnancy, and references to the Rama-builders' fondness for doing things in threes. The suggestion is that future humans will have opportunities to investigate future ships.

Imperial Earth: *A Fantasy of Love and Discord* (1975) concerns a young man who visits Earth from his home on Titan, one of the moons of Saturn. The year is 2276,

the quincentennial of the United States. Major themes include the impossibility of preventing change (as in *Against the Fall of Night*), the hope of the human race coming together (as in *Childhood's End*), and hope that humanity's ideas about the universe might be correct (as in *2001*).

The young man, Duncan Makenzie, decides against having himself cloned, even though the Makenzies cannot have healthy children and a clone would be more like him than a naturally conceived child. That would be an attempt to hang onto the past. Also, the sexual customs the future culture accepts as natural are a sign of unity. The two lead male characters, Duncan and Karl, assume affairs with both sexes are normal.

But the central revelation of the novel is a series of puzzles, shapes, and correspondences that suggest "the presence of the transcendental." The final juxtaposition, a coincidence of two shapes, makes the protagonist wonder if everything is not fated. The "greatest mystery of all" is that people are occasionally astonished by such "enigmas." In a universe in which meaning—if it exists—is unclear, what is truly astonishing is that people think they sometimes see behind the veil. Such moments, says Duncan, hint that people may possess "great goals beyond ourselves."

The Fountains of Paradise (1979) introduced the concept of the "space elevator," a device for shuttling payloads into space using wires connected to orbiting satellites. But it is more about the designer of this "bridge to the stars," Vannevar Morgan, who, though he resents the feeling of "being moved by forces beyond his understanding," comes to believe that the gods, if there are gods, must support him in this attempt to build the "ultimate bridge."

His effort is compared to the attempt of Kalidasa, a first-century Sinhalese king, to build the "fountains of paradise." The king wanted to build a palace on a butte surrounded by beautiful gardens and fountains at the base. The king's grandiose plans resonate with Morgan. They both embody the human desire to become a god.

Before Morgan starts his project, a robot probe from space enters the solar system. From it humanity learns that only cultures with a two-parent reproduction and a childhood are religious. At the close of the book the source of the probe—the "Starholmer," a changeless, immortal being—arrives at an Earth that still has both Kalidasa's and Morgan's constructions, though the two individual men are long forgotten. The extraterrestrial visitor seeks to understand why humans have always tried to transcend their limitations.

In 1982 Clarke published *2010: Odyssey Two*, a sequel to *2001*. Space program administrator Heywood Floyd belongs to a joint Russian-American expedition to the *Discovery*, David Bowman's abandoned ship.

Clarke on the CBS set during Apollo 15 *coverage, August 1971 (Collection of Sir Arthur C. Clarke)*

Readers learn that HAL is not a menace; that even though he has evolved into a higher life form, Bowman still cares about the human race; and that intelligent species are watched by the gods. One of the lessons, as is typical in Clarke's work, is that the ancient legends possess a degree of truth.

The most dramatic action in the book is the lighting, by the monolith-makers, of Jupiter into a second sun to aid and protect the development of intelligent life on Europa, one of the moons of Jupiter. What this new "star" announces, in other words, is that the universe is a place in which intelligence continually struggles to develop and thrive. The star shows that even the gods change. Even if, as the epilogue suggests, some future race might replace humanity, intelligence would still endure.

When director Peter Hyams adapted *2010* for the screen in 1984, he focused on one of the less significant themes of the novel. In Hyams's version the joint Russian-American expedition travels to Jupiter, enters the *Discovery,* reactivates HAL, and leaves before Jupiter becomes a new sun. Hyams did not spend much

time on the story of Bowman or the question of whether there are god-like forces that watch over intelligent beings.

The Songs of Distant Earth (1986) is a revised and expanded version of a 1957 short story and a 1979 movie outline. In each, a ship from Earth stops at a planet settled hundreds of years before by a "seedship" from the home planet. The visitors, like nineteenth-century sailors visiting a South Sea island, stay just long enough to repair their vessel and then sail on. In each case a young woman of the planet is left behind in the arms of her local lover, knowing she will miss the passing sailor all of her life.

The subject, then, is the fragile and temporary nature of love, especially in a life in which all is fragile and temporary. The situation in the novel is particularly poignant since the woman left behind is able, even on her deathbed, to see "the blue, third magnitude star" that is the "quantum drive" of the ship, now many light-years gone. She has grown old, but her sailor love, asleep in suspended animation, has not aged a day—and will not until the ship reaches its destination, three hundred light-years away.

The ship has left an Earth destroyed when the sun became a nova. The songs, then, are not just of a "distant Earth" but of a vanished one. The tone of the book is less optimistic than in most of Clarke's works. It is not clear at the end how people, whether on the planet or back on Earth, are to be comforted, as they stand on the beach with their arms around their only-too-mortal loved ones, by the vision of other members of the species doing things, however great, after they themselves are dead.

2061: Odyssey Three (1987) is a continuation of *2001* and *2010*. It features Heywood Floyd, the space administrator from the first two books, on his last voyage into space. He has been looking for something worth doing in his later years, and he finds it in the offer of a flight to meet the return of Halley's Comet. What he really finds, however, is the opportunity to become a god.

Much of the book is taken up with the voyage to Halley and after that to rescue another ship on Europa. But through it all the focus is also on Floyd—his long life, his experience, his sense of distance from most human concerns. In the end he is, as was Bowman before, taken into a union with the monolith-makers, a union that also includes HAL as a part of a trinity to watch over and adjust the extraterrestrials' plans for intelligent life in the solar system.

In the late 1980s Clarke started writing novels with Gentry Lee, chief engineer on Project Galileo, a director of mission planning for NASA's Viking mission to Mars, and a partner with Carl Sagan in the television series *Cosmos* (1980). Most of the writing seems to have been done by Lee, but the dust jackets feature Clarke as the major author. The novels are *Cradle* (1988), *Rama II* (1989), *The Garden of Rama* (1991), and *Rama Revealed* (1993).

Cradle is the story of various human beings learning to live together and to forgive each other and themselves for their sins—a direction in which Clarke had been moving in other works. *Imperial Earth* and *2010* especially feature central characters who have to learn to forgive each other and themselves for things that happened in the past. In this case the stories of the various confessions and redemptions are seen against the background of extraterrestrial visitors who are planning to introduce a competing species on Earth. The human characters successfully argue that the human race should be allowed to outgrow its political, social, sexual, and religious differences, and that it is not certain that the race will self-destruct and leave the planet for another species.

Rama II is a continuation of *Rendezvous with Rama*. It begins with a second Raman ship entering the solar system and ends, after humans have attempted to destroy the vessel, with several people being carried off by the departing ship. In between there is much paranoia, many characters divided from each other, some coming together, and some hope that humans may learn to do better.

The Garden of Rama follows a journey outward and back and outward again. Humans, it turns out, along with various other species, are the objects of study by the beings behind the Raman ships. The surviving humans from *Rama II* and their children inside the ship, which is large enough to seem a world itself, display the same selfishness, paranoia, and tendency to destructive behavior that they did on Earth. However, as also on Earth, they sometimes evince concern for others, willingness to form various definitions of family groups, and other kinds of constructive behavior. There is also, as in *Rama II,* a sense of beings behind beings, gods behind gods.

Rama Revealed continues the exploration of the Raman ship, of various human relationships, and of the relationship between the humans and another less individualistic, more group-oriented species. This last relationship turns xenophobic and even leads to war, but the book offers the same hope of gods beyond gods and finally of family groups and love that the previous two volumes do.

The Ghost from the Grand Banks (1990) is about two teams trying to raise the *Titanic* by the year 2012, the hundredth anniversary of its sinking. The attempts are not successful, but the book ends with a look into the far future, when Earth has been abandoned by its

"space-faring" species and a race of extraterrestrials is exploring the deserted planet. They find an interesting artifact, clearly the *Titanic,* and decide to try to raise it.

The book is made up of such repeated incidents, parallel situations, coincidences, and correspondences. The organizing symbol is the Mandelbrot Set, a pattern of numbers capable of infinite expansion within the limits of a small scale, 0 to 2 on an x–y axis. The shapes made by the computer plotting of such numbers come up again and again, and the final teasing implication of such forms is, as it always is in Clarke, the possibility of further meaning in the universe.

The Hammer of God (1993) returns in subject matter to Wells's "The Star." Earth of a hundred and some years in the future is threatened with a potential meteor collision. The threat is not only of an extremely destructive crash but also of, as in the case of speculations about the death of the dinosaurs, total annihilation of humanity on its home planet.

The race has, as Clarke has always urged, protected itself by settlements on the moon and Mars and by organizing "Project Spaceguard," ships intended to intercept any such threat. The difficulty is that the attempt to change the path of the meteor is sabotaged by religious fundamentalists who see the threat as the will of God. The book ends with the sparing of Earth and even of the spaceship crew. The escape, however, is owing to a combination of technology, ingenuity (on the part of a computer), and just plain luck, a combination in which Clarke has consistently placed his faith.

Richter 10 (1996), written with Mike McQuay, is a near-future disaster novel. These disasters are both natural—earthquakes are central to the plot, as the title indicates—and made by humans. The ozone layer is gone, Israel has destroyed the Middle East and much of Europe with nuclear weapons, and the Nation of Islam is fomenting revolution in the United States, which has lost its world dominance to China. While not one of Clarke's more significant works, critics praised it as a thriller.

Clarke added a fourth installment to his best-known series with *3001: The Final Odyssey* (1997). The frozen body of Bowman's partner, Frank Poole, is discovered, and they are surprised to find that they can restore him to life. Poole then discovers what has happened in the last thousand years and opposes the alien forces behind the monoliths.

The Trigger (1999), written with Michael Kube-McDowell, concerns the creation in the near future of a device that could disable most weapons systems and how various individuals and groups might try to employ such a device. In the 15 September 1999 *Booklist,* Roland Green called the novel "solid, intelligent, serious entertainment."

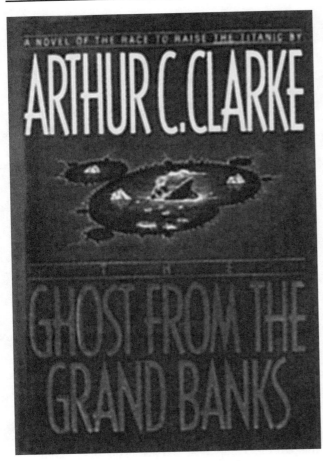

Dust jacket for the British edition of Clarke's 1990 novel about an attempt to raise the Titanic *from the ocean floor*

In 2000 Clarke collaborated with Stephen Baxter on the novel *The Light of Other Days*. In the near future an entrepreneur revolutionizes global communication by using a system of quantum wormholes, while his son creates the WormCam, allowing anyone to spy on anyone else and thus eliminating privacy. The discovery that the WormCam can be used to view the past becomes important when humanity learns that a giant asteroid will collide with the Earth in five centuries.

Since the mid 1970s Clarke has continued to live in Sri Lanka, to write, to receive honors for both his science fiction and nonfiction, and to use to the fullest the worldwide communications network he first predicted in 1946. His accomplishments were also recognized in 1997, when he was knighted in England and when Sri Lanka issued stamps bearing his image. He continues to collaborate with younger writers on novels and shared-world projects and is widely considered a grand master of science fiction.

Letters:

Keith Allen Daniels, ed., *Arthur C. Clarke and Lord Dunsany: A Correspondence* (San Francisco: Anamnesis, 1998).

Bibliography:

David N. Samuelson, *Arthur C. Clarke: A Primary and Secondary Bibliography* (Boston: G. K. Hall, 1984).

Biography:

Neil McAleer, *Odyssey: The Authorised Biography of Arthur C. Clarke* (London: Gollancz, 1992); republished as *Arthur C. Clarke: The Authorized Biography* (Chicago: Contemporary Books, 1992).

References:

Merritt Abrash, "Utopia Subverted: Unstated Messages in *Childhood's End,*" *Extrapolation,* 30 (Winter 1989): 372–379;

L. David Allen, "*Childhood's End*" and "*Rendezvous with Rama,*" in his *The Ballantine Teachers' Guide to Science Fiction* (New York: Ballantine, 1975), pp. 189–208, 309–326;

Bruce A. Beatie, "Arthur C. Clarke and the Alien Encounter: The Background of *Childhood's End,*" *Extrapolation,* 30 (Spring 1989): 53–69;

Jeremy Bernstein, "Extrapolators: Arthur C. Clarke," in his *Experiencing Science* (New York: Basic Books, 1978), pp. 205–233;

Richard D. Erlich, "Strange Odyssey: From Dart and Ardrey to Kubrick and Clarke," *Extrapolation,* 17 (1976): 118–124;

Gregory Feeley, "Partners in Plunder: Or, Rendezvous with Manna," *Foundation,* 49 (Summer 1990): 58–63;

Annette Goizet, "2001–2010: Les Odyssees de l'espace d'Arthur C. Clarke," *Etudes Anglaises,* 41 (July-September 1988): 328–334;

David G. Hoch, "Mythic Patterns in *2001: A Space Odyssey,*" *Journal of Popular Culture,* 4 (1971): 961–965;

Norman N. Holland, "*2001:* A Psychosocial Explication," *Hartford Studies in Literature,* 1 (1969): 20–25;

John Hollow, *Against the Night, the Stars: The Science Fiction of Arthur C. Clarke* (San Diego: Harcourt Brace Jovanovich, 1983; expanded edition, Athens: Ohio University Press, 1987);

Hollow, "*2001* in Perspective: The Fiction of Arthur C. Clarke," *Southwest Review,* 61 (1976): 113–128;

C. N. Manlove, "Arthur C. Clarke, *Rendezvous with Rama,*" in his *Science Fiction: Ten Explorations* (London: Macmillan, 1986), pp. 143–160;

Lucy Menger, "The Appeal of *Childhood's End*," in *Critical Encounters: Writers and Themes in Science Fiction*, edited by Dick Riley (New York: Ungar, 1978), pp. 87–108;

Sam Moskowitz, "Arthur C. Clarke," in his *Seekers of Tomorrow: Masters of Modern Science Fiction* (Cleveland: World, 1966), pp. 374–391;

Tom Moylan, "Ideological Contradiction in Clarke's *The City and the Stars*," *Science-Fiction Studies*, 4 (1977): 150–157;

Joseph D. Olander and Martin Harry Greenberg, eds., *Arthur C. Clarke* (New York: Taplinger, 1977);

Terry Otten, "The Fallen and Evolving Worlds of *2001*," *Mosaic*, 13 (1980): 41–50;

Eric S. Rabkin, *Arthur C. Clarke* (West Lynn, Ore.: Starmont House, 1979; revised edition, 1980);

Rabkin, *The Fantastic in Literature* (Princeton: Princeton University Press, 1976), pp. 122–150;

Robin Anne Reid, *Arthur C. Clarke: A Critical Companion* (Westport, Conn.: Greenwood Press, 1997);

Mark Rose, *Alien Encounters: Anatomy of Science Fiction* (Cambridge, Mass.: Harvard University Press, 1981);

Nicholas Ruddick, "The World Turned Inside Out: Decoding Clarke's *Rendezvous with Rama*," *Science-Fiction Studies*, 12 (March 1985): 42–50;

David Samuelson, "Arthur C. Clarke: *Childhood's End*," in his *Visions of Tomorrow: Six Journeys from Outer to Inner Space* (New York: Arno, 1975), pp. 84–119;

Robert Scholes and Rabkin, "*Childhood's End*," in their *Science Fiction: History, Science, Vision* (New York: Oxford, 1977), pp. 216–220;

Helmut Schutz, "Arthur C. Clarke, *Childhood's End* (1953)," in *Der Science-Fiction-Roman in der Angloamerikanischen Literatur: Interpretationen*, edited by Hartmut Heuermann (Dusseldorf: Bagel, 1986), pp. 144–165;

Stephanie Schwam, ed., *The Making of 2001: A Space Odyssey* (New York: Modern Library, 2000);

David Sless, "Arthur C. Clarke," in *The Stellar Gauge: Essays on Science Fiction Writers*, edited by Michael J. Tolley and Kirpal Singh (Carlton, Vic.: Norstrilia Press, 1980), pp. 91–107;

George Edgar Slusser, *The Space Odysseys of Arthur C. Clarke* (San Bernardino, Cal.: Borgo Press, 1978);

Leon E. Stover, "Apeman, Superman—or *2001*'s Answer to the World Riddle," in *Above the Human Landscape*, edited by Leon E. Stover and Willis E. McNelly (Pacific Palisades, Cal.: Goodyear, 1972), pp. 377–382;

Robert H. Waugh, "The Lament of the Midwives: Arthur C. Clarke and the Tradition," *Extrapolation*, 31 (Spring 1990): 36–53;

Mary S. Weinkauf, "The Escape from the Garden," *Texas Quarterly*, 16 (1973): 66–72.

Papers:

The two major archives of Sir Arthur C. Clarke's papers are the collection at Mugar Memorial Library, Boston University; and the "Clarkives," maintained by the author's brother Frederick Clarke in Dene Court, Taunton, Somerset, England.

D. G. Compton

(19 August 1930 –)

D. Douglas Fratz

BOOKS: *Too Many Murderers,* as Guy Compton (London: Long, 1962);

Medium for Murder, as Guy Compton (London: Long, 1963);

Dead on Cue, as Guy Compton (London: Long, 1964);

Disguise for a Dead Gentleman, as Guy Compton (London: Long, 1964);

High Tide for Hanging, as Guy Compton (London: Long, 1965);

The Quality of Mercy (London: Hodder & Stoughton, 1965; New York: Ace, 1965; revised, New York: Ace, 1970);

Farewell, Earth's Bliss (London: Hodder & Stoughton, 1966; New York: Ace, 1971);

And Murder Came Too, as Guy Compton (London: Long, 1966);

The Silent Multitude (New York: Ace, 1966; London: Hodder & Stoughton, 1967);

Synthajoy (London: Hodder & Stoughton, 1968; New York: Ace, 1968);

The Palace (London: Hodder & Stoughton, 1969; New York: Norton, 1969);

The Electric Crocodile (London: Hodder & Stoughton, 1970); republished as *The Steel Crocodile* (New York: Ace, 1970);

Chronocules (New York: Ace, 1970); republished as *Hot Wireless Sets, Aspirin Tablets, the Sandpaper Sides of Used Matchboxes, and Something That Might Have Been Castor Oil* (London: Joseph, 1971); republished as *Chronicules* [*sic*] (London: Arrow, 1976);

The Missionaries (New York: Ace, 1972; London: Hale, 1975);

The Continuous Katherine Mortenhoe (London: Gollancz, 1974); republished as *The Unsleeping Eye* (New York: DAW, 1974); republished as *Death Watch* (London: Magnum, 1981);

Twice Ten Thousand Miles, as Frances Lynch (London: Souvenir, 1974; New York: St. Martin's Press, 1974); republished as *Candle at Midnight* (New York: Dell, 1977);

D. G. Compton (photograph by Alexander Wilensky; from the dust jacket for the U.S. edition of Ascendancies, *1980)*

The Fine and Handsome Captain, as Lynch (London: Souvenir, 1975; New York: St. Martin's Press, 1975);

Stranger at the Wedding, as Lynch (New York: St. Martin's Press, 1976; London: Souvenir, 1977);

A Dangerous Magic, as Lynch (London: Souvenir, 1978; New York: St. Martin's Press, 1978);

A Usual Lunacy (San Bernardino, Cal.: Borgo Press, 1978);

In the House of Dark Music, as Lynch (London: Hodder & Stoughton, 1979; New York: Warner, 1983);

Windows (New York: Berkley, 1979);

Ascendancies (London: Gollancz, 1980; New York: Berkley, 1980);

Scudders Spiel (Munich: Heyne, 1985); published in English as *Scudder's Game* (Worcester Park, U.K.: Kerosina, 1988);

Die Herren von Talojz [The Masters of Talojz] (Munich: Heyne, 1986);

Radio Plays (Worcester Park, U.K.: Kerosina, 1988);

Ragnarok, by Compton and John Gribbin (London: Gollancz, 1991);

Nomansland (London: Gollancz, 1993);

Stammering: Its Nature, History, Causes and Cures (London: Hodder & Stoughton, 1993);

Justice City (London: Gollancz, 1994);

Back of Town Blues (London: Gollancz, 1996).

PRODUCED SCRIPTS: *Chez Nous,* radio, BBC, 1961;
Bandstand, radio, 1962;
Blind Man's Bluff, radio, BBC, 1962;
Fully Furnished, radio, BBC, 1963;
Always Read the Small Print, radio, 1963;
If the Shoe Fits, radio, 1964;
Mandible Light, radio, 1964;
A Turning Off the Minch Park Road, radio, BBC, 1965;
Time Exposure, radio, 1965;
The Real People, radio, 1966;
Island, radio, 1968;
The Respighi Inheritance, radio, BBC, 1973.

OTHER: "Bender, Fenugreek, Slatterman and Mupp," in *Interfaces,* edited by Ursula K. Le Guin and Virginia Kidd (New York: Ace, 1980);

"It's Smart to Have an English Address," in *The Road to Science Fiction, Volume 5: The British Way,* edited by James Gunn (Clarkston, Ga.: White Wolf, 1998), pp. 413–427;

"In Which Avu Giddy Tries to Stop Dancing," in *Starlight 3,* edited by Patrick Nielsen Hayden (New York: Tor, 2001).

SELECTED PERIODICAL PUBLICATIONS–
UNCOLLECTED: "The Profession of Science Fiction XVI: By Chance out of Conviction," *Foundation: The Review of Science Fiction,* 17 (September 1979);

"By Chance, Out of Conviction," by Compton and Jeffrey M. Elliot, *THRUST–Science Fiction in Review,* 18 (Winter/Spring 1982).

D. G. Compton is the author of several science-fiction novels written in the 1960s and 1970s that were characterized by their pensive and usually doleful tone, characters under debilitating stress, bleak near-future settings, and a deep concern for the moral dilemmas potentially created by new technology. Compton's science fiction received significant critical notice during those decades in the United States as well as in his native England for its depth of characterization, concern with mature themes, and rich prose style. His novels joined those of other British science-fiction authors of that period in having a sig-

nificant influence on many other writers within the science-fiction field.

Compton also wrote several non-science-fiction novels and radio plays and is one of the few successful writers in the genre to have entered without any background or knowledge of science-fiction literature. Indeed, Compton has stated that he set his early novels in an indeterminate near-future solely to distance them from reality so that he could feel safe in caring about them.

David Guy Compton was born on 19 August 1930 in London. His early life, which he has described as "estranged," appears to have had a profound effect on the themes and style of his science-fiction novels. Both of his parents, George and Margaret (Symonds) Compton, were actors, but he saw his mother seldom and his father not at all, and he was raised primarily by his Scottish maternal grandmother and a nanny. He developed a stammer as a child; the subject concerned him for years, and in 1993 Hodder and Stoughton commissioned him to write a nonfiction book on the topic. He decided to become a writer at an early age, and he was educated at Cheltenham College in Gloucester but never attended a university. He sought to write plays while still in school and began to write (but was unable to finish) his first novel during a difficult and traumatic eighteen months after he was conscripted into national service in March 1949. After he got out of the army in September 1951, his mother, who had no confidence that he could earn a living as a playwright, got him his first job as an assistant stage manager with a small theater company. The job lasted only a few months until he fell in love with Elizabeth (Tillotson) Taylor, the stage director's wife, whom he married soon after her divorce, in 1952.

Compton and Taylor (along with her first child) moved to a Cornish fishing village, where he intended to become a writer, and they lived in what he later described as a "romantically damp cottage." Their marriage rapidly soured but nevertheless lasted eighteen years, during which they had three children: Margaret, Hester, and James. Compton's career also did not flourish, a situation he later attributed to having, at the age of twenty-one, nothing to write about. As a result of that realization, he quit writing for ten years.

He and his family moved to London, where they lived on a houseboat. He had a succession of jobs, including office worker, salesman in a furniture store, and furniture maker. He later described this period as "jobs, nervous breakdowns, moves, more jobs." After moving to Devon and working as a door-to-door salesman, he decided to return to writing, trying his hand at radio plays. He found some moderate success but little money, so he began to write mystery and crime novels under the name Guy Compton. His big break came when German radio discovered him (through his Lon-

Gollancz
SF

THE
CONTINUOUS
KATHERINE
MORTENHOE

a new
science fiction novel by

D. G. COMPTON

author of
SYNTHAJOY

Dust jacket for Compton's 1974 novel, in which a man who has camera implants behind his eyes sets out to shoot a documentary about a dying woman (Richland County Public Library)

don agent, Peggy Ramsay, and a German translator who became interested in his work) and bought his backlog of plays done for the BBC in the early 1960s. These plays, often experimental, won a more enthusiastic reception in Germany than they had in Britain.

Compton has described himself in this period as a "spare-time writer" with "few ideas." But he came upon a "big idea" from which developed his first science-fiction novel, *The Quality of Mercy* (1965), about a genocidal plot to solve the problem of overpopulation using a biological/nuclear weapon. He had no background in genre science fiction, and the decision to market the book as science fiction was made by his editor. The novel focused primarily on the tensions among a group of military personnel who begin to learn of the plot, and although it was published in both Britain and the United States, it was not of the quality of his later novels and drew little notice. (A revised and improved version was published five years later, after his reputation became more firmly established.)

Still, even this mild commercial success spurred Compton to continue to write in that vein. After *The Quality of Mercy*, while Compton was working as a bank guard and part-time postman, his publisher offered him an advance for additional science-fiction novels. He decided to move further into what he believed to be the heart of the genre and set his next novel on Mars. *Farewell, Earth's Bliss* (1966) concerned a penal colony on Mars where misfit humans are sent from Earth and where (in a manner somewhat reminiscent of the work of Philip K. Dick, who is virtually the only other science-fiction author Compton has ever cited as influencing his work) fantasy and reality are often difficult to distinguish. Both of Compton's first two novels are written in a manner that makes the narrative difficult to follow, and both suffer from his lack of knowledge of science and the conventions of the genre. However, *Farewell, Earth's Bliss* was also published in the United States five years later.

His third science-fiction novel, *The Silent Multitude* (1966), is set in a deserted and crumbling future city on a dying Earth that has been attacked by spores from space that destroy concrete. In the novel the physical decay of humanity's technology thematically parallels the mental and physical decay of a small group of survivors. *The Silent Multitude* was in many ways similar to much of the work of J. G. Ballard, and the book so impressed American editor Terry Carr that the American edition preceded the British edition and was part of Carr's prestigious Ace Special line of science-fiction novels.

Compton's next novel, *Synthajoy* (1968), was the first to bring him significant notice both in England and the United States. It was also published as an Ace Special and was a complex novel concerning the development of a device to record emotional experiences from the human mind and play them back to another. The story is told from the point of view of the wife of the psychiatrist who developed (with the assistance of an electronics-savant radio shop owner) the mental recording device. It is a beautifully crafted and complexly structured novel told mainly in flashbacks as they occur to the protagonist during her psychiatric treatment following her conviction for murdering her husband. The true story is thus slowly revealed through random, almost hallucinatory episodes of recall by a far-from-reliable narrator. Compton's ability to handle so complex a task so successfully—*Synthajoy* may be his most compellingly readable novel—brought him the admiration of many other top authors in a science-fiction field that was striving toward higher literary standards and new narrative forms.

Carr and Donald A. Wollheim, founder of DAW Books, were among those impressed by Compton's work. In 1968 Robert Reginald of the academically oriented Borgo Press contacted Compton while working on a bibliography of his work and later published one of

Compton's unsold novels, *A Usual Lunacy* (1978), in which falling in love is found to be the effect of a virus.

After writing one final mystery novel, *The Palace* (1969), Compton began to write the science-fiction novels that firmly marked a place for him in the field. His next science-fiction novel, *The Electric Crocodile* (1970), involves an ultra-secret research institute that the protagonists, Dr. Matthew Oliver and his wife, Abigail, find is not what it seems. Slowly, Matthew learns the true story of the authorities' creation of a computer bank to monitor and interfere with the institute's work out of blind fear of technological progress. Some critics believe that the novel is possibly Compton's most accomplished work. *Chronocules* (1970) also involves an isolated research organization, this time set amid a crumbling society, with the researchers desperately trying to find a way to travel through time to escape into the future. Both *The Electric Crocodile* and *Chronocules* appeared on the Nebula Awards nominations list of the twenty-two best novels of 1970, and the former novel made the short list of the six best novels of the year.

In *The Missionaries* (1972) Compton took on religion for the first time, telling the story of a small group of aliens who arrive on Earth preaching a religion that is apparently absolutely correct and seeking to convert humanity to this one true faith. But humanity and its established religions react with fear and loathing, refusing to accept the "enlightenment."

Compton then wrote his most commercially and critically successful novel, *The Continuous Katherine Mortenhoe* (1974). Like many of his books, it was published under his chosen title only in England. The novel is set in a near-future world where most diseases have been cured and early deaths are rare. When Katherine Mortenhoe, a shy and reserved editor of computer-written fiction in her early thirties, learns she has one of the few incurable diseases, she and her timid husband are offered a chance to star in a television documentary chronicling her final days. She reluctantly agrees, but then ditches her husband and the television executives to become a disenfranchised indigent. The cameraman assigned to her, however, has had camera implants put behind his eyes, tapping into his optic nerve, and with the assistance of the producers (who have placed a tracer among Katherine's possessions) he becomes an indigent as well and befriends her. Over the next few weeks they travel together, and the nightly television series is, unbeknownst to its star, a strong commercial success. The cameraman, Roderick, grows to care for Katherine as their peregrinations lead to her own self-discoveries, and he finally makes an ethical decision to stop filming her. The novel has many flaws, including a narrative that is occasionally disjointed, but despite its relentless pessimism the novel often seems uplifting, as both protagonists discover themselves and finally decide that they can make their own decisions instead of flowing diffidently through life wherever it takes them. *The Continuous Katherine Mortenhoe* was included on the long list for the Nebula Award nominations but did not make the final short list for 1974, which included only four novels. It did, however, finish sixth in the Locus Awards, given by the science-fiction news magazine *Locus*.

The book was made into a movie in France in 1980 with the title *La Mort en direct* (*Deathwatch*), with Romy Schneider as Katherine, Harvey Keitel as Roderick, and Harry Dean Stanton as the television producer. Despite the low budget and the need to jettison more than half of the plot, the movie was successful in capturing the feel of Compton's novel. There are plans for a second movie version, this time from Italian director Alex Infascelli.

Despite the critical success of many of Compton's early books, they never sold well, either in England or the United States. His haunting but beleaguered characters, cynicism, and distrusting attitude toward technological advances ran counter to the usual competent protagonists and technophilia in science fiction. But these very traits, as well as his attention to characterization and human problems and his unusual narrative style, were what made Compton's novels a strong influence on other writers in the science-fiction field, including Judith Merril. Compton recalls that American editor Wollheim told him, "You may not sell many books, but the very best people will go to your funeral."

This lack of popular and financial success led Compton to "retire" as a science-fiction writer in the mid 1970s and earn a living by continuing to work full time as an editor in the Condensed Books department at *Reader's Digest* in London, a job he had begun in 1969. He had divorced his first wife in 1971, and in 1972 he married Carol Curtis Brown Savage, who was also working as an editor in London. He also, during the 1970s, wrote a series of Gothic romance novels under the pseudonym Frances Lynch. In the late 1970s he acquired Virginia Kidd as his American agent and was encouraged to write science fiction again.

In 1975 Compton had written a sequel to *The Continuous Katherine Mortenhoe* titled *Windows,* for which Kidd found a publisher in 1979. In this novel Roderick insists on the removal of his camera implants, choosing blindness over a continued life of invading the privacy of others. Much of the novel concerns the diverse reactions of others to his decision, and in the end he is forced to flee the country.

Compton's next science-fiction novel was *Ascendancies* (1980). It was an ambitious but mostly overlooked book wherein a strange substance begins to fall to Earth from space, and it turns out to be a cheap energy source,

Dust jacket for the U.S. edition of Compton's 1980 novel, in which an inexpensive, work-saving energy source causes people to hallucinate and disappear (Richland County Public Library)

attempts to become a writer. In the second article, Compton makes a telling statement regarding his science fiction:

> Admittedly, I'm no scientist, and this is a severe handicap. But the "science" in my stories has always been a metaphor for something else. If I write science fiction for one single reason, it's that I find looking at tomorrow a useful way of getting new perspectives on today.

By the start of the 1980s, Compton had left his native England to live permanently in the United States with his wife, herself an American. He wrote a new science-fiction novel, *Scudders Spiel,* which was first published in German in 1985 because British and American publishers initially showed no interest; once again the German market proved more receptive. The novel is about a near-future utopia of controlled population growth and free love brought on by the discovery of the ultimate contraceptive device. (One must assume that this novel was actually written before the early 1980s and the advent of AIDS.)

Several of his science-fiction novels of the 1960s and 1970s were republished in new paperback editions during the 1980s. In addition, a small press in England finally published the first edition in English of *Scudders Spiel* (as *Scudder's Game*) as well as a collection of his radio plays, in 1988. In 1991 Compton wrote, with British author John Gribbin, the near-future science-fiction novel *Ragnarok,* about a scientist who brings on a nuclear winter in an attempt to enforce disarmament; the novel was published only in Britain, and there has been no American edition to date. His next novel, *Nomansland* (1993), concerns a virus in the twenty-first century that makes women able only to conceive female children, while *Justice City* (1994) is a near-future treatment of the criminal justice system. Neither novel received much critical attention. *Back of Town Blues* (1996), a sequel to *Justice City,* is another mystery thriller featuring protagonist Alec Duncan, a black Scots policeman. Another collaboration with Gribbin, tentatively titled "Timeways," has been completed.

D. G. Compton will probably always be known as a writer's writer and one who came to the science-fiction field as much out of chance as out of conviction. Despite his lack of popular success, his work in the 1960s and 1970s (especially the novels *Synthajoy* and *The Continuous Katherine Mortenhoe*) had an important influence on many of the other authors in the field who were seeking to expand the scope of the field and bring to science fiction the mature characters and themes prevalent in the best of mainstream literature.

freeing people from most work. But strange side effects begin to occur, involving hallucinations and people disappearing. The story involves a woman whose husband disappears. She obtains a body from organized crime to show the insurance company to collect her husband's insurance, and the investigator who discovers her deception starts to blackmail her but then falls in love with her.

Most of what is known about Compton's life can be found in two autobiographical articles. The first, "By Chance, Out of Conviction," appeared in the British journal *Foundation: The Review of Science Fiction* in 1979. It focuses primarily on the financial ups and downs of his life as a science-fiction author. The second, a revised and expanded version of the first and published under the same title, appeared in the American magazine *THRUST—Science Fiction in Review* (1982). It provides much more detail regarding his childhood and early

Susan Cooper

(23 May 1935 –)

Amelia A. Rutledge
George Mason University

See also the Cooper entry in *DLB 161: British Children's Writers Since 1960.*

BOOKS: *Mandrake* (London: Hodder & Stoughton, 1964);

Behind the Golden Curtain: A View of the U.S.A. (London: Hodder & Stoughton, 1965; New York: Scribners, 1966);

Over Sea, Under Stone (London: Cape, 1965; New York: Harcourt, Brace & World, 1966);

J. B. Priestley: Portrait of an Author (London: Heinemann, 1970; New York: Harper & Row, 1971);

Dawn of Fear (New York: Harcourt Brace Jovanovich, 1970; London: Chatto & Windus, 1972);

The Dark Is Rising (New York: Atheneum, 1973; London: Chatto & Windus, 1973);

Greenwitch (New York: Atheneum, 1974; London: Chatto & Windus, 1974);

The Grey King (New York: Atheneum, 1975; London: Chatto & Windus, 1975);

Silver on the Tree (New York: Atheneum, 1977; London: Chatto & Windus, 1977);

Jethro and the Jumbie (New York: Atheneum, 1979; London: Chatto & Windus, 1980);

Foxfire, by Cooper and Hume Cronyn (New York: French, 1983; London: French, 1983);

The Silver Cow: A Welsh Tale (New York: Atheneum, 1983; London: Chatto & Windus, 1983);

Seaward (New York: Atheneum, 1983; London: Bodley Head, 1983);

The Selkie Girl (New York: Margaret McElderry, 1986; London: Hodder & Stoughton, 1987);

Tam Lin (New York: Margaret McElderry, 1991);

Matthew's Dragon (New York: Margaret McElderry/Macmillan, 1991);

Danny and the Kings (New York: Margaret McElderry/Macmillan, 1993);

The Boggart (New York: Margaret McElderry/Macmillan, 1993; London: Bodley Head, 1993);

Dreams and Wishes: Essays on Writing for Children (New York: Margaret McElderry, 1996);

Susan Cooper, 1999 (photograph by Jeffrey Cooper)

The Boggart and the Monster (New York: Margaret McElderry, 1997; London: Bodley Head, 1998);

King of Shadows (New York: Margaret McElderry, 1999; London: Bodley Head, 1999);

Green Boy (New York: Margaret McElderry, 2002; London: Bodley Head, 2002);

Frog (New York: Margaret McElderry, 2002; London: Bodley Head, 2002).

PLAY PRODUCTION: *Foxfire,* by Cooper and Hume Cronyn, Ontario, Stratford Festival Theatre, 1980; revised, Minneapolis, Guthrie Theatre, 1981.

PRODUCED SCRIPTS: *Dark Encounter,* television, 1976;

The Dollmaker, adapted by Cooper and Hume Cronyn from Harriette Arnow's novel, television, ABC, 13 May 1984;

Foxfire, adapted by Cooper from the play by Cooper and Cronyn, television, CBS, 13 December 1987;

A Promise to Keep, adapted by Cooper and Carleton Cuse from Jane Yarmolinsky's memoir, television, NBC, 1 October 1990;

George Balanchine's The Nutcracker, narration by Cooper, motion picture, Warner Bros., 1993;

To Dance With the White Dog, adapted by Cooper from Terry Kay's novel, television, CBS, 5 December 1993;

Jewel, adapted by Cooper from Bret Lott's novel, television, CBS, 7 February 2001.

OTHER: "Snoek Piquante," in *Age of Austerity,* edited by Michael Sissons and P. French (London: Hodder & Stoughton, 1963), pp. 35–54;

J. B. Priestley, *Essays of Five Decades,* edited by Cooper (Boston: Little, Brown, 1968);

"Escaping Into Ourselves," in *Celebrating Children's Books,* edited by Betsy Hearn and Marilyn Kaye (New York: Lothrop, Lee & Shepard, 1981), pp. 14–23;

"In Defense of the Artist," in *Signposts to Criticism of Children's Literature,* edited by Robert Bator (Chicago: American Library Association, 1983), pp. 98–108;

"My Links with Wales," in *Loughborough '83: Proceedings of the Sixteenth International Seminar on Children's Literature,* edited by Frank Keyse (Aberystwyth, Wales: Welsh National Centre for Children's Literature, 1984), pp. 79–81;

Nancy and John Langstaff, eds., *The Christmas Revels Songbook: In Celebration of the Winter Solstice,* introduction by Cooper (Boston: David R. Godine, 1985);

"Susan Cooper," in *Something About the Author. Autobiography Series,* 6 (Detroit: Gale, 1988), pp. 54–56;

"Harvesting the Wild Values," in *Literature and Hawaii's Children: Stories as Bridges to Magic Realms,* edited by Judith Kellogg and Hesse Crisler (Honolulu: University of Hawaii, 1992), pp. 22–23;

"Muffin," in *When I Was Your Age: Original Stories About Growing Up,* edited by Amy Ehrlich (Cambridge, Mass.: Candlewick Press, 1996), pp. 77–93.

SELECTED PERIODICAL PUBLICATIONS–
UNCOLLECTED: "A Love Letter to the *Horn Book Magazine,*" *Horn Book Magazine,* 50 (October 1974): 182–183;

"Address Delivered at the Children's Round Table Breakfast," *Texas Library Journal,* 52 (May 1976): 52–54;

"Newbery Award Acceptance Speech," *Horn Book Magazine,* 52 (August 1976): 361–372;

"A Dream of Revels," *Horn Book Magazine,* 55 (December 1979): 633–640;

"A Second Look: *The Nargun and the Stars,*" *Horn Book Magazine,* 62 (September–October 1986): 572–574;

"Preserving the Light," *Magpies,* 2 (May 1988): 5–9;

"How I Began," *New Welsh Review,* 2 (Spring 1990): 19–21;

"The 2001 May Hill Arbuthnot Honor Lecture," *Journal of Youth Services in Libraries,* 14, no. 4 (2001): 26–31.

Although Susan Cooper has lived in the United States since 1963, she considers herself, and is considered by her readers, to be a British writer of fantasy. All of her major fiction resonates with themes, settings, myths, and legends associated with Great Britain, especially her native Buckinghamshire, Cornwall, and Wales. She found it ironic that the American Library Association awarded her its highest honor for a children's book author, the John Newbery Medal, in 1976, its centennial year, for *The Grey King* (1975), the fourth book of her *Dark Is Rising* fantasy sequence. That series of five books, each an award winner, integrates the traditional lore of the British Isles with modern concerns. Her work, although commercially designated for a younger audience, exemplifies sophisticated mythopoeic writing not limited to that age group and is one of the major contributions to Arthurian fantasy of the 1970s.

Susan Mary Cooper, the daughter of John Richard and Ethel May (née Field) Cooper, was born in Burnham, Buckinghamshire, England, on 23 May 1935. Her father worked in the Great Western Railway offices and was an amateur pianist; her mother was a teacher. She has one younger brother, Rod, also a writer. Her childhood experiences of World War II as well as her yearly visits to Wales inform much of her major fiction. She attended Somerville College at Oxford and was the first woman to edit the university newspaper. After earning her M.A. in 1956, she subsequently entered a seven-year period as a journalist in London for the *Sunday Times.* In a 1976 author-information brochure published by Atheneum, Cooper admits that this work was deeply satisfying; she also compares it, in its effect on a young novelist, to Circe's island– "seductive, but death if you stay too long." Cooper came to the United States in 1963 when she married an American professor, Nicholas Grant; they lived in

Massachusetts and had two children, Jonathan (born in 1966) and Katharine (born in 1967). One of her nonfiction works, *Behind the Golden Curtain: A View of the U.S.A.* (1965), is a result of her new experiences as well as her journalistic career. Cooper and Grant divorced in 1983; she married the actor Hume Cronyn in 1996 and lives in Connecticut.

Cooper's first novel was a work of science fiction, *Mandrake* (1964), the story of a politician who unsuccessfully tries to rid the world of much of the human race with the help of "natural forces." It made no critical impression, and Cooper did not attempt further work in this genre, although a later novel, *The Boggart* (1993), employs elements of the youth subculture of computers.

Cooper is an advocate of fantasy for its capacity to provide social and ethical grounding in a world in which the impact of myth has been vitiated over time; this view is analogous to J. R. R. Tolkien's concept of "Recovery," one of the four functions of fantasy. Cooper's major fantasy deals with radically polarized forces in conflict, and such fantasy has been criticized, in general, as grounded in nostalgia for an outmoded, hierarchical worldview. Her fantasies counter this criticism to some degree by maintaining a tension between nostalgia and the inescapable yet difficult necessity for free choice.

Her work as a fantasy writer began with *Over Sea, Under Stone* (1965), a book that became the first of the *Dark Is Rising* sequence, although Cooper was not aware of its significance in that regard for nearly eight years. In the time between *Over Sea, Under Stone* and the rest of the sequence, Cooper completed a biography of J. B. Priestley and a children's novel, *Dawn of Fear* (1970), based on her experiences of bombing raids during World War II. Although this novel is not a fantasy, its depiction of a small boy's learning the meaning of fear, loss, and grief provides insight into the directness and power with which Cooper depicts human responses in her later work. She also notes that the war induced her to ponder the manifestations of conflict between good and evil in the world, which became the central issue in her fantasy sequence.

Over Sea, Under Stone, which takes place in Cornwall, focuses on a search for a chalice similar to the grail of Arthurian legend, although its significance is archaeological, without the religious overtones of the traditional stories. This grail functions as part of a code that will guide the finders to other objects of power that figure in the cosmic conflict worked out in the sequence as a whole. Cooper creates opposing forces representing the "Light" and the "Dark," whose struggles have been interwoven with human history, but which, in this sequence, are specifically located in the conflicts that determined historically the culture of the British Isles—

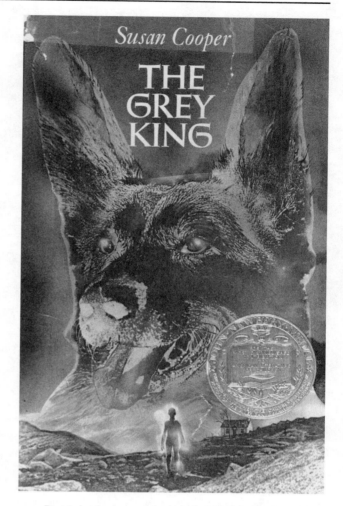

Dust jacket for the novel that won the 1976 Newbery Medal
(Richland County Public Library)

especially the Roman conquest and the Romano-Celtic resistance led by King Arthur. The direct representatives of the Dark and the Light are mythic—larger than life—as opposed to heroic figures, but their agents are always ordinary humans; in the first novel, the Light enlists the aid of the children Simon, Jane, and Barnabas Drew. They are guided by their "great-uncle," the scholar Merriman Lyon, whose Arthurian connections are slowly revealed through the rest of the sequence, beginning with Barnabas's insight into his true name, a modernization of Sir Thomas Malory's "Merlin."

Despite its Arthurian elements, *Over Sea, Under Stone* remains primarily an adventure story, as the children decipher the clues found on an ancient map while eluding the Dark's agents, who seem more like the antagonists of spy thrillers than the masters and agents of a cosmic tyranny. There is little to locate the story in the fantastic mode except the assertions of the Dark/

Light conflict. It remained for *The Dark Is Rising* (1973), the second and title book of the sequence, to show Cooper's mastery of fantasy in a contemporary setting. In *Dreams and Wishes: Essays on Writing for Children* (1996) Cooper explains that she did not have specific plans to continue developing the characters of *Over Sea, Under Stone* until, about five years later, a skiing trip inspired her decision "to write a book, set for the most part in thick snow like this, about a small boy who woke up one birthday morning and found he was able to work magic." A few years after that, rereading the passage in *Over Sea, Under Stone* about the Dark and the Light gave her the pattern for the rest of the series.

The second novel focuses on the coming of age of Will Stanton as the last of the Old Ones, the agents of the Light. The incursion of the magical into the mundane reality of a large Buckinghamshire family remains one of Cooper's best achievements. Will, the youngest of his family, but also the seventh son of a seventh son, experiences his empowerment by the Light both as terrifying and exhilarating: the former as strange energies build in concert with anomalous weather and strange visitations, the latter as he completes the intense initiation into his powers in a sequence of time-slip adventures as he absorbs the natural and mythic lore of the *Book of Gramarye*.

Each of the books in the series is anchored in a quest for a symbolic object; in *The Dark Is Rising* Will must find and link a set of symbols, each one a cross within a circle, forged or carved from stone, iron, bronze, gold, glass, and wood. Cooper also builds, gradually, a group of representatives of the Light; in *The Dark Is Rising* she introduces the Lady, Cooper's own representation of the archetypal feminine, especially the Wisewoman or Crone. Feminine presence in the series, except for Jane Drew, tends to be submerged in the general action. After her introduction, the Lady recedes into the background because of a rash act of Will's that depletes her powers, and although she is considered the strongest of the Light's agents, she figures only intermittently in the plot. *The Dark Is Rising* brought Cooper to the attention of the fantasy-reading public as the earlier book had not done. *The Dark is Rising* was a runner-up for the 1973 Boston Globe-Horn Book Award and a Newbery Honor Book in 1974. This novel and all of Cooper's subsequent fiction have been reviewed in major newspapers and in library journals.

The operative magic in *Greenwitch* (1974), third in the *Dark Is Rising* sequence, is that of the sea and fertility, figured in the female effigy of the Greenwitch, ritually constructed by Cornish women and committed to the sea by the men of the village. The Drew children return, and Jane's empathy with the Greenwitch allows the retrieval of the cipher that completes the code engraved on the grail that they found in the first book. *Greenwitch* is more compact than the other novels, and it is closer to folk tradition, differing from the others, which focus more on legend or fantastic invention. *Greenwitch* also brings the feminine element more into balance with the other elements of the stories, and it introduces more clearly the vulnerabilities of the agents—not only the humans, but those of the Light as well, as they struggle, despite their powers, with enigmas in much the same way as the human children.

Of all of the novels of the sequence, *The Grey King* is most characterized by narrative intensity and complexity, surpassing *The Dark Is Rising* in this respect. *The Grey King* won both the John Newbery Medal and the Tir na N'og Award, Wales's highest fantasy award, in 1976. Cooper carries the story into Wales, the home of Arthurian legend, and introduces Bran, actually the son of Arthur and Guinevere, brought forward in time by Merriman because of Guinevere's fear that Arthur will question his legitimacy. Bran, an albino and considered the natural son of one of the natives of the valley, is already set apart from his peers but is unaware of the heritage that makes him the Pendragon and proper bearer of one of the symbols of power.

Cooper complicates the narrative of *The Grey King* by including a history of human rivalry between Bran's foster father and Caradog Prichard, a neighboring farmer, whose intense hatred makes him, ultimately and disastrously, a vessel for the Dark. Also in this novel, Cooper offers her most explicit questioning of the ethics of the struggle. The speeches of the Welshman John Rowlands concerning the cold pragmatism of the Light in its use of human agents cannot be countered by Will, who can only acknowledge their accuracy. The denouement of the novel, although it follows the successful retrieval of the harp, crucial in Will's quest for the magical symbols, is starkly qualified by a series of concomitant catastrophes; in one instance, the Dark forces employ spectral foxes, the *Milgwn,* that take on the appearance of sheep-chasing dogs and lead Caradog Prichard to shoot Bran's dog in the boy's presence.

Cooper succeeds in the difficult task of bringing together all of the elements of the novels in the conclusion of the sequence, *Silver on the Tree* (1977). Only one narrative sequence—the time travel that occupies the Drew children while Will and Bran complete their quest for the crystal sword, Eirias—seems to slow the pace of the action; further, it adds little to the characterization of John Rowlands, who accompanies the children and has a crucial role to play at the climax of the story, and the partial elucidation of Caradog Prichard's fate in their own time seems superfluous. Once that point is past, the novel gains both poise and momentum, arriving at a conclusion that is, in the narrative logic of the sequence, as poignant as it is inevitable.

Cooper's sequence will inevitably be compared with the stories of Lloyd Alexander, Ursula K. Le Guin, and Alan Garner, or with J. K. Rowling and Philip Pullman. Such comparisons are both uncritical and reductive; what these writers have in common is a serious commitment to the power of storytelling and of fantasy, but their approaches differ. Although both Cooper and Garner use the motif of fantastic incursion, with the Old Ones Cooper solves one of the difficult problems of writing a fantasy that takes place in contemporary contexts. The Old Ones are not preternatural invaders or mythic reincarnations but human/Other, and the reader rarely forgets that Will is a child. Further, her Light/Dark conflict is embodied in each character in a way that Le Guin's art-magic, an operative substratum of quasi-scientific principles, is not. Finally, Cooper's work is distinguishable from these others by its ambivalence toward manipulation by the powers of benevolence, articulated explicitly from *The Dark Is Rising* throughout the sequence.

The Light, although clearly favored, is as dangerous in its ruthlessness as the Dark; its ethics and operations are explicitly opposed to the institutions of humanity, even when it works for their good, and her characters are forced to confront this fact. In a striking and disturbing scene in *The Dark Is Rising*, the local vicar is shown to be impotent against an attack of the Dark; only Will and his Sign prevail. Almost as disturbing is the enforced forgetfulness imposed on the children, except for Will, in the end—a last, high-handed gesture of the Light. It may be argued, however, that only thus can Cooper resist nostalgia for otherworldly rescue. Humankind is set free with the fearful gift of choice; Cooper thus shows the myth-based affirmation of human capabilities that she asserts is one of the great powers of fantasy.

Although Cooper has continued to produce works of fantasy, only *The Boggart* has a sequel—*The Boggart and the Monster* (1997). Her other novels have been single works such as *Seaward* (1983) and *King of Shadows* (1999), or retellings of traditional stories in picture-book format intended for younger readers. In a departure from her Celtic-based fantasies, she also wrote *Jethro and the Jumbie* (1979), the story of a small boy of the Caribbean, who, with the help of a local spirit, the Jumbie, persuades a relative to keep a promise. The tale is also distinguished by the characters' use of local dialect, but its core is Jethro's realization of the power of belief in forces outside of common-sense reality.

Seaward is a story of loss; both protagonists are seeking the parents they have lost, Westerly to political

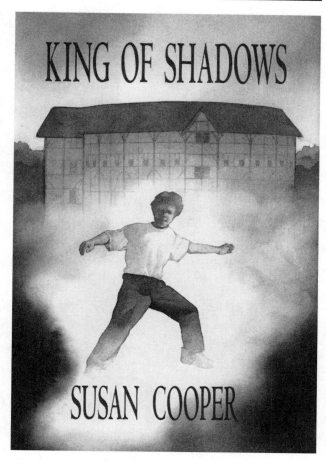

Dust jacket for Cooper's 1999 novel, in which a boy in a present-day production of A Midsummer Night's Dream *is transported back in time to a Globe Theatre production of the play during William Shakespeare's lifetime (Richland County Public Library)*

violence and Cally to illness. Their quest, in a world entered by Westerly through a hidden door and by Cally through a mirror, teaches them the value of life as it is lived in the face of death. The presentation of the characters is more balanced than in Cooper's earlier works; Cally is as important as Westerly and is even shown to have an advantage over him in an enigmatic episode with Snake, an embodiment of the life force, whose invitation to accept the sensuous nature of humanity she freely accepts as Westerly cannot. Offered a chance to enter the Celtic land of Promise, they reject a static afterlife for a life of contingency and promise.

The folktales of *The Silver Cow* (1983), *The Selkie Girl* (1986), and *Tam Lin* (1991) are Welsh, Irish, and Scottish, respectively. *The Silver Cow* is a story of selfishness punished; *The Selkie Girl* recasts the story of ill-fated love between a mortal and a seal-maiden or selkie; and *Tam Lin* gives a new frame to the traditional Scottish ballad of the fairy knight. The latter two are of particular interest in the role they give to female

Dust jacket for one of Cooper's 2002 novels (courtesy of the author)

self-determination: the selkie abandons her human family to return to her family in the sea, although the former are blessed by her favor; and Margaret, Cooper's name for the heroine of *Tam Lin,* is in rebellion against conventional feminine decorum.

The *Boggart* is the story of Emily Volnik and a Celtic sprite, a household mischief maker, who is accidentally transported in a piece of furniture from his castle in Scotland to Toronto when Emily's father, a theater director, inherits the castle and its effects. The boggart quickly realizes how profoundly displaced he is, as Emily and her family have no knowledge of Celtic folklore and hence no tolerance for his pranks. His discovery of how to manipulate electricity oscillates between exquisite special effects as he discovers a theatrical light machine and disaster as he manipulates traffic signals.

Cooper has a difficult negotiation to make between the world of modern preteens and ancient preternatural beings; the strain is evident in the almost-too-convenient presence of two members of the theater company who are of Celtic descent and thus

able to identify the boggart as the source of Emily's problems. There is also a tendency to depict Emily as passive, especially when the boggart's pranks lead to her being seriously considered the cause of poltergeist activities, but the resolution is both surprising and moving. *The Boggart and the Monster* is a simpler and more playful sequel, set among the lochs of Scotland, in which Emily, her brother Jessup, and their Scottish friend Tommy assist the boggart in rescuing his cousin, Nessie, trapped by his own shape-shifting in the form of the legendary monster, from an assortment of scientists.

Cooper says in her statement for *Something About the Author* (1988) that her impulse toward fantasy in the time between *Seaward* and *The Boggart* was directed to the theater, "which is itself a kind of fantasy." She has embodied her fascination with theater in *King of Shadows,* a time-shift fantasy that takes the young actor Nat Field from his work in a boys' theater production of *A Midsummer Night's Dream* back to a production of the play in William Shakespeare's time. Cooper deftly integrates the resolution of Nat's repressed personal tragedies with daily life in the Globe Theatre under actor and shareholder Richard Burbage when Shakespeare's plays were new. Shakespeare himself, who gives Nat the emotional support he needs, is an appealing and at times sentimentalized figure, but Cooper derives much of the narrative tension from the political risks Shakespeare takes in the productions of his plays.

Although the publication of stories such as *Matthew's Dragon* (1991), a short tale of a contemporary child and a dragon from his storybook, may imply a growing interest in writing for a somewhat younger audience, books such as the Boggart novels and especially *King of Shadows* suggest that Susan Cooper is exploring new contexts for continued work in the fantastic mode.

Interviews:

Raymond H. Thompson, "Interview with Susan Cooper," in his *Taliesin's Successors: Interviews with Authors of Modern Arthurian Literature,* The Camelot Project at the University of Rochester (2 July 1989) <http://www.lib.rochester.edu/camelot/intrvws/cooper.htm>;

Hazel Rochman, "The Booklist Interview: Susan Cooper," *Booklist,* 94 (15 September 1997): 226–227.

References:

Michael D. C. Drout, "Reading the Signs of Light: Anglo-Saxonism, Education, and Obedience in Susan Cooper's *The Dark Is Rising*," *Lion and the Unicorn: A Critical Journal of Children's Literature,* 21, no. 2 (1997): 230–250;

Emrys Evans, "Children's Novels and Welsh Mythology: Multiple Voices in Susan Cooper and Alan Garner," in *The Voice of the Narrator in Children's Literature: Insights from Writers and Critics,* edited by Charlotte Otten and G. Schmidt (New York: Greenwood Press, 1989), pp. 92–100;

Gwyneth Evans, "Three Modern Views of Merlin," *Mythlore: A Journal of J. R. R. Tolkien, C. S. Lewis, Charles Williams, General Fantasy, and Mythic Studies,* 17 (Summer 1990): 17–22;

Peter Goodrich, "Magical Medievalism and the Fairy Tale in Susan Cooper's *The Dark is Rising* Sequence," *Lion and the Unicorn: A Critical Journal of Children's Literature,* 12, no. 2 (December 1988): 165–177;

Valerie Krips, "Finding One's Place in the Fantastic: Susan Cooper's *The Dark Is Rising*," in *Functions of the Fantastic: Selected Essays from the Thirteenth International Conference on the Fantastic in the Arts,* edited by Joe Sanders (Westport, Conn.: Greenwood Press, 1995), pp. 169–175;

Lois R. Kuznets, "'High Fantasy' in America: A Study of Lloyd Alexander, Ursula Le Guin, and Susan Cooper," *Lion and the Unicorn: A Critical Journal of Children's Literature,* 9 (1985): 19–35;

Margaret K. McElderry, "Susan Cooper," *Horn Book Magazine,* 52 (August 1976): 367–372;

Nina Mikkelsen, *Susan Cooper* (New York: Twayne, 1998);

Raymond L. Plante, "Object and Character in *The Dark Is Rising*," *Children's Literature Association Quarterly,* 11 (Spring 1986): 37–41;

C. W. Sullivan III, "Traditional Welsh Materials in Modern Fantasy," *Extrapolation,* 28 (Spring 1978): 87–98;

Mary Harris Veeder, "Gender and Empowerment in Susan Cooper's *The Dark Is Rising* Series," *Children's Literature Association Quarterly,* 16 (Spring 1991): 11–15.

Papers:

An archive of Susan Cooper's papers is part of the Lillian H. Smith Collection, Toronto Public Library, Toronto, Ontario, Canada.

Richard Cowper
(John Middleton Murry Jr.)
(9 May 1926 –   )

Robert Galbreath
University of North Carolina at Greensboro

BOOKS: *The Golden Valley,* as Colin Murry (London: Hutchinson, 1958);

Recollections of a Ghost, as Colin Murry (London: Hutchinson, 1960);

A Path to the Sea, as Colin Murry (London: Hutchinson, 1961);

Breakthrough (London: Dobson, 1967; New York: Ballantine, 1969);

Phoenix (London: Dobson, 1968; New York: Ballantine, 1970);

Domino (London: Dobson, 1971);

Private View, as Colin Murry (London: Dobson, 1972);

Kuldesak (London: Gollancz, 1972; Garden City, N.Y.: Doubleday, 1972);

Clone (London: Gollancz, 1972; Garden City, N.Y.: Doubleday, 1973);

Time Out of Mind (London: Gollancz, 1973; New York: Pocket Books, 1981);

The Twilight of Briareus (London: Gollancz, 1974; New York: John Day, 1974);

Worlds Apart (London: Gollancz, 1974);

One Hand Clapping: A Memoir of Childhood, as Colin Middleton Murry (London: Gollancz, 1975); republished as *I at the Keyhole* (Briarcliff Manor, N.Y.: Stein & Day, 1975);

The Custodians and Other Stories (London: Gollancz, 1976);

Shadows on the Grass, as Colin Middleton Murry (London: Gollancz, 1977);

The Road to Corlay (London: Gollancz, 1978; enlarged, New York: Pocket Books, 1979; London: Futura, 1986);

Profundis (London: Gollancz, 1979; New York: Pocket Books, 1981);

The Web of the Magi and Other Stories (London: Gollancz, 1980);

Out There Where the Big Ships Go (New York: Pocket Books, 1980);

John Middleton Murry Jr., who writes science fiction under the pseudonym Richard Cowper (from the dust jacket for the U.S. edition of Clone, *1972)*

A Dream of Kinship (London: Gollancz, 1981; New York: Timescape/Pocket Books, 1981);

A Tapestry of Time (London: Gollancz, 1982; New York: Pocket Books, 1986);

The Story of Pepita and Corindo, published with *The Young Student* (New Castle, Va.: Cheap Street, 1982);

The Unhappy Princess, published with *The Missing Heart* (New Castle, Va.: Cheap Street, 1982);

The Tithonian Factor and Other Stories (London: Gollancz, 1984);

Shades of Darkness (Salisbury, Wiltshire: Kerosina, 1986);

The Magic Spectacles and Other Tales (Salisbury, Wiltshire: Kerosina, 1986).

OTHER: "Is There a Story in It Somewhere?" in *The Science Fiction Source Book,* edited by David Wingrove (New York: Van Nostrand Reinhold, 1984), pp. 74–75;

"Backwards Across the Frontier," in *The Profession of Science Fiction: SF Writers on Their Craft and Ideas,* edited by Maxim Jakubowski and Edward James (New York: St. Martin's Press, 1992), pp. 78–94.

SELECTED PERIODICAL PUBLICATIONS–UNCOLLECTED: "Foundation Forum: Problems of Creativity," by Cowper, Brian W. Aldiss, and Thomas M. Disch, *Foundation,* no. 13 (May 1978): 65–73;

"Yorcon Speech," *Vector,* no. 96 (December 1979–January 1980): 28–34;

"Apropos 'The White Bird of Kinship,'" *Vector,* no. 110 (October 1982): 6–12.

Richard Cowper, pseudonym of John Middleton Murry Jr., emerged in British science fiction in 1967 with the publication of *Breakthrough,* his first novel in that genre. In the two decades of his active science-fiction career, Cowper produced a distinguished body of work that is highly praised for its literary elegance. In "The Gulf and the Forest: Contemporary SF in Britain," Brian W. Aldiss cites Cowper among those who revivified the literary tradition of British science fiction in the 1960s and 1970s and returned the genre to the British literary mainstream. Eschewing the conventions of commercial science fiction–the preoccupation with action, conflict, and ideas at the expense of character–Cowper combines sensitive characterization (including frank relationships between the sexes) and evocative description with economical storytelling. He focuses typically on the struggles of a gifted individual to cope with unusual, often visionary or psychic, experiences that challenge commonsense understanding of reality. For Cowper, who has been strongly influenced by the English Romantics, especially William Blake and John Keats, the awakened imagination is a vehicle of human redemption through its capacity to transcend the limited grasp of reason and science. Far from being escapist, science fiction at its best helps to kindle the imagination. Cowper's major theme is redemption through the awakening of higher perception and living in accordance with reality thus revealed. Dreams, visions, precognition, and inner examination figure prominently in his writings as vehicles for exposing illusions about reality, time, free will, and human nature. Dreams are often major inspirations for his story ideas.

Born on 9 May 1926 in Abbotsbury, Dorset, England, the son of John Middleton Murry and his second wife, Violet Le Maistre, the future science-fiction author was registered at birth as John Middleton Murry Jr. He was soon given the nickname Colin, and he referred to himself thereafter by that name. All his non-science-fiction publications are signed as by Colin Murry or Colin Middleton Murry.

Colin Murry grew up in an exceptionally literary environment. The elder Murry was a noted literary critic, editor, social reformer, and erstwhile member of the D. H. Lawrence circle; his first wife had been Katherine Mansfield, who died in 1923. At age three or four Colin Murry played on the floor with H. G. Wells; as a boy he conversed with George Orwell. But his father was remote; his mother pointedly rejected him; and his father's third wife, a nurse whom he married only weeks after Violet's death in 1931, was an angry and vitriolic woman. Young Murry displayed little interest in literature, writing, or academics until later in life. He was sent away to boarding schools for his preparatory education, culminating at the rather experimental Rendcomb College, which he attended from 1937 to 1941. His two volumes of autobiography, *One Hand Clapping* (1975) and *Shadows on the Grass* (1977), record his troubled relationship with his father, as he sought his father's approval and recognition on the one hand and struggled for independence on the other. In 1944, when he was seventeen, a relaxation of pressure from his father suddenly released the younger Murry's creative energies, and he produced a torrent of short stories, fairy tales, verse, drawings, and paintings in a matter of weeks. His first published short story appeared in 1946 in a little magazine; a half-dozen more were published over the next two years, until the postwar little-magazine market dried up.

After service in the Fleet Air Arm of the British navy (1944–1947), Murry attended Oxford University on a government grant and graduated with a B.A. in English literature in 1950. That same year, he married Ruth Jezierski; they have two daughters, Jacqueline (born in 1954) and Helen (born in 1955). He obtained a teacher's diploma from Leicester University in 1951. His professional career thereafter was as a teacher of English, first as English master and later department head at Massada College, Brighton, Sussex (1952–1967), and then as department head at Atlantic College, Glamorgan, Wales (1967–1970).

He continued writing throughout the 1950s, but as rejection slips for his short stories multiplied, he shifted to novel writing. His first two attempts were rejected by publishers. The third, *The Golden Valley,* written in 1954, was largely autobiographical and accordingly not well received by his father. Finally published in 1958, a year after the elder Murry's death, it sold reasonably well and garnered some good reviews. However, his next two novels, *Recollections of a Ghost*

Murry and his future wife, Ruth Jezierski, in 1948 (from Shadows on the Grass, *1977)*

ence-fiction radio scripts were rejected by the BBC: one was seen as too horrifying, the other as too expensive to produce. A third script (not science fiction), "Taj Mahal by Candlelight," was rejected without explanation. However, a decade later the unrevised script won the BBC radio play competition (1965) and was broadcast. One science-fiction stage play was returned by Granada TV for "improvement."

Believing his literary career had reached an impasse, Murry gambled on a change of fortune by adopting the "Richard Cowper" pseudonym in 1964, presumably derived from the eighteenth-century English poet William Cowper, one of whose best-known quotations, "God moves in a mysterious way, his wonders to perform," appears in *Breakthrough* as "Science moves in a mysterious way, its wonders to perform." As Richard Cowper, Murry began concentrating on science fiction. His first effort, written in 1964, was the aptly titled *Breakthrough,* widely regarded as one of his best science-fiction novels. Even so, it too was rejected by several publishers before Dobson published it in 1967.

The decision to focus on science fiction, in retrospect, was not unexpected. Cowper himself has commented in "Backwards Across the Frontier," his contribution to "The Profession of Science Fiction" series in *Foundation* (November 1975; collected in 1992), that the seeds were probably sown in early childhood when he read fairy tales "voraciously," especially Hans Christian Andersen's and Andrew Lang's fairy-tale collections. He discovered H. G. Wells's science fiction at about the age of ten and never lost his enthusiasm for it. Later he went through phases of reading H. Rider Haggard, Arthur Conan Doyle, Karel Čapek, M. R. James, Richard Jefferies, John Buchan, and Sax Rohmer, although he admits that at no time in his adolescence did science fiction dominate his reading. He had written some fairy tales and several science-fiction scripts and plays, and his second and third published "straight" novels both included some paranormal elements. In short, as he put it in "Backwards Across the Frontier," for some time he had been "shuffling sideways and backwards into sf."

What is unusual about Cowper's entrance into professional science-fiction writing is how he did it. Unlike most of his contemporaries, both British and American, he served no apprenticeship whatsoever in writing for science-fiction magazines. He began immediately with a full-length hardcover novel and continued to emphasize the novel form thereafter. As of 1986, the date of his last published book, he had produced thirteen science-fiction and fantasy novels, as well as three short-story collections, all in hardcover, plus several chapbooks of fairy tales.

(1960) and *A Path to the Sea* (1961), made little impression. In 1963 he undertook a humorous treatment of sex that he thoroughly enjoyed writing. Considered too risky by his publisher, it appeared only in 1972, from a different publisher, as *Private View.* Murry also tried writing radio plays and full-length stage plays. Two sci-

Cowper is noted for the literary quality of his science fiction, with an emphasis on good writing, rounded characterizations (both male and female), credible dialogue, and the influence of landscape. He is sharply critical of market-driven formulaic science fiction typified by much of the American magazine market. Self-exploration is far more important to Cowper's writing than galactic exploration. The alien seldom manifests itself in the form of extraterrestrials and exotic otherworlds; it is far more likely to be found in the characters' interior lives, in their dreams, visions, and awakenings to realities beyond the empirical. In his editorial introduction to Cowper's "Backwards Across the Frontier" in *Foundation,* Peter Nicholls calls him "science fiction's poet of deja vu" for his ability "to evoke the mysterious landscapes of dreams . . . with precision and beauty, and to ponder their relation to our waking lives." Technology and gadgetry are peripheral to Cowper's fiction. Ideas are important, not so much in themselves as in how his characters react to them. An early reader of *Breakthrough* in manuscript thought it was a good novel about ESP but not good science fiction because the characters dominated the ideas. Cowper similarly does not write action adventure. The opening of Chapter 11 of *Breakthrough* is indicative:

> If this were a work of Science-Fiction I daresay events would at this point begin to move towards a rapid and theatrical climax in which Miss Bernstein, Doctor Dumpkenhoffer and I all found ourselves abducted, dragged on board an interstellar cruiser and winging our way via a hyper-space timewarp *en route* for Alpha Centauri. . . . The truth . . . is that nothing happened at all.

Ostensibly a story about ESP and other psi phenomena, *Breakthrough* is the first of Cowper's science-fictional explorations of human perception and human potential. "We've forgotten how to *see!*" one character exclaims, echoing Blake: "We see *with* not *through* the eyes." The theme is Romantic: Blake and Keats are quoted frequently, and the narrator, Jimmy Haverill, teaches English Romantic literature at Hampton University. His colleague, Dr. Dumpkenhoffer, is an American parapsychologist who tests students for paranormal abilities, especially precognition. One of his subjects, Rachel Bernstein, manifests heightened abilities in Haverill's presence. Haverill and Rachel discover that they also share disturbing mythic dreams. They struggle to understand what is happening to them and who they really are, a process paralleled by their growing love for one another. In time they discover that they are the last two survivors of an ancient race of Sky Children (from John Keats's *The Fall of Hyperion* [published in 1856], from which the epigraph to the novel is taken) whose pursuit of beauty ran afoul of self-destructive pride. Haverill learns that he is Haalar, who fled the Sky Children and hid among the people of Earth, while Rachel is Araaran, who has been searching thousands of years for Haalar to awaken him to his destiny and to deliver her message to humanity.

That message is manifested through electrical equipment, devised by Dr. Dumpkenhoffer and his assistant, Peter Klorner, that makes thoughts and past experiences visible. To Haverill the message is the image of the soaring, almost infinite Palace of the Sky Children; to Klorner it is a series of extraordinary mathematical equations; to Dumpkenhoffer it is "the face of God"–and he disappears shortly thereafter when he attempts to re-experience the message. More simply, the message is that humans possess the potential to realize the ultimate that is already within them. Haalar's sojourn on Earth has allowed sparks of his nature to mingle with humanity's. The joining of Haalar and Araaran and the delivery of the message may fan the sparks into a blaze.

There are elements in this story of the Gnostic myth of the messenger awakening those who are receptive to knowledge of their nature and destiny, as well as direct references to Adam and Eve and the Garden of Eden. What is pointedly lacking is the standard action-science-fiction convention that would make Haverill and Rachel into alien mutants or supermen. Nor is there an apocalyptic sense of revelation, of wonder, of the alien, such as is found in Arthur C. Clarke's *Childhood's End* (1953). *Breakthrough* refers more to the growth of human self-awareness than to the mutation of humanity into a new species.

Cowper submitted his second science-fiction novel, *Phoenix* (1968), at the request of his publisher. It continues Cowper's fascination with the themes of time and paranormal abilities, now transposed to the future. A young misfit ("the last Romantic," he calls himself) of the twenty-fourth century undergoes suspended animation for a few years to escape his problems. Instead, he awakens in a provincial England of the far future slowly recovering from the great epidemic some 1,500 years earlier. Society is organized in a manner astonishingly similar to late Roman times. A powerful church with an inner core of mind-reading priests vigorously combats heresy and thwarts the revival of industrial technology. The story line thereafter is a familiar one, of the protagonist's efforts to build a steam engine and of his involvement with a young heretic priestess with extraordinary paranormal powers. *Phoenix,* while less original than *Breakthrough,* is an enjoyable, well-told story that retains interest for its anticipation of the religious structure of Cowper's later White Bird of Kinship trilogy (also known as the Corlay trilogy).

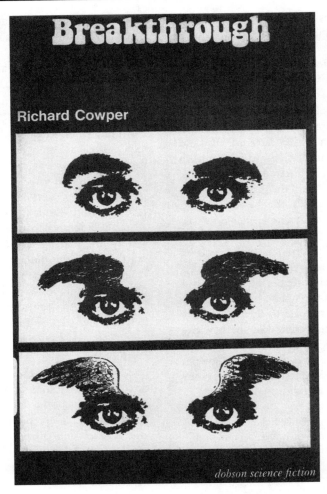

Dust jacket for Murry's first science-fiction novel, in which a young man and woman discover they are the last of an ancient race of Sky Children mentioned in John Keats's poem The Fall of Hyperion *(Richland County Public Library)*

Both *Breakthrough* and *Phoenix* sold well; both were also published in the United States by Ballantine, and *Phoenix* was a selection of the Science Fiction Book Club. Buoyed by this initial success, Cowper read an article by John Brunner in 1970 on the economic realities of writing science fiction in Britain and decided to try freelance writing for two years, the length of time the family could be supported by savings and his wife's income from teaching. The experiment ultimately proved successful, and from 1972 on Cowper gave his profession as freelance writer.

The road, however, was not always smooth. His third science-fiction novel, *Domino,* which had been written before the decision to freelance, was largely ignored upon publication in 1971. Although Cowper has described it in "Backwards Across the Frontier" as an "offbeat quasi-sf story," it deals with the traditional science-fiction theme of alternate futures. Christopher Blackburn's

involvement with genetics will eventually lead—like a row of dominoes falling over—to a genetically engineered slave society of utter degradation. Persons from this future society contact him in an effort to abort the entire timeline. The emphasis of the story is not on action and conspiracy but on Christopher's gradual development from outright skepticism to a new perception of reality that goes beyond mechanistic science and popular opinion. Unlike Cowper's first two novels, there was no American edition.

By contrast, his next novel—the first to be written during the experimental freelance period—was quite successful, according to Cowper. *Kuldesak* (1972) was accepted enthusiastically by Gollancz, which remained Cowper's publisher for the next decade; the novel was published the same year in the United States by Doubleday. *Kuldesak* depicts a future humanity that has lived underground for 2,000 years, dominated by intelligent machines and ignorant of the Earth's surface. According to alien Observers, humanity is about to enter a cul-de-sac, "a road along which no further progress is possible." A coming-of-age story, *Kuldesak* focuses on young Mel, who learns about the Outside, and Frankie, a telepathic girl with power over machine intelligences. They and their friends eventually make it to the surface and with the help of an alien Observer persuade God (the vast artificial intelligence to which humanity had surrendered its sovereignty) to lift the prohibition against going to the surface, offering the hope that humanity eventually will progress once more. *Kuldesak* is marred by a rather formulaic plot and characters and an annoying practice of using asterisks in place of "untranslatable" alien concepts.

Cowper next embarked on one of his major accomplishments in science fiction, *The Twilight of Briareus* (1974), a work that involved him more intensely than any of his other science-fiction novels. Pleased with the result, he was incredulous when it was initially rejected. Believing that commercial success would require him to produce a succession of *Kuldesak* clones, he decided to withdraw from writing altogether—but only after one final act, writing a savage parody of the crass science-fiction mind that would reject *The Twilight of Briareus*. The story took on a life of its own, however, and Cowper had great fun writing it. The result, *Clone* (1972), actually proved to be the book that gained him a popular audience both in Britain and in the United States, where it was selected by the Science Fiction Book Club.

Besides being a "breakthrough" novel, *Clone* represents another side of Cowper's writing, that of farcical satire, which appears again in *Worlds Apart* (1974) and *Profundis* (1979). *Clone* satirizes the superman story within the context of a ludicrous semidystopian society one hundred years in the future. Overpopulation is combatted by a Ministry of Procreation and by an organization of Samaritans who assist people with their suicides. Menial labor is performed by pious, well-spoken mutated chimps (except for those who have gone underground to work toward the dictatorship of the "proletariape"). Young Alvin and his three brothers are illegal human clones with highly unusual eidetic and paranormal abilities. When a youthful prank results in the accidental erasure of their memories, they are farmed out to foster homes. Alvin is raised by the chimps at a scientific station. He is completely ignorant of the world's ways, a Candide-like figure, whose utter innocence stuns those who encounter him. Alvin eventually recovers his memory and locates his brothers with the help of human and chimp allies. The collective paranormal power of the clones is sufficient to destroy or transform the world. The clones, however, do nei-

ther, other than to persuade the European powers that efforts to destroy them would only set off worldwide nuclear annihilation. Instead, the clones—now known collectively as "Adam"—retire into another dimension at the site of the original Garden of Eden, there to cultivate their own garden. The final message is typical Cowper: humanity sees only what it wants to see; people are not ready yet to realize that "they have it in them to be angels . . . that the earth's a paradise if they'll only see it."

Cowper followed *Clone* with *Time Out of Mind* (1973) which deals once again with time, heightened powers, and the nature of consciousness but is more of a conventional melodrama. In 1987 a young boy, Laurie, is warned in a vision by his future self that he must kill Piers Magobion. As an adult, Laurie, now an agent for the United Nations Narcotics Security, encounters a new drug that releases psychokinetic powers. To prevent it from being misused to establish the dictatorial society from which his future self came, Laurie must kill Magobion, who controls the drug and has developed immense psychokinetic power. At every step in his investigation, Laurie feels that he is reenacting something that has already taken place and that he himself belongs to past and future but not to the present (the epigraph to the book comes from T. S. Eliot's *Burnt Norton* [1936]: "Time present and time past / Are both perhaps present in time future"). This aspect, however, is not developed well, and much of the plot seems contrived, although the opening sequence of the vision and the fate of his future self are effectively rendered. Despite its greater affinity to genre conventions, *Time Out of Mind* was not published in the United States until eight years after its British publication.

In 1974 *The Twilight of Briareus* was finally published. Cowper's longest and most complex novel of heightened powers and human redemption, it also occasioned his later remark in "Backwards Across the Frontier" that what he said in it could only have been expressed through science fiction. To Cowper, science fiction is the literature of the imagination, and imagination means new perception. *The Twilight of Briareus* is a novel about the future awakening of new perception and the birth of a new humanity through shock, struggle, sacrifice, and the abandoning of illusion. The seemingly linear narrative structure of the novel, for example, is complicated by the frequent use of flashbacks, framing devices, dreams, and precognitions (which Cowper sometimes refers to as "flash-forwards"), as if to exemplify the view of the alien Briarians that "linear time is the biggest illusion of all."

The Twilight of Briareus is ultimately a debate over what it means to be human. Is humanity, or human nature, defined by biology or individual identity, by

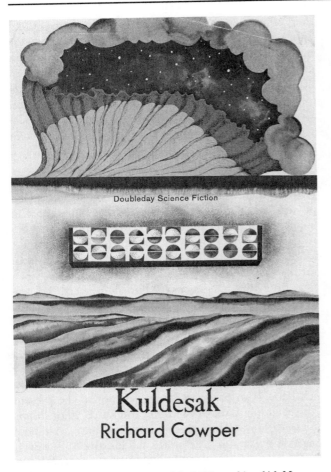

Doubleday Science Fiction

Kuldesak
Richard Cowper

Dust jacket for the U.S. edition of the 1972 novel in which Murry depicted a future world where humankind has lived underground for two thousand years (Richland County Public Library)

habits of perception or the potential for change? Both in the context of the story and in Cowper's own outlook, the survival of humanity depends upon how the question is answered. The key text is Blake's "All Things Exist in the Human Imagination." The culmination is a Christ-like act of self-sacrifice. The protagonist, Calvin Johnson, agonizes over the question of free will as biological instinct, alien manipulation, and indisputable precognition are all manifested.

The nearby supernova Briareus Delta causes massive climatic changes and loss of life on Earth in 1983. Within a few months, realization dawns that humanity has also become sterile. When the children already conceived reach puberty, it is clear that they too are sterile—they are the Twilight Generation. The assumption that the sterility was caused by radiation from the supernova is challenged by Calvin and Angus McHarty, an elderly maverick scientist. Working from a variety of clues, including reports of unusual dreams and visions, brainwave patterns, and

anomalous behavior, they hypothesize that what is happening is in fact an attempted takeover of humanity by aliens at the cellular level. Although the takeover is apparently benign, the human brain's instinctive and self-destructive response is to negate the will to live. Racial suicide is preferable at the deepest level of the hypothalamus to loss of identity as a species. As the takeover hypothesis becomes increasingly plausible, Calvin finds himself at the center of an internal "debate" between the instinctive, all too human fear of loss of identity and the more than human potential offered by the aliens. Calvin comes to believe that he is a "diplodeviant" in whom the human and the alien are balanced in such a way that he can fully respond to both sides of the dilemma. His "vote" will be decisive. Through Calvin's dreams, precognitions, travels, and journal entries from 1983 to 2001, the reader witnesses his struggle to recognize and then come to terms with the dilemma as his reason and his instinct are both transcended by a larger perception of reality stimulated by his surrender of self and receptiveness to visions from the aliens. This internal process of development itself suggests what the fusion of alien and human would produce: a larger and stronger whole symbolized by the Briareus ("strong") of Greek mythology, one of the giants first produced by Gaea (Earth) and Uranus (Heaven). Calvin's death shortly thereafter is accepted as the ultimate self-sacrifice and reassurance that such a fusion is possible. Human conception resumes, and a new generation is born with spiritual powers.

The Twilight of Briareus is arguably Cowper's best single science-fiction novel. It weaves together a great variety of experiences, characters, and clues into a unified whole focused in typical Cowper fashion on an individual's heightened response to universal questions concerning the nature of reality, time, free will, and identity. It is paradigmatic of Cowper's science fiction: human redemption or spiritual evolution is possible, but it is neither inevitable nor can it be engineered. It cannot be the result of natural evolution or alien intervention or experiments or even of conscious decision making. It is beyond reason and science to determine or even to understand. It takes place, if at all, within the individual through struggle, trust, sacrifice, and learning to see.

The Twilight of Briareus was well received in Britain and appeared in the United States as well, where it was also selected by the Science Fiction Book Club. The decade following its publication was an intensely productive period for Cowper. He first returned to satire with *Worlds Apart,* which continues his exploration of the nature of reality. He commented in "Backwards Across the Frontier" that he still had no idea what reality was, except that orthodox science was not of much help. *Worlds Apart* operates on the conceit that two characters at opposite ends of the universe are each writing a supposedly fictional account about the other. On Earth, George Cringe, a middle-aged schoolteacher, finds solace from his mundane existence by creating a science-fiction epic about the planet Agenor and his hero and heroine, Zil Bryn and Orgypp. Unknown to George, on the antimatter world Chnas, a being named Zil Bryn is writing *Shorge Gringe's Pilgrimage,* set on the planet Urth. Inevitably the two authors intersect—they are, after all, "contiguous enantiomorphic compatibles"—and manifest themselves on each other's world, causing mutual disorientation over what is reality and what is fiction. Once again Cowper connects reality to perception, and Blake's "All Things Exist in the Human Imagination" reappears as the epigraph. The dialogue is witty, and the plot is a clever send-up of self-reflexive fiction. But the humor of substituting Chnassian terms for English—"'Beauty is Hwyllth: Hwyllth Beauty,' That is all ye know on Chnas and all ye need to know"—soon wears thin. There was no American edition.

For two years after *Worlds Apart,* as Colin Middleton Murry, he devoted himself primarily to writing his autobiography, covering the years until his father's death in 1957: *One Hand Clapping* and *Shadows on the Grass.* Also, as Richard Cowper, he began to write short stories, eventually producing fourteen that were published between 1975 and 1984 and subsequently collected in three hardcover volumes, all published by Gollancz: *The Custodians and Other Stories* (1976), *The Web of the Magi and Other Stories* (1980), and *The Tithonian Factor and Other Stories* (1984). Thirteen of the stories thus collected had been published in the American *Magazine of Fantasy and Science Fiction,* despite Cowper's earlier criticisms of American commercial science fiction; the one remaining story, "The Tithonian Factor," appeared first in *Changes: Stories of Metamorphosis* (1983), an original anthology edited by Michael Bishop and Ian Watson. *The Magazine of Fantasy and Science Fiction* in that period was the most receptive of the American science-fiction magazines to literary quality, to fantasy, and to British authors (the April 1978 issue was a special all-British issue). His first two appearances in this periodical, "The Custodians" (October 1975) and "Piper at the Gates of Dawn" (March 1976), were each nominated for both the Hugo and Nebula awards. There were no American hardcover editions of his story collections, however, merely a single paperback selection of five tales (*Out There Where the Big Ships Go,* 1980). American book publishers did not see commercial viability in his short fiction.

The short works are in fact highly readable and absorbing, even though there is typically little or no action. Some are fantasy; some are science fiction; and several are modern versions of Victorian and Edwardian prototypes, complete with lost races, ancient manuscripts, and travelers' diaries. Nearly all are further explorations of Cowper's continuing preoccupation with reality and perception. "The Web of the Magi" (June 1980) is a Haggardesque tale of the discovery of a lost race in northwest Iran in 1886 who maintain the loom of Zurvan (Time) on which is woven—and unwoven—the pattern of destiny. A group of tourists unwittingly participate in an Incan rite of regeneration in "Incident at Huacaloc" (October 1981). Both stories ask which is the dream, which is reality? "The Hertford Manuscript" (October 1976) dates from 1665 yet purports to be the record of the final days of Wells's nineteenth-century Time Traveller. If the manuscript is genuine, what becomes of the concept of time? Is it "an endless snake with its tail in its own mouth, a cosmos in which the Past and the Future coexist and will continue to do so for all Eternity"? "Out There Where the Big Ships Go" (August 1979) tells about the alien game of Kalire, "the Gift from Beyond the Stars," brought back to Earth in the twenty-third century by the captain of the last starship. According to the aliens, attaining eligibility to play Kalire—which is simultaneously philosophy, religion, discipline, and game—involves taking "another step up the evolutionary ladder." Young Roger Herzheim learns that true mastery requires unlearning consensus views of reality.

In "What Did the Deazies Do?" (December 1982) a young boy discovers a puzzling M. C. Escher-like construction locked away in the cottage of the folk healer and reputed witch, Miss Deazie. It defies rational explanation. Years later Miss Deazie reveals that "it's what lets us be Deazies. That's what it *does.* It lets us in and out to do what we do." The youth realizes that "the kind of answers I was looking for would not have *been* answers at all in my sense of the word. They would have all been looking-glass answers and would never fit the questions of my world." Characteristically human responses of aggression and domination are exposed as obstacles to evolution, not advantages; in "Drink Me, Francesca" (April 1978), Peter Mahler is the one member of the Cygnus II expedition capable of opening himself to the alien and learning to perceive in new ways. A revealing classroom discussion of his journal two centuries later serves as the framework of the story.

"The Custodians" (October 1975), one of Cowper's most memorable short fictions, places Juvenal's question of who watches the watchers (*Quis custodiet ipsos custodes?*) within a context of ancient manuscripts, paranormal forces, and the nature of time and free will. Does foreknowledge imply determinism, or does it bring with it the responsibility to change the outcome?

*Dust jacket for the U.S. edition of the 1972 novel in which Murry satirized
the superman story with a farcical depiction of a
dystopian future society*

That is the question confronting the elderly Spindrift, the latest and perhaps the last in a chain of custodians at the abbey of Hautaire, who since the thirteenth century have possessed the ability to see impending crises of civilization "within the mind's eye." Might it be that what is foreknown is itself the product of limited human understanding and that to change the future would accordingly require a change in human perception? Is it already too late?

If "The Custodians" can be read as a cautionary tale, ending on a note of foreboding, the White Bird of Kinship trilogy ultimately reaffirms human redemption through new perception. It tells the story, set in a post-disaster future British Isles, of the origins, institutionalization, and eventual recovery of the intrinsic spiritual impulse of the new religion of the White Bird of Kinship. The saga, although referred to as a trilogy, is actually a series of seven stories: the original novella, "Piper at the Gates of Dawn"; *The Road to Corlay* (novel, 1978);

A Dream of Kinship (three interrelated stories, 1981); and *A Tapestry of Time* (two stories, 1982). The stories making up the latter two books were not published separately in magazines. Surprisingly, the original British editions of *The Road to Corlay* did not include "Piper at the Gates of Dawn." In a prefatory note to these editions, Cowper summarizes the novella, directs the interested reader to *The Custodians and Other Stories* for the text, and states that "ideally that tale should stand here as the prologue to the present one." All three Kinship volumes were published in the United States but only in paperback editions from Pocket Books, except for a Science Fiction Book Club edition of *The Road to Corlay*. "Piper at the Gates of Dawn" does appear as the prologue in the American and later British editions.

Although "Piper at the Gates of Dawn" was written in 1974 and is the first component of the series, the seed was already present much earlier in the concluding image of *Breakthrough*. Twelve years after the main events of the story, the young daughter of Haverill and Rachel has a powerful dream in which the long-vanished Dr. Dumpkenhoffer is manifested as an enormous white bird winging slowly into the distance against a backdrop of millions of stars. Haverill does not see how it could possibly be Dumpkenhoffer, although his daughter is adamant; yet, he admits, "I can't help feeling he would have acknowledged at least a spiritual kinship."

The Kinship series proper spans forty years, from 2999 until 3039, with framing texts from 3798–3799 and 3846. Much of England is underwater as a result of the "Drowning" of 2000 A.D., when carbon dioxide buildup melted the polar ice caps. The social and political pattern is medieval: seven small kingdoms, a landed aristocracy, and limited technology and education carefully controlled by the Established Church, which teaches that the Drowning was God's punishment for humanity's descent into scientific materialism. Much of this background must be pieced together by the reader—there is no systematic exposition until midway through the second book, *A Dream of Kinship*.

"Piper at the Gates of Dawn" takes place in the closing months of 2999, when apocalyptic expectations are rife, especially of the coming of the White Bird. Thirteen-year-old Tom, a musical prodigy on pipes created especially for him by the wizard Morfedd, travels to York with his great-uncle Peter of Hereford, ostensibly to enter the chapter school but in reality to keep his promise to Morfedd to be there at Christmas. On the way to York, Tom's extraordinary playing enchants and awakens all who hear him, enabling them to recognize a quality within themselves, a sense sometimes of intense longing and sadness, of reaching out toward something profound yet simple, "a vision of what might be" that brings feelings of both joy and loss. Tom knows how to find the right key to each individual through his music, but he also believes that "there's a master-key. . . . One to unlock the whole world. I call that key the White Bird." At the stroke of midnight on New Year's Eve in York, as Tom plays his "Lament for the White Bird" to a huge, expectant crowd, he is martyred, killed by the soldier Gyre, who takes the myth of the White Bird literally: that the Bird must be killed in order to live again. The Church claims Tom as one of its own, but his tale, the good news, is already being spread by Peter and Gyre.

The story is powerfully told. The wealth of detail creates a convincing atmosphere and delicacy of mood. As always, Cowper is not interested in theology or music or ideas for their own sakes, but rather in people's reactions to them. The quality of Tom's music and its effect is conveyed by skillful descriptions of the listeners' feelings and longings. Indeed, the extraordinary nature of these reactions is what later convinces

the skeptical Brother Francis that the Boy (as Tom is subsequently referred to) is authentic. "Even though I live for a thousand years I shall never meet another like him," says one witness, "for he took my heart from me and breathed his music into it and gave it back to me. . . . Oh you, holy men, how can you ever, *ever* hope to understand? . . . Tom is everywhere about you, just as he always has been and always will be. He came to show us what we have it in ourselves to be, and you blind priests killed him because you could not see what we saw!" At no point in the entire series does Cowper provide an exposition of the theology of the White Bird of Kinship. This omission is, of course, deliberate: neither Kinship nor redemption is reducible to articles of belief; each must be experienced directly.

Following the prologue, the main narrative of *The Road to Corlay* moves ahead to the year 3018, when the growing popularity of Kinship has alarmed the Church. Three characters are emphasized: Thomas of Norwich, a Kinsman who was baptized by Peter and who carries a precious document for safekeeping at the Kinship center of Corlay on the island of Brittany; Jane Thomson, born in the first minute after the Boy Tom was killed, who cares for Thomas of Norwich when he nearly drowns but senses another presence within him; and Brother Francis, who is sent out by the worried Archbishop to learn the truth about the Boy and is converted to Kinship. The title refers not only to the perilous journey of Thomas and Jane (the prophesied Bride of Time who is carrying Thomas's child) to reach Corlay after Kinship has been proscribed but also to Brother Francis's path from skepticism to belief, much on the model of Paul on the road to Damascus.

The story is clearly fantasy, not science fiction. Cowper himself says as much in his 1982 *Vector* article "Apropos 'The White Bird of Kinship'" about "Piper at the Gates of Dawn" at least. But in *The Road to Corlay* he does introduce a science-fictional narrative strand, with decidedly mixed results. The other presence Jane senses in Thomas of Norwich is revealed as one Michael Carver, a man from 1986 who is trapped in an out-of-body experience while participating in a scientific experiment partially conducted by Peter Klorner, Dr. Dumpkenhoffer's assistant in *Breakthrough*. Separate chapters depict the efforts of Carver's wife and associates to revive him. Nearly all critics are agreed that the effect of these chapters is jarring and disruptive of the mood created by the primary narrative, even though the double perspective provided by Carver/Thomas reinforces the contrast between spiritual and scientific modes of perception.

As a deliberate relaxation from the ardors of producing the first Kinship book, Cowper wrote *Profundis*, a black comedy. The title is the name of a huge subma-

Dust jacket for the 1974 novel that is widely considered Murry's best work of science fiction (Richland County Public Library)

rine that cruises the oceans of a post-nuclear-holocaust world until radiation levels subside. Within the microcosm of the ship, the bungling commander convinces himself that he is God the Father. Encouraged by the ship supercomputer in the role of the Holy Ghost, he plans a reprise of the New Testament, choosing as his Beloved Son one Tom Jones, an innocent whose picaresque adventures turn out to have unanticipated consequences. Neither Tom nor his adventures are more than mildly amusing. Although Cowper brings in redemption and psychical abilities, the farcical tone does little for them. *Profundis* is the weakest of Cowper's science-fiction satires, much less appealing than *Clone* or *Worlds Apart*. Even so, there was an American paperback edition in 1981.

Each of the three novellas in *A Dream of Kinship* focuses on a discrete historical moment in the evolution of Kinship. The first highlights a week in January 3019, when Corlay is burned by the Church, and Jane's son Tom—the third Thomas of the series, the Child of the Bride of Time—is born. The backlash against the Church hastens the spread of Kinship. The second novella moves ahead to 3029, when the social and political conflicts between the two faiths are coming to a head, and ten-year-old Tom returns to a rebuilt Corlay for further instruction. By 3038, the time of the third novella, Tom, now nearly eighteen, receives the powerful gift of his formidable spiritual heritage but also learns to recognize a terrifying darkness within himself that must be confronted. The gift of power carries its own responsibilities.

That lesson, however, is not fully comprehended. The first part of *A Tapestry of Time* moves forward to six critical months in 3039, when Tom realizes his destiny and the limitations of organized Kinship. Tom unleashes his full powers deliberately to kill two men who have raped his traveling companion and childhood friend, the girl Witchet. The price Tom pays for this misuse of his gift is Witchet herself. In seeking to recover her spirit from the Land of Shadows, he plunges deeper into his own darkness. From this rite of passage, he learns to accept his true self, thereby liberating himself and enabling him to create his Song of Songs. He accuses Brother Francis of clipping the wings of the White Bird, of turning it into a creed, "a thing of words" that is no longer real, but Francis cannot accept this view. Having no further need for the Boy's pipes, Tom buries them along with his music.

"The Cartwright Papers" concludes *A Tapestry of Time* and the Kinship series. It consists primarily of the journal of Robert James Cartwright, the scholar whose editorial introduction prefaces "Piper at the Gates of Dawn." It records the events in 3798–3799 leading to the discovery by Cartwright and his wife of the Boy's pipes and Tom's Song of Songs. The opening description of the New Year's Eve Service of 3798 at the cathedral of St. Francis in Oxford unobtrusively demonstrates that Francis's path, not Tom's, has been followed in the intervening centuries. The actual discovery of the artifacts is recorded in a much later memoir by Cartwright's wife, Margaret, who concludes that the recovery of the music and its playing has changed the human spirit forever. She reiterates Cowper's principal theme when she says of her husband that his ability to pursue the discovery ultimately derived from certain apparitional experiences that forced him "to question the truth of his own sensual perception, to allow his mind access to the possibility that there might exist a higher order of reality which transcends that of mere sense."

The Kinship books, for which Cowper is probably best known, gain in power when read consecutively, even though "Piper at the Gates of Dawn" can stand on its own. The complex interweaving of many details firmly links them together. The appearance of three successive Toms succinctly frames the sociological development of the new faith without belaboring the obvious parallels to the history of the Christian church. The visionary intensity of the books is magnified by the cumulative impact of the testimonies of those characters who experience firsthand the White Bird and the inspired music. The series falters only twice: the Michael Carver interludes in *The Road to Corlay* disrupt the otherwise almost lyrical mood, and the third Tom's sojourn in the Land of Shadows in *A Tapestry of Time* does not avoid formulaic fantasy. Critics agree that the series is compulsively readable and that it makes the reader care about the fate of the characters.

After *A Tapestry of Time* Cowper continued writing short stories—*The Tithonian Factor and Other Stories* was published two years later, and he also published a few of his early fairy tales in limited-edition chapbooks—but no further long fiction appeared until 1986. *Shades of Darkness* is Cowper's next novel and presumably brings closure to his writing career. It marks both a change in literary direction—the ghost story—and a change in publisher from Gollancz to Kerosina, a small specialist press. The novel is marginally fantasy: there are reports of ghosts and precognition, troubling dreams, an ad hoc exorcism, and strange words that mysteriously appear on the narrator's manuscript (and are seen at least once by another character). But *Shades of Darkness* is far more the story of a man finding himself, both creatively and romantically, by exorcising his own fears. The epigraph is from Samuel Johnson: "Fear . . . should not be suffered to tyrannise in the imagination." James Fuller, former journalist, rents an isolated cottage on the Essex coast, where he plans to write a novel exposing the political situation in Uganda, which he covered as a journalist and which cost him his job. The writing comes easily until unknown words appear in his manuscript, and the atmosphere becomes tense. He learns that a previous tenant of the cottage was tried and acquitted on the basis of self-defense for the murder of her houseboy in Kenya in 1953. Is her spirit now seeking peace? Fuller finally realizes that she did kill her houseboy, not in self-defense but in an attempt to kill

the darkness within herself. He recognizes the blackness in everyone, just as Tom does in *A Dream of Kinship*. He acts successfully to put matters right. The story is atmospheric, skillfully told, and interesting, but it is no more a "fright" story than Cowper's science fiction is action adventure or power fantasy.

Cowper has published no new fiction since 1986, even though the dust jacket of *Shades of Darkness* states that he was then at work on a new science-fiction novel. He also told David Wingrove in a 1979 interview that there were still a couple of "straight" novels that he wanted to write. His silence presumably indicates that he has said what he wanted to say. Peter Nicholls and John Clute in *The Encyclopedia of Science Fiction* (1993) surmise that the Kinship books "so clearly sum up RC's imaginative sense of a redeemed England that it is perhaps unsurprising that he has written relatively little since."

Throughout his career Cowper has consistently emphasized literary quality over genre conventions. He has moved easily across science fiction, satirical comedy, fantasy, and fairy tale. To him science fiction is simply a matter of emphasis, not different in kind from other fiction; what is important to him is not the genre of the book but how well written it is. The economy, grace, and sensitivity of his style, combined with his storytelling ability, are well suited to his thematic concerns with openness to inner experience, imagination as transcendence, and skepticism about reason and science.

Interview:

David Wingrove, "An Interview with Richard Cowper," *Vector*, no. 92 (March–April 1979): 3–8.

References:

Brian W. Aldiss, "The Gulf and the Forest: Contemporary SF in Britain," *Magazine of Fantasy and Science Fiction*, 54 (April 1978): 4–11;

Aldiss and David Wingrove, *Trillion Year Spree: The History of Science Fiction* (New York: Atheneum, 1986);

Wingrove, "The Rest Is Dreams: The Work of Richard Cowper," *Vector*, no. 92 (March–April 1979): 9–16.

Neil Gaiman

(*10 November 1960 –   *)

Joe Sanders

BOOKS: *Duran, Duran: The First Four Years of the Fab Five* (London & New York: Proteus, 1984);

Violent Cases, art by Dave McKean (London: Titan, 1987; Northampton, Mass.: Tundra, 1991);

Don't Panic: The Official Hitch-Hiker's Guide to the Galaxy Companion (London: Titan, 1988; New York: Pocket Books, 1988); revised with additional material by David K. Dickson as *Don't Panic: Douglas Adams and The Hitchhiker's Guide to the Galaxy* (London: Titan, 1993);

Good Omens: The Nice and Accurate Prophecies of Agnes Nutter, Witch, by Gaiman and Terry Pratchett (London: Gollancz, 1990); revised (New York: Workman, 1990);

The Sandman: The Doll's House, art by Mike Dringenberg and Malcolm Jones III (New York: DC Comics, 1990);

Black Orchid, art by McKean (New York: DC Comics, 1991; London: Titan, 1991);

The Sandman: Preludes and Nocturnes, art by Sam Kieth, Dringenberg, and Malcolm Jones III (New York: DC Comics, 1991; London: Titan, 1991);

The Sandman: Dream Country, art by Kelley Jones, Charles Vess, Colleen Doran, and Malcolm Jones III (New York: DC Comics, 1991);

Miracleman Book 4: The Golden Age, art by Mark Buckingham (Forestville, Cal.: Eclipse, 1992; London: EclipseGraphicNovels, 1993);

Signal to Noise, art by McKean (London: VG Graphics, 1992; Milwaukie, Ore.: Dark Horse, 1992);

The Sandman: Season of Mists, art by Kelley Jones, Dringenberg, Malcolm Jones III, Matt Wagner, Dick Giordano, George Pratt, and P. Craig Russell (New York: DC Comics, 1992; London: Titan, 1992);

The Sandman: A Game of You, art by Shawn McManus, Doran, Bryan Talbot, Pratt, Stan Woch, and Giordano (New York: DC Comics, 1993; London: Titan, 1993);

Angels and Visitations: A Miscellany (Minneapolis: Dream-Haven, 1993);

The Books of Magic, art by John Bolton, Scott Hampton, Vess, and Paul Johnson (New York: DC Comics, 1993);

The Sandman: Fables and Reflections, art by Kent Williams, McManus, Woch, Giordano, Duncan Eagleson, Vince Locke, Talbot, John Watkins, Buckingham, Jill Thompson, and Russell (New York: DC Comics, 1993; London: Titan, 1994);

The Sandman: Brief Lives, art by Thompson, Locke, and Giordano (New York: DC Comics, 1994; London: Titan, 1994);

The Sandman: World's End, art by Michael Allred, Gary Amaro, Buckingham, Giordano, Tony Harris, Steve Leialoha, Locke, Shea Anton Pensa, Alec Stevens, Talbot, Watkins, and Michael Zulli (New York: DC Comics, 1994; London: Titan, 1995);

Death: The High Cost of Living, art by Chris Bachalo, Buckingham, and McKean (New York: DC Comics, 1994; London: Titan, 1994);

Snow, Glass, Apples (Minneapolis: DreamHaven, 1994); revised as *Snow Glass Apples: A Play for Voices,* art by George A. Walker (Duluth, Ga.: Biting Dog Press, 2002);

The Tragical Comedy or Comical Tragedy of Mr. Punch, art by McKean (London: VG Graphics, 1994; New York: Vertigo/DC, 1995);

The Compleat Alice Cooper: Incorporating the Three Acts of Alice Cooper's The Last Temptation, by Gaiman and Alice Cooper, art by Zulli (New York: Marvel, 1995); republished as *The Last Temptation* (Milwaukie, Ore.: Dark Horse, 2000);

Angela, art by Greg Capullo and Mark Pennington (Anaheim, Cal.: Image, 1995; London: Titan, 1997); republished as *Spawn: Angela's Hunt* (Anaheim, Cal.: Image, 2000);

Sandman Midnight Theatre, by Gaiman and Wagner, art by Teddy Kristiansen (New York: DC Comics, 1995);

The Sandman: The Kindly Ones, art by Marc Hempel, Richard Case, D'Israeli, Kristiansen, Glyn Dil-

Neil Gaiman (photograph © 1996 by Kelli Bickman; from the dust jacket for the U.S. edition of Neverwhere, *1997)*

lon, Vess, Dean Ormston, and Kevin Nowlan (New York: DC Comics, 1996; London: Titan, 1996);

Neverwhere (London: BBC Books, 1996; New York: Avon, 1997);

The Day I Swapped My Father for 2 Goldfish, art by McKean (Clarkston, Ga.: Borealis/White Wolf, 1997);

Death: The Time of Your Life, art by Bachalo, Pennington, and Buckingham (New York: DC Comics, 1997; London: Titan, 1997);

The Sandman: The Wake, art by Zulli, Jon J. Muth, and Vess (New York: DC Comics, 1997; London: Titan, 1997);

Dustcovers: The Collected Sandman Covers, 1989–1997, commentary and a story by Gaiman, art by McKean (New York: Vertigo/DC Comics, 1997; London: Titan, 1997); republished as *The Collected Sandman Covers, 1989–1997* (New York: Watson-Guptill, 1997);

Smoke and Mirrors: Short Fictions and Illusions (New York: Avon, 1998);

Day of the Dead: An Annotated Babylon 5 Script (Minneapolis: DreamHaven, 1998);

Stardust: Being a Romance Within the Realms of Faerie, art by Vess (New York: DC Comics, 1998; London: Titan, 1998); text republished as *Stardust* (New York: Spike, 1999; London: Headline Feature, 1999);

Neil Gaiman's Midnight Days, by Gaiman and Wagner (London: Titan, 1999; New York: Vertigo/DC Comics, 2000);

The Sandman: The Dream Hunters, art by Yoshitaka Amaro (New York: DC Comics, 1999; London: Titan, 1999);

Green Lantern/Superman: Legend of the Green Flame (New York: DC Comics, 2000);

The Quotable Sandman: Memorable Lines from the Acclaimed Series (New York: DC Comics, 2000; London: Titan, 2001);

American Gods (New York: Morrow, 2001; London: Headline Feature, 2001);

Harlequin Valentine, art by Bolton (Milwaukie, Ore.: Dark Horse, 2001);

Murder Mysteries: A Play for Voices, art by Walker (Duluth, Ga.: Biting Dog Press, 2001);

Adventures in the Dream Trade, edited by Tony Lewis and Priscilla Olson (Framingham, Mass.: NESFA Press, 2002);

Coraline (New York: HarperCollins, 2002).

PRODUCED SCRIPTS: *Neverwhere,* by Gaiman and Lenny Henry, television, BBC2, 12 September–17 October 1996;

Signal to Noise, radio, BBC Radio 3, October 1996;

"Day of the Dead," television, *Babylon 5,* Turner, 11 March 1998;

Princess Mononoke, English adaptation of Hayao Miyazaki's Japanese screenplay, motion picture, Miramax, 1999.

RECORDINGS: *Warning: Contains Language,* readings by Gaiman, music by Dave McKean and The Flash Girls, CD, Minneapolis, DreamHaven 01-1957, 1995;

Neil Gaiman: Live at the Aladdin, videotape, Northampton, Mass., Comic Book Legal Defense Fund, 2001.

OTHER: *Ghastly Beyond Belief,* edited by Gaiman and Kim Newman (London: Arrow, 1985);

Now We Are Sick: A Sampler, edited by Gaiman and Stephen Jones (East Grinstead, U.K.: Neil Gaiman, 1986); republished as *Now We Are Sick: An Anthology of Nasty Verse* (Minneapolis: DreamHaven, 1991);

Temps, volume 1, edited by Gaiman and Alex Stewart (London: Roc, 1991);

The Sandman: Book of Dreams, edited by Gaiman and Edward E. Kramer (New York: HarperPrism, 1996; London: HarperCollins, 1996);

Samuel R. Delany, *The Einstein Intersection,* foreword by Gaiman (Hanover, N.H.: University Press of New England, 1998).

SELECTED PERIODICAL PUBLICATIONS–UNCOLLECTED: Review of Frank Miller, *Batman: The Dark Knight Returns, Foundation,* no. 38 (Winter 1986/1987): 87–91;

The Children's Crusade #1, art by Chris Bachalo and Mike Barreiro, DC Comics, December 1993;

The Children's Crusade #2, by Gaiman, Alison Kwitney, and Jamie Delano, art by Peter Snejbjerg, DC Comics, January 1994.

As Harlan Ellison describes it in his introduction to Neil Gaiman's *The Sandman: Season of Mists* (1992), the announcement that Gaiman's "A Midsummer Night's Dream" had won the award for Year's Best Story at the 1991 World Fantasy Convention produced a dramatic reaction: "all those artsy-fartsy writers and artists and critics sitting there expecting a standard-print short story to win, choked on their little almond cups as this renegade funnybook guy carted off the Diamond as Big as the Ritz. Much snorting through the nose. Much umbrage taken. Many dudgeons raised to new heights." Ellison goes on to describe rules being changed so that no comic-book story could ever be considered for the award in the future. Gaiman himself is less confrontational, mildly suggesting that much of the controversy was about how giving an award only to the writer of a comics script appeared to ignore the artist's contribution to the published story. Nevertheless, no writer for comic books has ever attracted as much favorable attention in as short a time as Gaiman has, and this phenomenon has at least perplexed many readers of standard-print fiction. Gaiman's career illustrates one of the main themes of his writing–a need to transcend categories, to respond to new possibilities.

The eldest of three children, Neil Richard Gaiman was born on 10 November 1960 in Portchester, England. His father, David Gaiman, owned a firm that manufactured vitamins, and his mother, Sheila (née Goldman) Gaiman, was a pharmacist. His mother was able to take a leave of absence from work during Gaiman's infancy, and one of his earliest memories is of himself and his mother playing with an alphabet carved out of wood. Gaiman has said that he always considered himself to be a writer; as he told Jessie Horsting in 1997, another of his first memories, from when he was about three years old, is of grabbing his mother and dictating a poem to her: "I was proud of it; I wanted it down on paper."

He remembers later nights spent "reading by whatever light came in by the hall" after he had been sent to bed. Along with the hardcover and paperback books he treasured, Gaiman was reading comic books. In particular, he remembers being given "a big box filled with mid-sixties Marvels and DC's" by a man who worked with his father. Even though he recognized that some comics were better than others, Gaiman loved the medium, and from then on his ambition was "to write American comics" because the stories were longer, more serious, and less child-centered than those in British comics.

Gaiman was educated at Ardingly College (1970–1974) and Whitgift School (1974–1977), but in 1977 he felt ready to begin writing professionally. After receiving "fairly enthusiastic" rejections for several short stories, he determined to become a freelance journalist so he could learn how the world of publishing worked. Through a combination of talent, luck, and nervy bluffing, he became a successful nonfiction writer for British men's magazines such as *Knave,* and once he established his presence as a journalist he was able to sell his earlier stories, several of which are reprinted in the collection *Angels and Visitations: A Miscellany* (1993). On 14 March 1985 he married Mary McGrath, with whom he has three children: Michael, Holly, and Maddy.

By the mid 1980s Gaiman was ready to return to fiction. It happened to be exactly the right time for a would-be writer of mainstream comics to approach that medium seriously. The industry was unusually open to experimentation, and even longtime monolith DC Comics was attempting to revitalize some of its prized characters. Alan Moore's innovative scripting for *Swamp Thing* (1983–1987) especially impressed Gaiman and convinced him that serious work could be done in the field. Reviewing another such experiment, Frank Miller's reworking of Batman, Gaiman observed in *Foundation* (Winter 1986/1987) that "The most important dreams, the most manipulable of cultural icons, are those that we received when we were too young to judge or analyze. The things that mattered–*really* mattered–when we were too young to discriminate have tremendous pressure to move us now." Gaiman is not disparaging the adult activities of analyzing and discriminating. But he also insists that among the commercial fabrications that fill many mainstream comic books–the outrageously muscled men throwing each other through buildings–can be found genuine, powerful evocations of fears and desires.

In 1986 Gaiman met art student Dave McKean, and the two began collaborating on comics, both "intoxicated by the potential of the medium"–as Gaiman wrote in an introduction to the 1991 American edition of *Violent Cases.* Their first work together was *Violent Cases,* serialized in *Escape,* a showcase for new British comics, and published in book form in late 1987. The narrator is a young man in dark sunglasses and a black T-shirt–a dead ringer for Gaiman's own public persona–who is trying to make sense of events that he remembers from when he was a young boy. "I don't want to gloss over the true facts," he tells readers. "Without true facts, where are we?" But "facts" turn out to be dubious, as the man remembers the boy encountering Al Capone's former chiropractor and discovering that grownups are as prone to uncertainty, emotional outbursts, and naive rationalizations as children. The boy is delighted, the grownup narrator perplexed, to see how "facts" change to fit an interpreter's needs.

Violent Cases attracted attention for both of its creators. After doing another collaboration with McKean as a kind of audition for DC Comics, the limited-run series *Black Orchid* (1988–1989, published in book form

in 1991), Gaiman was offered his choice of inactive DC characters to relaunch. He chose to write about the Sandman, though his version bore no resemblance to the earlier costumed crimefighter. Gaiman's *The Sandman* appeared monthly for seventy-five issues, until he brought the story to a conclusion; in an unusual move, DC acknowledged that the comic should end when the creator decided. Finishing the themes of *The Sandman* took roughly twice as long as Gaiman had intended when he began the project, but the magazine earned him multiple awards (including eight Eisner and three Harvey Awards) and widespread recognition as a writer. It also was a popular success, with the highest sales of any comic in the DC sub-imprint Vertigo, and it is the first mass-market comic to have all its issues still on sale in trade paperbacks. It continues to inspire side-bar stories, including two by Gaiman about Death's interaction with mortals.

Gaiman's enigmatic Sandman came into focus gradually over several issues following the debut of the comic in late 1988 (cover date January 1989). The character is first seen in the hands of occultists who have magically imprisoned him while attempting to trap Death. Neither they nor readers can guess the identity of this gaunt, shaggy-haired figure with piercing, dark eyes. When he finally escapes, he is revealed to be Dream, one of the family of beings called The Endless, along with Destiny, Destruction, the twins Desire and Despair, and Delirium (formerly Delight). They are older than the gods of humanity; in fact, they antedate humanity itself. They appear actually to have been created out of evolving intelligence, the fundamental process of thinking in categories. Dream–also known as Morpheus, Oneiros, Shaper, and other names besides the Sandman–rules the domain that humans enter when they leave their waking consciousness in order to approach the things they most hope for or dread.

That premise could have allowed Gaiman (and DC Comics) to do an endless series of short stories, and *The Sandman* did include several intervals of short tales, including the award-winning "A Midsummer Night's Dream," which was issue 19 in the series. Generally, however, Gaiman worked in larger units, story arcs that continued for several months (and that utilized the talents of different artists Gaiman selected) to show different aspects of the Sandman: protector of humans, destroyer of humans, passionate but vengeful lover, distant and unsympathetic father, and aloof immortal. Even though he exhibits such a variety of behaviors, Morpheus identifies himself with one narrow role. He sees himself as merely the embodiment of his duty. "I am not a man," he tells William Shakespeare in the last issue of *The Sandman.* "And I do not change." He is mistaken. When he says that, Morpheus is wrapped up in

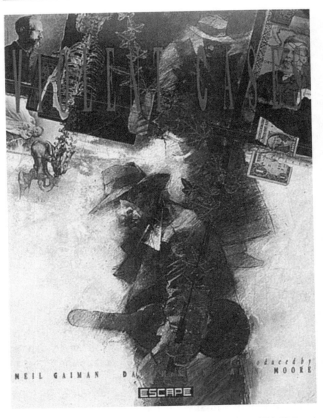

Cover for the first book publication of the comic book on which Gaiman collaborated with artist Dave McKean

Besides deserving attention for its subtle exploration of a complex theme, *The Sandman* is an example of how a serious writer can utilize the comics medium. Gaiman used the delay between issues to control his readers' absorption of details, especially in the long, methodically paced series of catastrophes leading to Morpheus's death in *The Kindly Ones*. He selected different artists for different stories—or sometimes for sections inside a given story—to emphasize various moods. And he utilized the cheeky looseness of comics to bring together an astonishing range of images; *The Sandman* considers, with equal sympathy and assurance, the personal and professional life of Shakespeare and the interpersonal dynamics of a convention of serial killers.

Soon after he began *The Sandman,* in 1990, Gaiman and his family relocated from England to the rural American upper Midwest, near Minneapolis. There he lives connected electronically to the publishing industry and an easy commute away from direct involvement in music and dramatic projects. Gaiman alternated his work on *The Sandman* with other material. In *Good Omens: The Nice and Accurate Prophecies of Agnes Nutter, Witch* (1990), a humorous collaboration with Terry Pratchett, the forces of Evil bungle switching the baby Antichrist for a human infant, so the spawn of darkness begins developing without supernatural tutors. Instead, he enjoys a pleasantly normal childhood. When, therefore, he is confronted by the Four Bikepersons of the Apocalypse with the demand that he accept his ordained role and bring the world to an end, the Antichrist considers the joys of destruction but finally replies that he is content with himself as he is, where he is, and does not feel bound by the ancient script outlined in Revelation. A subplot of the novel describes how a perfectly accurate (though somewhat jumbled) prophetic book eventually is destroyed because people decide they do not want to know exactly what to expect. So life will continue to amble along in its random way, for the Last Judgment has been indefinitely postponed.

In much the same way, "Murder Mysteries" (1992, collected in *Angels and Visitations*), perhaps Gaiman's best short story, moves from contemporary Los Angeles to the literal City of Angels. The narrator is approached by a strange drifter who tells the story of how, in his past as an angel, he was assigned the task of investigating the murder of another angel in Heaven. He discovered the love-deranged criminal and extinguished him utterly under God's approving gaze. Then, however, the law-enforcing angel rejected his role and his very existence of secure, unquestioning righteousness in Heaven. Now he offers humans forgiveness rather than justice; he gives peace to those who deserve punishment. Grasping why he is talking to the narrator

dreams of his own. Gaiman is remarkably successful at building and sustaining sympathy for a superhuman character who wields vast powers with appalling, almost desperate naiveté about what is really going on or who he truly is.

Eventually, *The Sandman* shows the protagonist's discovery that he cannot live with what he has imagined to be his basic nature. It is not so much that he welcomes profound change as that he begins to learn and accept the true facts about himself—his failure to sympathize and his willful narrowness, but also his potential ability to participate in the lives of others. And so he must act, even if it ends his existence as one of The Endless. In "The Tempest" (1996), the final Sandman issue, Morpheus also tells Shakespeare that "I am Prince of stories, Will; but I have no story of my own. Nor shall I ever." Again, he is wrong. Besides the obvious fact that he already is in a story, addressing the eavesdropping readers, Morpheus appears in the dreams of other characters during *The Wake* (1997), the volume collecting the Sandman stories set primarily after his death. In escaping his isolation, he has entered the realm of fiction and/or dreams himself.

and reflecting on his parting comment—"I never fell. I don't care what they say. I'm still doing my job, as I see it"—readers of "Murder Mysteries" are led to what Joe Sanders has called "an awareness of the unsolvable Mysteries of love and forgiveness." The story was adapted and published in 2001 as a play for voices.

Signal to Noise (serialized in *The Face,* a style and fashion magazine and then published as a graphic novel in 1992) echoes some of the themes of *The Sandman.* This collaboration with McKean deals with a fatally ill director who persists in finishing the script of a picture he knows he will not live long enough to actually get on film. After his death, as a friend reads the opening scene that shows credulous villagers panicking at the end of 999 A.D. because they think their world is about to come to an end, she sees the director in the crowd.

Miracleman is an unfinished project of interest. When Alan Moore handed the comic over to Gaiman (who worked on it from 1990 to 1993), he already had taken the superhero plot to its logical extreme—genuinely superhuman characters who see what a mess ordinary humans make of their lives would naturally choose to rule the world for what they consider humans' own good. Taking over at that point, in a series of slowly germinating scripts, Gaiman explored what that "utopia" would be like; it is one thing to identify vicariously with a superhuman being, but it is different to live with one.

The Tragical Comedy or Comical Tragedy of Mr. Punch (1994) is perhaps Gaiman and McKean's most impressive collaboration, a further exploration of the themes of *Violent Cases.* Although the narrator does not announce his concern with "true facts," that is precisely what he is looking for as he sorts through his memories of being a boy who is trying to figure out how to relate to other people. Should he pattern his behavior on that of the grownups around him? Or should he be trying to figure out how successful their relationships are—or whether they even want genuine relationships at all? In *The Tragical Comedy or Comical Tragedy of Mr. Punch* Gaiman explores more thoroughly how dreams work through deliberate invention to produce art; looking at the costume head of a badger after a performance of *Toad of Toad Hall* (1929), for example, the boy imagines himself putting it on so that he could "become the badger, a tiny stumbling thing with a huge head, uttering vast truths I dared not think as a child." This process of giving dreams a shape can be dangerous, for it has produced the selfish, vicious puppet Mr. Punch, thrust on generations of children by adults who want to excuse their own actions by saying that even children love violence. But though art can confuse its audience, Gaiman suggests, awareness of what it is and what it is doing gives people the only way to confront the struggling

forces within their natures. And so the adult narrator eventually turns away from Mr. Punch's jubilant promise that "everybody is free to do whatever they wish!": he says, "I left the churchyard then, shivering in spite of the May sunshine, and went about my life."

Besides acquiring considerable skill in comics scripting, Gaiman has done several works in more conventional prose. He has continued to explore the nature of dreams and art and how these can imprison or liberate a dreamer. In stories such as "Troll Bridge" (1993, collected in *Angels and Visitations*) and "Snow, Glass, Apples" (1994) and the poem "The White Road" (1995, both collected in *Smoke and Mirrors: Short Fictions and Illusions* [1998]), Gaiman reexamines traditional fairy-tale images and plots. What he discovers is that the labels of "victim" and "violator" depend on bystanders' perceptions, so the roles can be easily exchanged.

Among the works in which Gaiman turns his attention to more-modern tales, "One Life Furnished in Early Moorcock" (1994, collected in *Smoke and Mirrors*) pays tribute to another contemporary writer by showing a British schoolboy identifying passionately with Michael Moorcock's glamorous, doomed hero Elric. This tale shows how immature the boy's reworking of the stories is, but it also shows how those fantasies offer him escape from his powerlessness, while the people around him are spinning more selfish and less entertaining fantasies that they inflict on him. Exotic dreams help young Richard survive without hurting anyone else or being hurt too badly himself, until finally he has escaped this particular set of threats and can relax with a friend: "the two children sat alone in the gray twilight . . . and waited for the future to start." Finally, "The Goldfish Pool and Other Stories" (1996, collected in *Smoke and Mirrors*) is an allusive, illusive examination of commercial mythmaking. What seems to begin as a horror story about the superhuman glamor that Charles Manson briefly possessed actually becomes a meditation on human yearnings for magic to transform the mundane. Since the story is set in Hollywood, it largely shows how timid people may crave liberation through dreams but wind up rejecting it.

Gaiman turned to longer fiction in 1996 with his first novel, *Neverwhere,* written in conjunction with a BBC miniseries he scripted. Many of the characters and situations had been simmering in Gaiman's imagination for years, but the story turned out to be a much lighter piece than he intended. A glorious tale of wonderment and menace, it may best be compared to Robert Louis Stevenson's *Treasure Island* (1883) in its extravagant villainy and mega-heroic challenges. Readers have little doubt that stodgy young businessman Richard Mayhew will become a hero in the magical realm of London

Dust jacket for the U.S. edition of Gaiman's first novel, set in the shadowy world of "London Below" (Richland County Public Library)

Below. The fun is watching funny or frightening events jar him out of his comfortable rut. Even in this entertainment for a mass audience, Gaiman emphasizes that the villains are those who refuse to change, who insist on their own selfish, isolated fantasies. The novel surprised critics who had assumed Gaiman was just a comics writer.

His next long fiction was *Stardust: Being a Romance Within the Realms of Faerie* (1998), a tale that was intended to look like an illustrated Victorian children's book while appealing to a contemporary, adult sensibility. A young man escapes his mundane upbringing, though he does not find quite what he—or readers— expect in the world of magic. The book reworks the conventions of literary fantasy in order to remind readers that fulfilling one's expectations for love and/or revenge may be less satisfying than opening oneself to fresh experience. Charles Vess's illustrations complement Gaiman's text well, and the text-only version (done at the request of his prose-fiction publisher) gives

readers a much diminished experience. The novel received a Mythopoeic Award in 1999 for Best Novel for Adults.

American Gods (2001) is a much more substantial work, in physical bulk and emotional weight. The main plot thread shows a young drifter's growing involvement in what seems to be an impending magical war. On one side are the old gods, mostly immigrants to the new continent. On the other side are more contemporary objects of worship, mostly artifacts such as computers and television characters who have achieved an independent existence. Only one kind of supernatural power can survive, readers are told. But Gaiman intersperses the intrigue and violence with quiet, poignant scenes that show people interacting with the gods they have made or discovered; the novel is not simply about sweeping action but about what human beings truly need versus what they imagine they need— and how they sometimes can learn the difference. *American Gods* required Gaiman to develop the range of his prose considerably, and the quiet scenes of small-town life do not serve as mere intermissions in the action but are glimpses of everyday life that are vivid and sharply observed. The critical reception of the novel was overwhelmingly positive, and it was a national best-seller. Gaiman founded a website, <http://www.neilgaiman.com/>, to promote *American Gods* and frequently uses it to share his experiences and opinions.

Gaiman has also completed a short novel titled *Coraline* (2002), describing a girl who is dissatisfied with her parents until she meets the beings who are eager to replace them. According to Gaiman, adults who have read the manuscript think it is a horror story, much too disturbing to show children; children, on the other hand, find it a rousing adventure. His first book for younger readers, *The Day I Swapped My Father for 2 Goldfish* (1997), was listed by *Newsweek* as one of the best children's books of 1997.

At this point in his career no one can be sure what Neil Gaiman will do next. There are new stories to be told, as comic scripts, screenplays, or prose fiction, for readers willing to enlarge their attention to take in experiments in a wide range of media. As Gaiman said in a BBC interview following the broadcast of *Neverwhere:*

> When I was small, people would always tell me not to make things up. And they'd say "You're making that up!" and they'd say "You know what happens if you make things up!" And I never did. Gradually, as I've got older, I've found out what happens when you make things up—which is you have an awful lot of fun and you get to make television and books and comics, and people read them and enjoy them, and it gives you a tremendous amount of freedom of motion and just freedom to do things.

He concluded, in a slightly more serious tone, "What keeps me going is the fact that there are all these stories that nobody's ever heard before. And I know them, and I feel like it's my job to tell them to people."

Interviews:

Brian Hibbs, "Gaiman Interview with Brian Hibbs," 26 October 1989 <http://www.holycow.com/dreaming/lore/interview1.html>;

"Pratchett and Gaiman: The Double Act," *Locus,* no. 362 (March 1991): 4, 72–73;

Stanley Wiater and Stephen R. Bissette, "Neil Gaiman: A Man for All Seasons," in *Comic Book Rebels: Conversations with the Creators of the New Comics,* edited by Wiater and Bissette (New York: Donald I. Fine, 1993), pp. 186–198;

Gary Groth, "Neil Gaiman Interview," *Comics Journal,* no. 169 (July 1994): 54–108;

Dust jacket for Gaiman's 1999 novel, a reworking of the fairy-story genre as fiction for adults (Richland County Public Library)

Jim Fleming, "Radio Interview with Neil Gaiman," 31 May 1995 <http://www.holycow.com/dreaming/lore/interview3.html>;

Roger A. Ash, "A Talk with Neil Gaiman," *Worlds of Westfield–Interview,* 10 October 1995 <http://www.westfieldcompany.com/wow/int_002.html>;

Ash, "More Talk with Neil Gaiman," *Worlds of Westfield–Interview,* 10 October 1995 <http://westfield company.com/wow/int_004.html>;

Aaron Vanek, "Seasons in Hell," *Comics Scene,* no. 53 (November 1995): 54–58;

"Neil on AOL," 24 February 1996 <http://www.holycow.com/dreaming/lore/interview4.html>;

Jessie Horsting, "Neil Gaiman: So Long, Sandman," *Midnight Graffiti,* no. 8 (Winter/Spring 1997): 16–31;

James Lovegrove, "No More Worlds to Conquer," *Interzone,* no. 116 (February 1997): 17–20;

Neil Gaiman: Notes from the Underground, videotape, Seattle, Wash.: KCTS-TV, 1998;

"Neil Gaiman: Of Monsters and Miracles," *Locus,* no. 459 (April 1999): 4, 66–68;

Lyda Morehouse, "Neil Gaiman," *Science Fiction Chronicle,* 20 (May 1999): 7, 42;

George Khoury, "Gaijin Mononoke: An Interview with Neil Gaiman," *Creative Screenwriting,* 6 (November–December 1999): 63–65.

Bibliographies:

NGVB: Neil Gaiman Visual Bibliography <http://home town.aol.com/grandmoffzoe/neil/front.html>;

Lance Smith, "Neil Gaiman Bibliography," August 1996 <http://home.bip.net/rivieran/magian/bibliography/html>.

References:

Hy Bender, *The Sandman Companion* (New York: Vertigo/DC Comics, 1999);

Samuel R. Delany, "Neil Gaiman, I, II, and III," in *Shorter Views: Queer Thoughts and the Politics of the Paraliterary* (Hanover, N.H.: Wesleyan University Press, 1999), pp. 359–372;

Leonardo L. Flores, "Neil Gaiman and Comic Books: Collaborative Approaches to a Collaborative Form," M.A. thesis, Bowling Green State University, 1994;

David E. Goldweber, "The Function of Dreams and Stories in *The Sandman,*" *International Journal of Cartoon Art,* 3 (Spring 2001): 77–85;

A. David Lewis, "A New Frame for Comic Books: The Genuine Literary Value of the Comic Book Medium," <http://home.bip.net/rivieran/literature/essay1.html>;

Everitt Long, "Reading, Writing and Rendering in the World of Neil Gaiman's *The Sandman,*" M.A. thesis, University of Western Ontario, 1997;

Michael Niederhausen, "Signifying in Comic Books: Neil Gaiman's *The Sandman,*" M.A. thesis, Xavier University, 1999;

Joe Sanders, "Of Parents and Children and Dreams in Neil Gaiman's *Mr. Punch* and *The Sandman,*" *Foundation,* no. 71 (Autumn 1997): 18–32;

Richard Tuinstra, "The Life and Death of Wanda" <http://home.bip.net/rivieran/literature/wanda.html>.

Alan Garner

(17 October 1934 –)

Amelia A. Rutledge
George Mason University

See also the Garner entry in *DLB 161: British Children's Writers Since 1960, First Series.*

BOOKS: *The Weirdstone of Brisingamen: A Tale of Alderley* (London: Collins, 1960); revised as *The Weirdstone: A Tale of Alderley* (New York: Watts, 1961);

The Moon of Gomrath (London: Collins, 1963; New York: Walck, 1967);

Elidor (London: Collins, 1965; revised edition, New York: Walck, 1967);

Holly from the Bongs: A Nativity Play, text by Garner, photographs by Roger Hill, and music by William Mayne (London: Collins, 1966);

The Old Man of Mow, text by Garner and photographs by Hill (London: Collins, 1967; Garden City, N.Y.: Doubleday, 1970);

The Owl Service (London: Collins, 1967; New York: Walck, 1968);

Red Shift (London: Collins, 1973; revised edition, New York: Macmillan, 1973; revised again, London: Lions, 1975; revised again, London: Lions, 1977);

The Breadhorse (London: Collins, 1975);

The Stone Book (London: Collins, 1976; revised edition, New York: Collins World, 1978);

Granny Reardun (London: Collins, 1977; revised edition, New York: Collins World, 1978);

Tom Fobble's Day (London: Collins, 1977; revised edition, New York: Collins, 1979);

The Aimer Gate (London: Collins, 1978; revised edition, New York: Collins World, 1979);

Fairy Tales of Gold, 4 volumes (London: Collins, 1979); republished as *Alan Garner's Fairy Tales of Gold,* 1 volume (London: Collins, 1980; New York: Philomel, 1980)—comprises *The Girl of the Golden Gate, The Golden Brothers, The Princess and the Golden Mane,* and *The Three Golden Heads of the Well;*

The Lad of the Gad (London: Collins, 1980; New York: Philomel, 1981);

The Stone Book Quartet (London: Collins, 1983)—comprises *The Stone Book, Granny Reardun, Tom Fobble's Day,* and *The Aimer Gate;*

Alan Garner

Alan Garner's Book of British Fairy Tales (London: Collins, 1984; New York: Delacorte, 1984);

Potter Thompson, libretto by Garner, music by Gordon Crosse (London: Oxford University Press, 1985);

A Bag of Moonshine (London: Collins, 1986; New York: Delacorte, 1986);

Jack and the Beanstalk (London: HarperCollins, 1992; Garden City, N.Y.: Doubleday, 1992);

Once Upon a Time, Though It Wasn't in Your Time, and It Wasn't in My Time, and It Wasn't in Anybody Else's Time . . . (Vancouver: Raincoast, 1993; London & New York: Dorling Kindersley, 1993);

Strandloper (London: Harvill, 1996);

The Little Red Hen (New York: Dorling Kindersley, 1997);

205

The Voice That Thunders: Essays and Lectures (London: Harvill, 1997);

The Well of the Wind (New York: Dorling Kindersley, 1998);

Grey Wolf, Prince Jack and the Firebird (London: Scholastic, 1998).

PLAY PRODUCTION: *Holly from the Bongs,* Goostrey, U.K., Crown Inn Stable, 1966; revised version, Manchester Grammar School, 18 August 1999.

PRODUCED SCRIPTS: "Have You Met Our Tame Author?" radio, BBC, 1962;

"Elidor," radio, BBC, 1962;

"Four Hairy Herrings: A Short Survey of Nonsense," radio, BBC, 1962;

"Merlin's Isle," radio, BBC, 1963;

"In Case of Emergency," BBC, radio, 1964;

"Thor and the Giants," radio, BBC, 1965; revised, BBC, 1979;

"Loki and the Storm Giant," radio, BBC, 1965; revised as "Idun and the Apples of Life," BBC, 1979;

"Baldur the Bright," radio, BBC, 1965; revised, BBC, 1979;

The Owl Service, Granada Television, 21 December 1969 – 8 February 1970;

"One Pair of Eyes: . . . *All Systems Go* . . . ," television, BBC, 1972;

"Feel Free," television, 1974;

"My Delight," radio, BBC, 1978;

"Red Shift," television, BBC, 1978;

"Writer's Workshop: Places and Things," Thames Television, 1978;

"Lamaload," television, BBC, 1979;

"To Kill a King," television, BBC, 1980;

"Lurga Lom," television, BBC, 1980;

"Writer's Workshop: Images," Thames Television, 1980;

"The Edge of the Ceiling," Granada Television, 1980;

"The Stone Book," "Granny Reardun," "The Aimer Gate," and "Tom Fobble's Day," radio, BBC, 1980;

"Strandloper," television, BBC, 1981;

"Images," television, BBC, 1981;

The Echoing Waters, radio, BBC Radio 4, 25 December 2000.

OTHER: "Galgoid the Hewer," in *Winter's Tales for Children 2,* edited by C. Hillier (London: Macmillan, 1961);

"Feel Free," in *Miscellany 4,* edited by Edward Blishen (Oxford: Oxford University Press, 1967), pp. 1–9;

"How Finn Maccumhail Was in the House of the Rowan Tree Without Power to Stand or Leave to Sit Down," in *The Hamish Hamilton Book of Heroes,*

edited by William Mayne (London: Hamish Hamilton, 1967);

The Hamish Hamilton Book of Goblins, edited by Garner (London: Hamish Hamilton, 1969); republished as *A Cavalcade of Goblins* (New York: Walck, 1969);

"Introduction," in *Filming the Owl Service,* E., A., and K. Garner (London: Armada, 1970);

Untitled contribution, in John Rowe Townsend, *A Sense of Story: Essays on Contemporary Writers for Children* (London: Longman, 1971), pp. 117–119;

The Bellybag, libretto by Garner, music by Richard Morris, 1971;

The Guizer: A Book of Fools, edited by Garner (London: Hamish Hamilton, 1975; New York: Morrow, 1976); republished with revised introduction (London: Fontana Lions, 1980);

"Inner Time," in *Science Fiction at Large: A Collection of Essays, by Various Hands, About the Interface Between Science Fiction and Reality,* edited by Peter Nicholls (New York & London: Harper & Row, 1976), pp. 119–138;

"Rascally Tag," in *Jubilee Jackanory* (London: BBC, 1977);

"The Fine Anger," in *Responses to Children's Literature: Proceedings of the Fourth Symposium of the International Research Society for Children's Literature, 1978,* edited by Geoff Fox and Graham Hammond (New York: K. G. Saur, 1980), pp. 1–12.

SELECTED PERIODICAL PUBLICATIONS–UNCOLLECTED:

POETRY

"The Island of the Strong Door," *Aperture,* no. 82 (1979): 16–23.

FICTION

"In Case of Emergency," *Yorkshire Life,* Christmas Review (1967).

NONFICTION

"A Bit More Practice," *Times Literary Supplement,* 6 June 1968; republished in *The Cool Web: The Pattern of Children's Reading,* edited by M. Meek and others (London: Bodley Head, 1977), pp. 196–200;

"Real Mandrakes in Real Gardens," *New Statesman,* 1 November 1968, pp. 591–592;

"The Death of Myth," *New Statesman,* 6 November 1970, p. 606;

"A Librettist Speaks," *Music and Musicians,* 23 (January 1975): 20–21;

"Achilles in Altjira," *Children's Literature Association Quarterly,* 8 (Winter 1983): 5–10;

"Once Upon a Time," *Bulletin of the Centre for Children's Books,* 47 (1 January 1994): 153;

"Beyond the Tenth Kingdom," *School Librarian,* 42 (1 February 1994): 4.

In 1968 Alan Garner, defending his focus on the adolescent audience, asserted in "A Bit More Practice" that "This group of people is the most important of all, and selfishly, it makes the best audience. Few adults read with a comparable involvement." Yet, Aidan Chambers, a sympathetic reviewer, responded to Garner's most complexly structured novel, *Red Shift* (1973), by asserting in a 1973 *Horn Book* review that "Garner has given up any pretense of writing for children and is now writing entirely to please himself and those mature, sophisticated, literate readers who care to study his works." This disparity of perceptions seems to be inherent in Garner's career. He has progressed from an author of conventional fantasy in his first two works, *The Weirdstone of Brisingamen* (1960) and *The Moon of Gomrath* (1963), to become a writer whose work is engaging, powerful, and uncompromising in its artistry.

Alan Garner, son of Colin and Marjorie Garner, was born on 17 October 1934 in Congleton, Cheshire, England, into a family of laborers established there for generations. After several bouts with severe illnesses in early childhood, he attended Manchester Grammar School, probably the best secondary school in England, and then studied classics at Magdalen College, Oxford. He has described himself as the first educated member of his family and has throughout his career worked toward reintegrating the fragmentation resulting from an education that effectively cut him off from his background, linguistically and socially. He served in the British army, and in 1956 he married Ann Cook, with whom he has three children: Adam, Ellen, and Katharine. The marriage ended in divorce. In 1972 Garner married Griselda Greaves, with whom he has two children, Joseph and Elizabeth.

Garner turned away from a possible career as an athlete—transformed from a sickly child into a potential champion sprinter—and chose the isolated freedom of writing. His choice of audience was also conscious. In "A Bit More Practice" he said that "at the age of twenty-one, I could not imagine that I had anything worth saying to people twice my age," but once he realized that the traditional style and content appropriate for children's literature need not constrain him, he also did not deviate from that choice.

Garner's first novel, *The Weirdstone of Brisingamen*, has received little positive commentary from its author, and although some critics have spoken of its vigorous narration, even a brief synopsis demonstrates the awkwardness of the obviously derivative story. It is the tale of two children, Colin and Susan, living for a while in Garner's own Cheshire region, who discover that what seems merely to be a trinket is the charm that will enable the wizard Cadellin Silverbrow to awaken a group of sleeping knights destined to fight against a cos-

Dust jacket for the U.S. edition of Garner's 1967 novel, inspired in part by a story in the collection of Welsh folktales known as The Mabinogion *(Bruccoli Clark Layman Collection)*

mic foe. The title links the archaic definition of *weird* and the name Brisingamen, the necklace of the Norse goddess Freya. Garner admits that the characterization of the children was an experiment in aesthetic distancing that went wrong. He wanted the children to serve as minimally depicted focal characters for the action, but the result was excessively flat characterization. He claims that he was able to complete the sequel, *The Moon of Gomrath,* only after imagining a scene in which Colin would be strangled by one of the villains.

He was able to avoid this outcome in the finished work, and *The Moon of Gomrath* has hints of the powerful storyteller Garner has become. In this story, the children are again menaced by their former antagonists, and in one of their adventures, they awaken and are freed by nature-based magical forces, the Old Magic. The conclusion of the story is open-ended; the Old Magic cannot be confined. Garner did not continue the sequence, although it is possible to see reflections of the folk motif of the "sleeping hero," used in *The Moon of*

Gomrath, in the Sleeping Knight, the hero's goal in Garner's opera libretto *Potter Thompson* (1985).

Having gained some notice from the first two books, Garner began to earn additional income writing plays and program series for BBC radio. The need for accuracy and concise narrative had a salutary effect—he suggests in a 1970 interview, almost a too-restrictive one—on his prose. Henceforth, his dialogue and narrative took on a script-like clarity but also a compact elegance.

There is a temptation to see in Garner's first works the influence of J. R. R. Tolkien, but, as the critic Neil Philip points out, it is rather the case of the two authors using the same sources. Garner was trained as a philologist, as was Tolkien, but Garner read classics at Oxford, while Tolkien was a professor of Anglo-Saxon. Garner found that as a writer he was most strongly inspired by Celtic and Norse myth and legend; Tolkien admitted that Finnish and Old English were stronger influences on his work than the Celtic languages. In his first novels Garner's enthusiasm for the names from legend, particularly from the lists in "Kulhwch and Olwen" (circa 1100), one of the tales appended to the medieval Welsh *Mabinogion,* leads to awkward juxtapositions of Norse, Welsh, and even Pictish that become distracting oddities rather than the organic and functional languages Tolkien carefully developed.

Garner's third novel, *Elidor* (1965), is based on a story of the same name that he had used in a radio play in 1962. Four children are appointed to guard magical objects: a grail, a spear, a stone, and a sword that will restore the kingdom of Elidor from the Wasteland it has become. The children are co-opted by the ambiguous Malebron, the lame king of the land; only Roland, the youngest, succeeds in Malebron's ruthless testing of their resolve. The action of the story moves between the Alderley region and the working-class district and partially demolished slums of Manchester. The children defend the treasures with difficulty, and despite their efforts, their world is invaded by Malebron's enemies. They resist the invaders long enough for the final restorative act, the singing of a mortally wounded unicorn; the children return the treasures to a revitalized Elidor as the boundary between the realms is closed for the last time.

As in the earlier novels, the fantastic realm invades contemporary reality. For Garner, this grounding in the everyday is a sine qua non of responsible fantasy. As he said in 1970, "if you can make a unicorn believable in a back street of Manchester, along with the smell and touch of Manchester, then I think you are making people think about unicorns in a direct way and experiencing unicorns, not as pretty-pretty heraldic beasts, but as . . . terrifyingly potent sexual symbols."

Garner succeeds at his self-assigned task, but characterization is still a problem in *Elidor;* of the four children involved in the story, only Roland is fully realized. Garner has, however, integrated magic and "reality" more effectively than in the earlier works. The last line of the novel—"The children were alone with the broken windows of a slum"—has the finality of the end of a vision.

In the interval between the publication of *Elidor* and that of *The Owl Service* (1967), Garner continued his radio work with plays based on Norse mythology, but he also wrote a nativity play for the local school, *Holly from the Bongs* ("Bongs" is the name of a woodlot behind the Goostrey school), that was performed in 1965 and published in 1966; it later became the basis of an opera libretto. The play is a striking blend of medieval mystery play, especially *Secunda Pastorum* (The Second Shepherds' Play), amusingly figured in the shepherds' complaints with which *Holly from the Bongs* opens, and the traditional mummer's play, with which the destitute shepherds entertain the Christ Child (to Joseph's mild, although courteous, dismay). In 2000, Garner again revised the play, which was broadcast on BBC radio as *The Echoing Waters,* shifting the focus to Mary's distress at the persecution and death of her son. This version provides, as a dramatic climax, an antiphonal "Credo" in twelve languages that, in Garner's words, "froze the audience" in astonishment.

During this time Garner also wrote the text for *The Old Man of Mow* (1967), a photographic essay of two small boys' quest on the eponymous hill in Cheshire in search of the "Old Man." Their encounters are both mildly perilous (an irascible farmer's wife) and helpful (an old man who is not the Old Man of Mow), and the photographs, both color and black and white, form a quasi-cinematic sequence.

Although *The Owl Service,* Garner's best-known work to date, did not appear in print until 1967, its germ lay in an experience of 1961. A friend of Garner purchased a dinner service and noticed that the floral patterns, if manipulated properly, would represent owls. The flower/owl opposition suggested the story of Gwydion, Lleu Llaw Gyffes, Gronw, and Blodeuwedd from "Math, Son of Mathonwy," the "Fourth Branch" of the *Mabinogion.* In this story the young Lleu Llaw Gyfes, cursed never to wed a human woman, is given a wife made of flowers by his wizard uncles. The wife is later punished for taking a lover by being turned into an owl. "Flower-face" is one Welsh name for an owl; hence the owl-flower connection in Garner's story. Garner, after four years of thought and research, produced a tale in which the Celtic elements were not mere nomenclature but an inextricable thread of the tapestry. The narrative is one of adolescent psychological and sexual tensions, English/Welsh as well as class resentments, and ancient interfamilial feuds. The critical impact was both gratifying and dismaying. Predictably, there was dispute about its intended audience, but the book won both the Carnegie Medal and the Guardian Award; when it became required reading for school examinations, Garner was dismayed because of the chilling effects of compulsory reading and banal examination questions on young readers' enjoyment of his work.

The central characters are Alison and Roger, new step-siblings as a result of the remarriage of Roger's father to Alison's mother, a character who is present only as a manipulative force. The third character, Gwyn, is the son of the Welsh housekeeper, to whom he is held in thrall by the support she gives to the education that she hopes will elevate him above the working class. Gwyn's attraction to Alison is hopeless, but the true tension emerges with the discovery of a dinner service and Alison's obsession with tracing its floral pattern and forming paper owls. It slowly emerges that in each generation, a triangle of young people repeats the fateful story from the *Mabinogion*.

The resolution of the near-fatal conflict has been the source of much of the critical discussion of the novel. Garner's success lies in his avoiding banal reenactment, and his understated masterpiece is his Gwydion-figure: the laborer Huw, called Hannerhob (Halfbacon), whose fragmentary utterances, a blending of shrewdness and apparent imbecility, bind the legend with the mundane.

The Owl Service was filmed for television on location in Wales in 1969. The experience was unexpectedly traumatic for Garner, and he discussed it in an intense lecture, "Inner Time," that he gave in 1975 at the Institute for Contemporary Arts (ICA) in London. The focus of the lecture was intended to be science fiction and time, and Garner cast his address as a discussion of the psychological concept of the "engram," an encapsulated association, which, when repressed, can sometimes surface with explosive force. In a later lecture, "Fierce Fires and Shramming Cold," delivered in 1996 for World Mental Health Day, he spoke of his struggles with bipolar disorder. In both instances, his point has not been that his writing is confessional but that the pain that is sometimes a force behind creativity can pose serious risks and is a matter for treatment, not romanticizing.

In the intervals between novels, Garner has continued to edit story collections. *The Hamish Hamilton Book of Goblins* (1969) was the first in a continuing effort to preserve and re-present myth and legend to the contemporary audience. Many of the tales are English, but there are several Japanese and Native American legends; with these, Garner says, he feels an affinity that

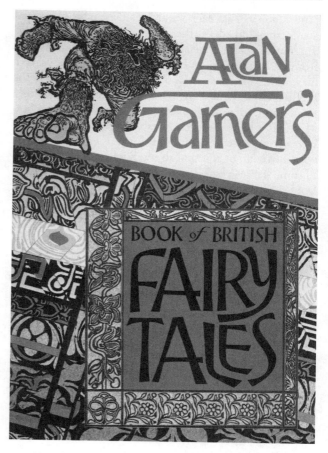

Dust jacket for the U.S. edition of Garner's 1984 retellings of classic children's stories (Richland County Public Library)

he does not for classical legends. Garner does not claim in any of his editions to be practicing systematic scholarship. Where older translations obscure the spirit of the text, he feels free to alter the translation; he describes his techniques as free adaptation or retelling and transposition, which is almost a re-creation of the story. He is meticulous, however, in providing notes that list his sources, including, in one instance, a notice issued in 1860 by the Japanese government, informing indigenous demons of the forthcoming visit of a government minister.

Despite its title, which inspired the invitation to speak at the ICA conference, *Red Shift* (1973) is not science fiction. Red shift, the spectrographic indication of the increasing speed of galaxies receding from one's vantage point, operates solely as a metaphor for the impossibility of fulfilling frustrated desires—time causes an exponential increase in the speed of loss.

Red Shift interlaces three narratives in segments ranging from nearly chapter length to the fragmentary speeches at the conclusion of the novel. Three young men, living in different centuries, possess briefly the same stone ax that each regards as talismanic. The men are further linked by their names: Macey (a regional diminutive of Thomas), a member of a renegade Roman military unit in England during the second century A.D.; Thomas, a Roundhead in the time of the English Civil War; and Tom, a contemporary youth. Each young man is characterized by mental instability: Macey is a berserker; Thomas is epileptic; and Tom is brilliant and neurotically sensitive. Each is involved with a woman of spiritual strength who encounters, and to some degree resists, male violence. In the two strands from the past there seems some hope of peace in a love relationship; this option is denied to the twentieth-century Tom.

The economical narrative is at the same time richly allusive; most obvious is Tom's self-conscious identification with mad Edgar of *King Lear* (1606); there are references as well to T. S. Eliot's *The Waste Land* (1922) and to the old Scottish ballad of Childe Roland and Burd Ellen. Garner deftly shades the transitions between each strand; the psychological bonds among the three young men are suggested by carefully crafted juxtapositions.

Macey's fits are exploited by his obsessed commander, who denies the demobilization of his regiment and continues the war against the Celts on his own. In a telling stroke, Garner lets his renegades speak the military slang of American GIs of the Vietnam era; their massacre of a village is a replay of My Lai and is also reflected in the historically recorded Royalist massacre of villagers in Bromely in 1643 that Thomas and Madge, his future wife, barely escape. The ravages of war are present in the contemporary narrative in the psychological savaging that Tom gives and receives in his home, as well as his increasingly violent demands on Jan, the young woman with whom he is able to experience love for the first time.

The personal bonds that permit some type of resolution of conflict wear thin through time—an additional connection to astronomical red shift. The first two couples survive military hostilities, but Tom's and Jan's lives are too fragmented to give them the resources to weather their difficulties. The bleakness of *Red Shift* is offset by the skill with which Garner creates aesthetic distance.

Critical response to the novel was intense and polarized. *Red Shift* displays the experimental techniques of the 1960s New Wave that affected the discourse of science fiction. Its complexity, especially the repeated use of untagged speech, was frequently cited as an obstacle to reader enjoyment, while other critics found in the novel the fiction of despair, unsuitable for adolescents. Garner continued to refine *Red Shift* after publication, and readers of critical discussions of the

novel need to be aware of the text to which the writer refers. Criticism based on the 1975 English edition mentions details not present in the earlier editions, including the 1973 American edition indicated by Neil Philip as Garner's preferred text.

Garner, in "Inner Time," mentions the flurry of creative activity that followed the publication of *Red Shift*. He composed a narrative poem, *The Breadhorse* (1975), based in part on Romany legend, and edited *The Guizer: A Book of Fools* (1975), his most wide-ranging collection of tales. *The Breadhorse* is the story of a boy who is always "it" in the children's game of "breadhorse," in which he must carry the others on his back. His release comes in a dream of a fabulous horse, and his ability to share his dream frees him from perpetual bondage to his role in the game.

Also in 1975 Garner converted *Holly from the Bongs* into an opera libretto and produced the libretto to the opera *Potter Thompson;* music for both operas was composed by Gordon Crosse. *Potter Thompson* is a story of reconciliation to ancient loss. The title character, the only adult role, is a potter alienated from his neighbors since he was jilted in his youth. On the night of the harvest festival of which he was once "harvest king" with his intended as his queen, he breaks down and undergoes a mythic underworld journey in which, after successive encounters with the four elements, his story is linked with a local legend of a sleeping king, who will be awakened by a hero. Potter Thompson realizes that the time to wake the destined hero is never now but in the future; he must be reconciled to the present. The text is fragmentary, but the musical interweaving of separate lines creates artistic coherence.

With the publication in the late 1970s of the four books that make up the Stone Book Quartet—a fictional family history that spans the time from the late nineteenth century to World War II—Garner completed a stage in his artistic development. He referred to these brief autobiographical stories as "the major work," since they imaginatively reconcile old tensions. The characters represent four generations of Garners and their trades, and each story focuses on an epiphany experienced by a child in his (or, in one case, her) relationship with the older generation.

In *The Stone Book* (1976), Mary, whose father builds churches, dreams above all of becoming literate. Her father, knowing that education will limit her chances of local employment, attempts to dissuade her. After testing her bravery, he sends her on a quest traditionally reserved for the eldest son in the family. In a neolithic cave beneath the hills, her moment of insight comes to her, and as a token her father gives her a split stone, enclosing a fossil and shaped into a "book." Her story is followed by the simpler one of her son, Joseph;

*Dust jacket for the 1998 book in which Garner depicts a young girl's efforts to undo a witch's spell
(Richland County Public Library)*

in *Granny Reardun* (1977) Joseph, who is illegitimate, is brought up by his grandmother, hence the title of the book. His dilemma is whether to follow in his stonemason grandfather's steps, and his epiphany shows the way to his own future.

Garner considers the next book he wrote, *Tom Fobble's Day* (1977), to be the masterpiece of the series. Chronologically, it concludes the sequence, focusing on Joseph's grandson, William, who loses his sled to a bully in a boys' game of forfeits. Joseph, on the last day of his life, builds William a new sled from parts of the forge and from his own great-uncle's demolished loom. William returns from his first ride in time to greet his dying grandfather with news of the perfection of the sled and to claim as his birthright his grandparents' wedding horseshoes, a "Tom Fobble's" forfeit that is also a sign of his accepting his place in the family's traditions.

The sequence is rounded out by *The Aimer Gate* (1978), which is the story of Robert, William's father. The story differs from the rest in that Robert makes no decision about himself, but he learns grim truths about the soldier's trade from the story of his soldier uncle's career. There is no mention of Robert in *Tom Fobble's Day,* so he remains the most shadowy of the characters.

In 1978 Garner gave a speech titled "The Fine Anger" that is a summation of his thoughts on the

recovery of the deracinated regional dialects of England. The Stone Book Quartet reclaims the West Mercian dialect from which he was severed by his education. Fully integrated into the tales, the dialect requires no glosses.

Since the Stone Book sequence, Garner has continued to preserve traditional stories by producing several collections of folk and fairy tales. *The Lad of the Gad* (1980) collects a series of tales of the "male Cinderella" type. A similar volume is *A Bag of Moonshine* (1986), which includes several "Dümmling" stories. (A Dümmling is an awkward or apparently foolish boy who ultimately triumphs over stronger or more-talented rivals.) *Alan Garner's Book of British Fairy Tales* (1984) not only collects classic tales such as "Mally Whuppy" but also includes one haunting tale, "The Green Mist," that Garner has reworked as a "dance-drama." The heroine, stricken with a wasting illness, wishes to live only so long as one of the first cowslips of spring; holding an early blossom plucked by a youth who loves her, she fades and dies. *Jack and the Beanstalk* (1992) and *Once Upon a Time, Though It Wasn't in Your Time, and It Wasn't in My Time, and It Wasn't in Anybody Else's Time . . .* (1993), a short assortment of tales, also consist of retellings.

Garner's next novel, *Strandloper* (1996), is based on the historical nineteenth-century Englishman William Buckley, who was transported to Australia on a charge of sedition and escaped captivity to be adopted by a native tribe, whose shaman he became. After living with his tribe for thirty-four years, he averted a massacre of English colonists, was granted a reprieve, and returned to his Cheshire village. Garner writes about his research in the 1996 essay "The Voice That Thunders" (collected in *The Voice That Thunders: Essays and Lectures,* 1997), but the most striking achievement of the novel rests in the cross-cultural imaginative sympathies conveyed in the language of vision. This complex novel moves from village church rituals grounded in ancient fertility myths, through the brutality of the sea passage and Buckley's near death, to Buckley's transformation and his final return to England. Readers familiar with *Red Shift* will see Buckley as similar in sensibility to the three Thomases of the earlier novel. The intense physical and emotional content of the novel is conveyed in the terse, concentrated prose that is Garner's hallmark; but some passages, such as the horrific shipboard narrative, are symphonic in complexity.

In *The Well of the Wind* (1998) Garner freely adapts traditional motifs in a tale of a young girl's persistence in defeating a witch and reuniting her long-separated family. Garner continues to evoke regional lore, since one of the phrases used in a country ritual in *Strandloper* is in this work both the witch's spell and its undoing.

Alan Garner continues to work on new projects. He provides no details, but *Strandloper* and *The Echoing Waters* promise future work of intensity and depth. He stands at the forefront of those contemporary writers who have mediated, in their creative work, the traditional folklore of England and Wales. In 2001 he was awarded an OBE (Officer of the Order of the British Empire) "for services to children's literature."

Interviews:

"Coming to Terms," *Children's Literature in Education,* 2 (March 1970): 15–29;

Aidan Chambers, "An Interview with Alan Garner," in *The Signal Approach to Children's Books,* edited by Nancy Chambers (Metuchen, N.J.: Scarecrow Press, 1981), pp. 276–328;

Raymond H. Thompson, "Interview with Alan Garner," in his *Taliesin's Successors: Interviews with Authors of Modern Arthurian Literature,* The Camelot Project at the University of Rochester, 12 April 1989 <http://www.lib.rochester.edu/camelot/intrvws/garner.htm>.

References:

Brian Attebery, "Myth and History: Molly Gloss's *Wild Life* and Alan Garner's *Strandloper,*" *New York Review of Science Fiction,* 13 (June 2001): 1, 4–6;

Grahaeme Barrasford-Young and John Matthews, eds., *Labrys Seven: Alan Garner Symposium* (London: Brans Head Books, 1981);

Eleanor Cameron, "*The Owl Service:* A Study," *Wilson Library Bulletin,* 44 (December 1969): 425–433;

Emrys Evans, "Children's Novels and Welsh Mythology: Multiple Voices in Susan Cooper and Alan Garner," in *The Voice of the Narrator in Children's Literature: Insights from Writers and Critics,* edited by Charlotte F. Otten and G. Schmidt (New York: Greenwood Press, 1989), pp. 92–100;

Iain Finlayson, "Myths and Passages," *Books and Bookmen,* 22 (November 1977): 74–79;

Peter J. Foss, "The Undefined Boundary: Converging Worlds in the Early Novels of Alan Garner," *The New Welsh Review,* 2 (Spring 1990): 30–35;

Labrys, special Garner issue, 7 (1981);

Ursula K. Le Guin, "No, Virginia, There Is Not a Santa Claus," *Foundation,* 6 (May 1974): 109–112;

Michael Lockwood, "'A Sense of the Spoken': Language in *The Owl Service,*" *Children's Literature in Education,* 23 (June 1992): 83–92;

Maria Nikolajeva, "The Insignificance of Time: *Red Shift,*" *Children's Literature Association Quarterly,* 14 (Fall 1989): 128–131;

Neil Philip, *A Fine Anger: A Critical Introduction to the Work of Alan Garner* (London: Collins, 1981; New York: Philomel Books, 1981);

Mavis Reimer, "The Family as Mythic Reservoir in Alan Garner's *Stone Book Quartet,*" *Children's Literature Association Quarterly,* 14 (Fall 1989): 132–135;

C. W. Sullivan III, "One More Time: The Conclusion of Alan Garner's *The Owl Service,*" *Journal of the Fantastic in the Arts,* 9, no. 1 (1998): 46–54;

Andrew Taylor, "Polishing Up the Pattern: The Ending of *The Owl Service,*" *Children's Literature in Education,* 23 (June 1992): 93–102;

Victor Watson, "In Defense of Jan: Love and Betrayal in *The Owl Service* and *Red Shift,*" *Signal: Approaches to Children's Books,* 41 (May 1983): 77–87.

Papers:

Brigham Young University in Provo, Utah, houses a collection of Alan Garner's manuscripts.

Jane Gaskell

(7 July 1941 –)

Elizabeth S. Davidson
University of South Carolina, Spartanburg

BOOKS: *Strange Evil* (London: Hutchinson, 1957; New York: Dutton, 1958);

King's Daughter (London: Hutchinson, 1958; New York: Pocket Books, 1979);

Attic Summer (London: Hodder & Stoughton, 1963; New York: Paperback Library, 1966);

The Serpent (London: Hodder & Stoughton, 1963; New York: Paperback Library, 1968); republished as two books, *The Serpent* (New York: St. Martin's Press, 1977) and *The Dragon* (New York: St. Martin's Press, 1977);

The Shiny Narrow Grin (London: Hodder & Stoughton, 1964);

The Fabulous Heroine (London: Hodder & Stoughton, 1965);

Atlan (London: Hodder & Stoughton, 1965; New York: Paperback Library, 1968);

All Neat in Black Stockings (London: Hodder & Stoughton, 1966);

The City (London: Hodder & Stoughton, 1966; New York: St. Martin's Press, 1966);

A Sweet, Sweet Summer (London: Hodder & Stoughton, 1969; New York: St. Martin's Press, 1972);

Summer Coming (London: Hodder & Stoughton, 1972);

Some Summer Lands (London: Hodder & Stoughton, 1977; New York: St. Martin's Press, 1979);

Sun Bubble: A Novel (London: Weidenfeld & Nicolson, 1990).

PRODUCED SCRIPT: *All Neat in Black Stockings,* by Gaskell and Hugh Whitemore, motion picture, Anglo-Amalgamated/Miron, 1969.

Tales of inhuman sentient creatures, distressed princesses, and mysterious lost lands, especially Atlantis, in the works of Jane Gaskell provide fare of interest to readers of both science fiction and fantasy. Nevertheless, except for such details as her version of ancient Atlantis having been separated from the Americas by science rather than magic, and the fact that her Earth has no moon because the former, prehistoric moon was pulled into the ocean a millennium or so before the events of the Atlantis tales, the science is of little more narrative use than as a perfunctory general setting. Gaskell herself prefers fantasy; in *Science Fiction and Fantasy Literature: A Checklist, 1700–1974* (1979) R. Reginald quotes Gaskell's comments about seeing science fiction as "a vehicle by so many pamphleteers whose interest is in lecturing us: telling us how we should achieve utopia, or how naughty we are to contaminate our earth." She adds that science fiction is "concerned with here and now while it's pretending to be concerned with space and time and miracle." Science fiction makes her feel "boxed-in"; fantasy, though perhaps less reassuring, "has more juice in it—more excess, more 'let's go. . . .' Fantasy is packed with nuance, flavour, weather, quest, far-off horizons. Fantasy revels in the setting-out on the journey." Although there have been negative or lukewarm comments about Gaskell's writing style, these are balanced by an emphasis on the richness of her imagination and the similarity of her style to that of writers of the picaresque novel, itself an episodic, loosely structured form of literature.

Gaskell was born Jane Gaskell Denvil on 7 July 1941, in Grange-over-Sands, Lancashire. Her parents, artist Andrew Gaskell Denvil and Edith Hackett Denvil, a teacher, educated their daughter at home. Walter E. Meyers, in his synopsis of Gaskell's Atlan series for *Survey of Modern Fantasy Literature* (1983), notes that she is also the "great-grandniece of the Victorian novelist Elizabeth Gaskell."

Gaskell's first novel, *Strange Evil,* was written when she was fourteen years old and published two years later, in 1957. It went mainly unnoticed, however, except for a couple of 1958 reviews, until 1979, when it was republished by Pocket Books, along with her other early novel, *King's Daughter* (1958), and her Atlan novels, including the last, *Some Summer Lands* (1977). Reviews in *Fantasiae* and *Isaac Asimov's Science Fiction Magazine* were brief but laudatory, not so much because of her age but in spite of it. *Strange Evil* is an adventure in a rather perilous unnamed fairyland in which the fairies are not some idealized creatures more beautiful than humans and somehow superior to them. They are instead rather mean-spirited, petty sex fiends—perhaps stereotypical of a fourteen-year-old's concept of sin. It is also dangerous to get to this parallel world: one does not fall into it by accident but somehow has to get to the top of Notre Dame and step off, seemingly into thin air. D. Keller notes in the July 1979 *Fantasiae* that this fairy-land is "vivid and concrete rather than mistily evocative and archetypal—it is palpably there, not dreamlike in the least. Furthermore, it is thoroughly thought through; social, economic and geographic consider-ations are all taken into account, nor is the supernatural and the mystic left out." Keller prefers *Strange Evil* to any of the books in Gaskell's Atlan series, objecting mostly to the "goshwow writing" that could have been improved by "a very thorough rewrite" because the "basis of the book is very much there."

Also completed and published in her teens is Gaskell's second fantasy, *King's Daughter,* which Baird Searles in *Isaac Asimov's Science Fiction Magazine* (Decem-ber 1979) saw as "something of a preliminary sketch for her great Atlan series." It is set in the same prehistoric time period as the series and is organized to emphasize the picaresque, episodic adventures of the runaway, beautiful Princess Bulinga, whose "biggest discovery is that there are no unalloyed heroes in the real world . . . no white knight types devoid of human greed or human fears."

Gaskell married truck driver Gerald Lynch on 10 May 1963. Two years later their daughter, Lucy Emma, was born; in 1968 the marriage ended in divorce. A former theater usherette in London, Gaskell worked during the 1960s as a novelist and as a feature writer for the *Daily Express* and the *Daily Mail,* London tabloid newspapers. Her journalism was published under the name Jane Gaskell Lynch.

When Gaskell's first Atlan novels were published during the 1960s, they appeared to be a trilogy: *The Ser-pent* (1963), *Atlan* (1965), and *The City* (1966). All later printings, however, have split *The Serpent* into two sepa-rate books, the first adventures keeping the original title and the remaining adventures retitled *The Dragon* (1977). Both refer to the mixed blood of Zerd, the fear-some Northern general, who is descended from a reptil-ian woman, and whose skin therefore is dark and is covered with soft, not at all disgusting scales. The mys-tique of Zerd's power and physique make him quite a sex object to many of the women in the series. In 1977 another novel, *Some Summer Lands,* was added to the Atlan tales. All of these novels are centered around a few main characters and are often overpopulated with many minor characters who are rarely if ever seen beyond one episode. They are set in a prehistoric era

somewhere between the time the first moon had fallen to Earth and the time its gravity captured the wander-ing orb that became the present moon—a time shared by dinosaurs, lizard men, ape men, and descendants of the gods, or at least people who believe they are so descended. Their location is identified by Gaskell in a foreword to *The Serpent* as the Americas and Atlan, an island cut off from those mainlands not only by water but also by some kind of mysterious vacuum barrier erected by the scientists of Atlan to protect them from just such problems as are about to occur in the series. The episodic organization takes the picaresque heroine, Cija (pronounced Key-a, according to Gaskell's fore-word), through adventures on foot, riding an ostrich-like bird, and by ship, often into some unpleas-ant situation that she manages to survive, sometimes in ways quite amusing to the reader if not to Cija. Gaskell's foreword is part of the fiction, creating a soon forgotten twentieth-century translator of Cija's diary. She maintains this pose throughout the first books but changes the point-of-view character in *Some Summer Lands* to Seka, the mute daughter of Cija and Zerd. The other main character is Smahil, the man to whom Cija is most strongly attracted sexually. Although he turns out to be her half brother, he fathers her eldest child, a mating that is acceptable to the mores of the people of Atlan (in that way similar to the royalty of ancient Egypt) but that is a cultural taboo to Cija, a forbidden union that she must continue to fight throughout all the novels once she has realized their blood bond.

In the fourth book, *The City,* Cija undergoes one more fertile mating, this one with Ung-g the ape man, and is pregnant as the novel ends. Although it requires some stretching of the imagination to see Cija, or any action-adventure hero, as a rounded character, Cija does show some change throughout these books, especially as she moves from naive adolescent virgin to victim of rape to mother. Also, though some reviewers have character-ized her as a heroine of sword and sorcery fiction, Cija seems inept with either a sword or a spell. These are not the means by which she survives—and Cija seems the quintessential survivor, escaping, though often damaged, the foul plans not only of enemies, including her father, but also the loving but manipulative plans of her friends, including her mother.

The premise for all of the novels is established in the first chapter of *The Serpent.* A somewhat inept, rebel-lious adolescent of seventeen, the goddess Cija is partic-ularly naive and self-centered. She has been raised in an isolated luxury, not only ignorant but actually lied to by her attendants and her mother about the true nature of the world. This pattern sounds similar to the fairy-tale motif of the princess in the tower who escapes her isolation to go far away with her true love. But the

Dust jacket for the U.S. edition of Gaskell's first novel, about a parallel world of mean-spirited faeries (Bruccoli Clark Layman Collection)

"wicked witch" who imprisons Cija is her mother, the Dictatress of their little kingdom, who is protecting her from two forces that would destroy her. One is her father, the supposedly celibate High Priest, who from her birth has tried to have this embarrassing evidence of his lack of celibacy destroyed. Like her father and like her half brother Smahil, another of the High Priest's indiscretions, Cija has extremely pale skin. The paleness of all three is noted at various times in the series. The second force that might destroy her is the force of public opinion about a prophecy made at her birth that through a marriage she will bring her people under foreign rule, a prophecy made by Ooldra, who, the reader later learns, has motives to make such a prophecy and to wish any heir to the Dictatress harm. Ooldra also turns out to be the mother of Smahil, who was raised by a foster family. Though protective custody is necessary for Cija's survival up to age seventeen, one of the lies she has been raised on makes her an unlikely candidate for the role her mother assigns her as a condition of her release. Although she has been brought up to believe that men are extinct (a belief that made her think Zerd, when she first saw him, was a

serving woman of her mother), Cija is ordered to go along with Zerd's army as a hostage, to seduce him into marrying her, and to kill him when they are alone on their wedding night. It does not seem to occur to the Dictatress, in her plots for the safety of her throne, that a Cija who has never even had any friends, female or male, should have any problems at all with such an assignment, that Ooldra should wish her daughter any harm that might lead her to prevent rather than prepare Cija's escape, or that Zerd, who already has not only a high-born Northern wife but also a beautiful mistress, might have all the female company he can deal with and still have time for an army.

The motif of the journey begins in the second chapter of *The Serpent* and continues to some extent throughout the rest of the books. It is a useful device for bringing Cija knowledge of the world (and various perils) that she could never have achieved in the isolation of her tower. Early in this journey she learns that Zerd is the strange "serving woman" whom she had seen from the window of her tower and with whom she had then conversed in a manner reminiscent of the scene between the aging Caesar and young Cleopatra in

Dust jacket for the 1977 U.S. edition of the first in the series of tales Gaskell set in the Americas and the mythical island of Atlan before the extinction of the dinosaurs (Bruccoli Clark Layman Collection)

George Bernard Shaw's *Caesar and Cleopatra* (1901). Zerd had been amused enough to demand her as one of the hostages, but that amusement seems to be the only emotion he has about her in the early parts of the journey. Most of the time she cannot even find him to try her untrained seductive techniques on him. Much of the time, also, she is forced into the company of several other young hostages from her country, who do not become her friends. The girls, in fact, become her rivals, one for Zerd and one for Smahil, who is one of the two male hostages. Cija is sexually attracted by Smahil and remains so throughout the novels; but even before she discovers he is her half brother, she prefers not to lose her independence to him and not to let him get in the way of her mission. Although Zerd marries her later in Atlan, the attraction to and repulsion from these two male characters continues to be a point of conflict for Cija.

In *The City,* Zerd is never present but still in Atlan, though expected to be coming soon to the city. Smahil and his other bed partners are in the city, however, and

manage to protect Cija from the High Priest out of motives of love and jealousy. Cija escapes the unholy love of the attractive Smahil because his jealous mistress brings Cija's mother and her troops to rescue Cija from her father rather than leaving that final rescue to Smahil. Cija seems more interested in her children than in the men who father them. Though the children's presence is not really necessary to most of her adventures, she cares for their well-being, especially that of the mute daughter, Seka. Though Cija is glad enough to see Zerd or Smahil at a moment when she needs one or the other of them to come to her rescue, afterward their demands on her, sexual or otherwise, often make the price of the rescue too high.

Searles commented in his review that the Atlan series might well be viewed as "the *underside* of heroic fantasy . . . while the heroes and generals are off battling armies and slaying dragons, the women, children, and poor folk are being raped and pillaged by those armies and eaten by those dragons." Cija's happiest moments are in the company of the common folk, but she can never remain with them long and can never be secure because of Zerd and Smahil.

Between the Atlan books, Gaskell wrote novels in other genres. Her attention turned to the psychologically crippled or deviant denizens of the London of the late 1960s. Unlike the greater staying power of her Atlan fantasies, however, the relevance of her realistic psychosocial black comedies is a phenomenon limited to the time of their production and probably apparent only to a cultural historian of the 1960s.

The Shiny Narrow Grin (1964) might be considered fantasy because it does include one (and possibly a second) vampire. The word "vampire" is never mentioned until the final chapter, but "the boy" does appear only at night, reacts in violently startled fear to the word "God" even used blasphemously, becomes nauseous on eating eggs seasoned with garlic, and never stays around to see the dawn. He may be no more than a figment of protagonist Terry's imagination, summoned to help her cope with having no one on whom she can truly depend. An adolescent who in her real world seeks meaningful relationships in sexual promiscuity, Terry may have created this vampire fantasy as a more hopeful alternative relationship. Her father, her mother, her mother's "fiancé," her schoolteacher, her steady boyfriend, and even her seemingly virginal roommate all disappoint her by their own promiscuity. By the last chapter Terry's roommate is pregnant by Terry's father. Therefore she is fascinated by "the boy," who does not smoke, drink, or do drugs, who has told her his real name is Terence, and who tells her, "I cannot destroy you without your permission." His final dematerialization is more like that of the Cheshire cat from the bewildered Alice of Lewis Carroll's *Alice's Adventures in Wonderland* (1865) than the flying away of a vampire in bat form: "The last she [Terry] saw of him was the eyes, the narrow shiny grin." Unlike Alice, Terry is not dreaming her horrors. Readers are left with no resolution to Terry's dilemma, to be lost in the sexually predatory world of father and human boyfriend or to seek escape from that reality with a vampire of her own imagination.

During the eleven-year gap between parts 4 and 5 of the Atlan series, Gaskell wrote a fantasy novel that reviewers compare to Anthony Burgess's *A Clockwork Orange* (1962) in its savagery. Its title, *A Sweet, Sweet Summer* (1969), in light of the blood and violence, is ironic: there is little that is sweet about it. England has been taken over by aliens, and there is no safety there any more. Frijja and her cousin Rat cope as best they can in this once-familiar world turned strange and threatening. The novel received a Somerset Maugham Award.

Sun Bubble (1990), though also labeled a fantasy, seems even less fantastic than *The Shiny Narrow Grin*, even considering that one of the most hopelessly over-sentimentalized wishes in daily life is that the love of a woman can redeem and win for her the handsome but ruined man she desires. Julia, the forty-something protagonist, a newswoman and a mother, is caught up in just such a situation, wishing on a pillowcase bearing the image of Cinderella's fairy godmother. The pillow-case is a gift from Cosima, the only friend whom she tells about her infatuation with Joey, an attractive but heroin-trapped alcoholic. Cosima terms the early, happy stages of a romance the "sun bubble." Julia is fascinated with the words: "A Sun Bubble. . . . As though one had been taken off for a while in a space craft. Except that it didn't feel like that. A bubble was finite. Julia wasn't in a capsule. She was in a slipstream of some kind perhaps. She felt as if she were being magnetized." Julia does begin an affair with Joey. Then her adolescent, pink-haired daughter gives away the pillow-case, and the magic vanishes from Julia's new relationship. Joey becomes physically abusive, even knocking out some of her teeth; nevertheless, when he dies, Julia looks for a spiritualist to reestablish her contact with him. A fairy godmother pillowcase and a spiritualist, however, prove thin mental stimulation for readers whom the Atlan tales have led to expect more.

Published in Gaskell's adolescent years, *Strange Evil* and *King's Daughter* seemed to herald the blossoming of a new talent for action-adventure fantasy. The move with her third novel to publishers Hodder and Stoughton began a halcyon fifteen-year period during which she produced the volumes for which she will be remembered: *The Serpent, The Dragon, Atlan, The City,* and *Some Summer Lands*. After the realistic *Sun Bubble,* however, Gaskell disappeared from the publishing scene, leaving the amusing, picaresque extrapolation of the Atlantis myth as her major contribution to fantasy.

Alasdair Gray

(28 December 1934 –)

Darren Harris-Fain
Shawnee State University

See also the Gray entry in *DLB 194: British Novelists Since 1960, Second Series.*

BOOKS: *The Comedy of the White Dog* (Glasgow: Glasgow Print Studio Press, 1979);

Lanark: A Life in Four Books (Edinburgh: Canongate, 1981; New York: Harper & Row, 1981; revised edition, Edinburgh: Canongate, 1985; New York: Braziller, 1985);

Unlikely Stories, Mostly (Edinburgh: Canongate, 1983; revised, 1997);

1982 Janine (London: Cape, 1984; New York: Viking, 1984);

The Fall of Kelvin Walker: A Fable of the Sixties (Edinburgh: Canongate, 1985; revised edition, Harmondsworth, U.K.: Penguin, 1986; New York: Braziller, 1986);

Lean Tales, by Gray, James Kelman, and Agnes Owen (London: Cape, 1985);

Alasdair Gray, Saltire Self-Portrait 4 (Edinburgh: Saltire Society, 1988);

Old Negatives: Four Verse Sequences (London: Cape, 1989);

McGrotty and Ludmilla; or, The Harbinger Report: A Romance of the Eighties (Glasgow: Dog and Bone, 1990);

Something Leather (London: Cape, 1990; New York: Random House, 1990);

Poor Things: Episodes from the Early Life of Archibald McCandless M.D., Scottish Public Health Officer (London: Bloomsbury, 1992; New York: Harcourt Brace Jovanovich, 1992);

Why Scots Should Rule Scotland (Edinburgh: Canongate, 1992); revised as *Why Scots Should Rule Scotland, 1997: A Carnaptious History of Britain from Roman Times until Now* (Edinburgh: Canongate, 1997);

Ten Tales Tall and True (London: Bloomsbury, 1993); republished as *Ten Tales Tall and True: Social Realism, Sexual Comedy, Science Fiction, Satire* (New York: Harcourt Brace, 1993);

A History Maker (Edinburgh: Canongate, 1994; revised edition, London: Penguin, 1995; San Diego: Harcourt Brace, 1996);

Alasdair Gray (photograph by Renate von Mangoldt)

Mavis Belfrage: A Romantic Tale with Five Shorter Tales (London: Bloomsbury, 1996);

Working Legs: A Play for People without Them (Glasgow: Dog and Bone, 1997);

Sixteen Occasional Poems, 1990–2000 (Glasgow: Morag McAlpine, 2000);

A Short Survey of Classic Scottish Writing (Edinburgh: Canongate, 2001).

PLAY PRODUCTIONS: *Dialogue,* Edinburgh, Pool Lunchtime Theatre, 1971;

Homeward Bound, Edinburgh, Pool Lunchtime Theatre, 1971;

The Fall of Kelvin Walker, Stirling, McRoberts Centre, University of Stirling, 1972;

The Loss of the Golden Silence, Edinburgh, Pool Theatre, 1973;

The Homecoming, Edinburgh, Pool Theatre, 1973;

McGrotty and Ludmilla, Glasgow, Tron Theatre, 1975;

Tickly Mince, by Gray, Tom Leonard, and Liz Lochhead, Glasgow, Tron Theatre, 1982; Edinburgh, The Pleasance, 1982;

The Pie of Damocles, by Gray, Leonard, Lochhead, and James Kelman, Glasgow, Tron Theatre, 1983; Edinburgh, The Pleasance, 1983;

Working Legs: A Play for People without Them, Cumbernauld, Scotland, Alpha Project, 1998.

PRODUCED SCRIPTS: *Under the Helmet,* television, BBC, 1965;

The Fall of Kelvin Walker, television, BBC 2, 1968;

Quiet People, BBC Radio Scotland, 1968;

Dialogue, BBC Radio, 1969;

The Night Off, BBC Radio, 1969;

Honesty, television, Scottish BBC Schools, 1970;

Thomas Muir of Huntershill, BBC Radio Scotland, 1970;

Dialogue, television, Granada, 1972;

Martin, television, Scottish BBC Schools, 1972;

Agnes Belfrage / Cholchis / Triangles, television, Granada, 1972;

Today and Yesterday, television, BBC Scotland, 1972;

The Man Who Knew about Electricity, television, BBC, 1973;

The Loss of the Golden Silence, BBC Radio Scotland, 1974;

The Harbinger Report, BBC Radio, 1975;

McGrotty and Ludmilla, BBC Radio, 1975;

Beloved, television, Granada, 1976;

Henry Prince, television, as Martin Green, Granada, 1976;

The Gadfly, television, Granada, 1977;

The Vital Witness, Scottish BBC Radio, 1979;

Near the Driver, radio, translated by Berndt Rullkotter, Westdeutscher Rundfunk, 1983; English version, BBC, 1988;

The Fall of Kelvin Walker, radio version, BBC Radio 4, 1986;

The Story of a Recluse, television, adapted from the story by Robert Louis Stevenson, BBC 2, 1987.

OTHER: Agnes Owens, *Gentlemen of the West,* postscript by Gray (Harmondsworth, U.K.: Penguin, 1986);

Five Scottish Artists, introduction by Gray (Gartocharn, U.K.: Famedram, 1986);

The Anthology of Prefaces, edited by Gray (Edinburgh: Canongate, 1989); revised and expanded as *The Book of Prefaces* (London & New York: Bloomsbury, 2000);

"The Wasting of Old English Speech and How a New Was Got," in *Acid Plaid: New Scottish Writing,* edited by Harry Ritchie (New York: Arcade, 1997), pp. 59–67.

SELECTED PERIODICAL PUBLICATIONS– UNCOLLECTED: "A Ghost Comes to Whitehill," as A.J.G., *Whitehill School Magazine,* 58 (1948): 21–22;

"The Wise Mouse," as Yarg, *Whitehill School Magazine,* 60 (1949): 10–11;

"What's Eatin' You, Hamlet?" as A.J.G., *Whitehall School Magazine,* 66 (1952): 20–22.

Social Realism, Sexual Comedy, Science Fiction, Satire, the subtitle to the American edition of Alasdair Gray's *Ten Tales Tall and True* (1993), could easily stand as a capsule description of the range of the author's work. He is best known as an experimental novelist and illustrator and as one of the leading literary figures of Scotland at the turn of the twenty-first century. Anthony Burgess once acclaimed him the best Scottish novelist since Sir Walter Scott. Gray has also gained some small measure of renown in the worlds of English-language science fiction and fantasy for his best-known novel, *Lanark: A Life in Four Books* (1981), which conjoins the conventions of those genres with those of the contemporary realistic novel.

Alasdair James Gray was born in the Riddrie neighborhood of Glasgow on 28 December 1934. His parents were Alexander Gray, a factory worker who made cardboard boxes, and Amy Fleming Gray. Gray's working-class family exposed him to liberal politics and the arts. His father was a socialist and read left-wing workers' publications. Family outings to plays and operettas were common; his mother sang with the nationally acclaimed Glasgow Orpheus Choir; and his father possessed complete sets of the plays of Henrik Ibsen and George Bernard Shaw.

In the early months of World War II, Gray moved north with his mother and younger sister, Mora Jean, to a farm in Auchterarder, where Gray experienced his first problems with asthma, which has plagued him throughout his life. The three moved again in 1940 to Stonehouse in Lanarkshire, and then the family lived together in Wetherby, Yorkshire, for the remainder of the war. Here, Gray's father managed a hostel for munitions workers, and Gray's formal education began as he attended a local religious school.

Self-portrait of Gray in an August 1955 letter to Robert Kitt (National Library of Scotland)

In 1946 the family returned to their home in Glasgow, where Gray attended primary school and then the Whitehill Senior Secondary School. The family's fortunes declined because his father was unable to return to a skilled trade position and had to take work as a laborer and then as a clerk. Gray's mother was forced to enter the workplace to supplement their finances.

Gray's persistent asthma contributed to his pursuit of intellectual and artistic activities rather than physical ones. He was not an outgoing youth, but he sang in choirs at school and church and participated in a literary debate club. During his childhood and adolescence he began writing and drawing. In a 1987 interview in *Contemporary Authors,* Gray said that his parents and most of his teachers encouraged his efforts, but his teachers "also told me I was unlikely to make a living by either of these jobs . . . "–a somewhat prophetic statement, given his later financial difficulties. Despite such warnings, he persisted in his efforts. In his youth, thanks to a BBC competition, he had his first experience with the media: reading poems and an adaptation of a fable from Aesop on a Scottish radio children's program. His reading ranged widely, including comic books and fantasy. At age fourteen he began publishing some of his fiction in *Collins Magazine for Boys and Girls,* and he started a work he called "Obby Pobbly," the earliest version of what emerged three decades later as *Lanark,* his first novel.

Also in the course of his formal education, Gray began to develop his talents as an artist, and after graduating from Whitehill in 1952, he made the decision to attend the Glasgow School of Art. During that same year his mother died. Except for a hospital stay because of his asthma, he remained at the art school until he earned his diploma in 1957, concentrating on murals while continuing to write. His literary efforts at this time included some shorter pieces that were later published in *Unlikely Stories, Mostly* (1983) and the book that became *Lanark,* which he was then calling "Thaw" and whose plot, Gray has claimed in interviews, was established in his head by this time.

Following his graduation from the Glasgow School of Art in 1957, Gray earned a Ballahouston Travelling Scholarship to study in Spain. While in Gibraltar in 1958, his asthma forced him to cut short his stay and return to Glasgow. He wrote about his Spanish travels in an essay later collected in *Lean Tales* (1985). Back in Glasgow, though he lacked training as an educator, he found work as an art teacher, and he was commissioned to paint murals at two houses of worship: a church in Glasgow, completed in 1962, and a synagogue in Crosshill.

In 1959 Gray began attending Jordanhill, a teacher-training college, in order to receive his teaching credentials. During the same year, he took part for the first time in political protests, a series of demonstrations organized by the Campaign for Nuclear Disarmament to protest a Polaris submarine base in Holy Loch. From that point onward he has remained active in working for nuclear disarmament.

In 1960 Gray took teaching jobs at two schools in Glasgow, Riverside and Wellshot Road. The following year, during a short stint as a nightclub comedian at the Edinburgh Festival, Gray met Inge Sørensen, and the two were married six weeks later, on 3 November. They settled in the Cowcaddens neighborhood of Glasgow, where their son, Andrew, was born in 1963. The couple was divorced in 1971.

In 1962 Gray gave up teaching to work full-time as a scene painter at the Pavilion Theatre, a position he abandoned in 1963 for a similar short-term job with the Citizens' Theatre. The year 1964 was difficult for Gray, who found it hard to sell his paintings and literary work. He had developed "Thaw" to the point at which he felt part of it could be published on its own, but the agents to whom he submitted the manuscript rejected it. This work later became book 1 of *Lanark.* Gray turned to public assistance to meet living expenses while he continued to work at painting and writing.

Gray's fortunes began to improve when his paintings and poetry became the subject of the BBC documentary *Under the Helmet,* filmed by Bob Kitts. Its broadcast in 1965 brought Gray greater recognition than he had hitherto achieved and allowed him to get off welfare and find work as a writer, artist, and part-time lecturer on art appreciation. In 1965 the BBC network bought his story *The Fall of Kelvin Walker,* airing it on television in 1968. Other efforts to sell television scripts were less successful, however, and by 1967 he found himself working in the library of the Glasgow Art School during the evenings after devoting himself to painting and writing by day. For the remainder of the 1960s Gray exhibited his work periodically but never experienced any great success.

Also frustrating were his continuing efforts on the novel that became *Lanark.* By the early 1970s books 1 and 3 were substantially complete, but he still had considerable work to do on turning the sprawling narrative into an ultimately coherent whole. During this time he joined a Glasgow writers' group led by Philip Hobsbaum. The support Gray received there and the friendships he made proved fruitful efforts, and he collaborated with several members of the group, including James Kelman, Tom Leonard, and Liz Lochhead.

In 1971 Gray's first stage play, *Dialogue,* was produced. He had greater success in 1973 with the professional production of his stage version of *The Fall of Kelvin Walker.* Until the late 1970s Gray continued to

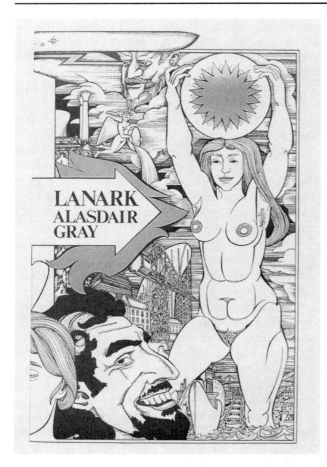

Dust jacket for Gray's first novel, which Anthony Burgess praised as "a shattering work of fiction in the modern idiom"

divide his time among painting, working on *Lanark,* writing television and radio scripts for the BBC, and part-time teaching. As early as 1973 Gray had interested a publisher in the still incomplete *Lanark.* They ultimately rejected the project, but in 1978 Canongate Press contracted with Gray for the novel and a collection of short stories. The book was published three years later, and in the meantime Gray continued to experience financial difficulties, while working as an artist-recorder at the People's Palace, a Glasgow museum, and as writer-in-residence at the University of Glasgow between 1977 and 1979.

Lanark was finally published in 1981. Subtitled *A Life in Four Books,* the novel depicts the life of Glasgow artist Duncan Thaw, both in mid-twentieth-century Scotland and in a fantastic, highly imaginative afterlife in which he assumes the name Lanark. It is here that the novel begins, nonchronologically, with book 3.

As the novel opens, a young man finds himself in a dark, nearly deserted city with nothing more than the clothes on his back and the contents of his pockets. He remembers next to nothing of his life before this moment, not even his name, and adopts the name Lanark from one of the few things he can recall. He receives money from an Orwellian government office and rents a room in a boardinghouse. After joining a bohemian group led by a man named Sludden, he meets Rima, a sullen young woman who eventually becomes his lover, even though at times she seems to hate him because she seems to have known him in his former life and can remember more than he can.

Along the way, readers are slowly introduced to the urban world of Unthank. Though it is different from the world of the reader, Unthank is in some ways not terribly fantastic or science-fictional. In many respects it is no different from any twentieth-century industrial city, though its extreme bleakness renders the novel akin to dystopian works—especially in the way that the ruling elite of Unthank preys on the citizens in their disintegrating society. A few elements of Unthank, however, render it fantastic: the almost complete absence of sunlight; the sudden disappearances of characters; the "dragonhide" disease that afflicts Lanark and Rima, turning their human flesh into reptilian scales and talons; and the mouths that grow on Rima's hand and that open out of the earth to swallow Lanark and deliver him to the Institute, a strange subterranean place that is half clinic, half laboratory. After he is cured of the dragonhide at the clinic, he is appointed to be a doctor, even though he knows nothing of how the Institute works or of how to deal with its fantastic "patients." He is confused and then outraged when he learns that the Institute derives its fuel and even its food from patients it has failed to cure—a parallel to the elite's exploitation of the masses in Unthank and, by extension later in the novel, in Scotland. He makes some progress by talking and reading to a "dragon," who turns out to be Rima. Once reunited, the pair plans their escape, which they attempt with the assistance of a mechanical oracle, who begins by telling Lanark who he was before arriving at Unthank.

After an interlude that explains the history of the voice behind the oracle, the novel moves into books 1 and 2, taking the reader from the beginning of Lanark's life as Duncan Thaw to his death at the end of book 2. Born in Glasgow and growing up in often sad and unpromising circumstances in bleak postwar Scotland, Thaw, like Gray, becomes an artist and writer. He wishes Glasgow could be reborn as a more beautiful city—a wish that is transposed into the moribund industrial dystopia of Unthank following his rebirth as Lanark.

While Thaw shows great artistic promise, his personal life is chaotic, and he remains an outsider. He longs to connect with women but does not know how to relate to them. Ultimately, in despair over the loss of an art project, he murders one of his girlfriends, Marjory Laidlaw, and then drowns himself.

Book 2, which ends with Thaw's suicide, leads to book 3, with which the novel began. The story then shifts to book 4, which resumes with Lanark and Rima's desire to escape the Institute and their further wanderings through this hellish benighted world. They travel through a strange zone or dimension where the passage of time defies the conventions of normal time. The best example of this aberration is the fact that, when Rima becomes pregnant, their son, Alexander, is born instantly.

After some time, Lanark and Rima return to Unthank. The city has changed somewhat, from a gray industrial city to a bustling commercial center filled with streets and highways lined with advertisements—a transition, John Crowley pointed out in his mixed review of *Lanark* (*New York Times Book Review,* 5 May 1985), that parallels the changes that have taken place in Glasgow during Gray's lifetime. Despite this development, however, Unthank is no less dystopian than before; it has merely changed, as has its leadership. The ambitious Sludden, who earlier had hoped to supplant the ruling elite, now governs Unthank. Rima, who was drawn to Sludden in book 3, leaves Lanark, taking their son, to be at Sludden's side. Nonetheless, Sludden convinces Lanark to come to the aid of Unthank when its destruction seems imminent, and though Lanark is unsuccessful, he achieves a final reconciliation with his lover and their son.

Just as Thaw had longed for Glasgow to be transformed into something more splendid, Lanark hopes to transform Unthank and devotes himself to that goal. Though the city remains in its declining state, Lanark achieves a sort of personal transformation through his commitment to other people. A man once afflicted with the dragonhide that symbolized his inability to love, he is now altered by relinquishing his selfish worldview and making strides toward a greater humanitarian attitude.

Then, before the novel ends, Lanark and the reader enter the "Epilogue," a dialogue between Lanark and a character who claims to be the author of the novel. This character asserts that Unthank is not only an underworld or afterlife, but also a text—specifically, the text of the novel whose conclusion the protagonist and the reader have reached. Thus, in a typically postmodern twist, world and text are shown to be one, and the "author" and Lanark debate how the story should end. Employing another postmodern technique, the novel also includes a footnoted discussion of its predecessors and "plagiarisms," among them such diverse authors as Lewis Carroll, James Joyce, and Kurt Vonnegut Jr. Earlier authors such as Dante and William Blake have also been noted as influences. Despite such influences, however, Gray's use of language and his voice are distinctly his own.

Lanark adroitly combines the realistic and the fantastic in such a way that the two complement one another. The social history of modern Scotland relates to the dystopian world of Unthank, and vice versa. Similarly, the inner life of Thaw/Lanark bears a strong relationship to his physical surroundings and experiences. Related to these strengths is the structure of the narrative itself. Gray is far from the first author to alter conventional chronology, but he makes better use of the out-of-sequence story line in *Lanark* than many other authors experimenting with narrative temporality. Starting the book in the strangeness of Unthank makes the beginning of the novel as unsettling for the reader as it is for its amnesiac protagonist, both of whom learn of Lanark's past at the same time. Finally, Gray's striking black-and-white illustrations evoke the darkness and strangeness of the worlds Thaw/Lanark inhabits but take nothing away from the reader's imagination of the scenes depicted in the novel, and Gray's unconventional indentation of paragraphs, similar to James Joyce's innovations in presenting dialogue, provides an appropriately unsettling effect.

Although some reviewers faulted the novel as overdeveloped and perhaps too allegorical, the critical reception of *Lanark* in Great Britain was generally positive. The most significant comment about the novel may have come from Anthony Burgess, who wrote in his *Ninety-Nine Novels: The Best in English Since 1939—A Personal Choice* (1984), "It was time Scotland produced a shattering work of fiction in the modern idiom. This is it." In addition, *Lanark* was nominated for the prestigious Booker Prize. In the United States the publisher of *Lanark,* Harper and Row, classified the novel as science fiction. Therefore, mainstream publications tended not to review it, while science-fiction magazines called it too "literary" and too far from genre science fiction or fantasy. Only after critics such as John Clute began promoting the novel as a significant work in the field did it begin to receive respect from American science-fiction readers.

Although the fantastic pervades *Lanark,* much of the novel is rooted in Gray's life in Scotland. For instance, the "Prologue" was influenced by Gray's childhood experiences at the farm where he and his family stayed briefly during World War II, while the chapter titled "The Hostel" drew on the hostel his father ran in Wetherby during the war. More broadly, the decline of the industrial economy of Scotland, which is a frequent topic in Gray's fiction, is reflected in the realistic portions of the novel set in contemporary Scotland and distorted through a fantastic lens in the dystopian world of Unthank.

The success of *Lanark* ensured that Gray's other writing projects were taken seriously. He completed *Unlikely Stories, Mostly* in 1981, and it was published in 1983. One of the stories in the collection, "The Star"—first published in 1951, when Gray was in his teens—concerns what happens when a boy catches a star and swallows it, thus revealing Gray's early interest in the fantastic. In "The Spread of Ian Nicol," a man engages in asexual reproduction by gradually dividing in two, like an amoeba. In "The Crank That Made the Revolution," another story that exhibits traces of science fiction or fantasy, the Industrial Revolution emerges from an eighteenth-century Scottish swamp where Vague McMenamy creates inventions to improve the efficiency of ducks and even his grandmother. Like many of Gray's works, the story satirizes the Scottish political situation and modern industrialism.

In 1984 Gray published his next novel, *1982 Janine*. The novel is not as fantastic as *Lanark*, but thanks to its drunken narrator, it possesses a similar hallucinogenic quality. Like *Lanark*, *1982 Janine* combines the personal and the political, though not on so broad a scale. In particular, *1982 Janine* addresses the issues of economic systems and pornography. Its treatment of the latter, through the sexually explicit fantasies of the narrator, has perhaps received more attention than Gray's treatment of the characters and themes in the novel.

Although *1982 Janine* did not receive as much attention as *Lanark*, its sales—combined with earnings from his earlier books and his artwork—enabled Gray to work full-time on his creative projects for a few years before he again found himself in financial difficulty, until he could receive an advance on another book. One such project was a return to an older work that had already been presented on stage and screen: an adaptation of *The Fall of Kelvin Walker* as a novel, published in 1985. Somewhat autobiographical, it concerns a young man from a strongly religious background trying to make his way in London. The following year Gray adapted it as a radio program for BBC Radio 4. While the story itself is not fantastic, Gray has indicated in interviews that the plot is derived from the story of Aladdin in *The Thousand and One Nights*.

Much of Gray's work in the late 1980s was devoted to performance art in one medium or another. His play *McGrotty and Ludmilla* was revived in Glasgow in 1986, while in 1987 *The Story of a Recluse* appeared on Christmas on the BBC 2 television channel. He also worked on a movie adaptation of *Lanark* and reported that he had completed the screenplay by 1989.

During the 1980s Gray also published *Alasdair Gray* (autobiography) in 1988, *Old Negatives* (poetry) in 1989, and in 1990 *Something Leather* (novel) and a novel version of *McGrotty and Ludmilla*. *McGrotty and Ludmilla*, like *The Fall of Kelvin Walker*, is a realistic story filled with social commentary, in particular the relationship and tensions between Scotland and England. *Something Leather* began as an expansion of a short story about June, a woman from Glasgow who begins a new direction in her life by shaving her head and dressing in leather. Other earlier efforts were adapted or revised to fill out the book. Reviewers tended to note that the origins of the book are apparent and that the individual stories do not cohere as a novel.

In general, Gray's writings from the late 1980s and early 1990s were not as well received as *Lanark*, either by readers or critics. Some felt that he had expended what he had to say in his first novel; others believed that he was less proficient in the more-realistic and focused fictions. However, novels such as *The Fall of Kelvin Walker* have had their admirers.

In 1991 Gray married Morag McAlpine, to whom he dedicated his next novel, *Poor Things: Episodes from the Early Life of Archibald McCandless M.D., Scottish Public Health Officer* (1992). This book fared better with the critics and received the Whitbread Award for Best Novel. As with many of Gray's works, it has at least one literary antecedent, in this case Mary Shelley's *Frankenstein* (1818).

Poor Things marks Gray's return to fantasy and science fiction. As in Shelley's novel, his story concerns the creation of a living human being from nonliving parts. There are several differences, however. While *Frankenstein* is set primarily in Germany in the early 1800s, *Poor Things* takes place in Scotland at the end of the nineteenth century. Victor Frankenstein makes a man, while the two medical students in Gray's novel, Archie McCandless and Godwin Baxter, create a woman. Their methods also differ: while Frankenstein composes his creature from parts of corpses, McCandless and Baxter create one life from two—a woman who committed suicide while pregnant is transformed into another person by the transplantation of the fetus's brain into the woman's skull.

The most significant difference between the two works is that Frankenstein makes his creation into a monster by turning against it and abandoning it, while the doctors in *Poor Things* try to nurture and educate their beautiful creation, whom they name Bella. This attempt proves a daunting task, given Bella's combination of adult physical maturity and infantile psyche. The result is a tale full of twists and turns leading to a typically Victorian resolution and one of Gray's most impressive fictional efforts.

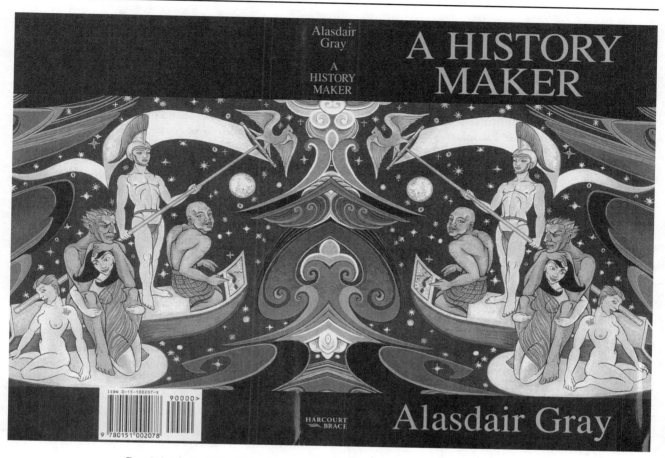

Dust jacket for the U.S. edition of the novel Gray set in Scotland during the twenty-third century
(Richland County Public Library)

Gray's books are replete with his own typography and illustrations, but perhaps *Poor Things* benefits the most from the inclusion of Gray's art. The many engravings and medical illustrations complement the story well, giving it the flavor of a nineteenth-century medical text and a Victorian novel.

The stories in Gray's next book, *Ten Tales Tall and True* (1993), are set in contemporary Scotland and represent both Gray the realist and satirist and Gray the writer of science fiction and fantasy, as is indicated by the subtitle *Social Realism, Sexual Comedy, Science Fiction, Satire.* The somewhat fantastic elements, however, play a secondary role to Gray's primary purpose: the exploration of the dynamics of relationships. Thus, as in *Lanark,* the fantastic is used in an almost allegorical fashion.

This tendency toward allegory is also present in Gray's next novel, *A History Maker* (1994), set in Scotland during the twenty-third century. Though this setting alone makes the novel science fictional, the future depicted here better resembles antiquity or the Middle Ages than any technological vision dreamed by most

science-fiction authors. Twenty-third-century Scotland is a world of clans and warfare, where the greatest threat to humanity is not a bomb but a virus. Still, Gray's futuristic society includes several elements that make *A History Maker* science fiction rather than historical fiction. Scotland and England are engaged in a series of border wars, in which the protagonist, Wat Dryhope, becomes a reluctant hero. While the setting often seems ancient or medieval, it is a world of machines, including the "public eye," an Orwellian device that both watches the populace and supplies them with information. Wat seeks to escape this machine-dominated life and the matriarchal society in which he lives, a desire that is complicated by his relationship with an unusual femme fatale. *A History Maker* critiques several aspects of modern society, in particular the nature of global politics and the increasing technology-induced alienation from a simple, more natural life.

Gray's social concerns are also evident in other works, especially *Why Scots Should Rule Scotland,* published in 1992 and revised in 1997. In this work dedicated to the cause of Scottish independence from

England, he also employs a science-fiction frame, as the work is presented as a history of Scotland from ancient times to the year 2020.

While Gray continues to publish a variety of fiction, ranging from the straight realism of the stories in *Mavis Belfrage* (1996) to more allegorical and fantastic efforts, he remains best known as the author of *Lanark*, one of the most ambitious English-language novels of the twentieth century—in science fiction or in any genre. He continues to be an important and influential figure in Scottish letters.

Interviews:

Carol Anderson and Glenda Norquay, "Interview with Alasdair Gray," *Cencrastus*, 13 (1983): 6–10;

Elizabeth C. Donaldson, "Alasdair Gray Talking," *Verse*, 1 (1984): 30–35;

Kathy Acker, "Alasdair Gray Interviewed," *Edinburgh Review*, 74 (1986): 83–90;

Sean Figgis and Andrew McAllister, "Alasdair Gray," *Bête Noire* (Spring 1988): 17–44;

Jennie Renton, "Alasdair Gray Interviewed," *Scottish Book Collector*, 7 (1988): 2–5;

Jean W. Ross, "Interview," *Contemporary Authors,* volume 126, edited by Susan M. Trosky (Detroit: Gale, 1989), pp. 142–144;

Frank Delaney, "Anarchy and Tradition in Disnaeland," *Sunday Times* (London), 1 July 1990, VIII: 8–9;

Francis Spufford, "The Perfect Marriage of Heaven and Hell," *Guardian* (Manchester), 2 September 1992, p. 33;

Mark Axelrod, "An Epistolary Interview, Mostly with Alasdair Gray," *Review of Contemporary Fiction,* 15 (Summer 1995): 106–115;

Keith Bruce, "Alasdair Gray Has Remarkable Visions," *Glasgow Herald,* 31 October 1995, p. 25.

Bibliographies:

Mark Axelrod, "An Alasdair Gray Checklist," *Review of Contemporary Fiction,* 15 (Summer 1995): 197–198;

Phil Moores, *Alasdair Gray: Critical Appreciations and a Bibliography* (London: British Library, 2001).

References:

Stephen Bernstein, *Alasdair Gray* (Lewisburg, Pa.: Bucknell University Press, 1999);

Anthony Burgess, *Ninety-Nine Novels: The Best in English Since 1939–A Personal Choice* (London: Allison & Busby, 1984);

Dominique Costa, "Decadence and Apocalypse in Gray's Glasgow—*Lanark:* A Postmodernist Novel," *Scotia,* 18 (1994): 22–34;

Costa, "In the Scottish Tradition: Alasdair Gray's *Lanark* and *1982 Janine,*" *Literature of Region and Nation,* 2 (November 1990): 2–7;

Robert Crawford and Thom Nairn, eds., *The Arts of Alasdair Gray* (Edinburgh: Edinburgh University Press, 1991);

Douglas Gifford, "Private Confession and Public Satire in the Fiction of Alasdair Gray," *Chapman,* 10 (Summer 1987): 101–116;

Gifford, "Scottish Fiction 1980–81: The Importance of Alasdair Gray's *Lanark,*" *Studies in Scottish Literature,* 18 (1983): 210–252;

Alison Lumsden, "Innovation and Reaction in the Fiction of Alasdair Gray," in *The Scottish Novel Since the Seventies: New Visions, Old Dreams,* edited by Gavin Wallace and Randall Stevenson (Edinburgh: Edinburgh University Press, 1993), pp. 115–126;

C. N. Manlove, "Alasdair Gray, *Lanark* (1981)," in his *Scottish Fantasy Literature: A Critical Survey* (Edinburgh: Canongate, 1994), pp. 197–213;

Phil Moores, *Alasdair Gray: Critical Appreciations and a Bibliography* (London: British Library, 2001);

Marie Odile Pittin, "Alasdair Gray: A Strategy of Ambiguity," in *Studies in Scottish Fiction: 1945 to the Present,* edited by Susanne Hagemann (Frankfurt: Peter Lang, 1996), pp. 199–215;

Review of Contemporary Fiction, special Alasdair Gray issue, 15 (Summer 1995);

Richard Todd, "The Intrusive Author in British Postmodern Fiction: The Cases of Alasdair Gray and Martin Amis," in *Exploring Postmodernism,* edited by Matei Calinescu and Douwe Fokkema (Amsterdam: Benjamins, 1987), pp. 123–137;

Beat Witschi, *Glasgow Urban Writing and Postmodernism: A Study of Alasdair Gray's Fiction* (Frankfurt am Main, Bern, & New York: Peter Lang, 1991).

Papers:

Alasdair Gray's papers are located in the Glasgow University Library, the Mitchell Library in Glasgow, and the National Library of Scotland.

M. John Harrison

(26 July 1945 –   )

Rob Latham
University of Iowa

BOOKS: *The Committed Men* (London: New Authors, 1971; Garden City, N.Y.: Doubleday, 1971);

The Pastel City (London: New English Library, 1971; Garden City, N.Y.: Doubleday, 1972);

The Centauri Device (Garden City, N.Y.: Doubleday, 1974; St. Albans: Panther, 1975);

The Machine in Shaft Ten and Other Stories (London: Panther, 1975);

A Storm of Wings. Being the Second Volume of the "Viriconium" Sequence, in Which Benedict Paucemanly Returns from His Long Frozen Dream in the Far Side of the Moon, and the Earth Submits Briefly to the Charisma of the Locust (London: Sphere, 1980; Garden City, N.Y.: Doubleday, 1980);

In Viriconium (London: Gollancz, 1982); republished as *The Floating Gods* (New York: Pocket Books, 1983);

The Ice Monkey and Other Stories (London: Gollancz, 1983);

Viriconium Nights (New York: Ace, 1984; revised, London: Gollancz, 1985);

Fawcett on Rock, as Ron Fawcett and John Beatty with Mike Harrison (London: Unwin Hyman, 1987);

Climbers (London: Gollancz, 1989);

The Luck in the Head, illustrated by Ian Miller (London: VG Graphics / Gollancz, 1991);

The Course of the Heart (London: Gollancz, 1992);

Signs of Life (London: Gollancz, 1997; New York: St. Martin's Press, 1997);

The Wild Road, by Harrison and Jane Johnson, as Gabriel King (London: Century, 1997; New York: Ballantine, 1998);

The Golden Cat, by Harrison and Johnson, as King (London: Century, 1998; New York: Ballantine, 1999);

The Knot Garden, by Harrison and Johnson, as King (London: Century, 2000);

Travel Arrangements: Short Stories (London: Gollancz, 2000);

Nonesuch, by Harrison and Johnson, as King (London: Century, 2001).

OTHER: "The Great God Pan," in *Prime Evil: New Stories by the Masters of Modern Horror,* edited by Douglas E.

Winter (New York: New American Library, 1988), pp. 105–125;

"The Gift," in *Other Edens II,* edited by Christopher Evans and Robert Holdstock (London: Unwin, 1988), pp. 151–172;

"The Horse of Iron and How We Can Know It and Be Changed by It Forever," in *Tarot Tales,* edited by Rachel Pollack and Caitlin Matthews (London: Legend/Century Hutchinson, 1989), pp. 51–69; republished in *The Year's Best Horror Stories XVIII,* edited by Karl Edward Wagner (New York: DAW, 1990), pp. 324–341.

SELECTED PERIODICAL PUBLICATIONS–
UNCOLLECTED:
NONFICTION
"A Literature of Comfort," *New Worlds,* 55 (September 1971); simultaneously published in *New Worlds Quarterly #1,* edited by Michael Moorcock (New York: Berkley, 1971), pp. 182–190;

"By Tennyson Out of Disney," *New Worlds,* 55 (December 1971); simultaneously published in *New Worlds Quarterly #2,* edited by Moorcock (New York: Berkley, 1971), pp. 185–189;

"The Black Glak," *New Worlds,* 55 (March 1972); simultaneously published in *New Worlds Quarterly #3,* edited by Moorcock (New York: Berkley, 1972), pp. 214–219;

"The Problem of Sympathy," *New Worlds,* 55 (June 1972); simultaneously published in *New Worlds Quarterly #4,* edited by Moorcock (New York: Berkley, 1972), pp. 5–11;

"Sweet Analytics," *New Worlds,* 58 (1975); reprinted in *New Worlds: An Anthology,* edited by Moorcock (London: Fontana, 1983), pp. 341–346;

"The Profession of SF," *Foundation: The Review of Science Fiction,* 46 (Autumn 1989): 5–13.

Of the major British writers associated with the magazine *New Worlds* in the 1960s and 1970s, M. John Harrison is one of the most consistently underrated.

M. John Harrison (photograph by Nicholas Royle; from the dust jacket for the U.S. edition of Signs of Life, *1997)*

Part of the problem lies in the fact that much of his best work has been of shorter length, and critical reputations are generally founded upon novelistic production. In a career of more than three decades (his first story appeared in 1966), Harrison has published eight solo novels, a rather paltry number compared to the vast outpourings of New Wave contemporaries Brian W. Aldiss, J. G. Ballard, and Michael Moorcock during the same period; post–New Wave writers such as Ian Watson and Iain M. Banks have easily eclipsed this total in considerably less time, which in part accounts for the greater critical visibility of their writing. Harrison has admitted in interviews that he finds novel-writing a difficult business, preferring the density and conciseness of novellas and short stories; in fact, the majority of his novels have been seeded by previously published free-standing tales—most gathered in his four collections, *The Machine in Shaft Ten and Other Stories* (1975), *The Ice Monkey and Other Stories* (1983), *Viriconium Nights* (1984), and *Travel Arrangements* (2000)—a process of expansion that indicates how structurally dependent all of the

author's work is upon the shorter forms. Moreover, not only has Harrison's career been animated by an antipathy toward the novel as such, but he also largely dismisses his first three novels—*The Committed Men* (1971), *The Pastel City* (1971), and *The Centauri Device* (1974)—as apprentice hackwork (a draconian assessment not shared by all critics), and he violently disparages the genres of science fiction and heroic fantasy within which his longer narratives, with the exception of his novels *Climbers* (1989), *The Course of the Heart* (1992), and *Signs of Life* (1997), have been positioned. All this background makes assessing Harrison's work a challenge, but one worth the effort, for he is arguably one of the best stylists that the British New Wave produced.

Michael John Harrison was born in the Midlands, England, on 26 July 1945, the son of Alan Spencer Harrison, an engineer, and Dorothy Lee Harrison, a clerk. He grew up in Rugby. In 1963 he worked briefly as a groom at Atherstone Hunt in Warwickshire before entering a teacher training college there, where he studied and taught for the next three years. Harrison admits, in the first of three interviews with Christopher J. Fowler for the journal *Foundation,* that college was for him merely "a refuge . . . somewhere to go other than a metal-worker's bench in the local factory," but that he resigned when he realized he would not have as much time for writing as he had hoped. At his next job, as clerk for a Masonic charity institute, Harrison spent most of his time writing stories on the backs of envelopes and not doing any work; this employment ended badly after an argument over a menial assignment. In 1968 Harrison joined *New Worlds* as its books editor, a position arranged by his friend, American science-fiction writer James Sallis, then a member of Moorcock's youthful, freewheeling editorial collective. As Harrison tells it, Sallis "dragged me round to Mike Moorcock's house one night at about three o'clock and said: 'This chap should be Books editor.' So Mike said something like: 'Oh, all right'—and I was." Although he sometimes worked part time as a publisher's reader to make ends meet, from this point forward Harrison essentially devoted himself to the writing and criticism of science fiction and fantasy, maintaining a conflictual relationship with these genres.

Harrison's view of contemporary science fiction and fantasy, as reflected in his many editorials for *New Worlds,* is scathing; taken together, these articles amount to one of the most consistent, sustained, and uncompromising interrogations of these genres ever produced by an insider—and they thus had more potent reverberations within the field than would similar condemnations originating in the broader culture. His 1975 essay "Sweet Analytics," published in one of the last regular issues of the magazine, summed up the stern verdict of this seven-year tenure, condemning the naive technophilic materialism of contemporary science fiction, which in Harrison's view functions as a degraded form of mythology, and linking it with popular fantasy, which similarly vends comforting myths to a mass audience. He feels their mutual fabrication of imaginary worlds—"the World of Tolkien, the World of Michael Moorcock, the Worlds of *Dune* and of *Star Trek,* to name only a few"—insidiously effaces the complexity of reality with the same "vast blotting-pad credulity" manifested in the dogmas of religious cults. The unsparing character of this critique was evidenced by Harrison's willingness to indict not only his editor's complicity in the general malaise but also his own, since he had himself contributed an early trilogy of stories to Moorcock's ongoing "Jerry Cornelius" series.

Harrison's earlier editorials and feature articles for *New Worlds* (sometimes published under the byline "Joyce Churchill") led up to this indictment. "By Tennyson Out of Disney" (1971) criticized the current enthrallment of fantasy to J. R. R. Tolkien's *The Lord of the Rings* (1954–1955), the narrative elements of which derived "not from the beautiful chaos of reality but from what amounts to other fictions . . . vicarious by hand-me-down, already twice-removed"; the boldness of the attack was buttressed by Harrison's extensive knowledge of the trilogy, which he cited chapter and verse. Science fiction took a similar cudgeling in "The Problem of Sympathy" (1972), where the fault was seen to lie not merely in a repetition of models but in a stunted emotive range, in the appeal of modern science fiction "to writers and readers who can feel more compassion for a machine . . . than a human being." Ultimately, both genres had been reduced to what he called "A Literature of Comfort" (1971), marked by "the repetition of form and content; careful rationalisation of any change in the status quo; a body of warm, familiar assumptions, reiterated from book to book and serving precisely the same purpose as 'once upon a time'"—in short, "shoddy, programmed pap." Whatever one may think of Harrison's dire assessments of the contemporary publishing scene, one can hardly argue with the fact that, as books editor for *New Worlds,* he was in a position to know; as he remarks in his first *Foundation* interview, "I would get possibly 70 or 80 books a month, which I read before they were sent out to reviewers. . . . It was a very quick transfer from being astonished to being appalled and finally to despair." Consequently, "it was very easy for me to slip into a deliberate and active cynicism, rather than a passive cynicism. That was how my style of *New Worlds* criticism developed: as a polemical, anarchistic, iconoclastic, deliberate refusal to accept almost anything that was put in front of it."

Throughout this period of disillusionment, Harrison was also a practicing writer in these genres, publishing four books and many uncollected stories. Not surprisingly, this participation was fraught with irony and paradox—and not a little cynicism, both active and passive. Harrison refers to "the schizoid process that any sf writer who starts simply as a writer has to go through, to produce work that will on the one hand satisfy him and on the other satisfy what he conceives to be the science fiction public." In the author's somewhat harsh view, his first three novels do not succeed at resolving this dilemma adequately. Deliberate attempts to ape prevalent genre models, *The Committed Men* is a post-holocaust story; *The Pastel City* is sword and sorcery; and *The Centauri Device* is space opera. All three embarrass Harrison now, but for different reasons.

According to Harrison, *The Committed Men,* while "less generic" and thus "more honest than the next two," is still "very poorly conceived and structured." Its honesty, in Harrison's view, lies in its unremitting bleakness, its refusal to offer the reader comfort. At the time of its writing, Harrison still maintained—a view shared by most of the major *New Worlds* writers—that science fiction, despite being deformed by commercial pressures, nonetheless possessed a vitality that much mainstream fiction lacked, and that a cross-pollination between the two literary breeds might—as Harrison puts it in his 1971 review-article "The Black Glak"—"mature the one and invigorate the other." In his first *Foundation* interview, published in 1981, Harrison continued to maintain this belief in the "dynamism" of science fiction, a restless energy and a boldness of surmise that contemporary mainstream fiction—"immobile, nerveless"—desperately needed. The main strength of the best science fiction, for Harrison, was its "peculiar sense of incompleteness," its ability to "*suggest* a fantasy world . . . then leave the reader to puzzle over the rest and fill in the gaps"; this dynamic cognitive engagement contrasted both with the stolid torpor of the mainstream and the comforting banality of conventional genre fiction. Harrison's involvement with *New Worlds* was an expression of his belief that "science fiction needs to be radically changed from the inside by people who will not compromise," and *The Committed Men,* for all its rather cynical positioning within the hoary British tradition of futuristic disaster stories, was his best early effort to realize the innate promise of science fiction; however, the calculated ellipticism of its vision and the grimness of its emotional palette, combined with its admitted stylistic and structural flaws, made its reception within the field problematic.

The Committed Men is set in a near-future Britain devastated by an unspecified catastrophe—most likely the fallout of a nuclear exchange, since environmentally induced mutations figure prominently in the action. National political structures and social institutions have largely collapsed, and human culture has fragmented into local despotisms ruled by petty tyrants. The story relates the strange quest of a tatterdemalion assortment of spiritual losers—Wendover, a bitter, aging doctor; Morag, a feral waif; Harper, a brooding, crippled teenager; and Arm, a dwarf—to convey a mutant baby from its birthplace in a grimy shantytown to its fated rendezvous with a mysterious tribe of its own kind subsisting in the wilds south of London. Along the way, in a series of picaresque incidents strongly reminiscent of Ballard's absurdist disaster stories (an admitted influence), this motley crew becomes involved in a senseless squabble between a military junta and a roving band of guerilla anarchists, is captured by a Kafkaesque regime of senile bureaucrats inhabiting ruined high-rises, and must manage a bloody escape from a barbarous religious commune run by a power-mad nun in a hovercraft. The resolution of the tale is enigmatic, despairing, and oddly hopeful at the same time, as an exhausted, moribund humanity symbolically passes the torch to a new breed of (literally) tough-skinned, hardy mutations. Beneath the surface of the sometimes silly plot, Harrison grapples with an ambitious metafictional theme: the wandering "road" the protagonists travel is compared with the illusory linearity of narrative itself, its pretense to lead the reader on a destined quest when in fact, as one of the chapter titles declares, "destination is a state of mind." But, as Harrison's remarks about the botched structure of the book suggest, this reflexive theme hardly provides a sufficient alibi for the obvious failings of the narrative as a narrative.

Despite these problems, the novel shows emotional honesty, as Harrison has also remarked, an uncompromising dourness befitting its portrait of entropic decay. Many mainstream review outlets in Britain praised this stark mordancy of spirit—novelist Francis King, in the *Sunday Telegraph,* proclaimed that it had been "a long time since a first novel so full of poetry, sardonic humour and despairing vision has come my way"—but science-fiction commentators were less kind. In a review of the American edition in the December 1972 issue of *The Magazine of Fantasy and Science Fiction,* American science-fiction writer Joanna Russ complained that the "psychological subtleties of dreary suffering, accurate as they were, only bored me." *The Committed Men* was indiscriminately lumped with other "depressing" minor products of the British New Wave, leading Harrison, in his first *Foundation* interview, to brood over the "fact that a complex, unromantic story is still impossible to sell, and a simple, sentimental one will sell immediately." Again, the "Literature of Comfort" had rejected the painful truths of what Harrison was slowly coming to define as a "Literature of Compassion": "Genuine compassion only exists on a one-to-one basis, between author and character, or between one character and another. . . . Compassion goes out the window when you start having great sweeps of ideation about things. . . . Science fiction is very prone to that." Consequently, following the rejection of his bleak but compassionate first novel by the genre, Harrison, in what he now identifies as a frankly cynical move, wrote the heroic fantasy *The Pastel City.*

The fact that *The Pastel City* has become Harrison's most popular with genre readers openly galls him. Written in haste ("because I had words with NEL about the deadline"), purposely in imitation of "the Tolkien-based, Moorcock-based type of fantasy," and with "tongue . . . securely anchored in the cheek," the book became the author's best-seller within the field, was hailed by genre fans and writers alike (including Moorcock, Ursula K. Le Guin, and Philip José Farmer), and is the only title of Harrison's to receive an entry in Frank Magill's canonical surveys of science-fiction and fantasy literature. It is possible to appreciate both sides in this situation: one can certainly grasp the reason for the popularity of this book, given its lush evocation of a weird far future, and one can understand Harrison's bitterness, because he was capable of so much more than the novel displays.

The tale is set in Viriconium, a decadent feudal empire built upon the ruins of the Afternoon Cultures, the technological high point of civilization. Remnants of that technology—energy weapons, aircraft—remain active, but their mechanisms are unintelligible to contemporary humanity; many more wonders lie hidden in the wastes of the Great Rust Desert to the north of Viriconium. These instruments, once salvaged, prove political wild cards in the War of the Two Queens for control of the empire; when Canna Moidart, pretender to the throne of Viriconium, unearths an army of unstoppable killer robots, she descends on the capital city and unseats the legitimate queen, Methvet Nian. Summoning the aid of her late father's scattered knights—tegeus-Cromis, a swordsman and poet; Tomb the Dwarf, an engineer; and Birkin Grif, a hard-drinking warrior—Methvet mounts a campaign to regain her throne. They are aided in this quest by the mysterious Cellur, an immortal survivor of the Afternoon Cultures, who directs them to an underground bunker purportedly to destroy the vast organic brain that animates the robots by remote control. In fact, this brain is also the repository of the souls of the Afternoon Culture; and Tomb, using knowledge secretly transmitted to him by Cellur, not only deactivates the robots but also raises an army of Reborn Men who, with their superior knowledge, easily defeat Canna Moidart and her minions. Methvet is restored to power, and tegeus-Cromis, the sullen viewpoint character for most of the story, returns to his isolated tower, far from the festive capital of Viriconium, where he broods alone.

Such a summary, while it conveys the generic quality of the major events and characters, does not really do justice to the texture of the novel, which is, despite some sketchy writing, exotic. Larded into the fairly standard quest-fantasy plot are moments of descriptive beauty—for example, the mutated fauna encountered in a bog of decomposing metal, or Cellur's swarming flock of mechanical birds; but the hastiness of the general composition overwhelms these passages. Still, Harrison felt that, while the majority of sword and sorcery is "rubbish" because it is "written too quickly," the form "could perhaps be made to work by conscientious writers with some time on their hands." *The Pastel City* is now of interest primarily for establishing a fictive venue sufficiently resonant with possibility to permit more leisurely excursions in the future.

The success of his slickly contrived second novel after the failure of his ambitious, if flawed, first sent Harrison into a lengthy depression. As he succinctly put it in the first *Foundation* interview, "I sat and looked at a wall for a couple of years. . . . I'd begun to realize that there wasn't any point in writing science fiction if you wanted to say anything, or if you wanted to be a good writer." His next novel, *The Centauri Device*, paradoxically manages to be both meaningful science fiction and a frivolous space opera knock-off. Harrison acknowledges its indebtedness to American science-fiction writer Alfred Bester in its baroque plotting, but he also cites William S. Burroughs and Thomas Pynchon as influences on its style and social vision. The plot, typical for the subgenre, is a pell-mell race around and beyond the galaxy, as the protagonist, John Truck, seeks his racial destiny—his mother was Centauran, a rare survivor of humanity's genocide of her species in a brutal war—amid the star-spanning machinations of the Israeli World Government (IWG), the Union of Arab Socialist Republics (UASR), the Openers religious sect, and the Interstellar Anarchists. The historical background of these various political entities is shadowy at best—at times Harrison's exposition reads like a pastiche of a Burroughsian parody of science fiction. The only obvious thread of connection with contemporary realities is the survival of twentieth-century Cold War ideologies into this twenty-fourth-century milieu: the IWG have inherited the mantle of American capitalism, while the UASR are the heirs of Soviet Marxism. Harrison's contempt for the competitive power-lust of their militant systems of belief is unmitigated, and it extends to encompass the Openers as well, fanatical devotees of radical techniques of body manipulation. All these groups place adherence to dogma before the sanctity of the individual and are thus capable of all manner of atrocities; "the whole point about belief in systems," as Harrison remarks, "is that "you have to kill and maim and repress and indoctrinate to make them work. It's the trap of ideological solutions."

Against these apostles of ideology, Harrison contrasts the Anarchists, a cadre of warrior aesthetes whose code of behavior evokes the late-Victorian decadents—a connection cemented not only by the fact that their spiritual leader is named Swinburne Sinclair-Pater but also by a whole raft of allusions to Symbolist and Pre-Raphaelite poetry and aesthetic theory. As Harrison has commented, "I believe in art for art's sake, especially when confronted with politics." Still, for all the obvious sympathy of their depiction, Harrison remains aloof from endorsing any general movement; the main strength of his narrative is its intense and unwavering absorption in the mundane existence of its bumbling antihero John Truck—one-time drug dealer, second-rate

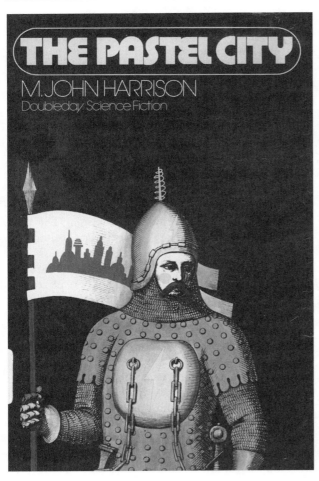

Dust jacket for the U.S. edition of Harrison's second novel, the most popular of his books (Richland County Public Library)

smuggler, and born loser—as he stumbles through a minefield of warring factions. These groups are hunting Truck because his Centauran heritage genetically enables him to operate the eponymous Centauri Device, a mysterious weapon coveted by all sides. Cornered at the end and bleeding to death, Truck, who has come to represent all the disenfranchised souls manipulated by political systems, activates the device—and promptly blows up the galaxy.

The tension in this novel between Harrison's evolving Literature of Compassion, with its commitment to discrete, downtrodden individuals, and the science-fiction Literature of Comfort, with its sweeping fairy-tale resolutions, is condensed in the paradox of its explosive climax; as Harrison remarks, "It's a contradiction in terms, that he [Truck] should ever, as a loser, be put in that position. Because losers don't—they die of hypothermia in bus shelters. They will never have the power." Again, as with *The Pastel City,* elements of descriptive brilliance

enliven an essentially generic story, a fact observed by American science-fiction writer Avram Davidson in his review of *The Centauri Device* in the May 1975 issue of *The Magazine of Fantasy and Science Fiction:* "Christ, this man writes brilliantly. I'm not sure what he might write like if he had a better theme than this one (James Bond out of Baudelaire)—blow all our minds out the window, maybe." That Harrison himself clearly saw the novel as a dead end and yearned for a fresh direction was proven by the fact that, as he admits in his third *Foundation* interview, he turned down a "four book space opera contract" that would permit him to mine the same vein. Despite Harrison's distaste for *The Centauri Device,* the novel has been largely responsible for spawning a series of space-opera pastiches in British science fiction; Colin Greenland, for example, has acknowledged its influence on his highly regarded work *Take Back Plenty* (1990). For Harrison, though, it was only in his shorter stories written during the 1970s that he began to shake off the fetters of genre plotting and partly realize his literary ideals.

Many of the tales in *The Machine in Shaft Ten and Other Stories* provided the narrative supports for the author's early novels: "Ring of Pain" (1971) evoked the fragmented postholocaust landscape explored at greater length in *The Committed Men;* long passages from "The Lamia and Lord Cromis" (1971) were incorporated into *The Pastel City;* and the central event of "The Machine in Shaft Ten" (1972; originally published as by Joyce Churchill) was reconfigured in *The Centauri Device.* Moreover, a few of the stories strangely confused the narrative topoi of those books: "Events Witnessed from a City" (1975) reintroduced the characters of *The Pastel City* under different guises, while "The Bringer with the Window" (originally published as "Lamia Mutable" in *Again, Dangerous Visions* [1972], edited by Harlan Ellison) intersected with both that novel and *The Centauri Device,* as Birkin Grif confronted a member of the Opener sect. This conflation of elements was less a calculated effort to draw Harrison's various worlds into consistent relationship than it was a kind of sport: "let the reader try to figure it out for himself," says Harrison in his first *Foundation* interview; "The more confused he becomes, the happier I will be."

The tales gathered in Harrison's first two collections, produced between 1968 and 1982, represent the author's most important work of the period. In the first volume, "London Melancholy" (1969) stands out as an eerie science-fiction adventure set in a desolate future where mutated humans are hunted by a telepathic race of alien insects. Some of the early stories are all too clearly under the spell of Ballard in their impacted elusiveness and their obsession with the theme of bizarre transformation—"Visions of Monad" (1968) is one example. "Running Down" (1975), however—included in both *The Machine in Shaft Ten and Other Stories* and his second collection, *The Ice Monkey and Other Stories,* slightly revised for the latter—shows Harrison stepping forward into a literary terrain all his own. This classic tale of the doomed friendship between a crippled man and his embittered college friend, who literally destroys everything he touches, contributes to the ongoing investigation of the concept of entropy that exercised the *New Worlds* cohort, as many commentators have remarked. But, as Harrison stresses, "the story isn't 'about' entropy. . . . what the story is 'about' is compassion. . . . Entropy is the science fictional metaphor which reflects and elucidates the subject-matter." Harrison is more inclined to use the term "Gothic" to describe the effect of "Running Down," not only because of its horrific charge but also because "the central image infects every single part of the action"—as opposed to the more instrumental deployment of metaphor in science fiction. Writing the tale was a breakthrough for Harrison, a vindication of his conviction that a Literature of Compassion could be articulated within a genre framework. Still, as he bitterly points out, "I'd like to have it on record that the first publication of 'Running Down,' which is my best story, and into which I put a great amount of work and a great deal of my life and a great deal of whatever talent I do have, earned me £50. And *that's* why I have to write rubbish."

The other tales in *The Ice Monkey and Other Stories* continue to mine this new "Gothic" vein. "The Incalling" (1978) is an ambiguous and disturbing tale of "a grubby little ceremony" of "crude urban magic" carried out against the backdrop of a morally vacant modern London; it connects with "Running Down" in its empathic portrait of a poisoned friendship, and it points ahead to *The Course of the Heart.* "Egnaro" (1981) explores similar terrain in its paranoiac evocation of a "secret country, a place behind the places we know"—the eponymous Egnaro—which links, again, two disgruntled friends in a scenario of urban despair. The title story (1980) depicts the fallout of yet another such friendship, as the narrator visits the resentful wife of a deceased rock-climbing companion; it also prefigures the central situation of *Climbers.* This repetition of a specific kind of relationship—the antagonistic yet inescapably dependent friendship between two luckless men—has, Harrison admits, an autobiographical dimension, as does the blighted urban wasteland in which their baffled camaraderie plays out. As Harrison remarked in a brief note for an entry in *Contemporary Authors* (1975), his early writing years "living frugally in the bleak 'bedsitter' belt of London's Tufnell Park and Camden Town—an area of one-roomed cold water apartments full of Irish expatriots, junkies and broken gas meters"—left

him with a lingering fascination, and a deeply ambivalent feeling, for the urban dispossessed; the losers who grapple confusedly with one another in his stories reflect, as he admits in his first *Foundation* interview, "people I actually know and for whom I find it difficult to feel compassion, because their very misery makes them unlikable: their failures and weaknesses suck down and damage everyone around them." To depict these sorts of people in this wasted environment with genuine empathy is a hard challenge for a Literature of Compassion, but in the stories gathered in his second collection, Harrison succeeds. In many ways, *The Ice Monkey and Other Stories* remains his best book.

Its success lies as much in its stylistic accomplishment as in its emotional or thematic resonance. Harrison evolves, in *The Ice Monkey and Other Stories,* a neo-Gothic style that might best be described as an eroded, hallucinatory lyricism. This form of writing manifests Harrison's persistent interest in "prose cadencing. I don't write so much to a grammar or a syntax as to a cadence." He adds that this "stylistic interest separates me from the other *New Worlds* writers. . . . the new wave was not a stylistic revolution, except for me." While his contemporaries developed a fresh register of ideas and themes in science fiction, Harrison instead pursued a precision of language linked to a specific emotional tone of resigned compassion. When he turned again, after a lengthy hiatus, to the writing of novels with *A Storm of Wings* (1980) and *In Viriconium* (1982), he deployed this style to profound effect.

These novels return to the far-future landscape first evoked in *The Pastel City* but now with a greater thematic and stylistic sophistication; for nearly a decade in the late 1970s and early 1980s, Harrison devoted himself to the meticulous reworking of this fictive milieu, drawing out the shadings and subtleties that *The Pastel City,* with its generic quest structure, had glossed over. In fact, so committed was Harrison to this project of revision that he extensively emended "The Lamia and Lord Cromis" for the British edition of *Viriconium Nights;* in his second *Foundation* interview Harrison suggests that he plans one day to revise *The Pastel City* in ways "which might offend traditional readers . . . quite heavily, I think." For a writer so stridently opposed to the popular practice of articulating a monolithic "World," this persistent returning to Viriconium might seem contradictory. Yet, as Harrison stresses in the Author's Note to *The Floating Gods,* the American edition of *In Viriconium,* "Viriconium was never intended to be the same place twice. . . . The very streets shift, from story to story. All that remains . . . is a whisper of continuity." As it stands now, and as it surely will in any further reshufflings of material, the Viriconium sequence displays the author's sly insurgency against the representational conventions of genre world-building: rather than a mimetic unity, Harrison has conjured an elliptical metafiction that subtly "hints at things."

Harrison suggests the metaphysical rationale behind this narrative agnosticism in his first *Foundation* interview: "Could it be that at the end of time the only thing that matter and space in their horrible sort of tired and entropic form could do is to vaguely attempt to repeat or partially repeat one or two significant symbolic events?" This metaphysic formalizes the author's conviction that truly serious fantasy—unlike its generic variants, with their helpful provision of charts and glossaries—should have the uneasy effect of "dragging the reader into a maze without a map and leaving the bugger there." Thus, iconic characters appear under different guises, and suffer incongruous fates, from story to story; the topography of Viriconium itself shifts, becoming an unknowable labyrinth, "shattered and fragmentary, tumbled into hard meaningless patterns of light and shade, blue and grey and faded gamboge, grainy of texture and difficult of interpretation." Harrison's invocation of the obscure color gamboge in this quotation from *A Storm of Wings* points to a major linguistic strategy underlying the author's depiction of his far-future dreamscape, one shared by American science-fiction writer Gene Wolfe in his *Book of the New Sun* tetralogy (1980–1982): the use of an extensive vocabulary of recondite extant words. By deploying terms such as lampyrine, nitid, albescent, elytra, induviate, phthisis, and craquelure, Harrison manages to give a semantic specificity to the most surreal exoticism. Indeed, Harrison has identified his method, in *A Storm of Wings* specifically, as deriving from the Imagism of Ezra Pound and T. S. Eliot: virtually every sentence is embedded with precise yet resonant figures that generate an allegorical shimmer around the main story.

As in *The Pastel City,* the surface plot is fairly generic: a race of telepathic insects—refugees from "London Melancholy," the central situation of which the novel reworks—infiltrates Viriconium, transmuting humans into locusts. Once again a quest is mounted by Methvet Nian—this time mobilizing Cellur, Tomb the Dwarf, Reborn Man Alstath Fulthor, and Galen Hornwrack, a scruffy assassin who stands in for tegeus-Cromis, now dead—to squelch the invasion. Harrison's dense fretwork of figuration, however, gives this basic story multiple meanings. The pervasive insectile imagery, for instance, evokes "a sickening rumour of otherness" that suggests at once the alien intractability of nature, the excruciating uncertainty of communication, and the disturbing lure of the shadow self. Under this weight of metaphor, linguistic and characterological identity fragment into a kaleidoscope of possibility, a theme vivified in the fate of Benedict Paucemanly, the

former airship pilot who returns from a trip to the moon transfigured into a wayward alien oracle. Describing Paucemanly's eccentric mental processes, Harrison might almost be defining the effects of his prose: "a thought received with the clarity of a sensation—hard, complex, resonant," yet also "subtly awry," aphasic, subject to "a dubious lyricism." With its proliferation of bizarre incidents, the novel is, as the author remarks in his first *Foundation* interview, "a very chaotic book"; but it is also a rich one. Harrison affirms that *A Storm of Wings* is the first novel he has written "that is wholly M. John Harrison."

Just as he achieved this distinctive voice with *A Storm of Wings,* however, he turned in a different direction in his subsequent fiction. While the novel culminated a trend toward baroque imagism in Harrison's work, it also left him "desperately looking around for a simpler way of saying things." As a result, his next book in the Viriconium sequence, though it retains the playful metafictional frame, is much more sparely written. His goal was "to strip the prose down," the author avers; "the events should be enough in themselves." The events of *In Viriconium* are deceptively simple: a mysterious, floating "plague zone" has afflicted the city with entropic dissolution; against this backdrop, a young portrait painter, Ashlyme, plots to smuggle his artistic idol, the languidly consumptive Audsley King, out of the sequestered zone, a scheme that is alternately abetted and undermined by The Grand Cairo, a pompous, murderous dwarf whose agents enforce the quarantine. Yet, this simple structure manages to support allegorical freight: as Harrison observes in his second *Foundation* interview, the contrast between Ashlyme's pallid waffling and The Grand Cairo's ferocious recklessness represents the political conflict between "liberal paralysis and fascist hysteria . . . the paradox of our time." At another level, aesthetic rather than political, Audsley King's doom crystallizes the fate of the modern artist, afflicted by the energy-sapping pall of commercialism and sycophancy, her youthful iconoclasm waning into a quiescent sentimentality.

On the one hand, this aesthetic allegory continues Harrison's fascination with the historical avant-garde first evidenced in *The Centauri Device;* on the other hand, it displays an intriguing autobiographical element. According to Harrison, the disaffected bohemians of *In Viriconium* also represent "the real driving force behind the so-called new wave, and *New Worlds.* The sort of artist who believes that *he* should decide what he produces, not the audience or the publisher." For all its humor and satirical moments, it is "a bitter little story" of alienation and the frustration of ambition. The tale had a hard time finding a publisher; the original novella, written in 1980, was eventually expanded for book publication in 1982. As if in confirmation of Harrison's grim allegory of the genre publishing scene, the novella was included in the American edition of *Viriconium Nights*—along with seven other Viriconium stories, including the unrevised "Lamia and Lord Cromis"—a collection that appeared while Harrison was extensively rethinking the framing and ordering of the tales for the subsequent British edition. The decision by Ace Books to cash in on the growing reputation of the Viriconium novels—then being reprinted in the United States by Pocket Books under their prestigious Timescape imprint—by lumping all the extant stories into an indiscriminate mass, without waiting for the revisions, effectively pre-empted stateside publication of Harrison's edited text, which has remained unavailable to American readers for more than a decade. The British edition of *Viriconium Nights,* however, is one of Harrison's most impressive accomplishments.

The British *Viriconium Nights* displays, in microcosm, the process by which the author converted the stolid trappings of genre fantasy into the elusive icons of a mercurial metafiction. Harrison's growing interest in structuralist and poststructuralist literary theory, especially its questioning of traditional boundaries between content and form, provided a guiding method—as it did for American science-fiction writer Samuel R. Delany, in his series of heroic fantasies set in Nevèrÿon (1979–1988). Harrison consistently exposes the illusory nature of all fixed boundaries: at the surface level of image, Viriconium becomes, like one of Italo Calvino's *Invisible Cities* (1972), both imaginary and "real," both a hallucinatory realm of otherness and a metaphorical repetition of human history and culture; at the discursive level of form, the "stories . . . interpenetrate one another. They contain one another as shells . . . in a topological twist which would involve an infinity of possible boundaries . . . a continual interweaving and interpenetration of the versions of Viriconium." The individual parts—each crafted with deceptive stylistic simplicity, lending a quality of folklore to tales such as "The Luck in the Head" and "Strange Great Sins"—thus add up to a densely complicated whole, making of Viriconium a textual "space which appears to be limited from the outside but from the inside is delimited to infinity."

Despite this infinite expanse of possibilities, by the mid 1980s Harrison had grown weary of Viriconium. His theoretical insights, however, provided clues for a more general expansion of his literary ambitions. He came to perceive that the undecidable boundary between surface and story had a real-world analogue: human experience, too, is like an "onion which when you strip one skin off you reach only another. . . . somehow we make life from moment to moment for ourselves, and

Dust jacket for Harrison's 1983 collection of short fiction, which includes "Running Down," the work Harrison considers his best story (Richland County Public Library)

between ourselves. That, to me, is the most unbelievably precious thing." This realization, combined with the corollary perception that the boundaries between "fantasy" and "reality" are also tenuous and permeable, allowed Harrison to imagine ways of expanding his Literature of Compassion in new directions. Thus, in the middle of the decade, he began work on two large-scale projects—a "documentary fiction" about rock-climbing and a "metaphysical thriller"—which eventually became *Climbers* and *The Course of the Heart.*

For all their many differences, these two works share a structural logic that mingles elements of realism and fantasy. They are set wholly in the contemporary world, and they include substantial "documentary" material—a term Harrison prefers to "autobiographical" because, although both texts incorporate incidents and characters from the author's life, these elements are observed with detachment and worked over, not simply experienced. "It is fiction by the manipulation of not-fiction," Harrison remarks in his second *Foundation* interview. And, for all their rootedness in the mundane world, both novels are "fantastic" in the sense that they depict efforts to escape from that world, to grapple with and defy its boundaries. In *Climbers* this escape takes the form of obsessive rock-climbing; in *The Course of the Heart,* of magical practices. Both works follow quests by the main characters to, in Harrison's words, "escape from that sense of hopelessness, pointlessness, and alienation" that deforms modern life and to find a transcendent, liberating "moment of ecstasy." Since these moments, when gained, are fleeting, and since their price in terms of physical and emotional suffering is great, both quests end as ambiguous failures—as opposed to the more conventional quests of Harrison's previous genre fantasies, which had ended as ambiguous successes. The main difference in these novels is that, rather than merely "making things up" as he did previously, his "documentary" method provides "a terrific authenticity. . . . I now seem to be inventing reality from a much more acceptably moral or ethical base."

The sense of authenticity generated by *Climbers* in particular is striking, which is not surprising given Harrison's extensive background as an amateur rock-climber. The form of the novel is a series of gripping anecdotes related by the first-person narrator and linked by recurrent images and themes. The central thematic connection is the psychic pathology that compels Harrison's climbers to their crazy feats. Harrison further confirmed in his third *Foundation* interview (conducted in 1992) that he, like his characters, "was caught in my own philosophical and experiential trap" during the planning and early writing of *Climbers:* "I was frightened to be a person. I wanted to be a text, or a discourse, not a human being." By late 1985 "the personal pressure on me of that sort relaxed" when he fell in love and realized that "being obsessed with rock and mountains . . . is just another text, it's just another way of pretending that you're not living." This perception enabled him to devote himself more to the literary depiction, and less to the terrifying actuality, of rock-climbing. The result is what most critics, as well as Harrison himself, view as his best stand-alone novel.

Harrison continues to enjoy the sport occasionally, but his relationship with the climbing community—cemented in 1987, when he ghost-wrote the nonfiction book *Fawcett on Rock* for Ron Fawcett, one of Britain's top climbers—became controversial when his novel was published because some climbers found the use of rock climbing as a literary metaphor rather pretentious, and some individuals felt they were being mocked in Harrison's depictions of certain characters. Repeating his youthful iconoclastic status within science fiction, Harrison found himself at "the centre of a radical new wave of climbing writing," and *Climbers* became the first work

of fiction ever to win the Boardman-Tasker Award for Mountain Literature. This encomium, combined with the brisk sales of the book, gave Harrison a sudden status as a serious writer, respected by mainstream critics and courted by mainstream publishers. Harrison had moved back to London in the mid 1980s in order to be with his lover—following several years of self-exile in Holmfirth, in the rocky Midlands of England—and this relocation allowed him to enjoy his fresh celebrity to the full, moving in contemporary literary circles and giving public readings at bookstores and conventions.

The Course of the Heart is more obviously a fantasy than *Climbers,* since it deals with the efficacy of magic and culminates with an apparently supernatural intrusion into the mundane world. However, it shares with *Climbers* not only an obsession with transcending boundaries—an implicitly "fantastic" theme in both cases—but also the marked emphasis on "documentary" elements. Not only does Harrison include material generated by his trip to Eastern Europe during the mid 1990s, but the central relationship between the nameless narrator and his sullen, down-at-heel college chum, Lucas Medlar, carries forward Harrison's personal preoccupation with the tensions of pathological friendships. (The novel also continues Harrison's reliance on previously published tales as the underpinnings of his longer works, expanding upon his 1988 novelette "The Great God Pan" and incorporating a revamped version of "The Quarry," a short story included in *The Ice Monkey and Other Stories*.) In this case, the warped friendship has led to a mutual entanglement with a strange, sleazy necromancer named Yaxley, whose attempts to contact a mystical realm known as the "Pleroma" poison all their lives. Perhaps the most afflicted is Lucas's wife, Pam Stuyvesant, who begins to suffer harrowing hallucinations that slowly sap her spirit; as an anodyne, the couple evolve an elaborate historical fantasy of the "Coeur," a utopic heartland destined to emerge from the Pleroma to redeem the fallen world.

Much of the plot details the narrator's wandering course between squalid black magic and whimsical reverie, between his reluctant apprenticeship with Yaxley and his compassion for his troubled friends. Meanwhile, he is himself beset by mystical emanations, but these prove more soothing than those that plague Pam and Lucas, consisting of the overpowering scent of roses and the vision of a "green woman," a sensual nature goddess. Near the end, these manifestations coalesce in a moment of seeming epiphany, in which the Coeur appears to grant its redemption; but the novel closes ambiguously, with the narrator concluding that it had only been "an embarrassment, a ghost, a hyperaesthesia of middle age . . . cruel and undependable."

The Course of the Heart brings to fruition several strands in Harrison's career. It shows that the narrative momentum of genre can be combined with the concerns of mainstream literature, and it does so by further refining the "Gothic" mode the author first essayed in the tales collected in *The Ice Monkey and Other Stories*. It also, in its exploration of painfully frayed but still essential human connections, represents Harrison's most potent effort yet at realizing a Literature of Compassion. In the relationship between the narrator and Pam, Harrison feels he has written effectively about an emotional bond of frustrated but enduring love, a theme he has visited again in *Signs of Life* (1997)–based, as is so often Harrison's practice, on a previous story, "Isobel Avens Returns to Stepney in the Spring" (1994).

Signs of Life is the story of the fraught relationships uniting two vaguely intellectual, bohemian, middle-aged couples: Mick Rose, the mordant narrator; the love of his life, Isobel Avens; his best friend and business partner, Choe Ashton; and Christiana Spede, the on-again, off-again lover of both Mick and Choe. Mick is a disaffected loner who realizes the emotional hollowness of his life only when he meets the earthy, impulsive Isobel; up until that time, his closest bond had been with Choe, a punkish thrill-seeker with whom he runs a fly-by-night courier service. Choe is another vivid portrait in Harrison's gallery of fascinating losers, a figure based–according to a 1997 interview with Harrison published in the British magazine *Interzone*–on a childhood friend whose aspiration to be a movie stuntman led him to court danger with a naive insouciance. Choe's fondness for hard drugs and fast motorcycles (preferably in combination) raises reckless amorality to an art form. Mick, helplessly entranced with his friend's avid self-destruction, permits himself to be drawn into a series of shady enterprises, including ferrying medical waste to secret dumping sites and transporting illicit materials for outlaw biotechnology firms with names like FUGA-OrtheGen and GenEx Plc International. Choe's dubious connections lead them to newly entrepreneurial post–Soviet Hungary, where they become embroiled with a group of creepy gangsters who lure them into trafficking in human specimens.

Isobel, too, is drawn into their schemes but for her own reasons. Obsessed with dreams of flight, she becomes the guinea pig for a biological experiment that leads Harrison's novel over the edge of realism into the explicitly supernatural. Her final transformation into a sickly bird-woman hybrid, evoked with a chilling matter-of-factness, is among the major accomplishments of Harrison's career: what might have seemed merely bizarre or even silly is instead conveyed with an agonizing pathos. Moreover, the technological framework supporting this gothic effect brings to an appropriate culmination Harrison's itinerant genre

Dust jacket for the U.S. edition of Harrison's 1997 novel, in which a woman obsessed with flying is transformed into a bird-woman hybrid (Richland County Public Library)

career: part science fiction, part horror story, part mainstream novel, *Signs of Life* is distinctly Harrisonian in its vision, a mature work by a self-confident writer. The response it has received among critics suggests that Harrison is poised, finally, to achieve genuine crossover success.

During the late 1980s and 1990s, as Harrison was perfecting his novelistic craft, he also began to stretch himself in other directions. In 1991, as part of his return to London literary society, he began reviewing fiction regularly for *TLS: The Times Literary Supplement*, where he has continued the iconoclastic posture of his *New Worlds* days, generally preferring the intricate metafictions of mainstream talents such as John Barth to the work of genre figures such as William Gibson, which Harrison scathingly compared to a "comic strip" (in a review of Gibson's 1993 novel *Virtual Light*). At the same time, Harrison was publishing a series of strange, moody, fragmented short stories, which were eventually collected in *Travel Arrangements* (2000). Several of these stories–in particular "The Gift" (1988) and "The

Horse of Iron and How We Can Know It and Be Changed by It Forever" (1989)—carry to an even more radical extreme the insights Harrison gleaned from contemporary literary theory—insights he affirms explicitly in his piece titled "The Profession of SF" that appeared in *Foundation* in 1989, where he cites with approval formalist and structuralist critics such as Victor Shklovsky and Gérard Genette.

In his third *Foundation* interview, Harrison claims that he "wanted to write about . . . the idea of the random and the determined"—the interplay of chance and structured elements—and in "The Horse of Iron and How We Can Know It and Be Changed by It Forever" particularly, with its use of the tarot deck as a controlling metaphor, he has found a perfect structural device. Harrison had already shown, in *In Viriconium,* the effectiveness of the tarot as a structuring concept, but "The Horse of Iron and How We Can Know It and Be Changed by It Forever" is even more subtly crafted, a metafictional collage showing how narratives may be shuffled and redealt endlessly, an arbitrary play of shifting signifiers whose only value is the mundane life readers make of them. "The Horse of Iron and How We Can Know It and Be Changed by It Forever" is New Wave science fiction crossbred with the avant-garde fictions of Walter Abish and Lynne Tillman. With other hauntingly elliptical tales such as "Anima" and "Seven Guesses of the Heart," it establishes Harrison as a major craftsman of the contemporary literary short story.

Harrison is one of the most fecund talents to have emerged from the British New Wave—a movement he helped to propel forward. As he commented in his first *Foundation* interview, "*New Worlds*—the new wave—was an attempt by science fiction writers to free themselves from their own audience. For a while, it looked as if we might escape, and even take some of the audience with us." But genre science fiction and fantasy proved recalcitrant to radical innovation, and a "counter-revolution" set in, reaffirming traditional themes and motifs. Judging by the evidence of his varied, thematically challenging, and stylistically accomplished fiction, however, M. John Harrison continues to move beyond the boundaries.

Interviews:

Christopher J. Fowler, "The Last Rebel: An Interview with M. John Harrison," *Foundation: The Review of Science Fiction,* 23 (October 1981): 5–30;

Andy Darlington, "M. John Harrison: The Condition of Falling," *Vector,* 122 (1984): 3–5;

Paul Kincaid, "A Young Man's Journey From Viriconium," *Vector,* 135 (December 1986/January 1987): 9–10;

Kincaid, "M. John Harrison Interview," *Interzone,* 18 (Winter 1986/1987): 31–32, 58;

Fowler, "On the Edge: The Last Holmfirth Interview with M. John Harrison," *Foundation: The Review of Science Fiction,* 57 (Spring 1993): 7–25;

Fowler, "A Detective Fiction of the Heart: The First London Interview with M. John Harrison," *Foundation: The Review of Science Fiction,* 58 (Summer 1993): 5–26;

Nicholas Royle, "The Committed Man," *Interzone,* 122 (August 1997): 31–34.

References:

John Clute, "M. John Harrison," in his *Look at the Evidence: Essays and Reviews* (Liverpool: Liverpool University Press, 1995), pp. 430–435;

David Pringle, "The Centauri Device," in *Science Fiction: The 100 Best Novels,* edited by Pringle (New York: Carroll & Graf, 1985), pp. 165–166.

Robert Holdstock

(2 August 1948 –   )

W. A. Senior

BOOKS: *Legend of the Werewolf,* as Robert Black (London: Sphere, 1976);

Eye among the Blind (London: Faber & Faber, 1976; Garden City, N.Y.: Doubleday, 1977);

Earthwind (London: Faber & Faber, 1977; New York: Pocket Books, 1978);

Shadow of the Wolf, as Chris Carlsen (London: Sphere, 1977);

The Bull Chief, as Carlsen (London: Sphere, 1977);

Necromancer (London: Futura, 1978; New York: Avon, 1980);

Raven, Swordsmistress of Chaos, by Holdstock and Angus Wells, as Richard Kirk (London: Corgi, 1978; New York: Ace Fantasy, 1987);

The Satanists, as Black (London: Futura, 1978);

A Time of Ghosts, as Kirk (London: Corgi, 1978; New York: Berkley, 1987);

Alien Landscapes, by Holdstock and Malcolm Edwards (London: Pierrot, 1979; New York: Mayflower, 1979);

The Horned Warrior, as Carlsen (London: Sphere, 1979);

Lords of the Shadows, as Kirk (London: Corgi, 1979; New York: Ace, 1987);

Space Wars: Worlds and Weapons, as Steven Eisler (London: Octopus, 1979; New York: Crescent, 1979);

The Alien World: The Complete Illustrated Guide, as Eisler (London: Octopus, 1980; New York: Crescent, 1980);

Tour of the Universe: The Journey of a Lifetime—The Recorded Diaries of Leio Scott and Caroline Luranski, by Holdstock and Edwards (London: Pierrot, 1980; New York: Mayflower, 1980);

Cry Wolf, as Ken Blake (London: Sphere, 1981);

Magician: The Lost Journals of the Magus Geoffrey Carlyle, by Holdstock and Edwards (Limpsfield, U.K.: Dragon's World, 1982; Topsfield, Mass.: Salem House, 1985);

Where Time Winds Blow (London: Faber & Faber, 1982; New York: Pocket Books, 1982);

In the Valley of the Statues (London: Faber & Faber, 1982);

The Untouchables, as Black (London: Sphere, 1982);

Richard Holdstock (photograph from the dust jacket for the U.S. edition of Mythago Wood, *1985)*

Operation Susie, as Blake (London: Sphere, 1982);

You'll Be All Right, as Blake (London: Sphere, 1982);

The Stalking, as Robert Faulcon (London: Arrow, 1983; New York: Charter, 1987);

239

Realms of Fantasy, by Holdstock and Edwards (Limpsfield, U.K.: Paper Tiger, 1983; Garden City, N.Y.: Doubleday, 1983);

The Talisman, as Faulcon (London: Arrow, 1983; New York: Charter, 1987);

Elite: The Dark Wheel (Cambridge, U.K.: Acornssoft, 1984);

The Ghost Dance, as Faulcon (London: Arrow, 1984; New York: Charter, 1987);

Lost Realms, by Holdstock and Edwards (Limpsfield, U.K.: Dragon's World, 1984; Salem, N.H.: Salem House, 1984);

The Shrine, as Faulcon (London: Arrow, 1984; New York: Charter, 1988);

The Hexing, as Faulcon (London: Arrow, 1984; New York: Charter, 1988);

Bulman (London: Futura, 1984);

Mythago Wood (London: Gollancz, 1984; New York: Arbor House, 1985);

Thorn (Birmingham: Birmingham Science Fiction Group, 1984);

John Boorman's "The Emerald Forest" (New York: Zoetrope, 1985);

One of Our Pigeons Is Missing (London: Futura, 1985);

The Labyrinth (London: Arrow, 1987; New York: Charter, 1988);

Lavondyss: Journey to an Unknown Region (London: Gollancz, 1988; New York: Morrow, 1989);

The Fetch (London: Orbit, 1991; New York: Warner, 1992); republished as *Unknown Regions* (New York: Roc, 1996);

The Bone Forest (London: HarperCollins, 1991; New York: Avon, 1992);

The Hollowing (London: HarperCollins, 1993; New York: Penguin, 1994);

Merlin's Wood; or, The Vision of Magic (London: HarperCollins, 1994);

Ancient Echoes (London: HarperCollins, 1995; New York: Roc, 1996);

Gate of Ivory (London: HarperCollins, 1997); republished as *Gate of Ivory, Gate of Horn* (New York: Roc, 1997);

Celtika: Book One of the Merlin Codex (London: Simon & Schuster, 2001);

The Iron Grail: Book Two of the Merlin Codex (London: Simon & Schuster, 2002).

OTHER: "Microcosm," in *New Writings in SF 20,* edited by John Carnell (London: Corgi, 1972);

"The Darkness," in *New Writings in Horror and the Supernatural 2,* edited by David A. Sutton (London: Sphere, 1972);

"Ash, Ash," in *Stopwatch,* edited by George Hay (London: New English Library, 1974);

"On the Inside," in *New Writings in SF 28,* edited by Kenneth Bulmer (London: Sidgwick & Jackson, 1976);

Encyclopedia of Science Fiction, consulting editor (London: Octopus, 1978);

"High Pressure," in *Pulsar 2,* edited by Hay (London: Penguin, 1979);

Stars of Albion, edited by Holdstock and Christopher Priest (London: Pan, 1979);

"Ocean of Sound," in *Peter Davison's Book of Alien Monsters,* edited by Peter Davison (London: Sparrow, 1982);

Other Edens, edited by Holdstock and Christopher Evans (London: Unwin, 1987);

Other Edens 2, edited by Holdstock and Evans (London: Unwin, 1988);

Other Edens 3, edited by Holdstock and Evans (London: Unwin, 1989);

"The Ragthorn," by Holdstock and Garry Kilworth, in *The Year's Best Fantasy and Horror, Fifth Annual Collection,* edited by Ellen Datlow and Terri Windling (New York: St. Martin's Press, 1992);

Kilworth, *Hogfoot Right and Bird-Hands,* introduction by Holdstock (Cambridge, Mass.: Edgewood, 1993);

"Infantasm," in *The Merlin Chronicles,* edited by Mike Ashley (London: Raven, 1995; New York: Carroll & Graf, 1995), pp. 110–129.

Born on the Romney Marsh, in Hythe, Kent, on 2 August 1948, to Robert and Kathleen Holdstock, Robert Paul Holdstock is the eldest of five children who grew up in a lively, busy household. His father, a policeman, worked various shifts and was frequently absent during the day but "was brilliant at compensating when he was around," as Holdstock told Catie Cary in an interview for *Vector* (October/November 1993). Holdstock's parents read to him often, and he himself began to read at about age three and began writing stories as early as age eight or nine. He cites as early influences C. S. Lewis's Narnia fantasies, the Westerns his grandfather left around, and the novels of H. Rider Haggard, Jules Verne, and H. G. Wells. His other grandfather, a gardener in Kent, taught him gardening and an appreciation of the land and nature. An obsessive researcher and reader, he lists as other predominant influences medieval romances; folklore and folk songs, especially Celtic; and works in the Arthurian tradition: *Gawain and the Green Knight;* the writings of Sir Thomas Malory, Alfred Tennyson, T. H. White, and Rosemary Sutcliffe; and even such historical works as Aubrey Burl's *Prehistoric Avebury* (1979). As an adult he has held a variety of odd jobs, including stints as a construction worker, a slate miner in Wales, and a banana-boat man. Perhaps the greatest influence on his literary career, however, comes from his background as a medical researcher after he graduated from the University College of North Wales with a B. Sc. in 1970 and the London School of Hygiene and Tropical Medicine in 1971 with an M.Sc. in medical zoology. These conjoined influences—an early fascination with storytelling, a passion for the beauty and power of nature and the land, and his scientific training—give rise to and are reflected in the primary concerns and impulses of Holdstock's fiction.

Holdstock has been an enthusiastic editor and writer of nonfiction along with his science-fiction and fantasy novels and short stories. He served as consulting editor to the *Encyclopedia of Science Fiction* in 1978, co-edited the anthology *Stars of Albion* (1979) with Christopher Priest, and collaborated with Christopher Evans to produce the *Other Edens* anthologies (1987, 1988, and 1989). His picture books, in conjunction with Malcolm Edwards, include *Alien Landscapes* (1979), *Tour of the Universe: The Journey of a Lifetime—The Recorded Diaries of Leio Scott and Caroline Luranski* (1980), *Magician: The Lost Journals of the Magus Geoffrey Carlyle* (1982), *Realms of Fantasy* (1983), and *Lost Realms* (1984).

During his early writing career in the 1970s, Holdstock began publishing what one reviewer called "hasty commercial efforts," mostly of the sword-and-sorcery type, under various noms de plume. At the same time he dabbled in novelizations of motion pictures and television programs: as Robert Black, he redacted two horror movies, *Legend of the Werewolf* (1976) and *The Satanists* (1978), as well as two television novelizations, *Bulman* (1984) and *One of Our Pigeons Is Missing* (1985); under his own name he published another movie novelization in 1985, *John Boorman's "The Emerald Forest."* As Richard Kirk, at times with Angus Wells, he wrote *Raven, Swordsmistress of Chaos* (1978), *A Time of Ghosts* (1978), and *Lords of the Shadows* (1979). Other early novels include, under the pseudonym of Ken Blake, *Cry Wolf* (1981), *The Untouchables* (1982), *Operation Susie* (1982), and *You'll Be All Right* (1982). As Chris Carlsen, he created the "Berserker" series, a quasi-Arthurian trilogy notable for its unflinching brutality: *Shadow of the Wolf* (1977), *The Bull Chief* (1977), and *The Horned Warrior* (1979). As Robert Faulcon, he continued this trend in a dark fantasy series shot through with graphic violence; under the rubric "Nighthunter," it includes *The Stalking* (1983) and *The Talisman* (1983), both later published as *The Stalking* (1987); *The Ghost Dance* (1984) and *The Shrine* (1984), both combined as *The Ghost Dance* (1987); and *The Hexing* (1984) and *The Labyrinth* (1987), again both combined as *The Hexing* (1988). Many of his works have never been published in the United States, and others, such as *The Bone Forest* (1991), had short runs on bookstore shelves.

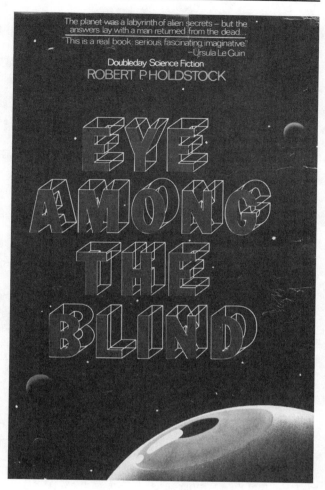

Dust jacket for the U.S. edition of Holdstock's 1976 novel, which introduces many of the themes on which he has elaborated in subsequent works (Richland County Public Library)

In his first true science-fiction novel, *Eye among the Blind* (1976), Holdstock introduces many of the themes that inform his later works: humanity's relationship to its environment, the impersonal and oblivious brutality of nature, the figure of the alien and the question of human alienation, and the malleability of time, evolution, and the dimensions of both the human intellect and unconscious. *Eye among the Blind* begins as a standard science-fiction novel, in which humans have landed on a distant, troubled planet, Ree'hdworld, with its own intelligent form of life, and it treats the typical issues of human intervention with alien species, including the problems of galactic colonialism and the limitations of scientific inquiry and human understanding. At the start of the novel the researcher Robert Zeitman (whose name, translated as "time-man," is a pun suggesting Holdstock's theme) returns to Ree'hdworld to reconcile with his estranged wife, Kristina, and to probe further the mysteries of the planet. Zeitman is accompanied by Kevin Maguire, a blind man who supposedly died seven hundred years before and has unaccountably risen from the dead because of a call from the planet or some force on it.

Zeitman finds the planet in turmoil as colonial authority breaks down and the natives grow hostile to the crowds of tourists invading their world while reports of ghosts on the planet, the mythic Pianhmar, increase. He also discovers his wife has taken an alien as her lover and has begun to enter into a mental symbiosis with that race. Zeitman, under the mystical guidance of Maguire, learns that the Pianhmar were once a powerful species that came to a cultural peak and then began a process of devolution, a pattern of Holdstock's that looks to the past for answers, not to the future, as in H. G. Wells's novels. In conjunction, a mental disease called the Fear has begun to decimate human populations on many planets; humans seem to have reached a point at which a god-like power or some evolutionary force of the universe has begun to destroy them, primarily as a result of their inability to fit into the universe and adapt to it. The return to nature, the importance of a species' place in the proper biosphere, and the metaphysics of death and life are all scrutinized as Zeitman realizes that the Pianhmar still exist in a hidden valley from whence their spirits emerge to metamorphose into Ree'hd and later the primitive Rundi. In this early work are precursors to other figures and themes of the later works: the obsessed scientist (a figure who often shares both Holdstock's age and his intellectual tenacity); the incomprehensible, hidden alien; and the conundrum of the nature of time. The Pianhmar foreshadow the mythogenesis of *Mythago Wood* (1984).

Holdstock's second, richer novel, *Earthwind* (1977), continues many of the concerns of the first, while it develops others that later find more mature expression in the Mythago novels. As Paul Kincaid comments in "Touching the Earth: The Fiction of Robert Holdstock" (*Vector,* October/November 1993), this book "has the first overt showing of the obsessions with myth and ritual which have become the most significant factors shaping his work." In *Earthwind,* survivors of a colonizing expedition to the planet Aeran have regressed to a stone-age culture with artwork and tumuli reminiscent of those on Earth (and similar to underground painting and artwork depicted in *Eye among the Blind*), particularly in Neolithic culture (a result of Holdstock's research in Ireland while he was writing the book). Elspeth Mueller, a member of a fringe group studying odd phenomena and cultures, arrives on Aeran about the same time as a quasi-military group from the paranoid, repressive federation that has demanded both ultimate authority over all cultures and ultimate obedience in the face of extreme penalties. The ship's rationalist, a shamanic figure named Peter Ashka (akin to Maguire in *Eye among the Blind),* attempts to

mediate between the shipmaster, Karl Gorstein; Elspeth; and the local clans, and so again the perspectives and goals of the scientist, bureaucrat, visionary, and primitive conflict. Ashka and Elspeth discover that primitive rock paintings follow the same pattern as scientific graphs of earth energy; here Holdstock clearly begins to mesh scientific inquiry with humanity's unconscious relationship to the natural world. Central to the mythology of the Aerani is also the Earthwind, a flow of seemingly supernatural air from deep in the earth, which their art also illustrates in parallel to a physical energy flow.

As usual, Holdstock does not explain his symbols or figures; he relies instead on their suggestive power and their appeal to the collective unconscious, drawing on images from early Earth cultures and asserting their universality. Peter Ashka, for instance, uses the Chinese *ching* to direct and augment his inquiries but finds its analogue in the Aerani holy man's oracle of the Earthsong, both of which affirm the essential oneness of the universe. Both are also thrown into relief by matching computer projections, as Holdstock continues to combine myth, mysticism, science, and evolution.

Moreover, the enigma of the relativity of time also becomes an issue, as it was in *Eye among the Blind,* for just as the Pianhmar live in a temporal construct of their own, so the creatures of Aeran live in a world where time is flexible and mercurial, not linear. Kincaid notes that "this idea of time not flowing in the conventional straight line but like a wind, gusting and swirling, is exquisitely original." Creatures who seem to teleport actually flex time, not space, and the effect of the planet on the human brain reverts people to an earlier primitive state in which the brain regains the connection between its higher functions and the unconscious time center lost over the course of evolution. Complicating each of the "beyonders'" problems is the fact that the longer one remains on Aeran, the more one's mind erodes, erasing all memories and conceptions of self. Elspeth and Gorstein survive and assimilate the effects of the Earthwind, returning to a more primeval harmony with the planet and becoming stone-age Aerani, adept in the savage world. As such, Gorstein is a forerunner of many of the characters whom Ryhope Wood transmutes in the Mythago books, particularly Christian Huxley.

In *Where Time Winds Blow* (1982) Holdstock examines many of the same themes from a slightly different perspective. Again, the setting is a planet hostile to humanity with an indistinct, mythical alien presence. Human obsession and curiosity once more form the driving motives of the action. VanderZande's World draws men and women from all over known space because of the time winds, gusts of power that sweep down canyons and deposit relics from other ages and then rage through and change the land and its temporal reality again. As in the previous novels, the planet is an unfamiliar and forbidding place to humans: not only is its atmosphere acrid, capable of searing the human retina in a short period of time, but indistinct forces and elements of the biosphere dull human emotion to empty people of any of the vibrancy that first impelled them to the world.

The novel is divided into four sections that follow the main characters as they explore VanderZande's World in search of treasure and themselves: Lena Tanoway and Leo Faulcon, two lovers gradually losing their sense of themselves; Kris Dojaan, an idealist (like Elspeth Mueller) who has come to search for a brother, lost to the time winds, whom he emphatically believes is still alive; and their supervisor, Commander Ensavlion, another of Holdstock's obsessed scientists (like Gorstein, George Huxley from *Mythago Wood,* and Alexander Lytton from *The Hollowing,* 1993). Each searches passionately for the knowledge to discover and enter a personal Shangri-la. Faulcon loses both Lena and Kris to the time winds and is ostracized because he refuses to commit suicide, a practice born, like others, of pure superstition among the people of VanderZande's World. Eventually, he submits himself to the time winds but is sent back by the power that controls them, at which point much of the mystery is solved; Faulcon journeys to a distant valley, the source of the power, and enters a quasi-mythical world controlled by forces (like the Pianhmar) beyond human comprehension.

Where Time Winds Blow examines the fitness of humanity, both morally and physically, to occupy worlds other than Earth. VanderZande's World has several moons, one of which exerts a peculiar, half-comprehended effect on humans; it also has an odd atmospheric effect called a *fiersig,* which alters emotions and creates rage and depression; its fauna live in odd symbiotic combinations utterly foreign to Earth zoology. In view of these characteristics, Holdstock's medical degrees and interest in biospheres informs his presentation of humanity's attempts at colonization in these three novels, yielding a pessimistic verdict. Greed, stupidity, arrogance, and hubris damn humans' attempts to coexist with other species and with one another, while physical limitations—biological, chemical, and genetic, for example—doom attempts by humankind to accommodate themselves to alien worlds and vice versa. In *Where Time Winds Blow* a group of settlers called the Manchanged have undergone radical surgery and bodily revision in order to survive on the planet without oxygen masks, protective suits, and other technologies; yet, they live a precarious, hardscrabble existence trying to farm genetically altered crops in a hostile environment. All others, who live encapsuled in atmosphere suits, closed vehi-

Dust jacket for the U.S. edition of the novel that won the 1984 World Fantasy Award (Richland County Public Library)

cles, and sealed, movable cities (the largest of which is called Steel City), isolate themselves from the planet and its dangers and hold the Manchanged in contempt. Although there is no regression to the atavism so prominent in much of Holdstock's other work, *Where Time Winds Blow* still leaves readers with a picture of humankind's lack of understanding of the forces of the universe and its probable unfitness, as a species, to inhabit or control much of it.

The 1984 World Fantasy winner *Mythago Wood,* based on a novelette of the same title (published in *The Magazine of Fantasy and Science Fiction,* September 1981) earned Holdstock his first major commercial success under his own name. Set in the 1940s in Gloucestershire, the novel combines Celtic and pre-Celtic folklore, Jungian archetypes, and modern technology, a mix of old mythic patterns with a powerful mythopoesis and a shifting, mercurial natural world. Although adjudged a fantasy novel, it is, as Brian W. Aldiss and David Wingrove comment in *Trillion Year Spree: The History of Science*

Fiction (1986), a work that "attains much of its power from its science fictional mode." In an article in *Extrapolation* (Summer 1993) Carroll Brown avers that it "is not truly a fantasy novel, but science fiction" and argues that "Holdstock examines the process of myth and its role in modern society as he attempts to reintegrate myth and its apparent displacer, science." His observation that "Holdstock conflates science, its paradigms, and its 'myths'" to examine mythology and to remarry "these two seemingly disparate elements" agrees with the assessment in John Clute and Peter Nicholls's *The Encyclopedia of Science Fiction* (1993) that in *Mythago Wood* Holdstock's "two careers suddenly and thankfully converged in a tale whose elaborate proprieties of rationale are driven by narrative energies and an exuberance of language previously restricted to his Berserker novels, written as Chris Carlsen."

Other factors buttress the classification of the novel as science fiction. *Mythago Wood* in particular adheres to a careful chronological construction through the presentation of particular dates in Steven Huxley's narrative and in journals, letters, and other accounts that support his, much in the manner of Mary Shelley's *Frankenstein* (1818), to which the novel alludes in several places. Trains and train schedules, airplanes and fuel expenses, and electric lights and kerosene lamps are all included to create a technological underpinning to the action. In a passage that looks back to the energy patterns in *Earthwind,* Huxley reads in his father, George's, journal of "an energy associated with all the life that grew there. He had found a spiral vortex around each tree, and those spirals bounded not just trees, but whole stands of trees, and glades." Christian Huxley explains to his puzzled brother that "The old man believed that all life is surrounded by an energetic aura," which he mapped and measured.

Yet, the basic narrative and flavor remains that of fantasy, for the story involves a quest into the "perilous realm" where time runs differently and people are changed by their experiences. The setting of the novel, Ryhope Wood, although only several square miles in area, encompasses all time and huge landscapes, and it is a psychomachic representation of George Huxley's mind; the action of the novel is an odyssey through an inner space as dimensionless as outer space. As in most fantasy, characters enter the magical land and confront external representations of internal fears, powers, qualities, and limitations, and one of Holdstock's talents is to inspire that mainstay of fantasy, wonder—in this case, wonder in human relationships past, present, and future to the outer world.

In *Mythago Wood* Holdstock pursues his exploration of humanity's relationship with its environment and his inquiry into the human heart of darkness, but he has moved from the alien planets of his pure science-fiction novels into a realm composed of anthropological, mythical, and psychological impulses. In Ryhope Wood, one of the few remnants of the British forest primeval, the characters move into a primitive world filled with incarnations and vestiges of both cultural and personal dreams; as a result they confront the primitive within themselves and reestablish lost ties with the world and rituals superseded by modern mechanized life. George Huxley's sons' consequent entry into this land, where legends and forgotten archetypes spring alive from Huxley's interaction with the energy of the wood, thus recalls a standard pattern of folklore and fantasy, for both visit the boundary where the physical world abuts that other world of timeless wonder and possibility. In the interview with Cary, Holdstock states that he has "been obsessively interested in Earth Magic (not the New Age Version, but in the power of people and places), the symbols, the icons with which we mark territory." The genius in the Mythago books lies in the power of the storytelling as Holdstock admixes the ancient places and figures of myth and Earth magic with a science-fiction explanation of their nature, something he began in *Earthwind,* to demonstrate their mutual compatibility.

A further change from the purely science-fiction writings is Holdstock's concern in all the Mythago books with families, particularly fathers and children. In a review of *The Hollowing* in *Interzone* (December 1993), John Clute wrote that "The story is the story Holdstock tells best, and tells most often: The tale of the Lost Child searching for its Parent, or whose parent is searching for it." Like Charles Dickens, he generally excludes the mother as an effective or important figure and sets the father at the center, much as in his novelization of Boorman's *The Emerald Forest,* which appeared shortly after *Mythago Wood.* Literally and symbolically, Steven and Christian's story tells of their desire both to revolt from yet join with their estranged father. In *Lavondyss: Journey to an Unknown Region* (1988), Tallis Keeton must search for her older half brother, who is tied closely to her by their father's love. In *The Hollowing* Richard Bradley's entry into Ryhope Wood is motivated by his son Alex's disappearance, the result of Tallis's father returning from the wood after searching for his missing daughter. In addition, the wisdom-figure of the shaman or old man, who directs the children, slips in and out of the stories: Huxley himself; Edward Wynne-Jones trapped in the wood; Tallis's grandfather, Owen Keeton; old Gaunt the caretaker; and then Ralph Vaughan Williams the composer. Holdstock frames three narratives—the desire to claim the father's love, the need to supplant him, and the need for his protection and acceptance—in relationships absent in his previous novels.

The word *mythago* comes from "myth imago" and indicates "the idealized form of a myth creature," which develops in ancient unspoiled woodlands when the need arises, generated by a shared collective unconscious; mythagos "grow from the power of hate, and fear, and form in the natural woodlands." Holdstock reminds readers that there is magic in the earth, magic of, by, and for the earth, and that humanity lost and must recover it. In *Mythago Wood* George Huxley begins to generate mythagos in Ryhope Wood, estranging himself from his family and becoming bound by the world he half creates. The strange land inside the wood leads back through time to an Eden or Heaven, and Huxley desires to discover its secrets and experience the epiphany it offers. When Christian, the older son, intrudes and competes with him for the wood and the Guinevere archetype that each projects, battle begins. Then Steven returns from his convalescence after World War II, and all three members of the family yield to the call of the wood, which is in part themselves.

Myth circles within myth: the story of the conflict of father and son instigates the rivalry of the brothers for a beautiful woman, which leads to the epic journey to the lost land and incorporates the convention of the sidekick. After Christian kidnaps Guiwenneth, Steven, with the help of the aviator Harry Keeton, sets off to reclaim her, tracking Christian through the constantly changing wood and trying to make sense of the various stories and legends it contains. Once again, Holdstock's interest with the past, with humankind's return to an earlier, more primal, more natural state emerges as he concomitantly examines the process of mythmaking itself. Christian becomes a brutal, primitive invader, adept with all manner of weapons, the Outsider (perhaps symbolizing Christianity) whom other (pagan, Bronze Age) cultures fear, while Steven becomes the avenging younger brother who in legend overcomes and supplants the evil elder. Keeton notes of him that he too has become "increasingly adept with sword and spear" and that "Steven has become a myth character himself!" As both move toward Lavondyss, trailed by their father in the form of the primal Urscumug (the boar-shaped "first hero"), they traverse cultural settings from a medieval fort to a Roman villa to Bronze Age villages to earlier hunter-gatherer encampments and meet various figures, including a shell-shocked Tommy from World War I; mailed, medieval knights; and earth-daubed storytellers from prehistoric times. Along the way Holdstock weaves in folktales and myths, many of Celtic stock, as the primary characters merge into the secondary world.

In the end, at the gate of fire that marks the boundary to Lavondyss, Christian falls, fulfilling a

Dust jacket for the U.S. edition of the second novel in the Mythago Wood series (Richland County Public Library)

prophecy, albeit from an unpredictable source, and Steven discovers, in fairy-tale fashion, that the father he sees as a beast does love him and makes him a promise that he will return with Guiwenneth from Lavondyss. In the coda to the novel, another strand of folklore that runs inseparably through the story, a warrior awaits the return of his beloved at her father's grave, and a legendary figure from an early part of the story names the valley "Where the Hunter Waits." The hunter is Steven himself—thus endowing Steven with his own place in the legend; the story has not ended. Holdstock, in all the Mythago books, constantly defeats expectations and leaves much unresolved or unclear. Perhaps because his characters, like people in real life, can never know the whole story, he mimics reality in his narrative strategy so that the reader too is left with questions and doubts but is also left wanting more.

Lavondyss, the second of the Mythago novels, provides some answers to the questions raised in *Mythago*

Wood. Set several years after the previous novel, *Lavondyss* shifts to a different protagonist, Tallis Keeton, Harry's half sister, and her obsession with the wood that calls to her as it did to Harry and to her dead grandfather. Through local legend, visions, seemingly spectral visitations and portents, letters, and journals, Tallis begins to understand what Ryhope Wood is and what it contains. After reading part of one of the journals in the Huxleys' now overgrown lodge, she tells her father that Harry is close, "But he's in the wrong part of the Otherworld. . . . He's lost in hell and he needs me to go to him."

This comment reveals a substantial change in Holdstock's presentation of his magical world. First, his central character is a girl, not a woman like Elspeth in *Earthwind;* second, her father's adoration of her contrasts markedly with George Huxley's abandonment of his family because of his obsession, and it strengthens the link to her half brother. Third, the tone in *Lavondyss* shifts from the heroic and romantic to something darker and more sinister, a reminder of the earlier dark fantasies. The Ryhope Wood of the first novel held its perils and dangers but could not be construed as a hell, whereas from the start of *Lavondyss,* shadows and death dominate, starting with Owen Keeton, who dies in the snow, peering through a gateway into the heartlands of Ryhope but lacking the knowledge and the youth to enter. One of Tallis's first views through a gateway shows her a handsome warrior dying at the base of a tree while carrion birds pick at corpses and scarecrow figures wander among the dead.

Through Tallis and her discoveries and subsequent journey into the wood, Holdstock reveals more of its puzzling nature. Tallis's manufacture and use of masks representing elemental forms allow her to see into the wood, to understand its entrances and guards. Little by little, she begins to penetrate and to explain to her father what she knows about the wood. Later, in fact, as a young woman lost for years with Scathach, an incarnation of the warrior she first saw, she meets Edward Wynne-Jones, Huxley's companion, who has been long lost in Mythago Wood. He explains to her much of what he has learned about the wood since he has lived there. Like Steven and Christian, her search for a lost loved one leads her to become part of the legends that understructure Ryhope, and part of her task is to understand the stories she is told, some of which hark back to *Mythago Wood.* Furthermore, she too becomes a teller of tales, and Kincaid notes that "in her name we not only get echoes of the ancient tale-teller Taliesin but also of the point Holdstock is emphasising, about the creative nature of myth and its inspirational role in the creative process long after its ritualistic role is forgotten."

Tallis, for instance, meets Scathach in the company of one of the Jagud, the mythic band of warriors originally responsible for Guiwenneth (again Holdstock insinuates linked legends in the form of an early Round Table and a mix of the Guinevere and Celtic princess legends). She explains the oolering men, who are able to open "gateways" to the "otherworld" and whom George and Steven Huxley referred to as *shamiga.* They function as guardians of the "hollowings," places of passage into the woods. She runs across references to earlier characters, including Harry, and the mythagos spawned by them in their passages through the wood. She meets Wynne-Jones's children, including Tig, generated out of the leaf mold of the forest, a mythago raised from Wynne-Jones's unconscious. All of these discoveries and revelations complicate readers' understanding and perception of the setting. Ryhope Wood is not simply the faerie of high fantasy; it is an Escherian world where loops turn on themselves and disappear or reappear impossibly.

Tallis's own story includes a chapter in which she dies, is absorbed by the forest, grows into a tree, falls to the ground, becomes a totem, and witnesses the release of Harry, as a blind neolithic boy, from Lavondyss, which has become a place of horror, murder, and interminable ice and storm. She then returns to herself in the wood, survives to become the elder of a primitive tribe filled with her children and grandchildren, and dies when Harry, still as he was when he entered the wood as a young man, comes to claim her. Yet, at the instant she dies as an old woman, a thirteen-year-old Tallis climbs back through the hollowing through which she originally entered, to reassure her anxious father that she is safe and to let him lead her home. Readers are left wondering which ending to accept. Perhaps both are possible, revealing Holdstock experimenting yet again with the mythmaking process and the question of the flexibility of time.

The third Mythago novel, *The Hollowing,* picks up several years after the action of *Lavondyss.* Holdstock continues his major themes and concerns but also continues to stretch his scope. The usual preliterate and mythic Celtic and northern figures appear, but he adds North American Indian myths, classical Greek heroes, and Indo-European figures. Clute comments that "the long sequence featuring Jason and the Argonauts . . . is in fact a tour de force of seeming easeful but in fact extremely sophisticated fabulating." Central to the story are forms of the tales of Sir Gawain and various trickster figures. The characters around whom the novel is built are no longer simply inhabitants who live on the fringe of the wood; they are scientists and anthropologists living in, exploring, and conducting experiments on the wood, including a massive Frenchman, Arnauld Lacan; a Native American, Helen Silverlock; a pair of Finns; and the leader of the group, a Scot named Alexander Lytton. Yet, they are linked to previous characters by the fact that their explorations into the wood are journeys in search of parts of themselves.

The main plot, however, details a father's search for his lost child. When James Keeton stumbles out of the wood after several years of searching for Tallis, the one person he responds to is Alex Bradley, a young friend of his daughter's. Upon Keeton's death, Alex disappears, and several years later Helen confronts his father, Richard, with the news that he is still alive, lost in Ryhope Wood and beginning to assert his own nightmares and fears in the form of mythagos, ultimately destabilizing the wood. Alex has created himself a refuge in his mythago of Gawain's Green Chapel (another conflation of myths in its pagan elf-mound form and its later Christian incarnation), and his dreams and nightmares are eating away at the symbolic fabric of George Huxley's unconscious creation. Thus, the natural lack of compassion of the wood itself merges with the menace of the Jabberwock and its cousins to produce a place that springs from the human unconscious and yet is alien.

In *The Bone Forest,* a collection of eight previously published short stories, one can see Holdstock experimenting with various approaches to his primary subjects. In the novella "The Bone Forest" he goes back in time before the action of the Mythago novels to tell more of the story of George Huxley, his obsession with Ryhope Wood, and the disintegration of his relationship with his family. Told in Huxley's voice, it details his first entries into Ryhope and his generation of a mythago ghost, or double. A story first published in *The Magazine of Fantasy and Science Fiction* (1986), "Thorn" treats the conflict between older nature culture and worship and Christianity as Thomas the mason, torn between the two, chisels the face of the old god, at its insistence, into a wall of the new church. Written as a forerunner to the tale of Taliesin, "Time of the Tree" narrates the passage of time from the point of view of an elm as it watches seasons, animals, and peoples come and go. In "The Shapechanger" the Gawain mythago appears in a different form than in *The Hollowing,* and the action of *Ancient Echoes* (1995) is foreshadowed.

Ancient Echoes is perhaps Holdstock's most profound and brutal book. While the other novels and stories recount grim experiences and savage places and times, this novel is filled with cruelty that exceeds even the ferocious early sword-and-sorcery books. As a boy, Jack Chatwin falls into trance-like visions in which he witnesses a man and woman he calls the Greyface and Greenface fleeing from others; he is seeing back through time to the plight of two outcasts who have left their city. As the same time, John Garth, who "dowses" for ancient cities, comes to Chatwin's hometown, meets Jack, and enlists him in his quest to find the ghost city he calls Glanum, which rides a wave of time from which it surfaces into different eras. Angela Harris, a classmate, is fascinated by Jack's ability and the physical symptoms, such as a halo of energy, that evidence it. Jack and Angela grow apart as young adults but later come together again, marry, and have a daughter, Natalie.

Angela has become a researcher and with her group begins a series of physical and psychological tests on Jack as he dreams his way into the slippage of time that he has experienced. While there, he helps the woman Greenface to escape her pursuers, separating her from her brother, but in return Greyface finds his way into Jack's world as a spirit and threatens Natalie. He will permit the girl to live only if Jack returns his sister, so Jack, like the Huxleys in Ryhope Wood, must venture into this shifting world to find Greenface and save someone beloved to him. His adventures in many ways parallel those of the earlier books and use the same interfaces of time, nature, culture, and humanity. *Ancient Echoes,* however, involves bitter marital strife, prolonged suffering, despicable slaughter, grotesque tortures, and incomprehensible forces grinding lives as they pass. In the end Jack lives in two worlds, drawn by the magic of one and held by love of his daughter and the demands of the other.

It must be noted that these novels are not simple commercial sequels that visit the same terrain or inject the same shopworn clichés of fantasy; each builds from the previous but develops and bends off in different directions, luring the reader with the promise of new psychological landscapes within the limited external geography of Ryhope Wood and similar settings. Robert Holdstock has several undisclosed projects in mind for the future, but the majority take place in the world of mythagos.

Interviews:

Catie Cary, "Robert Holdstock: Interview," *Vector* (October/November 1993): 3–6;

Stan Nicholls, "Robert Holdstock: Plays with His Cerebral Cortex," in his *Wordsmiths of Wonder* (London: Orbit, 1993), pp. 99–110;

Charles N. Brown, "Robert Holdstock: Lost Landscapes, Grand Obsessions," *Locus,* 36 (April 1996).

References:

Carroll Brown, "The Flame in the Heart of the Wood: The Integration of Myth and Science in Robert Holdstock's *Mythago Wood*," *Extrapolation,* 34 (Summer 1993): 158–172;

Paul Kincaid, "Touching the Earth: The Fiction of Robert Holdstock," *Vector* (October/November 1993): 7–9.

Fred Hoyle

(24 June 1915 – 20 August 2001)

Salvatore Proietti
Università degli Studi di Roma "La Sapienza"

BOOKS: *Some Recent Researches in Solar Physics* (Cambridge: Cambridge University Press, 1949);

The Nature of the Universe (Oxford: Blackwell, 1950; New York: Harper, 1950; revised edition, Oxford: Blackwell, 1960; New York: Harper, 1960);

A Decade of Decision (London: Heinemann, 1953); republished as *Man and Materialism* (New York: Harper, 1956; London: Allen & Unwin, 1957);

Frontiers of Astronomy (London: Heinemann, 1955; New York: Harper, 1955);

The Black Cloud (London: Heinemann, 1957; New York: Harper, 1957);

Ossian's Ride (London: Heinemann, 1959; New York: Harper, 1959);

A for Andromeda, by Hoyle and John Elliot (London: Souvenir, 1962; New York: Harper, 1962);

Astronomy (London: Macdonald, 1962; Garden City, N.Y.: Doubleday, 1962);

A Contradiction in the Argument of Malthus (Hull: Publications Committee, University of Hull, 1963);

Fifth Planet, by Hoyle and Geoffrey Hoyle (London: Heinemann, 1963; New York: Harper & Row, 1963);

Star Formation (London: Her Majesty's Stationery Office, 1963);

Andromeda Breakthrough, by Hoyle and Elliot (London: Souvenir, 1964; New York: Harper & Row, 1964);

Of Men and Galaxies (Seattle: University of Washington Press, 1964; London: Heinemann, 1965);

The Asymmetry of Time (Canberra: Australian National University, 1965);

Encounter with the Future (New York: Trident, 1965);

Galaxies, Nuclei, and Quasars (New York: Harper & Row, 1965; London: Heinemann, 1966);

Nucleosynthesis in Massive Stars and Supernovae, by Hoyle and William A. Fowler (Chicago: University of Chicago Press, 1965);

Man in the Universe (New York: Columbia University Press, 1966);

October the First Is Too Late (London: Heinemann, 1966; New York: Harper & Row, 1966);

Element 79 (New York: New American Library, 1967);

Rockets in Ursa Major, by Hoyle and Geoffrey Hoyle (London: Heinemann, 1969; New York: Harper & Row, 1969);

Seven Steps to the Sun, by Hoyle and Geoffrey Hoyle (London: Heinemann, 1970; New York: Harper & Row, 1970);

The Molecule Men and The Monster of Loch Ness: Two Short Novels, by Hoyle and Geoffrey Hoyle (London: Heinemann, 1971; New York: Harper & Row, 1971);

The New Face of Science (New York: World, 1971);

From Stonehenge to Modern Cosmology (San Francisco: Freeman, 1972);

The Inferno, by Hoyle and Geoffrey Hoyle (London: Heinemann, 1973; New York: Harper & Row, 1973);

Nicolaus Copernicus: An Essay on His Life and Work (London: Heinemann, 1973; New York: Harper & Row, 1973);

Action-at-a-Distance in Physics and Cosmology, by Hoyle and J. V. Narlikar (San Francisco: Freeman, 1974);

Into Deepest Space, by Hoyle and Geoffrey Hoyle (New York: Harper & Row, 1974; London: Heinemann, 1975);

Astronomy and Cosmology: A Modern Course (San Francisco: Freeman, 1975);

Astronomy Today (London: Heinemann, 1975); republished as *Highlights in Astronomy* (San Francisco: Freeman, 1975);

Energy or Extinction? The Case for Nuclear Energy (London: Heinemann, 1977; second edition, London & Exeter, N.H.: Heinemann Educational, 1979);

The Incandescent Ones, by Hoyle and Geoffrey Hoyle (London: Heinemann, 1977; New York: Harper & Row, 1977);

On Stonehenge (London: Heinemann Educational, 1977; San Francisco: Freeman, 1977);

Fred Hoyle (photograph from the dust jacket for Home Is Where the Wind Blows, *1994)*

Ten Faces of the Universe (London: Heinemann, 1977; San Francisco: Freeman, 1977);

The Cosmogony of the Solar System (Cardiff: University College Cardiff Press, 1978; Short Hills, N.J.: Enslow, 1979);

Lifecloud: The Origin of Life in the Universe, by Hoyle and Chandra Wickramasinghe (London: Dent, 1978; New York: Harper & Row, 1979);

The Westminster Disaster, by Hoyle and Geoffrey Hoyle, edited by Barbara Hoyle (London: Heinemann, 1978; New York: Harper & Row, 1978);

Diseases from Space, by Hoyle and Wickramasinghe (London: Dent, 1979; New York: Harper & Row, 1979);

Commonsense in Nuclear Energy, by Hoyle and Geoffrey Hoyle (London: Heinemann Educational, 1980; San Francisco: Freeman, 1980);

The Origin of Life, by Hoyle and Wickramasinghe (Cardiff: University College Cardiff Press, 1980);

The Physics-Astronomy Frontier, by Hoyle and Narlikar (San Francisco: Freeman, 1980);

The Relation of Astronomy to Biology (Cardiff: University College Cardiff Press, 1980);

Steady-State Cosmology Re-Visited (Cardiff: University College Cardiff Press, 1980);

Evolution from Space, by Hoyle and Wickramasinghe (London: Dent, 1981; New York: Simon & Schuster, 1982);

Ice: The Ultimate Human Catastrophe (London: Hutchinson, 1981; New York: Continuum, 1981);

The Quasar Controversy Resolved (Cardiff: University College Cardiff Press, 1981);

Space Travellers: The Bringers of Life, by Hoyle and Wickramasinghe, edited by Barbara Hoyle (Cardiff: University College Cardiff Press, 1981; Hillside, N.J.: Enslow, 1982);

The Universe: Past and Present Reflections (Cardiff: University College Cardiff Press, 1981);

Copernicus: Narrative and Credo, libretto by Hoyle, music by Leo Smit (New York: Fischer, 1982);

The Energy Pirate, by Hoyle and Geoffrey Hoyle (Loughborough, U.K.: Ladybird, 1982);

The Giants of Universal Park, by Hoyle and Geoffrey Hoyle (Loughborough, U.K.: Ladybird, 1982);

The Frozen Planet of Azuron, by Hoyle and Geoffrey Hoyle (Loughborough, U.K.: Ladybird, 1982);

The Planet of Death, by Hoyle and Geoffrey Hoyle (Loughborough, U.K.: Ladybird, 1982);

The Anglo-Australian Telescope (Cardiff: University College Cardiff Press, 1982);

Facts and Dogmas in Cosmology and Elsewhere (Cambridge & New York: Cambridge University Press, 1982);

The Universe According to Hoyle (Hillside, N.J.: Enslow, 1982);

Why Neo-Darwinism Does Not Work (Cardiff: University College Cardiff Press, 1982);

Proof That Life Is Cosmic, by Hoyle and Wickramasinghe (Sri Lanka: Institute of Fundamental Studies, 1982);

The Intelligent Universe: A New View of Creation and Evolution (London: Joseph, 1983; New York: Holt, Rinehart & Winston, 1984);

Flight (Loughborough, U.K.: Ladybird, 1984);

From Grains to Bacteria, by Hoyle and Wickramasinghe (Cardiff: University College Cardiff Press, 1984);

Comet Halley (London: Joseph, 1985; New York: St. Martin's Press, 1985);

Living Comets, by Hoyle and Wickramasinghe (Cardiff: University College Cardiff Press, 1985);

The Small World of Fred Hoyle (London: Joseph, 1986);

Viruses from Space and Related Matters, by Hoyle, Wickramasinghe, and John Watkins (Cardiff: University College Cardiff Press, 1986);

Archaeopteryx, the Primordial Bird: A Case of Fossil Forgery, by Hoyle and Wickramasinghe (Swansea, U.K.: Davies, 1986);

Cosmic Life-Force, by Hoyle and Wickramsinghe (London: Dent, 1988; New York: Paragon, 1990);

The Theory of Cosmic Grains, by Hoyle and Wickramasinghe (Dordrecht, Netherlands & Boston: Kluwer, 1991);

Our Place in the Cosmos: The Unfinished Revolution, by Hoyle and Wickramasinghe (London: Dent, 1993);

The Origin of the Universe and the Origin of Religion (Wakefield, R.I.: Moyer Bell, 1993);

Home Is Where the Wind Blows: Chapters from a Cosmologist's Life (Mill Valley, Cal.: University Science, 1994; Oxford: Oxford University Press, 1997);

Lectures on Cosmology and Action at a Distance Electrodynamics, by Hoyle and Narlikar (River Edge, N.J.: World Scientific, 1996);

Life on Mars? The Case of a Cosmic Heritage, by Hoyle and Wickramasinghe (Redland, U.K.: Clinical Press, 1997);

Mathematics of Evolution (Memphis, Tenn.: Acorn, 1999);

A Different Approach to Cosmology: From a Static Universe through the Big Bang towards Reality, by Hoyle, Narlikar, and Geoffrey Burbidge (Cambridge: Cambridge University Press, 1999; New York: Cambridge University Press, 2000).

OTHER: *Fundamental Studies and the Future of Science,* edited by Chandra Wickramasinghe, foreword by Hoyle (Cardiff: University College Cardiff Press, 1984);

Astronomical Origins of Life: Steps toward Panspermia, edited by Hoyle and Wickramasinghe (Dordrecht, Netherlands & Boston: Kluwer, 1999).

PRODUCED SCRIPT: *A for Andromeda,* television, by Hoyle and John Elliot, BBC, 3 October–14 November 1961;

The Andromeda Breakthrough, television, by Hoyle and Elliot, BBC, 28 June–2 August 1962.

When Fred Hoyle published his first science-fiction novel, *The Black Cloud,* in 1957, he was already a distinguished and world-famous scientist and teacher, on his way toward a prestigious astronomy chair at Cambridge, and about to join the research staff of the cutting-edge observatory of the Mount Palomar radio telescope. Both his literary and his scientific careers thrived until his death in 2001. Among the many British scientists who have tried their hand at science fiction, Hoyle is the most important. His science-fiction output was steady for decades, along with a prodigious production of scholarship and popularizations in various fields of science. The quality of this output made him one of the principal figures in pre–New Wave British science fiction.

Fred Hoyle was born in Bingley, Yorkshire, in 1915, the son of Ben Hoyle, a wool merchant, and Mabel Pickard Hoyle. He was educated at Cambridge, where he started teaching in 1939. In effect, his biography is closely related to his academic career, with his full professorship beginning in 1958 and his post as director of the Institute of Theoretical Astronomy, which he held between 1966 and 1972, when he retired. He also taught physics and astronomy at the California Institute of Technology, Pasadena, and at Cornell, while earning a long list of honorary degrees, visiting professorships, and prizes and awards from academic and scientific institutions around the world. He was made a Fellow of the Royal Society in 1957 and was knighted in 1972. He married Barbara Clark in 1939, and the couple had a son, Geoffrey, born in 1942, and a daughter, Elizabeth Jeanne. Geoffrey Hoyle had an important role in his father's literary career; starting with *Fifth Planet* in 1963, the two collaborated on thirteen books. Hoyle, in 1962 and 1964, also collaborated on two novels with television scriptwriter John Elliot. The importance of collaboration in Hoyle's science-fiction career seems to represent his effort to extend the scientific ideal of teamwork to literary activity. The whole trajectory of his career is indeed marked by a stubborn refusal to accept any split or separation between humanistic and scientific culture.

In Hoyle's nonfiction one can clearly detect an attempt to escape from the specialized context of academic writing: he wrote scholarly works and textbooks published by prestigious university presses, but also books of popularization aimed at the larger public; in Britain, Hoyle soon became a familiar radio and television personality as a popular expert in the fields of astronomy and cosmology. He emphasized the speculative, even visionary, aspect of scientific inquiry: for him astrophysics and theoretical physics became cosmology and at times cosmogony, always in an attempt to be both rigorous and provocative. As an astronomer and cosmologist he championed, starting with his 1950 book *The Nature of the Universe*—which summarized research Hoyle conducted with Bondi and Thomas Gold, culminating in breakthrough papers published in 1948—the "steady-state theory" of the creation and development of the universe, in opposition to the dominant Big Bang theory (a term Hoyle is credited with coining as mockery). Quite often, the speculative dimension in some of Hoyle's works assumes the tone of a narrative hypothesis, offering stories or histories of various celestial bodies, the solar system, the galaxy, and the universe.

Some works are admittedly visionary; for example, *Of Men and Galaxies* (1964) casts severe doubts on the possibility of interstellar travel but stresses the possibility of an exchange of information with hypothetical alien species; there could even be a galactic library or information point that could help Earth learn, in its future progress, from the history of other worlds. Hoyle's notoriety also benefited from his books on subjects of popular science, from dinosaur fossils to the Stonehenge mystery. In other cases he directly tackled political issues, for example, in his advocacy of nuclear energy. Occasionally, Hoyle's works seem to present science-fiction hypotheses as scientific fact. *Diseases from Space* (1979) and later works, for example, warn of comets carrying incubated viruses and spreading diseases across space. Similarly dubious are those books that attack Charles Darwin's theory of evolution in the name of a sort of secular creationist thesis, such as *Evolution from Space* (1981). Life and intelligence are too complex to be the mere result of accidental processes; Hoyle imagines the beginning of life on a planet as the result of cosmic clouds, under the influence of a superior intelligent agency: not a god, but an incommensu-

Dust jacket for the U.S. edition of the first novel Hoyle wrote with his son, Geoffrey Hoyle (Richland County Public Library)

rably powerful entity, who is carrying out a plan in the known universe.

As a science-fiction writer Hoyle bridges scientific romance and more recent generations. As a scientist-writer he is a part of a tradition in British science-fiction history, beginning with H. G. Wells and including biologists J. D. Bernal and J. B. S. Haldane, which was a strong influence on Olaf Stapledon and Aldous Huxley. After World War II, only a handful of writers—such as Hoyle, Arthur C. Clarke, and Patrick Moore (and, to an extent, J. G. Ballard)—share this background. More recently, British science fiction has largely been the domain of authors with a humanistic background, presenting—especially in the New Wave avant-garde—science and scientists as negative or irrelevant forces. Hoyle has come to represent, for many critics, "traditional" and obsolete values such as escapism, scientism, and didacticism, and his characters have been criticized as lacking in psychological depth. He is, in other words, much in the same position as Isaac Asimov in the United States; a popular personality and a best-selling author beyond the confines of the genre "ghetto," he has been often neglected or dismissed by critics and reviewers as a "commercial" author. Most of his novels have remained continuously in print in Penguin paperbacks. Hoyle is definitely not an avant-garde writer, and he relies heavily on a more-or-less Victorian realist framework. Furthermore, much like Asimov, his writings show their strengths and qualities when considered broadly, while closer scrutiny often highlights stylistic flaws and weaknesses. As a rule, his protagonists are scientists and intellectuals whose inquisitive curiosity leads them to tackle some sort of mysterious or unexpected event. In their ensuing puzzle-solving endeavors, their certainty and self-confidence are shattered or at least seriously affected. In Hoyle's novels there is no intellectual conqueror of the universe. Instead, all inquiries meet a degree of resistance and recalcitrance from their targets, and there is always a price to pay for the acquisition of knowledge. This knowledge always brings new questions. Hoyle stresses the political and economic context of scientific research; also, contrary to the stereotypes of "hard" science fiction, an extreme emphasis is placed on the role of information (including information sciences). In this sense he distances himself from positivist rationalism and comes closer to contemporary anxieties.

In *The Black Cloud,* Hoyle's first novel and one of his best, the puzzle revolves around a sentient cloud of cosmic gas. The first half of the book chronicles in detail the independent, exciting process of discovery of a cosmic intruder by British and American teams of astronomers. An eventual joint effort dispels all doubts: the immense gaseous globe is heading for the sun; the effects are going to be apocalyptic. The reaction of both governments is narrow-minded; with social control their top priority, their only preoccupation is secrecy. Cambridge astronomer Chris Kingsley, leader of the British team, cynically suspects that he and his collaborators are about to be confined or imprisoned; through negotiations and maneuvers he establishes, under his direction, a center for researching the cloud. The international brain trust is locked with its high-tech equipment in the new base of Nortonstowe, Gloucestershire. Nortonstowe becomes indispensable as a monitoring and communication center—the only one able to avoid interference from the cloud—when a heat wave, followed by a long freeze, kills a quarter of the world's population. The scientists hypothesize that the cloud is sentient, based on its otherwise inexplicable movements and activities. Dialogue is successfully established; the cloud, astonished at finding intelligent life on a planetary surface, learns English and is fed the *Encyclopaedia Britannica.* Its mind owes its enormous efficiency to its modular structure; made of countless components, it

works and handles information through radiation signals, can expand indefinitely, and is virtually immortal. A crisis erupts when, after showing their intention to take over Nortonstowe, the U.S. and Soviet governments attack the cloud with nuclear missiles. The cloud, warned by Kingsley, returns the missiles to their senders, wiping out a few more cities, and announces its intention to leave the solar system. Urged by Kingsley, the cloud agrees to try to reprogram a human brain in order to make possible the downloading of the concepts and information in its possession. Kingsley and another volunteer die of massive "mental overload." Kingsley is eventually made the scapegoat for all public hostility, as a sort of fanatic Victor Frankenstein, and the truth of the cloud remains a secret.

This novel (especially the early chapters) introduces what is probably Hoyle's stylistic trademark: his use of long expository sections—usually in dialogue form—full of mathematical disquisitions and formulas. His emphasis is always on scientific work, portrayed as full of sweat and toil, never as automatic or effortless. The result is an attenuation of the boundaries between fiction and nonfiction. Hoyle also juxtaposes a variety of other genres, mixing the disaster novel in the vein of John Wyndham or John Christopher with a first-contact story and alternating witty conversation pieces, action-adventure scenes, and sweeping, god-like views à la Stapledon. Facing the interstellar uninvited guest is an international community of scientists, mostly Anglo-Saxon (British, American, Australian) but with a Russian astronomer. The group also includes a doctor (the ostensible author of the manuscript), a musician (who apparently becomes Kingsley's girlfriend), a historian, a painter, and even a politician (a science-educated liaison with the British authorities). This motley crew is indicative of Hoyle's stance: neither a nationalist nor a technocrat in the stricter sense, he believes in science as the potential harbinger of a transitional culture founded on rational method and speculative open-mindedness, without anthropocentrism and without the petty concerns driving the powers that be. Nortonstowe is precisely a community built on these principles that can best engage in the inevitable clash with the power-driven, irrational "literary mind" of politicians and the military. Kingsley's "mathematical mind" is, on the other hand, based on post- Einsteinian and post-Heisenbergian cognitive horizons, allowing for no such concept as a detached observer facing a passive object of observation. This horizon is literalized in the cloud, virtually immaterial (gaseous and radiant) in nature, but nevertheless posing a strenuous resistance to earthly presence and activities. Furthermore, in this novel there is no such thing as pure or ivory-tower research; rather, scientists must, at all steps, face pressures from military and political establishments trying to control, contain, and even thwart their efforts. The opposition between the Nortonstowe group and the rest of the world elite is ultimately simplistic, and Kingsley is too much of an individualist. In this sense, the characters go against the ideals of teamwork and reasonableness they embody. These contradictions are emphasized in Hoyle's preface disclaiming full identity of views with them and make for both added suspense and complexity of characterization. *The Black Cloud* is not a utopian novel and does not propound any dubious blueprint for the establishment of a scientific oligarchy of rulers. Its outcome is both successful, in that Earth is saved, and failed, in that two of the heroes die, while new questions are opened: the cloud is in its turn inquiring into the existence of even higher life-forms. Ultimately, the planet is left with the never-ending task of further choices, like Kingsley's group, between the alternatives of liberating creativity and deadly self-interest.

This didacticism makes also for the main flaws of the novel. Hoyle evidently had an audience in mind: the beginning of mass education was creating a new public of mainly young readers with more than a sprinkling of scientific background, in part already engaged professionally in technology-related jobs or at least fascinated by contemporary advances. The mathematical formulas in the novel are not beyond the reach of high-school students, and there is something adolescent about this group of big minds who seem to have no interests besides math and physics. The only moment of apparent nonscientific activity occurs when Kingsley recites two lines of love poetry to pianist Ann Halsey (which perhaps implies that Halsey's grandson, to whom Dr. O'Neill has willed his manuscript, is also Chris's descendant). Despite this naive element, *The Black Cloud* remains a landmark in British science fiction.

After Hoyle's thoughtful debut, *Ossian's Ride* (1959) seems a slight setback. The novel describes the rise of Ireland to the status of a world superpower, thanks to the action of a secretive megacorporation, the Industrial Corporation of Eire (ICE). ICE gathers together a top team of scientists and accumulates huge profits by marketing a method for extracting minerals from low-concentration soil, a cheap line of contraceptive pills, and a commercially viable chain of nuclear reactors, all in an incredibly short time. The secrecy of ICE and Ireland seems impenetrable, and the British government tries to infiltrate mathematician Thomas Sherwood, a harmless-looking Cambridge graduate, into ICE. In Ireland he encounters a Kafkaesque, police-state atmosphere, with inquisitive immigration officers and policemen, shadowy secret agents, curfews, and death squads. A priest he meets makes a parallel

with Nazism; in this case, though, neither police nor scientists seem to be in control: "They're all slaves," members of "an army" without visible leaders.

On the other hand, Sherwood sees the renewed Dublin as an ideal city, with streamlined, twenty-story high-rises made of glass and metal and immersed in peaceful parks. Eventually, an ICE representative offers him a job, pitching the corporation as "an organization run by scientists" who "serve only science itself." In the company town of Caragh, a half-million ICE employees live in a garden city ("the city of the third millennium, the city of the future"). Whereas the "older style of civilization" was based on "mineral deposits," Sherwood is told, humanity is moving toward a "second phase" based on "information as a violently explosive social force"; the wealth or poverty of a country will be determined by "the possession of an effectively unlimited source of energy," namely, the information under control of ICE. In the last chapter Sherwood discovers that a group of space aliens are in charge of the organization. They left their planet because of increasing heat but did not send their physical bodies through space. Instead, they chose to imprint the information ("the electronic part") of their mind patterns onto human brains. The human mind is "a small computer" that cannot accommodate all of the aliens' abilities; still, they have managed "to pass on some memory" of themselves, in order "to avoid a complete oblivion." Sherwood is so fascinated that he decides to join them.

The novel is for the most part a spy thriller in the style of Ian Fleming, with shoot-outs and fistfights, high-tech gadgetry and romantic subplots; science-fiction elements are limited to the ending and little else. The novel again stresses the role of scientists. While *The Black Cloud* updates its urban gentlemen for the age of quantum physics, however, *Ossian's Ride* imagines a near-future (1970) world of transnational corporations like the Japanese *zaibatsus*. This portrayal is the most realistic extrapolation of the novel: ICE is not an underground assembly of crooks, but a legitimate enterprise on the verge of rendering meaningless the notion of national and popular sovereignty. In Ireland there is already no distinction between state and corporation, and the latter has taken over all security and administrative functions. With its monopolistic control of immaterial goods such as technological processes, ICE seems to have replaced democratic procedures, and, indeed, the whole sphere of politics, with a technocracy. As a scientist, Sherwood seems all too willing to give up Kingsley's liberal ideal of intellectual autonomy from the questionable actions of the power structures. He constantly and unblinkingly accepts regimentation, first under his government and in the end in the ICE structure. Sherwood constantly chooses security and cutting-

Dust jacket for the U.S. edition of Hoyle's 1966 novel, in which the Earth becomes "unstuck in time" and different phases of past, present, and future exist simultaneously (Richland County Public Library)

edge knowledge over freedom and responsibility. He perceives the aliens as benevolent, although their rule in Eire is dictatorial and violent, their rhetoric is imbued with a sort of social Darwinism, and the world economic order they have helped create is as ruthless as the old one, with a widening gap between rich and poor regions. Sherwood states his intention to work for the glory of humanity, hoping that eventually the human species will find a way to survive bodily and not just in electronic spirit. Still, the novel leaves too many unanswered questions that challenge the aliens' benevolent status, particularly with respect to what happened to the minds of the people into whom the aliens have projected themselves.

A refusal to consider people as disposable is instead one of the forces driving the protagonist of *A for Andromeda* (1962), Hoyle's first collaborative novel. Co-authored with John Elliot, like the sequel *Andromeda Breakthrough* (1964), it is the novelization of a BBC

television serial; a few years later, the series was also adapted by science-fiction writer and editor Inisero Cremaschi for an Italian RAI-TV serial, starring two major stage actors: Luigi Vannucchi as the Hemingwayesque protagonist, John Fleming, and Paola Pitagora as the glacial synthetic girl, Andre. The Italian series ensured Hoyle's fame in that country; to date, editor and critic Gianni Montanari is the author of the longest comprehensive treatment of Hoyle's fiction, in his *Ieri, il futuro: Origini e sviluppo della SF inglese* (Yesterday, the Future: Origin and Development of English Science Fiction, 1977). The author's death was covered thoroughly by Italian radio and newspapers.

A for Andromeda reworks many of Hoyle's earlier themes, particularly those concerning first contact with distant aliens, scientific teamwork, and ambiguous multinationals. British radio astronomers detect interstellar signals coming from the Andromeda nebula, and computer scientist Fleming decodes them enough to understand that some unknown entity is emitting blueprint information for a mega-computer; this machine would then elaborate the rest of the data. Fleming persuades the government to let him use the military installations of Thorness, Scotland, to build the machine. Two main obstacles appear immediately: the military and the politicians want to try to use the information in the Cold War, and a transnational cartel called Intel is infiltrating the project in order to get hold of marketable patents.

The alien machine starts a life-synthesizing program, proceeding from a DNA molecule to a cell and then a blob of protoplasm. Eventually, it hypnotizes a lab assistant into touching two mysterious high-voltage terminals; the woman is killed, but now the computer has the information it needs to create a human life. Andre, the synthetic girl, who can mentally communicate with the computer through the terminals, grows up and learns at an incredible rate. At this point, the military takes over and has Andre and the computer work on antimissile technology, while closing with Intel for a joint venture on the financial sides of these interstellar gifts. Fleming is scared of the implications of the events: an alien agency now has Earth in its hands, using violent methods and questionable allies. He attempts to seduce Andre, hoping to stir, through emotional reactions, a feeling of autonomy in her. He is finally successful, although the computer inflicts repeated "punishments" on the girl. They destroy the machine and run away, but Andre apparently dies during the escape.

Again, the thrilling and exhilarating process of scientific reasoning is presented side by side with its wider contexts, from professional jealousy (mathematicians feel they are "purer" researchers than engineers, with biologists somewhere in the middle, and so on) to profit-seeking mentality (one of the main participants in the project is killed after being exposed as an Intel spy). These scientists must continually face the responsibility for the consequences of their work. The most important relationship is that between Fleming and the alien creations, the computer and Andre. What scares him about the machine he has enthusiastically helped to build is the virtual impossibility to pull the plug on it. It has a will and an agenda of its own, beyond human control or consent; its ruthlessness is evident in its repeated killings and in its sadistic violence toward the girl; for him, the computer is a "fifth column" whose "corrupting" presence is endangering the future of humanity. With his pacifist leanings, his heavy drinking, and his continual emotional outbursts, he is the most complex human character in Hoyle's fiction. He and Andre embody two opposite poles—emotional sensuality versus distant coldness—as even her physical appearance reinforces: narrator and characters describe her as an icy blonde goddess. She is a new Frankenstein monster, and her monstrosity is above all defined by her lack of an independent will. Rather than the computer commanding the girl, the two exist as a cyborg-like complex, wherein they are telepathically linked. The most interesting variation on the Frankenstein motif is that both the creature and her immediate creator (biochemist Madeleine Dawnay) are women, and in effect there are, for once, many women in the Thorness research community. In his seduction efforts Fleming is clever and passably crude: he skillfully socializes Andre into earthly gender roles (he teaches her to wear perfume, for example, and to style her hair) and almost unfailingly treats her like a puppet. At least for a while, he only wants the computer to see her as a faulty component. He is also applying some basic scientific common sense; for him, all materials, including organic life, have specific patterns of resistance and reaction. Thus he appeals to bodily sensuality (or perhaps a caricature thereof) in order to induce feelings of independent self-awareness in the girl. By contrast, the computer wrongly assumes that organic creatures behave just like electronic components. As in Mary Shelley's *Frankenstein* (1818), however, the creature's self-awareness results in death.

Hoyle and Elliot never show what Andre's life as a free agent could be like, even though she is duly resurrected in *Andromeda Breakthrough*. Whereas the former novel was a skillful fusion of the science-fiction and thriller genres, in the sequel (as in *Ossian's Ride*) the sensationalistic elements take over at the expense of science fiction. These genre and thematic oscillations are typical of Hoyle's early career. Here, the Intel transnational consortium (again, like ICE in *Ossian's Ride,* compared to Nazism) first duplicates the computer in an imagined

Middle Eastern country called Azaran and then kidnaps Fleming, biologist Dawnay, and Andre (who has survived many hours underwater without drowning). The goal of Intel is world domination through the possession of the superior alien technology. Struggling for space with a muddled series of coups, murders, and conspiracies, the science-fiction element involves the computer's inadvertent unleashing of nitrogen-eating bacteria, which shortly causes climatic and environmental devastation and threatens to destroy life on Earth; Andre and the computer synthesize an anti-agent, while all secret services pool together and dismantle Intel.

Andre settles with Fleming in Azaran, after persuading him that the Andromeda aliens are benevolent and worth working for. She shows him a television image of the aliens, "monstrous elongated shapes . . . without movement, without eyes, just brains," and tells him that humans' animal nature leads inevitably to cycles of catastrophes and illusory triumphs: pure mind and disembodiment is the best of all possible states. He gives up the idea of destroying the machine's memory with "input negative," one of the first computer viruses to appear in science fiction. In other words, whereas *A for Andromeda* had insisted on a recuperation of the body, as complementary and not incompatible with rationality, *Andromeda Breakthrough* asserts bodiless reason. Also, whereas in the first novel Andre's discovery of the body and of selfhood had resulted from both experiences of pleasure (with Fleming) and of pain (with the computer), in the sequel she is in constant pain (from her near-death experience and her burned hands and degenerative metabolic collapse, all computer-generated afflictions) and almost works herself to death in mind-to-mind contacts with the computer. As for selfhood and individuality, Fleming says he is scared of her identity as "mechanical doll," but constantly refers to her as "man-made *femina sapiens*" and as a "normal piece of human chemistry" with no will of her own ("the girl is nothing without the machine"), in need of a "repair kit" for her wounds. He fixes her and joins her in relinquishing free agency to the aliens: a despairing and disturbing choice for contemporary science, away from the military-industrial complex and toward wishful, uncontrollable benefactors.

The overall quality of Hoyle's production remained above average until the mid 1970s. In 1963 he published *Fifth Planet,* his first collaboration with his son, Geoffrey. Astronomer Hugh Conway, brilliant but with a messy private life, discovers an inhabitable planet, Achilles, in a solar system that is somehow approaching Earth's. The Russian and American expeditions are victims of inexplicable events, from landing accidents to death and madness-inducing visions, but manage to return. Conway's cheating wife rushes to the

Dust jacket for Hoyle's 1969 novel, in which humans become involved in a war between two alien species (Richland County Public Library)

deathbed of her astronaut lover, and an alien entity invades her body. The alien-possessed Cathy, more likable than her fully human version, reveals good intentions toward Earth. In order to dissuade the world from an arms-race escalation that is clearly leading to nuclear war, she gives all humanity a terrifying vision of what a nuclear holocaust could be like. Earth authorities decide to reconsider their belligerence but keep chasing the alien. After she commandeers a spaceship, Conway chooses to follow her. The Hoyles' message is again clear: human authorities (politicians, the military, and in this case also the press) are not to be trusted; scientists, with their reliance on cool reason, can act as mediators and entrust human destiny to benevolent alien supervision. In *Fifth Planet* this theme is expressed through the healing powers of the telepathic alien visions. The two "visionary" scenes are the best moments of the book, first with the American and Soviet crews becoming overwhelmed by their own guilty consciences and Cold War prejudices, and then with the shocking collective experience of the nuclear holocaust. This novel is a confident homage to the role of science fiction as a purveyor of cautionary warnings.

Hoyle's *October the First Is Too Late* (1966) introduces elements of time travel and parallel worlds. An unknown modulated signal from space has an incredible time-disrupting effect: different phases of Earth's past, present, and future (or possible futures) come to exist simultaneously on different parts of the planet. The action therefore includes episodes in the present, in classical Greece, in Europe during World War I, and in various future space-times, including an unspecified period during which the Earth is dying. The novel is far removed from "hard" science fiction, even in Hoyle's peculiar version; the protagonist/narrator is not a scientist but a musician, although his friend and sidekick throughout the story is a Nobel Prize–winning mathematician. The story unfolds through various explorations and adventures, following the two characters as they try to make sense of what happened and exploring the possibilities and limits of art and science as cognitive tools, either alone or in collaboration. In this original treatment of an original idea, no final answer is given either on the origin and possible purposes of the phenomenon or on the superiority of either art or science. Both are successful, and both are limited, in an overall pattern that may be compared to the writings of Stanisław Lem and Arkady and Boris Strugatsky, despite a few scenes of crude and melodramatic action and romantic subplots.

In this picaresque novel the whole planet becomes (as Donald Lawler has pointed out, borrowing a phrase from Kurt Vonnegut's *Slaughterhouse Five*, 1969) "unstuck from time." The crucial episode occurs when the two Wellsian time travelers are caught in a future utopia in Mexico reminiscent of Edward Bellamy's *Looking Backward* (1888); the placid, ethereally perfect descendants tell them that the history of Earth has followed, throughout its course, a cyclical rise-and-fall pattern, with wondrous civilizations repeatedly destroying themselves because of greed, war, overpopulation, and pollution. These utopians thought they had broken the pattern, but an appalling vision of a never-ending "Plain of Glass" and other indications all show unequivocally a future without human life on Earth. Their choice is resignation: they do not try to find out how the time warp occurred and whether this dreadful outcome can be averted. The musician decides to remain permanently there, sharing their feeling of hopelessness but judging the era as worth living in for an artist, while the scientist decides to get back to his own time in order to fight present ills. Hoyle offers no clues as to whose interpretation might be more correct. The utopians' past includes recognizable historical incidents, but British authorities have (in the most grotesque sequence of the novel) managed to impose peace on war-ridden 1917 Europe. Thus, maybe history can now be rewritten for the better, or maybe humans must make do with what they have in sight. History and the future, in this paradoxically most hopeful of Hoyle's novels, are open-ended: all depends on human actions and intentions.

In 1967 Hoyle published his only collection of short stories, *Element 79*. This book presents a darkly comic side to the author and includes some fantasy and supernatural tales. In the latter, scientific knowledge and human action normally have the upper hand, and the devil is cheated at his own game by a scientist who wins professional fame ("Pym Makes His Point") or scared off by cunning aliens disguised as a human woman ("Welcome to Slippage City"). In "Cattle Trucks" a reborn and capricious Greek god rushes away from the contemporary, technology-dominated United States, while in "A Jury of Five" the theory involving Erwin Schrödinger's cat becomes the basis for a contemporary ghost story.

The science fiction Hoyle presents in the collection resembles closely the black "social science fiction" of William Tenn, Fredric Brown, or Robert Sheckley: in "The Zoomen" a crew of proud humans becomes unwilling specimens for an interplanetary zoo; in "The Magnetosphere" a stolid English nobleman turns astronaut and prevents the useless destruction of a peaceful planet; in "Agent 38" Earth astronauts are captured by Venusian ufologists; in "The Martians" Martians annihilate humans, without the need for any physical strike, by playing on the dynamics of gender roles; in "Blackmail" animals become a major target for television ratings and reclaim their rightful place in Earth's culture; and in the title story a gold meteorite has surreal effects on the world economy and human relations. These are all apologues, exposing arrogant human assumptions against the larger scheme of things provided by science-fiction conventions. There are also two more-affirmative tales: in the fantasy "Judgment of Aphrodite" the Greek goddess asserts her emotional and sexual superiority over both masculine deities from past history and an unlikable creature who is trying to defeat them all, while in "The Operation" a child escapes a horrifying dystopia based on eugenics and brainwashing. Both stories present protagonists who wittily fuse physical and intellectual features and provide a playful hope for their respective worlds.

Until 1985 all of Hoyle's novels are collaborations with Geoffrey Hoyle. *Rockets in Ursa Major* (1969), originally a play for children, produced in London in 1962, and its sequel, *Into Deepest Space* (1974), are interesting variations on the space-opera subgenre. Earth becomes involved in a galactic war between two powerful species. A formerly imperialistic, and now repentant, alien species is being chased across the universe by one of their former subjects, now turned mercilessly genocidal. In this transparent (if one-sided) allegory of the postcolonial fate of Britain, Earth heroes and benevolent aliens first chase the villainous Yelas out of the solar system, then, faced with their returning threat, start a pursuit that leads them in a voyage through relativistic time that resembles Poul Anderson's *Tau Zero* (1970). After traveling across the universe, an Earthman and three sterile aliens land on an uninhabited Earth of the future, with no chance of establishing a new colony and no way of knowing of the outcome of the war. In the Hoyles' refusal of traditional formulaic reassurances, this overly melodramatic saga finds a mature and problematic conclusion.

In *Seven Steps to the Sun* (1970) the Hoyles return to the time-travel motif. Utilizing the shaky narrative frame of a shadowy mastermind (and science-fiction fan) projecting a hapless writer in a series of leaps into the future, they offer some powerful dystopian visions. The sequence of increasingly dictatorial nightmares of computerized social control and crushing conformism ends with global war and the almost total extermination of humanity. According to the brooding narrator, the beginning of the world's downward spiral is associated with uprisings in 1968 and "anarchy"; this statement of right-wing politics may be a key to the pessimism the novel expresses.

A similar political outlook informs *The Inferno* (1973). The scientist protagonist of this novel has to cope with global disaster, the result of a radiation wave from a quasar. Top physicist Cameron, disappointed by the self-serving reflex attitudes of the prime minister and other authorities, decides to retreat to his native Scottish Highlands to await death there with his wife. Unexpectedly, he and a few more people survive the heat wave, followed by a long, freezing darkness of unknown origin. In his native valley Cameron establishes an iron-fisted rule, overtly presenting himself as successor of traditional Scottish clan chiefs. Eventually, he finds grounds to hypothesize that an alien entity might have provided a way to screen part of the radiation, thus saving at least a portion of humanity. He also reunites with his wife, who had left him in horror at his liberal use of capital punishment, even for petty thefts. This novel reveals Scottish nationalism as part of the Hoyles' background. Most disturbingly, however, this neo-feudal system is presented as logical and rational, a return to natural tribal harmony after the hypocritical parenthesis of modern democracy. Cameron will be the superior overseer of his community, just as the alien entity has supervised the survival of humanity, sacrificing all it takes to preserve the new clan. In this reactionary rendering of the disaster novel, the unchecked rule of the superior intellect is upheld as an actual blueprint for political action.

The other novels by the Hoyles are forgettable. *The Molecule Men and The Monster of Loch Ness* (1971), *The Incandescent Ones* (1977), and *The Westminster Disaster* (1978) all include conspicuous digressions on cosmological and astrophysical theory, as well as overwhelming doses of melodramatic adventures in dystopian scenarios and space opera; *The Incandescent Ones* includes effectively portrayed aliens from the planet Jupiter. The diminishing quality of Hoyle's writing seems to coincide with the increasing focus on pseudoscience that marks his nonfiction. In 1982 the Hoyles also co-authored four entertaining science-fiction novels for juveniles(the "Professor Gamma" series): *The Energy Pirate, The Giants of Universal Park, The Frozen Planet of Azuron,* and *The Planet of Death.*

Hoyle's last novel, *Comet Halley* (1985), is a solo effort that fictionalizes his speculations on comets as living beings. He offers his usual portrait of the scientific community, with its endless struggle for independence and for funding, and presents a totally new collaboration with political authorities. In accordance with the Wellsian dream of world government under the League of Nations, Hoyle assigns the role of a "good" political body to the United Nations, making Secretary General Kurt Waldheim one of the main characters. Dubiously, Waldheim is made into a member of the team (led by a Cambridge scientist named Isaac Newton) that first formulates the intelligent-comet hypothesis. The comet emerges as a "third superpower," willing to provide ways out of both the limits of the current world system based on nation-states and the strictures of post-Keynesian welfare states (which all of the characters loathe). False nuclear alarms and mysterious illnesses put NATO and the Soviet Politburo in their place, while a meteorite falls on the North Pole, melting the icecap and bringing about eternal spring on the planet (the fate of coastal and subtropical regions is left unconsidered). Hoyle thus ended his novel-writing career with the prospect of a rosy future in a laissez-faire cosmos: the universe knows how to take care of itself, and sooner or later it will take care of Earth and of humanity.

After his retirement in 1972, Fred Hoyle lived in the Lake District and later in Bournemouth, on the south coast of Britain, where he died in 2001. Despite a few disappointments, Hoyle produced a significant body of fiction, which includes at least three important works, *The Black Cloud, A for Andromeda,* and *October the First Is Too Late.* His grasp of science as cognitive method, his pioneering emphasis on information theory, and his portrayals of both scientists and aliens have combined to produce many interesting and problematic fictions. His success as a best-selling author deserves to be matched by further critical attention.

References:

Donald L. Lawler, "*October the First Is Too Late,*" in *Survey of Science Fiction Literature,* volume 4, edited by Frank N. Magill (Englewood Cliffs, N.J.: Salem House, 1979), pp. 1,574–1,582;

Gianni Montanari, *Ieri, il futuro: Origini e sviluppo della SF inglese* (Milan: Nord, 1977), pp. 138–152;

Patrick Parrinder, "Scientists in Science Fiction: Enlightenment and After," in *Science Fiction Roots and Branches,* edited by Rhys Garnett and R. J. Ellis (London: Macmillan, 1990), pp. 57–78;

Giorgio Spina, *Utopia e satira nella fantascienza inglese* (Genoa: Tilgher, 1974), pp. 81–87;

Brian Stableford, "*The Black Cloud,*" in *Survey of Science Fiction Literature,* volume 1, edited by Magill (Englewood Cliffs, N.J.: Salem House, 1979), pp. 228–232;

Patricia S. Warrick, *The Cybernetic Imagination in Science Fiction* (Cambridge, Mass.: MIT Press, 1980), pp. 173–174.

Garry Kilworth

(5 July 1941 –   )

Darren Harris-Fain
Shawnee State University

BOOKS: *In Solitary* (London: Faber & Faber, 1977; New York: Avon, 1979);

The Night of Kadar (London: Faber & Faber, 1978; New York: Avon, 1980);

Split Second (London: Faber & Faber, 1979; New York: Warner, 1985);

Gemini God (London: Faber & Faber, 1981);

The Songbirds of Pain: Stories from the Inscape (London: Gollancz, 1984);

A Theatre of Timesmiths (London: Gollancz, 1984); published as *Theater of Timesmith* (New York: Warner, 1986);

Tree Messiah: A Collection of Short Poems (Newport, Wales: Envoi, 1985);

Highlander, as Garry Douglas (London: Grafton, 1986);

Witchwater Country (London: Bodley Head, 1986);

Spiral Winds (London: Bodley Head, 1987);

The Wizard of the Woodworld (London: Dragon, 1987);

Abandonati (London: Unwin, 1988);

Cloudrock (London: Unwin, 1988);

The Street, as Douglas (London: Grafton, 1988);

Trivial Tales (Birmingham: Birmingham SF Group, 1988);

The Voyage of the Vigilance (London: Armada, 1988);

Hunter's Moon: A Story of Foxes (London: Unwin Hyman, 1989); republished as *The Foxes of First Dark* (New York: Doubleday, 1990);

In the Hollow of the Deep-Sea Wave: A Novel and Seven Stories (London: Bodley Head, 1989);

The Rain Ghost (New York: Scholastic, 1989);

Dark Hills, Hollow Clocks: Stories from the Otherworld (London: Methuen, 1990);

Midnight's Sun: A Story of Wolves (London: Unwin Hyman, 1990);

The Drowners (London: Methuen, 1991);

The Third Dragon (New York: Scholastic, 1991; London: Hippo, 1991);

Frost Dancers: A Story of Hares (London & New York: HarperCollins, 1992);

Standing on Shamsan (London & New York: HarperCollins, 1992);

Garry Kilworth (photograph by Mark Cummins; from the dust jacket for The Foxes of First Dark, *1990)*

Angel (London: Gollancz, 1993; New York: Forge, 1996);

Billy Pink's Private Detective Agency (London: Methuen, 1993);

Hogfoot Right and Bird-Hands (Cambridge, Mass.: Edgewood, 1993);

In the Country of Tattooed Men (London: Grafton, 1993);

The Oystercatcher's Cry, as F. K. Salwood (London: Headline, 1993);

Archangel (London: Gollancz, 1994);

The Phantom Piper (London: Methuen, 1994);

The Saffron Fields, as Salwood (London: Headline, 1994);

The Electric Kid (New York: Bantam, 1994);

The Brontë Girls (London: Methuen, 1995);

House of Tribes (London: Bantam, 1995);

The Ragged School, as Salwood (London: Headline, 1995);

Cybercats (London: Bantam, 1996);

A Midsummer's Nightmare (New York: Bantam, 1996);

The Raiders (New York: Bantam, 1996);

The Roof of Voyaging (London: Orbit, 1996; Boston: Little, Brown, 1996);

The Princely Flower (London: Orbit, 1997; Boston: Little, Brown, 1997);

The Devil's Own: Sergeant Jack Crossman and the Battle of the Alma, as Douglas (London & New York: HarperCollins, 1997);

The Gargoyle (London: Heinemann, 1997);

Thunder Oak (London: Corgi, 1997);

Castle Storm (London: Corgi, 1998);

The Drummer Boy (London: Heinemann, 1998);

Heavenly Hosts v. Hell United (London: Mammoth, 1998);

Land-of-Mists (London: Orbit, 1998; Boston: Little, Brown, 1998);

The Lantern Fox (London: Mammoth, 1998);

The Valley of Death: Sergeant Jack Crossman and the Battle of Balaclava, as Douglas (London & New York: Harper Collins, 1998);

Hey, New Kid! (London: Mammoth, 1999);

Shadow-Hawk (London: Orbit, 1999; Boston: Little, Brown, 1999);

Windjammer Run (London: Corgi, 1999);

Soldiers in the Mist: Featuring Sergeant Jack Crossman, as Douglas (London & New York: HarperCollins, 1999);

Gaslight Geezers (London: Corgi, 2001).

OTHER: "The Black Wedding," in *Other Edens,* edited by Robert Holdstock and Chris Evans (London: Unwin, 1987);

"The Silver Collar," in *Blood Is Not Enough: 17 Stories of Vampirism,* edited by Ellen Datlow (New York: Morrow, 1989);

"Snake Dreams," in *Tarot Tales,* edited by Rachel Pollack and Caitlin Matthews (London: Legend, 1989; New York: Ace, 1996);

"The Woodman's Enigma," in *Haunting Christmas Tales* (London: Scholastic, 1991; New York: Scholastic, 1993);

"The Cave Painting," in *Omni Best Science Fiction Two,* edited by Datlow (Greensboro, N.C.: Omni, 1992), pp. 195–218;

"Confessions of a Bradbury Eater," in *The Profession of Science Fiction: SF Writers on Their Craft and Ideas,*

edited by Maxim Jakubowski and Edward James (New York: St. Martin's Press, 1992), pp. 154–160;

"The Borgia Brats," in *Now We Are Sick: An Anthology of Nasty Verse,* edited by Stephen Jones and Neil Gaiman (Minneapolis: DreamHaven, 1994);

"Nerves of Steel," in *New Worlds 4,* edited by David Garnett (London: Gollancz, 1994);

"Cherub," in *Heaven Sent: 18 Glorious Tales of the Angels,* edited by Martin H. Greenberg and Peter Crowther (New York: DAW, 1995);

"Masterpiece," in *Ruby Slippers, Golden Tears,* edited by Datlow and Windling (New York: Morrow, 1995), pp. 33–53;

"Wayang Kulit," in *Best New Horror 6,* edited by Jones (London: Raven, 1995; New York: Carroll & Graf, 1995);

"The Goatboy and the Giant," in *Fantasy Stories,* edited by Mike Ashley (London: Robinson, 1996);

"Oracle Bones," in *Touch Wood,* edited by Crowther (New York: Warner, 1996);

"Attack of the Charlie Chaplins," in *New Worlds,* edited by Garnett (Clarkson, Ga.: White Wolf, 1997);

"The Sculptor," in *The Best of Interzone,* edited by David Pringle (New York: St. Martin's Press, 1997), pp. 44–66;

"The Trial of Hansel and Gretel," in *Black Swan, White Raven,* edited by Datlow and Windling (New York: Avon, 1997), pp. 104–121;

"Mirrors," in *Sirens and Other Daemon Lovers,* edited by Datlow and Windling (New York: HarperPrism, 1998), pp. 59–70;

"The Frog Chauffeur," in *Silver Birch, Blood Moon,* edited by Datlow and Windling (New York: Avon, 1999).

SELECTED PERIODICAL PUBLICATIONS—UNCOLLECTED: "The Final Assassin," *Isaac Asimov's Science Fiction Magazine,* 9 (January 1985);

"Image in a Dark Glass," *Twilight Zone Magazine* (July/August 1985);

"The Lost Garden of Enid Blyton, Beatrix Potter, Lucy Atwell and the Rest of the Lads of the 32nd Parachute Regiment," *Isaac Asimov's Science Fiction Magazine,* 9 (March 1985);

"Angel's Eyes," *Twilight Zone Magazine* (July/August 1986);

"Paper Moon," *Omni* (1987);

"Ifurin and the Fat Man," *Magazine of Fantasy and Science Fiction,* 76 (March 1989);

"Bowmen in the Mist," *Magazine of Fantasy and Science Fiction,* 76 (June 1989);

"Hamelin, Nebraska," *Interzone,* 48 (June 1991);

"Fossils," *Interzone,* 69 (March 1993);

"Punctuated Evolution," *Crank!* 1 (Fall 1993);

"Black Drongo," *Omni,* 16 (May 1994);

"The Council of Beasts," *Interzone,* 111 (September 1996);

"The Bare Rock and the Vulture: Gwyneth Jones Interviewed," *Interzone,* 136 (October 1998);

"Death of the Mocking Man," *Interzone,* 147 (September 1999).

Garry Kilworth came to professional writing relatively late in life, in his thirties, even though he wrote his first book, an unpublished story for younger readers, when he was twenty. But he has since made up for lost time with a prolific output of stories and novels covering a wide array of genres and types, from science fiction, fantasy, and horror to books for children and young adults. He has done so under his own name and using a handful of pseudonyms. Along the way he has gained a reputation as a solid writer of interesting stories, both fantastic and realistic. Although he initially gained a reputation as a science-fiction writer, it would be more accurate to call Kilworth a fantasist, given his fascination with mythologies, both traditional and invented.

Garry Douglas Kilworth was born on 5 July 1941 in York. His parents were George Kilworth, a sergeant with the Royal Air Force, and Joan Kilworth, née Hodges, a bookkeeper. As an Air Force brat, Kilworth moved frequently with his parents and two brothers and ultimately attended twenty-two different schools—an experience that informed his 1999 children's novel *Hey, New Kid!* One of his favorite childhood homes was in Aden (formerly South Yemen), where he read widely and identified with Rudyard Kipling's Kim. Twice during his childhood he almost died: once in England, when the floods that ravaged the southeastern portion of the country covered their house, and he and his family were rescued seven hours later; and again in the Arabian peninsula when he and a friend became lost in the desert and were rescued two days later. At fifteen he entered the Royal Air Force Training School, and three years later he joined the Royal Air Force, becoming a cryptographer (although he later accepted the pacifist teachings of the Society of Friends, popularly known as the Quakers). Successful at breaking and creating codes, he attained the rank of sergeant cryptographer and was stationed in various places around the world during more than a decade in the service, working in half a dozen different countries. When he was twenty-one, he married Annette Bailey, a social worker and therapist, with whom he had two children, Richard and Chantelle. After seventeen years of service, he left the military in 1974, the same year his career as a professional writer began with the publication of his story

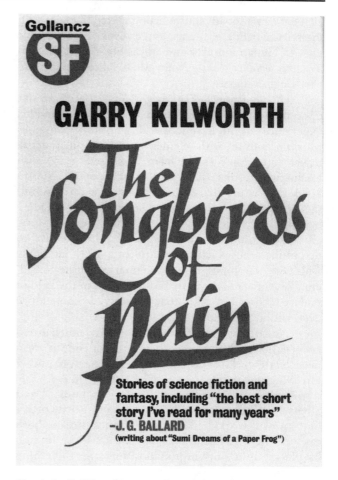

Dust jacket for Kilworth's 1984 collection of short fiction, which includes his story about a time traveler who journeys to Judea to witness the life of Jesus firsthand (Richland County Public Library)

"Let's Go to Golgotha!" in the *Sunday Times,* where it won a contest for best science-fiction story sponsored by the *Times* and by the publisher Gollancz. He did not devote all of his energies to writing until later, however; between 1974 and 1982 he also worked as an executive at Cable and Wireless after earning a diploma in business from Southwest London Polytechnic. Though based in London, this job also took him around the world, including three years in Hong Kong. During that time Kilworth continued to write, and his first published novel, *In Solitary,* appeared in 1977.

In Solitary concerns a decimated human population on an Earth centuries into the future. Their numbers have been severely diminished by the harsh rule of their alien overlords, avian beings who have governed the planet for more than four hundred years. The plot focuses on the efforts of a group of humans to rebel against their alien masters. Two aspects of Kilworth's science-fiction novels are present in this work: a strong element of action-adventure fiction mixed liberally with the science-fiction elements, and a distinctly pessimistic view of human morality and efficacy that John Clute in *The Encyclopedia of Science Fiction* (1993) labels "an identifiably English dubiety."

His next novel, *The Night of Kadar* (1978), draws upon both Kilworth's interest in science fiction and his experiences in the Islamic world. The story combines Muslim culture with elements such as interstellar travel and people raised from frozen embryos, with fascinating results. Just as the philosopher Martin Heidegger wrote that human beings are thrown into the world and must establish a sense of personal identity and authenticity, so the characters here are literally cast into an alien environment and are forced to determine who exactly they are. In a 1991 interview with Gwyneth Jones, Kilworth remarks that he considers *The Night of Kadar* to be his best work in the field of science fiction but adds that it received scant notice even within the field.

Nor did his next few novels receive much attention, either within science fiction or outside it. *Split Second* (1979) links a contemporary person and a Cro-Magnon, while *Gemini God* (1981), like *In Solitary,* deals with the relationship between humans and aliens. While neither is among Kilworth's best-known works, like much science fiction both explore the question of what it means to be human by placing humanity in juxtaposition with something else, something other.

Kilworth's first collection of short stories, *The Songbirds of Pain: Stories from the Inscape,* was published in 1984. It includes his debut story, "Let's Go to Golgotha!" Like Michael Moorcock's novel *Behold the Man* (1969), it is a time-travel narrative in which the protagonist goes to ancient Judea to witness the story of Jesus of Nazareth firsthand.

Also in 1984 Kilworth published *A Theatre of Timesmiths.* The novel is an example of a recurring motif in several science-fiction works: a futuristic closed world in which the inhabitants do not realize the true nature of their environment or its history. The environment in this story is completely enclosed by an enormous wall of ice. All is relatively well until another common motif, the breakdown of technology—in this case, computer failure—leads the characters to confront a new situation and the challenges it brings. This development then leads to discoveries about who they are and how they came to be in this situation. While the trappings are thus familiar to readers of science fiction, Kilworth is inventive in his treatment of his topics. Also, the characters' search for identity is reminiscent of his earlier novel *The Night of Kadar.*

Feeling undereducated despite his wide reading and extensive travels, Kilworth decided to attend King's College of the University of London, earning an honors degree in English literature in 1985. In 1986 he composed a novelization of the motion picture *Highlander* (1986) under the pseudonym Garry Douglas—which he also has employed for his horror novel *The Street* (1988) and his historical military novels *The Devil's Own* (1997), *The Valley of Death* (1998), and *Soldiers in the Mist* (2000). While *Highlander* is not an original work, and likely one done for commercial reasons, Kilworth nonetheless lists it on his website, <http://www.garry-kilworth.co.uk>, rather than disowning it. The novel, like the movie, tells the story of a sixteenth- century Scottish warrior, Connor MacLeod, who learns that he belongs to a race of immortal beings and becomes involved in a battle of good versus evil with the wicked Kurgan, a battle that culminates in contemporary New York City.

Also in 1986, Kilworth published his first book-length work for younger readers, *Witchwater Country.* As with several of his later juveniles, such as *The Drowners* (1991), he places the action of the story in southeast England, where he resides. He draws extensively on local folklore and superstitions in this tale of the marshes of Essex, haunted with all kinds of supernatural beings, most specifically the witches who inhabit the bottom of a pond in the region. The children who are the center of the novel must learn how to deal with them. Similar themes are explored in *The Wizard of the Woodworld* (1987) and its sequel, *The Voyage of the Vigilance* (1988), although both are closer to conventional fantasy than to the supernaturalism of *Witchwater Country.*

In addition, *Witchwater Country* includes a passage that might suggest why Kilworth, soon after its publication, turned most of his attention to writing for children and young adults: childhood ends, one character remarks, "with the death of fantasy." If fantasy and science fiction in part are dedicated to evoking a sense of wonder in readers, it is not surprising that a writer interested in cultivating such a sense might devote more of his efforts to writing for an audience in whom such a sense is still fresh.

In his 1987 novel *Spiral Winds* Kilworth returned to a more familiar setting, Aden, infusing this story placed in one of his childhood homes with supernatural elements drawn from Middle Eastern culture. He returned to this setting again in *Standing on Shamsan* (1992).

Like *Highlander,* Kilworth's novel *Cloudrock* (1988) focuses on conflict between two characters, in this case brothers. As in *A Theatre of Timesmiths,* the setting is an enclosed environment in which the citizens erroneously believe that their limited world is the extent of the universe—in this case, an atoll elevated from the surrounding land after the ocean has disappeared. However, Kilworth is more interested in exploring the dynamics of the brothers' relationship and the nature of their internal and external conflicts rather than going into great detail about their world. In general, Kilworth in his science fiction focuses more on individuals and their societies rather than on matters of science or technology.

This concern with the individual is also true of another 1988 novel, *Abandonati.* The setting is more familiar—London—but also somewhat strange, as the city has changed considerably in this near-future time. While not exactly a dystopian work, the novel nonetheless does not depict a bright future for England or for Earth in general. Those who can afford to do so have left the planet, leaving only the "derelicts" or "abandonati." In *Abandonati,* unlike some of Kilworth's other science-fiction efforts, there is much more emphasis placed upon the setting in addition to the characters and their conflicts.

Cloudrock and *Abandonati* come at the end of what could be called the first half of Kilworth's literary career, in which he focused primarily on science fiction. Since the late 1980s he has turned more toward fantasy and toward writing for younger audiences. While some of his work from this later period falls under the category of science fiction, the second half of his career has been dominated by other kinds of writing.

Such a clear and convenient break, of course, does not exist, as the two periods in actuality overlap. For example, his novel *Witchwater Country,* which employs fantasy elements and is aimed at younger readers, was published in 1986, two years before his last science- fiction novels. However, it is generally correct to say that in 1988 he basically stopped writing science fiction, and in 1989 he began publishing fantasy and children's books predominantly. One novel stands as an interesting interlude between these two phases of Kilworth's career, a horror novel titled *The Street,* published under the pseudonym Garry Douglas.

He began his shift to children's literature with a series of animal fantasies: *Hunter's Moon: A Story of Foxes* (1989), published in the United States as *The Foxes of First Dark* (1990); *Midnight's Sun: A Story of Wolves* (1990); and *Frost Dancers: A Story of Hares* (1992). All are good examples of animal fantasy, in which common animals are given human characteristics while retaining their animal natures. The books are laudable for Kilworth's commitment to depicting the lives of the animals realistically despite the fan-

Dust jacket for the U.S. edition of Kilworth's 1993 novel, in which angels cast out from Heaven take refuge in San Francisco (Richland County Public Library)

tasy element of granting them human intelligence and awareness. Kilworth's animal fantasies have often been compared to Richard Adams's *Watership Down* (1972).

Also in 1989 Kilworth published a horror novel for young adults called *The Rain Ghost.* Steve Winston, lost during a school outing, finds a beautiful old dagger on a mountain. Fascinated with the dagger, he later researches its history and learns that the mountain where he was rescued was the site of an ancient massacre, and that he had pulled the dagger from the hands of a long-dead Rain Warrior. Fascination turns to horror when the Rain Warrior begins to haunt Steve, and Kilworth does a good job of creating tension within the story while keeping his younger audience in mind. This audience is also considered in other aspects of the story, which expands from dark fantasy to include traditional concerns in young-adult literature such as relationships with peers and first love.

Kilworth followed *The Rain Ghost* with two collections of stories: a collection for adult readers, titled *In the Hollow of the Deep-Sea Wave* (1989), and another for young adults, titled *Dark Hills, Hollow Clocks* (1990). The stories in *Dark Hills, Hollow Clocks* all fall under the heading of fantasy, yet demonstrate considerable variety. The book includes a ghost story, but there are also tales involving traditional fantasy figures such as dragons and wizards as well as more unconventional inventions such as living scarecrows. Several of the stories are drawn from various folktales around the world. Reviewers praised the collection for its inventiveness along with the conversational nature of the stories, which helps to evoke the atmosphere of folktales.

Kilworth has continued to produce short stories in a variety of genres, some of which are collected in *Hogfoot Right and Bird-Hands* and *In the Country of Tattooed Men,* both published in 1993. One of his more notable stories is a novella called "The Ragthorn," a 1992 collaboration with Robert Holdstock. The story is about the search, via a variety of sources, for the biblical Tree of Life. It later received several honors, including the World Fantasy Award and the British Science Fiction Association Award.

Kilworth then published another novel for young adults, *The Drowners*. Initially the book reads like historical fiction rather than fantasy: set in early-nineteenth-century Hampshire, the story concerns Tom's and Jem's apprenticeships to the Master Drowner, who oversees engineers attempting to irrigate farms through a complex network of channels and sluices. Tom dies trying to save a lady from drowning, and Jem succeeds Tom as apprentice, but before he can learn the trade, the Master Drowner dies as well. At this point Kilworth blends the historical with the supernatural, as Tom returns as a ghost and teaches Jem and the farmers how to manage the system and avert the flooding that threatens the farms. Reviewers praised the novel for its narrative skills and its use of an obscure bit of history, and it received a Carnegie Medal Commendation.

Southeastern England is also the locale for *Billy Pink's Private Detective Agency* (1993). While the title might suggest a contemporary children's story featuring a youthful detective such as Donald J. Sobol's Encyclopedia Brown, the story is actually set in Essex during the nineteenth century, and the detective is not a boy genius but a sentient will o' the wisp.

Kilworth returned to fiction for adults with *Angel* (1993) and its sequel, *Archangel* (1994). Both are examples of the author's comfort with a variety of genres, combining as they do elements of fantasy, horror, and crime noir. *Angel* establishes the situation: as a result of a civil war in heaven, some of the cast-out angels (now demons) are hiding on Earth—San Francisco, to be specific. The deaths of innocents bring in the human detectives, who ultimately learn that humans are in the crossfire of a cosmic battle between good and evil. In *Archangel* the epic story continues, shifting to London.

Also in 1993 Kilworth began a series of realistic novels set in rural England, for which he used the pseudonym F. K. Salwood, the maiden name of one of his grandmothers. He has referred to *The Oyster-catcher's Cry* (1993), *The Saffron Fields* (1994), and *The Ragged School* (1995) as his "Country Sagas."

The Phantom Piper (1994) is a skillful blending of elements from the legend of the Pied Piper of Hamelin and from William Golding's *Lord of the Flies* (1954). In Canlish Glen, a village in the Scottish Highlands, a phantom piper lures not the children but the adults away into the hills and into another time with his eerie bagpipe music. This event leaves the children alone, as in Golding's novel, and they are forced to run their world on their own. There the comparisons end, as Kilworth's vision of the kind of life children might have without adults is not as dark as Golding's, and in fact the children manage rather well. As the author remarked in an interview in the 27 October 1994 issue of the Glasgow *Herald*, "There are so many books in which children regress when left to their own devices and I wanted to do something different because I think on a practical level children are very resourceful." For instance, in the book the children often assume the occupations of their parents. Only the intrusion of adults into the village—two men named Tyler and McFee—brings trouble serious enough for the children to disrupt their parent-free existence to search for the missing adults and the music that will bring them back. Furthermore, they discover that unless they can do so by Hogmanay, the Scottish New Year, the adults will die. The result is a suspenseful adventure story that at the same time raises interesting questions about the relationship between children and adults.

Another young-adult novel of 1994, *The Electric Kid,* is considerably different in nature. Inspired both by Kilworth's background in science fiction and his experiences in the Philippines, watching homeless children scrabble for a living from garbage dumps in Manila, the novel is set in 2061, a dismal time following an economic collapse, and is about two young teens, Blindboy and Hotwire, who earn a livelihood from the trash dumps. Blindboy possesses the ability to "hear" electronic impulses, even from devices buried under mounds of refuse, while Hotwire has an uncanny ability to repair even the most damaged

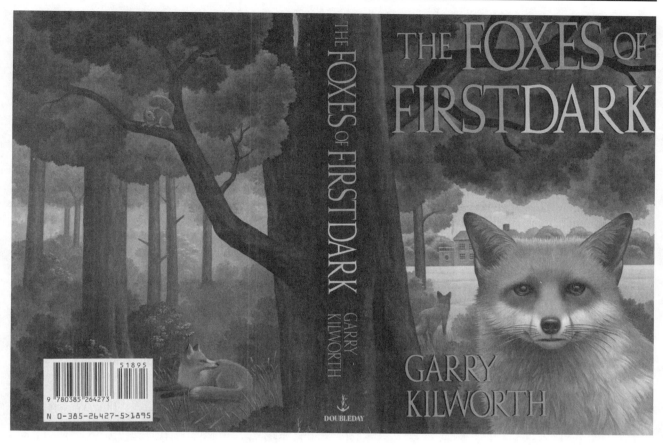

Dust jacket for the U.S. edition of Hunter's Moon *(1989), one of Kilworth's animal-fantasy novels for children*
(Richland County Public Library)

abandoned equipment. With his finding skills and her repair skills, the duo are able to survive in a rather hostile environment, and their circumstances do not impair their sense of humor. The novel then twists into a tale of adventure when the pair is kidnapped by a crime syndicate that wishes to exploit their skills. Critics praised *The Electric Kid* for its strong characterization, original setting, and effective plotting, encouraging Kilworth to describe the further adventures of Blindboy and Hotwire in a sequel, *Cybercats* (1996).

The Brontë Girls (1995) was originally intended as an adult novel. However, the book did not fit neatly into any particular genre—a limitation within publishing for adults that Kilworth has criticized in interviews—and so he marketed it for young adults without changing the nature of the story. Given its intriguing premise, adult publishers were unsure how the book could be marketed. Three sisters—Anne, Charlotte, and Emily—live on an isolated farm in the twentieth century. Are they being raised by a father obsessed with the Brontës who desires to escape the

contemporary world? Or are they the actual Brontë sisters, fantastically transplanted from Victorian times to more than a century hence? The concept is ingenious, but what carries the novel is Kilworth's subtle exploration of family dynamics, especially the role of parents in shaping their children's lives. In addition, the reader is presented with a thought-provoking juxtaposition of past and present.

Kilworth returned to animal fantasy with *House of Tribes* (1995). The protagonist is a mouse named Pedlar, and the plot is both conventional and innovative—conventional in sending Pedlar from his comfortable home on a journey to another world, and innovative in the details of this particular world. The voices of the ancestors send Pedlar from the Hedgerow to the House. After long travels, he reaches the House, which he finds is fought over by competing tribes of other animals. While most of the tribes claim certain parts of the House, there is still much conflict among them until they reach an agreement to unite against their common enemy: the nudniks. The nudniks, whom readers will identify as the humans who occupy the House, are a source of considerable frustration and fear to the various tribes, so they come to the only logical conclusion—drive them out. Thus begins an adventure that is both exciting and humorous, as the assorted animals of the tribes attempt to evict their human pests and their pets, two cats and a mouse who are allied with the nudniks.

In 1996 Kilworth published *A Midsummer's Nightmare,* which brings the fairies of William Shakespeare's *A Midsummer Night's Dream* (1595–1596) into the modern world—or rather, brings the modern world to them. Over the years, developers have encroached into Sherwood Forest, where the fairy king and queen Oberon and Titania, their servant Puck, and the other fairies have resided for centuries. This intrusion eventually drives them from their native forest in search of another that might better allow them space for their magical ways. They decide to get there by bus, with the assistance of Sid, a young mechanic they take captive, who teaches Titania the rules of the road. With the fairy queen at the wheel, off they go, a band of merry pranksters beyond Ken Kesey's wildest dreams. Especially amusing is when they are joined by a group of New Age believers on their way to Stonehenge.

But, as in Shakespeare's classic play, all is not fun and games. For instance, enthralled with a human baby, Titania steals it from a pram, which provokes outrage and fear throughout England, along with a nationwide search. Finally, Titania is forced to do battle with another legendary figure, the evil Morgan le Fey, and their combat is both exciting and terrifying. But as in Shakespeare, in the end all is mended, and the fairies can once more live in peace.

The Roof of Voyaging (1996) is the first volume of a young-adult series called "The Navigator Kings." Set in Polynesia at an unspecified time, the novel concerns the adventures of Kupe. Initially sailing in search of a monstrous octopus, he becomes embroiled in a series of strange adventures along with more conventional political struggles. Kilworth also adds a supernatural element with the gods of Polynesian myth intervening in human affairs. This novel introduces the Land-of-Mists, which becomes more important in the next two novels of the trilogy.

In *The Princely Flower* (1997) the narrative shifts to Kieto, who is destined to conquer the Land-of-Mists. To do so he must confront those who control the island, Europeans with horses and iron weapons. For assistance he decides to enlist Maori warriors from far away, which launches him and his companions on an epic sea voyage that takes them to, among other places, Easter Island. As in *The Roof of Voyaging,* the supernatural is present, in the form of gods and

fairies, who along with the human antagonists help to create the excitement of the narrative.

The trilogy concludes with *Land-of-Mists* (1998). After confronting the fierce Maori in *The Princely Flower,* Kieto has convinced them to join his cause and wrest control of the Land-of-Mists from the Europeans who have occupied it. Reminiscent of Homer's *Iliad,* the story sets up a war between two factions aided by the involvement of the gods.

The three novels that comprise "The Navigator Kings" are noteworthy for Kilworth's interesting combination of history and fantasy and for his use of a mythology that is considerably different from the standard European inspirations of Western fantasy. In addition, he does so in such a way as to appeal to younger readers for whom such material would likely be foreign.

Kilworth returns to European sources for his 1997 young-adult fantasy *The Gargoyle.* A lonely boy befriends a stone gargoyle that comes to life with each full moon. Their friendship turns to adventure when the two set off in the night to find the boy's missing mother—a search complicated by the fact that they have only a short time before the gargoyle reverts to stone.

In 1997 Kilworth began "The Welkin Weasels," a series of animal fantasies for younger readers. The first novel of the series, *Thunder Oak,* establishes that the stoats rule over the weasels, who band together with the protagonist, Sylver, to rebel against the stoats' power. At first their activities are limited to small weapons such as slingshots—deviating from much animal fantasy, the creatures in these stories not only are sentient but also develop tools. However, the stoats are better armed, and the outlaws see little hope of succeeding until Sylver creates an unusual plan. The stoats and the weasels all live in a place called Welkin, which was abandoned years ago by human beings. His plan is to lure the humans back to Welkin and employ their help in ridding themselves of the stoats' tyranny.

The story is continued in *Castle Storm* (1998), which details Sylver's quest, led by the clues he gathered from *Thunder Oak,* to find the long-missing humans. As in *House of Tribes,* the structure of the story is a familiar fantasy plot—the epic quest of a small group of unlikely heroes. The next clue as to where the humans may be found resides in an ancient castle, so the interest of the book lies not in the completion of their quest but in the various adventures along the way. In addition, back home at Welkin the situation has been complicated by the arrival of the rats, who are as rapacious as the stoats they seek to overturn.

In *Windjammer Run* (1999) the band of weasel outlaws led by Sylver finally encounters humans; but their quest will not be complete until they locate the humans who left Welkin years before they were born. Their voyage takes them from land to the sea, riding aboard a human ship. Much of the adventure comes from a series of chases. The stoats, concerned that the weasels might be successful in luring humans back to Welkin, send Sheriff Falshed after them; his efforts to stop them are complicated humorously by his extreme seasickness. Sylver and his gang are also chased by the rats, who falsely believe that the weasels are after a pirate treasure. While all the books in the series are humorous, perhaps *Windjammer Run* is the funniest, yet like the others it is filled with excitement and adventure.

The next novel in the Welkin Weasels series, *Gaslight Geezers* (2001) introduced a new story arc, the first of a trilogy set in Victorian times. In *Gaslight Geezers* Sylver's descendant Montagu Sylver is a weasel detective intent on solving a mystery involving a lemming prince and on foiling an anarchist plot.

The children's novel *The Lantern Fox* (1998) combines a treatment of a childhood problem—in this case, extreme shyness—with a fantastic premise. April, who would rather be alone than have to deal with people, discovers a lantern fox, a magical creature that glows like a lantern. This quality makes the fox an easy prey for hunters, so April takes it home with her and hides it in her room. Much of the interest of the plot comes from her attempts to keep her discovery hidden from her family, but in the meantime she becomes transformed by the fox's magical powers and learns to relate better to other people.

Shadow-Hawk (1999) is another fantasy for young adults. The setting is a rainforest, specifically the Kingdom of the Sun Bear. Like many fantasies, the story involves a quest. The characters long to find seven ancient heads left by the Punan in the Kingdom of the Sun Bear, thereby acquiring great wealth, but naturally this task is not easy. Their adventures thus pit them against challenges both natural and supernatural, against ferocious forest animals and angry spirits and gods, as well as each other. Also looming over the whole affair is the Shadow-Hawk, which consumes the souls of men.

Although Kilworth has not risen to the upper ranks of British fantasy and science fiction, he is a well-respected writer with diverse interests who ably juggles the worlds of fantasy, science fiction, and horror as well as books for children, adolescents, and adults. In addition to receiving many awards, he has also been the subject of a fan magazine produced by Mike Stone called *Spiral Words*. Happily settled in rural Essex, he continues to maintain a prolific output in a variety of forms. As Jones notes in her interview with Kilworth, "He's a writer who deserves a lot more recognition."

Interviews:

Gwyneth Jones, "Garry Kilworth," *Strange Plasma*, 5 (February 1991);

Jennifer Cunningham, "Essex Man and Glasgow Woman Remind Us of Importance of Our Native Tongues: Standing the Pied Piper on His Head," *Herald* (Glasgow), 27 October 1994, p. 12.

David Langford

(10 April 1953 –   )

D. Douglas Fratz

BOOKS: *The Necronomicon,* by Langford, George Hay, Robert Turner, and Colin Wilson (St. Helier, U.K.: Spearman, 1978);

War in 2080: The Future of Military Technology (Newton Abbott, U.K.: David & Charles/Westbridge, 1979; New York: Morrow, 1979);

An Account of a Meeting with Denizens of Another World, 1871, as William Robert Loosley and edited by Langford (Newton Abbott, U.K.: David & Charles, 1979; New York: St. Martin's Press, 1980);

Facts and Fallacies: A Book of Definitive Mistakes and Misguided Predictions, by Langford and Chris Morgan (Exeter, U.K.: Webb & Bower, 1981; New York: St. Martin's Press, 1981);

The Space Eater (London: Arrow, 1982; New York: Pocket Books, 1983);

The Science in Science Fiction, by Langford, Peter Nicholls, and Brian Stableford (London: Joseph, 1982; New York: Knopf, 1982);

Micro Mania: The Whole Truth about Home Computers, by Langford and Charles Platt (London: Gollancz, 1984);

The Leaky Establishment (London: Muller, 1984);

The Third Millennium: A History of the World, AD 2000–3000, by Langford and Stableford (London: Sidgwick & Jackson, 1985; New York: Knopf, 1985);

The TransAtlantic Hearing Aid (Chichester, U.K.: Inca, 1985);

Earthdoom! by Langford and John Grant (London: Grafton, 1987);

Platen Stories (Cambridge: Conspiracy '87, 1987);

Critical Assembly: The First 50 White Dwarf Review Columns (Reading, U.K.: Ansible Information, 1987);

The Dragonhiker's Guide to Battlefield Covenant at Dune's Edge: Odyssey Two (Birmingham, U.K.: Drunken Dragon Press, 1988);

Critical Assembly II (Reading, U.K.: Ansible Information, 1992);

Let's Hear It for the Deaf Man, edited by Ben Yalow (Framingham, Mass.: NESFA Press, 1992);

David Langford (photograph from the dust jacket for the U.S. edition of War in 2080: The Future of Military Technology, *1979)*

expanded as *The Silence of the Langford,* edited by Yalow (Framingham, Mass.: NESFA Press, 1996);

Irrational Numbers (West Warwick, R.I.: Necronomicon Press, 1994);

The Unseen University Challenge: Terry Pratchett's Discworld Quizbook (London: Vista, 1996);

Pieces of Langford, edited by John and Eve Harvey (Tonwell, U.K.: Auld Lang Fund Press, 1998);

A Cosmic Cornucopia, text by Langford, art by Josh Kirby (London: Paper Tiger, 1999);

Guts, by Langford and Grant (Gillette, N.J.: Wildside Press, 2001);

Through an Empty House of Stars: Reviews and Essays 1980–2001 (Gillette, N.J.: Wildside Press, 2002);

The Wyrdest Link: A Terry Pratchett Discworld Quizbook (London: Gollancz, 2002).

Edition: *The Complete Critical Assembly* (Gillette, N.J.: Wildside Press, 2001).

PRODUCED SCRIPT: *Strange Objects: Fact and Fiction,* radio, BBC Radio 4, 1983.

OTHER: "Heatwave," in *New Writings in SF 27,* edited by Kenneth Bulmer (London: Sidgwick & Jackson, 1975);

"Takeover," in *The Eighth Armada Ghost Book,* edited by Mary Danby (London: Armada, 1976);

"Accretion," in *Andromeda 2,* edited by Peter Weston (London: Futura, 1977);

"At the Corner of the Eye," in *The Tenth Fontana Book of Great Horror Stories,* edited by Danby (London: Fontana, 1977);

"Connections," in *Andromeda 3,* edited by Weston (London: Futura, 1978);

"The Still Small Voice Inside," in *Pulsar 1,* edited by George Hay (London: Penguin, 1978);

"Sex Pirates of the Blood Asteroid," in *Aries 1,* edited by John Grant (Newton Abbott, U.K.: David & Charles, 1979);

"Training," in *Thor's Hammer,* edited by Reginald Bretnor (New York: Ace, 1979);

"The Chess Set," in *The Twelfth Armada Ghost Book,* edited by Danby (London: Armada, 1980);

"Cold Spell," in *The Thirteenth Armada Ghost Book,* edited by Danby (London: Armada, 1981);

"The Final Days," in *Destinies 3:1,* edited by Jim Baen (New York: Ace, 1981);

"Sacrifice," in *Destinies 3:2,* edited by Baen (New York: Ace, 1981);

"Transcends All Wit," in *Pictures at an Exhibition,* edited by Ian Watson (Cardiff, U.K.: Greystoke Mobray, 1981);

"Semolina," in *Peter Davison's Book of Alien Monsters* (London: Hutchinson/Sparrow, 1982);

"Lukewarm," in *Alien Encounters,* edited by Jan Howard Finder (New York: Taplinger, 1982);

"Under the Bedclothes," in *The Fourteenth Armada Ghost Book,* edited by Danby (London: Armada, 1982);

"3:47 AM," in *The Gruesome Book,* edited by Ramsey Campbell (London: Piccolo, 1983); reprinted in *The Year's Best Horror Stories XII,* edited by Karl Edward Wagner (New York: DAW, 1984);

"In the Place of Power," in *Beyond Lands of Never,* edited by Maxim Jakubowski (London: Unwin, 1984);

"Notes for a Newer Testament," in *Afterwar,* edited by Janet Morris (New York: Baen, 1985); republished in *White Dwarf,* 91 (July 1987);

"In a Land of Sand and Ruin and Gold," in *Other Edens,* edited by Christopher Evans and Robert Holdstock (London: Unwin, 1987);

"The Facts in the Case of Micky Valdron," in *Dark Fantasies,* edited by Chris Morgan (London: Legend, 1989);

"The Motivation," in *Arrows of Eros,* edited by Alex Stewart (London: New English Library, 1990); reprinted in *The Year's Best Horror Stories XVIII,* edited by Wagner (New York: DAW, 1990);

"A Surprisingly Common Omission," in *Drabble II: Double Century,* edited by Rob Meades and David B. Wake (Harold Wood, U.K.: Beccon, 1990);

"Ellipses," in *More Tales from the Forbidden Planet,* edited by Roz Kaveney (London: Titan Books, 1990);

"What Happened at Cambridge IV," in *Digital Dreams,* edited by David B. Barrett (London: New English Library, 1990);

"Waiting for the Iron Age," in *Tales of the Wandering Jew,* edited by Brian Stableford (Sawtry, U.K.: Dedalus, 1991);

"Leaks," in *Temps,* edited by Neil Gaiman and Stewart (London: Roc, 1991);

"The Arts of the Enemy," in *Villains!* edited by Mary Gentle and Kaveney (London: Roc, 1992);

"If Looks Could Kill," in *Eurotemps,* edited by Stewart (London: Roc, 1992);

"The Lions in the Desert," in *The Weerde II: The Book of the Ancients,* edited by Gaiman and Kaveney (London: Roc, 1993);

"Christmas Games," in *Christmas Forever,* edited by David G. Hartwell (New York: Tor, 1993);

Contributing editor, *The Encyclopedia of Fantasy,* edited by John Clute and Grant (London: Orbit, 1997).

SELECTED PERIODICAL PUBLICATIONS— UNCOLLECTED:

FICTION

"Imbalance," *Ad Astra,* 4 (June 1979);

"Understudy," *Practical Computing* (October 1979);

"Turing Test," *Practical Computing* (April 1980);

"Law of Conservation," *Ad Astra,* 10 (June 1980);

"Friendly Reflections," *Practical Computing* (February 1982);

"Hearing Aid," *Practical Computing* (October 1982); republished with corrections, *Phoenix Magazine* (August 1983) and *Knave* (1984);

"Too Good to Be," *Imagine,* 3 (June 1983);

"Statement of a Minor Offender," *Knave* (June 1984); republished in *Best of Knave* (1985);

"Sidetrack," *Knave* (August 1984);

"Wetware," *What Micro?* (November 1984);

"Cube Root," *Interzone,* 11 (Spring 1985) republished in *Interzone: The Third Anthology,* edited by John Clute, David Pringle, and Simon Ounsley (London: Simon & Schuster, 1988);

"The Power of the Frog," *White Dwarf,* 74 (February 1986);

"Blit," *Interzone,* 25 (September/October 1988); republished in *Interzone: The Fourth Anthology,* edited by Clute, Pringle and Ounsley (London: Simon & Schuster, 1989);

"A Snapshot Album," *Interzone,* 43 (January 1991);

"Encounter of Another Kind," *Interzone,* 54 (December 1991);

"Blossoms That Coil and Decay," *Interzone,* 57 (March 1992).

NONFICTION

"Fission Fragments" (column), *Ad Astra* (1979–1981);

"SF for the People: A New SF Magazine, Anyone?" *Vector,* 103 (August 1981);

"Ian Watson Interviewed," *Science Fiction Review,* 11 (February 1982);

"Interview with John Sladek," *Science Fiction Review,* 12 (February 1983); republished as "Sladek at Random: John Sladek Interviewed," *Vector,* 112 (1983);

"Hey Prestel: Electronic SF," *SFWA Bulletin,* 17 (Spring 1983);

"Critical Mass" (column), *White Dwarf* (1983–1988); *GamesMaster International* (1990–1991);

"Critical Hits" (column), *GM* (1988–1990);

"Dispatches from the UFO Wars," *Interzone,* 40 (October 1990);

"Slightly Foxed" (column), *Million,* 1991–1993; *Interzone,* 51 (September 1991);

"A Gadget Too Far," *New Worlds,* 2 (August 1992);

"Ansible Link" (column), *Interzone,* 1992–1993;

"The Editor My Destination," *QUANTUM,* 43/44 (Spring/Summer 1993);

"Different Kinds of Darkness," *The Magazine of Science and Science Fiction* (January 2000).

David Langford is one of the most popular commentators in the field of science fiction and fantasy, as well as the author of many science-fiction, fantasy, and horror stories and one science-fiction novel. He has also co-authored several books on topics related to popular science, futurology, and microcomputers. He has become best known in both England and the United States for his humorous essays and book reviews (many of which have been published first in science fiction fanzines circulated to only a few hundred fans), for which he has received fifteen Hugo Awards.

David Rowland Langford was born in South Wales on 10 April 1953 to Denis George Langford, an accountant, and Catherine Alice (née Lenta) Langford. He received an honors degree in physics at Brasenose College, Oxford, in 1974, and a master's degree there in 1978. He worked as a physicist at the Atomic Weapons Research Establishment at Aldermaston from 1975 until 1980. He has since been a freelance author and lives with his wife, Hazel (née Salter, a civil servant whom he married in June 1976), in a large old house in Reading. He is the owner, formerly in partnership with fellow author Christopher Priest, of a software company called Ansible Information.

Langford became active in British science-fiction fandom in the early 1970s, writing for various fanzines. In 1976 he began publishing *Twll-Ddu,* a fanzine that featured his humorous writings about fandom, conventions, and other topics often only tangentially related to science-fiction literature. His best-known fanzine, *Ansible,* was begun in 1979 and is still in existence (after a four-year hiatus, 1987–1991). His light, humorous, but often insightful style earned him a growing popularity, first in the United Kingdom and then the United States, among the several hundred fans and professionals most active in the inner core of science-fiction fandom. By 1979 he was widely considered one of the best writers of such "fannish" material and began receiving regular nominations for Hugo Awards for Best Fanzine and/or Best Fan Writer.

Langford also began writing science fiction in the early 1970s. His first published story was "Heatwave," published in 1975 in the twenty-seventh volume of Kenneth Bulmer's long-running British anthology series, *New Writings in SF.* He followed with several more science-fiction and horror short stories over the next few years but received little critical success until the 1979 publication of "Sex Pirates of the Blood Asteroid," a humorous story that utilized Langford's distinctive wit and was nominated for the British SF Association Award for best short story; it was reprinted in *Penthouse* in 1980, his first short-fiction publication in the United States. His most successful science-fiction short story in the 1970s was "Training" (1979), his first story printed in an American anthology.

In the late 1970s and early 1980s Langford also wrote or collaborated on several books. His first book was called *The Necronomicon* (1978) and was a hoax reconstruction and critique of this "lost" occult book. It was written with several other British authors and was never published in the United States. His first book to gain an American edition was *War in 2080: The Future of Military Technology* (1979), a popular science book that utilized his knowledge from working as a weapons physicist.

His next two books heralded Langford's interest in pseudoscience and weird beliefs. The first was titled *An Account of a Meeting with Denizens of Another World, 1871* (1979), a realistically written fiction account allegedly from a recently discovered manuscript by William Robert Loosley, a Victorian man who encountered a UFO one evening near his home in Buckinghamshire. The book includes "Loosley's" firsthand account, written the day after the encounter and hidden away in a desk (where it lay undiscovered for one hundred years); historical photos of Loosley and his family, his house, and family grave site (supposedly uncovered during Langford's research); and a lengthy commentary by Langford that seeks explanations of Loosley's observations. Langford wrote this last section in such an earnest-but-just-slightly-skeptical manner that the book was almost certainly considered genuine by many who read it and were unfamiliar with Langford's odd sense of humor. This book later gained some interesting notoriety (at least within the science-fiction field) when in 1989 well-known American author Whitley Strieber summarized the same account in one of his best-selling books wherein he described an account (supposedly based on a true incident) of a visitation by alien visitors. Langford's next book, written with Chris Morgan, was a nonfiction book, *Facts and Fallacies: A Book of Definitive Mistakes and Misguided Predictions* (1981).

The Space Eater (1982), Langford's only science-fiction novel, incorporated a revised version of his story "Training." *The Space Eater* is a traditional science-fiction adventure novel about a soldier in a future world where high-technology "anomalous" physics experiments are threatening the very fabric of space-time, altering the physical constants that make stars and matter stable. The protagonist, Ken Jacklin, is a military veteran who has become expert at enduring excruciating pain, sustaining extensive physical damage, and then being slowly regenerated back to fighting form. Anomalous physics made all kinds of superweaponry and matter transmitters possible before scientists discovered (but carefully hid from the public) that its widespread use was causing instability in stars throughout Earth's sector of the galaxy, filling the sky with supernovae and even endangering the sun. The plot involves the protagonist's assignment to be matter-transmitted to a far star (where a now-isolated settlement of humans had long ago been transmitted) to stop their new anomalous physics experiments that are once again endangering space-time. The reason he is chosen is his ability to face pain and death without undue psychological trauma; the only safe matter transmitter can open up a hole 1.9 centimeters wide at best. The protagonist and his female partner must face the gruesome procedure of being physically cut into small strips and transmitted, then reassembled and regenerated by the robots at the other end of the transmitter.

Published as part of the prestigious Pocket Books Timescape program in the United States, *The Space Eater* was an ambitious and rather successful book, owing to its original physics, fast-moving plot,

Paperback cover for the expanded edition of Langford's 1992 collection of critical essays

and believable protagonist. It did suffer, however, from many of its key elements being less than logically justified. Langford made no attempt to explain how soldiers were able to avoid sustaining brain damage during the war training and battle exercises, nor why those going through the matter transmitter could not be put to sleep or otherwise anesthetized before transmission. For that matter, slicing a human brain into 1.9-centimeter pieces would obliterate all memory, even if the brain could be reassembled and repaired. The book therefore has much in common with many science-fiction novels in seeking to cover up logical and scientific inconsistencies with a plot too fast paced to allow too much scrutiny. (These types of inconsistencies in the science fiction of other authors have actually provided the basis for many of Langford's best and most humorous critical writings.)

Also in 1982 Langford collaborated with Peter Nicholls and Brian Stableford on a large, illustrated book called *The Science in Science Fiction*, which utilized Nicholls's encyclopedic knowledge of science fiction,

Paperback cover for the horror-novel parody Langford described as "resolutely tasteless"

Stableford's knowledge of biology, and Langford's knowledge of physics to present extensive descriptions of the known and speculative science most commonly used in science-fiction literature and movies. The book won the Special European SF Award in 1984 as well as a Spanish award for best translated work in 1987. Langford wrote four of the twelve chapters, covering cosmological physics, warfare and natural disasters, artificial and altered human intelligence, and bad science and misguided predictions. In 1985 Langford completed, with Stableford, his most ambitious project: an illustrated future history of humankind, titled *The Third Millennium: A History of the World, AD 2000–3000.* The narrative, written as if by historians from the year 3000, relates in great detail all of the political, technological, and sociological changes that occurred in the millennium. Although Langford and Stableford's vision is extremely upbeat (especially considering that both are British), it is often conservative regarding the pace of technological and social change. The effects of computers on society, for example, have already outstripped

those speculated for the next hundred years. The progress and changes they predicted might have made more sense if their history covered only a couple hundred years instead of a thousand.

Although *The Space Eater* was his only serious science-fiction novel, Landford continued to produce serious short stories, both science fiction and horror, throughout the 1980s and into the 1990s. Many of his stories, however, were never published in the United States, perhaps because they often feature subjects and writing styles somewhat inaccessible to many American readers. "Transcends All Wit" (1981), for instance, is an enigmatic dream-like narrative that makes little sense outside of the context of the anthology in which it appeared. "Lukewarm" (1982) was a more successful story, although its human-telepath-narrated sections were not written clearly enough to contrast properly with the strange alien-stream-of-consciousness sections. Later stories such as "Blit" (1988), "A Snapshot Album" (1991), "Encounter of Another Kind" (1991), and "Blossoms That Coil and Decay" (1992), all published in the British magazine *Interzone,* ranged widely in subject and theme but were written in a slightly too-obscure British literary style. More interesting was "Notes for a Newer Testament" (1985), a postnuclear-war story in which already backward local Britons fend off invading hordes through use of the remnants of high-tech weaponry; although the story is a bit colloquial, the concept keeps reader attention. His most successful story in this period was "Cube Root" (1985), which won the British SF Association Award for best short story. Langford also wrote several good horror stories in the 1980s, among the most notable being "3:47 AM" (1983).

Some of his best short stories in the 1990s have featured mystery elements, including "Leaks" (1991) and "If Looks Could Kill" (1992), both science-fiction mysteries with the former having the same setting as *The Leaky Establishment* (1984), Langford's satire of British nuclear research. "The Lions in the Desert" (1993) and "Christmas Games" (1993) are variations on the locked-room mystery. Only occasionally has Langford been able to carry the straightforward, easily readable style of his nonfiction into his fiction.

He was, however, able to convey his outrageous but erudite British humor in some of his fiction, and Langford's best-known fiction is in a satirical or humorous mode. Most of his spoofs, first published between 1984 and 1988, were collected in *The Dragonhiker's Guide to Battlefield Covenant at Dune's Edge: Odyssey Two* (1988). The book includes outrageous parodies of fiction by Piers Anthony, Isaac Asimov, Lewis Carroll, The Brothers Grimm, Frank Herbert, William Hope Hodgson, Michael Moorcock, E. E. Smith, A. E.

van Vogt, and James White, along with an introduction that parodies Harlan Ellison. Langford also collaborated with John Grant (a pseudonym of British author/editor Paul Barnett) in 1987 on a world-shattering spoof disaster novel, *Earthdoom!,* which received mixed reviews. A second humorous novel written with Grant, *Guts,* which Langford describes on his website <http://www.ansible.demon.co.uk/biblio.html> as a "bowel-wrenching spoof horror novel, resolutely tasteless," was written in the late 1980s but not published until 2001.

Langford's most successful writing, however, has been his nonfiction written for various periodicals in the science-fiction field, ranging from fanzines to professional magazines. Most of his work for fanzines is only tangentially related to science fiction. His work for professional magazines such as *SFX* and *Interzone* and semiprofessional journals such as *Foundation, SF Commentary, Quantum,* and *The New York Review of Science Fiction* has consisted primarily of critical literary reviews combining both wit and insight into what makes for good (and bad) science fiction. One of Langford's specialties is noting stupid errors in logic and bad writing. Much of his best fan and critical writing has been collected in small-press collections, including *The TransAtlantic Hearing Aid* (an account of his trip to the United States for the 1980 World Science Fiction Convention), *Platen Stories* (1987), *Critical Assembly* (a 1987 indexed collection of his book review columns written for a gaming maga-

zine), *Let's Hear It for The Deaf Man* (1992, nominated for a Hugo Award as Best Non-Fiction) and *Critical Assembly II* (1992).

Langford also ghost-edited and is credited for coauthoring the second edition of John Clute and Nicholls's *The Encyclopedia of Science Fiction* (1993), one of the most important volumes yet published covering the science-fiction genre, and was a contributing editor for Clute and John Grant's *Encyclopedia of Fantasy* (1997). He has been chosen as Guest of Honor at many conventions (as far away as Boston, Minneapolis, Finland, Florida, Melbourne, and Portland, Oregon), where his humorous talks are considered highlights of those events. In 2002 Langford received the New England Science Fiction Association's Skylark Award, presented annually in memory of E. E. Smith to honor notable contributions to science fiction.

Few writers with Langford's talent have produced so much of their writing for such limited audiences, and it would be easy to question why Langford has expended so much time and effort on nonpaying, small-circulation fanzines. But Langford appears to do his best writing when he is most comfortable in his knowledge of his audience, and he is thoroughly familiar with the inner core of science-fiction fandom. He may yet turn his talents to writing popular fiction and allow a larger audience to enjoy his distinctive and penetrating wit.

Tanith Lee

(19 September 1947 –   )

Maureen F. Moran
Brunel University

BOOKS: *The Betrothed* (Sidcup, U.K.: Slughorn Press, 1968);

The Dragon Hoard (New York: Farrar, Straus & Giroux, 1971; London: Macmillan, 1971);

Animal Castle (New York: Farrar, Straus & Giroux, 1972; London: Macmillan, 1972);

Princess Hynchatti and Some Other Surprises (London: Macmillan, 1972; New York: Farrar, Straus & Giroux, 1973);

The Birthgrave (New York: DAW, 1975; London: Futura, 1977);

Companions on the Road (London: Macmillan, 1975);

Don't Bite the Sun (New York: DAW, 1976);

The Storm Lord (New York: DAW, 1976: London: Futura, 1977);

The Winter Players (London: Macmillan, 1976);

Drinking Sapphire Wine (New York: DAW, 1977);

Volkhavaar (New York: DAW, 1977; London: Hamlyn, 1981);

East of Midnight (London: Macmillan, 1977; New York: St. Martin's Press, 1978);

Companions on the Road and The Winter Players: Two Novellas (New York: St. Martin's Press, 1977; London: Bantam, 1979);

Vazkor, Son of Vazkor (New York: DAW, 1978); republished as *Shadowfire* (London: Futura, 1978);

Quest for the White Witch (New York: DAW, 1978); republished as *Shadowfire 2: Quest for the White Witch* (London: Futura, 1979);

The Castle of Dark (London: Macmillan, 1978);

Night's Master (New York: DAW, 1978; London: Hamlyn, 1981);

Death's Master (New York: DAW, 1979; London: Hamlyn, 1982);

Electric Forest (New York: DAW, 1979; London: Hamlyn, 1983);

Shon the Taken (London: Macmillan, 1979);

Drinking Sapphire Wine (Incorporating Don't Bite the Sun) (London: Hamlyn, 1979); republished as *Biting the Sun* (New York & London: Bantam, 1999);

Tanith Lee (photograph from the dust jacket for
The Book of the Mad, *1993)*

Sabella; or, The Blood Stone (New York: DAW, 1980; London: Unwin, 1987);

Kill the Dead (New York: DAW, 1980; London: Legend, 1990);

Day by Night (New York: DAW, 1980);

Sometimes, After Sunset (Garden City, N.Y.: Doubleday, 1980)–comprises *Sabella; or, The Blood Stone* and *Kill the Dead;*

Unsilent Night (Cambridge, Mass.: NESFA Press, 1981);

Lycanthia; or, The Children of the Wolves (New York: DAW, 1981; London: Legend, 1990);

Delusion's Master (New York: DAW, 1981; London: Arrow, 1987);

The Silver Metal Lover (Garden City, N.Y.: Doubleday, 1981; London: Unwin, 1986);

Prince on a White Horse (London: Macmillan, 1982);

Cyrion (New York: DAW, 1982);

Red as Blood; or, Tales from the Sisters Grimmer (New York: DAW, 1983);

Sung in Shadow (New York: DAW, 1983);

Anackire (New York: DAW, 1983; London: Futura, 1985);

The Beautiful Biting Machine (New Castle, Va.: Cheap Street, 1984);

Tamastara; or, The Indian Nights (New York: DAW, 1984);

The Wars of Vis (Garden City, N.Y.: Doubleday, 1984)—comprises *The Storm Lord* and *Anackire;*

Night Visions 1, by Lee, Charles L. Grant, and Steve Rasnic Tem, edited by Alan Ryan (Niles, Ill.: Dark Harvest, 1984); republished as *Night Visions: In the Blood* (New York: Berkley, 1988);

The Gorgon and Other Beastly Tales (New York: DAW, 1985);

Days of Grass (New York: DAW, 1985);

Dark Castle, White Horse (New York: DAW, 1986)—comprises *The Castle of Dark* and *Prince on a White Horse;*

Delirium's Mistress (New York: DAW, 1986; London: Arrow, 1987);

Dreams of Dark and Light: The Great Short Fiction of Tanith Lee (Sauk City, Wis.: Arkham House, 1986);

Night's Sorceries (New York: DAW, 1987; London: Legend, 1988);

Tales from the Flat Earth: The Lords of Darkness (Garden City, N.Y.: Doubleday, 1987)—comprises *Night's Master, Death's Master,* and *Delusion's Master;*

Tales from the Flat Earth: Night's Daughter (Garden City, N.Y.: Doubleday, 1987)—comprises *Delirium's Mistress* and *Night's Sorceries;*

The White Serpent (New York: DAW, 1988);

The Book of the Damned (London: Unwin, 1988; Woodstock, N.Y.: Overlook Press, 1990);

The Book of the Beast (London: Unwin, 1988; Woodstock, N.Y.: Overlook Press, 1991);

Madame Two Swords (West Kingston, R.I.: Donald M. Grant, 1988);

Women as Demons: The Male Perception of Women Through Space and Time (London: Women's Press, 1989);

Forests of the Night (London: Unwin Hyman, 1989);

A Heroine of the World (New York: DAW, 1989; London: Headline, 1994);

The Blood of Roses (London: Legend, 1990);

The Secret Books of Paradys 1 & 2 (New York: Guild America Books, 1991)—comprises *The Book of the Damned* and *The Book of the Beast;*

Black Unicorn (New York: Atheneum, 1991; London: Orbit, 1994);

Into Gold (Eugene, Ore.: Pulphouse, 1991);

The Book of the Dead (Woodstock, N.Y.: Overlook Press, 1991);

Dark Dance (New York: Dell, 1992; London: Macdonald, 1992);

Heart-Beast (London: Headline, 1992; New York: Dell, 1993);

Personal Darkness (London: Little, Brown, 1993; New York: Dell, 1994);

Elephantasm (London: Headline, 1993; New York: Dell, 1996);

The Book of the Mad (Woodstock, N.Y.: Overlook Press, 1993);

The Secret Books of Paradys 3 & 4 (New York: Guild America Books, 1993)—comprises *The Book of the Dead* and *The Book of the Mad;*

Nightshades: Thirteen Journeys into Shadow (London: Headline, 1993);

Darkness, I (London: Little, Brown, 1994; New York: St. Martin's Press, 1995);

Eva Fairdeath (London: Headline, 1994);

Gold Unicorn (New York: Atheneum, 1994; London: Orbit, 1995);

Vivia (London: Little, Brown, 1995);

Reigning Cats and Dogs (London: Headline, 1995);

Louisa the Poisoner (Berkeley Heights, N.J.: Wildside Press, 1995 [i.e., 1996]);

When the Lights Go Out (London: Headline, 1996);

The Gods Are Thirsty (Woodstock, N.Y.: Overlook Press, 1996);

Red Unicorn (New York: Tor, 1997);

Faces Under Water (Woodstock, N.Y.: Overlook Press, 1998);

Law of the Wolf Tower (London: Hodder Children's Books, 1998); republished as *Wolf Tower* (New York: Dutton, 2000);

Voyage of the Bassett: Islands in the Sky (New York: Random House, 1999);

Saint Fire (Woodstock, N.Y.: Overlook Press, 1999);

The Secret Books of Venus 1 & 2 (New York: SFBC Fantasy, 1999)—comprises *Faces Under Water* and *Saint Fire;*

Wolf Star Rise (London: Hodder Children's Books, 2000); republished as *Wolf Star* (New York: Dutton, 2001);

White as Snow (New York: Tor, 2000);

Queen of the Wolves (London: Hodder Children's Books, 2001); republished as *Wolf Queen* (New York: Dutton, 2002);

A Bed of Earth (The Gravedigger's Tale) (Woodstock, N.Y.: Overlook Press, 2002).

PRODUCED SCRIPTS: "Bitter Gate," radio, *The Monday Play,* BBC, 20 June 1977;

"Red Wine," radio, *Thirty Minute Theatre,* BBC, 3 December 1977;

"Death Is King," radio, *The Monday Play,* BBC, 17 September 1979;

"Sarcophagus," television, *Blake's 7,* BBC, 3 March 1980;

"The Silver Sky," radio, *Saturday Night Theatre,* BBC, 9 August 1980;

"Sand," television, *Blake's 7,* BBC, 23 November 1981.

OTHER: "Eustace," in *The Ninth Book of Pan Horror Stories,* edited by Herbert van Thal (London: Pan, 1968), p. 252;

"Sun City," in *Young Winter's Tales 3,* edited by Marni Hodgkin (London: Macmillan, 1972); reprinted in *Fantasy Stories,* edited by Mike Ashley (London: Robinson Children's Books, 1996), pp. 291–322;

"Cold Spell," in *Young Winter's Tales 7,* edited by Hodgkin (London: Macmillan, 1976), pp. 118–131;

"In the Balance," in *Swords Against Darkness III,* edited by Andrew J. Offutt (New York: Zebra Books, 1978), pp. 91–96; reprinted in *The Year's Best Fantasy Stories: 5,* edited by Lin Carter (New York: DAW, 1980);

"The Sombrus Tower," in *Weird Tales #2,* edited by Carter (New York: Zebra Books, 1981), pp. 243–256; reprinted in *Weird Tales: The Magazine That Never Dies,* edited by Marvin Kaye (Garden City, N.Y.: Science Fiction Book Club, 1988), pp. 129–137;

"As Time Goes By," in *Chrysalis 10,* edited by Roy Torgeson (New York: Doubleday, 1983), pp. 39–52; reprinted in *The 1984 Annual World's Best SF,* edited by Donald A. Wollheim and Arthur W. Saha (New York: DAW, 1984), pp. 178–192;

"The Pale Girl, The Dark Mage, and the Green Sea," in *Moonsinger's Friends: An Anthology in Honor of Andre Norton,* edited by Susan M. Shwartz (New York: Bluejay Books, 1985), pp. 74–76;

"Love Alters," in *Despatches from the Frontiers of the Female Mind,* edited by Jen Green and Sarah Lefanu (London: Women's Press, 1985), pp. 60–73;

"The Minstrel's Tale," in *Invitation to Camelot: An Arthurian Anthology of Short Stories,* edited by Parke Godwin (New York: Ace, 1988), pp. 19–29;

"Foolish, Wicked, Clever and Kind," in *Arabesques: More Tales of the Arabian Nights,* edited by Shwartz (New York: Avon, 1988), pp. 42–72;

"Ceres Passing," in *Hidden Turnings: A Collection of Stories Through Time and Space,* edited by Diana Wynne Jones (London: Methuen, 1989), pp. 12–24;

"The Three Brides of Hamid-Dar," in *Arabesques 2,* edited by Shwartz (New York: Avon, 1989), pp. 89–106;

"Don't Get Lost," in *Dark Fantasies,* edited by Chris Morgan (London: Legend, 1989), pp. 210–218; reprinted in *100 Twisted Little Tales of Torment,* edited by Stefan Dziemianowicz, Robert Weinberg, and Martin H. Greenberg (New York: Barnes & Noble, 1988);

"Exalted Hearts," in *Grails: Quests, Visitations and Other Occurrences,* edited by Richard Gilliam, Greenberg, and Edward R. Kramer (Atlanta: Unnameable Press, 1992), pp. 53–60; reprinted in *Grails: Visitations of the Night,* edited by Gilliam, Greenberg, and Kramer (New York: Roc, 1994);

"Snow-Drop," in *Snow White, Blood Red,* edited by Ellen Datlow and Terri Windling (New York: Morrow, 1993), pp. 106–129;

"Unnalash," in *Xanadu,* edited by Jane Yolen and Greenberg (New York: Tor, 1993), pp. 46–61;

"The Witch of the Moon," in *The Ultimate Witch,* edited by Byron Priess and John Betancourt (New York: Dell, 1993), pp. 40–58;

"The Champion," in *Xanadu 3,* edited by Yolen (New York: Tor, 1995), pp. 173–178;

"She Sleeps in a Tower," in *The Armless Maiden and Other Tales for Childhood's Survivors,* edited by Windling (New York: Tor, 1995), pp. 42–45;

"Felixity," in *Sisters in Fantasy,* edited by Shwartz and Greenberg (New York: Penguin, 1995), pp. 183–206;

"Saxon Flaxen," in *Ancient Enchantresses,* edited by Kathleen M. Massie-French, Greenberg, and Gilliam (New York: DAW, 1995), pp. 67–77;

"Introduction" and "Age," in *The Ultimate Dragon,* edited by Preiss, Betancourt, and Keith R. A. DeCandido (New York: Dell, 1995), pp. 5–10;

"La Dame," in *Sisters of the Night,* edited by Barbara Hambly and Greenberg (New York: Warner Aspect, 1995), pp. 112–125; reprinted in *The Year's Best Fantasy and Horror: Ninth Annual Collection,* edited by Datlow and Windling (New York: St. Martin's Press, 1996), pp. 332–340; reprinted in *Girls' Night Out: Twenty-Nine Female Vampire Stories,* edited by Dziemianowicz, Weinberg, and Greenberg (New York: Barnes & Noble, 1997);

"King's Mage," in *The Merlin Chronicles,* edited by Ashley (New York: Carroll & Graf, 1995; London: Raven Books, 1995), pp. 255–264;

"The Beast," in *Ruby Slippers, Golden Tears,* edited by Datlow and Windling (New York: Morrow, 1995), pp. 16–32;

"The World Well Lost," in *Warrior Enchantresses,* edited by Massie-French and Greenberg (New York: DAW, 1996), pp. 13–29;

"Flowers for Faces, Thorns for Feet," in *Twists of the Tale: Cat Horror Stories,* edited by Datlow (New York: Dell, 1996), pp. 328–366;

"Cain," in *Dying For It: More Erotic Tales of Unearthly Love,* edited by Gardner Dozois (New York: Harper-Prism, 1997), pp. 25–45;

"The Pandora Heart," in *Don't Open This Book!* edited by Kaye (Garden City, N.Y.: Guild America Books, 1998), pp. 83–105;

"Wolfed," in *Sirens and Other Daemon Lovers,* edited by Datlow and Windling (New York: HarperPrism, 1998), pp. 35–47;

"Living Hell," in *Barlowe's Inferno,* art and text by Wayne D. Barlowe (Beverly Hills: Galerie Morpheus International, 1998), pp. 7–9;

"Kiss Kiss," in *Silver Birch, Blood Moon,* edited by Datlow and Windling (New York: Avon, 1999), pp. 8–24.

SELECTED PERIODICAL PUBLICATIONS–UNCOLLECTED:

POETRY

"Memorial Stone: 1945," *Dragonfields,* no. 4 (Winter 1983): 26.

FICTION

"Sleeping Tiger," *Dragonbane: Tales of Heroic Fantasy,* no. 1 (Spring 1978): 6, 8–9, 11–12; reprinted in *The Year's Best Horror Stories, Series VII,* edited by Gerald W. Page (New York: DAW, 1979), pp. 59–66; reprinted in *After Hours,* 1 (Winter 1989);

"The Third Horseman," *Weirdbook,* no. 14 (Spring 1979): 56–58;

"Goldenhair," *Fantasy Macabre,* no. 1 (September 1980): 4, 6–8;

"Beauty Is the Beast," *American Fantasy,* 2 (Fall 1986): 20–23; reprinted in *The Year's Best Fantasy Stories: 13,* edited by Arthur W. Saha (New York: DAW, 1987);

"Death Dances," *Weird Tales,* 50 (Spring 1988): 133–140; reprinted in *Best of Weird Tales,* edited by John Betancourt (New York: Barnes & Noble, 1995);

"The Kingdoms of the Air," *Weird Tales,* 50 (Summer 1988): 103–129; reprinted in *The Chronicles of the Holy Grail,* edited by Mike Ashley (New York: Carroll & Graf, 1996), pp. 228–263;

"Zelle's Thursday," *Isaac Asimov's Science Fiction Magazine,* 13 (October 1989): 53–63; reprinted in *Isaac Asimov's Robots,* edited by Gardner R. Dozois and

Sheila Williams (New York: Ace, 1991); reprinted in *Isaac Asimov's Skin Deep,* edited by Dozois and Williams (New York: Ace, 1995);

"A Night on the Hill," *After Hours,* 2 (Summer 1990): 3–4;

"Venus Rising on Water," *Isaac Asimov's Science Fiction Magazine,* 15 (October 1991): 76–95;

"The Winter Ghosts," *Weird Tales,* 53 (Winter 1991–1992): 87–91; reprinted in *100 Fiendish Little Frightmares,* edited by Stefan Dziemianowicz, Robert Weinberg, and Martin H. Greenberg (New York: Barnes & Noble, 1992);

"The Lily Garden," *Weird Tales,* 53 (Spring 1992): 62–66, 68–69; reprinted in *Weird Tales: Seven Decades of Terror,* edited by Betancourt and Weinberg (New York: Barnes & Noble, 1997);

"Ondralume," *Magazine of Fantasy & Science Fiction,* 83 (August 1992): 92–103;

"Winter Flowers," *Isaac Asimov's Science Fiction Magazine,* 17 (June 1993): 44–46, 48–50, 52–54, 56–58, 60–62, 64–67; reprinted in *Isaac Asimov's Vampires,* edited by Dozois and Williams (New York: Ace, 1996);

"Antonius Bequeathed," *Weird Tales,* 54 (Spring 1993): 54, 56, 58–59;

"The Persecution Machine," "Mirror, Mirror," and "One for Sorrow," *Weird Tales,* 54 (Spring 1994): 12–18, 25–27, 68–82;

"The Story Told by Smoke: From *The Journals of St. Strange,*" *Realms of Fantasy,* 1 (February 1995): 23–31, 77;

"These Beasts," *Magazine of Fantasy & Science Fiction,* 88 (June 1995): 56–66;

"Edwige," *Isaac Asimov's Science Fiction Magazine,* 19 (July 1995): 40–42, 44–46, 48–52;

"Tiger I," *Isaac Asimov's Science Fiction Magazine,* 19 (December 1995): 122–131;

"Doll Skulls," *Realms of Fantasy,* 2 (February 1996): 61–67;

"Death Loves Me," *Realms of Fantasy,* 2 (August 1996): 40, 42–47;

"The Werewolf," *Worlds of Fantasy and Horror,* 1 (Summer 1996): 17–18, 20–23;

"The Reason for Not Going to the Ball (A Letter to Cinderella from Her Stepmother)," *Magazine of Fantasy & Science Fiction,* 91 (October/November 1996): 83–91; reprinted in *The Year's Best Fantasy and Horror: Tenth Annual Collection,* edited by Ellen Datlow and Terri Windling (New York: St. Martin's Press, 1997), pp. 45–49;

"The Sequence of Swords and Hearts," *Worlds of Fantasy & Horror,* 1 (Winter 1996–1997): 12–22;

"Old Flame: From *The Journals of St. Strange,*" *Realms of Fantasy,* 3 (February 1997): 33–39, 68;

"After I Killed Her," *Isaac Asimov's Science Fiction Magazine,* 21 (July 1997): 92–102;

"The Lady of Shalott House," *Realms of Fantasy,* 4 (October 1997): 51–54;

"The Girl Who Lost Her Looks," *Interzone,* no. 128 (February 1998): 21–26;

"I Bring You Forever," *Realms of Fantasy,* 4 (June 1998): 44, 46–49, 84;

"Yellow & Red," *Interzone,* no. 132 (June 1998): 14–20; reprinted in *The Mammoth Book of Best New Horror: Volume 10,* edited by Stephen Jones (London: Robinson, 1999; New York: Carroll & Graf, 1999), pp. 220–237;

"Jedella Ghost," *Interzone,* no. 135 (September 1998): 6–14; reprinted in *The Year's Best Science Fiction: Sixteenth Annual Collection,* edited by Dozois (New York: St. Martin's Press, 1999), pp. 72–86; reprinted in *The Mammoth Book of Best New Science Fiction: 12th Annual Collection,* edited by Dozois (London: Robinson, 1999);

"Flower Water," *Weird Tales,* 55 (Summer 1998): 15–19;

"All the Birds of Hell," *Magazine of Fantasy & Science Fiction,* 95 (October/November 1998): 10–32; reprinted in *The Best from Fantasy and Science Fiction: The Fiftieth Anniversary Anthology,* edited by Edward L. Ferman and Gordon Van Gelder (New York: Tor, 1999), pp. 209–232;

"Stars Above, Stars Below," *Weird Tales,* 55 (Fall 1998): 14, 16–18;

"The Sky-Green Blues," *Interzone,* no. 142 (April 1999): 6–18;

"Unlocking the Golden Cage," *Weird Tales,* 55 (Spring 1999): 56, 58–65;

"Where Does the Town Go at Night?" *Interzone,* no. 147 (September 1999): 7–17;

"Scarlet and Gold," *Weird Tales,* 55 (Summer 1999): 51–56;

"Vermilia," *Dreams of Decadence,* no. 9 (Fall 1999): 17–24;

"An Iron Bride," *Weird Tales,* 56 (Winter 1999/2000); 62, 64–66;

"The Eye in the Heart," *Magazine of Fantasy & Science Fiction,* 98 (March 2000): 37–40;

"The Woman in Scarlet," *Realms of Fantasy,* 6 (April 2000): 30, 32–37, 71.

NONFICTION

"Paint's Master," *Realms of Fantasy,* 3 (February 1997): 56–61.

Tanith Lee has written more than 50 novels, some 250 shorter works, episodes for television series and radio plays, poems, and books for younger readers. Her work is science fiction and fantasy, but she distinctively blends many popular subgenres, including horror, dark fantasy, and sword-and-sorcery fiction. Her tone is equally diverse, from the barbaric sensuousness of her epic fantasy to the caustic spareness of some of the short stories and the sly humor of her revisionist treatment of fairy tales. Traces of myths, legends, and folktales underpin her narratives, which draw on such wide-ranging cultural topoi as European monsters (such as the vampire and werewolf) and Indian myth. Some of the fiction speculates on varied future worlds (of the highest technological sophistication or postholocaust degradation and decay). However, Lee is equally imaginative in her heroic fantasy, focusing on the degenerate remnants of great civilizations; she also reinterprets historical periods such as Renaissance Italy, Victorian England, and the 1960s Mediterranean beau monde. She elaborates the more grotesque features of these periods with speculative additions of her own in increasingly erotic and violent explorations of the nature of identity and personal freedom. More renowned in the United States than in her native Great Britain, Lee has received several awards for her work.

Lee was born on 19 September 1947 in London, England, the daughter of Bernard and Hylda (née Moore) Lee. Her parents were professional dancers, and Lee's schooling was disrupted by family traveling. As she stated in a 1989 interview with Stan Nicholls, homework distracted her from "the fantasy projection of my inner world." Although she was initially slow learning to read (perhaps because of dyslexia), by age eight she was engrossed by classic fairy tales such as those of Hans Christian Andersen. She recalls in the Nicholls interview the subversive fairy tales her mother told her: "in her stories the prince married the wicked witch in the end!" This predilection for the macabre and the disruption of expectations can be traced in her own adult work. By nine she had started writing her own stories and produced several horror stories as a teenager (some of which were later published).

Lee attended Catford Grammar School in London and was inspired there by some of her teachers, particularly in English, religion, and history. The influence of these disciplines on her work is evident. Broad religious and ethical issues emerge in her themes, such as the battle against oppressive forces and the ambivalent exploration of the individual's desire for self-determination and personal power. Religious images, narratives, and allusions also permeate her work, although their effect is frequently unorthodox and radical, challenging conventional Christian belief. Lee's commitment to history is perhaps the most important legacy from her secondary-school experience. Her characters and their environments are carefully delineated, and her work demonstrates the historian's interest in significant lives. Lee makes the link between fantasy and history in her interview with Nicholls: "To my mind a good fantasy novel reads like a good historical novel . . . It's all about people. That's what I want to write about, and what I care about." She reinforces this point in an interview for *Locus* in 1998, in which she asserts "all lives are important, all people are important, because everyone is a book." She has also expressed a dislike of the term "fantasy," preferring to define her work as historical fiction, though dealing, perhaps, with different kinds of historicality.

After finishing high school, Lee attended Croydon Art College for a year and subsequently worked as a file clerk, waitress, shop assistant, and librarian. Her desire, however, was to write. For Lee, writing goes beyond a worthwhile career. She sees it as an integral part of her personality and the best expression of her psychic energy. She has termed the creative process "like being possessed . . . an instinctive drive" in her interview with Nicholls. These metaphors suggest something of her total submission to the world or image that grips her imagination; this immersion usually results in a formidable, rapid output (about one hundred pages a month) despite her production of drafts in longhand, retyped by herself. Her work rarely needs significant rewriting, and she has the ability to work on several pieces simultaneously. Lee approaches the development of individual narratives systematically, often with the help of her husband, John Kaiine, a British artist and writer whom she met in 1987 and married in 1992.

Lee's first significant published work, *The Betrothed* (1968), was privately printed so a friend could try his printing press; Lee recalls on her website <http://www.tanithlee.com>, "I think 6 copies in all were printed." The story demonstrates many characteristic features of her horror fantasies, including an interest in the use and abuse of the body. Its fairy-tale plot recalls "The Lady of Shallot," Rapunzel, and similar tales of love and entrapment. The flame-haired heroine, Genesta, with her realistic desires, is a standard Lee type in her combination of innocence, strong sexuality, and need for love. Beside her, the male figures of lover and tyrant are insignificant. Also typical is the evocative, even Gothic language; intense imagery not only gives authenticity to the landscape but hints ominously at the tragedy to come. Lee indicates on her website that she decided "to use not only elements of ideas and storyline from *The Betrothed,* but also small pieces of actual writing" in her 2002 novel *A Bed of Earth (The Gravedigger's Tale).*

While still at her parental home in her late teens Lee began to write children's books with fantasy and

Dust jacket for the 1979 novel in which Lee blended elements of Christopher Marlowe's Dr. Faustus, George Bernard Shaw's Pygmalion, *and Mary Shelley's* Frankenstein *(Richland County Public Library)*

fairy-tale structures and themes. When she worked as an assistant librarian, several of her stories were accepted for publication, but when the publishing firm had financial difficulties, publication was shelved. Finally her first novel, *The Dragon Hoard* (1971), was published, followed in 1972 by *Animal Castle,* a picture book, and *Princess Hynchatti and Some Other Surprises,* a collection of stories featuring a range of princesses and princes and their unusual adventures. Both *The Dragon Hoard* and *Princess Hynchatti and Some Other Surprises* have some interest for students of Lee's work since they demonstrate her ability to deal with fantasy motifs ironically and comically. They also reveal themes that recur in Lee's adult fiction: challenging quests; the triumph of courage, benevolence, and love; the need to test dreamworlds and private fantasies against reality; and the abuses and benefits of the nonmaterial world of sorcery and enchantment. Standard fairy-tale devices all figure, but Lee's perspective sometimes has unusual effects. The stories in *Princess Hynchatti and Some Other Surprises* show a characteristic delight in reversing reader and character expectations. But overall the stories endorse conventional values of kindheartedness, good sense, and initiative.

With the American publication of her first adult novel, *The Birthgrave* (1975), Lee became a full-time professional writer. This lengthy blend of heroic fantasy and science fiction is the first text in the Birthgrave Trilogy and establishes Lee's capacity to use, deepen, and extend the conventions of popular genre fiction. The work was nominated for the 1975 Nebula Award for best novel, and critics compared her scope and vision to that of Andre Norton and Ursula K. Le Guin, singling out her vivid characterizations and expressive prose. The novel derives much of its swashbuckling energy from the motifs of sword-and-sorcery writing, blending violence, sex, and magic.

Lee does develop the formula, however. Her questing protagonist is an albino "goddess" who is the only survivor of a superior Lost Race, a decadent, cruel civilization wasted by plague. She awakens many years later under a volcano, unaware of her identity and convinced she is cursed, destined to blossom into evil and bring destruction to all she encounters. Impelled nonetheless by an "instinct for freedom," she flees her underground tomb and encounters barbaric cultures who are both impressed and threatened by her superior powers. The goddess is not a passive heroine subordinate to male adventurers. Her prowess is demonstrated by her ruthless will, her fighting skills, and her display of physical competence (in a deadly chariot race, for example). She is also archetypally female. In her dreams and intuitions she reveals her mystical sensitivity; she is both a victim and a reluctant healer who discovers her capacity to overcome death.

In addition to characterization, the vivid background and the skillful plotting contribute to the appeal of the novel. The plot is episodic but swift paced, and the denouement is unusual, integrating sword and sorcery with science fiction. Her powers seemingly exhausted, the heroine summons aid telepathically from a spaceship. With the help of its vast computer, she learns the truth of her identity and the abusive history that made her doubt herself and even feel evil. The end point of her quest unifies her dark and positive selves. Only then can her power be used responsibly and be controlled; only then does she realize her beauty and accept her lonely vocation to advance the civilization.

In 1975 Lee also published a second novel for young people, *Companions on the Road,* a bleaker work intended for a somewhat older readership. Two sets of companions feature in the work—the mercenary Havor and two thieving comrades who steal a magical chalice when looting after battle, and three undead riders who

pursue them for its return. As with much of her work, the real interest is the drama of the inner self. Havor undergoes a rite of passage to attain maturity and self-knowledge. He is saved by the loving ghosts of a family for whom he had sympathy and by his ability to pity the creatures of the Dark as strange, corrupted souls. The lesson is that good and evil co-exist in the difficult, complex reality of adult experience.

A similar seriousness characterizes Lee's next young-adult novel, *The Winter Players* (1976), which uses standard fantasy types: an enchanted, ambivalent stranger (Grey), held in a spell by the wandering spirit of an evil priest (Niwus) and their opponent, a young virgin priestess, Oaive, guardian of secret lore and relics. Grey's theft of the Bone relic compels Oaive to journey to retrieve it; gradually Grey becomes the object of her quest in a narrative using time travel to link past, present, and future. The novel links redemption to the process of maturation, suggesting that the difficult choices of adulthood involve self-denial but that this denial does not preclude self-fulfillment.

Lee's adult publications in 1976 draw again on science fiction and heroic fantasy but show her capacity to innovate technically and deal with contemporary issues. *The Storm Lord* introduces another epic fantasy trilogy, the Wars of Vis. Like *The Birthgrave,* this novel charts the education of a god figure and interrogates the nature and exercise of power. Again Lee laces her fast-moving, complex plot with violent adventures, passionate and perverse sexuality, mystery, and the supernatural. But unlike her earlier fantasy, *The Storm Lord* develops its themes of identity in a more detailed social world where class, race, and political authority are explored. Lee's parallel universe, the continent Vis, with its different cultures and races, is richly imagined; but its alien features do not disguise its earthly parallels. The semidivine hero is Raldnor, the product of the rape of a Lowland temple girl by Rehdon, the Storm Lord and King of Dorthar, a member of the "master race." Raldnor sets out to free his people, the Lowlanders, from Amrek and his "Dragon Guards." Raldnor's journey is constantly deflected, but his encounters with other cultures needing liberation redouble his determination and draw out his god-like powers. Gradually Raldnor unites Amrek's enemies, frees the downtrodden nations, and destroys Amrek's regime. With no taste for ruling, Raldnor returns to his humanity, rescues his beloved, and moves off with her into the jungle.

Political and cultural enslavement is explored quite differently in *Don't Bite the Sun* (1976) and its sequel, *Drinking Sapphire Wine* (1977), seen by several reviewers as original in depicting oppression in a hedonistic future completely controlled by advanced technology. Lee switches from heroic fantasy to a colloquial self-conscious discourse and an invented slang appropriate to her shape-shifting teenage heroine and "Jang," the adolescent subculture. The book echoes Aldous Huxley's *Brave New World* (1932) and Anthony Burgess's *A Clockwork Orange* (1962) in its dystopian treatment of a regulated society that encourages self-indulgence but reserves "Personality Dissolution" for serious deviance and independence. The novel offers a different perspective on Lee's central theme of identity formation, dramatizing the ways in which identity is largely constructed and maintained by society unless the urge for freedom is strong, in which case individuals will pursue it at any cost. Lonely and bored, the heroine takes on a male body and seeks adventure and love but is sentenced to Personality Dissolution when she kills a man in a duel. Instead she chooses exile and asserts her identity by developing a counterculture that recognizes and satisfies human needs. The transformation of the wasteland into a site of healing and fertility validates the revolt against pressures to conform.

Volkhavaar (1977) takes Lee's interest in love, identity, and power in new directions. Motifs of supernatural and occult fantasy combine in an investigation of the capacity of loyalty and selfless love to overcome brutality and hate. The structure of the novel supports the thematic tensions so that the separate plots involving the three main characters are gradually interwoven and brought together for a final battle against evil. Each plot uses the concept of metamorphosis to explore desire and its relation to truth and illusion. In the end, love is identified as the supreme motive, but the novel also shows how humans make gods in the image of their own desires, a theme to which Lee later returns.

The power of the dispossessed and insignificant is also a feature of *East of Midnight* (1977), another young-adult novel. The initiation of a rebellious slave boy, Dekteon, into a new world by his master, Zaister, becomes an exploration of relations between gender and power. Two parallel worlds exist—the harsh, patriarchal sun-world of Dekteon and a moon-governed matriarchy where the "Lord of the City" periodically replaces her male "sun" consort to ensure the vitality and fertility of the kingdom. Zaister, a consort, is unwilling to be sacrificed and magically swaps places with Dekteon. For Dekteon the women's world is dream-like and unreal. He cannot comprehend the women's "off-hand authoritarianism," believing they should be "dependent on men for their strength, for security and for children." Zaister is equally discomfited by Dekteon's rough world. In the end Dekteon rescues Zaister and restores male confidence in the right to kingship.

Dust jacket for Lee's 1986 collection of short fiction, which was nominated for a 1987 World Fantasy Award (Richland County Public Library)

Lee also wrote fantasy and science-fiction scripts in the late 1970s and early 1980s. "Bitter Gate" (1977), broadcast by the BBC, was Lee's first radio play, retelling Odysseus' return to Ithaca and reunion with Penelope from a feminist angle. "Red Wine" (1977), another BBC radio play, forays into vampire legend but with a witty twist on conventions. The ancient vampire, Constantine, lures young secretaries to his remote Gothic mansion to feed on their blood. His latest victim vanquishes him with scorn and mockery, however, for she is herself a vampire—but in a modern mode exploiting science and reason to improve rather than vanquish the myth.

In 1978 Lee completed one trilogy, published the first novel in a new sequence, and continued writing for children, all using different subgenres of fantasy but still showing her concern with self-discovery, power, and sexuality. *The Castle of Dark,* for older children, uses traditional fairy-tale motifs to explore the nature of evil. The plot invites readers to wonder whether evil might not simply be "the misunderstanding of men."

Vazkor, Son of Vazkor (1978) and *Quest for the White Witch* (1978) complete the Birthgrave Trilogy. The two novels rework such familiar themes as self-acceptance and personal discovery, although now from a male perspective. The main narrative impetus of the sequels is again the metamorphosis from savage to redeemer. Vazkor is the ambitious, sadistic tyrant against whom the heroine of *The Birthgrave* battled and by whom she has a son. Tuvek, Vazkor's son, begins his adventures motivated by revenge. But his search for his origins transforms him into a new Vazkor, wise, powerful, and with an ability to heal and nurture. His quest parallels that of Oedipus, but for Lee, maternal incest results in new insights into the just use of sexuality and power and reasserts the value of a matriarchal culture.

Night's Master (1978), the first volume in a series titled Tales from the Flat Earth: The Lords of Darkness, marks a new departure for Lee conceptually and stylistically. The mythic aspect of fantasy predominates, rather than the formulaic plots and characters of heroic or adventure fantasy. Something of the oral tradition underpinning myth and legend is also captured through the use of an authoritative storyteller, but one who can admit that storytellers are liars. The narrative structure, which at times takes the form of interlinked short stories and at others of meandering episodic plots, has reminded critics of the *Arabian Nights Entertainment* or uncanny Celtic tales. While *Night's Master* has been criticized for fragmentation and uneven quality, it was nominated for the 1979 World Fantasy Award.

Lee's portrayal of an ancient alternate Earth in this series is interestingly subversive. These books feature a time when the Earth was flat and demons and mortals interacted. In the Upperearth, gods sleep or are at best indifferent to human troubles; mortals exist on Flat Earth; and the demonic Lords of Darkness (from Underearth and Innerearth) interact with them there. Each novel in the series features a different Lord of Darkness, but perhaps these shape-shifting trickster figures represent elements of the human unconscious, for their actions challenge fixed laws. *Night's Master* features Azhrarn, Prince of Demons, who uses his erotic charm to ensnare men and women. He emerges, paradoxically, as a Christ-like savior of humanity who dies and is reborn, rescuing humans threatened by the hatred he accidentally created. But his motives are so mixed that the reader will likely see the novel as a deconstruction rather than an endorsement of the Christian mythos.

Death's Master (1979), winner of the 1980 August Derleth Award (the British Fantasy Award for best novel), continues the series and has been praised by critics for its strange, dark sensuality and rich prose. The novel focuses on Uhlume, Lord Death, and two children, Zhirem and Simmu, each with magical powers. The children become the pawns of Azhrarn and Uhlume, engaged in a struggle for supremacy that threatens to result in the death of Death. By the end, an uneasy equilibrium has been re-established.

Electric Forest (1979) is science fiction, but Lee blurs genre boundaries so that the novel also seems a macabre blend of Christopher Marlowe's *Dr. Faustus* (1604), George Bernard Shaw's *Pygmalion* (1916), and Mary Shelley's *Frankenstein* (1818). The novel might be read as the rite of passage of a girl into adulthood, but it also interrogates the cultural demand for conformity, exploitative cultural norms, and imperialism in both personal and public areas. Magdala Cled lives on a planet where almost everyone is beautiful, but she is rejected because she is ugly and deformed. Claudio Lorro offers her beauty, not for her soul, but her consciousness, for Lorro wants to involve her in his experiment in Consciousness Transferal. With her body sustained in a life-support capsule, Magdala's consciousness is implanted in a body Claudio has created. His intent is to entrap individuals in android bodies that can then be put to use. Reviewers responded enthusiastically to the story with its unexpected revelations.

In the same year Lee published *Shon the Taken,* a novel for older children that explores the value of difference by exposing the ignorance of superstition and prejudice. The adolescent Shon belongs to a primitive tribe whose language does not permit distinctions to be made. During a night in the forest, Shon encounters the legendary, faceless Crow's People (or Death's Children). When he returns he is tested as one possessed or "taken" by Death and hence cursed. That he now represents "the Other" is confirmed when he denounces the shaman, walks on air, and demonstrates sophisticated linguistic skills. Although the reader gradually discovers a "rational" explanation, neither Shon nor his tribe can initially account for the phenomena, and he flees. As an outcast he seeks to avenge his plight by destroying Death himself. Guilt, the acceptance of responsibility, and sympathy for strangeness or difference become Shon's legacy.

Another encounter with death can be found in Lee's third radio play, "Death Is King," a historical fantasy set in 1340 as the Black Death swept Europe. Lee also composed the songs that accompanied the broadcast. The drama offers a series of hallucinatory vignettes exploring the paradoxical relationships of life, love, and death, finally suggesting that life, not death, is king. The duke's virgin daughter, isolated in the tower to protect her from the plague, gradually succumbs to Death's logical and soothing suggestions to admit him. For Death, entry into life guarantees mortality and thus his supremacy. But she comes to realize only life offers love and artistic endeavors—both of which deny Death by sustaining the world.

Several works published by Lee in 1980 show her moving into new areas of fantasy to explore themes of monstrousness, difference, and unnaturalness. *Sabella; or, The Blood Stone* and *Kill the Dead* draw on archetypal horror figures to this end. *Sabella* is a futuristic vampire novel set on Mars with erotic overtones as well as grim realism. By placing the monstrous in the context of a conventional youthful initiation plot as the young, female vampire, Sabella, learns how to live "safely" on colonized Mars, Lee allows the unconventional and outcast to gain reader interest and sympathy. Ominously, however, Sabella learns that she can survive only with the support of one like her—another alien of the same species and predispositions. Moreover, the resolution shocks the reader, who has identified with the sharp-witted, well-meaning heroine. Sabella acts as instinct drives her, overriding sentimentality. Lee reminds readers that true difference is alien and incomprehensible, testing the capacity for tolerance and acceptance.

Kill the Dead, though not one of Lee's more significant novels, nonetheless is noteworthy for its use of revenants and vampirism to explore issues of the divided self. Parl Dro, a ghost-killer who dispatches ghosts to their proper realm, is haunted by the vengeful Ciddey Soban, the sister of a ghost he has "slain." The revenants feed on the energy of the living to materialize more and more concretely. Both Parl Dro and Myal Lemayal, a diffident minstrel who has a love-hate relationship with the ghost-slayer, are subject to this power and are drawn to Ghyste Mortua, the place of the dead alive. Parl Dro bests Ciddey by convincing her that her self-hatred has been her hell, but not before she recognizes Parl Dro as a ghost himself, killed by the husband of a woman he seduced. Myal is the product of that union and initially the source of the psychic energy that Parl Dro requires to materialize.

Parl Dro lives in a continual state of psychic conflict. Part of him desires to live and part wishes to drive the ghost-self back to its proper otherworld. In the end a Jungian balance is struck between these orderly and disruptive aspects of the self. His son has literally and figuratively become his reason for living. Lee suggests that the fluidity and fragmentation of humans' psychic identities are both stimulated and held in check by love.

Day by Night, Lee's last novel published in 1980, offers another variation on the theme of divided identities. But it may also be read as an ironic, disturbing deconstruction of fantasy as a consumer product and entertainment. Set on a planet that does not rotate and therefore has "bright" and "dark" sides and separate cultures unknown to each other, the novel employs a

Paperback cover for the 1989 novel Lee set in a fantasy world that resembles Europe at the turn of the nineteenth century (Richland County Public Library)

story within a story to dramatize its central themes. Vitra Klovez is a fantasy writer whose entertaining tales please the masses on the dark side of her planet. Her latest story is about a woman like herself on the sun side who is framed for attempted murder by a disappointed suitor. Lee creates a self-reflexive text interrogating the nature of fiction, the power of dreams and desires, and the indeterminable nature of reality.

Lee's science-fiction scripts for radio and television in 1980 and 1981 also probe the lessons to be learned from the clash of cultures. In "The Silver Sky" (1980), broadcast by the BBC as a science fantasy for radio, Paul Baxter, a time-dimension researcher from Earth, collides with Elzereth, a traveler from a parallel world of strawberry-pink seas and silver-grey skies. They fall in love, but their rescue brings tragedy. The play suggests a relationship among past, present, and future that destroys conventional notions of time, instead positing a continuum of interconnected moments, subjectively interpreted as past or future by their human participant.

Lee also provided scripts for two episodes of the BBC television show *Blake's 7,* a cult science-fiction soap opera about a band of Earth renegades who try to overthrow the evil totalitarian regime of Earth Forces Federation. Her episode "Sarcophagus" (1980), which includes a song composed by her, deals with the possession of a telepathic member of the renegades through an alien spell. "Sand" (1981) involves an evil Federation genius searching a hostile alien planet for its energy source and encountering Tarrant, an impulsive member of Blake's crew. They must collaborate to outwit the vampiric life-force of the planet. Both scripts deal with characteristic Lee themes of loyalty, domination, and power, but "Sand" is particularly interesting, showing Lee's ability to give some psychological depth to major characters in the series.

Lee has also been a prolific writer of science-fiction, fantasy, and horror short stories and novellas. These tend to be published in magazines in the field and often are later anthologized. In 1981, in conjunction with her February appearance as Guest of Honor at Boskone XVIII in Boston, Lee published *Unsilent Night,* collecting two stories and ten poems. The stories, "Sirriamnis" and "Cyrion in Wax," examine the limitations of power based on malign magic.

However, in *Lycanthia; or, The Children of the Wolves* (1981) Lee presents a more ambivalent portrait of the monstrous and malign. *Lycanthia,* like *Sabella* and *Kill the Dead,* takes as its central motif a traditional horror image—in this case, the werewolf. Yet, the confrontation between the shape-shifting, unknowable Luc and Gabrielle de Lagenay and the sophisticated Christian Dorse is not a conventional battle between the demonic and the good. Indeed, Dorse seems the increasingly unnatural figure as his relationship with the wolf-children develops. It is Dorse who has been the wolf, feeding on their strangeness, energy, and integrity to sustain his self-indulgent life.

Delusion's Master (1981), the third volume in the Flat Earth series, introduces another Lord of Darkness: Chuz, Prince of Madness. It opens a narrative that links this volume and the next two books in the sequence. Jasrin, who has abandoned her baby to its death, has been locked in a tower by her husband, has gone mad, and is visited by Chuz. She tells him she desires that her husband should also become mad, and so he seems to do, aspiring to build the Tower of Babyheln to seize immortality from heaven. His venture fails, but hundreds of years later Jasrin still haunts her tower while pilgrims worship the gods there. Azhrarn, disguised as

a prophet, predicts that a Lord of Darkness will save humanity. But the main thrust of the novel is Azhrarn's love for the beautiful priestess Dunizel. If the Tower of Babyheln recalls the Old Testament, then Dunizel offers a New Covenant based on love and self-sacrifice. The volume concludes with Azhrarn's declaration of war on Chuz and his removal of his and Dunizel's child to Underearth, away from Chuz's interest.

As the series developed, critics became more enthusiastic, praising *Delusion's Master* for its unconventional approaches to sex and sensuality, its compelling treatment of violence and revenge, and its vibrant prose. The novel transforms elements of Western and Asian myth, fairy tales, and high and popular culture to create an erotic vision of fantastic loves and careless cruelty. The reader is not positioned to sympathize with or judge the characters, but to observe with awe and horror the power of those dark forces that might be termed the "underside" of conscious reality.

The Silver Metal Lover (1981) seems a traditional science-fiction romance but again reverses expectations. Lee's world of urban horror and technological brilliance suggests the sterile quality of the emotional and spiritual life of the future. This narrative of a lonely rich girl and her love for a handsome robot has its sentimental dimension, but the novel also subverts generic and gender stereotypes. Silver is neither a bionic monster nor a coldly rational alien. If anything he is a "new man," gentle and artistic, programmed to please. His love for Jane humanizes him. She is also transformed, becoming a brave and selfless woman. Unlike the peripheral females of some robot tales, she is no passive victim of an alien force raging out of control. She—not the male scientist—is the creative mage, bringing the robot to full life as Frankenstein could not. Moreover, Silver's humanity is realized only when he moves beyond his scientifically managed state, becoming more like a "feeling" woman and less like a "thinking" man. And while Lee introduces the theme, common to the robot subgenre, of society's misplaced fear and punishment of a "rogue" species—neither human nor machine—the resolution suggests destruction of the feared Other is not so easy. Love, not technology and scientific advance, is the only source of meaningful continuity and real strength.

In *Prince on a White Horse* (1982), another narrative for older children, Lee parodies the heroic chivalric fantasy. Her questing prince is an amnesiac, bemused by the strange world in which he finds himself, beset by enchanters, talking animals, and strange monsters, and hailed as "the Looked-for Deliverer." Lee endorses values of selflessness, loyalty, and hope through the modest prince's surrealistic, at times almost comic, ordeals. He vanquishes the evil force of Nulgrave (Despair) and learns the secret of his identity. His origin is in another world, but he is content to remain in his new society and accept the challenge of restoring it. Another narrative of initiation and maturation, the work equates adulthood not simply with responsibilities but with the joy and confidence achieved through self-knowledge.

As Lee's reputation grew (particularly in the United States), further collections of her short stories appeared. *Cyrion* (1982) includes seven stories, a novella, two prologues, an epilogue, and linking material. Critical reception was mixed. For some critics the stories were predictable, the writing clichéd, the situations incredible, and the suggested linkages difficult to follow. Others admired her rich fantasy, plots of mystery and violence, and fabulous sword-wielding hero. Still others have perceived an interesting disruption of readers' expectations in Cyrion's encounters with a variety of obstacles from magic to monsters. Lee's handling of sexual perversity and androgyny introduces sexual exoticism and ambiguity into heroic-fantasy and detective formulas, darkening the standard gender classifications typically upheld in sword and sorcery.

Red as Blood; or, Tales from the Sisters Grimmer (1983) is another collection of short stories and novellas, most of which had been previously published. Her revisionist fairy tales, perhaps more accessible than Angela Carter's *The Bloody Chamber and Other Stories* (1979), undermine conventional attitudes toward sex, gender, and even spiritual values inscribed in classic folk and fairy tales. Snow White, for example, is recast in vampire mode; the prince who wakes her is a Christ figure. "Black as Ink" presents a modernized treatment of the swan-maiden tale. "The Golden Rope" inverts the Rapunzel story, giving phallic associations to Jaspre's incarcerating tower and suggesting that knowledge and sexual experience are linked. New versions of Cinderella (with a charming stepmother) and Beauty and the Beast (a science-fiction rewriting) are included. These stories use fantasy to explore the sinister and cruel. *Red as Blood* was nominated for the 1984 World Fantasy Award for best anthology or collection.

A similar revisionism, as well as Lee's interest in the fantastic reconstruction of historical periods and settings, is evident in *Sung in Shadow* (1983), a reworking of *Romeo and Juliet* (1597). Like William Shakespeare's play, the novel explores issues of fate, love, and death in an alternate Renaissance Italy. Lee's reconception of Shakespeare's narrative "aslant" introduces a powerful ambivalence into her treatment of love, which brings both death and superhuman transformation. *Sung in Shadow* has been praised for its vivid passion and flamboyance and its elaboration of secondary characters.

Lee's developing insistence on horror and decadence, on the disruption of conventional boundaries

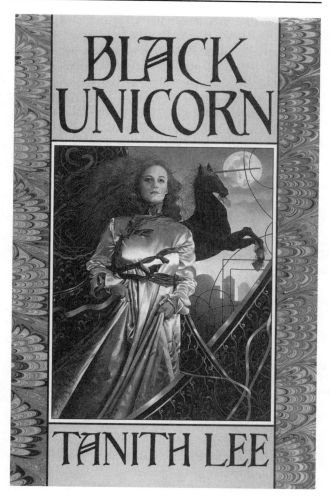

Dust jacket for Lee's 1991 novel for young adults, the first book in a fantasy series featuring a sixteen-year-old girl with the almost magical ability to mend objects (Richland County Public Library)

and differences, is maintained differently in *Anackire* (1983), the second volume in the Wars of Vis cycle. Ostensibly the sequel to *The Storm Lord,* this novel continues the history of Vis with a return to traditional heroic fantasy. Just as *The Storm Lord* critiques systems of class and racial oppression, so *Anackire* exposes similar themes. Sorcerous postmortem births, family rivalry, and civil war are woven together to reinforce two themes: the magic of the force of life and the need for trust in and reliance on the self. Lee suggests that abnormality and cruelty are the result of the suppression or distortion of natural desire or its transposition into possession. Woman's intuitive and mystical sensitivities depend on her acknowledgment of and pleasure in the body, rather than its denial.

In 1984 a limited illustrated edition of the vampire novelette *The Beautiful Biting Machine* was followed by a collection of seven stories, *Tamastara; or, The Indian*

Nights. The former offers a darkly erotic glimpse into sensual perversity and the corruption at its core. The latter mixes fantasy, horror, and science fiction and reflects Lee's strong engagement with Indian culture, though she has only "mentally" inhabited that country. The topics of the stories range from Indian myths to a tale about Indian actors. A shared short-story collection with material by Lee, Charles L. Grant, and Steve Rasnic Tem, *Night Visions 1* (1984) was nominated for the 1985 World Fantasy Award for best anthology or collection. It includes four new tales by Lee, including "The Vampire Lover" and "The Hunting of Death: The Unicorn," which exploits religious allegory in depicting three perspectives on the fabulous unicorn and its links with perfection, sacrifice and redemption, and death.

The Gorgon and Other Beastly Tales (1985) has a loose bestiary motif to unite the eleven stories. "The Gorgon," which won the 1983 World Fantasy Award for best short story, takes as its premise the revelation of the reality behind a local myth. "La Reine Blanche" is based on a familiar fantasy situation—a young virgin queen is imprisoned in a tower; in this case her spirit is freed by a raven. "Draco, Draco" shifts to the magical activity of dragon slaying. The writing style is less prone to the slippage from the lush to the overblown and pretentious that occasionally mars her longer fiction.

Lee's *Days of Grass,* her last major publication in 1985, is a bleak science-fiction vision of a postapocalyptic world. Driven underground by invading aliens, humans have lived for centuries in hiding. The proposed leader-redeemer is Esther, a girl on the verge of womanhood. Her hallucinatory encounter with the Master alien is powerful, but seems detached from the first part of the novel. Esther's ordeal reinforces that maturity involves confronting one's deepest fears and desires. More disturbing and unexpected, perhaps, is the model of leadership Esther assumes. She is not a benevolent and caring savior; she seems to feel little for her people, who are in some ways as alien to her as the conquering invaders.

Delirium's Mistress (1986), the fourth volume in the Flat Earth series, focuses on a rather different female protagonist with a quest. The main character is Azhriaz, the demon-mortal child of Azhrarn and Dunizel, who pledges herself to her father's cause, discrediting the gods. She instructs humanity on the indifference of the gods and provokes the deities. Azhriaz concludes her battle with the gods by promising to embrace a mortal death. As she approaches death, Azhrarn visits her. His plan to create Azhriaz as a tool "to be my curse upon the world" has failed, and he renounces his use of humanity as a plaything. While the series has con-

cerned itself to this point with extremes of power and its moral or immoral use, *Delirium's Mistress* offers a new model: true power lies in casting off power for love.

Dreams of Dark and Light: The Great Short Fiction of Tanith Lee (1986) reprints several of Lee's most significant stories and displays Lee's diversity as a fantasy writer. It was nominated for the 1987 World Fantasy Award for best anthology or collection. Ranging from the ghostly exploration of three manifestations of Lady Death in "Elle est Trois, (La Mort)," winner of the 1984 World Fantasy Award for best short story, to the science-fiction vampire story "Nunc Dimittis" (nominated for the 1984 World Fantasy Award for best novella), the stories adapt traditional plots and archetypes to explore such themes as the attractiveness of death, sexual perversity, and psychological obsessions. For example, "Bite-Me-Not; or, Fleur de Fur" is an alternative reading of the vampire legend, confronting its sexual overtones. Lee's creation of the vampire race as "pitiless fallen angels," a community with its own culture, is imaginative.

The final volume of the Flat Earth series, *Night's Sorceries* (1987), was also nominated for the 1988 World Fantasy Award for best collection. The seven short stories present material extraneous to the other volumes but loosely connected. "Dooniveh, the Moon" is a fairy tale about a monk who journeys to the moon on a winged horse given to Azhriaz and about the wedding of the Moon Queen and Sun King. The most important story is the last, "The Daughter of the Magician," recounting the tale of a sorcerer who resurrects Azhriaz's soul. Reincarnated as a young girl, she is sacrificed to a monster but finally recognizes that the monster is no alien but only a different part of the gift from the suitor who gave the winged horse. The ending reaffirms the importance of love to mortals and demons and makes explicit the mysterious but natural links between love and death established in *Delirium's Mistress.* Azhrarn's early prophecy, that a Lord of Darkness would save humankind, is fulfilled.

Lee's concluding volume of the Wars of Vis, *The White Serpent* (1988), lacks the mythic elements of the Flat Earth series. However, in completing the narrative of power struggles that characterize the history of Vis, Lee shapes a complex narrative about origins. Throughout the Vis series, identities hinge on borders and distinctions, but Lee makes a case for the value of transgression. Full humanity resides not in opposition and differentiation but in openness to different perspectives and the capacity to adopt different positions through life.

More significant for Lee's canon is the appearance in 1988 of the first two volumes in the Secret Books of Paradys series, *The Book of the Damned* and *The*

Book of the Beast. They represent a watershed for Lee's reputation as a writer of traditional heroic fantasy, speculative fiction, and dark fantasy. More popular in the United States than in her native United Kingdom, Lee's full-length fiction had, up until this point, normally appeared first in the United States and usually some years later (if at all) in Britain. However, the publication of the controversial *The Book of the Damned* and *The Book of the Beast,* with their unorthodox explorations of religion and sexuality, altered this pattern. The books revel in the macabre, violent, and perverse; the narratives are frequently surreal and hallucinatory.

Paradys has associations with Paris as well as paradise, but a Paris that is historically fluid (stories are set in different historical periods ranging from the Roman occupation to the twentieth century) and where the boundaries between the natural, material world and the supernatural, and between the moral and immoral, are eroded. Erotic relationships between sensitive mortals and demons, ghosts, and shape-shifters are central, as are themes of metamorphosis, infection, sexual violence, and revenge. Sexual experience and knowledge are frequently linked. The atmosphere evoked is horrific and sinister, and readers may feel this place must be the "paradise" of damned souls.

The Book of the Damned includes three novellas. In "Stained with Crimson," a surrealistic vampire tale, a ruby scarab passed to the protagonist introduces a cluster of images associated with blood and demonic avengers from ancient cultures. This story of sexual ambiguity and exchange dramatizes the perverse effects of repressing the "Other" self within. "Malice in Saffron: Le Livre Safran" has a medieval setting, peopled with dwarves and grotesques. Raped by her stepfather and disowned by her stepbrother, Jehanine enters a convent but at night adopts the persona of a sadistic male brigand, Jehan. She uses this position to murder all who abuse her, particularly any who epitomize the evil associated with masculinity. Moved by the suicide of a sympathetic nun and a disturbing vision, Jehan reverts to her female persona and nurses the ill when plague strikes. Locked in a plague house with her stepbrother, she offers an amazing sacrifice to feed him. This narrative moves far beyond simple themes of revenge, guilt, and penance. The volume concludes with "Empires of Azure: Le Livre Azur," set in the twentieth century but with roots in Roman times. A journalist is approached by a female impersonator who tells her of his impending death and invites her to investigate his secret. It emerges that he has been possessed by the hermaphrodite Roman-Egyptian sorceress Tiy-Amonet (or Tuamon).

The Book of the Beast is a series of linked episodes. The "sins" of one generation infect the next, so that

Dust jacket for the last novel of the series that established Lee's reputation in the United Kingdom (Richland County Public Library)

eventually the culpable and the innocent are similarly destroyed. A prostitute gives a Roman centurion an amulet, which he grinds up and swallows, hoping to change his fortunes. Instead he allows the demon who cursed the stone to be absorbed by his body and transmitted by intercourse through the generations. Only men manifest the infection, transformed into monstrous beast-men, tortured by sexual frenzy. David Cowperthwaite reads the text as a "parable about AIDS," and Lee captures the sense of uncontrollable panic, guilt, and intolerance that contaminates Paradys in the wake of the "infection."

While embarking on a major series of novels, Lee continued to be a prolific writer of fantasy and horror short fiction. The Parisian novella *Madame Two Swords* (1988) was followed in 1989 by two collections, *Women as Demons: The Male Perception of Women Through Space and Time* and *Forests of the Night.* As the title *Women as Demons* suggests, this volume is concerned with exploring myths of woman, particularly her association with "a mythology of darkness, corruption and the uncanny" as well as purity. Lee indicates that she finds the Demonic Woman an attractive and glamorous villain. The counterpart of this archetype is the Satanic Male, as much a construct of the fantasies of women as the wish fulfillment of the male. Lee, however, does not seek to perpetuate such myths. Rather, her stories analyze them—their history, their potency, and their inadequacy. Nor does she seek to set new myths in their place. Instead she demonstrates how psychic strength drawn from inner forces (both dark and light) is "entirely legitimate and self-expressive," although not necessarily resulting in moral action or appropriate as part of daily life.

Lee's stories draw widely on a range of cultures, settings, fairy-tale models, and fantasy subgenres. Some offer witty turns on traditional formulas to evoke sympathy for the figure of the vengeful, haunting woman; in "The Unrequited Glove," for instance, a poltergeist is created from the pain of rejection. "Into Gold" weaves together classical myth, Egyptian sorcery, and Arthurian legend to show the tragedy of misreading woman's benevolent and healing powers as evil. Some stories focus on the male fear and misunderstanding of women's bodies ("The Truce"); others explore male fantasies of women such as that of Oedipal incest ("Discovered Country").

Among the most important stories in the volume are "The Demoness" and "Northern Chess." Both feature women of action who usurp male roles to save and protect. In the former a sweet, strong girl, Siandra, seizes her knight's sword and beheads the infatuated demoness who pursues him. But the reader is finally directed to sympathize with the dismembered creature whose dust will continue to wait and desire in vain. "Northern Chess" is an upbeat subversion of the Amazon theme and a witty deconstruction of sexist language. Jaisel, a girl-knight, arrives in a barren land that is cursed by a magician. Only the destruction of his castle will restore the nation's health. Jaisel faces its Gothic horrors where all other knights fail because of the literal terms of the sorcerer's spell: the castle cannot "be taken by any man." Jaisel's modest view that "Any woman might have achieved this thing" conveys a new vision of women's power.

Forests of the Night collects twenty short works, including "The Gorgon" and "Elle est Trois, (La Mort)," and offers eight new pieces out of the twenty. Some of the bleak science-fiction tales such as "A Madonna of the Machine" and "Crying in the Rain" are noteworthy. In the former Lee attacks the automated world of the future in which humans evolve into the regulating Machine, becoming its Soul. Only "deviant" visions of life, love, and nature can disrupt the smooth functioning of the Machine, while disturbing

the half-trance of the human drones who tend it. "Crying in the Rain," influenced by the Chernobyl nuclear disaster, creates a future world of mutation, deterioration, and death.

From this point in her career, Lee's major works are primarily horror and dark fantasy, with a few excursions into heroic and romantic fantasy centering on the psychological and moral development of an adolescent heroine. Of the latter, some critics regard *A Heroine of the World* (1989) as one of Lee's most satisfying works. Set in a fantastic world akin to late-eighteenth- or early-nineteenth-century Europe, the novel encompasses a world in conflict. The heroine, Aradia, becomes a pawn in political intrigue, a captive of invaders. She is guided to her destiny primarily by her devotion to Thenser, a Byronic hero whose political loyalty is uncertain. Sexual passion is an important factor in the power games underpinning the plot. In the end Aradia fulfills her destiny as a heroine by her belief in Thenser and her determination to live. There is no supernatural fantasy; instead, the novel proposes an alternate reality imbued with decadent Gothic details.

Lee returns to traditional horror fantasy in *The Blood of Roses* (1990), ostensibly a variation on familiar vampire themes. However, the main thematic focus is its alternative perspective on Christianity. The origin of the vampires lies in the destruction of the Lord Tree in the mysterious Wild Wood, the center of a primeval nature worship demanding blood sacrifice. Opposed to this "natural" religion is the devotion to a crucified Christus, a worship based on distorted and fragmented texts, the property of sinister priests. Sympathy is maintained throughout for the displaced religion and the vampires it has produced, while Christianity's concern with blood sacrifice might be interpreted as a decadent, inadequate mimicry of vampiric and pagan rituals. Some have seen the tangled plot as irritatingly directionless, but the disturbing power of Lee's deconstruction of Christianity and of religious belief and ritual must be acknowledged.

In 1991 Lee produced the first novel in a fantasy series for young adults. *Black Unicorn* features a spunky, witty, sixteen-year-old heroine, Tanaquil, the daughter of a desert sorceress and an unknown father. While Tanaquil has no power as an enchantress, she has an almost magical capacity to mend objects. By putting together a collection of bones she restores a beautiful black unicorn that she follows, accompanied by a talking peeve, a bewitched desert animal. She reaches the kingdom of Prince Zorander, her true father. His city is a place of great riches and horrendous poverty where "Everything preys on everything else." Tanaquil is able to mend a magical gate between worlds to allow the unicorn to return to its own Perfect World. Although she and the peeve follow, they return to their own world when they realize their presence blights perfection. The novel shows a more humorous side of Lee while presenting a variation on her theme of the female savior.

In the same year, *The Book of the Dead* (1991) provided the third volume in the Secret Books of Paradys. This collection of eight Gothic short stories is based on the graveyard and crypt and investigates aspects of the lives of those buried there. The stories are macabre, characterized by decadence and violence.

Dark Dance (1992), the first novel in the Blood Opera sequence, continues the Gothic, decadent themes of *The Book of the Dead*. Set in a dismal, contemporary Britain, it opens depicting the life of Rachaela Day, a cold woman with a dreary job. Her father's family, the Scarabae, entices her to reside in their eerie, isolated Gothic mansion. Impossibly old, variegated, and peculiar, the Scarabae treat Rachaela as their curiosity, their possession, and their child. She in turn is mesmerized by their home and the family's mysterious powers and inexplicable behavior. She meets her father, the impossibly young Adamus, and is attracted to him, despite her fear that the Scarabae are vampires seeking her genes to survive. She eventually yields to him, is bitten and impregnated, and escapes. Their child, Ruth, is alien and demonic. When Ruth returns to the Scarabae, Rachaela follows, jealous of her daughter's incestuous betrothal to Adamus. Suicide, murder, and the destruction of the house follow. In this first novel of the series, Lee strikes a curious tone, blending the mundane and the Gothic. The survival of the uncanny Scarabae, remnants of some remote shadowy past, and their intrusion into Rachaela's present aptly symbolize the return of the repressed. The overall effect is disturbing.

Heart-Beast (1992) is a conventional horror fantasy with metamorphoses, exotic Middle Eastern connections, ancient Egyptian sorcery overlaid with Oedipal themes, class conflict, and hints of bestiality. Daniel Vehmund, who killed his father for abusing his mother, is in exile in the East. Contaminated by a potion containing a cursed diamond, he is transformed at full moon into an evil, bear-like, wall-climbing killing machine who mainly victimizes men. He returns to the family farm, kills his cruel brother, and develops an obsessive passion for Laura, the wife of the local landowner. Their struggle for mastery forms the main action.

Much of Lee's work from 1993 draws its inspiration from re-creating and refashioning particular historical moments and sites such as 1980s Britain, Victorian Kent, and the 1960s Mediterranean world of high fashion and indulgence. However, the relationship between violence and self-discovery remains cen-

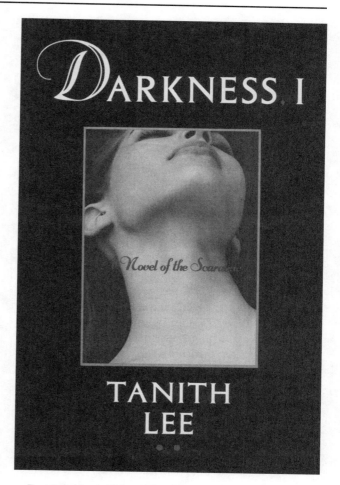

Dust jacket for the U.S. edition of the 1994 novel in Lee's "Blood Opera" series, about a clan of incestuous vampires (Richland County Public Library)

tral in her writing for adults. Her later dark fantasy and horror maintain Lee's concern with personal development and with exploring power, freedom, and responsibility on an individual level rather than with large-scale forces. She invites readers to compare social and cultural systems of exploitation and oppression and personal victimization.

Personal Darkness (1993) continues the Blood Opera sequence with the psychotic Ruth on a killing spree in 1980s Britain. Rachaela still lives with the surviving Scarabae, who now resemble the awesome undead from an ancient world, or possibly alien gods. Another line of the family is introduced to wean Ruth from her blood-lust. Like the other novels in the sequence, this one is characterized by lush sensual details and strange eroticism, both contrasting with and highlighting themes of alienation, rejection, and loss.

Elephantasm (1993) is another erotic spectacle, with a background drawn from Indian myth. In an alternate Victorian world of urban slums, prostitution, rural wilderness, and supernatural eruptions, the hero-ine, Annie Ember, is left alone when her prostitute sister is hanged for murdering an abusive husband. Annie goes into service for a rapist and murderer who has made a fortune as a soldier in India and whose wealth allows him to retire to Kent and build a fantastic rajah's palace. Flashbacks, scene shifts, and bizarre episodes disorient the narrative until the supernatural vengeance of a wronged culture expunges the man's corruption. Obsession, guilt, lust, and greed are the underlying emotions the novel explores, but Lee also offers a cultural critique in the parallels she suggests between imperialism and the sexual enslavement and domination of women.

The Book of the Mad (1993) concludes the Secret Books of Paradys. In this volume Lee emphasizes connections between three parallel worlds in which the characters act: Paradise, Paradis, and Paradys. The bizarre linking of past and future adds to a sense of oppression. In Paradis, Leocadia, an artist, is framed and condemned for murder as a maniac. In Paradys, Hilde develops an obsessional crush on an actor and is sent to an asylum. Past, present, and future are handled as fluid concepts, without clear-cut boundaries. Lee's portraits of asylum life are compelling. She draws effectively on historical detail to explore the irrational desire of the "keepers" to brutalize and dehumanize the inmates.

Nightshades (1993) consists of the novella *Nightshade* and twelve previously published short stories. The novella is predictable, with the horror derived more from personal obsessions and desire than from fantasy per se. The other stories more clearly fall into fantasy and horror modes. Among the most significant are "The Mermaid" (an effective representation of a legendary archetype taken literally), "After the Guillotine" (a postmortem fantasy suggesting that people's afterworlds accord with their earthly beliefs), "A Room with a Vie" (a terror tale featuring the "murder" of a seaside bedroom and the putrescent aftermath), and "The Devil's Rose" (a realistic tale).

Eva Fairdeath (1994), a postapocalypse novel set in a world of global pollution, madness, and despair, was originally written in 1973. Eva Belmort, an albino mutant, escapes from her village by following a shadowy murderer. They establish a bizarre relationship, which is challenged when Eva takes an additional lover. Throughout the novel Lee explores the complex motivations that sustain human relationships. Eva's process of maturation involves a gradual acceptance that she cannot control and imprison another's heart or soul for her own security. Lee's inventiveness can be seen in her refusal to resolve the dilemmas of the novel easily. She offers two

endings, but it might be argued that the only meaningful escape from this nightmare existence is death.

The more lighthearted *Gold Unicorn* (1994) is a sequel to *Black Unicorn* and continues the adventures of Tanaquil, the mender-witch. This time she must save her world from Lizra, her half sister, who intends to renew the world as its benevolent dictator. Lizra has created a mechanical Golden Unicorn to bring perfection to the earth, but her strategy for its use involves violence and subjugation. In the course of their adventures they are transported to an imaginatively re-created hell, ruled by the god of war. Oily, mechanical polluted landscapes and warring tribes help Lizra see beyond the desire to conquer and rule to the corruption inevitably following such a project. The main theme lies in its exploration of true power and leadership. Overall the novel explores the nature of true power, leadership, and freedom.

The last volume to date in the Blood Opera Sequence, *Darkness, I* (1994), reveals a further transformation of the vampire Scarabae, several of whom now seem heroic figures in the cruel, mad world of everyday reality. Rachaela has a second child, Anna, a girl of strange lineage, aging quickly. Anna falls prey to the monster Cain, a blood-obsessed outcast of the Scarabae, who kidnaps her as part of his plot to steal children in order to re-create his sadistic ancient Egyptian world. Anna is to be his child-bride. Rachaela's triumph is to know herself, finally, as Scarabae.

In addition to the novella *Louisa the Poisoner,* an historical fantasy, Lee produced two major novels in 1995, both continuing her exploration of power, sexual perversity, and redemption. *Reigning Cats and Dogs* uses the alternate Victorian fantasy community of Black Church to explore the release and subjugation of evil desires. Lee evokes a Dickensian underclass of scavengers, hustlers, and prostitutes and mingles them with surprising commercial and technological developments and powers of supernatural and monstrous destruction released from ancient Egypt and the world of death. The protagonist, Saul, is an intelligent but damaged man who seeks revenge for his traumatic sexual abuse and betrayal as a child. Only Grace, a kind prostitute and psychic healer, can resist and defeat the forces of evil. For her the body and sexual desire are natural, not tools of persecution and domination, and she uses sex to revive Saul, whom she loves, as the Egyptian goddess revived her lord-god. Their ecstasy coincides with the frenzied self-destruction of the evil forces that had stepped into the world from the darkness. Saul is released but still has to pay for his past murderous revenge, while Grace turns to healing others.

Vivia (1995) combines the warring adventures of competing kingdoms from historical fantasy and the vampire tradition of horror fiction in a further exploration of psychosexual relationships and the nature of fulfillment. Vivia escapes from her mad father's brutality, the ineffectual religion of Marius Christ, and the encroaching plague and uprising to an underground cavern. There she is seduced and bitten by King Death, a vampire prince, a demon, and yet the source of all pleasure and completion. Her adventures as a vampire focus on her ability to exert her power over others. Yet despite her ability to survive and subdue, Vivia remains unsatisfied. While she seeks a man who can be simultaneously father, benefactor, and lover, her curse is that she inevitably destroys the beings on whom she depends. In the end, only King Death satisfies her dream. Vivia's fulfillment lies in her maternal role. Her ability to make another creature happy gives her greater peace than her longing for sustenance. Self-acceptance, the ability to see within oneself darkness as well as light and thus to acknowledge the difference of others, becomes the key to fulfillment.

When the Lights Go Out (1996) has a contemporary setting against which Lee represents a familiar theme of adolescent self-discovery along with her interest in the enlightenment to be gained from the "underside" of reality. Hesta Web leaves home and moves in with a group of squatters, junkies, and beggars in a seaside resort. The novel deals with origins and the ways in which identities are fashioned. Moreover, the self-knowledge and self-acceptance marking true maturity give a power akin to magic. Hesta finally emerges as a typical Lee goddess-priestess, healing and dispensing justice.

In a different way violence and power underpin *The Gods Are Thirsty* (1996), set during the French Revolution. In some ways, though, the research threatens to overpower the story. More successful has been Lee's return to previous narratives and genre models. *Red Unicorn* (1997) is the third Tanaquil volume; the dystopia the heroine encounters raises interesting questions about the self's darker side, as she encounters the violent Tanakil, her mirror image. The first volume in another series for young adults followed in 1998 with *Law of the Wolf Tower,* short-listed for the Guardian Children's Fiction Award. Like many of Lee's young-adult novels, this book encourages deeper understanding of the need for independence, which often conflicts with institutional demands for conformity and the law, which can seem cruel. The orphan-slave Claidi is an apt protagonist for the journey to self-awareness, self-acceptance, and sound judgment. Her story continues in *Wolf Star Rise* (2000) and *Queen of the Wolves* (2001).

"Jedella Ghost" (1998), a science-fiction story, was nominated for the 1999 British Fantasy Award for best short fiction. Lee also embarked on a new series of

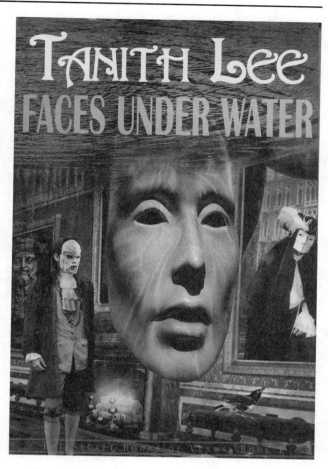

Dust jacket for the 1998 novel with which Lee began a series set in an alternate version of eighteenth-century Venice (Richland County Public Library)

linked novels reminiscent of the Secret Books of Paradys. *Faces Under Water* (1998) is set in eighteenth-century "Venus," an alternate Venice where pleasure-seeking camouflages a grotesque world of violent death and black magic. The second novel of the series followed in 1999. While the first volume drew on water, *Saint Fire* relates its elemental motif to the inner fire of Volpa, a Joan of Arc figure inhabiting a medieval Venus. Like Lee's other slave-heroines, Volpa harbors a secret power that can destroy her abusers but can be exploited. Whether this factor makes for a saintly or demonic representation of woman is one of the ambiguities Lee teases readers to consider. Third in the series, *A Bed of Earth (The Gravedigger's Tale)* is set in a Renaissance Venus and, as Lee says on her website, "contains a guest appearance by Cesare Borgia."

Lee's work for young people continues to attract commercial interest. *Voyage of the Bassett: Islands in the Sky* (1999) is a children's book set partly in Victorian London and partly in a magical world of centaurs and other mythical creatures. It is based on characters from James C. Christensen's *Voyage of the Basset* (1996).

Despite occasional unevenness, Tanith Lee has established herself as a major figure in fantasy and horror, and she is beginning to attract scholarly interest. Her complex, engaging plots, vivid protagonists, and imaginative alternate worlds have secured her a cult readership in America. Lee's ability to blend and challenge traditional fantasy formulas and popular genre conventions fits well with her questioning of cultural values and orthodox expectations concerning leadership and authority, sexuality and the body, and religious belief. As she suggests in her short story "Love Alters," the "natural intellectual, spiritual *truthful* urge" is always to "the recognition of one's own self in another," even when that means embracing the darkness.

Interviews:

Darrell Schweitzer, "Interview: Tanith Lee," *Fantasy Newsletter* (November 1981): 12–15;

Stan Nicholls, "Letting Go of the Here and Now: Tanith Lee Interview," *Fear* (October 1989), pp. 16–19;

Peter Garratt, "Unstoppable Fate: Tanith Lee Interview," *Interzone,* no. 64 (October 1992): 23–25;

"Coffee Shop: Tanith Lee Interview," *After Hours,* 7 (Winter 1995): 42–43;

Charles N. Brown, "Tanith Lee: Love and Death and Publishers," *Locus,* 40, no. 3 (April 1998): 4–5, 76.

Bibliography:

Jim Pattison and Paul A. Soanes, *Daughter of the Night: A Tanith Lee Bibliography* (Toronto: Gaffa Press, 1993); updated and published as a website, May 1997: <http://www3.sympatico.ca/jim.pattison/index.htm>.

References:

"A Celebration of Tanith Lee," *Dragonfields,* no. 4 (1983): 12–25;

M. R. Collings, "Words and Worlds: The Creation of a Fantasy Universe in Zelazny, Lee and Anthony,"

in *The Scope of the Fantastic,* edited by R. A. Collins and H. D. Pearce (Westport, Conn.: Greenwood Press, 1985), pp. 173–182;

David Cowperthwaite, ed., *Tanith Lee: Mistress of Delirium* (Stockport: British Fantasy Society, 1993);

Larry W. Gasser, "Feminism and Tanith Lee's *The Birthgrave,*" *Harbinger,* 1 (Spring 1976): 5–7;

Charles L. Grant, "Tanith Lee," in *World Fantasy Convention 1984,* edited by Charles de Lint (Ottawa: Triskell Press, 1984), pp. 55–57;

Mavis Haut, *The Hidden Library of Tanith Lee: Themes and Subtexts from Dionysos to the Immortal Gene* (Jefferson, N.C.: McFarland, 2001);

Lillian Heldreth, "Tanith Lee's Werewolves Within: Reversals of Gothic Tradition," *Journal of the Fantastic in the Arts,* 2 (Spring 1989): 15–24;

Sarah Lefanu, "Robots and Romance: The Science Fiction and Fantasy of Tanith Lee," in *Sweet Dreams: Sexuality, Gender and Science Fiction,* edited by Susannah Radstone (London: Lawrence & Wishart, 1988), pp. 121–136;

Maureen Moran, "Anarchic Spaces in Sword and Sorcery Fiction," Diegesis: The Journal of the Association for Research in Popular Fictions, 4 (Summer 1999): 41–50;

Kitty Perdone, "Blood Sisters," *Midnight Graffiti,* no. 4 (Fall 1989): 46–50;

Lea Silhol, "Elle est trois, une lecture symbolique du vampirisme chez Tanith Lee, Freda Warrington et Storm Constantine," in *Vampire: Portraits d'une Ombre,* edited by Silhol (Montpellier, France: Editions de L'Oxymore, 1999);

Silhol, "Venin, Velours, Vitrail, l'écriture vampirique chez Storm Constantine, Tanith Lee, Freda Warrington," in *Visages du Vampire,* edited by Barbara Sadoul (Paris: Dervy, 1999);

Jeannette C. Smith, "The Heroine Within: Psychological Archetypes in Tanith Lee's *A Heroine of the World,*" *Extrapolation,* 39 (Spring 1998): 52–56;

Donald A. Wollheim, "Profile: Tanith Lee," *Weird Tales,* 50 (Summer 1988): 43–44.

Michael Moorcock

(18 December 1939 –   )

William J. Collins

See also the Moorcock entries in *DLB 14: British Novelists Since 1960* and *DLB 231: British Novelists Since 1960: Fourth Series.*

BOOKS: *Caribbean Crisis,* by Moorcock and James Cawthorn as Desmond Reid (London: Fleetway, 1962);

The Stealer of Souls and Other Stories (London: Spearman, 1963; New York: Lancer, 1967; revised edition, New York: DAW, 1977);

Stormbringer (London: Jenkins, 1965; New York: Lancer, 1967; revised edition, New York: DAW, 1977);

The Sundered Worlds (London: Roberts & Vinter, 1965; New York: Paperback Library, 1966); republished as *The Blood Red Game* (London: Sphere, 1970);

The Fireclown (London: Roberts & Vinter, 1965; New York: Paperback Library, 1967); republished as *The Winds of Limbo* (New York: Paperback Library, 1969; London: Sphere, 1970);

Warriors of Mars, as Edward P. Bradbury (London: Roberts & Vinter, 1965; New York: Lancer, 1966); republished as *The City of the Beast,* as Moorcock (New York: Lancer, 1970; London: New English Library, 1971);

Blades of Mars, as Bradbury (London: Roberts & Vinter, 1965; New York: Lancer, 1966); as *The Lord of the Spiders,* as Moorcock (New York: Lancer, 1970; London: New English Library, 1971);

The Barbarians of Mars, as Bradbury (London: Roberts & Vinter, 1965; New York: Lancer, 1966); republished as *The Masters of the Pit,* as Moorcock (New York: Lancer, 1970; London: New English Library, 1971);

The Twilight Man (London: Roberts & Vinter, 1966; New York: Berkley, 1970); republished as *The Shores of Death* (London: Sphere, 1970; New York: Dale, 1978);

The Deep Fix, as James Colvin (London: Roberts & Vinter, 1966);

Michael Moorcock (photograph from the dust jacket for the U.S. edition of Mother London, *1989)*

Printer's Devil, as Bill Barclay (London: Roberts & Vinter, 1966); revised as *The Russian Intelligence,* as Moorcock (Manchester, U.K.: Savoy, 1980);

Somewhere in the Night, as Barclay (London: Roberts & Vinter, 1966); revised as *The Chinese Agent,* as Moorcock (London: Hutchinson, 1970; New York: Macmillan, 1970);

The Jewel in the Skull (New York: Lancer, 1967; London: Mayflower, 1969; revised edition, New York: DAW, 1977);

293

The Wrecks of Time [bound with *Tramontane*, by Emil Petaja] (New York: Ace, 1967); revised as *The Rituals of Infinity* (London: Arrow, 1971; New York: DAW, 1978);

The Final Programme (New York: Avon, 1968; London: Allison & Busby, 1969; revised edition, London: Fontana, 1979);

Sorcerer's Amulet (New York: Lancer, 1968); republished as *The Mad God's Amulet* (London: Mayflower, 1969; revised edition, New York: DAW, 1977; London: Fontana, 1979);

Sword of the Dawn (New York: Lancer, 1968; London: Mayflower, 1969; revised edition, New York: DAW, 1977);

The Secret of the Runestaff (New York: Lancer, 1969); republished as *The Runestaff* (London: Mayflower, 1969; revised edition, New York: DAW, 1977);

The Ice Schooner (London: Sphere, 1969; New York: Berkley, 1969; revised edition, London: Harrap, 1985);

Behold the Man (London: Allison & Busby, 1969; New York: Avon, 1970);

The Black Corridor, by Moorcock and Hilary Bailey (London: Mayflower, 1969; New York: Ace, 1969);

The Time Dweller (London: Hart-Davis, 1969; New York: Berkley, 1971);

The Singing Citadel (London: Mayflower, 1970; New York: Berkley, 1970);

The Eternal Champion (London: Mayflower, 1970; New York: Dell, 1970; revised edition, New York: Harper & Row, 1978);

Phoenix in Obsidian (London: Mayflower, 1970); republished as *The Silver Warriors* (New York: Dell, 1973);

A Cure for Cancer (London: Allison & Busby, 1971; New York: Holt, Rinehart & Winston, 1971; revised edition, London: Fontana, 1979);

The Warlord of the Air (London: New English Library, 1971; New York: Ace, 1971);

The Knight of the Swords (London: Mayflower, 1971; New York: Berkley, 1971);

The Queen of the Swords (London: Mayflower, 1971; New York: Berkley, 1971);

The King of the Swords (London: Mayflower, 1971; New York: Berkley, 1971);

The Sleeping Sorceress (London: New English Library, 1971; New York: Lancer, 1972); revised as *The Vanishing Tower* (London: New English Library, 1972; New York: DAW, 1977);

The Dreaming City (New York: Lancer, 1972); revised as *Elric of Melniboné* (London: Hutchinson, 1972);

An Alien Heat (London: MacGibbon & Kee, 1972; New York: Harper & Row, 1972);

Breakfast in the Ruins (London: New English Library, 1972; New York: Random House, 1974);

The English Assassin (London: Allison & Busby, 1972; New York: Harper & Row, 1972; revised edition, London: Fontana, 1979);

The Jade Man's Eyes (Brighton, U.K. & Seattle: Unicorn Bookshop, 1973);

Elric: The Return to Melniboné (Brighton & Seattle: Unicorn Bookshop, 1973);

The Bull and the Spear (London: Allison & Busby, 1973; New York: Berkley, 1974);

Count Brass (London: Mayflower, 1973; New York: Dell, 1976);

The Champion of Garathorm (London: Mayflower, 1973; New York: Dell, 1976);

The Oak and the Ram (London: Allison & Busby, 1973; New York: Berkley, 1974);

The Sword and the Stallion (London: Allison & Busby, 1974; New York: Berkley, 1974);

The Land Leviathan (London: Quartet, 1974; Garden City, N.Y.: Doubleday, 1974);

The Hollow Lands (New York: Harper & Row, 1974; London: Hart-Davis, MacGibbon, 1975);

The Distant Suns, by Moorcock and Philip James (James Cawthorn) (Llanfynydd, U.K.: Unicorn Bookshop, 1975);

The Quest for Tanelorn (London: Mayflower, 1975; New York: Dell, 1976);

The Sailor on the Seas of Fate (London: Quartet, 1976; New York: DAW, 1976);

The Time of the Hawklords, by Moorcock and Michael Butterworth (London: Wyndham, 1976; New York: Warner, 1976);

The Adventures of Una Persson and Catherine Cornelius in the Twentieth Century (London: Quartet, 1976); republished with *The Black Corridor* as *The Adventures of Una Persson and Catherine Cornelius* (New York: Dial, 1979);

Moorcock's Book of Martyrs (London: Quartet, 1976); republished as *Dying for Tomorrow* (New York: DAW, 1978);

Legends from the End of Time (London: W. H. Allen, 1976; New York: Harper & Row, 1976);

The End of All Songs (London: Hart-Davis, MacGibbon, 1976; New York: Harper & Row, 1976);

The Lives and Times of Jerry Cornelius (London: Allison & Busby, 1976; New York: Dale, 1979);

The Condition of Muzak (London: Allison & Busby, 1977; Boston: Gregg Press, 1978);

Sojan (Manchester, U.K.: Savoy, 1977);

The Transformation of Miss Mavis Ming (London: W. H. Allen, 1977); republished as *A Messiah at the End of Time* (New York: DAW, 1978);

The Weird of the White Wolf (New York: DAW, 1977; London: Panther, 1984);

The Bane of the Black Sword (New York: DAW, 1977; London: Panther, 1984);

Epic Pooh (London: British Fantasy Society, 1978);

Gloriana; or, The Unfulfill'd Queen (London: Allison & Busby, 1978; New York: Avon, 1979);

The Real Life of Mr Newman (Worcester, U.K.: A. J. Callow, 1979);

The Golden Barge (Manchester, U.K.: Savoy, 1979; New York: DAW, 1980);

The Great Rock 'n' Roll Swindle (London: Virgin, 1980);

My Experiences in the Third World War (Manchester, U.K.: Savoy, 1980);

The Entropy Tango (London: New English Library, 1981); republished with *The Lives and Times of Jerry Cornelius* as volume 2 of *The Cornelius Chronicles* (New York: Avon, 1986);

The Steel Tsar (London: Mayflower, 1981; New York: DAW, 1982);

The War Hound and the World's Pain (New York: Simon & Schuster, 1981; London: New English Library, 1982);

Byzantium Endures (London: Secker & Warburg, 1981; New York: Random House, 1982);

The Brothel in Rosenstrasse (London: New English Library, 1982; New York: Carroll & Graf, 1987);

The Retreat from Liberty: The Erosion of Democracy in Today's Britain (London: Zomba, 1983);

The Laughter of Carthage (London: Secker & Warburg, 1984; New York: Random House, 1984);

The Opium General and Other Stories (London: Harrap, 1984); abridged as *The Alchemist's Question* in volume 3 of *The Cornelius Chronicles* (New York: Avon, 1987);

Elric at the End of Time (London: New English Library, 1984; New York: DAW, 1985);

The Crystal and the Amulet (Manchester, U.K.: Savoy, 1986);

The Dragon in the Sword (New York: Ace, 1986; London: Grafton, 1987);

The City in the Autumn Stars (London: Grafton, 1986; New York: Ace, 1987);

Letters from Hollywood (London: Harrap, 1986);

Mother London (London: Secker & Warburg, 1988; New York: Harmony, 1989);

Fantasy: The 100 Best Books, by Moorcock and Cawthorn (New York: Carroll & Graf, 1988);

The Fortress of the Pearl (London: Gollancz, 1989; New York: Ace, 1989);

Wizardry and Wild Romance: A Study of Heroic Fantasy (London: Gollancz, 1989);

Casablanca (London: Gollancz, 1989);

Cover for a 1965 issue of the magazine in which Moorcock published his novella about a misfit who travels back to the time of Jesus and takes his place as Messiah

The Revenge of the Rose (London: Grafton, 1991; New York: Ace, 1991);

Jerusalem Commands (London: Cape, 1992);

Hawkmoon (London: Millenium, 1992; Clarkston, Ga.: White Wolf, 1995);

Von Bek (London: Millenium, 1992; Clarkston, Ga.: White Wolf, 1995);

Sailing to Utopia (London: Millenium, 1993; Clarkston, Ga.: White Wolf, 1997);

Blood: A Southern Fantasy (New York: Morrow, 1994; London: Millenium, 1995);

Fabulous Harbors: A Sequel to Blood (New York: Avon, 1995; London: Millenium, 1995);

Lunching with the Antichrist: A Family History, 1925–2015 (Shingletown, Cal.: Ziesing, 1995);

The War amongst the Angels: An Autobiographical Story (New York: Avon, 1996; London: Millenium, 1996);

Tales from the Texas Woods (Dripping Springs, Tex.: Mojo, 1997);

King of the City (New York: Scribner, 2000);

Silverheart, by Moorcock and Storm Constantine (London: Simon & Schuster, 2000);

The Dreamthief's Daughter: A Tale of the Albino (New York: Warner, 2001).

PRODUCED SCRIPT: *The Land That Time Forgot,* motion picture, by Moorcock and James Cawthorn, American International Pictures / Amicus Productions, 1974.

OTHER: *The Best of New Worlds,* edited by Moorcock (London: Roberts & Vinter, 1965);

Robert Harris, *The LSD Dossier,* ghostwritten by Moorcock (London: Roberts & Vinter, 1966);

Langdon Jones, ed., *The New SF,* preface by Moorcock (London: Hutchinson, 1969);

Best SF Stories from New Worlds, edited by Moorcock (8 volumes, London: Panther, 1967–1974; 6 volumes, New York: Berkley, 1968–1971);

The Inner Landscape, edited by Moorcock (London: Allison & Busby, 1969);

The Nature of the Catastrophe, edited by Moorcock and Jones (London: Hutchinson, 1971);

Before Armageddon: An Anthology of Victorian and Edwardian Imaginative Fiction Published Before 1914, edited by Moorcock (London: W. H. Allen, 1975);

"Mal Dean," in *New World 8,* edited by Hilary Bailey (London: Sphere, 1975);

"Modern Metaphors," in *J. G. Ballard: The First Twenty Years,* edited by James Goddard and David Pringle (London: Bran's Head Books, 1976);

England Invaded: A Collection of Fantasy Fiction, edited by Moorcock (London: W. H. Allen, 1977; New York: Ultramarine, 1977);

"New Worlds: A Personal History," in *Foundation,* 15 (January 1979): 5–18;

"Wit and Humor in Fantasy," in *Foundation,* 16 (May 1979): 16–22;

New Worlds: An Anthology, edited by Moorcock (London: Fontana, 1983);

"Aspects of Fantasy," in *Exploring Fantasy Worlds: Essays in Fantastic Literature,* edited by Darrell F. Schweitzer (San Bernardino, Cal.: Borgo Press, 1985);

The New Nature of the Catastrophe, edited by Moorcock and Jones (London: Millenium, 1993).

From his beginnings as a writer of science fiction and heroic fantasy in the early 1960s through his long, idiosyncratic, unclassifiable novels of the 1980s and 1990s, Michael Moorcock has been compared, variously but rarely adversely, with Charles Dickens, William S. Burroughs, Donald Barthelme, Thomas Pynchon, and Jorge Luis Borges. As editor of the British speculative-fiction magazine *New Worlds* from 1966 to 1971, Moorcock was perhaps the dominant force for change in New Wave science fiction, the attempt to introduce experimental modernist and postmodernist techniques into what Moorcock and his associates viewed as an ossified genre. Since the 1980s he has moved away from the realm of overt fantasy to become an acclaimed novelist of urban life with his Dickensian novel of the London Blitz and its survivors, *Mother London* (1988), and his Between the Wars tetralogy (1981–   ).

Michael John Moorcock was born in Mitcham, Surrey, a suburb of London, on 18 December 1939. As a young child, he remembers, he witnessed the Blitz of London during World War II, and, as some critics have noted, his observations contributed to his later ability to portray carnage, both in a fantastic realm of sorcery and in the real world of the twentieth century. His father, Arthur Moorcock, a draftsman who did not serve in the war, abandoned the family in 1945, leaving the author's mother, June (Taylor) Moorcock, to raise her somewhat rebellious child, who was expelled from one school and cut so many classes at another that in 1950 he failed his eleven-plus exams, the examinations given to British schoolchildren at the end of elementary school to determine what form of secondary education they should receive.

Moorcock's boredom with school may be traced to his early reading ability. Before his formal schooling began, he was already reading both juvenile and adult fiction. By the age of ten he was producing hand-done, carbon-copied "magazines" (including one titled "Outlaw's Own"), so his mother entered him in Pitman College, a business school that she hoped would prepare him for a career in journalism. During his stay at Pitman, which he left when he was fourteen, Moorcock continued to produce fanzines, one for Edgar Rice Burroughs enthusiasts and another for collectors of the Old Boy Books and *Boys' Own Paper* fiction.

Having lost his first job, at a shipping company, for insulting the manager's mistress, the fifteen-year-old Moorcock joined the publishing house Harold Whitehead and Partners, where his amateur writing (sometimes on company time, with company equipment) was encouraged. By the time he was sixteen, he was selling freelance material to his employer, and at seventeen he became editor of their magazine *Tarzan Adventures,* for which he wrote his first longer sword-and-sorcery fantasy story, "Sojan," published in book form in 1977 with other juvenilia and brief essays on his later work.

After Moorcock made *Tarzan Adventures* more sophisticated than its longtime readers liked, Whitehead decided to turn it into a pure comic-strip magazine, and Moorcock resigned in protest. After a few months living the bohemian life in Paris, he returned to

Dust jacket for the 1969 British edition of the first novel in Moorcock's tetralogy about "multiversal"
traveler Jerry Cornelius (Richland County Public Library)

London in 1958 and took a job at Amalgamated Press
(later Fleetway) writing detective thrillers for the Sexton
Blake Library and comic-book continuity for strips featuring characters such as Tarzan, Billy the Kid, Robin
Hood, and the Three Musketeers. He also began to
experiment with what he called "non-generic fiction,"
that is, fiction challenging the preconceived boundaries
of whatever genre in which it was nominally set. The
term might validly be applied to nearly all his subsequent fiction.

Moorcock's first serious writing included three
novels: "Duel Among the Wine-Green Suns," a
science-fiction-based tale; "The Quest of Jephraim
Tallow," an allegory featuring a misshapen social outcast (the first of a long line of "outsider" protagonists)
who rejects love, power, and honor in the monomaniacal pursuit of a mysterious golden barge that forever
sails just outside his ability to catch it (published in
paperback as *The Golden Barge* in 1979); and *The Eternal Champion* (published in book form, 1970), part of
which first appeared in a fanzine and which originates

one of the controlling devices of practically all of his
heroic fantasy, science fiction, and postmodernist multiversal fiction.

Moorcock worked for the Sexton Blake Library
for two years, leaving when the publishers
demanded that he encorporate xenophobic attitudes
toward Germans and Russians into his comic-strip
continuity. By that time he had sold his first "adult"
story, "Peace on Earth," a collaboration with Barrington J. Bayley, to the British science-fiction pulp
magazine *New Worlds,* edited by E. J. Carnell. Following a trip to Scandinavia for mountain climbing (one
of his hobbies), he began to freelance, writing articles
and comic-strip continuity, specializing in historical
and mythological themes. At Carnell's invitation, he
also began a series of linked novelettes featuring the
first of the Eternal Champion figures to appear in a
professional magazine, Elric of Melniboné. The first
of these novelettes was "The Dreaming City," which
appeared in the June 1961 issue and was published in
book form in 1972.

Moorcock also contributed to *Science Fantasy* and *Science Fiction Adventures,* sister publications of *New Worlds.* Published in 1962, his first long science-fiction story, a two-part serial novel titled "The Sundered Worlds" and "The Blood Red Game" (published in paperback under the first title in 1965 and under the second in 1970), introduced the concept of the "multiverse," which he later expanded and incorporated into the sagas of the Eternal Champion in his various incarnations.

In the multiverse (based on the time theories of J. B. Dunne) past, present, and future coexist in all their infinite possibilities. What might have happened, but did not in the temporal reality Moorcock and his readers share (an Axis victory in World War II, Moses drowning in the Nile as a baby, a star across the galaxy going nova, deciding this morning to wear blue socks instead of brown ones), did happen in some version of the infinite possible pasts and forever altered the direction of a given continuum, whether personal, planetary, or universal. Just as there are an infinite number of pasts, so those pasts have generated an infinite number of presents, which will generate an infinite number of futures.

In developing the concept of the multiverse over the next several years, Moorcock added his own corollary to Dunne's theories: all these pasts, presents, and futures coexist simultaneously, rather than flowing diachronically (that is, over a period of time as, for example, the alternative continua do in Jorge Luis Borges's short story "The Garden of Forking Paths"). Furthermore, outside the planal dimensions of the coexistent multiverse, there exist entities that seek to influence the direction of all time, either toward Chaos or toward Law. These entities seek to throw off the Cosmic Balance, which requires a measure of both Law and Chaos for equilibrium. Moorcock has equated Chaos with Romanticism, individualism, the Dionysian; Law with Classicism, obedience, the Apollonian. If, in a particular plane of the multiverse, one of the forces becomes overwhelming, the Cosmic Balance is so upset that that continuum ceases to exist. In order to forestall this eventuality (usually brought on by the Lords of Chaos), a single, superhuman figure must arise to combat the Gods. This hero, with avatars in every plane of the multiverse, is the Eternal Champion.

Arguably the most interesting of the many avatars of the Eternal Champion, and the most representative, is the first, Elric of Melniboné. Elric inhabits a version of Earth in what appears to be the distant past. He is the last emperor of an alien race of superhumanoids who once held weaker humanity in slavery, but, having grown bored with conquest, they have retired to their Dragon Kingdom, allowing humans to establish nations and commerce throughout the rest of the (geographically unrecognizable) globe.

Though the Elric stories owe a great deal in form to Robert E. Howard's Conan the Barbarian, Moorcock has never been satisfied merely to entertain readers with tales of violence, sex, and sorcery for their own sake as, to an extent, Howard and many of his imitators have through the years. Moorcock has said that Elric, metaphorically, "*was* me (the me of 1960–1, anyway)." Indeed, Moorcock has often stated that many of his plots are metaphoric representations of his personal relationships and those of his close friends.

Elric was also conceived as almost the opposite of the Conan figure: he is an albino, an oddity even among his own superhuman race, given strength through the possession of his sinister, sentient sword Stormbringer, a gift from the Lord of Chaos, whom Elric serves. The sword must drink not only the blood but also the souls of those it slays, and when it is, in Elric's hands, in a killing frenzy, even he cannot control it.

Elric is also an intellectual oddity among his people. He is fascinated with the proliferating human race and equivocal about the violence and cynicism of humans and his own people. Though he nominally serves a Lord of Chaos, he repeatedly questions his own motives and decisions, and, in an agonizing way searches for some personal peace, which constantly eludes him. He is constantly aware of his apartness, constantly seeking balance in a world growing more chaotic.

After his creation of Elric, Moorcock's output began to appear in almost every issue of Carnell's three pulp magazines. Soon another avatar of the Eternal Champion made his debut, a present-day Londoner, John Daker, who inhabits the body of Erekosë and other avatars, his curse being that he alone of the Champions remembers his incarnations. In one novelette he crosses the dimensions of the multiverse to battle side by side with Elric, thus setting up a pattern of linkages among characters and Moorcock's various series that grew in ever more bewildering fashion, to the point that it is impossible not to be slightly confused while reading almost any of the sagas of the Eternal Champion in their final (often somewhat rewritten) form.

Contributing regularly to Carnell's magazines and selling freelance nonfiction and comic strips elsewhere, Moorcock tried to settle down, marrying Hilary Bailey in September 1962 and going to work writing advertising for the Liberal Party. He lost his party job in yet another clash with a superior, and in 1964 it appeared that *New Worlds* and *Science Fantasy,* his major markets, might soon fold. (*Science Fiction Adventures* had already ceased publication in 1963.) At the last minute, the remaining magazines were sold to the Roberts and Vinter Company, and on the recommendation of retiring editor Carnell, Moorcock was hired to edit *New Worlds*.

A year earlier, he and fellow *New Worlds* contributor J. G. Ballard had put together a dummy issue of a new kind of science-fiction magazine, which would incorporate–along with traditional science fiction–works that employed avant-garde and postmodernist fictional techniques, the model being one of Ballard's favorite authors, William S. Burroughs, but no publisher had been interested. In the pages of *New Worlds,* Ballard also called for science-fiction writers to "abandon outer space for inner space." Under Moorcock's editorship, *New Worlds* began to feature an increasing quantity of avant-garde material. Much of the first such fiction seems to have been eccentric for its own sake rather than experimental, and Moorcock began to receive criticism for his "indulgence" of such work. Yet, soon a cadre of genuine science-fiction revolutionaries were drawn to its pages. In addition to Ballard, whose stories for the magazine (collected as *The Atrocity Exhibit,* 1969) perhaps best exemplify the far edge of New Wave, writers such as Brian W. Aldiss, Harlan Ellison, Thomas M. Disch, Samuel R. Delany, and Moorcock's spouse, Hilary Bailey, began contributing to the magazine. In the United States, Judith Merril called attention to the new movement with articles and the anthology *England Swings SF* (1968), and science-fiction fans and writers became polarized into pro- and anti–New Wave factions.

Moorcock's earliest venture into the movement he helped create came in the early days of 1965 with his first Jerry Cornelius novel, *The Final Programme* (published in book form in 1968), based–as some sharp observers noted–on the same plot as the first two Elric stories but set in a multiversal version of contemporary Britain. The Cornelius character, in varying guises, appeared throughout most of Moorcock's fiction until his move into large-scale urban novels in the 1980s, and even in these books his mother (in the multiversal fiction) is a main character.

Cornelius is a trickster hero, a hip innocent in a chaotic world. His first name echoes that of Jeremiah, author of the Old Testament book of Lamentations, and the noun *jeremiad* that denotes a literary work of prolonged lamentation or complaint designed to evoke the reader's pity for the protagonist. This description fits the malleable Cornelius of the central tetralogy, four peripheral novels and collected short stories that form The Cornelius Chronicles, but it hardly describes the Cornelius character who pops in and out of the Eternal Champion sagas with variations on the Cornelius name. This character, self-described as "the companion

Dust jacket for the 1972 novel that helped to convince mainstream critics that Moorcock was not just a science-fiction writer

of champions," serves the function of lending a bit of lightness and comedy to the overbearing sense of relentless fate that looms for Eternal Champions such as Elric, Erekosë, and Corum. Nor does the description fit the holy innocent Jherek Carnelian, protagonist of the Dancers at the End of Time trilogy.

At the same time as his foray into what *New Worlds* was calling "speculative fiction" (to differentiate it from traditional science fiction but to retain the traditional abbreviation *SF*), Moorcock wound up the Elric series in *Stormbringer* (1965) with the cataclysmic extinction of all life on that plane by the Champion's sinister sword and abandoned the John Daker/Erekosë avatar on a wintry plane, far from the eternal city of Tanelorn (a nodal point coexisting in all the spheres) and from his lost love, Ermizhad. At his publisher's behest, he wrote–under the pen name Edward P. Bradbury–a trilogy of novels unabashedly modeled on Edgar Rice Burroughs's John Carter of Mars series. He also began a new tetralogy, The High History of the Runestaff, set in an alternative future in which the evil scientists of

Granbretan seek to extend their negative adherence to Law toward global domination. They are opposed by Dorian Hawkmoon, Duke of Köln, who survives the implantation of a brain-eating jewel in his forehead to defeat the Granbretanians and, alone among the avatars of the Eternal Champion, retire in a balanced world to the joys of marriage and family.

Yet, Moorcock's most important 1965 publication was his novella "Behold the Man" (later expanded to novel length and published as a book in 1969). The story is about a neurotic misfit, Karl Glogauer, who travels back in time to biblical Judea, where he discovers that Jesus is a drooling idiot and his mother, Mary, is a slut. Glogauer's assumption of Jesus' public role as Messiah has been described by Colin Greenland as an act of "masochistic self-fulfillment." The novella won Moorcock a Nebula Award from the Science Fiction Writers of America and a British Science Fiction Association Award, and the work brought him to the attention of the mainstream novelist and critic Angus Wilson, who became the first establishment critical voice extolling Moorcock's unpredictable fiction.

Trouble for *New Worlds* began to surface again in 1966, when the distributor for the publishing company went bankrupt. Through the efforts of Brian Aldiss, a British Arts Council Grant of £200 a year allowed publication of the magazine to continue as ownership went from one publisher to another, including one named (aptly, according to Moorcock) Stoneheart. By 1968 Moorcock was not only editor but sole publisher of the magazine, which had abandoned its traditional digest size for an 8" x 10" format. During these years he completed the Runestaff series, wrote *The Ice Schooner* (1969), a conventional science-fiction novel (albeit with a doomed, Byronic hero), and completed an agreement with the U.S. publisher Avon Books for the continuation of the Jerry Cornelius series. He also published in *New Worlds* "The Pleasure Garden of Felipe Sagittarius," which he considers pivotal in forming the basis for his distinctive approach to postmodernist science fiction as he practiced it in The Cornelius Chronicles and *Breakfast in the Ruins* (1972).

"The Pleasure Garden of Felipe Sagittarius" takes place in a Berlin whose police chief is Otto von Bismarck; one of his assistants is a likable but sexually repressed captain, Adolf Hitler, who is tricked by the insane biologist Sagittarius into killing a prostitute named Eva Braun. In most alternate histories—for example, Philip K. Dick's *The Man in the High Castle* (1962), which takes place in an Axis-occupied United States—one of the major stylistic challenges is the successful embedding in the narrative of enough information to allow the reader to locate and understand the point at which the alternative continuum has branched

off from the reader's (in Dick's novel, the assassination of Franklin D. Roosevelt in 1935). Moorcock consciously refuses the reader this consolation. In a short explanation included in *Sojan,* he explains the decision by saying that in one of his stories the "internal logic is straightforward; the . . . characters know exactly what they are talking about. To 'explain' all this, to editorialise, would break the mood, break the dramatic tensions. . . . The apparent obscurity should not confuse the reader because the narrative should be moving so rapidly that he shouldn't care if he doesn't understand every reference." Moorcock later went well beyond this approach in his postmodernist works. Writing in *Isaac Asimov's Science Fiction Magazine* (April 1994), Norman Spinrad compared Moorcock's approach to jazz, in which the "riffs," or variations on a tune (that is, the plotline), need not include the tune itself, that "rather than *describe* the phenomenological surface of reality 'realistically,' prose could convey its inner landscape *allusively,* in the manner of poetry."

Initially, Moorcock applied the internally allusive theory of composition to a series of vignettes (collected in 1976 as *The Lives and Times of Jerry Cornelius*) in which Cornelius inhabits various planes of the late-twentieth-century multiverse. From one vignette to another, Cornelius is tall, short, middle sized; a fearless hero, a coward, a nonentity; a lover, a user, a victim; and a liberal, a conservative, an opportunist, a bigot. His adventures take place in competing versions of China, India, Czechoslovakia, Nazified Europe, and a Time Centre that plays a part in several future series. Furthermore, Moorcock began to intercalate both real and (at least for humans' continuum of the multiverse) spurious documentation, in the form of quotations, bibliographic references, advertisements, and untrustworthy author-omniscient statements.

The year 1969 was pivotal for Moorcock, both in the direction he would be forced to take as a writer and for his finances. Never much of a businessman, he failed to incorporate the magazine he took over as its publisher. His distributors were becoming fearful of public outcry from conservative readers, who deplored the irreverent treatment of established religion, morality, and political philosophy in *New Worlds*. They were particularly outraged by the serialization of Norman Spinrad's *Bug Jack Barron* (1969), with its literal metaphor of capitalism as cannibalistic, and Harlan Ellison's "A Boy and His Dog," in which the starving protagonist has to choose between killing and eating his lover or his telepathic hound. National distributors began to send back vast quantities of *New Worlds* without parceling them out to local distributors. In London, the editorial staff began selling copies on the street.

Financially responsible for the debts of the magazine, Moorcock found himself required to produce more of the staple fare that brought in the most money, his heroic fantasies. He was temporarily forced to leave further contemporary multiversal adventures in postmodern style to other writers (later collected in the anthology *The Nature of the Catastrophe,* 1971). A contact with Ace Books resulted in a rare work of futuristic science fiction, *The Black Corridor* (1969), plotted and written with his wife, Hilary Bailey, though Ace published it under Moorcock's name alone.

The Black Corridor begins with a clichéd theme, the flight of a small group of chosen humans from an Earth threatened with destruction. (In typical Moorcock fashion, the threat is of anarchic chaos.) Yet, the narrative soon becomes a disturbing investigation of possible madness, leaving the reader at the conclusion unsure as to whether the ship's captain is a mass murderer, the prisoner of his crew, or a madman guiding a frozen-sleep crew across the void to nowhere.

In late 1969 Moorcock turned the editorship of *New Worlds* over to Charles Platt. The magazine ceased publication as a periodical with issue number 200 in April 1970. (A memorial "Good Taste Issue" was sent to subscribers, with a complete index, in 1971.) Moorcock rewrote or recobbled uncollected sections of the Elric saga for paperback publication, resurrected John Daker, and began a trilogy featuring yet another unmuscular, introspective, intellectual alien, Prince Corum Jhaelen Irsay, forced to take up a sword (another sinister one) to right the cosmic balance. Moorcock also managed to deliver the second of the Jerry Cornelius novels, *A Cure for Cancer* (1971).

The first novel of the tetralogy, *The Final Programme,* is limited largely to an alternate, late-1960s London in which Jerry, a hip genius whose Unified Field Theory lay safely in the Vatican Library, wages a fratricidal private war for the incestuous love of his sister Catherine, at the conclusion of which Catherine lies dead, encased in ice, while Jerry has merged with Miss Brunner, a contemporary vampire who lives by draining her victims of their DNA, into a hermaphroditic superhuman. Readers of *A Cure for Cancer* find themselves in the middle of the multiverse. Jerry is no longer a hermaphrodite; now he is black. His brother Frank, whom Jerry has killed, is alive, but Catherine is still dead and frozen. Miss Brunner is now male and a captain in the U.S. Army, which occupies England. (Moorcock had printed on the title page, "This book has an unconventional structure.") The plot, though confusing, is relatively linear and, except at fairly clear points, confined to a single alternate plane of the multiverse. Jerry possesses a "black box" that affords passage through the multiverse, but it feeds on the DNA of its

Dust jacket for the U.S. edition of the first volume in the "Dancers at the End of Time" trilogy (1972–1976), whose protagonist is the last natural-born human on an Earth populated by superhuman aliens (Richland County Public Library)

victims, a technological version of Elric's soul-stealing sword Stormbringer.

In *A Cure for Cancer* Moorcock continued his fascination with the capacity of the human race for relentless inhumanity. For him, the one way to preserve sanity is to view the carnage with compassionate irony. Moorcock has said that one of the frustrations of writing heroic fantasy lies in the difficulty of introducing ironic commentary into it, aside from the cosmic tragic irony that dogs the Eternal Champion. In his travels through the infinite variations on the late twentieth century, however, Jerry Cornelius brings an immediacy and a hip cynicism to catastrophe, which has led more than one critic to call Jerry "a hero for our time." Like Elric and Erekosë, and later Corum, Jerry always aims too high and is thus eternally forced into compromise in a world where all who surround him have already compromised themselves. Jerry believes in personal liberty in a world (rather, a series of worlds) under assault from political, theological, military, and economic forces—as well as from corrupt individuals who have taken the easy way out by giving in to these forces. Readers may be shocked at some of Jerry's ideals and actions (his consistent efforts to make love with his sister, for example), but his occasional epiphanic triumphs, his will to continue, and his sense of the ironic contrast with the petty aims of the forces arrayed against him, validate his ideals.

Perhaps to balance the dark vision of *A Cure for Cancer,* Moorcock turned in *The Warlord of the Air* (1971) to a more limited, traditional version of alternate history. In this novel, the first of his Bastable trilogy (1971–1981), Oswald Bastable, a British officer serving in the Raj in 1902, is trapped in a cave and emerges into a 1973 in which Great Power cooperation has prevented the world wars and made the globe safe for European imperialism. Moorcock captured both an authentic Victorian writing style and the deceptive complexity of a basically decent man infected by the prevailing Victorian idea of "the white man's burden" and approval of colonialism. Moorcock is at his most playful in this Bastable trilogy, introducing familiar historical figures in unfamiliar roles (such as Colonel T. E. Shaw advising Chinese rebels, Joseph Conrad as a dirigible captain, and Ronald Reagan as a racist scoutmaster); yet there is a serious undercurrent as Bastable, confronted with undeniable moral qualities in women, blacks, and Asians, is forced to rid himself of his external sense of superiority as a white male and discover whether he has in him qualities equal to those not of his race or sex.

Late in 1971 the three novels of the Swords Trilogy, the adventures of Prince Corum of the Silver Hand, were published almost simultaneously. The first, *The Knight of the Swords* (1971), won the 1972 British Fantasy Award, and Moorcock was given the 1972 Best Writer Award.

Moorcock's fiction took a new turn early in 1972 with the first volume of his Dancers at the End of Time trilogy, *An Alien Heat.* This curiously gentle, comedic pastorale involves a small group of superhumans who populate the Earth, using power rings that draw on the remaining energy of the collapsing universe to entertain themselves by creating whatever they can imagine on their spacious grounds. This infinite capacity, however, has stultified their ability to create true art, to experience powerful emotions, or to comprehend any morality beyond self-satisfaction. The occasional time travelers who arrive at the end of time are usually put in one or another of the immortals' curio collections. Jherek Carnelian, the last natural-born human, experiences an unfamiliar emotion when he is introduced to Mrs. Amelia Underwood, an accidental time traveler from a version of Victorian England.

In the Dancers at the End of Time trilogy, Moorcock provided an original problem with time travel. Some who arrive at the end of time find it impossible to return to their original times and planes of the multiverse; others, including Mrs. Underwood, are snatched back by an elastic side effect, and Jherek goes after her. The humor of this first volume lies in the play of ideas between Mrs. Underwood and Jherek, who—as the last "expert" on nineteenth-century England (his hobby)— almost wills himself into falling in love with Mrs. Underwood, to her consternation. Jherek points out with some logic that at the end of time she is in fact a widow by several million years, but Mrs. Underwood's Victorian principles preclude her recognizing her feelings toward Jherek. Moorcock has a passion for the Victorian period and obviously understands its attractions and its self-delusions. In the Dancers at the End of Time trilogy he played with the concepts of self-denial, romantic love, honor, and duty with sweet, rather than savage, irony.

Moorcock's second major novel of 1972, *Breakfast in the Ruins,* brought him to the attention of the British literary establishment. They may have avoided or ignored his heroic fantasy background, but his Arts Council grant, the censorship battles over *New Worlds,* and the publication of "Behold the Man" and the first two volumes of the Cornelius Chronicles had alerted the establishment to his potential importance. *Breakfast in the Ruins* and the third Cornelius novel, *The English Assassin,* also published in 1972, convinced critics that Moorcock was a significant voice in contemporary fiction.

The structure of *Breakfast in the Ruins* is Cornelian in scope. An alternate Karl Glogauer, a lower-middle-class bore, is picked up by an urbane African diplomat, who takes Karl to his hotel, where they spend a week in lovemaking, growing more sadomasochistic as the nights progress. Interspersed with descriptions of their sexual activities are chapters concerning alternate Karls, usually children, witnessing or taking part in scenes of violence from the Paris Commune of 1871 to the 1946 Irgun rebellion against British rule in Palestine. Following each of Karl's multiversal disasters, Moorcock adds a "What Would You Do?" segment, posing questions to the reader involving unanswerable moral dilemmas, the making of a choice among alternatives in which each involves a betrayal of someone.

The English Assassin was the most challenging Jerry Cornelius novel yet. At the conclusion of *A Cure for Cancer,* the multiversal key, the black box, had dropped into its own "possibility field," a fact that may help the literal minded to approach the bewildering structure of the third and fourth volumes in the tetralogy, both of which take place in simultaneous multiple manifestations of the multiverse. Characters die and, to no one's surprise,

Dust jacket for the 1981 novel Moorcock set during the Thirty Years War (Richland County Public Library)

return a few chapters later; they change lifestyles with no apparent memory of having been other than who they are at a given point. In fact, all save Jerry, Catherine (alive again), and the ubiquitous time traveler Una Persson are killed by naval gunfire at the conclusion of *The English Assassin* but turn up again with simultaneous conflicting lives throughout the fourth volume, *The Condition of Muzak* (1977).

Again Moorcock interspersed the chapters with both real and fictitious documentary material, much of it concerning the deaths of children. Again the world and most of its inhabitants are vile, treacherous, and with no motives save the basest self-interest. Jerry, heretofore the trickster, is curiously passive in most of his planal incarnations. If, as Colin Greenland has suggested in *The Entropy Exhibition* (1983), the black box eats DNA, it may have debilitated Jerry throughout much of the multiverse.

New Worlds had been revived as a quarterly paperback and by 1973 was being edited by Hilary Bailey, with whom Moorcock had just amicably separated. The magazine began to publish shorter Moor-

cock stories featuring various secondary characters in the Dancers at the End of Time trilogy, much as it had published the Jerry Cornelius vignettes a few years earlier. A movie version of *The Final Programme* appeared in 1973. Moorcock, who had been involved with it only at an early stage, disliked it, finding that the sense of irony in the novel had been removed from the motion picture and replaced with an overemphasis on psychedelic technogadgetry. His literary production in 1973 included reviving the two avatars of the Eternal Champion whom he had left in peace and quiet, Dorian Hawkmoon and Corum of the Silver Hand.

In the Chronicles of Corum trilogy—*The Bull and the Spear* (1973), *The Oak and the Ram* (1973), and *The Sword and the Stallion* (1974)—the hero is called forward in time, appearing on his own gravemound, to defend humanity against a group of Chaos Lords trapped in this plane after a great shift in the multiverse. They are wreaking havoc on humanity even as they rot away, deprived of the life-giving force of their lost dwelling beyond time and space. The Chronicles of Corum are a bit more carefully written than the Swords Trilogy, though there are far too many miraculous rescues of an apparently defeated and doomed Corum, thanks to the chance appearance of benevolent, semidivine creatures who then have to explain their presence, past, and interest in the events in which they interfere. This defect appears in most of Moorcock's heroic fantasy, but it reveals itself strongly as a fault only if one reads large quantities of Moorcock's romances in a short time.

Hawkmoon reappears in the Chronicles of Castle Brass series, finding that multiversal meddling on the part of renegade Granbretanian scientists has changed history and left him an unmarried, childless traitor rather than a happily married hero. As with Elric, Erekosë, and Corum, Hawkmoon's quest leads (in the third volume of the trilogy) to fabled Tanelorn, at the crossroads of the multiverse. With his writing subject to increasingly positive, understanding evaluations by the critical mainstream in England, Moorcock seems to have been determined to put behind him the Eternal Champion, at least in his heroic fantasy aspects. The first of the Castle Brass novels, *Count Brass* (1973), is well plotted, but the second, *The Champion of Garathorm* (1973), seems padded. Its central conflict—in which the Eternal Champion as a woman warrior temporarily shares Hawkmoon's consciousness and frees her people from one of the temporally stranded Granbretanian scientists—has little to do with Hawkmoon's plight.

Readers expecting a definitive conclusion to the four aspects of the Eternal Champion had to wait almost two years for the final volume, *The Quest for Tanelorn* (1975), dedicated to "all the many readers who wrote and asked for this particular book." In Tanelorn the four avatars of the Champion are united once more, in a battle against insane gods, a scene that had already appeared, in part, from Elric's and Corum's perspectives, in volumes dedicated to their histories. Though Moorcock later turned again to some of his Eternal Champion avatars, the series as such ended here. When Moorcock becomes the subject of a full-scale biography, the personal metaphors woven into the mythic avatars of the Eternal Champion may prove the various series to be literarily richer than they have seemed so far. Several critics, among them Patricia Marx in *SFRA Review* (1993), have alluded to a parallel metaphorical content relating to British politics and social issues during the decade in which most of the novels were written, another potential avenue of critical endeavor.

A more-contemporary version of the Eternal Champion, the unwilling cross-time traveler Oswald Bastable, reappeared in 1974 in *The Land Leviathan,* a bleaker, angrier book than *The Warlord of the Air.* In *The Land Leviathan* Bastable follows an African conqueror destroying a virulently racist United States. Again balancing darkness and light, Moorcock published almost simultaneously *The Hollow Lands,* the second volume of the Dancers at the End of Time trilogy. In this novel there is much good humor, even a bit of Keystone Kops slapstick, in Jherek Carnelian's pursuit of the immovable Mrs. Underwood back to her nineteenth-century London and in cameo appearances by H. G. Wells, George Bernard Shaw, and Frank Harris; yet, the book has less inventiveness, less philosophical give-and-take, and less gently ironic commentary on the interplay between Victorian duty and End-of-Time license than the first volume.

In 1975 Moorcock published *The Quest for Tanelorn,* the conclusion to the Chronicles of Castle Brass, and collaborated with James Cawthorn (writing as "Philip James") on a science-fiction novel, *The Distant Suns.* It was much more a year for Moorcock the rock musician. He had for some time been associated with the British rock band Hawkwind, as well as his own group, The Deep Fix, which issued its only long-playing disc, *The New Worlds Fair,* on the United Artists label. (Single 45s were released in 1980 and 1982.)

In 1976 Moorcock completed a sidebar to the Cornelius Chronicles, *The Adventures of Una Persson and Catherine Cornelius in the Twentieth Century.* It is a more linear work than the main series had become, with its alternate-history time explained by Moorcock as editor of Mrs. Persson's papers. (He had used the device in the Bastable novels and employed it again with the von Bek series and the Between the Wars novels.) Una and Catherine, who becomes a substantial character for the first time, visit, separately and together, various times and multiversal planes of the present century. Una's adventures are largely involved with scenes of war and carnage; Catherine's are mostly with perverse, violent males. Aside from the secondary plot in *The Champion of Garathorm,* it is Moorcock's first work with female central characters, who are a welcome change from the succession of beautiful, enchanted, doomed princesses that the requirements of heroic fantasy had forced on the Eternal Champion sagas, or the twisted, perverse vampires of the early Cornelius Chronicles. Additionally, the work offers the first extended version of Jerry and Catherine's mother, the loud, cheerful, bawdy, uneducated Cockney who later dominates the thoughts of Colonel Pyat in the Between the Wars tetralogy.

Legends from the End of Time, a collection of unconnected adventures of the Dancers at the End of Time, preceded the November 1976 publication of *The End of All Songs,* the concluding volume of the trilogy. More inventive than its immediate predecessor, this novel includes sharp social commentary in the person of Mrs. Underwood's fundamentalist husband, transcendent heroism in Jherek's saving the immortals from the heat death of the universe, and romantic pathos in his decision to renounce his powers in order more fully to experience the lost emotion of romantic love.

Readers drawn to the series by favorable mainstream reviews may justifiably have been confused by the appearance of Una Persson and Oswald Bastable of the Guild of Temporal Adventurers and might entirely have missed a fairly sinister hint about Lord Jagged's possible connection to the multiversal battle between Law and Chaos in the heroic fantasies. Moorcock's crossover characters have always made comprehension difficult for new readers; to savor all the ironies one must read practically all Moorcock's novels in sequence.

The Jerry Cornelius tetralogy came to a conclusion in 1977 with *The Condition of Muzak,* an epic of multiversal defeat for the protagonist, in which he relives, with variations, most of the events of the preceding novels, with negative results. In the two most extended recurring narratives, Jerry is humbled and broken in surroundings both elegant and squalid. In the first, at a grand ball attended by practically every major character in Moorcock's fiction, Jerry exhaustedly relinquishes his persona as Harlequin, the trickster hero, and instead appears in the archetypal garb of Pierrot, the eternal loser. As he confesses to a recurring minor character, Flash Gordon Garvin, "I used to believe I was Captain of my own Fate. Instead, I'm just a character in a bloody pantomime."

In the other recurring sequence, Jerry inhabits a 1970s London familiar to the reader. Ladbroke Grove, which has been Jerry's castle/fortress/hideaway in other continua, is a seedy slum. Jerry, an inarticulate but not unintelligent teenager, finds solace only in the amateur rock band he heads. His brother is a small-time swindler, his mother an alcoholic, his sister Catherine a tart. At the climax of this continuum, he is offered a free concert at which a record producer will be present, but he arrives high on drugs, and the makeshift stage collapses during his first number.

The power and pessimism of *The Condition of Muzak* caused Angus Wilson, long a Moorcock supporter, to compare him, in *The Observer* (3 April 1977), to Joyce Cary, Raymond Chandler, Bernard Shaw, Ronald Firbank, and John Dos Passos, and to write insightfully of Moorcock's ability to convey a powerful sense of despair that "Violence in these books is real, absurd, and shameful." Certainly the continuing horror of the Vietnam War, the social chaos and rising

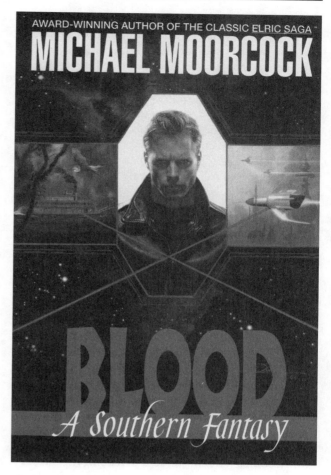

Dust jacket for Moorcock's 1994 novel, set in an American South run by African Americans and Hispanics (Richland County Public Library)

racism of 1970s Britain, the author's memory of more-decent human relationships during the Blitz, the recent examples of the Holocaust, and the continuing Stalinist/Maoist repression of individual destiny all found a home in the postmodern catalogue of hopes dashed, pride crushed, indifference glorified, and inhumanity rampant as depicted in the Cornelius Chronicles.

The Condition of Muzak won *The Guardian* Fiction Prize for 1977. The tetralogy as a whole was praised as having a Dickensian flavor. Moorcock no longer had to worry about being stereotyped as a genre-bound author, but his financial situation remained such that he continued to mine his past for publishable material. An Elric rewrite, *The Weird of the White Wolf,* appeared simultaneously with *The Condition of Muzak* and was followed in the same year by *Sojan,* a collection of his 1950s juvenilia, ostensibly a children's book.

Early in 1978, the British Fantasy Society published *Epic Pooh,* a short extract from an unpublished critical monograph on the nature of fantasy. In this booklet Moorcock reacted against the avoidance of psychological mimesis in what he calls "consolatory" fantasy, fantasy that avoids political and psychological engagement on any sophisticated metaphorical level, settling instead for a simplistic good/evil moral world with no shades of gray, a world without ambiguities in which good, despite terrible hardships, must eventually triumph. J. R. R. Tolkien and his imitators are Moorcock's chief targets. He describes their moral world as no more complex than that of A. A. Milne, creator of Winnie-the-Pooh.

Colin Greenland, in *DLB 14,* quotes Moorcock on his aim in fiction: "to find equilibrium between unchecked Romanticism ('Chaos') and stifling Classicism ('Law') and successfully to combine the scene and idea which inform the epic/romance with psychological demands of the modern novel." With *Gloriana; or, The Unfulfill'd Queen* (1978), he perhaps came closer to his ideal even than in the Cornelius Chronicles. Written in William Morris–like pseudo-Elizabethan–with Edmund Spenser's *The Faerie Queene* (1590–1596) as an obvious model—*Gloriana* takes place in a modern but Elizabethan London that is the capital of the Empire of Albion, which was founded by refugees from Troy and now extends around the world. The work is pervasively influenced by an absence that renders the Elizabethan (or Glorianan) court unsettling and strange to the reader: there is no hint of Christianity present. Richly complex in conspiracy, psychology, pageantry, and intrigue, the novel, like "The Pleasure Garden of Felipe Sagittarius," unfolds amid its own internally consistent logic. Unlike the Cornelius Chronicles, it develops its narrative within a single multiversal plane, though not without occasional allusions to a multiplicity of continua and some characters with names familiar from other Moorcock fiction. Reviewing the novel for *The Sunday Times Magazine* (5 November 1978), Philip Oakes described it as "an audacious retelling of *The Faerie Queene* in which Chivalry ends up with a pie in the face and a knife in the back, and Vice triumphs over Virtue, but is seen to be the ideal and eternal tool for pragmatists."

In 1978 Moorcock was divorced from Hilary Bailey, and in May of that year he married artist Jill Ritches, a marriage that lasted only two years. During 1979–1981 Moorcock published some minor Corneliana, including another formally postmodern novel, *The Entropy Tango* (1981). The appearance of a weak third adventure of Oswald Bastable, *The Steel Tsar* (1981), with its dedication "To my creditors, who remain a permanent source of inspiration," seemed to suggest a necessary retreat from the critically praiseworthy to the immediately profitable.

Another reason for Moorcock's relative silence must have been his work on the first volume of a long-planned tetralogy, initially called "Between the Wars." By the time *Byzantium Endures* appeared in 1981, that series title had grown to "Some Reminiscences of Mrs. Cornelius Between the Wars." However, it turns out not to be the reminiscences of Mrs. Cornelius, here a younger version of the coarse, ignorant, charismatic mother of Catherine in *The Adventures of Una Persson and Catherine Cornelius in the Twentieth Century*. Rather, with Moorcock taking again the role of editor within the text, the tetralogy so far is the reminiscences of one Maxim Pyatnitski, "Colonel Pyat," assembled from boxes of manuscript in several languages that were foisted on "Moorcock" as a reward for his having included Mrs. Cornelius, Col. Pyat's only friend, in some of his fiction.

If the reader believes him, Pyatt was brought up in prerevolutionary Russia, endured the Bolshevik takeover, lived and prospered in Istanbul, Paris, Hollywood, Benito Mussolini's Rome, and Adolf Hitler's Berlin prior to World War II. He claims to have been—among other things—a trailblazing inventor, military genius, linguist, and movie maker. He is also a Jew whose anti-Semitism is unrelenting, a homophobe who has carried on a "Dionysian" affair with a Russian aristocrat, a pederast who detests pederasts, and a con man who is forever being duped. In short, he is one of the most irredeemably self-deluding characters ever to take center stage in a major literary work.

A Colonel Pyat had appeared in minor roles in many of the multiversal planes of the Cornelius Chronicles. In Between the Wars he is grounded in a recognizable twentieth century as protagonist of a Balzacian epic that stretches to many more than a million words. If Pyat has one redeeming quality, it is that he is a survivor. Between the Wars is essentially a picaresque novel (its division into four volumes being an obviously necessary, but arbitrary, result of its great length), and Moorcock has taken a writerly challenge to keep readers interested in the adventures and the survival of a racist, sexist, self-deluding, equivocating hypocrite.

One of the fascinations of the tetralogy lies in sorting out fact from fiction in Pyat's first-person narrative. He must certainly be a linguist of great skill; Moorcock assures the reader that, except for some passages in what appears to be a personal code, Pyat writes in English, French, German, Russian, Greek, Italian, Yiddish, and Turkish in various places. But should the reader take Pyat's word that as a teenager he invented a successful one-person flying machine and that as a prisoner of the Cossacks he put together

Dust jacket for Moorcock's 1995 collection of short stories about the family he introduced in The War Hound and the World's Pain
(Richland County Public Library)

a death ray? *Byzantium Endures* and its sequels *The Laughter of Carthage* (1984) and *Jerusalem Commands* (1992) bewilderingly mix passages in which it appears that Pyat must be telling the truth, passages in which he seems to be deluding himself even as he gives readers enough information to realize it, passages in which he deludes himself so fully that for the time being readers are taken in, and passages in which he appears to be acting as one of the great liars of literature.

Another strength of the work lies in Moorcock's fascination with urban settings. Focusing for much of his literary career on the primitive cities and lush castles of heroic fantasy, he made the multiversal versions of London characters themselves in the Cornelius Chronicles. Writing about Pyat, Moorcock is free to conjure up prerevolutionary Kiev, Odessa, and St. Petersburg; Istanbul (which the Graecophile Pyat obstinately calls Constantinopol) of the postwar period; and Memphis, Tennessee, San Francisco, Hollywood, and Cairo during the 1920s. With Dickensian detail Moorcock describes the sounds and smells, the atmosphere of the cafés and restaurants, the opu-

lence of the mansions, the squalor of the slums, and the routes of the tram cars. In *Byzantium Endures,* he proved that he could take a conventional form, the big urban novel, invest it with an originality and unpredictability that is distinctly his, and call attention to this new aspect of his work with critical success.

The War Hound and the World's Pain (1981) appears to be an attempt to combine adventure with philosophical challenge: seeking to explain the absence of God from and the increasing inhumanity in the world. Set amid the horrors of the Thirty Years War (1618–1648), the novel follows a mercenary knight, Ritter Konrad von Bek, through his employment by a seemingly repentant Lucifer to retrieve the Holy Grail and mediate a truce between Lucifer and God in which both will agree to withdraw from interference in humanity's struggle to civilize itself. Lucifer has become repelled by the excesses of his followers, both conscious and unknowing. His rebellion was the antithetic response of individualistic Chaos to the overbearing rule of universal Law. In his fall, he restored the Cosmic Balance, but he has become disgusted with the extent to which humanity has taken his example of Chaos. Von Bek succeeds in his quest, and Lucifer, though unsure of God's response, withdraws from human affairs. Or does he? Moorcock's Lucifer is Miltonic in his supernatural beauty and knowledge, but is the Prince of Lies telling von Bek the truth? Implicit in the question is whether or not humanity is responsible for the increasingly chaotic world, or whether Lucifer has once more deceived a good man. Moorcock leaves no clues.

Eroticism has played a part in almost all Moorcock's work, except perhaps for his early science-fiction novels. There are long passages of eroticism in the Cornelius Chronicles and in *Byzantium Endures*. In Moorcock's short novel *The Brothel in Rosenstrasse* (1982), however, eroticism is central. Set in Mirenberg, the fictitious middle-European seat of the von Bek family, at the close of the nineteenth century, the novel follows Rickhardt von Bek, no Grail warrior but a decadent voluptuary, in his affair with his sixteen-year-old mistress, Alexandra. Von Bek appears at once a realistically portrayed debauched sensualist and an allegorical figure representing the detached self-centeredness of the European aristocracy as the world swept toward violent social change, radically inhuman methods of warfare, and general decay. Even in his old age, wasted and dying, the impoverished aristocrat narrating the story shows no remorse for the erotic monomania that brought him and his lover disaster.

In September 1983, during a year in which he published no books, Moorcock married Linda Mullens Steele. The following year he produced the second installment of Pyat's memoirs, *The Laughter of Carthage*. With this title and the announcement of the titles of the concluding volumes, one can put together a sentence that illustrates Pyat's twisted worldview, "Byzantium endures the laughter of Carthage; Jerusalem commands the vengeance of Rome." For Pyat, Byzantium stands for the triumph of a holy, white, Christian Orthodox state, banisher of the red revolution from Mother Russia and the defiling Turk from greater Greece; Carthage is the antithesis, the unholy, nonwhite, Jewish-oriental East that schemes to reduce white Orthodox Christianity to its own debased level. Furthermore, for Pyat, the cooperation of Jerusalem (another, specifically Jewish manifestation of Carthage) influences and bribes the spiritually weak western, non–Orthodox Christianity, Rome, in its pursuit of world degradation.

The Laughter of Carthage is a somewhat funnier book than *Byzantium Endures,* which follows Pyat not only through the idyll of tsarist Russia but also through the horrors of Bolshevik terrorism, anarchist pillage, Cossack rape, and White Russian violence. Now Pyat is at the height of his career (or so he tells the reader), hobnobbing with Parisian financiers, becoming a spokesman for the Ku Klux Klan, befriending the Mafia boss of San Francisco, and breaking into moving pictures in Hollywood.

Some critics were becoming uneasy, despite the continuing brilliance of Moorcock's powers of description and inventive picaresque storytelling. Reviewing the novel for *The Washington Post* (23 December 1984), Angus Wilson wrote that "there is a serious danger for an author who creates such a hero: that in bringing alive with sympathy the divine idiocy of his character, the devil's advocacy inherent in so many of his views may be insufficiently stressed." Valentine Cunningham, in *TLS: The Times Literary Supplement* (7 September 1984), worried that "even one reader can take seriously this sinister monstrosity Moorcock has so vigorously spawned, even for a moment." Moorcock can at least take pride in having created a character so vividly evil that, rarest of reactions in the late twentieth century, critics are frightened by him.

Work on the remaining Pyat sequels and on the Dickensian novel Moorcock had longed to write occupied much of the next five years, during which time he also turned out several heroic fantasies, presumably for the financial reward rather than out of any overwhelming desire to return to the multiverse of Elric and Erekosë. The collection *Elric at the End of Time* (1984) was billed by its publishers as "The Seventh Book of Elric of Melniboné," but in fact it includes only one work not already collected in *Sojan:* the title novelette, a self-parody in which Elric's version of doomed heroism is viewed as quaint by the Dancers at the End of Time.

The Dragon in the Sword (1986) allowed Erekosë/John Daker an alternative, less bittersweet fate than that allotted to him at the conclusion of *The Quest for Tanelorn,* perhaps indicating that Moorcock had grown tired of seeking an overall unity for the essentially concluded Eternal Champion sagas. *The City in the Autumn Stars* (1986) returns to the von Bek family and Mirenberg at the time of the French Revolution, equaling the sense of wonder in *The War Hound and the World's Pain* but lacking any of its philosophic content.

Mother London, Moorcock's third big mainstream work, appeared in 1988, evoking further favorable comparisons to Charles Dickens. The protagonists are three Londoners who experienced the Blitz during their youth and are, in the late 1970s, outpatients at a mental clinic: David Mummery, a failed writer obsessed with the arcana of his city; Mary Gasalee, who spent fifteen years in a coma after her house was destroyed in an air raid; and Joseph Kiss, a Falstaffian bon vivant who keeps apartments all over the city, the better to experience the individuality of its myriad sectors and to discover their secrets. Moorcock has written of secret cities in his fantasy novels and of the real secrets of the great Western cities in the Pyat novels. In *Mother London* both the public and secret Londons are palpable—a secret London, not the realm of the necromancer or the criminal, but of the observant connoisseur.

With the character of Mary Gasalee, Moorcock appears to be experimenting with a bit of magic realism. During her coma, Mary has not aged. When she awakes, though near forty, she still looks twenty. She has retained in her mind the subject matter of comic books, pulp magazines, and movie magazines one of her attendants has read aloud to her during her coma, but she needs years to adjust to the social changes that the war and its aftermath have wrought in England.

Using a temporal tapestry shifting from the 1940s to the 1970s and shifting the third-person point of view among the three major characters, Moorcock peoples his London with a collection of likable eccentrics that is perhaps surpassed only by Dickens. If there is anything un-Dickensian about *Mother London,* it must be the lack of menace that Dickens brings to so much of his work. Paradoxically, Moorcock is known for his ability to bring evil alive (as critical reaction to Pyat as protagonist attests); yet, his novel whose model is Dickens rather more closely resembles a work by Anthony Trollope in the essential gentleness of its narrative. There is some tragedy, and one main character dies sadly, but the overpowering sense is of the benevolence of London itself, a far cry from the evil city of the Cornelian multiverse. Reviewing the novel for *The Listener* (23 June 1988), Nigel Andrew wrote, "If this wonderful book does not finally convince the world that he [Moorcock] is in fact one of our very best novelists and a national treasure, there is no justice."

In 1989 and 1991 Moorcock published two more Elric novels, *The Fortress of the Pearl* and *The Revenge of the Rose,* again billed by publishers as sequels in the Elric saga. They are in fact "prequels," relating adventures of Elric during his wanderings among the human tribes long before he destroyed his own universe. It is perhaps a measure of the raw power of the original 1961–1965 series that, unlike the many successful prequels in science-fiction and fantasy series by other writers, *The Fortress of the Pearl* and *The Revenge of the Rose* seem somehow drained of their vitality by the reader's knowledge of Elric's—and humanity's—destiny on that plane. Readers know he will survive to destroy the universe. In both novels Moorcock does, however, play

more overtly than in earlier heroic fantasy with the use of allegory. In *The Fortress of the Pearl,* for example, Elric must successfully negotiate a series of seven dream landscapes: Dreams-in-Common, Old Desires, Lost Beliefs, Forgotten Love, New Ambition, Madness, and a final nameless one where the Fortress of the Pearl lies. Political, personal, Jungian, and Freudian interpretations may all have relevance to Elric's journey.

Pyat's adventures extend to the end of the 1920s in *Jerusalem Commands* (1992), wherein the wandering anti-Semitic Jew, flying across the United States to meet his mistress when readers last glimpsed him, encounters the American hobo life of the Depression and adds Alexandria, Luxor, and the Sahara Desert to his geographic reminiscences. Critics seemed to be tiring of Pyat's incessant vileness, no matter how comic the situations in which Moorcock places him. John Clute, a longtime friend of Moorcock's, who had justified *The Laughter of Carthage* as "sustained brilliance . . . [in which] the underlying moral grasp never seriously falters" (*The New Statesman,* 7 September 1984), complained that in *Jerusalem Commands* Pyat's "charade collapses" (*The Observer,* 24 July 1992).

In *The Laughter of Carthage,* Pyat buys a thirteen-year-old Armenian prostitute who resembles his lost teenage love, Esme; educates her erotically and academically; and leaves her in the care of his treacherous business partners in Paris. The scene in *Jerusalem Commands* that appears to have most disturbed commentators involves Esme's rape in Egypt, during the filming of what Pyat has envisioned as a motion picture to challenge those of D. W. Griffith, but which has degenerated into a big-budget porn movie. After three-quarters of a million words, some of Moorcock's faithful readers have tired of Pyat. Yet, others, reading more clinically, still assert that Moorcock successfully keeps readers interested in a totally vile human being through three long novels.

The Vengeance of Rome, yet to be published, may offer some method of understanding Pyat's virulent personality. In *Jerusalem Commands* Pyat writes, "There is a state of terror so absolute that it becomes an unconscious way of life. . . . It would be obscene to pass moral judgement on anyone who was ever exposed to it." Looking ahead to the fact that the announced conclusion of Pyat's memoirs takes place during the Holocaust, Mark Sanderson, writing in *TLS: The Times Literary Supplement* (10 July 1992), speculates that perhaps Pyat is speaking of himself, that the racial and sexual phobias of his after-the-fact interpretation of his life may actually have their genesis in the Nazi camps.

Whatever the content of *The Vengeance of Rome,* it would appear that Pyat will have to speed up the pace of his narrative. The half million words of *The Laughter of Carthage* and *Jerusalem Commands* have moved Pyat only from 1919 to 1929. Still to come are already-mentioned adventures in Mussolini's Italy and Hitler's Germany, as well as the long-promised revelation concerning Pyat's eventual sexual congress with Mrs. Cornelius.

In the mid 1990s Moorcock and his American-born third wife moved to the United States and settled outside of Austin, Texas. This new locale gave new inspiration to his fiction, especially in the books *Blood: A Southern Fantasy* (1994) and *Tales from the Texas Woods* (1997). *Blood* is set in an alternate South where "Anglos" are the minority, and African Americans and Hispanics are calling the shots. Moorcock ties in this world with his multiverse, and the characters' gambling brings them into contact with other planes of reality. *Tales from the Texas Woods* is a collection of stories in which the reality of Western life merges with the pulp fantasies of the Westerns Moorcock read as a child along with, once again, the multiverse (including a Native American warrior who happens, like some other Moorcock heroes, to be an albino). The volume also includes some of Moorcock's nonfiction, including "About My Multiverse" and "How Tom Mix Saved My Life."

Another significant collection is *Lunching with the Antichrist: A Family History, 1925–2015* (1995), linked stories that continue the ongoing saga of the von Beks. As in so much of Moorcock's fiction, these characters are seeking something, a grail of one kind or another. Also the stories again reveal Moorcock's interest in history and travel, as they are set in a wide variety of times and places. Despite the von Beks' assorted supernatural adventures, the stories are rooted in the real life of the twentieth century (and a bit beyond).

The stories in *Fabulous Harbors* (1995) are related not only to each other but also to *Blood* and to a third volume in this loose trilogy, the novel *The War amongst the Angels* (1996). The tales in *Fabulous Harbors*, told at a party, concern such familiar characters as Jerry Cornelius, Elric, and the von Beks, and they make for almost casual reading, although familiarity with the characters and their complex histories and relationships is certainly helpful. In contrast, *The War amongst the Angels* is a complicated postmodern fantasy, connecting Moorcock's family to the von Beks and exploring, through an experimental structure, these characters' relationships with each other and with history.

Moorcock's novel *King of the City* (2000) is set in a London slightly altered from that of the reader's reality. The protagonist, photographer, and rock musician Dennis Dover, comes of age during the 1960s, shaped by the vibrant city around him. He also falls in love with Rosie Beck, a Temporal Adventuress much like other Moorcock characters. Once more the historical and the fantastic intertwine in a story that includes much social commentary. Also in 2000, Moorcock collaborated with Storm Constantine on *Silverheart,* a fantasy thriller.

In *The Dreamthief's Daughter: A Tale of the Albino* (2001) Moorcock returned to familiar territory with yet another novel featuring an albino warrior. The albino mentioned in this title, however, is not Elric but rather Ulric von Bek. He survives the devastation of the first half of the twentieth century and goes on to fight the Nazis, learning in the process that the struggle against fascism is only part of a much larger conflict between good and evil. Thus, though the full connection is never made explicit, Ulric is connected to the multiverse and the Eternal Champion, especially Elric.

Since 1960 Moorcock has been one of the major figures of British fantasy and science fiction, notable for his role in the development of experimental New Wave and for his prolific efforts that expanded the possibilities of these genres, both stylistically and conceptually. He is also important for helping to bring science fiction and fantasy to the attention of the mainstream literary establishment in England and for showing that these genres can possess genuine literary merit. While much of his work has been commercially oriented, there is no doubt of Moorcock's literary qualities.

Interviews:

"*The Eildon Tree* Interview—Michael Moorcock," *Eildon Tree,* 1, no. 2 (1976): 4–8;

Paul Walker, *Speaking of Science Fiction: The Paul Walker Interviews* (Oradell, N.J.: Luna, 1978);

Ted Butler, "*Algol* Interview: Michael Moorcock," *Algol,* 15 (Winter 1978): 29–32;

Ian Covell, Interview with Michael Moorcock, *Science Fiction Review,* 8 (January 1979): 18–25;

Charles Platt, "Michael Moorcock," in his *Who Writes Science Fiction?* (Manchester: Savoy, 1980), pp. 233–242; republished as *Dream Makers: The Uncommon People Who Write Science Fiction* (New York: Berkley, 1980), pp. 97–104;

Moorcock and Colin Greenland, "Conversations," in *Death Is No Obstacle* (Manchester, U.K.: Savoy, 1993).

Bibliographies:

Andrew Harper and George McAuley, *Michael Moorcock: A Bibliography* (Kansas City, Mo.: T-K Graphics, 1976);

Paul C. Allen, "Of Swords and Sorcery: 5," *Fantasy Crossroads,* 13 (1978): 31–40;

A. J. Callow, *The Chronicles of Moorcock* (London: Callow, 1978);

Richard Bilyeu, *The Tanelorn Archives: A Primary and Secondary Bibliography of the Works of Michael Moorcock, 1949–1979* (Manitoba: Pandora's Books, 1981).

References:

Brian Appleyard, "Fiction of the Future," *Times* (London), 18 June 1988, p. 20;

Michael Ashley, "Behold the Man Called Moorcock," *Science Fiction Monthly,* 2 (February 1975): 8–11;

Peter Caracciolo, "Michael Moorcock," in *Twentieth Century Science Fiction Writers,* second edition, edited by Curtis C. Smith (Chicago: St. James Press, 1986), pp. 519–522;

John Clute, "The Repossession of Jerry Cornelius," introduction to *The Cornelius Chronicles,* volume I (New York: Avon, 1977);

John Dean, "'A Curious Note in the Wind': The New Literary Genre of Heroic Fantasy," *New Mexico Humanities Review,* 2 (Summer 1979): 34–41;

David Glover, "Utopian Fantasy in the Late 1960s: Burroughs, Moorcock, Tolkien," in *Popular Fiction and Social Change,* edited by Christopher Pawling (New York: St. Martin's Press, 1984);

Colin Greenland, *The Entropy Exhibition: Michael Moorcock and the British "New Wave" in Science Fiction* (London: Routledge & Kegan Paul, 1983);

William H. Hardesty, "A Nomad of the Time Streams: Moorcock's Oswald Bastable," in *Selected Proceedings of the 1978 Science Fiction Research Association National Conference,* edited by Thomas J. Remington (Cedar Falls: University of Northern Iowa, 1979);

Dave McFerran, "The Celtic Incarnation," *Dark Horizons,* 29 (1985): 33–37;

Peter Nicholls, "Michael Moorcock," in *Science Fiction Writers,* edited by E. F. Bleiler (New York: Scribners, 1982), pp. 449–457;

David Pirie, "The Chaos Machine of Michael Moorcock," *Time Out,* 17 (September 1971): 49–51;

Charles Platt, Introduction to *The Condition of Muzak* (Boston: Gregg Press, 1978);

Norman Spinrad, Introduction to *The Final Programme* (Boston: Gregg Press, 1976);

Nick Totten, "Culture Shock," *Spectator,* 9 April 1977, pp. 21–22;

Ralph Willett, "Moorcock's Achievement and Promise in the Jerry Cornelius Books," *Science-Fiction Studies,* 3 (1976): 75–79;

Papers:

There are collections of Michael Moorcock's manuscripts at the Bodleian Library, Oxford University, and the Sterling Library, Texas A & M University.

Alan Moore

(18 November 1953 –   )

Jefferson M. Peters
Fukuoka University

BOOKS: *Alan Moore's Shocking Futures* (London: Titan, 1986);

D. R. & Quinch's Totally Awesome Guide to Life, art by Alan Davis (London: Titan, 1986);

Alan Moore's Twisted Times (London: Titan, 1987);

Alan Moore's Maxwell the Magic Cat (London: Acme, 1987);

Saga of the Swamp Thing, art by Stephen R. Bissette and John Totleben (New York: DC Comics, 1987);

Watchmen, art by Dave Gibbons (New York: DC Comics, 1987; London: Titan, 1987);

Batman: The Killing Joke, art by Brian Bolland (New York: DC Comics, 1988; London: Titan, 1988);

Miracleman: Book One: A Dream of Flying, art by Garry Leach and Davis (Forestville, Cal.: Eclipse, 1988);

Big Numbers, issues 1–2, art by Bill Sienkiewicz (Northampton, U.K.: Mad Love, 1990);

Miracleman: Book Two: The Red King Syndrome, art by Chuck Beckum, Rick Bryant, Davis, John Ridgway, and Rick Veitch (Forestville, Cal.: Eclipse, 1990);

Miracleman: Book Three: Olympus, art by Totleben (Forestville, Cal.: Eclipse, 1990);

Swamp Thing: Love and Death, art by Alfredo Alcala, Bissette, Shawn McManus, Ron Randall, Totleben, and Veitch (New York: DC Comics, 1990);

V for Vendetta, art by David Lloyd (New York: DC Comics, 1990; London: Titan, 1990);

The Complete Ballad of Halo Jones, art by Ian Gibson (London: Titan, 1991);

A Small Killing, art by Oscar Zarate (London: VG Graphics/Gollancz, 1991);

The Complete Bojeffries Saga, art by Steve Parkhouse (Northampton, Mass.: Tundra, 1992);

From Hell: Book One: The Compleat Scripts, art by Eddie Campbell, edited by Bissette (Baltimore: Borderlands Press, 1994);

Lost Girls: Book One, art by Melinda Gebbie (Northampton, Mass.: Kitchen Sink Press, 1995);

Lost Girls: Book Two, art by Gebbie (Northampton, Mass.: Kitchen Sink Press, 1996);

Alan Moore (photograph from a 2000 issue of Top 10*)*

Voice of the Fire (London: Gollancz, 1996);

Superman: Whatever Happened to the Man of Tomorrow? art by George Perez, Kurt Schaffenberger, and Curt Swan (New York: DC Comics, 1997);

Alan Moore's Songbook, art by various artists (Westland, Mich.: Caliber, 1998);

The Birth Caul, art by Campbell (Paddington, Australia: Eddie Campbell Comics, 1999);

Bloodfeud, by Moore, Tony Daniel, and Kevin Conrad (London: Titan, 1999);

Voodoo: Dancing in the Dark, art by Michael Lopez and Al Rio (La Jolla, Cal.: Wildstorm Productions, 1999);

From Hell: Being a Melodrama in Sixteen Parts, art by Campbell (Paddington, Australia: Eddie Campbell Comics, 1999; London: Knockabout Comics, 2000);

WildCATs Homecoming, art by Travis Charest (New York: DC Comics, 2000);

Tom Strong, volume 1, art by various artists (La Jolla, Cal.: America's Best Comics, 2000);

Top 10, art by Gene Ha and Zander Cannon (La Jolla, Cal.: America's Best Comics, 2000);

Promethea, volume 1, art by J. H. Williams III (La Jolla, Cal.: America's Best Comics, 2000);

The League of Extraordinary Gentlemen, volume 1, art by Kevin O'Neill (La Jolla, Cal.: America's Best Comics, 2001);

Swamp Thing: The Curse, art by Alcala, Bissette, Randall, Totleben, Veitch, and Woch (New York: DC Comics, 2001);

Swamp Thing: A Murder of Crows, art by Alcala, Bissette, Randall, Totleben, Veitch, and Woch (New York: DC Comics, 2001);

Promethea: Collected Edition, volume 2, art by Williams (La Jolla, Cal.: America's Best Comics, 2001);

Snakes and Ladders, art by Campbell (Paddington, Australia: Eddie Campbell Comics, 2001);

Skizz, art by Jim Baikie (London: Titan, 2002);

Tom Strong, volume 2, art by various artists (La Jolla, Cal.: America's Best Comics, 2002);

Tomorrow Stories, art by various artists (La Jolla, Cal.: America's Best Comics, 2002);

Captain Britain, art by Davis (New York: Marvel Books, 2002);

Swamp Thing: Earth to Earth, art by Alcala, Totleben and Veitch (New York: DC Comics, 2002);

Top 10, book 2, (La Jolla, Cal.: America's Best Comics, 2002).

RECORDINGS: *Birth Caul (Shamanism of Childhood),* by Moore, David J, and Tim Perkins, CD, Charrm, 1996;

The Moon and Serpent Grand Egyptian Theatre of Marvels, by Moore, J, and Perkins, CD, Cleopatra, 1996;

Brought to Light, by Moore and Gary Lloyd, CD, Codex, 1997;

The Highbury Working: A Beat Seance, by Moore and Perkins, CD, RE:, 2000;

Angel Passage, by Moore and Perkins, CD, RE:, 2002.

OTHER: "A Hypothetical Lizard," in *Liavek: Wizard's Row,* edited by Will Shetterly and Emma Bull (New York: Ace, 1987), pp. 143–181;

AARGH! (Artists Against Rampant Government Homophobia), edited by Moore (Northampton, U.K.: Mad Love, 1988);

Shadowplay–The Secret Team, art by Bill Sienkiewicz, published with *Flashpoint–The La Penca Bombing,* as told to Joyce Brabner and Thomas Yeates, as *Brought to Light: A Graphic Docudrama* (Forestville, Cal.: Eclipse, 1989; London: Titan Books, 1989).

SELECTED PERIODICAL PUBLICATIONS–UNCOLLECTED: "For the Man Who Has Everything," art by Dave Gibbons, *Superman Annual,* 11, DC Comics, 1985;

"On Writing for Comics," part 1, *Comics Journal,* 119 (January 1988): 91–95;

"On Writing for Comics," part 2, *Comics Journal,* 120 (March 1988): 99–102;

"Come On Down," art by William Wray, *Taboo,* 1 (1988): 12–20;

"Warpsmith: Ghostdance," art by Garry Leach, *A1,* book 1 (1989): 8–14;

"The Bowing Machine," art by Mark Beyer, *RAW,* 2 (1991): 155–162;

1963, books 1–6, art by Stephen R. Bissette, Chester Brown, Dave Gibbons, John Totleben, Jim Valvano, and Rick Veitch, Image Comics, 1993;

Violator, issues 1–3, art by Bart Sears and Mark Pennington, Image Comics, 1994;

Supreme, issues 41–56, art by various artists, Image Comics / Awesome Entertainment, 1996–1998.

Because of the quality of his prose, the fertility of his imagination, and the range and power of his subjects, narrative techniques, and themes, Alan Moore has become one of the most important writers in the British and American comics industry of the 1980s and 1990s. Before Moore made his mark on comics, writers were far less important than artists to the medium, which was widely perceived as illiterate trash for kids. Moore's work has helped establish a greater balance between writing and art in comics and has dramatically increased the audience for, and aesthetic value of, the medium.

Perhaps the most striking thing about Moore's work is its diversity: in mood (terror, wonder, humor), style (scientific language, ornate prose, spare poetry), genre (fantasy, science fiction, and erotica), and audience (adults desiring serious literature, boys thirsting for high-adrenaline adventure). Although his work is marked by a variety of themes such as environmental disaster, fantasy and reality, and self-exploration, his most important theme is anarchy, which he defined in a 1990 interview with Gary Groth as a "revolution" starting "with people making choices about their own personal liberty, their own personal responsibility." His rejection of coercive power and affirmation of anarchy lie behind his expansion of constricting genres; his reinvention of existing characters; his modification of scripts to suit the artists with whom he

Paperback cover for the 1990 collected edition of the comic book on which Moore collaborated during 1982–1989 (Collection of Jason Paddock)

collaborates; his condemnation of censorship; his avoidance of celebrity and comics conventions; his creation of plots, characters, and themes; and his vision of the vital role of art. Moore believes that "the political function" of his art is to provide readers with different worldviews to encourage them to form their own, which is "necessary if you're going to survive in a changing world."

Because Moore knows that personal anarchy alone could lead to selfishness, he also writes about healthy connection—empathy and love—between different humans, species, and cultures. He has used pictorial or textual overlap from one scene to the next to build a "synchronicity" between seemingly disparate characters, as he explains in his 1988 article "On Writing for Comics." He also presents a stunningly varied host of characters, among them monsters, supermen, prostitutes, artists, and children. Because these characters possess "the denominator of basic humanity," as he points out in "On Writing for Comics," his readers have the opportunity to empathize with different beings.

Moore generally protects his privacy, declining to reveal many personal details. An exception is his three-part interview in *The Comics Journal* with Groth, "Big Words" (October 1990–February 1991), which provides most of the known biographical information about him. Alan Moore was born on 18 November 1953 to working-class parents Sylvia Doreen and Ernest Moore in Northampton, England, where he has lived all his life. In his youth his family was "traditionally poor" and lived in a low-income "Council House" rented from the government and lacking a bathroom. Moore grew up reading comic books and science-fiction novels and, when still young, realized that he would most enjoy an artistic career. At seventeen Moore's formal education terminated when he was expelled from his Northampton grammar school because the headmaster deemed him a bad influence and sent letters to art schools and colleges to warn them that Moore would "undermine the moral fabric" if given the chance. His early artistic education occurred roughly from age fifteen to eighteen, when he participated in the informal Northampton Arts Lab, where he learned to treat art mechanically (as posing technical problems to be solved), to value creative freedom, and to begin to understand the strengths of literature and painting. After grammar school, Moore worked at various menial jobs ranging from "skinyard" laborer processing the hides of slaughtered animals to office invoice clerk. He and his wife, Phyllis, were married in 1974, and the couple has two daughters.

In 1978, when Moore's wife became pregnant with their first child, he decided to attempt a career in comics. Moore's first comics job was writing and drawing two strips of his own invention (though published under the name Kurt Vile): *Roscoe Moscow* (March 1979–July 1980), "a surreal private eye" parody, and *The Stars My Degradation* (July 1980–February 1982), a science- fiction comedy, for the British rock-music weekly *Sounds*. At the same time, he began to write and draw *Three Eyes McGurk and His Death Planet Commandos* (December 1979 in *Dark Star*) and *Maxwell the Magic Cat* (August 1979–October 1986), a "five-frame gag strip in a local newspaper" published under the name Jill de Ray. Moore's goal was simply to do the best job he could and to enjoy what he did. He worked on such strips for "two or three years," as he told Groth, and despite the fact that he now feels they are "repulsive bilge," they provided him a small living and "a hands-on education in comic strips."

These early strips also taught Moore that, because it took him too long to draw pictures and because he was not talented enough to execute them well anyway, to earn a living in comics he would have to focus on writing. In 1980 he did his first commercial-comics work with stories for British Marvel's *Doctor Who Weekly/Monthly* (June 1980–October 1981) and for the *Future Shocks* section of

2000 A.D. (July 1980–August 1983). These early works are notable for their first hints of the imagination and irrepressible humor (ranging from black to silly and caustic to affectionate) which have leavened most of Moore's later, more serious works.

Moore's desire has always been to write and create his own comics without interference from publishers, and his move in March 1982 to work for the British comic anthology *Warrior* was a step in that direction. At *Warrior* Moore began the first two of his major works: *Marvelman* (1982–1990) and *V for Vendetta* (1982–1989).

With *Marvelman*, begun in 1982 in *Warrior* and moved as *Miracleman* (the title changed under legal pressure from Marvel Comics) in 1984 to Eclipse Enterprises in America, where it was completed in 1990, Moore revised the superhero genre. His original intention was to take a simple 1950s-era superhero and place him in the brutal 1980s. The early episodes later collected in *Miracleman: Book One: A Dream of Flying* (1988) and *Miracleman: Book Two: The Red King Syndrome* (1990) introduced human depth and complexity into the superhero genre. The boundary blurred between villains and heroes; black-and-white moral issues became ambiguous; and the story satirized its own genre. Mike Moran, a paunchy middle-aged man who has forgotten that he is also Miracleman, recollects his other identity and journeys insecurely toward self-knowledge. He learns that Miracleman is a "cellular replicate" of himself created in 1954 via alien technology and that his superhero past is a juvenile comic-book fantasy designed to enable a branch of British air force intelligence to control his superhuman powers. Although Moran and Miracleman ostensibly share the same consciousness, their bodies, only one of which may occupy our continuum at a time, are so different that Moran comes to feel more inadequate and Miracleman less human. The story reaches a controversial climax in *The Red King Syndrome* when Moran's wife graphically gives birth to Miracleman's baby: "a head, protruding from inside her. It looks so hideous, beautiful, absurd, awesome . . . here is blood. Here is violence . . . redeemed by love, by this pure act of creation. . . . These are the moments when we are real."

Whereas the first part of the *Miracleman* cycle revised the superhero genre with an infusion of humanity, the final part, collected in *Miracleman: Book Three: Olympus* (1990), presented what Moore told Groth were his "last words on the super-hero," pushing the genre to its inhuman conclusion. After Moore renders the horrible effects of a brawl between supermen—"there's never been a heaven not built on human bones," Miracleman muses—Miracleman makes Earth a utopia where there is no violence, hunger, or pollution; where Charles Manson runs a care group for children; Andy Warhol is resurrected and duplicated eighteen times; and anyone may become a god.

This utopia may seem wonderful, but it is not human, and Moran effectively commits suicide and leaves the brave new world to Miracleman.

Throughout the *Miracleman* saga Moore uses superheroes to explore difficult questions: What do people want from their gods? Are the costs of using power to improve the world worth the effort? Can humans ever create a utopia? As Mikal Gilmore says in the introduction to *Olympus,* the *Miracleman* series is a work that "changed popular culture, that helped revivify one of its most complex and interesting storytelling mediums [comics], and that also helped return new depth and imagination to an industry turned for too long toward prosaic visions and conservative methods."

In *V for Vendetta,* which Moore began in 1982 in *Warrior* and completed in 1989 for DC Comics, a fascist state rules the England of 1997. In the first pages a poor girl, Evey, tries to sell her body. The man she awkwardly propositions is a policeman, and he and his corrupt colleagues are about to rape and murder her when an eerie figure in a cape and a smiling Guy Fawkes mask rescues her, quoting *Macbeth* and killing three policemen in the process. The rescuer then shows Evey his work: the Houses of Parliament explode, and fireworks light the sky in a V. The mystery man, V, takes Evey to his hideout, which is filled with works of art. V is an artist-anarchist who "performs" the destruction of the state to offer the members of his audience the chance to become their own masters.

Although the work began as a stylish pulp adventure assignment given to Moore by his editor, *V for Vendetta* transcended its genre and challenged its readers to think. What are the strengths and weaknesses of anarchy and fascism? Do humans want to be free? Should one hurt people one loves in order to liberate them? How much violence can be used in a good cause? At the heart of the graphic novel is a letter written on toilet paper five years before the narrative present by Valerie, a lesbian actress who because of her sexuality was imprisoned in a concentration camp, tortured, and given lethal experimental hormone therapy. Despite her experiences, Valerie retained "the last inch" of her integrity and compassion: "I don't know who you are, or whether you're a man or woman. . . . But I love you." Before dying she delivered the letter to the unknown person in the next cell, transforming him into V, and five years later he gives it to Evey, transforming her in turn. V is insane, and Evey rejects his violence, yet after undergoing his harrowing and liberating education she replaces him as a creative V.

Moore began a third series at *Warrior* that he also later completed for an American publisher, *The Complete Bojeffries Saga* (1983–1992). Moore uses the Bojeffries family of "supernormal" monsters to satirize "the really *stupid* bits of England": Council Houses, racist organizations,

*Cover for a 1984 issue of the comic-book series on
which Moore collaborated during 1984–1986*

punk nihilists, and naughty postcards. Although he continued writing for British comics such as *2000 A.D.* (including *The Ballad of Halo Jones* [July 1984–April 1986] and *D.R. & Quinch* [April 1983–Summer 1985]), when *Warrior* collapsed in the early 1980s, Moore went on to create his most influential work yet for the American comics industry via mail from Northampton.

His first American success came when, late in 1983 (starting with issue 20), he took over *Saga of the Swamp Thing,* a poorly selling DC Comics horror title. Moore decided to work on *Saga of the Swamp Thing* (later shortened to *Swamp Thing*) because with the money came freedom; as he told Stanley Wiater and Stephen R. Bissette in a 1993 interview, "It was like having practiced swimming in the local municipal baths, and then being suddenly given the entire Atlantic Ocean to play in." When Moore left *Swamp Thing* in 1987 after issue 64, he had won several awards and written more than one thousand pages of innovative, horrifying, and beautiful stories that revitalized the comic and the genre, more than doubled the market for the title, and influenced several top comics writers (including Neil Gaiman and Jamie Delano).

Despite the loose nature of serial work, Moore's *Swamp Thing* opus coheres as a graphic novel chronicling Swamp Thing's journey through an American Gothic landscape and the universe on his quest for knowledge of himself and his world, always centered by his love for Abby Cable. The saga opens with Moore's reinvention of the Swamp Thing as a vegetable consciousness who, devastated when he learns that he is not human, sinks alone into his swamp. The cycle ends when Swamp Thing, having learned that he is an Earth elemental, chooses not to transform the Earth into an Edenic cornucopia and retreats again into the swamp, this time with Abby. Within this frame Moore writes diverse subplots, from horror involving demons and Patagonian sorcerers to science fiction consisting of mental space travel and a point at which all times and places are viewed at once. Moore explores political themes (pollution, sexism, racism) and philosophical ones (love and fear, life and death, good and evil, fantasy and reality).

Many issues are memorable. The necrophiliac incest of issue 29, "Love and Death" (October 1984), was so disturbing that the issue, as well as subsequent ones in the series, was published without the Comics Code Authority's Seal of Approval—rare for a mainstream comic up to that time. In issue 34, "Rite of Spring" (March 1985), Abby and Swamp Thing have cosmic sex, fusing their linked minds with the natural pulses of the world. And issue 60, "Loving the Alien" (May 1987), offers a union of artistic and scientific languages in text and images that depict Swamp Thing's rape by a bioclockwork entity. After being violated with "fine-bore needles of hollow diamond" and acid, Swamp Thing falls "past the tubes of tinted crystal that were already sluicing his codes and his chemicals towards the vats below, where they were analyzed, synthesized and mass produced, channeled along the uterine duct system to be sprayed across my ova-orchards in a fine and fertile mist." The entity thinks, "If he understood that he was loved, that would be enough." In addition to its impact on comics, *Swamp Thing* "was a great learning process" that removed Moore's artistic "manacles," as he told Wiater and Bissette, and led to his award-winning masterpiece, *Watchmen* (1986–1987).

Watchmen ushered in a new era for Moore of ambitious, tightly crafted graphic novels. Moore's setting is the New York City of an alternate history marked by the presence of superheroes. One of them, the Comedian, has just been murdered as the story begins. As the mystery deepens, Moore introduces other superheroes such as Rorschach, Nite Owl, and Ozymandias. Some are retired, others neurotic, and all are quite human, except Dr. Manhattan, an omnipotent being who mentally manipulates matter. It develops that one of the superheroes has initiated a plot to kill millions to make world peace. To this story Moore adds a second—that of a pirate comic book in which the protagonist and his horrible adventure mirror the characters and plot of the "real" world of *Watchmen.*

Watchmen is a comic book about comic books, a study of the flawed people compelled to become heroes,

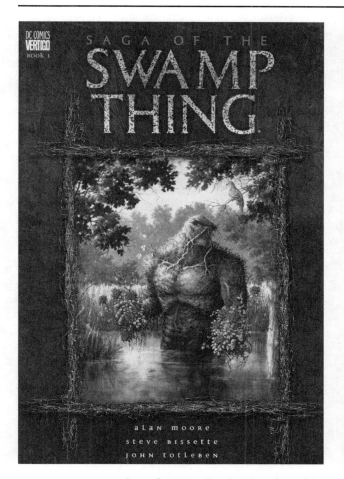
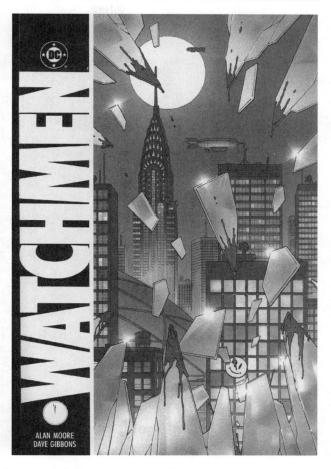

Covers for 1987 collected editions of two of the comic books on which Moore worked during the 1980s
(left: Collection of John Lyles; right: Collection of Jason Paddock)

an examination of how such beings would deform society, a satire of American politics and culture, a transcendental science fiction, and a meditation on free will and determinism. It shows how people subjectively "scrawl" meaning on the world, questions the use of power to force one's visions onto other people, and asserts the need for love amid the emptiness of existence.

The complexity of the work partly derives from Moore's use of different perspectives for various characters, none of which he obviously validates. And the textual and pictorial density of *Watchmen* displays an aesthetic control and impact that could be achieved only in comics but that never before had been to that degree. For example, a close-up of the insane sailor from the pirate comic book eating a bloody seagull is followed on the next page by an identically composed close-up of a superhero eating a cooked chicken leg. Such details economically achieve many effects: they make transitions between scenes; create irony; demonstrate the interconnectedness of people and their potential to be insane or sane; and provide an intellectually stimulating experience as readers become sensi-

tive to signs and search for meaning with the characters. *Watchmen* revised mainstream comics, won a 1988 Hugo Award, and was cited in *The Encyclopedia of Science Fiction* (1993) as "one of the central sf novels of the 1980s."

Batman: The Killing Joke (1988), a strong comic that uses the similarities between Batman and the Joker to discuss the thin line separating sanity from insanity, and *V for Vendetta* concluded Moore's work for DC Comics during this period of his career, as he became unhappy with the company's treatment of its creators and the medium. He felt that in order to continue growing as an artist, he needed to be free from marketplace and publisher pressures to churn out superhero work; he believed that the superhero genre had ended for him with *Watchmen* and *Olympus,* because it would only contaminate with violence, adventure, and costumes the human themes he wanted to pursue. In 1987 Moore left his lucrative and secure job with DC and in 1988 founded a publishing company, Mad Love.

This phase of his career in the late 1980s and early 1990s, free from mainstream comics, included extraordi-

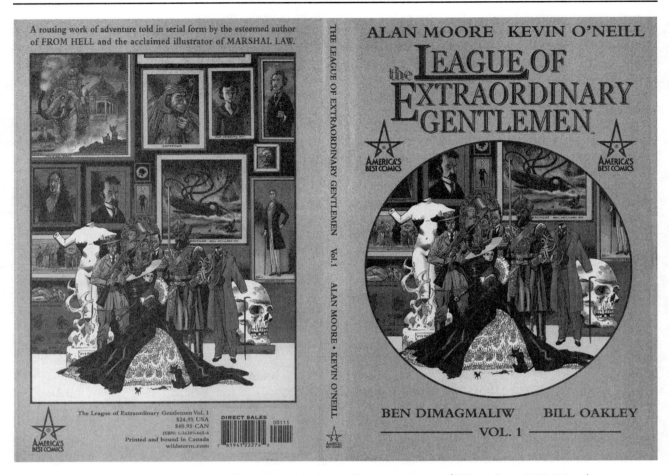

Dust jacket for the 2001 collected edition of a comic-book series Moore wrote in 1999 (Richland County Public Library)

narily diverse projects. His first work for Mad Love was contributing to, editing, and publishing an anthology comic called *AARGH! (Artists Against Rampant Government Homophobia)* in 1988. For Eclipse he wrote the graphic docudrama *Shadowplay–The Secret Team* (1989), in which a diseased bald eagle with a blood-filled briefcase relates CIA history. For Gollancz he wrote *A Small Killing* (1991), in which artist Timothy Hole journeys into his past to acknowledge his first cruel act and his betrayal of his aesthetic idealism for money. In this same period Moore began his most ambitious projects: *From Hell* (1989–1998), *Big Numbers* (1990), and *Lost Girls* (beginning in 1991).

Winner of multiple Eisner and Harvey awards for best serialized story and best writer, *From Hell* is a meticulously researched historical graphic novel about Jack the Ripper's dissection of prostitutes in Victorian London. Moore critically analyzes the intertwining roles played by myth, history, and symbols in shaping human lives. Moore's Jack the Ripper, the Royal Physician Sir William Gull, performs Masonic magic to solidify male dominion over women by eviscerating prostitutes along ancient lines of masculine power in London, laying down new lines of

misogynist myths and symbols that continue to mark modern society. *From Hell,* at more than 700 pages in the collected edition (including maps, epilogues, and appendices), is an achievement of awful grandeur. *From Hell-Book One: The Compleat Scripts* (1994) provides a fascinating look into Moore's creative process, and a movie adaptation of *From Hell* was released in 2001.

With *Big Numbers* Moore began a projected 480-page, twelve-chapter graphic novel about "ordinary" Hamptonshire people (including a poet, a history teacher, mental-hospital outpatients, and characters created by dice in a game called "Real Life") who have been "damaged" by twentieth-century life. The fragmented characters are unified via fractal mathematics: behind the chaos of life lies a beautiful pattern. Although *Big Numbers* is complex, it displays a new simplicity in Moore's storytelling, free from elements he believes are distractions in his earlier work: thought balloons and narration captions, rich prose, and obvious pictorial and textual connections. Moore believes *Big Numbers* includes his best work, but it ceased production when artist Bill Sienkiewicz left after the second issue was published.

Joanna Page, Heather Graham, and Johnny Depp in the 2001 movie version of From Hell *(20th Century-Fox)*

Lost Girls is an erotic fantasy with an intriguing premise. Alice, Wendy, and Dorothy, heroines of children's fantasy novels written by men, meet as adults in a decadent art nouveau hotel in Austria on the eve of World War I. As the three women become romantically involved with each other, through opium and sex they begin to remember their childhood fantasies. *Lost Girls* is a work of comics erotica emphasizing place, character, and story and exploring relations between sex, art, fantasy, and reality.

Moore's mainstream comics work such as *Watchmen* raised the standard for quality in comics writing. It also helped to spawn a legion of violent superhero comics lacking his irony, humor, narrative skill, and the sense of wonder of the comics he read as a boy. In a 1992 interview with Groth titled "Mainstream Comics Have, at Best, Tenuous Virtues," Moore said that mainstream superhero comics are like crack cocaine because the plot, imagination, and character have been refined out, leaving only a chemical rush. To instill some charm and story back into superhero comics, to enjoy himself, to escape his role as pure artist of difficult alternative comics, and to earn money for the less marketable projects close to his heart, Moore has been writing a plethora of stories for mainstream companies since 1993. Apart from occasional works such as his three-issue *Violator* series (1994), a repul-

sive, over-the-top parody of violent superheroes for Image Comics, his mainstream work has fulfilled his goals.

In 1993, for example, Moore wrote *1963,* an affectionate six-issue parody of 1963 Marvel superhero comics. Each issue includes hilarious and wondrous heroes, plots, and settings, fictional fan letters, Cold War posturing, allusions to 1963-era American culture, and ads for imaginary tacky products. Moore told Wiater and Bissette that *1963* was "refreshing in the midst of my more demanding projects." Beginning at Image in August 1996 with issue 41 and finishing at Awesome Entertainment in February 1998 with issue 56, Moore wrote *Supreme,* wherein he recovered the wonder of the *Superman* comics of his boyhood by creating a "retro-techno" world around the hero Supreme, including Radar the Hound Dog Supreme and a villain named Optilux, who seeks to transform all matter in the universe into pure light. *Supreme* won the 1997 Eisner Award for best writing.

Moore's fiction shares the themes of his comics. For example, "A Hypothetical Lizard" (first published in *Liavek: Wizard's Row,* 1987), is a dark, baroque fantasy story about obsessive love. *Voice of the Fire* (1996) is an historical novel consisting of twelve short stories. Each story occurs in a different era (from 4000 B.C. to 1995 A.D.) with a different first-person narrator speaking in a distinct voice (including a simple boy with his own transformed English, a witch, a poet, a murderer, and Moore himself). The stories are unified by the main character of the novel: Moore's hometown, Northampton. Like the best history, *Voice of the Fire* shows how the incidents and people of the past shape the present. Like the best horror, it teaches that some of the most horrible things of all can originate within the human mind. Like the best fantasy, it reveals human truths via supernatural metaphors. And like the best literature, it demonstrates the power of language to make the world new.

In 1999, when Moore launched the America's Best Comics (ABC) imprint, he entered a period of intense productivity fueled by his becoming a "magician" able to access the magical nature of consciousness, perception, and artistic creation. As he explained to Simon Lewis in a 2001 interview, "To me, creativity and magic are pretty much the same thing . . . I've got a lot of energy from somewhere. I feel that a lot of this energy is a result of the areas of consciousness that magic has taken me into." *The League of Extraordinary Gentlemen,* a limited series Moore concluded in 1999, is a thriller in which Mina Harker, Alan Quatermain, Captain Nemo, Griffin (the Invisible Man), and Dr. Jekyll (and Mr. Hyde) must protect England from a villain possessing Cavorite, the gravitation-proof and hence highly dangerous substance created by the scientist Mr. Cavor in H. G. Wells' *The First Men in the Moon* (1901). Also in 1999 for ABC, Moore began four continuing titles that parody, subvert, and refresh the mainstream superhero genre: *Tom Strong* (artist: Chris Sprouse), a nostalgic and parodic fusion of elements of Doc Savage, Tarzan, and Superman; *Top 10,* an insertion of the television police drama into Neopolis, a city populated by every kind of superhero imaginable; *Tomorrow Stories,* an anthology of short stories written by Moore and drawn by various artists using distinct, often nonmainstream styles and techniques; and *Promethea,* an ambitious amalgam of "popular, esoteric, and historical references" that Rich Kreiner calls "Moore's most sweeping post-modern reclamation project yet," as it traces the magical education of college student Sophie Bangs in her role as the latest incarnation of the superwoman Promethea, the imagination made flesh and the gateway between the material and immaterial worlds. Moore's goal with his ABC line, he told Simon Lewis in a 2001 interview, is to invigorate the mainstream comics industry by writing superhero comics of superior quality and thereby "to fold in" radical and experimental "ideas from the perimeters" and to "branch out into different areas" and "get comics back to the diversity that they used to have."

Although he has recorded CDs, done performance art, and written fiction, Moore's chief passion remains comics because the medium fuses pictures and words into a potent and as yet relatively untapped language. As Wiater and Bissette say in *Comic Book Rebels: Conversations with the Creators of the New Comics* (1993), Moore is "unique in that his work as a writer has organically enlivened and wholly elevated what is possible in comics as a form of literature." Throughout his career Moore's writing has focused on anarchy, empathy, and knowledge of history and self. In a short time he grew from a writer of superhero comics about the human condition into an author of widely different genres who explores themes of human relevance with ever-increasing ambition, complexity, and imagination.

Interviews:

Neil Gaiman, "Moore about Comics," *Knave,* 18, no. 3 (1986): 38–41;

Gaiman, "A Portal to Another Dimension," *Comics Journal,* 116 (July 1987): 80–87;

Bob Stewart, "Synchronicity and Symmetry," *Comics Journal,* 116 (July 1987): 89–95;

Gary Groth, "Interview," *Comics Journal,* 118 (December 1987): 61–72;

Groth, "Big Words, Part One," *Comics Journal,* 138 (October 1990): 56–95;

Groth, "Big Words, Part Two," *Comics Journal,* 139 (December 1990): 78–109;

Groth, "Big Words, Part Three," *Comics Journal,* 140 (February 1991): 72–85;

Groth, "Mainstream Comics Have, at Best, Tenuous Virtues," *Comics Journal,* 152 (August 1992): 89–100;

Stanley Wiater and Stephen R. Bissette, *Comic Book Rebels: Conversations with the Creators of the New Comics* (New York: Donald I. Fine, 1993), pp. 161–173;

Simon Lewis, "Alan Moore's ABCs," *Comics Journal,* 231 (March 2001): 29–31.

References:

Gregory Cwiklik, "The Tingler: *Violator* #1–3," *Comics Journal,* 176 (April 1995): 41–43;

Leon Hunt, "Destination: Planet Thatcher: *Big Numbers* and *St. Swithin's Day,*" *Comics Journal,* 138 (October 1990): 45–52;

Rich Kreiner, "Superish Woman: *Promethea,*" *Comics Journal,* 231 (March 2001): 32–34.

Charles Platt

(26 April 1945 –   )

D. Douglas Fratz

BOOKS: *Garbage World* (New York: Berkley, 1967; London: Panther, 1968);

Highway Sandwiches, by Platt, Thomas M. Disch, and Marilyn Hacker (N.p.: Privately printed, 1970);

The Gas (New York: Ophelia Press, 1970; Manchester, U.K.: Savoy, 1980; revised, Port Townsend, Wash.: Loompanics Unlimited, 1996);

The City Dwellers (London: Sidgwick & Jackson, 1970); revised as *Twilight of the City: A Novel of the Near Future* (New York: Macmillan, 1977);

The Image Job (New York: Ophelia Press, 1971);

The Power and the Pain (New York: Ophelia Press, 1971);

Planet of the Voles: A Science Fiction Novel (New York: Putnam, 1971);

T-Shirting: A Do-It-Yourself Guide to Getting It on Your Chest (New York: Hawthorn Books, 1975);

Outdoor Survival (New York: Watts, 1976);

A Song for Christina, as Blakely St. James (Chicago: Playboy, 1976);

Sweet Evil (New York: Berkley, 1977);

Christina Enchanted, as St. James (Chicago: Playboy, 1980; London: Arrow, 1987);

Dream Makers: The Uncommon People Who Write Science Fiction (New York: Berkley, 1980); republished as *Who Writes Science Fiction?* (Manchester, U.K.: Savoy, 1980);

Using WP-6502 (New York: Dwo Quong Fok Lok Sow, 1980);

Love's Savage Embrace, as Charlotte Prentiss (New York: Jove, 1981);

Christina's Touch, as St. James (Chicago: Playboy, 1982);

Dream Makers Volume II: The Uncommon Men & Women Who Write Science Fiction (New York: Berkley, 1983);

Double Delight, as Aston Cantwell (New York: Warner, 1983);

Tease for Two, as Cantwell (New York: Warner, 1983);

BASIC without Maths (London: Zomba, 1984);

Graphics Guide to the Commodore 64 (Berkeley, Cal.: Sybex, 1984);

Charles Platt

The Whole Truth Home Computer Handbook (New York: Avon, 1984); revised by Platt and David Langford as *Micro Mania: The Whole Truth about Home Computers* (London: Gollancz, 1984);

Artificial Intelligence in Action: Commodore 64 (New York: Trillium Press, 1985);

More from Your Micro (New York: Avon, 1985);

Less Than Human, as Robert Clarke (New York: Avon, 1986); as Platt (London: Grafton, 1987);

How to Be a Happy Cat, by Platt and Gray Jolliffe (London: Gollancz, 1986; Pittstown, N.J.: Main Street Press, 1987);

Dream Makers: Science Fiction & Fantasy Writers at Work (New York: Ungar, 1987; London: Xanadu, 1987)—comprises material from *Dream Makers: The Uncommon People Who Write Science Fiction* and *Dream Makers Volume II: The Uncommon Men & Women Who Write Science Fiction;*

Piers Anthony's Worlds of Chthon: Plasm (New York: New American Library, 1987; London: Grafton, 1988);

Free Zone (New York: Avon, 1989);

When You Can Live Twice as Long, What Will You Do? And 99 Other Questions You May Have to Answer . . . Sooner Than You Think (New York: Morrow, 1989);

Piers Anthony's Worlds of Chthon: SOMA (New York: New American Library, 1989; London: Grafton, 1990);

The Silicon Man (New York: Bantam, 1991);

Children of the Ice, as Prentiss (New York: New American Library, 1993);

People of the Mesa, as Prentiss (New York: New American Library, 1995);

Children of the Sun, as Prentiss (New York: New American Library, 1996);

Protektor (New York: Avon, 1996);

Anarchy Online (New York: Black Sheep Books, 1996; New York: HarperPrism, 1997);

The Island Tribe, as Prentiss (New York: HarperPrism, 1997);

The Ocean Tribe, as Prentiss (New York: HarperPrism, 1999);

Loose Canon (Gillette, N.J.: Wildside Press, 2001);

Enrob Annual Report 2001, by Platt and Erico Narita (New York: ReganBooks, 2002).

OTHER: "The Total Experience Kick," in *The Best SF Stories from New Worlds 2,* edited by Michael Moorcock (London: Panther, 1968; New York: Berkley, 1968);

"The Disaster Story," in *The Best SF Stories from New Worlds 3,* edited by Moorcock (London: Panther, 1968; New York: Berkley, 1968);

"Direction," in *The New SF,* edited by Langdon Jones (London: Hutchinson, 1969);

"The Rodent Laboratory," in *The Best SF Stories from New Worlds 5,* edited by Moorcock (London: Panther, 1969; New York: Berkley, 1969);

"Lone Zone," in *The Best SF Stories from New Worlds 7,* edited by Moorcock (London: Panther, 1971);

"A Cleansing of the System," in *New Worlds Quarterly 3,* edited by Moorcock (London: Sphere, 1971; New York: Berkley, 1972);

New Worlds 6, edited by Platt and Moorcock (London: Sphere, 1973); republished as *New Worlds 5* (New York: Avon, 1974);

"New York Times," in *Orbit 11,* edited by Damon Knight (New York: Putnam, 1973);

"Family Literature," in *New Worlds Quarterly 5,* edited by Moorcock (London: Sphere, 1973);

"The Motivation Chart," in *New Worlds Quarterly 5,* edited by Moorcock (London: Sphere, 1973);

New Worlds 7, edited by Platt and Hilary Bailey (London: Sphere, 1974); republished as *New Worlds 6* (New York: Avon, 1975);

Moorcock, *The Condition of Muzak,* introduction by Platt (Boston: Gregg Press, 1977);

R. A. Lafferty, *The Devil Is Dead,* introduction by Platt (Boston: Gregg Press, 1977);

Philip K. Dick, *The Zap Gun,* introduction by Platt (Boston: Gregg Press, 1979).

SELECTED PERIODICAL PUBLICATIONS–
UNCOLLECTED:
FICTION

"One of Those Days," *Science Fantasy* (December 1964–January 1965);

"Cultural Invasion," *New Worlds* (November 1965);

"The Failures," *New Worlds* (January 1966);

"A Taste of the Afterlife," *New Worlds* (September 1966);

"Expressing the Abstract," *New Worlds* (July 1967);

"Fun Palace–Not a Freakout," *New Worlds* (March 1968);

"Id," *New Worlds* (March 1969);

"The Responsive Environment," *New Worlds* (May 1969);

"Star Haven," *Magazine of Fantasy and Science Fiction* (January 1982);

"Dark Desires," *Pulphouse* (July 1992).

NONFICTION

"The Sexual Gothic Private Eye Caper," *New Worlds* (July 1969);

"An Editor's Day," *Science Fiction Review,* 40 (August 1970): 17–18;

"So You're Immortal, So What?" *Harper's,* 246 (1477) (June 1973): 9;

"Love Thy Publisher: The Asimov Method," *Science Fiction Review,* 29 (January–February 1979): 36–37;

"None So Blind," "A Feudal Future," and "Cheap Thrills," *Patchin Review,* 3 (January 1982): 20–24, 46–48, 52–53;

"Who Is Arnold Klein?" and "How to Write Like Hugo Gernsback," *Patchin Review,* 6 (March–May 1982): 42–43, 44–45;

"A Junkyard of Dreams," *Patchin Review,* 4 (April–June 1982): 15–17;

"Do Androids Dream of Philip K. Dick?" *Horizon,* 25 (July–August 1982): 38–42;

"Keith Laumer: A Profile," *Science Fiction Review,* 45 (Winter 1982): 8–11;

"Notes from Baltimore," *Science Fiction Review,* 49 (November 1983): 8–10;

"Viewpoint: In Defense of the Real World," *Isaac Asimov's Science Fiction Magazine,* 7 (November 1983): 53–66;

"The Fiction They Deserve," *Science Fiction Review,* 50 (Spring 1984): 12–13;

"The Decline of Fiction," *Science Fiction Review,* 51 (Summer 1984): 20–21;

"In Search of Surprises," *Isaac Asimov's Science Fiction Magazine,* 8 (December 1984): 33–40;

"Profile of Rudy Rucker," *Magazine of Fantasy & Science Fiction,* 67 (December 1984): 18–24;

"The Pompous Rose," by Platt and Gregory Benford, *Patchin Review,* 7 (March 1985): 3–8;

"Frank Herbert: Interview," *Stardate,* 1 (October 1985): 11–17;

"A Hard Look at Hardcovers," *THRUST–Science Fiction & Fantasy Review,* 25 (Winter 1986): 17–18;

"The Insanity Offense," *THRUST–Science Fiction & Fantasy Review,* 26 (Spring 1987): 19–20;

"On Science Fiction: Ackermania," *Magazine of Fantasy & Science Fiction,* 74 (May 1988): 93–98;

"On Alfred Bester," *Interzone,* 23 (Spring 1988);

"Destination: Gloom," *Interzone,* 24 (Summer 1988);

"Two Kinds of Censorship," *Interzone,* 25 (September–October 1988);

"Inside Science Fiction: Inscrutable Science Fiction," *Magazine of Fantasy & Science Fiction,* 75 (November 1988): 93–99;

"The War Bores," *Interzone,* 26 (November–December, 1988);

"An Unnecessarily-Detailed Report on the 1987 Worldcon," *THRUST–Science Fiction & Fantasy Review,* 29 (Winter 1988): 5–8;

"The Triumph of Whimsey," *Interzone,* 27 (January–February 1989);

"Inside Science Fiction: How to Live Forever," *Magazine of Fantasy & Science Fiction,* 76 (April 1989): 81–85;

"The Vanishing Midlist," *Interzone,* 29 (May–June 1989);

"Taking Liberties," *THRUST–Science Fiction & Fantasy Review,* 33 (Spring 1989): 5–6;

"The Rape of Science Fiction," *Science Fiction Eye,* 5 (July 1989): 44–49;

"In Purely Commercial Terms," *Interzone,* 30 (July–August 1989);

"The Missing Middle of Science Fiction," *THRUST–Science Fiction & Fantasy Review,* 34 (Summer 1989): 5–6;

"Inside Science Fiction: Down Among the Dead," *Magazine of Fantasy & Science Fiction,* 77 (September 1989): 85–89;

"Homage to Narcissism," *Interzone,* 31 (September–October 1989);

"Report from Utopia," *Interzone,* 33 (January–February 1990);

"The Special Case of Bantam Spectra," *Science Fiction Eye,* 6 (February 1990): 19–22;

"Participative Fiction," *Interzone,* 34 (March–April 1990);

"Quantum Fiction: A Blueprint for Avoiding Literary Obsolescence," *New York Review of Science Fiction,* 20 (April 1990);

"Fairly Rich, Fairly Quick," *Interzone,* 36 (June 1990);

"Inside Science Fiction: Too Many Books," *Magazine of Fantasy & Science Fiction,* 79 (July 1990): 65–70;

"The Island Mentality," *Interzone,* 39 (September 1990);

"Beyond Science Fiction," *Interzone,* 40 (October 1990);

"Alfred Bester's Tender Loving Rage," *Science Fiction Eye,* 9 (November 1991): 30–34;

"Who Needs Privacy?" *Science Fiction Eye,* 10 (June 1992): 69–72;

"Freeze!" *Science Fiction Eye,* 11 (December 1992): 61–66;

"The Teflon Fantasist," *QUANTUM–Science Fiction & Fantasy Review,* 43/44 (Spring/Summer 1993): 19–20;

"Upstream," *Science Fiction Eye,* 12 (Summer 1993): 29–34;

"Life & Death in SF," *Non-Stop Science Fiction Magazine,* no. 1 (1993);

"Inside Science Fiction: Trading Data with Dead and Digital," *Magazine of Fantasy & Science Fiction,* 86 (March 1994): 33–39;

"Wrist Voodoo," *Interzone,* 83 (May 1994);

"In Search of Science Fiction," *Interzone* (July 1994);

"Why Hypertext Doesn't Really Work," *New York Review of Science Fiction* (August 1994);

"The Selling of SF," *Interzone* (November 1994);

"The Tenacity of Fiction," *Interzone* (January 1995);

"The Soviet Space Auction," *Science Fiction Eye,* no. 14 (Spring 1996);

"The Ides of Lust," *Non-Stop Science Fiction Magazine,* no. 3 (1997).

Charles Platt has had a lengthy career in science fiction as an author of stories and novels, as an editor of magazines and books, as a skilled interviewer of other

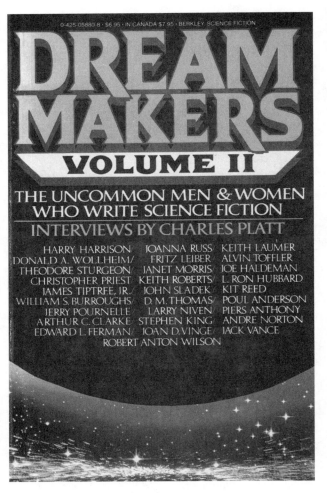

Paperback cover for Platt's second collection of interviews, which won a
Locus Award for best nonfiction (Thomas Cooper Library,
University of South Carolina)

divorce: to Leah Wallach in 1971, and to Nancy Weber in 1976; the only child mentioned in that source is a daughter, Rose, from the second marriage.

Platt has since confirmed that he was born Charles Michael Platt in London to Maurice and Marjorie (Hubbard) Platt on 26 April 1945, moving to the small town of Letchworth at the age of five. In the Winter interview Platt described his childhood as "typical of a science-fiction writer": he read voraciously, was not popular, and preferred intellectual pastimes to sports. He began writing comic strips at age seven, and by age eighteen he was writing science-fiction stories, which he tried to sell to *New Worlds*. In 1963 Platt began studying economics at Cambridge University, but he soon dropped out and moved to London. There he played keyboards with several little-known rock groups while writing, working for *New Worlds,* and working part-time as personal assistant to the publisher at Clive Bingley Limited.

Platt's first published science-fiction story, "One of Those Days," appeared in the British magazine *Science Fantasy* in 1964, but he did not begin to make a name for himself until he became associated with Michael Moorcock and *New Worlds* in 1965, during the height of its influence in the British New Wave movement. Platt spent several years with *New Worlds* as a designer and production manager, becoming the editor when Moorcock left the magazine in 1969. During this period Platt continued writing his own science fiction. Beginning in the mid 1960s, he wrote several short stories per year, which were published in *New Worlds*.

Platt's first novel was *Garbage World* (1967), a clever work, although its inventiveness is somewhat harmed by its heavy use of scatological humor. The novel depicts a degenerate society on an asteroid that serves as the garbage dump of the solar system. In his later comments on the novel, Platt has said that it satirizes the obsessive packrat nature of science-fiction fans and collectors. A small production company in New York bought the movie rights in 1995.

Platt moved in 1970 from London to New York, where he still maintains a residence, and he became increasingly prolific as a writer, both within the science-fiction genre and elsewhere. One of his most ambitious efforts was *The City Dwellers* (1970), in which he collected and revised several shorter works. This effort was further revised and expanded as *Twilight of the City: A Novel of the Near Future* (1977). The setting of these novels, also written with a New Wave sensibility, is a dying New York City. Neither version received substantial critical attention, especially the more serious *Twilight of the City*. Equally unsuccessful was *Planet of the Voles: A Science Fiction Novel* (1971), a New Wave satire of

science-fiction authors, and as a critic. Under his own name and various pseudonyms, he has written in other genres, including suspense, erotica, and nonfiction computer reference books; but he is best known for his contributions to science fiction.

In an interview with Douglas E. Winter, included in Platt's *Dream Makers Volume II: The Uncommon Men & Women Who Write Science Fiction* (1983), Platt admitted that he "can never take anything totally seriously"; one result has been that he has allowed various contradictory biographical details to appear in sources such as the dust-jacket copy of his books. Different references list him as having been born in Hertfordshire, Scotland, Tehran, or "a small English village," in 1943, 1944, 1945, or 1949, with a variety of parents; he has also been called "the adopted son of Lord Platt," a famous English physician (who is, in fact, his uncle). Some sources state that he is divorced, with two sons born in the early 1970s, but another source lists two marriages, both ending in

space opera that Platt wrote in one week upon arriving in New York.

Platt's early work also included eight hard-core pornographic novels, published under the *Playboy* house pseudonym Blakely St. James and the pseudonym Aston Cantwell, in addition to his own name. Although there were some fantasy-genre elements in several of these books, particularly *Sweet Evil* (1977), the only one with a strong science-fiction premise was *The Gas* (1970), a post-apocalypse satire that was initially considered too obscene to publish in England. A 1980 British edition published by Savoy Books was seized by the Director of Public Prosecutions and subsequently withdrawn by the publisher. Platt also wrote historical romances as Charlotte Prentiss beginning in 1981.

After moving to New York, Platt became a science-fiction editor for the paperback firms Avon Books from 1972 to 1974 (resigning when the firm rejected Philip K. Dick's *Flow My Tears, the Policeman Said* [1974] on the basis of its title) and Condor Publishing from 1977 to 1978. He also taught courses in science fiction, technology, computer programming, and writing at the New School for Social Research and at Staten Island Community College. In 1986 he returned to book publishing with Franklin Watts, where he helped to produce quality hardcover editions for authors such as Brian W. Aldiss, Rachel Pollack, and John Shirley. He remained with Watts until 1988.

Platt had been active in science-fiction fandom since the late 1960s, and he published his own fanzines and wrote for many others. He began to develop a reputation as a critic with strong views and little inhibition in stating them. After moving to the United States, Platt increased his nonfiction output and was published in science-fiction fanzines and semiprofessional magazines on both sides of the Atlantic. He became established as a fan and critic who often engaged in "feuds" with other professionals in the field. Platt also became a well-known personality at conventions, where his pranks (such as collecting money from participants who hired "Agents of Pie Kill" to hit author and editor Ted White with a pie in the face) became legendary.

Platt began interviewing science-fiction authors in the late 1970s as he traveled around the United States. His interviewing style was personal, but he also freely presented his opinions in his profiles. These interviews garnered his first real critical attention. They were collected in two books, *Dream Makers: The Uncommon People Who Write Science Fiction* (1980) and *Dream Makers Volume II: The Uncommon Men & Women Who Write Science Fiction*. A combined 1987 volume added some extra material. Reflecting the changing nature of the field in the 1970s and 1980s, many complained that all but one of the authors interviewed in the first volume were male; for the second volume, Platt made sure that several female authors were included. Both *Dream Makers* volumes received Hugo Award nominations as the best nonfiction books of the year, and the second volume won the Locus Award for best nonfiction. By the mid 1980s Platt was widely considered the best and most influential interviewer in the science-fiction field.

Platt also continued in the 1980s to write criticism. He began publishing his own magazine, *The Patchin Review,* in 1980. Many science-fiction readers associated the magazine with Platt's opinionated and satirical commentary, both under his own name and attributed to a variety of pseudonyms. Platt's playfulness was gradually replaced by a more serious attitude in his position as critic. By the mid 1980s he regularly produced essays in venues ranging from most of the professional American science-fiction magazines and the British science-fiction publication *Interzone* to several respected semiprofessional journals, among them *THRUST* (later retitled *QUANTUM*), *Fantasy Review, Science Fiction Chronicle,* and *Science Fiction Eye.* Before the 1980s were over, Platt's stature as a science-fiction critic had risen considerably. Much of Platt's best commentary on science fiction from this period, and through the 1990s, was collected in a small-press book, *Loose Canon* (2001).

Platt continued to develop his prankster reputation, despite his otherwise respectable image. He often self-published his most irreverent commentary, which included gossip columns by "Gabby Snitch" in which Platt recited in frank terms the inside gossip among those in the science-fiction field. This practice engendered only minor controversies when it was read by a few hundred fans and professionals, but that controversy increased in 1984 when the column was picked up by *Science Fiction Chronicle,* with a circulation of several thousand. Andrew Porter, editor and publisher of the *Science Fiction Chronicle,* had to drop the Snitch columns when disgruntled subscribers began cancelling their subscriptions. One classic Platt prank of this period occurred in 1985, when he wrote a review (at the suggestion of the review editor) of a nonexistent soft-core pornographic book, "*Love Lessons* by John Wilson," alleging that Wilson was a pseudonym of Stephen King. The hoax article, published in the April 1985 issue of *Fantasy Review,* drew angry letters from King and threats from King's lawyer.

Also in the 1980s, Platt returned to writing novels. *Plasm* (1987) and *SOMA* (1989) were contributions to Piers Anthony's "shared world" of Chthon. *Less Than Human* (1986), which Platt wrote as Robert Clarke (jokingly hoping that readers might think he was related to Arthur C. Clarke), is a science-fiction satire about an android in a degenerate New York in 2010. *Free Zone* (1989) is also satirical, ridiculing virtually every science-fiction cliché in the field.

Paperback cover for Platt's 1991 novel, in which he demonstrated his knowledge of early 1990s microcomputer technology (Richland County Public Library)

Platt's next novel is perhaps his most accomplished effort at serious science fiction. *The Silicon Man* (1991), published as a Bantam Spectra Special, exhibits Platt's extensive knowledge of early microcomputer technology, also shown in the books on computers and artificial intelligence he wrote in the 1980s. The novel, though written as a thriller, realistically portrays the idea of downloading a human consciousness into an environment created by a computer. An FBI agent follows the source of a sophisticated weapon circulating through the black market back to a scientific team working for a defense contractor. These scientists actually belong to a conspiracy aimed at achieving immortality through the transfer of consciousness to computers, which involves destroying the brain. The scientists "translate" the FBI agent to protect their plans, which leads to a surprising revelation.

With *The Silicon Man* Platt became one of a handful of science-fiction authors who really understood computers well at the time. A reviewer for the *Washington Post Book World* (31 March 1991) noted that "Platt has read a good deal about computer science and biology, and presents his research with gung-ho enthusiasm." In *The New York Times* (21 April 1991) another reviewer called the narrative "compelling" as well as "philosophically and psychologically penetrating." *The Silicon Man* was republished in hardcover in 1993, and again in paperback in 1997.

Protektor (1996) also deals with computers, but in a far-future static eutopia where humans on one hundred thousand worlds are benevolently ruled by vast computer networks programmed to protect an immortal, self-indulgent humanity. The plot involves a computer expert assigned to solve problems caused by hackers seeking to destroy the governing system of one planet. The novel, in several thematic and stylistic aspects, is an homage to two of Platt's "literary heroes," Alfred Bester and Dashiell Hammett.

In the 1990s Platt became intensely interested in cryonics, a speculative technology to freeze people immediately after death in the hope that future generations will be able to revive and cure them. After working for the Alcor Foundation, managing their public relations, he was one of the founders of CryoCare Foundation in 1994; he served as the vice president of the organization for three years and subsequently became its president, a position he still holds. Strangely, the concept of cryonics has played only a small role in Platt's science fiction. He also has continued writing about computers and contributing frequent articles to *Wired* magazine. His 1996 book *Anarchy Online* explores issues of crime and pornography on the Internet; an editorial reviewer for Amazon.com called this work "absolutely a must-read for anyone concerned about cyberspace matters" and added, "Although he possesses an insider's knowledge of the insiders, Platt steps back sufficiently to get a useful and thought-provoking perspective."

Charles Platt has contributed to science fiction as an author, editor, interviewer, and critic. His fiction has ranged from satire to serious works, but he has no plans to contribute further to the field, since, in his words, "it has deteriorated exactly as I predicted in *The Patchin Review*, in 1980." Perhaps his most valuable role may be as a writer of nonfiction, both as an interviewer and as a commentator. Many would argue that his presence in science fiction has substantially improved the field.

Interview:

Joe Magee, "The Charles Platt Interview," *Non-Stop Science Fiction Magazine,* no. 2 (1995).

Christopher Priest
(14 July 1943 –   )

Frederick M. Burelbach
SUNY College at Brockport

See also the Priest entries in *DLB 14: British Novelists Since 1960* and *DLB 207: British Novelists Since 1960, Third Series.*

BOOKS: *Indoctrinaire* (London: Faber & Faber, 1970; New York: Harper & Row, 1970; revised edition, London: Pan, 1979);

Fugue for a Darkening Island (London: Faber & Faber, 1972); republished as *Darkening Island* (New York: Harper & Row, 1972);

Inverted World (London: Faber & Faber, 1974; New York: Harper & Row, 1974);

Real-Time World (London: New English Library, 1974);

Your Book of Film-Making (London: Faber & Faber, 1974);

The Space Machine: A Scientific Romance (London: Faber & Faber, 1976; New York: Harper & Row, 1976);

A Dream of Wessex (London: Faber & Faber, 1977); republished as *The Perfect Lover* (New York: Scribners, 1977);

An Infinite Summer (London: Faber & Faber, 1979; New York: Scribners, 1979);

The Making of the Lesbian Horse (Birmingham, U.K.: Birmingham Science Fiction Group, 1979);

The Affirmation (London: Faber & Faber, 1981; New York: Scribners, 1981);

The Glamour (London: Cape, 1984; Garden City, N.Y.: Doubleday, 1985; revised edition, London: Abacus, 1991; revised again, London: Touchstone, 1996);

Mona Lisa, as John Luther Novak (London: Sphere, 1986);

The Last Deadloss Visions (London: Privately printed, 1987; revised, 1988); expanded and republished as *The Book on the Edge of Forever* (Seattle: Fantagraphics, 1994);

The Quiet Woman (London: Bloomsbury, 1990);

Seize the Moment: The Autobiography of Helen Sharman, by Priest and Helen Sharman (London: Gollancz, 1993);

Running Tall, by Priest and Sally Gunnell (London: Bloomsbury, 1994);

Christopher Priest (from James Gunn, The New Encyclopedia of Science Fiction, *1988)*

The Prestige (London: Touchstone, 1995; New York: St. Martin's Press, 1996);

The Extremes (London: Simon & Schuster, 1998; New York: St. Martin's Press, 1999);

The Dream Archipelago (London: Earthlight, 1999);

David Cronenberg's eXistenZ, as Novak (London: Pocket Books, 1999);

The Separation (London: Scribner, forthcoming 2002).

Editions: *Omnibus 1* (London: Earthlight, 1999)—comprises *The Space Machine* and *A Dream of Wessex;*

Omnibus 2 (London: Earthlight, 1999)—comprises *Inverted World* and *Fugue for a Darkening Island.*

PRODUCED SCRIPTS: *The Space Machine,* BBC Radio 4, 1979;

Return to the Labyrinth, HTV, 1981;

The Watched, Thames TV, 1984;

The Glamour, BBC Radio 4, 1993.

OTHER: *Con,* fanzine, edited by Priest, 1964;

"The Interrogator," in *New Writings in SF 13,* edited by John Cannell (London: Dobson, 1969), pp. 45–76;

"The Ersatz Wine," in *Best SF Stories from New Worlds 6,* edited by Michael Moorcock (London: Panther, 1970; New York: Berkley, 1971);

"The Invisible Men," in *Stopwatch,* edited by George Hay (London: New English Library, 1974), pp. 125–136;

"Men of Good Value," in *New Writings in SF 26,* edited by Bulmer (London: Sidgwick & Jackson, 1975), pp. 29–49;

"The Suburbs My Destination," in *The View from the Edge: A Workshop of Science Fiction Stories,* edited by George Turner (Carlton, Australia: Norstrilia Press, 1977), pp. 14–19;

"The Negation," in *Anticipations,* edited by Priest (London: Faber & Faber, 1978; New York: Scribners, 1978);

"Swimming against the Stream," in *Envisaged Worlds,* edited by Paul Collins (St. Kilda, Australia: Void Publications, 1978), pp. 1–2;

"New Wave Science Fiction," in *The Encyclopedia of Science Fiction,* edited by Robert Holdstock (London: Octopus Books, 1978), pp. 162–173;

"Whores" and "Afterword," in *Stars of Albion,* edited by Priest and Holdstock (London: Pan, 1979);

"British Science Fiction," in *Science Fiction: A Critical Guide,* edited by Patrick Parrinder (London & New York: Longman, 1979), pp. 187–202;

"The Agent," by Priest and David Redd, in *Aries 1,* edited by John Grant (Newton Abbot, England: David & Charles, 1979), pp. 69–101;

"The Cremation," in *Andromeda 3,* edited by Peter Weston (London: Dobson, 1979), pp. 101–131;

Deadloss, fanzine, edited by Priest, 1980–1984;

"Landscape Artist: The Fiction of J. G. Ballard," in *The Stellar Gauge: Essays on Science Fiction Writers,* edited by Michael J. Tolley and Kirpal Singh (Carlton, Australia: Norstrilia Press, 1980), pp. 187–196;

"The Miraculous Cairn," in *New Terrors 2,* edited by Ramsey Campbell (London: Pan, 1980), pp. 11–55;

"The Ament," in *Seven Deadly Sins,* edited by Elizabeth Troop (London: Severn House, 1985), pp. 109–143;

H. G. Wells, *Christina Alberta's Father,* introduction by Priest (London: Hogarth Press, 1985);

Wells, *Mr. Britling Sees It Through,* introduction by Priest (London: Hogarth Press, 1985);

John Wyndham, *The Midwich Cuckoos,* introduction by Priest (London: Penguin, 2000);

"The Discharge," in *Sci.Fi.com,* edited by Ellen Datlow (2002).

SELECTED PERIODICAL PUBLICATIONS–UNCOLLECTED:

FICTION

"Conjugation," *New Worlds,* 169 (December 1966): 69–72;

"Impasse," *SF Impulse,* 12 (February 1967): 95–97;

"Charlie Was a Bastard," *Oz Magazine,* 41 (March/April 1972): 8–9;

"Static Gravity," *Omni,* 1 (April 1979): 76–79;

"In a Flash," *Interzone* (September 1995);

"The Cage of Chrome," *Interzone* (June 2000).

NONFICTION

"Science Fiction Magazine Survey," *Zenith Speculation,* 5 (June/July 1964): 17–20;

"New Wave–Prozines," *Zenith Speculation,* 8 (March 1965): 9–11;

"Migrant Angel," *Vector,* 41 (December 1966): 7–12;

"The Tankless Task of Thinking," *Vector,* 50 (July 1968): 10–14;

"Nothing Like the Sun," in *Vision of Tomorrow,* 1 (July 1970): 16–23;

"Foundation Forum, Part II; Science Fiction: Form versus Content," by Priest and Ian Watson, *Foundation,* 10 (June 1976): 55–65;

"The Profession of Science Fiction: Overtures and Beginners," *Foundation,* 13 (May 1978): 51–56;

"Wells's Novels, Imagination or Thought?" *Wellsian* (September 1978): 14–24;

"News for High-Octane Water Lilies," *Matrix,* 22 (February 1979): 3–7;

"Writing a Novel? Do!" *Focus* (Autumn 1979);

"Outside the Whale," *Vector,* 97 (April 1980): 5–14;

"Meetings with Remarkable Men," *Vector,* 98 (June 1980): 4–11;

"The Authentic Voice," *Focus,* 4 (Spring 1981): 4–5;

"Into the Arena: The Barrel: Hell Creatures of the Third Planet," *Vector,* 109 (April 1982): 22–26;

"Novel Contracts," *Focus,* 6 (Autumn 1982): 15–22;

"Crouching in Cheadle," *Vector,* 112 (1982): 25–29;

"Best of Young British," *Bookseller,* 2 July 1983, pp. 44–45;

"Venture into the Stodgy," *Bookseller,* 3 September 1983, pp.1097–1099;

"Books and the Box," *Bookseller,* 5 November 1983, pp. 1894–1895;

"Mucking About in Bytes," *Focus,* 10 (February 1985): 26–28;

"Leave the Forgotten to the Night," *Vector,* 127 (August/September 1985): 9–10;

"Peoria my destination," *Interzone* (November/December 1988): 33–34;

Review of *Christopher Priest* by Nicholas Ruddick, *Foundation,* 50 (Autumn 1990): 94–101;

"A Room without a Desk: Without a Suit," *Focus* (December 1990);

"Out of the Temple," *Interzone* (August 1994): 37–39;

"Pax Ortygia," *Interzone* (October 1994): 52–54;

"A Retreat from Reality," *Vector,* 206 (July/August 1999).

Perhaps the best words to describe Christopher Priest's work are those he himself used in his essay "British Science Fiction" (1979) to describe the genre as a whole: "literate and fresh, displaying qualities of landscape, irony, language and subtlety that any other nation, English-speaking or otherwise, would find hard to match." Since his first novel, *Indoctrinaire* (1970), his focus has been on the interface between the "real" world and the one that the mind creates. For a fiction writer, the relationship between these worlds is particularly problematical, and Priest uses a variety of narrative styles and points of view in exploring it. Many of his characters are themselves writers, and the infinite-regress effect of having characters create fictions within fictions affords Priest a range of opportunities to call into question the nature of reality. Once linked with New Wave writers—according to Nicholas Ruddick, Priest coined the phrase—Priest declared his independence from this group and closed the gap between science fiction and "mainstream" fiction while opening both to postmodern speculation and self-reflexivity.

Christopher McKenzie Priest was born on 14 July 1943 in Cheadle, Cheshire, outside Manchester, England, to Walter MacKenzie and Millicent Alice (Haslock) Priest. Educated at an elementary school in Manchester and then at Manchester Warehousemen Clerks' Orphan School, he joined a London firm of accountants in 1959, beginning a training program that continued until he was dismissed in 1965. By 1962 he had become fascinated by science fiction and joined the British Science Fiction Association; particularly impressed by the work of J. G. Ballard, he published a short-lived fanzine, *Con,* in 1964 and began a series of letters and essays for *Zenith Speculation* in addition to early stories that did not sell. From 1965 to 1968 he worked for several companies as an assistant accountant or junior manager, selling his first story in 1965 and marrying Christine Merchant in 1968, when he became a full-time writer. From 1969 to 1971 he wrote a column, "View of Suburbia," for *Speculation,* criticizing the contemporary science-fiction scene, and his 1969 story "The

Interrogator" became the germ of his first novel, *Indoctrinaire.* He was a part-time lecturer in science fiction at the University of London from 1973 to 1978, a regular early attender at the Milford Science Fiction Writers' Conference after its United Kingdom branch was established in 1972, and reviews editor for *Foundation* from 1974 to 1977, contributing several essays and reviews of books by such authors as Lester del Rey, Bob Shaw, and Arthur C. Clarke. Associated in the 1960s and 1970s with the British New Wave in science fiction, he wrote an essay on the movement for the *Encyclopedia of Science Fiction* (1978), but he felt that the movement, which had started as a revolution in thinking, degenerated into a stylistic affectation. In 1979 *Vector* published a special Christopher Priest issue, including some of his stories and critical comments on his work, and in the same year Priest gave a Guest of Honor address, "Meetings with Remarkable Men," to Novacon in Birmingham, England. Divorced from Christine Merchant in 1974, he subsequently married science-fiction writer Lisa Tuttle in 1981. The marriage ended in 1987. In 1988 he married American-born Laura-Lee McClure, who writes science fiction as Leigh Kennedy. They have two children: Simon Walter and Elizabeth Millicent, twins born in 1989. The Priests live in Hastings, East Sussex.

Priest's early stories give little indication of the extraordinary stylist he became. In "The Run" (1965)—included in his collection *Real-Time World* (1974) in, as he says, "all its pristine melodrama"—Senator Robbins is forced by a crowd of unemployed and unemployable "juvies" into a "chicken run" in which he can choose between stopping his car or running over their bodies. Just as he stops, an atomic bomb destroys all the juvies; only being in his car saves the senator. The attempt at suspense is unconvincing, as is the characterization. Other early stories collected in *Real-Time World* include "Breeding Ground" (1970), a dark comedy about a spaceship salvager tormented by space mites, and "The Perihelion Man" (1970), which Priest calls "an attempt to write a kind of story I had never done before (and haven't done since): the man who gets in a spaceship to go somewhere to do something." What this unlikely hero does is save Earth from a thermonuclear threat posed by aliens: he blows them up with their bombs. Closer to later themes are Priest's 1970 stories "Double Consummation," in which characters use "transition drugs" to switch their lifestyles and partners so as to live double lives, and "Fire Storm," which Priest says "contains threads of many of my themes in sf." In "Fire Storm" Captain Maast, in charge of a training exercise first to restore a city

Dust jacket for Priest's 1972 novel, in which African refugees encounter racism in England (Richland County Public Library)

and then to destroy it, wants to get as close to the action as possible, eventually immolating himself along with the city. Later stories in the collection are consistent with themes developed in Priest's novels: "The Head and the Hand" (1972), frequently anthologized, is a chilling story about a voyeuristic public getting pleasure from watching a performer amputate parts of his own body, culminating with his head; "Real-Time World" (1972) concerns scientists in an observatory, who think they are studying life on a remote planet, slightly displaced in time, but are really the subjects of an experiment, observed by one of them, on the effects of depriving them of news; and "A Woman Naked" (1974) concerns a woman, afraid of rape because she must live naked for six months as punishment for adultery, who finds that the real mental rape begins when she is required to tell a courtroom full of men the details of her affair.

Voyeurism and displacement in both time and mind are themes found in Priest's first novel, *Indoctri-*

naire. Elias Wentik, a research chemist, has been experimenting with a drug designed to aid in indoctrinating people by opening their minds to easy belief in their own fantasies and others' statements. Suddenly he finds himself in a surrealistic prison somewhere in the Brazilian jungle, subject to unintelligible interrogations by an officer and bizarre behavior by guards. Attempting to flee, he is rescued by Dr. Jexon, who tells him that the date is two centuries later, that poison gases derived from Wentik's research are causing hallucinations and personality changes, and that Wentik should find an antidote or return through time to destroy his work before it can be wrongly used. Since Wentik has been ingesting his own drug, however, how much of all this adventure is real? The novel has been criticized as unfocused, with weak characterization, but its suspenseful development of hallucinatory images, reminding some readers of Franz Kafka and Alain Robbe-Grillet, powerfully communicates the mental isolation of someone who resists indoctrination. Although Priest's later novels explore questions of perception and imagination much more subtly, with horror effects that remind one of Henry James's *The Turn of the Screw* (1898), this early novel firmly established him as a writer in the British vein of science fiction, thoughtful and stylish, as contrasted with the American emphasis on technological man in a hard-edged world.

Priest's next novel, *Fugue for a Darkening Island* (1972), takes risks with a tricky subject. Millions of African refugees, victims of nuclear war in Africa, have come to England, where they encounter militant racism that leads to civil war. Middle-class liberal Alan Whitman, caught up in these events, finds his marriage, family, and own identity fragmenting just as the British Isles are. Whitman is increasingly isolated, darkened mentally and morally, and in flight from emotional ties, and his ontogeny recapitulates the phylogeny of English society in the novel. The concept of "fugue" governs the physical action of the novel, the mental and emotional estrangement of its characters, and the contrapuntal style of the writing. Although capable of being seen as a satire on British insularity, racism, and sexual inhibitions, this novel is much more a study of psychological escape from commitment. Initially praised by critics, including Theodore Sturgeon, as thoughtful, tragic, and important, and translated into at least five languages, the novel won the John W. Campbell Jr. Memorial Award but has faded into obscurity since its 1979 republication by Pan.

Priest's third novel, *Inverted World* (1974), has retained the popularity (especially in France) that it achieved on first publication, possibly because it is Priest's closest approximation to "hard" science fiction. Priest's novel is more a study of how differing perceptions create different realities than it is an investigation of the peculiar effects of living on a planet constructed as a hyperboloid. Priest's interest in mathematics led him into considering what living on a world constructed by rotating a hyperbolic curve in space would be like, but he turns the thought experiment into a continuation of ideas taken up in his two previous novels: indoctrination into a worldview inconsistent with a differing reality, and movement through space that is also movement through time and mind. In the novel, Helward Mann has just come to maturity and left the crèche, being inducted into one of the guilds that are responsible for keeping Earth City moving along steel rails in an attempt to stay at a space-time "optimum." Time is measured in miles forward into the future or backward into the past, and the inhabitants of the city (those who are allowed outside) perceive peculiar physical effects as

they move backward and forward. Curiously, Helward perceives these effects in the "tooks" (local inhabitants who are engaged as laborers and breeding stock), but the tooks do not perceive them in themselves. Already two perceptions of reality are manifest, and a third is introduced by Elizabeth Khan, a nurse working in a took village, who tells Helward that Earth City is actually in Europe on planet Earth, and that his perceptions are distorted because of an artificially produced dilation effect that existed for centuries but does so no longer. Helward must attempt to come to terms with the difference between his sensory experience and his intellectual and emotional responses to Elizabeth and her views; the open-ended conclusion of the novel leaves his resolution of the conflict in doubt. Like *Fugue for a Darkening Island,* the novel can be seen as a satire on English insularity and closed-mindedness, but it is much subtler. The reader is led by Helward's first-person narrative to accept his perceptions and rationalizations as true; the introduction of differing narrative voices and viewpoints is as disturbing to the reader as it is to Helward, leading to a questioning of all the "truths" and the ways of reaching them that one takes for granted. By creating several fictions within fictions, Priest has dramatized the problems of relativity in the psychological, moral, and social spheres as well as in physics. Although the novel was nominated for a Hugo Award for Best Novel and won a British Science Fiction Association Award in 1975, early reviews indicate that even sensitive readers such as Peter Nicholls and Brian Stableford did not detect all that Priest was doing in the novel.

To relax from the disturbing implications of these three novels, or perhaps as an experiment in adopting a different worldview himself, Priest next wrote *The Space Machine: A Scientific Romance* (1976), an homage to H. G. Wells that, in a somewhat Victorian style, incorporates some of the events of *The Time Machine* (1895) and *The War of the Worlds* (1898) and even a character named Mr. Wells. This good-humored novel, which sold badly and received mostly negative reviews in England but won the Australian Ditmar Award for Best International Fiction, follows the careers of commercial traveler Edward Turnbull and Amelia Fitzgibbon, amanuensis to inventor Sir William Reynolds, as they ride Sir William's time machine (which turns into a space machine) to Mars, get involved in a revolution of slaves against their cannibalistic masters, and return to Earth on one of the Martian invaders' ships. There they encounter Mr. Wells and help him reconstruct the time machine (the original has vanished with its inventor into the future) in order to combat the Martians, who eventually succumb to terrestrial microbes, leaving Mr. Wells to write their story and Edward and Amelia to enjoy their love together. The novel gains a great deal of humor from the reader's contemporary perception of the naive Victorian characters' inhibitions, but the ability of the characters to adjust their attitudes and behavior to the changes they face is instructive when compared with the intransigence of characters in previous Priest novels. At the same time, the metafictional quality of the novel, its consciousness of the invented/inverted nature of all worldviews, is suggested in Priest's comment in his 1978 article "Wells's Novels, Imagination or Thought?" that *The Space Machine* "is a novel about a false past, one where Wells's novels came true."

A Dream of Wessex (1977), Priest's fifth novel, returns to the interface between "dream" and "reality," or between two worlds equally perceived as "real." Set in a near future in an imaginary Wessex, the novel is centered on a project designed to determine the extent to which human minds can cooperate in creating a world different from their contemporary one. Thirty-nine "dreamers" voluntarily isolate themselves from their overcrowded, violent, industrially polluted world to enter, in a laboratory under Maiden Castle, a consensual hypnotic semiparadise in which Dorchester, separated from the mainland by earthquakes that have produced a tidal bore, is a haven for surfboarders and craftspeople. The central character, Julia Stretton, seeking escape in the project from her dominating former lover Paul Mason, forms a mutually satisfying attachment to David Harkman inside the projection, but her worried superiors bring her "back" to encounter the latest addition to the project team—Mason. Although aware that the projection is not "reality," Julia finds it much preferable to the world that Mason dominates, while at the same time Harkman learns that his dreamworld is being "edited" by forces beyond his control. Eventually all three characters choose to inhabit different variations of the projection, never to return to the "real" world. The novel therefore focuses on how human beings create the "realities" they inhabit and the relationships among these "realities." In one sense an allegory of fiction writing, the novel is conscious of its metafictionality as well as its psychological and philosophical speculations on the nature of reality. Criticized by some writers for having flat characters, the novel has been accused of not being science fiction—an accusation that would not bother Priest. As complex fiction within the Proustian tradition, however, the novel teases the reader with myriad possible interpretations.

During the next few years, Priest wrote a group of short stories, collected in *An Infinite Summer* (1979),

that were set in the Dream Archipelago, an imaginary string of islands, politically neutral but each with distinctive characteristics, located south of a mainland split into two warring nations. One of these stories, "The Watched," was nominated for a Hugo Award in 1978. "Palely Loitering"–which is not part of the Dream Archipelago sequence–was nominated for a Hugo and won the British Science Fiction Association's Best Short Fiction Award for 1979. Both "The Watched" and "Palely Loitering" develop the theme of voyeurism with erotic overtones that can be seen in such previous stories as "A Woman Naked" and "The Head and the Hand." Another story from the Dream Archipelago group, "The Negation," initially published in the anthology *Anticipations* (1978), edited by Priest, has a special relationship to his novel *The Affirmation* (1981). In "The Negation" Dik, a young soldier-poet patrolling the border wall between warring countries, encounters Moylita Kaine, the author of his favorite novel, *The Affirmation*. She explains to him the symbolism in her novel, especially that of the wall between its two main characters that one of the characters fails to climb and so remains a failed romantic. Arrested for writing and giving to Dik a seditious story titled "The Negation," Kaine is imprisoned and interrogated, while Dik, whom she has told to "climb the wall" and become a poet, returns to his sentry duty. At the end of Priest's story, Dik, under the influence of hallucinatory gas that both sides use as a weapon, either climbs the wall into the enemy territory or encounters an enemy soldier who has climbed the wall into his own; it is not clear which. The anguish of choosing, of affirming one course of action while negating another, relates to both living and writing; this existentialist angst is central to *A Dream of Wessex* as well as to these stories and to Priest's next novel, *The Affirmation*.

This novel, with settings in both contemporary England and the fictive Dream Archipelago, is the account of a writer trying to create/re-create/stabilize his identity by writing the fictionalized story of his life as a "truer" statement than the one his memory provides him. Having just lost his father and his apartment, and having broken up with his girlfriend, thirty-one-year-old Peter Sinclair secludes himself in a friend's country cottage, paints one room white, and begins his story, assigning different names to his girlfriend, his sister, her husband, and to the altered landscape of the Dream Archipelago. In his account, he has won a prize: athanasia, an operation that will grant him almost immortal life but deprive him of his memory. Undergoing the operation, he depends on his (previously written) life story to reimplant his memories and therefore his identity. However, the

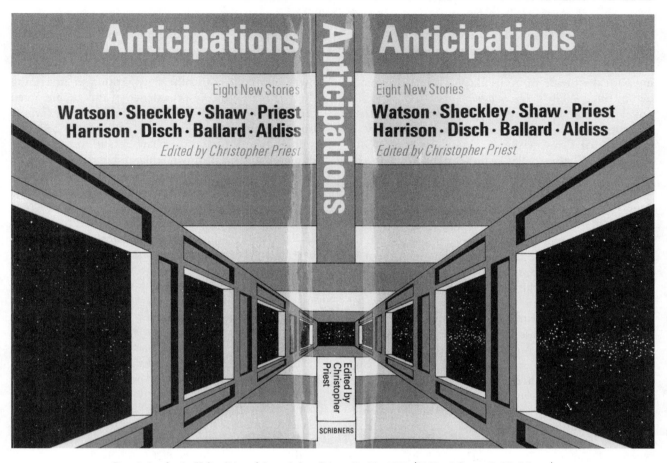

Dust jacket for the U.S. edition of the anthology Priest edited in 1978 (Richland County Public Library)

data of "fact" and of "fantasy" intermingle—his "real" girlfriend and his "fantasy" girlfriend especially interchange roles—so that neither he nor the reader knows which is which. Priest's novel ends with the same incomplete sentence that Sinclair's narrative does, developing a circularity that asks the questions: What is reality? What is fantasy? What is memory? What is identity? The novel is ultimately frustrating and inconclusive but fascinating, and it won an Australian Ditmar Award for Best International Fiction in 1982.

Equally self-involved and fascinatingly frustrating is *The Glamour* (1984), which Priest regards as forming a triptych with *A Dream of Wessex* and *The Affirmation*. Insisting on the spelling *glamour* to express the ambiguity of the arcane and Hollywood meanings of the word, Priest has written another mystery of a man's search for his own identity. Richard Grey, a freelance news photographer, is recovering in a convalescent home after having been injured by an Irish Republican Army bomb that has caused him to lose his memory and, with it, his past identity. His psychiatrist, using hypnosis, causes him not to see a

woman who is in the room; this experiment is eerily repeated later when a girlfriend, Susan, tries to fill in his missing memories, including the fact that she and he both have "glamour," the ability to become unnoticed and even invisible to others. She also reveals that she is haunted by another lover, Niall, who has even stronger glamour. Richard finds all this information hard to believe and does not truly remember it, even though she demonstrates, in situations also involving voyeurism. He also finds the triangle—Niall, Susan, and himself—unendurable. Various discrepancies in Richard's returning memories of his time with Susan and her own account of this period, including a postcard that he remembers having sent her but which he later finds among his own possessions, raise questions about the relationships between memory, reality, and fiction. Finally, Niall reveals that he has been writing the whole account and that Richard and Susan are characters within the fiction he has been creating. The novel reveals the malleability of truth and fiction, of memory and perceptions of reality, and asks to what extent humans create and edit themselves by selective memory and imagination. Or are they the product of other people's views? Is the postmodern technique of reader response limited to critical theory, or is it a creative mechanism in the real world? Although he is working with the theme of invisibility, a staple of science fiction since Wells's *The Invisible Man* (1897), Priest's novel can be considered science fiction only by stretching the boundaries of the genre. But that is exactly what Priest wishes to do; in his essay "Outside the Whale" (1980) he explained why he resigned from the Science Fiction Writers of America and attacked the Nebula Awards process as well as American chauvinism in science fiction and the coarsening of the genre.

Priest's novel *The Quiet Woman* (1990) is also on the fringes of science fiction, set in a small town in Wiltshire that has been largely evacuated because of a nuclear reactor accident in France. The main character, Alice Stockton, who writes biographies of women under her former married name, Alice Hazledine, has had her latest manuscript confiscated by the Home Office for no apparent reason. While hoping to hear from her agent about publication and pay, she learns that her quiet, grandmotherly neighbor Eleanor Hamilton has been murdered. This news increases Alice's previous desire to write a biography of Eleanor, who wrote popular, gentle children's fiction yet was active on the Campaign for Nuclear Disarmament. Eleanor's death brings Alice into contact with Gordon Sinclair (also known as Peter Hamilton), who claims to be Eleanor's younger son, her husband and elder son having been killed in a Ferris-wheel accident years previously. Gordon narrates some parts of the novel in the first person, and readers learn that he is a daydreamer and an information manager who has weird experiences, such as seeing huge, spinning cylinders that make circles in the ground and then fly out of sight. Consequently, readers never know what parts of his narrative, including explicit sadomasochistic sex activities with Alice Hazledine, are factual. Nor do they know for sure whether he uses his access to computers to destroy Alice's credit rating and reputation, nor whether he is really Eleanor's son, nor whether, as seems possible, he is the one who murdered her. Other parts of the novel are narrated in the third person from Alice Stockton's point of view; these present a much different Alice, a healthily sensual divorcée who rejects Gordon but enters into a relationship with Tom Davies, a technical writer and editor. Because all of the characters are writers, editors, and/or information managers, they manipulate the evidence in ways that leave readers unsure, as in previous Priest novels, about objective fact within the fiction. There is a quiet horror in the power of technology, especially computers, to alter identity by editing official and economic records. The emphasis throughout the novel is on creating and editing one's own life or those of others by writing or imagining them. Because of the prevalence of this theme, even the "happy" ending in which Alice apparently winds up in contented association with Tom becomes ambiguous. Although the characters in this novel are dynamic and well drawn, this ambiguity shades the reader's belief in their reality while, at the same time, it raises Priest's typical speculations about the relationship of fact to fiction.

Priest's next novel, *The Prestige* (1995), returns to the world of illusions. A journalist, convinced he has an unknown twin somewhere, searches for him but instead discovers that he is descended from a stage magician who, a century earlier, had perfected an illusion of instantaneous "transportation" from place to place. The journalist encounters a young woman who, coincidentally, is descended from his ancestor's bitter rival who had developed the same trick. In both the present and the past, the characters try to discover the secrets of these illusions. *The Prestige* displays characteristic Priestian ambiguity, complete with literary allusions to *The Invisible Man,* Robert Louis Stevenson's *The Strange Case of Dr. Jekyll and Mr. Hyde* (1886), and other classic science fiction and fictionalized science fact (such as the presence of inventor and electrical engineer Nikola Tesla). The novel won the 1995 James Tait Black Memorial Prize for Fiction and the 1996 World Fantasy Award for Best Novel. As in *The Glamour,* the title of *The Prestige* reflects Priest's concern with appearance and reality, especially that "magically" created by art. Priest's art is both intellectual and complex in characterization.

In 1998 Priest published *The Extremes,* a novel focusing on an FBI agent whose husband is killed. Haunted by her loss, she explores a kind of virtual-reality program that allows her to relive the event from a variety of perspectives, drawn from witnesses' memories. The reviewer for *The Independent* (London) said of the novel, "Swift, haunting, cruel and kind, *The Extremes* is a guidance manual for the maze we face," and *SFX* called the novel "A vital contribution from a key British writer." *The Extremes* won the BSFA award and was nominated for the Arthur C. Clarke award.

Priest returned to familiar territory with *The Dream Archipelago* (1999), a collection of six linked stories, further exploring the fantasy landscape of *An Infinite Summer* and *The Affirmation.* Also in 1999, he pseudonymously published a novelization of David Cronenberg's science-fictional film *eXistenZ* (1999).

His next novel, *The Separation,* will be published in late 2002.

Christopher Priest is a significant figure in British fantasy and science fiction. His individual style, his imaginative ideas, and his unwillingness to abide by standard genre conventions have earned ever-increasing critical acclaim.

Interviews:

Charles Platt, "Christopher Priest," in his *Dream Makers,* volume 2 (New York: Berkley, 1983), pp. 25–33;

Johan Thielemans, "Interviews with Chris Priest and Jack Vance," in *Just the Other Day,* edited by Luk De Vos (Antwerp: Restant, 1985), pp. 481–494;

Lisa Appignanesi, Interview with Brian Aldiss and Christopher Priest, *The Anthony Roland Collection of Films on Art* [VHS videotape] (London & Northbrook, Ill.: Institute of Contemporary Arts Video, 1986);

David Langford, "Christopher Priest Interview," *Ansible,* September 1995 <http://www.ansible.demon.co.uk/writing/cpriest.html>;

Graham Dickson, "A Quick Chat with Christopher Priest," *Richmond Review* <http://www.richmondreview.co.uk/features/priestint.html>;

Paul Kincaid, "Throwing Away the Orthodoxy," *Vector,* 206 (July/August 1999).

References:

Hélène Auffret, "Science Fiction bien tempérée ou l'Art de la Fugue," *Etudes Anglais,* 36 (April/September 1983): 181–196;

Max Duparray, "Itinéraires iteratifs: Reécrire le voyage fantastique à la fin du XXe siècle: *The Affirmation,* de Christopher Priest," in *Le Voyage Romantique et ses reécritures,* edited by Christian La Cassagnère (Clermont-Ferrand: Faculté des Lettres et Sciences Humaines de Clermont-Ferrand, 1987), pp. 289–298;

John Fletcher, "Cultural Pessimists: The Tradition of Christopher Priest's Fiction," *International Fiction Review,* 3 (January 1979): 20–24;

Hélène Greven-Borde, "Utopie et science-fiction: le discours des bâtisseurs de cités," *Etudes Anglais,* 41 (July/September 1988): 272–290;

Paul Kincaid, "Mirrors, Doubles, Twins: Patterns in the Fiction of Christopher Priest: 1. In the Dreamtime," *Vector,* 206 (July/August 1999);

Kincaid, "Mirrors, Doubles, Twins: Patterns in the Fiction of Christopher Priest: 2. In the Realtime," *Vector,* 209 (January/February 2000);

Kincaid, "Only Connect: Psychology and Politics in the Work of Christopher Priest," *Foundation,* 52 (Summer 1991): 42–53;

Ludmila Lashku, "The Marriage of Fantasy and Psychology in the Works of Christopher Priest," *Foundation,* 50 (Autumn 1990): 52–60;

Marianne Leconte, "Les Ilots obsessionels de Christopher Priest," in *Le Livre d'Or de la Science Fiction: Christopher Priest,* edited by Leconte (Paris: Presses Pocket, 1980), pp. 7–37;

Nicholas Ruddick, *Christopher Priest* (Mercer Island, Wash.: Starmont, 1989);

Ruddick, "Out of the Gernsbackian Slime: Christopher Priest's Abandonment of Science Fiction," *Modern Fiction Studies,* 32 (Spring 1986): 43–52;

David Wingrove, "Legerdemain: The Fiction of Christopher Priest," *Vector,* 93 (May/June 1979): 3–9.

Keith Roberts

(20 September 1935 – 5 October 2000)

F. Brett Cox

BOOKS: *The Furies* (London: Hart-Davis, 1966; New York: Berkley, 1966);

Pavane (London: Hart-Davis, 1968; expanded edition, Garden City, N.Y.: Doubleday, 1968);

The Inner Wheel (London: Hart-Davis, 1970; Garden City, N.Y.: Doubleday, 1970);

Anita (New York: Ace, 1970; London: Millington, 1976; expanded edition, Philadelphia: Owlswick Press, 1990);

The Boat of Fate: An Historical Novel (London: Hutchinson, 1971; Englewood Cliffs, N.J.: Prentice-Hall, 1974);

Machines and Men: Science Fiction Stories (London: Hutchinson, 1973);

The Chalk Giants (London: Hutchinson, 1974; abridged edition, New York: Putnam, 1975);

The Grain Kings: SF Stories (London: Hutchinson, 1976);

The Passing of the Dragons: The Short Fiction of Keith Roberts (New York: Berkley, 1977);

Ladies from Hell (London: Gollancz, 1979);

Molly Zero (London: Gollancz, 1980);

Kiteworld (London: Gollancz, 1985; New York: Arbor House, 1986);

The Lordly Ones (London: Gollancz, 1986);

Kaeti and Company (Salisbury, U.K.: Kerosina, 1986; Berkeley Heights, N.J.: Wildside, 2000);

Kaeti's Apocalypse (Salisbury, U.K.: Kerosina, 1986);

Gráinne (Salisbury, U.K.: Kerosina, 1987);

A Heron Caught in Weeds: Poems, edited by James Goddard (Salisbury, U.K.: Kerosina, 1987);

Irish Encounters: A Short Travel (Salisbury, U.K.: Kerosina, 1988);

The Natural History of the P.H. (Salisbury, U.K.: Kerosina, 1988);

The Road to Paradise: A Novel (Salisbury, U.K.: Kerosina, 1988);

The Event (Scotforth, U.K.: Morrigan, 1989);

Winterwood and Other Hauntings (Scotforth, U.K.: Morrigan, 1989);

Kaeti on Tour (London: Sirius, 1992);

Lemady: Episodes of a Writer's Life (San Bernardino, Cal.: Borgo Press, 1997).

Keith Roberts, 1986 (from Locus, *November 2000)*

SELECTED PERIODICAL PUBLICATIONS–UNCOLLECTED: "The Chalk Giant: Reflections by Keith Roberts," *Vector,* no. 132 (June/July 1986): 6–8;

"Kaeti and Kerosina," *Vector,* no. 132 (June/July 1986): 9–11;

Letter to the editor, *Ansible,* 78 (January 1994);

Drek Yarman, Spectrum SF, no. 1 (February 2000): 4–59; no. 2 (April 2000): 37–63; no. 3 (July 2000): 79–137);

"Virtual Reality," *Spectrum SF,* no. 4 (November 2000): 81–105.

American author and editor Gardner Dozois has called Keith Roberts "one of the most powerful talents to enter the field in the past thirty years," while Canadian author and academic Douglas Barbour, writing in the 1986 edition of *Twentieth-Century Science Fiction Writ-*

ers, considers Roberts "the Thomas Hardy of Science Fiction." British editor Malcolm Edwards declared Roberts's best-known work, *Pavane* (1968), "one of the finest SF novels ever written" (*Ansible,* November 2000), and American author and critic Algis Budrys pronounced Roberts "the best English SF writer" (*The Magazine of Fantasy and Science Fiction,* February 1978). Despite such high praise, Roberts has been, as Dozois notes, a "severely underappreciated author." Aside from three British Science Fiction Association Awards (for the short stories "Kitemaster" and "Kaeti and the Hangman" and the novel *Gráinne,* 1987), two nominations for the Science Fiction Writers of America Nebula Award (for the novellas "The God House" and "The Tiger Sweater"), and one nomination for the Hugo Award of the World Science Fiction Convention (for the short story "The Lordly Ones"), he did not receive any major science-fiction honors. After 1985 almost all his books appeared only in small-press British editions, and after 1977 only three of his books were published in the United States.

Part of the reason for Roberts's lack of commercial success may be found in Budrys's comment that "Keith Roberts at anything less than novel length can do it all." Historically, science-fiction writers have advanced their craft through short fiction and their careers through novels. Only a small handful of writers, most notably Ray Bradbury and Harlan Ellison, have become well known without regularly producing novels. Of Roberts's twenty-four published books, only seven are full-length novels, and of these, all but two— *The Furies* (1966) and *Gráinne*—are constructed from shorter works. (*Molly Zero* [1980] is an expansion of an earlier novella.) Indeed, as Nicholas Ruddick has noted, Roberts's longest and most ambitious books—*Pavane, The Chalk Giants* (1974), and *Kiteworld* (1985)—are not really novels as such, but "story cycles" in the manner of Arthurian tales. As Ruddick also says, Roberts was never overly concerned with generic boundaries, producing "writerly" texts that are "full of discontinuities with which one must struggle to make a meaning"— hardly a formula to achieve popular acclaim. Moreover, the most successful British science-fiction writers, such as Arthur C. Clarke or Brian W. Aldiss, maintain a certain degree of internationalism in their work. For Roberts, on the other hand, England is not merely the country of his birth, but the subject and sensibility of his fiction, a characteristic that may limit its appeal to the American mass market. To his credit, Roberts seldom strayed from his determinedly intricate, even problematic, narratives or his profound sense of place, creating a substantial body of work that includes some of the most powerful and literate science-fiction writing ever produced.

Keith John Kingston Roberts was born in Kettering, Northamptonshire, on 20 September 1935, to Lance John Kingston Roberts and Laura Ellen Well Roberts. His father was in the cinema business; his mother was a nurse. After receiving the National Diploma in Design from the Northampton School of Art in 1956, Roberts studied at Leicester College of Art in 1956–1957 and subsequently held several art-related jobs, including work at animated-movie studios and an advertising agency. His background in art informs his writing in his painterly attention to landscape detail and his frequent use of characters who are artists.

After establishing himself as a writer, Roberts continued to pursue a career as an artist, designing most of the cover art for the British magazine *Science Fantasy* (later titled *SF Impulse*) during the mid 1960s. (He also served as associate editor of the magazine in 1965–1966 and as editor from 1966 until its demise in 1967.) Roberts also illustrated his own stories and stories by other writers in Michael Moorcock's *New Worlds Quarterly* during the 1970s, and he illustrated several of his own books.

Roberts's first published story, "Escapism," which appeared in the September 1964 issue of *Science Fantasy,* marked the beginning of an extremely prolific period that lasted into the mid 1970s. During this time, Roberts published dozens of stories, some under pseudonyms, and most found their way, in one form or another, into the eight books he had published by 1976.

Roberts's preoccupation with his native land became something seldom found in science fiction: a vision, not of conservative or reactionary politics, but of a genuine historical conservatism. For Roberts, history was a wheel that inevitably returned to its beginning; as Paul Kincaid has observed, Roberts's imaginary futures likewise "roll around in great circles to, at best, the same point." In that sense, there is, in the long run, nothing to worry about: as the title character of *Gráinne* observes, "What's done can never be undone. It's always there." Yet, at Roberts's point in the circle, the second half of the twentieth century, there were forces at work that threatened to sunder human beings from their past and their individual selves. To deal with these forces, which have the potential of creating nuclear disaster or Orwellian bureaucracy, is to make moral choices that will carry humanity into the future and affect the final outcome, but it is also to acknowledge, or discover, the earlier time and place from which one sprang. For Roberts, this point of origin was ancient Britain, especially as embodied in the mythic landscape of southwest England. As he stated in "The Mayday" (included in *Anita,* 1970),

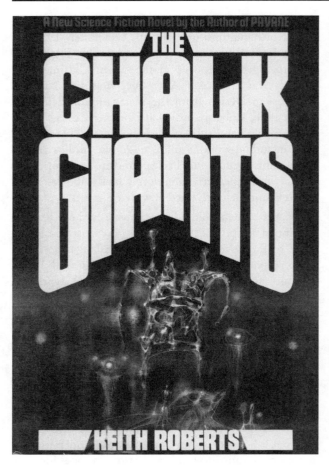

Dust jacket for the abridged, U.S. edition of Roberts's 1974 novel, about the re-emergence of British civilization after a nuclear war (Richland County Public Library)

The West Country was thick with magic; she heard the soundless roaring of the hills as they butted the sea, felt the rage of giants lying buried, all buckled and distorted by the strata, their pictures carved above them like x-rays in the turf. Old voices rang from barrows atop windy downs, thudded from underground where fossils lay like coiled watch springs in the rocks. She sensed the power of the Great Henge away to the north, the dumb stone anger of Corfe; and from far in the west, where the place names clashed and tinkled like ancient weapons, came the blue shouting of the Great One, the Thing men sometimes called Merlin.

Roberts expresses this prelapsarian impulse not only through his rich evocations of his native landscape but also through his other obsession: the recurrent figure of a woman variously known as the Ultimate Woman, the Multi-Girl, or the Primitive Heroine; a pure or nearly pure Celt, beautiful, intelligent, rebellious, who embodies the landscape of Britain even as that landscape embodies the wheel of history.

All these concerns are present, in somewhat embryonic form, in Roberts's first novel, *The Furies*. An homage to the school of British disaster novels exemplified by the works of John Wyndham, *The Furies* depicts a contemporary Britain under siege by aliens. After nuclear-bomb tests gone awry loosen them from their hidden observations of Earth, these beings assume the form of giant wasps and lay waste to England and its inhabitants. The novel follows the artist- narrator and a small group of survivors as they fight the wasps, witness the near-total destruction of their country, and finally win out, after the aliens collapse under the built-in limitations of the life form they have assumed. *The Furies* is an unexceptional example of its subgenre, marked by neither great originality nor insight, and it is of interest chiefly as an initial statement of Roberts's main concerns: England under threat, ordinary individuals whom extreme circumstances have forced to make fundamental choices, and, in the character of Pete, the first incarnation of the Primitive Heroine.

With his second novel, *Pavane,* Roberts clearly established himself as a major voice in science fiction, and it is largely on that novel that his reputation has rested. The prologue sets up a world in which Elizabeth I was assassinated; the Spanish Armada was victorious; and the Western world has remained under the absolute domination of the Catholic Church through the twentieth century. In this world, technology has developed only at the pleasure of the Church; the chief means of long-distance transportation and communication are steam-powered, trackless locomotives and an intricate network of semaphore towers. One of the chief pleasures of the book lies in Roberts's detailed and ingenious working out of these alternate technologies and their consequences. For example, the semaphore network gives rise to an elite Guild of Signallers, the only group able to operate largely outside the umbrella of the Church. However, Roberts's main concern is not with the hardware of this world or its political and religious infrastructure, but the people who inhabit it. Each of the stories in the *Pavane* cycle tells of individuals and their responses to the exigencies of their world: Jesse Strange, whose obsession with a barmaid drives him to build a shipping empire; Brother John, an artist-monk who rebels against the Church after being forced to record the horrors of the Inquisition; and Lady Eleanor, who defends Corfe Castle against the incursions of the Church and sparks her own rebellion. The narrative movement of *Pavane* is toward an emancipation from the oppressive rule of the Catholic Church.

The coda to *Pavane* implies that the novel describes not an alternate history of the modern world, but a future history taking place after the collapse of the present civilization, replicating–but not literally repeating–the progress of an earlier time. Thus, the attempts of the Church to retard the growth of technology are aimed at averting a repetition of earlier disasters: "Did she oppress? Did she hang and burn? A little, yes. But there was no Belsen. No Buchenwald." Roberts has admitted that this discontinuity between prologue and coda is "a structural flaw," and critics have disagreed as to whether *Pavane* is an "alternate" or "future" history, and to what extent, if any, this ambiguity is a weakness in the novel.

Roberts's inspiration for *Pavane* was a barmaid's claim that she was the reincarnation of Lady Mary Bankes, who defended Corfe Castle during the siege of 1643, and in Roberts's words, the novel was fueled by "the sheer contrast between that great growing ruin and the modern tourists." The result is Roberts's most powerful evocation of Eternal England, whose citizens are aided in their revolt against an oppressive Church by fairies of the heath, who retain the ancient knowledge that ruled before the Church and whose central image is the iconic Corfe Castle, which "seemed to ride not a hill but a flaw in the timestream, a node of quiet from which possibilities might spread out as limitless as the journeyings of the sun."

Roberts's next novel, *The Inner Wheel* (1970), is reminiscent in structure and subject matter of Theodore Sturgeon's *More Than Human* (1953); each is composed of three loosely linked novellas that deal with aspects of the linking of disparately "gifted" people into a single gestalt intelligence. In Roberts's novel, "The Inner Wheel" introduces Jimmy Stringer, a young artist who retreats to a small town in the south of England and encounters the gestalt intelligence as a hostile force from which he rescues Anne, the woman he has come to love. "The Death of Libby Maynard" is the life history of the gestalt's telepath, while in "The Everything Man" Jimmy and Anne are reconciled with the gestalt and work actively with it to forestall the world's descent into nuclear war. In "The Death of Libby Maynard" the first-person portrait of a telepath coming to terms with her extraordinary and alienating ability is quite powerful, but the other two sections of the novel demonstrate none of the lyric power, compelling characterization, or conceptual audacity of *Pavane,* and the novel as a whole cannot be counted a success.

Roberts abandoned science fiction while holding on to his obsessions in his next novel, *The Boat of Fate* (1971), an historical novel set in Roman Britain. With *The Chalk Giants,* however, Roberts picked up where he left off with *Pavane,* producing a novel that recalls the earlier book in both structure and theme. In fact, Roberts labeled *The Chalk Giants* a "black *Pavane*." As in the earlier novel, the initial movement in *The Chalk Giants* stems from unrequited passion–in this case, that of the relentlessly unexceptional Stan Potts for the beautiful Martine. In the first two sections of the novel Stan, Martine, and several of her bohemian friends attempt to escape a looming disaster that threatens England. In the third section the disaster–a nuclear war–has happened, and the remainder of the book traces the re-emergence of civilization in stories governed by the central image of the prehistoric chalk carvings of the British uplands (which, for the people of postapocalypse Britain, are the "giants" of the preapocalypse) and the "Multi-Girl" Martine, who recurs throughout the novel in various guises, such as acolyte, priestess, and crone. By the end of the final section, there is a promise of resolution among the warring factions, as the victorious King Marck stands in the shadow of Corfe Gate.

The Chalk Giants is complicated by the presence of linking sections between the main stories. In these links, set before the catastrophe, Stan Potts is caught in a traffic jam and experiencing a series of visions that seem to foretell the events of the main narratives. Thus, the novel is not merely a string of related stories but a complex and indeterminate narrative that is both future history and individual dream, taking the reader far into a future that recapitulates the past only to return the reader to exactly where he or she started, as the final linking section is a restatement of the first. Perhaps this complexity contributed to the extremes of critical response to the novel. Writing in *The New York Times Book Review* (14 September 1975), Gerald Jonas found the book "too ambitious" but "far more successful than it has any right to be." Ruddick has argued that *The Chalk Giants* is Roberts's best work, but other critics agree with David I. Masson, who titled his review of the novel "A Bloody Muddle" (*Foundation,* March 1975). Complicating the reception of the novel still further is the fact that it was published in the United States with the first two sections and all the linking material removed. *The Chalk Giants* does indeed include much writing of exceptional power and beauty, especially in the first two postapocalypse sections, "Monkey and Pru and Sal" and "The God House." However, a story cycle is only as strong as its stories. *Pavane* is regarded as a classic, in part because its individual stories are uniformly excellent, read together or separately. The final sections of *The Chalk Giants*–"The Beautiful Ones," "Rand, Rat, and the Dancing Man," and "Usk the Joke-man," which together make up more than half the book–may not be quite the "dismal Celtic fiction" they were labeled by *TLS: The Times Literary Supplement,* but they never really transcend the sword-and-sorcery aesthetic from which they are so heavily drawn, and the conceptual audacity of the linking sections is not enough to offset this weakness. *The Chalk Giants* is an

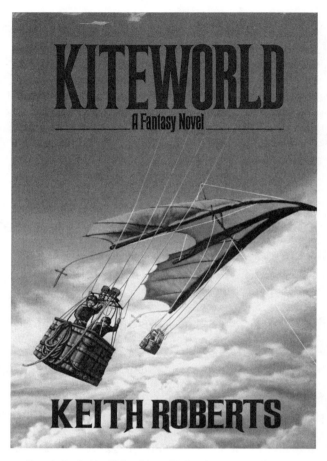

Dust jacket for the U.S. edition of Roberts's 1985 novel, set in a postapocalypse, preindustrial England (Richland County Public Library)

searing study of the primal forces of good and evil. Also appearing in this period was *Anita* (1970), a collection of linked stories about a witch. Although of varying quality, they skillfully present Roberts's views on contemporary England.

By the late 1970s Roberts had produced a substantial and ambitious body of work. Except for *Pavane* and *The Chalk Giants,* however, little of it had received much critical attention, and none of the books had been a great commercial success. Roberts was disappointed by this turn of events and outraged by the cuts in the American edition of *The Chalk Giants.* In a 1986 interview, he claimed that its publishers had "destroyed the book, and . . . also destroyed my American reputation." As a result, Roberts wrote less and turned increasingly to graphic art and advertising to make a living. The stories in *Ladies from Hell* (1979), all of which appeared in periodicals between 1975 and 1979, perhaps reflect these circumstances in their loosely shared background of an England that has either become—or is about to become—a Stalinist nightmare. In "Our Lady of Desperation," for example, so-called nonproductive people—such as artists—are taxed in excess of their total income and are assigned Overseers to monitor their work. In the best story of the collection, "The Big Fans," this dystopian element is relegated to the background, and Roberts combined his two greatest strengths in a story about an intricately detailed, high-tech wind-power project that rips a hole in the fabric of time and briefly warps the main characters back to ancient Britain. The tales in Roberts's last major collection of independent stories, *The Lordly Ones* (1986), are more diverse in background, tone, and overall quality. The title story, however—the first-person account of a slow-thinking man who continues his duties as a public-toilet attendant even after an unspecified, society-leveling catastrophe— is elegant and moving. This story and "Weihnachtsabend" are arguably Roberts's best individual works of short fiction.

Roberts's novel *Molly Zero* continues to treat his major themes but with a noticeably different formal approach. Unlike *Pavane* and *The Chalk Giants, Molly Zero* comprises six chapters forming a continuous narrative and making brilliant use of a second-person point of view. The background is the dystopian England that lies behind the stories in *Ladies from Hell.* This England enjoys a certain bottom-line prosperity, but its promising children are removed to Orwellian (if not Foucauldian) kibbutzim, and the country is under constant martial law. The novel is the story of Molly's coming of age as she and her rebellious boyfriend escape from their school and make their way through the various levels of British society, ending up as terrorists engaged in a futile attempt to undermine the state. Though *Molly*

admirable book and crucial to an understanding of Roberts's work, but it is only a mixed success.

At the same time Roberts was producing the stories that became his second, third, and fourth novels, he was also writing many independent stories, most of which were collected in *Machines and Men* (1973) and *The Grain Kings* (1976). (Some stories from each of these collections were republished in *The Passing of the Dragons: The Short Fiction of Keith Roberts,* 1977.) Roberts's stories that attempt more traditional science fiction and fantasy, such as the humorous "Boulter's Canaries" or the Asimovian "Synth," are for the most part unmemorable. Of far greater interest are stories such as "I Lose Medea," with its dream-like depiction of ordinary people caught up in an unexplained conflict; "The Grain Kings," a novella remarkable for its detailed extrapolation of combines the size of small cities, as well as for its unsettling misogynistic protagonist; and the extraordinary "Weihnachtsabend," which provides the alternate history of an England that capitulated to Nazi Germany before the start of World War II as a background to a

Zero is as obviously indebted to George Orwell and Anthony Burgess as *The Furies* is indebted to Wyndham, Roberts crafted a strikingly effective narrative. As Paul Kincaid has noted in his review of *Molly Zero* (*Vector,* October 1980), the novel is not only Molly's personal odyssey but also a survey of English society of the 1950s (as Molly gets a day job and lives with a stable middle-class family), 1960s (as Molly travels with a caravan of free-spirited gypsies), and 1970s (as Molly resides in a grim London and traffics with political terrorists). Molly is arguably Roberts's finest creation: another incarnation of the Primitive Heroine, but, unlike Martine or Gráinne, she is a flawed, sympathetic human being who never fades into archetype. Of all Roberts's "underappreciated" fiction, *Molly Zero,* his best-crafted novel, is perhaps his most unjustly neglected book.

Five years passed between *Molly Zero* and Roberts's next novel, *Kiteworld,* which returns to the structure and, to some extent, the plots of *Pavane* and *The Chalk Giants.* Once again, the novel is set in a postholocaust landscape–England, more or less–in which civilization has rebuilt itself to approximately pre-industrial levels while being ruled by an authoritarian religious bureaucracy. In *Kiteworld* the holocaust was nuclear, and the society that emerges is centered around a vast Kitecorps, elite forces whose motorless, tethered aircraft guard the realm against the Demons–barely remembered ICBMs–as well as mutants who inhabit an irradiated frontier. All in some way connected with the kites, the large cast of characters plays out intertwining personal dramas that, cumulatively, lead to increased dissent from the Church Variant and the promise of a less insular society.

While much of a piece with *Pavane* and *The Chalk Giants, Kiteworld* is a more conventional narrative than the earlier novels. The technology and sociology of the kite system are presented in acute detail–"worldbuilding" in the classic sense. This attention to detail combines with characters far more individuated than the iconic figures of *The Chalk Giants* to make *Kiteworld* more accessible to the general reader than much of Roberts's other work.

Yet, despite its reader-friendly elements, *Kiteworld* remains a dark book. The explicit, primal sexuality of *The Chalk Giants* becomes violent and appetitive in *Kiteworld,* in which the Lady Kerosina procures adolescent boys and girls, and the doomed Manning expresses his incestuous passion for his autistic sister, Tan, by beating her unconscious when he catches her with another man. As Ruddick notes, the true demons the Kites guard against are not from without but from within: "the self-destructive urge that once laid waste the world." Roberts shows greater compassion toward his characters in *Kiteworld* than in *The Chalk Giants,* to the point of constructing a deus ex machina ending that removes them from harm and suggests a sequel. The two most powerful characters in the book, Tan and Lady Kerosina, are further incarnations of the idealized Primitive Heroine: at one point, Manning describes his sister as "perfection . . . The First Woman of the myth, from whom sprang all the world." Yet, the women who incarnate this primal Female are afflicted with autism and pedophilia, making an already problematic strategy of characterization even more suspect.

By the mid 1980s, continued lack of commercial success and critical notice caused Roberts to threaten to give up writing altogether. In 1984, however, Anthony Burgess listed *Pavane* in his *Ninety-Nine Novels: The Best in English Since 1939*–a tribute that, according to Roberts, "got me back into print." Then, however, Roberts's career took a different turn. With one exception, the eleven books and chapbooks he produced after *The Lordly Ones* were all published by British small presses, most frequently Kerosina Books, which takes its name from a character in *Kiteworld.* As if to emphasize this turn away from mainstream commercial publishing, the books of this period were increasingly nongeneric, including poetry (*A Heron Caught in Weeds,* 1987), travel writing (*Irish Encounters,* 1988), and commentary on his own work (*The Natural History of the P.H.,* 1988), as well as a contemporary adventure-suspense novel (*The Road to Paradise,* 1988) and a collection of ghost stories (*Winterwood and Other Hauntings,* 1989). His two major works of the period–the novel *Gráinne* and the Kaeti stories (1986–1992)–turned the narrative discontinuities of his earlier work into self-referentiality, both to Roberts's biography and the biographies of his fictional creations.

It is intriguing that *Gráinne,* the most confessional and least generic of Roberts's works, is also his only award-winning novel. The protagonist, Alistair Bevan, refers to himself in the third person as he tells his life story to officials in a hospital where he is a patient. "Alistair Bevan" was one of Roberts's pseudonyms, and the first half of the novel is apparently taken from Roberts's own life. Bevan grows up in a small English town with a kindly father who runs a cinema (as did Roberts's father) and a harsh, tyrannical mother whom Bevan refers to as "the Mother"; he attends art school, works for an advertising agency, and becomes a free-lance writer. Bevan is haunted by Gráinne, a Celtic beauty with whom he has had a brief affair and who is, for him, "the ultimate Woman." In the second half of the book, Gráinne becomes a media celebrity and founds a self-help movement that points Britain in a different direction than it might otherwise have gone. As Bevan's inquisi-

THE Lordly ONES

A new collection by the author of **KITEWORLD**

KEITH ROBERTS

Dust jacket for the collection that features Roberts's story about a restroom attendant who continues doing his job after a major, unspecified catastrophe (Richland County Public Library)

tor puts it in the final sentence, "The next ten thousand years are going to be most interesting."

Gráinne is in many ways a culmination of the themes of Roberts's work. The brooding concern with the once and future England is pushed back to the nation's Celtic origins. Gráinne is named for a figure from Irish myth who bewitched her lover and caused him to betray his king. The penultimate action of the novel takes place as Bevan goes on a vision quest to Ireland. The indeterminacy of *The Chalk Giants* is taken to new extremes in *Gráinne* as Bevan's story is related in fragmentary memories whose veracity is by no means guaranteed. Gráinne is the ultimate incarnation of the Primitive Heroine, and the novel is, as critic John Clute noted in *Look at the Evidence* (1995), "an anguished submission to Woman as intoxicant and succubus, and as savior of these Isles one day." This aspect is both the strength and the weakness of the novel and perhaps of Roberts's work as a whole. J. G. Ballard once advised

writers to "trust your obsessions"; in doing so, Roberts frequently produced work of visionary power. Nonetheless, to turn a female human being into Woman, and to turn Woman into Savior, is a tricky business at best; unlike Lady Eleanor or Molly Zero, Gráinne is a symbol rather than a character.

A far more interesting character is Kaeti. The stories in *Kaeti and Company* (1986), *Kaeti's Apocalypse* (1986), and *Kaeti on Tour* (1992) present a cast of recurrent characters much like an acting troupe. In fact, in the linking sections with which Roberts connects his stories, the characters are referred to as "actors," and Kaeti converses directly with the author. ("'Who's the other girl?' she said. 'New actress,' I said. 'One-off. Guest performance.'") Such self-referentiality can easily degenerate into the coy mutterings of an author talking to himself because no one else is listening, but in this case the device does have a unifying effect on the stories, which otherwise do not portray Kaeti or her "cast" in any consistent fashion. Stories such as "Kaeti's Nights" (in *Kaeti and Company*) and "The Tiger Sweater" (in *Kaeti on Tour*) are some of Roberts's best fiction. Kaeti, although unquestionably another incarnation of the Primitive Heroine, is a more real and engaging character than Martine or Gráinne, and Roberts's obvious affection for his creation is well earned. And more than any other Roberts work, except perhaps *Molly Zero,* the Kaeti stories give a clear sense of the author's feelings about his country at the end of the twentieth century, feelings that are elegiac at best and depressed at worst. According to Clute, "the final sense of the book is that the vaudeville dance from world to world is, in the end, sisyphean. . . . *Kaeti on Tour* is a lament for the dying" (*The New York Review of Science Fiction,* July 1993).

In 1990 Roberts was diagnosed with multiple sclerosis; complications from the disease resulted in amputation of both his legs and prolonged stays in a residence hospital. The January 1994 issue of the British science-fiction newsletter *Ansible* published excerpts from a bitter letter in which, publicly acknowledging his illness for the first time, Roberts declared himself a "has been at the age of fifty-eight. . . . in effect I died in March 1990. . . . Having got myself blacklisted by the Establishment, it was unlikely I would ever publish again, in English at least; but this would not have been permitted anyway. In the Mother of Democracies, cripples are naturally not allowed to earn; that would be to rise above their station." Though these are the words of a man who does not expect to live much longer, Roberts survived for six years after writing this letter, during which time he published two final works.

In 1997 the American specialty publisher Borgo Press brought out *Lemady: Episodes of a Writer's Life,* a memoir whose "episodes," arranged in no particular chronological sequence, interweave Roberts's comments on writing, publishing, art, and his careers in all three with brief narratives about his travels around England with Lemady, the woman who "informed all but a couple of my books." Roberts's comments on his work are often of interest. He claimed that his work after *The Furies* was seldom really science fiction, and his thoughts on writing and art reveal a writer determined to avoid both "The determined hopelessness of the kitchen sink school" and "the steely hygiene of romantic fiction." The sections concerning Lemady, however, although arguably the "neatly drawn and perfectly captured vignettes" the dust-jacket copy declares them, are presented with a clinical detachment that leaves the reader with no real sense of who Lemady is, or if Roberts regards her, finally, as anything other than a muse. In 2000 a new British magazine, *Spectrum SF,* serialized *Drek Yarman,* a sequel to *Kiteworld,* and published "Virtual Reality," a novelette featuring Norma, the daughter of Roberts's earlier heroine Kaeti. Neither *Lemady* nor the magazine fiction received any significant notice within the science-fiction community. On 5 October 2000, Roberts died of complications from pneumonia and bronchitis.

Keith Roberts's career is an object lesson in the dangers faced by authors who remain true to their visions even though they are unappreciated by wide audiences. While not wholly successful work, *The Chalk Giants, Kiteworld,* and *Gráinne* remain far richer and more interesting than many award winners, and his best work—*Pavane, Molly Zero,* "Monkey and Pru and Sal," "Weihnachtsabend," "The Big Fans," and "The Lordly Ones"—stands among the best science-fiction works produced. In 2000 *Pavane* was republished in both the United States and United Kingdom, and several of Roberts's other books were made available in the United States by the "print-on-demand" publisher Wildside Press. Admirers of Roberts's fiction hope this event signals an increase in attention to the work of a gifted writer.

Interviews:

Paul Kincaid, "Of Men and Machines: Keith Roberts Interviewed," *Vector,* 108 (1982): 6–12;

Charles Platt, "Keith Roberts," in his *Dream Makers II: The Uncommon Men and Women Who Write Science Fiction* (New York: Berkley, 1983);

Kincaid, "Mosaic of Words: An Interview of Keith Roberts," *Vector,* 132 (June/July 1986): 2–5.

References:

John Clute, *Look at the Evidence: Essays and Reviews* (Brooklyn, N.Y.: Serconia, 1995), p. 21;

Gardner Dozois, Introduction to "The Lady Margaret," in *Modern Classics of Science Fiction,* edited by Dozois (New York: St. Martin's Press, 1991), pp. 196–197;

L. J. Hurst, "A Timeless Dance: Keith Roberts' *Pavane* Re-Examined," *Vector,* no. 124/125 (April/May 1985): 17–19;

Paul Kincaid, "Future Historical: The Fiction of Keith Roberts," *Steam Engine Time,* no. 3 (December 2001): 20–24;

Kincaid, "Second Glance," *Vector,* no. 126 (June/July 1985): 11;

Bernie Peek, "Exercises in Landscape: An Overview of the Works of Keith Roberts," *Vector,* no. 132 (June/July 1986): 12–13;

Nicholas Ruddick, "Flaws in the Timestream: Unity and Disunity in Keith Roberts' Story-Cycles," *Foundation,* 45 (1989): 38–49; "Flaws in the Timestream, Part Two," *Foundation,* 46 (1989): 14–26; "Flaws in the Timestream (Conclusion)," *Foundation,* 47 (1989–1990): 33–42.

Arthur Sellings
(Arthur Gordon Ley)
(31 May 1911 – 24 September 1968)

Gina Macdonald
Nicholls State University

BOOKS: *Time Transfer and Other Stories* (London: Joseph, 1956);

Telepath (New York: Ballantine, 1962); republished as *The Silent Speakers* (London: Dobson, 1963);

The Uncensored Man (London: Dobson, 1964; New York: Berkley, 1967);

The Quy Effect (London: Dobson, 1966; New York: Berkley, 1967);

Intermind, as Ray Luther (New York: Banner, 1967); as Arthur Sellings (London: Dobson, 1969);

The Long Eureka: A Collection of Short Stories (London: Dobson, 1968);

The Power of X (London: Dobson, 1968; New York: Berkley, 1970);

Junk Day (London: Dobson, 1970).

OTHER: "The Mission," in *A.D. 2500: The Observer Prize Stories, 1954* (London: Heinemann, 1955);

"The Outstretched Hand," in *The Best of New Worlds,* edited by Michael Moorcock (London: Compact, 1965);

"Gifts of the Gods," in *New Writings in SF 9,* edited by John Carnell (London: Dobson, 1966); republished as *New Writings in SF 7* (New York: Bantam, 1971);

"The Power of Y," in *SF Reprise 12,* edited by Moorcock (London: Compact, 1966);

"That Evening Sun Go Down," in *Gods for Tomorrow,* edited by Hans Stefan Santesson (New York: Award, 1967);

"The Last Time Around," in *New Writings in SF 12,* edited by Carnell (London: Dobson, 1968);

"The Trial," in *New Writings in SF 15,* edited by Carnell (London: Dobson, 1969);

"The Key of the Door," in *New Worlds Quarterly No. 2* (London: Sphere, 1971);

"Starting Course," in *The Best of British SF 2,* edited by Mike Ashley (London: Futura, 1977).

SELECTED PERIODICAL PUBLICATIONS–UNCOLLECTED: "The Boys from Vespis," *Galaxy Science Fiction* (February 1954);

"The Departed," *Galaxy Science Fiction* (August 1954);

"The Cautious Invaders," *Imagination,* 5 (October 1954);

"Cry Wolf," *Nebula Science Fiction,* 17 (July 1956);

"The Masters," *New Worlds,* 17 (July 1956);

"The Warriors," *New Worlds,* 17 (August 1956);

"Armistice," *Nebula Science Fiction,* no. 18 (November 1956);

"Fresh Start," *New Worlds Quarterly,* 21 (July 1957);

"The Well-Trained Heroes," *Galaxy Science Fiction* (June 1964);

"The Tinplate Teleologist," *Worlds of Tomorrow,* 3, no. 3 (1965);

"Crack in the Shield," *Magazine of Fantasy and Science Fiction,* 34 (January 1968);

"The Legend and the Chemistry," *Magazine of Fantasy and Science Fiction,* 36 (January 1969);

"The Dodgers," *Fantastic,* 18 (April 1969): 11–19.

Arthur Sellings was a respected British scientific researcher and science-fiction writer, noted for his studies of human adaptability in the face of physical, psychological, and cultural challenges–especially those involving reconsideration of a priori premises and adjustment to frightening shifts of perception, alien races, and alien environments. His carefully crafted science fiction deals with extrasensory perception, generational starships, travel among dimensions or times, antigravity, the transforming power of drugs, memory transfer, genetic engineering, mutation, collective racial memory, and postholocaust nightmares. His novels are particularly notable for their convincing characterization, compelling plots, irony, and humor. Critics have praised their "precision," "vision," and "insight."

Though Sellings's real name is sometimes listed as Robert Arthur Ley, most sources, including his wife, call him Arthur Gordon Ley. In addition to the pseudonym Arthur Sellings, he used the pen names Ray Luther and Martin Luther. There is also some disagreement about his birth date. His wife has said he was born in 1911, but 1921 is listed in some sources. The son of Kent Ley and Stella Grace (Sellings) Ley, Arthur Sellings was born and raised in Tunbridge Wells, Kent, spent most of his life there, and died in Worthing, Sussex. He married Gladys Pamela Judge on 18 August 1945. A long-time book dealer, art dealer, and antiquarian, Sellings worked from 1955 to 1968 as a scientific researcher for the British government. He had already written science-fiction short stories in the early 1950s, but his scientific research inspired longer, more memorable fiction.

Sellings's stories are set in troubling times, such as eras of holocaust or alien confrontation, and they feature scientific advances that could prove more dangerous than beneficial. Exploring human reactions to the unfamiliar and unknown, on Earth and in outer space, he conceived of humankind's essential self—in both its strengths and its weaknesses—as remaining basically intact despite a gradual evolution in anatomy, intellectual capabilities, culture, and custom. His future humans may take unrecognizable, apparently alien, physical forms, but their inner selves seem familiar to the reader. Sellings's fiction speculates about the human potential for development of characteristics such as telepathic and telekinetic abilities, shape changing (like that in American Indian legends), and psychic skills capable of spanning dimensions or altering reality. Sellings's heroes may initially seem ordinary, but they prove extraordinary in their commitment and determination. Whether men of integrity or anti-authoritarian rascals, they have adventuresome minds and accept intellectual challenges that others ignore.

Sellings first explored science-fiction themes in short stories, some of which were collected in *Time Transfer and Other Stories* (1956) and *The Long Eureka: A Collection of Short Stories* (1968) while others remain scattered. Some of these early stories are only borderline science fiction. For example, "The Scene Shifter" (first published in *Star Science Fiction Stories No. 5* [1959]; collected in *The Long Eureka*), describes a major Hollywood movie studio, Mammoth, in a panic because recent releases have been travesties of the originals. The studio sleuth finally tracks down the culprit: a long-time movie fan who, fed up with uninspired, cliché-ridden motion pictures, has been mentally projecting onto celluloid what he wants to see; his latent telepathic skills awaken similar skills in others. Two stories collected in *Time Transfer*, "The Figment" (*Fantastic Universe*, February 1955) and "The Haunting" (*Authentic*, no. 38 [1953]), are ghost stories, with the "ghost" in the first a

Dust jacket for the British edition of Sellings's 1962 novel, published in the United States as Telepath (Richland County Public Library)

human stuck in another dimension and that of the second an astral projection with dire warnings from the future. Often these stories include a comic touch, as in "The Long Eureka" (*Science Fantasy*, no. 26 [1959]), in which the discoverer of an immortality elixir spends four hundred years trying to convince humans his elixir works; he finally discovers that his only believers are an alien race of immortals. In "The Boy Friends" asexual Vesian visitors, disguised as attractive males, deal with human male jealousy by assuming stunning female shapes. In "The Escape Mechanism" (*Fantastic Universe*, August 1955; collected in *Time Transfer*) a skeptical psychiatrist unwittingly helps a henpecked husband escape to bliss in another dimension, while in "One Across" (*Galaxy*, May 1956; collected in *The Long Eureka*) an obsessed crossword-puzzle addict solves a puzzle that flings him into a barren fourth dimension and the hands of a nineteenth-century feminist with designs on his genes. Cross-cultural misunderstandings also produce humor. The aliens in "Control Room" (collected in *Time Transfer*) are disdainful of human achievement, which they constantly misinterpret, but they are frightened away by pinball machines, which they mistake for highly sophisticated space-control systems. In "Pentagram" (collected in *Time Transfer*) the human clusters, an urban division of labor carried to extremes, find the self-sufficiency of single-unit country people sexually stimulating but ultimately terrifying.

Some of Sellings's short stories focus on robots and androids. In "Trade-In" (collected in *The Long Eureka*) an aging robot, replaced by an updated series, has twenty-one days to find a financial backer or join the scrap heap; his discovery of latent artistic talents both makes and breaks his new patron. Sometimes the stories take a humorous view of robots putting human workers out of business. In "Categorical Imperative" (first published as "The Category Inventors," *Galaxy*, February 1956; collected in *Time Transfer*) humans who have lost jobs to robots must find themselves previously nonexisting job titles. While on a drinking binge two disgruntled failures invent "Umbrological Parallax Tracer" and "U.P. Co-relator," titles that earn them a new office, a steady salary, and the chance to discover a new science. The stories also express concerns about the relationships of humans and robots. "Starting Course" (in *The Best of British SF 2*, 1977) traces the integration of androids into society, while in "The Proxies" (*If*, October 1955; collected in *Time Transfer*) robots are the only representatives of Earth in space travel. Because human contact with aliens encourages the worst of human colonialist tendencies, the robots in "The Proxies" must anticipate and counter such negatives, thus compelling humankind to live up to the high ideals instilled in robot programming. "A Start in Life" (*Galaxy*, September 1954; collected in *Time Transfer*) describes a nightmarish possibility: a plague on a starship wipes out the entire adult population and leaves five-year-old children unharmed and without human supervision. Their rearing and training is left to robots during a preprogrammed journey destined to last several lifetimes.

Several of Sellings's stories involve amnesia. A telepathic, amnesiac alien in "From Up There" (collected in *Time Transfer*) is in despair because he cannot convince humans that he is from another planet, but then a pretty bohemian persuades him to accept his fate and to get on with living, even amid human oddities. In "Blank Form" (*Galaxy*, July 1958; collected in *The Long Eureka*) a psychiatrist helps an amnesiac alien capable of reflexive shape-changing to discover its original form and its latent memories. The amnesiac protagonist of "Homecoming" (collected in *The Long Eureka*) is a space explorer who has been in suspended

animation for hundreds of millions of years. In addition to coping with the physical challenges created by so long a "sleep," he must deal with the horror of learning that the world he once knew and the battles he fought no longer exist, nor does his physical "life" as previously defined. He must spend his future among aliens, a psychologically unnerving situation, but one he is resilient enough to endure.

Other Sellings stories also explore the psychological difficulties of space travel and alien encounters. In "The Well-Trained Heroes" (*Galaxy*, June 1964; collected in *The Long Eureka*) dangerous urban tensions are produced by claustrophobia and mass dreams of escape to space at a time when space travel is no longer a viable possibility. An elite squad of space cadets (most of whom have never been in space) has been trained to predict, assess, and control trouble through a form of psychological warfare that involves the self-sacrifice of team members who redirect hatred and violence to themselves. Those few ingenious enough to see through the ploys of the scapegoats are immediately enlisted in the service. "The Last Time Around" (*New Writings in SF 12*, 1968) depicts the human implications for space travelers of the difference between subjective and objective time. The narrator of "Birthright" (*New Worlds*, November 1956; collected in *The Long Eureka*) has been genetically engineered for mining uranium on a high-gravity planet, and the story explores the cruelties of genetic engineering for the purpose of space colonization and the power of racial memories. In turn, "The Age of Kindness" (*Galaxy*, November 1954; collected in *Time Transfer*) demonstrates the cruelty of kindness toward the physically deformed at a time of genetically engineered "perfection." The living memories of humans are captured in a time warp and put on continuous replay in "Jukebox" (*Fantastic Universe*, December 1955; collected in *Time Transfer*). In "The Dodgers" (*Fantastic*, April 1969) a clever race of humanoids set in a hostile environment has developed time travel as an everyday survival skill, while "Verbal Agreement" (*Galaxy*, September 1956; collected in *The Long Eureka*) demonstrates how a futuristic traveling salesman confronts a highly advanced telepathic society that is contemptuous of his painfully noisy, uncontrolled thoughts and learns to adapt its citizens to his needs—through poetry. Overall, Sellings's short fiction is touching, intellectually stimulating, and always entertaining.

Throughout Sellings's stories and novels a well-developed protagonist is forced to deal with the unexpected against a backdrop of political intrigue, powerful military complexes, and competition for power. This protagonist is often an artist with special powers of perception and intuition. When faced with frightening conspiracies or unthinkable possibilities, he first doubts his sanity and then decides to test the reality of his perceptions. Setting up a series of rational tests, he eventually learns to face new concepts, deal with new powers, or adjust to changing realities. His flexibility and adaptability help him to achieve an understanding of his strange perceptions or discoveries, to adjust to them, and ultimately to accept the responsibilities they bring. These protagonists, whether human or alien, are characterized in detail, with the comments of minor characters rounding out the picture. Usually Sellings defines a character through conflict or opposition, particularly with a member of the opposite sex.

The short story "The Wordless Ones" (collected in *Time Transfer*)–with its male dreamers who awaken the telepathic powers latent in human females and produce a sexual dichotomy on Earth that is the mirror image of that on their planet–paved the way for *Telepath* (1962), also published as *The Silent Speakers* (1963). In this novel unsuspected telepathic powers produced by mutant genes transform human relationships. Once discovered, these powers are developed to provide a means for preserving racial memories from generation to generation. This ability proves particularly valuable for far distant space travel during which normal records, even computerized records, might be destroyed or lost. *Telepath* captures the shock of new experience and explores the complex human psychological responses to telepathic invasion of privacy.

In *The Uncensored Man* (1964) a psychiatrist helps a defense-department nuclear physicist use LSD and psilocybin to respond to puzzling messages from a higher dimension that is inhabited by sympathetic, challenging multipersonality beings who represent the merging of human memories and experiences. The novel is the first of Selling's works to explore the use of drugs to transfer humans to another dimension, encounters with powerful, Jungian collective lifeforms, and humanity's latent faculties of levitation, telepathy, and other hidden psychological powers. In *The Uncensored Man* the mental powers and memories of dead humans, a matrix of energy assembled in another dimension, are an integral power ready to help humans of the earthly dimension discover a racial memory that is stored unused and unacknowledged in infant minds. In the physicist-hero this memory awakens psychic superpowers that he uses responsibly to save humanity's from self-destruction, thus protecting both dimensions.

The Quy Effect (1966), set in 1973, begins with a bang that shatters windows, decimates a laboratory building, and sends its originator, Mr. Quy, flying three hundred feet from its center. Mr. Quy is a womanizing septuagenarian, a scalawag who has spent a lifetime

Dust jacket for Sellings's 1964 novel, in which a nuclear physicist takes mind-altering drugs to communicate with beings in a higher dimension (Richland County Public Library)

tinkering with offbeat projects and inventing an assortment of gadgets, some useful, some not. He has come close to breakthrough discoveries in the past, only to find some other scientist just a step ahead of him. Now he has finally invented a new form of power inspired by superconductors and the DNA molecule and based on antigravity; of course, no one believes him.

The novel explores the aging scientist's struggle to perfect and publicize his invention, despite the skepticism of colleagues and family. The night watchman, Charlie, praises "old Quy" for not being like the "status-hogging stuffed-shirts" who never got "their lily-white hands dirty" and for instead eating in the workers' canteens (when he occasionally remembers meals) and engineering a blast whose size would make any working man proud. Quy's lack of class of consciousness and his unconventional obsessions make credible his conflicts with the national scientific establishment and his final acceptance by a freer-spirited foreign power.

Dust jacket for Sellings's 1968 novel, in which any material object, including people and works of art, can be duplicated by a process called "transdimensional multiplying" (Bruccoli Clark Layman Collection)

At the same time *The Quy Effect* explores the conflict between freewheeling father and conventional son, who tries to have the father institutionalized; the close ties of grandfather and grandson, who share a sense of adventure and a drive to break new ground; and the camaraderie of old friends, who have shared economic and emotional ups and downs. A successful antigravity flight under the auspices of the Israeli government opens the possibility at the end of the book for speedy, nontraumatic, long-distance space travel and perhaps another discovery based on the secrets of life hidden in the DNA molecule.

Intermind (1967) combines science fiction with the international spy story. Dominic Ryder—an attractive, fit, James Bond type—can immobilize a pack of trained killer dogs with his bare hands, identify the opposition from seemingly insignificant clues, resist bribes, and withstand torture. He works for INDEX, an international data-exchange organization with high ideals and the best of motives in Cold War battles. The research division of INDEX has already made scientific breakthroughs to facilitate company goals, advances such as an antitruth vaccine to help protect captured operatives. At the start of the story, however, the unexpected death of a booby-trapped agent compels INDEX to test an experimental technique: memory transfer by spinal-tap injection of brain fluid. After the initial nightmare of experiencing the operative's death in his own mind, Ryder discovers that alcoholic drinks in particular open his mind to flashes of intuitive understanding gleaned from the dead man. These range from seeing shared acquaintances through strange eyes and understanding compulsions that are not his own to knowing suddenly the right word to say in Turkish. He also learns that to trace the dead agent's final steps he must go to Istanbul and then to the small town of Banlahir on the road to Izmir. There he learns of another scientific breakthrough, an electronically transmitted, crystal-based telepathy machine that, in the wrong hands, could be used to manipulate an unsuspecting populace. Thus, the novel not only explores the exciting potential value of organically enhanced forms of telepathy but also warns of the threat of its abuse in the hands of the unscrupulous.

The Power of X (1968) is set in 2018, a time in which synthetic flesh may be used to create convincing disguises; a brontium-headed atomic-boring machine makes tunnel building an easy feat; and a European moon base is a launching pad for distant exploration. The novel examines the disturbing repercussions of an expensive and carefully regulated process called "plying," short for "Transdimensional Multiplying." By this process any material object, including valuable works of art, can be duplicated perfectly up to twenty times by laser cutting the exact copies from what is thought to be a space continuum. Thus, the novel examines the meaning of "authentic," asking if a new, scientifically reproduced Chagall, Rembrandt, or Monet is any less artistic or less valuable than the original, and if the ability to divine the original might change the balance of value. Since plying can also reproduce living matter (a process forbidden by law), the novel also provides an interesting view on cloning. A living president is exactly reproduced, but the clone has a weakened will and a confused psychological vagueness that makes him easily manipulated into acting against values and beliefs that are an integral part of the original's character. The hero of *The Power of X,* a "divvy" who can distinguish imitation from original by feeling the electric charges given off, enjoys running an art gallery and is proud of his special powers of "serendipity" that have made him successful in the art trade. He is offended at politicians who would exploit a scientific breakthrough and sacrifice a respected, heroic president for their own ambitious ends. Though at times confused and alienated, he acts heroically in conspiracy with trusted friends and family to rescue the "original" president and thereby to save the nation. The ending raises interesting questions about the relationship of time and space and the dangers of employing scientific "miracles" without adequate testing and consideration of their implications for the future.

On 24 September 1968, Sellings died suddenly and unexpectedly of a heart attack. Critics considered his posthumously published novel, *Junk Day* (1970), his best book, praising its intriguing investigations of character and its powerful theme. *Junk Day*, a postholocaust story of survival, is set in the 1980s in a London that has been reduced to rubble and infested by vipers and rats. The novel depicts humankind's tentative efforts to recover from madness, to throw off the shock of wholesale destruction, rebuild community, and restore order. Its hero, Douglas Bryan, whom some critics identified with Sellings himself, is an artist driven to create; its heroine is Veronica, a former novice whose convent no longer exists. The novel explores and defines basic human values and questions at what point survival becomes too costly. It sets human individuality against social engineering and opposes the views that "might makes right" and that scientific training leads to superior solutions to human problems.

Junk Day opposes a traumatized, humanistic artist against two sorts of villains—the junkman, a tough, lower-class bully who runs a protection racket and rules the junk pile that is London with an iron fist, and the cynical, overweening international scientists who manipulate and use the junkman to help them set up a new world order in which they play God, reconditioning humanity and remaking society to fit their distorted vision of social planning. The artist values individuality, community, creativity, and rebellion against imposed authority. The junkman looks to the past and values power, brute force, and possessions for their own sake. The scientists claim a higher cause and a greater intellect but are basically junkmen with a sophisticated vocabulary, "social therapists" to brainwash "negative" individualists, and superior weapons to enforce their will. Allusions to Greek myth and the Bible, sympathetic descriptions of the psychologically traumatized, and a peculiar mix of cynicism and idealism raise this novel far above pulp fiction.

Arthur Sellings's fiction is suspenseful, handling clever plotting and wry twists with discipline and restraint and displaying his sensitivity to the give-and-take of ordinary conversation. The humanistic dominates science in his fiction, which argues that the unknown cannot be denied or ignored; instead it must be faced and dealt with responsibly.

Brian M. Stableford
(25 July 1948 –)

Elizabeth S. Davidson
University of South Carolina, Spartanburg

BOOKS: *Cradle of the Sun* [bound with *The Wizards of Senchuria,* by Kenneth Bulmer] (New York: Ace, 1969); published separately (London: Sidgwick & Jackson, 1969);

The Blind Worm [bound with *Seed of the Dreamers,* by Emil Petaja] (New York: Ace, 1970); published separately (London: Sidgwick & Jackson, 1970);

The Days of Glory: Dies Irae I (New York: Ace, 1971; London: Quartet, 1974);

In the Kingdom of the Beasts: Dies Irae II (New York: Ace, 1971; London: Quartet, 1974);

Day of Wrath: Dies Irae III (New York: Ace, 1971; London: Quartet, 1974);

To Challenge Chaos (New York: DAW, 1972);

The Halcyon Drift (New York: DAW, 1972; London: Dent, 1974);

Rhapsody in Black (New York: DAW, 1973; London: Dent, 1975);

Promised Land (New York: DAW, 1974; London: Dent, 1976);

The Paradise Game (New York: DAW, 1974; London: Dent, 1976);

The Fenris Device (New York: DAW, 1974; London: Pan, 1978);

Swan Song (New York: DAW, 1975; London: Pan, 1978);

Man in a Cage (New York: John Day, 1975);

The Face of Heaven (London: Quartet, 1976); expanded as *The Realms of Tartarus* (New York: DAW, 1977);

The Florians (New York: DAW, 1976; Feltham, U.K.: Hamlyn, 1978);

The Mind-Riders (New York: DAW, 1976; London: Fontana, 1977);

Critical Threshold (New York: DAW, 1977; Feltham, U.K.: Hamlyn, 1979);

The Mysteries of Modern Science (London: Routledge & Kegan Paul, 1977; Totowa, N.J.: Littlefield, Adams, 1980);

Wildeblood's Empire (New York: DAW, 1977; Feltham, U.K.: Hamlyn, 1979);

Brian Stableford (photograph from the dust jacket for The Hunger and Ecstasy of Vampires, *1996)*

The City of the Sun (New York: DAW, 1978; Feltham, U.K.: Hamlyn, 1980);

The Last Days of the Edge of the World (London: Hutchinson, 1978; New York: Berkley, 1985);

A Clash of Symbols: The Triumph of James Blish (San Bernardino, Cal.: Borgo Press, 1979);

Balance of Power (New York: DAW, 1979; London: Hamlyn, 1984);

The Paradox of the Sets (New York: DAW, 1979);

The Walking Shadow (London: Fontana/Collins, 1979; New York: Carroll & Graf, 1989);

Optiman (New York: DAW, 1980); republished as *War Games* (London: Pan, 1981);

The Castaways of Tanagar (New York: DAW, 1981);

Masters of Science Fiction: Essays on Six Science Fiction Authors (San Bernardino, Cal.: Borgo Press, 1981); revised and enlarged as *Outside the Human Aquarium: Masters of Science Fiction* (San Bernardino, Cal.: Borgo Press, 1995);

Journey to the Center (Garden City, N.Y.: Doubleday, 1982); revised and expanded as *Journey to the Centre* (London: New English Library, 1989);

The Science in Science Fiction, by Stableford, Peter Nicholls, and David Langford (London: Joseph, 1982; New York: Knopf, 1983);

The Gates of Eden (New York: DAW, 1983; London: New English Library, 1990);

Future Man: Brave New World or Genetic Nightmare? (New York: Crown, 1984; London: Granada, 1984);

The Third Millennium: A History of the World, A.D. 2000–3000, by Stableford and Langford (London: Sidgwick & Jackson, 1985; New York: Knopf, 1985);

The Cosmic Perspective and Custer's Last Stand (Polk City, Iowa: Chris Drumm, 1985);

Scientific Romance in Britain, 1890–1950 (London: Fourth Estate, 1985; New York: St. Martin's Press, 1985);

The Sociology of Science Fiction (San Bernardino, Cal.: Borgo Press, 1987);

The Empire of Fear (London: Simon & Schuster, 1988; New York: Carroll & Graf, 1991);

The Way to Write Science Fiction (London: Elm Tree Books, 1989);

The Werewolves of London (London: Simon & Schuster, 1989; New York: Carroll & Graf, 1992);

Warhammer: Zaragoz, as Brian Craig (Brighton, U.K.: GW Books, 1989; New York: Simon & Schuster, 2002);

Warhammer: Plague Daemon, as Craig (Brighton, U.K.: GW Books, 1990);

Invaders from the Centre (London: New English Library, 1990);

The Centre Cannot Hold (London: New English Library, 1990);

Sexual Chemistry: Sardonic Tales of the Genetic Revolution (London: Simon & Schuster, 1991);

Warhammer: Storm Warriors, as Craig (Brighton, U.K.: GW Books, 1991);

The Angel of Pain (London: Simon & Schuster, 1991; New York: Carroll & Graf, 1993);

Dark Future: Ghost Dancers, as Craig (Brighton, U.K.: GW Books, 1991);

Slumming in Voodooland (Eugene, Ore.: Pulphouse, 1991);

Young Blood (London: Simon & Schuster, 1992);

The Carnival of Destruction (New York: Carroll & Graf, 1994; New York & London: Pocket Books, 1994);

Firefly: A Novel of the Far Future (San Bernardino, Cal.: Unicorn & Son, 1994);

Opening Minds: Essays on Fantastic Literature (San Bernardino, Cal.: Borgo Press, 1994);

Algebraic Fantasies and Realistic Romances: More Masters of Science Fiction (San Bernardino, Cal.: Borgo Press, 1995);

Serpent's Blood: The First Book of Genesys (London: Legend, 1995);

Fables and Fantasies (West Warwick, R.I.: Necronomicon, 1996);

The Hunger and Ecstasy of Vampires (Shingletown, Cal.: Mark V. Ziesing, 1996);

Salamander's Fire: The Second Book of Genesys (London: Legend, 1996);

Chimera's Cradle: The Third Book of Genesys (London: Legend, 1997);

Writing Fantasy and Science Fiction, and Getting Published (London: Teach Yourself, 1997; Chicago: NTC, 1998);

Glorious Perversity: The Decline and Fall of Literary Decadence (San Bernardino, Cal.: Borgo Press, 1998);

Yesterday's Bestsellers: A Journey through Literary History (San Bernardino, Cal.: Borgo Press, 1998);

Inherit the Earth (New York: Tor, 1998);

Architects of Emortality (New York: Tor, 1999);

The Dictionary of Science Fiction Places (New York: Fireside/Wonderland, 1999; London: Simon & Schuster, 1999);

Fountains of Youth (New York: Tor, 2000);

Year Zero (Mountain Ash, Wales: Sarob, 2000);

Warhammer: The Wine of Dreams, as Craig (Nottingham, U.K.: A Black Library Publication of Games Workshop Publishing, 2000);

Warhammer 40,000: Pawns of Chaos, as Craig (Nottingham, U.K.: A Black Library Publication of Games Workshop Publishing, 2001);

The Cassandra Complex (New York: Tor, 2001);

The Eleventh Hour (Gillette, N.J.: Wildside Press, 2001);

Dark Ararat (New York: Tor, 2002).

OTHER: "The Sun's Tears," in *The 1975 Annual World's Best SF,* edited by Donald A. Wollheim, with Arthur W. Saha (New York: DAW, 1975), pp. 128–139;

"The Engineer and the Executioner," in *The 1976 Annual World's Best SF,* edited by Wollheim, with Saha (New York: DAW, 1976), pp. 135–148;

"Marriage of Science and Fiction: The Emergence of a New Fiction," in *Encyclopedia of Science Fiction,* edited by Robert Holdstock (London: Octopus, 1978), pp. 18–27;

"2018 A.D. or The King Kong Blues," "334," "Across the Zodiac: The Story of a Wrecked Record," "The Angel of the Revolution," "Before the Dawn," "The Black Cloud," "The Black Flame," "Caesar's Column," "Children of the Atom," "Cities in Flight," "The Clockwork Man," "The Cornelius Chronicles," "Cosmicomics," "Darkening Island," "Darkness and Dawn," "Deep Waters," "The Drought," "Emperor of the If," "Fear and Typewriter in the Sky," "The Ghost of Guy Thyrle," "The Hampdenshire Wonder," "Herovit's World," "Ice," "Inverted World," "The Knights of the Limits," "The Legion of Time," "The Lensman Series," "The Lost World," "Lumen," "The Mortgage on the Brain," "Nightwings," "The Paradox Men," "The Philosopher's Stone," "The Poison Belt," "The Purple Cloud," "The Riddle of the Tower," "Ring Around the Sun," "The Rose," "Saurus," "Seed of Light," "The Short Fiction of J. G. Ballard," "The Short Fiction of Jorge Luis Borges," "The Short Fiction of Judith Merril," "The Short Fiction of William Tenn," "Sinister Barrier," "The Skylark Series," "Symzonia," "Syzygy," "They'd Rather Be Right," "The Three Stigmata of Palmer Eldritch," "Through the Looking-Glass," "A Time of Changes," "Twenty Thousand Leagues Under the Sea," "Who?" "The Wind from Nowhere," "The World Below," and "The Yellow Danger," in *Survey of Science Fiction Literature,* 5 volumes, edited by Frank Magill (Englewood Cliffs, N.J.: Salem, 1979);

Contributing editor, *The Encyclopedia of Science Fiction,* edited by Peter Nicholls (London: Granada, 1979; New York: Doubleday, 1979);

"Algebraic Fantasies: The Science Fiction of Bob Shaw," in *Bob Shaw,* British Science Fiction Writers, no. 1, edited by Paul Kincaid (Kent, U.K.: British Science Fiction Association, 1981), pp. 6–31;

"Science Fiction between the Wars: 1918–1938," in *Anatomy of Wonder: A Critical Guide to Science Fiction,* second edition, edited by Neil Barron (New York: R. R. Bowker, 1981);

"Clark Ashton Smith," "David H. Keller," "Fritz Leiber," "J. G. Ballard," "L. Sprague de Camp," and "Philip K. Dick," in *Science Fiction Writers: Critical Studies of the Major Authors from the Early Nineteenth Century to the Present Day,* edited by E. F. Bleiler (New York: Scribners, 1982);

"Man-Made Catastrophes," in *The End of the World,* edited by Eric S. Rabkin, Martin H. Greenberg,

and Joseph D. Olander (Carbondale: Southern Illinois Univerity Press, 1983), pp. 97–138;

"Aphrodite," "Arachne," "Atlantida," "Back to Methuselah," "Baron Munchhausen's Narrative of His Marvellous Travels and Campaigns in Russia," "A Beleaguered City," "Christmas Stories," "Chronology of Modern Fantasy Literature," "The Citadel of Fear," "The Connecticut Yankee in King Arthur's Court," "A Crystal Age," "The Deryni Trilogy," "The Devil in Crystal," "Dream," "Elsie Venner," "Eroticism and the Supernatural," "Fafhrd and the Gray Mouser," "Fantazius Mallare and The Kingdom of Evil," "Frankenstein; or, The Modern Prometheus," "The Gardens of Delight," "The Gees Series," "The Ghost Pirates," "The Green Isle of the Great Deep," "The Green Man," "Green Mansions," "The Happy Prince and Other Tales and A House of Pomegranates," "The Heads of Cerberus," "His Monkey Wife; or, Married to a Chimp," "Humour and Fantasy," "Jirel of Joiry," "The King in Yellow," "Kwaidan," "Little, Big," "The Lost Continent," "Lost Horizon," "The Lost Traveller," "The Magic Skin," "The Master and Margarita," "Moonchild," "Morwyn; or, The Vengeance of God," "Mr. Weston's Good Wine," "The Mythology of Fairie," "The Napoleon of Notting Hill," "Nephele," "On Wings of Song," "One of Cleopatra's Nights," "The Other Side of the Mountain," "Our Ancestors," "The Passion of New Eve," "Portrait of Jennie," "The Revolt of the Angels," "Ringstones and Other Curious Tales and The Doll Maker and Other Tales of the Uncanny," "A Romance of Two Worlds," "St. Leon," "The Saragossa Manuscript," "The Short Fiction of Balzac," "The Short Fiction of Bloch," "The Short Fiction of Boucher," "The Short Fiction of Heard," "The Short Fiction of Lee," "The Short Fiction of Smith," "Spirite," "The Supermale," "The Tarzan Series," "These Mortals," "The Three Immortals," "Thunder on the Left," "The Twilight of the Gods," "Undine," "Upsidonia," "The Vampires of Alfama," "The Violet Apple and the Witch," "Voyage to Faremido and Capillaria," "The Wandering Jew," "The Weigher of Souls," "The Werewolf of Paris," "When the Birds Fly South," "Witchcraft," "The Wolf-Leader," "The Wonderful Visit," and "The Worm Ouroboros," in *Survey of Modern Fantasy Literature,* 5 volumes, edited by Magill (Englewood Cliffs, N.J.: Salem, 1983);

"The Politics of Evolution," in *Shiel in Diverse Hands: A Collection of Essays* (Cleveland: Reynolds Morse Foundation, 1983), pp. 369–394;

"Alien Ecologies," "Aliens," "Disasters," "ESP," "Galactic Empires," "Inner Space," "Magic," "Man and Machine," "Media," "Parallel Worlds and Alternate Histories," "Religion and Mythology," "Sex and Sensuality," "Space Travel," "Time Travel," and "Utopia and Dystopia," in *The Science Fiction Source Book,* edited by David Wingrove (New York: Van Nostrand Reinhold, 1984; Harlow & Essex, U.K.: Longman, 1985);

"Anatole France," "Charles Dickens," "Eden Phillpotts," "F. Anstey," "Fritz Leiber," "J. D. Beresford," "J. M. Barrie," "John Cowper Powys and T. F. Powys," "L. Sprague de Camp and Fletcher Pratt," "Marie Corelli," "Robert Hichens," "Theodore Sturgeon," and "Théophile Gautier," in *Supernatural Fiction Writers: Fantasy and Horror,* edited by E. F. Bleiler (New York: Scribners, 1985);

"The Modern Period: 1964–1986," in *Anatomy of Wonder: A Critical Guide to Science Fiction,* third edition, edited by Barron (New York: R. R. Bowker, 1987);

"And He Not Busy Being Born . . . ," in *Interzone: The 2nd Anthology: New Science Fiction and Fantasy Writing* (New York: St. Martin's Press, 1987), pp. 77–84; also in *The Road to Science Fiction, Volume 5: The British Way,* edited by James Gunn (Clarkston, Ga.: White Wolf, 1998), pp. 608–622;

"The Growth of the House of Usher" and "The Man Who Loved the Vampire Lady," in *The Year's Best Science Fiction: Sixth Annual Collection,* edited by Gardner Dozois (New York: St. Martin's Press, 1989), pp. 64–83, 355–374;

"The Magic Bullet," in *The 1990 Annual World's Best SF,* edited by Wollheim, with Saha (New York: DAW, 1990), pp. 32–51;

"The British and American Traditions of Speculative Fiction," in *Contours of the Fantastic: Selected Essays from the Eighth International Conference on the Fantastic in the Arts,* edited by Michele K. Langford (New York: Greenwood Press, 1990), pp. 39–47;

The Dedalus Book of Decadence: Moral Ruins, edited by Stableford (Sawtry, U.K.: Dedalus, 1990);

"The Nineteenth Century, 1812–99" and "From Baum to Tolkien, 1900–56," in *Fantasy Literature,* edited by Barron (New York: Garland, 1990), pp. 62–222;

"Early Modern Horror Fiction, 1897–1949" and "The Later Gothic Tradition, 1825–96," in *Horror Literature,* edited by Barron (New York: Garland, 1990), pp. 58–159;

"The Magic of the Movies," in *Science Fiction and Fantasy Book Review Annual 1990,* edited by Robert Collins and Robert Latham (New York: Greenwood Press, 1991), pp. 99–108;

The Dedalus Book of British Fantasy: The 19th Century, edited by Stableford (Sawtry, U.K.: Dedalus, 1991);

"Innocent Blood," in *Tales of the Wandering Jew: A Collection of Contemporary and Classic Stories,* edited by Stableford (Sawtry, U.K.: Dedalus, 1991);

"Salomé," "The Woman in the Mirror" (as Brian Craig), and "Self-Sacrifice" (as Francis Amery), in *The Dedalus Book of Femmes Fatales: A Collection of Contemporary and Classic Stories,* edited by Stableford (Sawtry, U.K.: Dedalus, 1992);

Rémy de Gourmont, *The Angels of Perversity,* translated by Stableford as Amery (Sawtry, U.K.: Dedalus, 1992);

The Second Dedalus Book of Decadence: The Black Feast, edited by Stableford (Sawtry, U.K.: Dedalus, 1992)–includes works translated by Stableford as Amery;

"The Innsmouth Heritage," in *Shadows over Innsmouth,* edited by Stephen Jones (Minneapolis: Fedogan & Bremer, 1994; London: Gollancz, 1997);

Jean Lorrain, *Monsieur de Phocas,* translated by Stableford as Amery (London: Dedalus, 1994; New York: Hippocrene, 1994);

"The New Wave, Cyberpunk, and Beyond: 1963–1994," by Stableford and Michael M. Levy, in *Anatomy of Wonder 4,* edited by Barron (New York: R. R. Bowker, 1995), pp. 222–377;

"Frankenstein and the Origins of Science Fiction," in *Anticipations: Essays on Early Science Fiction and Its Precursors,* edited by David Seed (Liverpool: Liverpool University Press, 1995; Syracuse, N.Y.: Syracuse University Press, 1995), pp. 46–57;

Contributing editor, *The Encyclopedia of Science Fiction,* edited by Nicholls and John Clute (New York: St. Martin's Press, 1995);

"Les Fleurs du Mal," in *The Year's Best Science Fiction: 12th Annual Collection,* edited by Dozois (New York: St. Martin's Press, 1995);

"Mortimer Gray's History of Death," in *The Year's Best Science Fiction: 13th Annual Collection,* edited by Dozois (New York: St. Martin's Press, 1996);

Contributing editor, *The St. James Guide to Fantasy Writers,* edited by David Pringle (New York: St. James, 1996);

S. Fowler Wright, *S. Fowler Wright's Short Stories,* foreword by Stableford (Ludlow, U.K.: FWB, 1996), pp. 8–18;

"To Bring in Fine Things: The Significance of Science Fiction Plots," in *Visions of Wonder: The Science Fic-*

tion Research Association Anthology, edited by David G. Hartwell and Milton T. Wolf (New York: Tor, 1996), pp. 669–675;

"Outside the Human Aquarium: The Fantastic Imagination of Clark Ashton Smith," in *American Supernatural Fiction: From Edith Wharton to the Weird Tales Writers,* edited by Douglas Robillard (New York: Garland, 1996), pp. 229–252;

"Sang for Supper: Notes on the Metaphorical Use of Vampires in *The Empire of Fear* and *Young Blood,*" in *Blood Read: The Vampire as Metaphor in Contemporary Culture,* edited by Joan Gordon and Veronica Hollinger (Philadelphia: University of Pennsylvania Press, 1997), pp. 69–84;

"The House of Mourning," in *Year's Best SF 2,* edited by Hartwell (New York: HarperPrism, 1997);

"Fantasy in the Nineteenth Century, 1812–1899," "Early Modern Horror Fiction, 1897–1949, 1900–1956," and "From Baum to Tolkien," in *Fantasy and Horror: A Critical and Historical Guide to Literature, Illustration, Film, TV, Radio, and the Internet,* edited by Barron (Lanham, Md.: Scarecrow Press, 1999), pp. 73–198;

Paul Féval, *Vampire City,* translated and edited by Stableford (Mountain Ash, Wales: Sarob, 1999);

"Chanterelle," in *Black Heart, Ivory Bones,* edited by Ellen Datlow and Terri Windling (New York: Avon, 2000); republished in *Year's Best Fantasy,* edited by Hartwell and Kathryn Cramer (New York: HarperCollins, 2001);

"Sheena," in *The Vampire Sextette,* edited by Marvin Kaye (Garden City, N.Y.: GuildAmerica, 2000);

Féval, *Knightshade,* translated and edited by Stableford (Mountain Ash, Wales: Sarob, 2001);

"The Last Supper," in *Year's Best SF 6,* edited by Hartwell (New York: HarperCollins, 2001);

"Snowball in Hell," in *The Year's Best Science Fiction: Eighteenth Annual Collection,* edited by Dozois (New York: St. Martin's Press, 2001);

Lorrain, *Nightmares of an Ether-Drinker,* translated by Stableford (Carlton, U.K.: Tartarus Press, 2002);

Camille Flammarion, *Lumen,* translated by Stableford (Middletown, Conn.: Wesleyan University Press, 2002).

SELECTED PERIODICAL PUBLICATIONS– UNCOLLECTED:

FICTION

"Riding the Tiger," *Interzone,* 68 (February 1993): 44–56;

"Burned Out," *Interzone,* 70 (April 1993): 48–58;

"Busy Dying," *Magazine of Fantasy & Science Fiction,* 86 (February 1994): 138–160;

"What Can Chloë Want?" *Isaac Asimov's Science Fiction Magazine* (March 1994): 74–82;

"The Scream," *Isaac Asimov's Science Fiction Magazine* (July 1994);

"The Tree of Life," *Isaac Asimov's Science Fiction Magazine* (September 1994): 14–20;

"The Age of Innocence," *Isaac Asimov's Science Fiction Magazine* (June 1995): 88–100;

"Out of Touch," *Isaac Asimov's Science Fiction Magazine* (October 1995): 82–99;

"The Skin Trade," *Isaac Asimov's Science Fiction Magazine* (November 1995): 218–229;

"The Pipes of Pan," *Magazine of Fantasy & Science Fiction,* 92 (June 1997): 69–91;

"The Gift of the Magi," as Francis Amery, *Interzone,* 122 (August 1997): 35–37;

"The Piebald Plumber of Haemlin," *Interzone,* 130 (April 1998): 15–19.

NONFICTION

"Machines and Inventions: Deus Ex Machina, SF and Technology, II," *Vector,* 67/68 (Spring 1974): 51–63, 79;

"The Social Role of SF," *Algol,* 12 (Summer 1975): 23–26;

"William Wilson's Prospectus for Science Fiction: 1851," *Foundation,* 10 (June 1976): 6–12;

"Opening Minds," *Vector,* 76/77 (August/September 1976): 14–17;

"The Needs and Demands of the Science Fiction Reader," *Vector,* 83 (September/October 1977): 4–8;

"The Significance of Science Fiction," *Spectrum,* 148 (1977): 7–9;

"The Science Fiction of James Blish," *Foundation,* 13 (May 1978): 12–43;

"Science Fiction and the Image of the Future," *Foundation,* 14 (September 1978): 26–34;

"Notes towards a Sociology of Science Fiction," *Foundation,* 15 (January 1979): 28–41;

"Social Design in Science Fiction," *Amazing,* 52 (February 1979): 4–5, 119–124;

"Future between the Wars: The Speculative Fiction of John Gloag," *Foundation,* 20 (October 1980): 47–64;

"Realistic Romances of Edgar Fawcett," *Foundation,* 24 (February 1982): 23–48;

"Politics of Evolution: Philosophical Themes in the Speculative Fiction of M. P. Shiel," *Foundation,* 27 (February 1983): 35–60;

"Against the New Gods: The Speculative Fiction of S. Fowler Wright," *Foundation,* 29 (November 1983): 10–52;

"Marxism, Science Fiction and the Poverty of Prophecy: Some Comparisons and Contrasts," *Foundation*, 32 (November 1984): 5–14;

"Slaves of the Death Spiders: Colin Wilson and Existentialist Science Fiction," *Foundation*, 38 (Winter 1986–1987): 63–67;

"Is There No Balm in Gilead? The Woeful Prophecies of *The Handmaid's Tale*," *Foundation*, 39 (Spring 1987): 97–100;

"A Few More Crocodile Tears?" Foundation Forum: Feminism and SF, *Foundation*, 43 (Summer 1988): 63–72;

"Henceforward: SF in the Theatre," *New York Review of Science Fiction*, no. 7 (March 1989): 1, 3–4;

"The Plausibility of the Impossible," Foundation Forum, *Foundation*, 46 (Autumn 1989): 58–64;

"On 'On the True History of Science Fiction,'" *Foundation*, 47 (Winter 1989–1990): 29–30;

"The Profession of Science Fiction, 42: A Long and Winding Road," *Foundation*, 50 (Autumn 1990): 28–51;

"The World SF Conference in Chengdu," *Foundation*, 53 (Autumn 1991): 46–52;

"Adolf Hitler: His Part in Our Struggle; A Brief Economic History of British SF Magazines," *Interzone*, 57 (March 1992): 17–20;

"C. S. Lewis and the Decline of Scientific Romance," *New York Review of Science Fiction*, no. 45 (May 1992): 1, 8–12;

"The Redemption of the Infimal," *New York Review of Science Fiction*, no. 52 (December 1992): 1, 3–8;

"How Should a Science Fiction Story End?" *New York Review of Science Fiction*, no. 78 (February 1995): 1, 8–15;

"Discotheque for the Devil's Party: Black Metal, Pagan Rock and the Tradition of Literary Shamanism, Part 1," *New York Review of Science Fiction*, no. 86 (October 1995): 1, 8–13;

"Pioneer Award Acceptance Speech, 1996," *SFRA Review*, 225 (September/October 1996): 29–31;

"The Third Generation of Genre Science Fiction," *Science-Fiction Studies*, 23 (November 1996): 321–330;

"Creators of Science Fiction, 9: Fritz Leiber," *Interzone*, 123 (September 1997): 31–34;

"Creators of Science Fiction, 10: Hugo Gernsback," *Interzone*, 126 (December 1997): 47–50;

"The Advantages of Amateurism," *Interzone*, 129 (March 1998): 59;

"Speculative Fiction in Europe and America: The Past and the Future," *New York Review of Science Fiction*, 10 (March 1998): 1, 8–12;

"Science Fiction in the Seventies," *Vector*, 200 (July/August 1998): 21–24;

"Last and First Man: Tomorrow's Adam and Eternity's Eve," *New York Review of Science Fiction*, 11 (February 1999): 1, 8–11;

"Pilgrim Award Acceptance, 1999," *SFRA Review*, 241 (August 1999): 10–11;

"James White: Understanding the Alien," *New York Review of Science Fiction*, 12 (January 2000): 1, 6–7;

"The Final Chapter of the Sociology of Science Fiction," *Foundation*, 79 (Summer 2000): 41–58;

"Davy's Dream," *New York Review of Science Fiction*, 13 (January 2001): 1, 4–8;

"How Should a Science Fiction Story Begin?" *Journal of the Fantastic in the Arts*, 12, no. 3 (2001): 322–333.

Brian M. Stableford has been one of the most active writers and critics of science fiction and fantasy since the last quarter of the twentieth century. He has done extensive research on the topic, which has resulted in such works as *Scientific Romance in Britain, 1890–1950* (1985). In his fiction, Stableford envisions interesting alien ecosystems and alternate forms of social organizations on planets far removed in space and time. His fiction stresses the importance of individual and group moral responsibility for decisions that, even if they cannot change things as they are, can and do influence things as they might become.

Though he began by writing simple adventure in the early Ace and DAW fiction series, Stableford also experimented fairly early with questions about the nature of reality in works such as *Man in a Cage* (1975) and *The Walking Shadow* (1979). The Fallen Angels trilogy, the Genesys trilogy, and later series, including works such as *Inherit the Earth* (1998), are much more sustained investigations about what reality is and should be. Though Stableford abandoned his teenage attempts at short fiction for the more lucrative serial-novel form, he has recently returned to writing stories, with some excellent results. Some of his short fiction displays moments of insight with great vividness. Stableford's current fiction, long and short, is both entertaining and thought-provoking.

Born 25 July 1948 in Shipley, Yorkshire, Brian Michael Stableford is the son of William Ernest Stableford, an aircraft designer, and Joyce Wilkinson Stableford, a schoolteacher and later a hypnotherapist. His education included earning a B.A. in biology in 1969 and a D.Phil. in sociology in 1979, both from the University of York. After some years as a freelance writer, Stableford accepted a position teaching sociology at the University of Reading. Outside his regular sociology course load, he also taught interest groups in science-fiction and fantasy literature. In 1987 he was awarded the International Association for the Fantastic in the Arts Scholarship Award for his

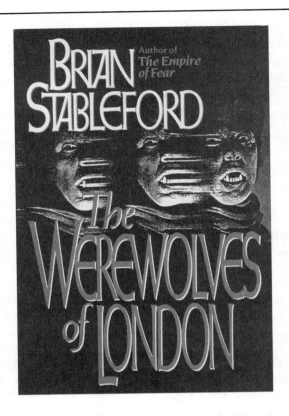

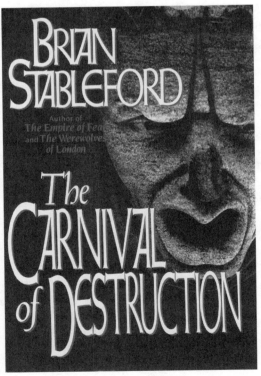

Dust jackets for the U.S. editions of the novels in Stableford's "Fallen Angels" trilogy
(Richland County Public Library)

nonfiction contributions to fantasy and science fiction. His novel *The Realms of Tartarus* (1977) was nominated for a Nebula Award, and six of his short stories for 1993 are in the Honorable Mention list of *The Year's Best Science Fiction, Eleventh Annual Collection*, edited by Gardner Dozois. His short stories have been well represented on this list in Dozois's subsequent collections. In 1994 Stableford also appeared as a guest science-fiction author on the speculative science television series *Future Quest*. In 1996 he was awarded the Pioneer Award and in 1999 the Pilgrim Award, both from the Science Fiction Research Association. He has two children, Leo Michael and Katharine Margaret. He and his wife, Roberta Jane Cragg (R. J. Rennie), whom he married on 16 May 1987, live in Reading, England.

Although he had an interest in writing science fiction as a child, having published "The Earth and the Moon, a Poem" in 1957, at age nine, in the *Manchester Evening News,* Stableford began his writing career in earnest with the publication of two Ace doubles in 1969 and 1970 and of his first trilogy in 1971. Stableford's first works are, by his own admission, rapidly written action adventures, by which he hoped to earn money instead of taking the types of jobs more frequently available to a college student on break. The two Ace doubles are *Cradle of the Sun* (1969) and *The Blind Worm* (1970). *Cradle of the Sun* already shows an interest in the survival instinct, or lack of it, in intelligent species. *The Blind Worm* deals with mutated life on an Earth of the future, with a machine intelligence, and with a journey in search of understanding.

Next, in 1971, Ace published Stableford's first series, the *Dies Irae* trilogy. The parts of this trilogy are *The Days of Glory, In the Kingdom of the Beasts,* and *Day of Wrath,* all dealing with the war between humans and genetically engineered beast-men, secretly set against each other by Heljanita the toymaker, another kind of being with marvelous technological skill. Based on the *Iliad* and the *Odyssey* by Homer, these works "achieve a borrowed mythic quality that usually rises above his writing imperfections," according to B. A. Fredstrom, who also judges these fledgling works entertaining, with "a certain sweep and imaginative grandeur reminiscent of some of the old 'space operas.'" These first novels were rapidly written for the mass-market appeal of a paperback publisher with little thought for revision, but already, in addition to the desire to entertain, Stableford's interests in transmuting the elements of old stories, in genetic engineering and evolution, and in man (or beast-man) against machine are present in his fiction.

DAW, another paperback line, began publishing works by Stableford in 1972 with *To Challenge Chaos,* which uses elements from the myth of Orpheus. With *The Halcyon Drift* (1972), DAW began publication of a six-part series, followed by *Rhapsody in Black* (1973), *Promised Land* (1974), *The Paradise Game* (1974), *The Fenris Device* (1974), and *Swan Song* (1975). These space operas—though the protagonist spends a lot of time on strange planets in most of them—are linked by the main character, Grainger; by the invader of Grainger's mind; and by the ship called the *Hooded Swan.* Grainger is a misanthropic version of the stereotypical loner forced into action on behalf of others. His main redeeming feature is his excellent piloting, especially in his mastery of the *Hooded Swan,* a hybrid of human and alien technology. One other interesting concept first explored in the series is the definition and value of a shared mind, a concept used much more extensively in some of Stableford's later fiction. The shared mind could also be a manifestation of a split personality, though more matter-of-fact and less dramatic than the personality examined in *Man in a Cage.*

Stableford began to develop a reputation as a scholar of science fiction starting in 1973 with reviews and articles in the periodicals *Vector, Algol, Foundation,* and *Spectrum.* Though he has since written book-length studies, he continues to publish nonfiction in such periodicals. One essay, "The Social Role of SF," originally published in *Algol* (1975), shows his focus shifting and widening from his undergraduate field, biology, to his graduate field, sociology. In 1975 he also published two more works, a short story and another novel. "The Sun's Tears" is a quest story in which Colfax finds the titular precious stones, "shining gems found only in the deepest mines of a few hot-cored worlds," only to lose a paradise that sounds like the land of the lotus-eaters from the *Odyssey.* Familiarity with this paradise breeds not necessarily contempt but boredom. He had begun the quest to try to win a girl, Siorane, from her abusive father, Orgoglio (an allusion to a giant who represents Pride in Edmund Spenser's *The Faerie Queene* [1590]), even though he did not know Siorane or give any thought to her wishes. When he returns to Orgoglio with the gemstone, Colfax no longer wants Siorane; he just wants to find his way back to paradise. The "oracles" of this story are a people called Gallacellone, who tell him exactly how to find the gemstone but also tell him about his paradise: "If it exists . . . , then it is beyond your power to find it again." The futility of Colfax's quest is inherent.

Man in a Cage is a mind puzzle with no clear plot, character development, setting, or theme, and this lack of clarity is the point of its symbolism, the insight to be gained from the stream-of-conscious point of view of narrator Harker Lee, the paranoid-schizophrenic, homicidal maniac. *Man in a Cage* is based on the ostensible premise that if interstellar space flight drives sane men mad or kills them, then it might not be fatal to a man already demonstrably insane; at the end of the novel an alert reader wonders if Lee has been sent to Proxima Centauri space at all, an effect that perhaps should be expected in a novel beginning and ending with sections headed "MADMAN'S DANCE." Even the typesetting of the contents pages is a part of the story, delineating visually the three irregularly interwoven narrative strands. The "MADMAN'S DANCE" section, an apparently rambling fantasy, consists of seventeen chapters that seem to encompass human history as it might be seen on a cosmic scale. Yet in the chapter "MADMAN'S DANCE: In the Prison of My Dreams" the determination to survive is the most directly stated: "However much you hate me, I'm not going to die tonight. Not for you, not for anyone."

The sections designated in italics as *Cage of Darkness* are a kind of diary kept by Lee, annotated by his psychiatrist, Dr. Jenny Segal. These twelve sections include most of his references to block C, called Canaan, in which he and other homicidal maniacs have been imprisoned. The seemingly most realistic sections are the fourteen segments designated in boldface type as **Titan Nine,** the name of the interstellar mission for which Lee, like a commodity, has been taken from imprisonment in block C to imprisonment on the site of the Titan project. In the **Titan Nine** sections, communication is an issue. Lee is not allowed to send or receive letters, while Lindquist, who came back catatonic from Titan Eight, has undergone "a sort of metamorphosis of the mind"; and in the last **Titan Nine** segment, "Where No Man Has Gone Before, Beyond the Split Infinitive"–an ironic allusion to the *Star Trek* television series–radio contact is reestablished with Lee, although days later than expected. Whether Lee has really been anywhere or has really succeeded in his mission is called into question, however; an oversimplified answer or resolution would have destroyed the mystery at the heart of the novel. In the last "MADMAN'S DANCE" chapter, "Adeste Fidelis, Laete Triumphantes," Segal seems to be trying to call him out of a fantasy, and he does not even seem to notice, much less to respond.

Stableford's fiction published in 1976 includes three novels and a short story. One of the novels, *The Face of Heaven,* was the first in a trilogy commissioned by Quartet, which went bankrupt before the other two books appeared. American publisher Donald A. Wollheim combined the three volumes into one as *The Realms of Tartarus.* The second novel, *The Florians*

(the first volume of the Daedalus Mission series), is a return to action-adventure fiction set at a space colony. The third, *The Mind-Riders,* is, in part, an action-adventure novel but also explores a narrative device common in fantasy and science fiction that Stableford has included in many works: mind-sharing. The protagonist, Ryan Hart, controls a video-simulated boxer, providing emotions for avid television viewers who want to feel as though they are participants in dangerous situations while remaining safe at home. The interesting element, however, is not so much the overt action as the conflict in the mind of the protagonist over which emotions and how much of them he wants to share.

The short story "The Engineer and the Executioner," included in *The 1976 Annual World's Best SF,* begins with a seemingly straightforward statement: "'My life,' said the engineer. 'It's mine.'" Yet the life in question is not the engineer's own state of being but an ecosystem that has been developed in a laboratory inside the asteroid Lamarck. The executioner is a robot sent to destroy the project by driving the asteroid into the sun. The engineer creates a breach in the chamber containing the Lamarck life system, however, which then provides for its own survival: "With vegetable efficiency, they began to dissolve the airlock." By the time the asteroid passes the orbits of Mars, Earth, and Venus, the Lamarckian life-forms are free. Beyond the orbit of Mars their threat to Earth's ecosystem was improbable; inside the orbit of Venus the solar winds make it probable that human life will be destroyed by the invading species. Those who have sent the robot have insured the doom of Earth as they know it. The biological engineer, though absorbed and destroyed as an individual, defeats the mechanical construct sent to destroy his new creations.

In *The Realms of Tartarus* the peoples of the future Earth do not exist on the same physical plane. Bringing them into contact with one another provides the conflict for this adventure. C. J. Cherryh, in a January 1978 article for *Galileo,* has noted that *The Realms of Tartarus* uses "a theme . . . explored in imaginative fiction since the unknown author of *Gilgamesh* first set stylus to clay; the descent to Hell and the ascent to Heaven." The creation of Euchronia, the seemingly ideal civilization on the sky platform, has only covered up the poisoned world below, without repairing the damage to the environment that had made the sky platform necessary in the first place.

The voyages of the starship *Daedalus,* whose mission is to seek out and reestablish contact with lost Earth colonies in space, are the link in another Stableford series of six novels for DAW, comprising *The Florians, Critical Threshold* (1977), *Wildeblood's Empire* (1977), *The City of the Sun* (1978), *Balance of Power*

(1979), and *The Paradox of the Sets* (1979). Some of the colonies appear to be lost, some appear utopian, but all have some hidden flaw, some danger that must be confronted and resolved by the crew of the *Daedalus,* especially genetic biologist Alexis Alexander. On the last mission they find evidence of another intelligent species from elsewhere in the universe, but these are not first-contact stories. Reviews in science-fiction journals were much harsher in their judgment of the *Daedalus* novels than those in more general sources. Of the fifth book, *Balance of Power,* Keith Justice, in *Science Fiction & Fantasy Book Review* (May 1979) observed that, although "this is a nice mixture of action and sociological speculation," the novel is flawed: "Stableford's fiction is always well-crafted and entertaining, but ultimately lightweight." The reviewer for *Library Journal* (15 January 1979) found *Balance of Power* "one of those rare sf novels in which a thoughtful, almost contemplative approach to a new world coexists with a very successful action-packed plot."

Most of Stableford's fiction has been science fiction or science fantasy rather than fantasy of the fairy-tale variety. The children's tale *The Last Days of the Edge of the World* (1978) involves a land of enchantment, an exchange of riddles, an old magician, the magician's beautiful daughter, and a clever apprentice. Unlike in conventional fairy tales, however, this land of enchantment is in a terrible mess: the unenchanted land is on the brink of economic disaster; the beautiful daughter—competent and courageous—has no use for marriage to a prince; the whole mess can be straightened out only by banishing magic from the world altogether; and the brave young couple, saved by common sense and preparation, are rewarded with college scholarships rather than marriage.

In Stableford's unusual novel *The Walking Shadow* he takes a look at the theatricality of televangelism against the cosmic scale of evolution of life on planets that ultimately have no place for individual intelligence, be it human, alien, or both working together. There is a hint that human survival may be possible in another dimension if some of the humans learn to remain there rather than returning to the reality stream they have left for a while. Paul Heisenberg, whose last name suggests an allusion to physicist Werner Heisenberg and his Uncertainty Principle, is a popular evangelist who, along with others, is "fished" out of the time-stream by some unknown agency desiring to preserve some of humankind. Heisenberg thus becomes a prophet in different points in time, ever further apart. One of the followers who enters the story at Heisenberg's first reawakening into the time flow, Rebecca, becomes a kind of love interest. A machine, which helps him as

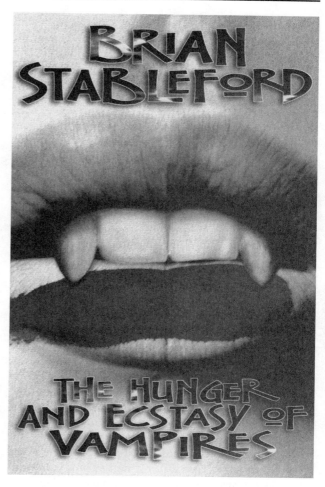

Dust jacket for the 1996 novel in which Stableford's narrator tells an audience that includes Oscar Wilde, H. G. Wells, and Nikola Tesla about his travels to a future time in which vampires have gained control over Earth and conquered the stars (Richland County Public Library)

he recovers from the effects of the first jump, also is important at the end of the novel. Meanwhile, individual intelligence is inevitably being displaced and absorbed into something called "third phase" life, in some ways reminiscent of the life-forms that will absorb Earth in "The Engineer and the Executioner." The place where the time-jumpers are in between times of reawakening is a place of great pain, but perhaps in that pain is revelation, the way into the new dimension. At last, even the machine cannot save Paul and Rebecca from the imminent absorption by the third-phase life. When they time-jump for the last time, even their frozen forms disappear. The conclusion of the novel suggests that they are the last humans to find their way across the threshold of a new dimension, although this final escape may be as much a delusion as Heisenberg's preaching had been a delusion of the masses.

First published by DAW as *Optiman* (1980), *War Games* (1981) is another action-adventure tale set on a remote planet. The "optiman" is a genetically engineered super warrior. The war games are many-leveled conflicts between humans and other aliens who have been "seeded" throughout space by former intelligent beings, also at war with one another. *The Castaways of Tanagar* (1981) is also an action adventure. Several cryogenically frozen criminals from Tanagar are sent across space to Earth to try to understand and cope with the changes in society, including concepts of morality, since the planet was abandoned by the humans who colonized Tanagar. Though Tanagar is too humane a society to execute its criminals, it is not too humane to put them at risk on this "new" Earth.

Journey to the Center (1982) is another action-adventure tale, set on and under the surface of the planet Asgard. In the novel Stableford uses the motif of a hollow world (in this case an alien artifact) and questions the nature of humanity through the practical and cynical Mike Rousseau and the android Myrlin, who has survived a war in space. Groups of space police and criminals embark on equally determined hunts deep into the core of Asgard. *The Gates of Eden* (1983), another action adventure, has a main character, Leander Caretta, whose memories of his nightmarish childhood complicate his efforts to come to grips with a shape-shifting native populace who stand in the way of their planet being available for human colonies.

In 1985 Stableford and co-author David Langford published *The Third Millennium: A History of the World, A.D. 2000–3000,* a futurist speculation that, though technically not fiction, could be enjoyed as such by those who are interested in the development of Earth in its next thousand years. As with any such extrapolation tied to specific dates, certain parts of it have become irrelevant because of events in the later 1980s and 1990s that changed the basis on which Stableford and Langford established their future history. In his review for the *Futurist* (September/October 1986), Burnham P. Beckwith noted that the world population, extrapolated as having risen to five billion in 2000, has already exceeded that number.

Also in 1985 Stableford's major contribution to the literary history of Britain was released. *Scientific Romance in Britain, 1890–1950* is a thorough study of a crucial sixty years in the development of speculative fiction. Stableford distinguishes scientific romance as a specifically British form of speculative literature that differs from science fiction, the American form, in terms of choice of subjects and of methods of developing those subjects. Different amounts of involvement in the conflict of ideas between Christians and followers of Charles Darwin, different reactions to World War I, and different publication realities contributed to the divergent results of these two beginnings of science fiction. The two lines of development did not converge until the aftermath of World War II.

Though originally presented in September 1978 to the University of York as his doctoral thesis, *The Sociology of Science Fiction* was not made easily available until its publication by Borgo Press in 1987, nine years later. Questions of the literary merit of the works Stableford uses in the study are beside the point. He limits the works he considers to those sold as science fiction and is interested in them on two counts: their popularity in the marketplace and their representation of "notions which are typical of their time." Whereas other sociologists of literature have been more concerned with insights gained from realistic fiction, Stableford believes that science fiction "may actually be more revealing of people's attitudes to social change than fiction dedicated to the description and evaluation of contemporary social situations."

Although *The Empire of Fear* (1988) was marketed as a horror novel and is about vampires, including Dracula, it really belongs to the subgenre of science fiction concerned with alternate history. Stableford's main character, Noell Cordery, is a scientist of the early seventeenth century. The cause of vampirism is not supernatural but extraterrestrial; it is a sexually transmitted "disease" with both desirable and undesirable effects. Though the disease confers an extremely long and healthy life (though Attila, still living, might remind a reader rather forcibly of Jonathan Swift's immortal but bitter Struldbrugs from *Gulliver's Travels,* 1726), it also lowers the male sex drive.

The first part of the novel, "The Man Who Loved the Vampire Lady," was also published in short-story form. The main characters of the section are the mortal Edmund Cordery, Noell's father, and his vampire love, the Lady Carmilla. Edmund has developed the microscope, which becomes Noell's chief tool in understanding that vampirism is a natural phenomenon. Edmund is apparently the first non-vampire to learn that vampirism is transmitted by blood and semen, and he uses the knowledge that the disease can be so transmitted to poison his own bodily fluids with plague and thus infect his vampire mistress in an attempt to protect his son and his microscope.

Noell's flight from the agents of vampire Richard the Lionhearted eventually takes him to a trading colony on the coast of Africa. With the invitation of African vampires and the help of an intelligent

Uruban youth, Ntikima, who is one of the Ogbone, a secret society, and in training to be a healer, he goes to Adamawara in the heart of the continent. To save his friends, Ntikima must assume the mask of Shango, the lord of the lightning and special patron of Adamawara. Because of this change he much later becomes the leader of his people. Noell, on the other hand, the first man to understand scientifically what began in Adamawara and has spread across Europe, is immune; he dies after being tortured by the Pope, also a vampire, as a condemned religious heretic. In the epilogue to the novel, vampirism is the rule rather than the exception, unless a person is unfortunate enough to have Cordery's Syndrome. The terror is gone, and "emortality," as vampirism is known, has become a sanitized medical process. Vampirism produces sterile physical matings, emortality is a process of emotionally sterile blood donations, and only one woman who has survived from that age to the far future realizes there has been anything of value lost.

After his study of sixty years of British scientific romance, Stableford developed a scientific romance of his own, ultimately writing it in trilogy form in response to the advice of his publisher. The result is the three Fallen Angels novels, *The Werewolves of London* (1989), *The Angel of Pain* (1991), and *The Carnival of Destruction* (1994). The basic premise of this trilogy has to do with the adaptability of the atheistic human mind in the face of evidence that does not fit its preconceptions. What if such a view suddenly has to come to grips with fallen angels capable of performing verifiable acts of creation and of interfering in the lives of humankind? The werewolves in the three novels—including the important characters Pelorus and Mandorla—appear mostly in their human form and, more important, are a deliberate creation of one of the seven fallen angels, Machalalel.

The main character, David Lydyard, is a young man in the first book, a medical researcher and father of a young family in the second, and a septuagenarian in the third. His mentor, then father-in-law, Sir Edward Tallentyre, is an optimistic Victorian atheist who sees no fear in his generation's loss of faith but rather experiences a great sense of wonder at the idea of being a tiny speck in a vast universe. He imparts this sense to David and to some extent his practical common sense to his granddaughter Nell. However, when David is possessed by one of the angels, Bast, Tallentyre's atheism is gravely tested. Eventually David uses the powers of analysis that Tallentyre has fostered in him to tie together all of his experiences with the fallen angels and come to an understanding of their true nature, which is not really supernatural at all.

Other characters are influenced by and try to understand the angels but are hindered by blind spots in their own nature. Luke Capthorn, later Asmodeus, understands only the brutish aspects of turn-of-the-century Satanic cults. The biochemist Jason Sterling is blinded by his monomania to discover the key to a healthy longevity or even immortality itself. A madam, Mercy, survives prostitution to thrive with relish on the business and theatrical aspects of prostituting others. The pride of Jacob Harkender, Lydyard's main nemesis, leads him to mistake the nature of the angel he has brought to consciousness, Zelophelon, and in the two latter books he does not manage to achieve the fullness of Lydyard's understanding. The special creations of the angels, Gabriel Gill, Hecate, the Clay Man, and the werewolves, are interesting false solutions to the angels' attempt to understand the nature of humanity and to determine if human intelligence is of any value to their survival. On the contrary, their links to humans nearly destroy them. As with *Man in a Cage,* the reader ultimately has to consider the possibility that all of these strange interactions are simply the result of delirium on the part of one of the characters.

The nonfiction *The Way to Write Science Fiction* (1989) includes an autobiographical preface and twelve chapters that discuss not only problems of constructing the science-fiction story, such as plot, characterization, and extrapolation, but also the practicalities of making a living while trying to market the product. Also in 1989 Stableford began a new project—the Warhammer series, under the pseudonym Brian Craig—including the novels *Warhammer: Zaragoz* (1989), *Warhammer: Plague Daemon* (1990), and *Warhammer: Storm Warriors* (1991), as well as several short stories in anthologies. *Dark Future: Ghost Dancers* (1991) is set in the universe of another Games Workshop product. This game tie-in work follows the conventions of the relevent war games rather than his own creations; nevertheless, he attempts to put the forces of "Chaos" in a more favorable light, as a deliberate subversion of the worldview in these game universes.

In the late 1980s Stableford began to experiment more with the short-story form. One of his short stories, "The Growth of the House of Usher," is a parody that is at once a compliment to Edgar Allan Poe and a future vision of bioengineering to produce a kind of self-sufficient living container that the friend of Roderick Usher must not flee from in horror but must preserve. Some of Stableford's stories, including "The Growth of the House of Usher," are collected in *Sexual Chemistry: Sardonic Tales of the Genetic Revolution* (1991). Two of his short stories, "The Cosmic Perspective" and "Custer's Last Stand," were published together in 1985, back-to-back in an imitation of the old Ace doubles. "Custer's Last Stand" is a curious piece of metafiction, in which author Marcus Custer undergoes a period of writer's block while being picketed by characters from his fiction, who are also harassing him on the telephone.

Five of Stableford's uncollected stories from 1993 introduce some interesting ideas and metaphors. "Riding the Tiger," published in the February 1993 issue of *Interzone,* involves people in dangerous undertakings, but the person riding the tiger here is an immortal shape-shifter who in saving his sister makes it possible for a terrorist to steal an antidote for germ warfare. "Burned Out," published in the April issue of *Interzone,* involves the search for survivors of a burned-out laboratory for genetic engineering, a terrorist act used by the scientists to cover their secret experiments. "The Flowers of the Forest," published in the June 1993 issue of *Amazing,* deals with a symbiosis of intelligent plant and animal, from the point of view of a space-faring human who has had to be specially adapted to work on a planet. In the light of those adaptations, the fact that his coworker has become part of a tree is not frightening but intriguing, with "unique evolutionary potential in it."

"Carriers," first appearing in *Isaac Asimov's Science Fiction Magazine* (July 1993) links a "man who came back from Mars," the practice of blood farming, and a young woman and her daughter by virgin birth being chased by government agents. Janine (the mother) and Emma (the child) carry a gene that makes males unnecessary for human reproduction. Bowring was unable save his friends on the Mars mission, and he is unable help Janine and Emma now. He is able to help Janine understand the entrapment of heredity and environment, however. "The Facts of Life," also from *Isaac Asimov's Science Fiction Magazine* presents an unusual underlying metaphor: God as a child in a dysfunctional family and the created world as a science project made to escape a combative family atmosphere. From December 2020 to December 2021 Benjy escapes the escalating quarrels of his stepmother and father by nurturing a terrarium of two life-forms that are at last learning to coexist peacefully. The experiment is ended by his father's destruction of the experiment after the failure of his marriage. In spite of his desolation, however, Benjy escapes again.

Another project in the 1990s was Stableford's work for Dedalus Press as an editor, author, and translator of some works from French to English. A couple of these collections include one or more of his short stories: "Innocent Blood" in *Tales of the Wandering Jew* (1991), and "Salomé" under his name as well as "The Woman in the Mirror" under the Brian Craig pseudonym and "Self-Sacrifice" under the Francis Amery pseudonym in *The Dedalus Book of Femmes Fatales* (1992).

Having previously tried his hand successfully at writing about vampirism in *The Empire of Fear* and having immersed himself in the fin de siècle decadence of the 1890s, Stableford explored vampirism further in two novels and a short story, *Young Blood* (1992), *The Hunger and Ecstasy of Vampires* (1996), and "Sheena" (2000). *Young Blood* and *The Hunger and Ecstasy of Vampires* are more centered on philosophy, on questions about the nature of reality and fantasy and what distinguishes them from one another, and on what survival of the fittest means in terms of vampires and human beings as two different evolutionary branches in the development of intelligent life on Earth. *The Hunger and Ecstasy of Vampires,* a philosophical tale set in 1895, has none of the overt action of *The Empire of Fear.* It is more of a thought puzzle, with literary and historical allusion playing a major part in the characters selected for Professor Edward Copplestone's narration of his dream vision. Oscar Wilde, H. G. Wells, Nikola Tesla, two characters rather like Sherlock Holmes and Dr. Watson, and Count Lugard (Dragul, spelled backwards) are Copplestone's audience for the frame narrative. Members of this unlikely gathering react to one another and to the situation, providing some conflict to the narrative. The effect on Count Lugard is, however, the most thought-provoking. This mysterious foreigner, picked up by Wilde in his nightly rambles and thus included in the group of Copplestone's guests, is the only one who understands the significance of what Copplestone has seen in his three "timeshadow" trips to the future. The vampires are the fitter of the two species in the distant future; they dominate the Earth and conquer the stars. Count Lugard begins his new mission to protect this future by destroying the evidence that the great investigator and his medical friend collect in an attempt to show what Lugard really is and that Copplestone's tale is reality rather than a series of drug-induced fantasies. *The Hunger and Ecstasy of Vampires* is part of a portmanteau novel; the other two parts, "The Black Blood of the Dead" (1997) and "The Gateway of Eternity" (1999), have been abridged serially in *Interzone.*

Stableford's next fictional effort, the Genesys trilogy, ventures again to a planet far from Earth and significantly different. The native life-forms evolved from land rather than sea, thus incorporating more mineral substances than Earth creatures. The planet's return to an active, progenerative phase of its life cycle presents its inhabitants with an unknown challenge, forcing the main characters into

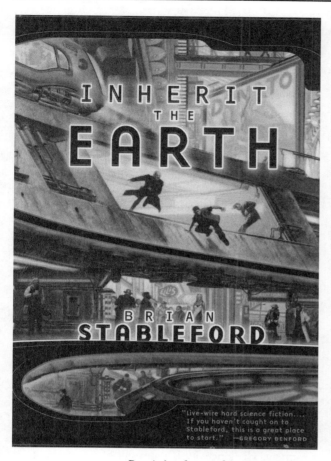
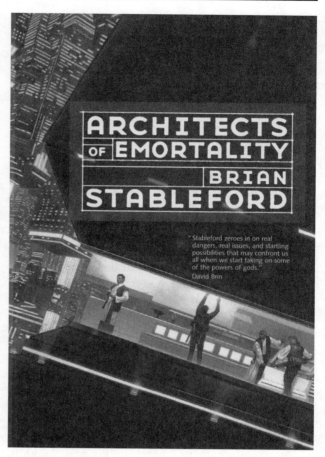

Dust jackets for two of the novels in which Stableford addresses the human desire for emortality,
a term he uses to denote a state of extended youthful longevity
(Richland County Public Library)

unsought alliances with one another. The Genesys novels comprise *Serpent's Blood: The First Book of Genesys* (1995), *Salamander's Fire: The Second Book of Genesys* (1996), and *Chimera's Cradle: The Third Book of Genesys* (1997). "Serpents" and "salamanders" refer literally to two of the indigenous species of Genesys, given these names in the distant past by the first human explorers, who borrowed some of their genetic structure to incorporate in that of the human colonists to increase their chances of survival on their new home world when they were left to survive or die. "Chimeras" refer to a forgotten adult stage of the indigenous species that recurs once every thousand years, enabling them to fly to the heart of their world, the "cradle," for their death/recombination/rebirth. The humans, in spite of their genetic modification, have to arrive at their destinations in a more pedestrian way, although one member of the quest does have a thrilling ride to his transformation via kidnap by manticore and ingestion, modification, and regurgitation by that part of the planet itself.

The Genesys trilogy is organized as an episodic quest made up of diverse characters from different parts of the planet, most of whom complete their quest in one way or another. The main character and original quester is a self-exiled prince, Andris Myrasol, from the land situated the farthest north from the legendary Chimera's Cradle. Yet, his participation in this quest with some of the other main characters is not at first as a leader but as a fugitive. Myrasol escapes early in *Serpent's Blood* from the same experience that becomes the fulfillment of his quest by the end of *Chimera's Cradle:* he becomes a contented, talking tree in one of the gardens of the "cradle." One of the other, minor questers who arrives at the same destination, the head of the drone from the "human" anthill, is less satisfied. The drone becomes forever trapped in the branches of Myrasol, now a philosophical but asexual tree.

Paul J. McAuley, in *Interzone* (August 1997), wrote that the trilogy "founders on reefs of explication." K. V. Bailey, in *Foundation,* suggested that the Genesys trilogy should be placed more "toward the fantasy end of the generic scale." Nevertheless, Bailey also wrote of how well "Stableford's biological inventiveness permeates successive landscapes of the journey." "Biological inventiveness" also underlies the premise of a self-aware planetary intelligence that takes stock of itself every thousand years and is perhaps also itself a genetic engineer of sorts, transforming the bearers of information back to the Chimera's Cradle. The chimerical forms of the serpents and salamanders are depicted in their varieties. One adult form is winged, making its journey to one of the parts of the chimera's cradle with none of the ground hazards encountered by questers such as Myrasol. Stableford's spelling of *Genesys* suggests a double meaning to the quest. Like quests in general, it has a mythic significance (the journey to the heart of the source of life) and a biologic significance (the attempt to discover the genetic systems of this environment).

Stableford's novels *Inherit the Earth, Architects of Emortality* (1999), *Fountains of Youth* (2000), and *The Cassandra Complex* (2001) address the human craving for "emortality," a term used earlier in *The Empire of Fear* to distinguish the state of extended youthful longevity from immortality, the inability to die. In the four later books this longevity is not linked to vampirism. Added to the common theme of the desirability of youthful longevity is the theme of the survival value of removing reproduction from human biological functions, thus sidestepping the grim prophecies of nineteenth-century economist Thomas Malthus. The first three novels have as a given that children are no longer the result of sexual intercourse and that many adults now form a cooperative "marriage" to parent a child through the formative years. In *Inherit the Earth* the main character, Damon Hart (born Damon Helier), has been raised by four parents. In *Fountains of Youth* Mortimer Gray is the child of eight parents and his friend Emily of even more.

Inherit the Earth involves multiple kidnappings and possible murders of Damon's biologist parents and even of Damon himself, with speculations about what possible terrorist groups could be behind them. Longevity in this novel has been achieved through extensive use of nanotechnology, but already there is a growing awareness that this longevity involves a rejuvenation process that can be repeated only a finite number of times before senility and death result. The "authentically young," a term used frequently in *Inherit the Earth* and *Architects of Emortality,* deliberately court injury to test their nanotechnology to its limits. Damon has recently moved past his rebellious phase as a street fighter for virtual-reality entertainment when he has to unravel the mystery of who wants to harm his remaining foster parents and destroy the reputation of his biological father, Con-

rad Helier, the man whose discovery of artificial wombs insured the survival of the human race in the aftermath of a worldwide plague of sterility. By the final chapter Damon and the readers realize that the events have not been staged by terrorists but by corporations who want to maintain control of technological and biological developments and therefore to stabilize human society.

Architects of Emortality is a murder mystery, and the instruments of death are genetically engineered flowers. Literary allusion abounds, from the chief crime investigators being named Hal Watson and Charlotte Holmes through the man who is ultimately responsible for the murders being called both Rappaccini and Moreau. The woman who delivers the flowers, therefore, is Rappaccini's "daughter," and the island on which the murders were planned is "the island of Dr. Moreau." Another allusion lies in the name of the rival genetic engineer of flowers, Oscar Wilde, who models much of his love of the showmanship of his life on that of his nineteenth-century namesake. Almost always talking nonstop, Wilde is the one who gives most of the explanations and interpretations of the biological extrapolations and their societal significance.

One of the three main characters, Wilde is not "authentically young" like the other two, but he has just undergone his third and final possible rejuvenation treatment. His longevity is the result of nanotechnology. Holmes, another of the three main characters, is "authentically young." Her probable longevity is also based on nanotechnology. Michael Lowenthal, also "authentically young," is the product of a later system. His future longevity is based on a recent breakthrough in genetic engineering called the Zaman transformation, which will give him youthful longevity far beyond that possible for Oscar or Charlotte. He has been sent as a special observer to the murder investigation by the MegaMall, the corporate "descendant" of the manipulative corporations of *Inherit the Earth.* These three eventually discover that the ultimate murder "victim" is an island genetically engineered by Rappaccini's father, a once-promising scientist who was on the track of something like the Zaman transformation, but whose intellectual timidity sidetracked him into safer inquiries, dooming the elder Rappaccini to the limited longevity of nanotechnology. The use of Charlotte, Michael, and Oscar to solve this mystery gives Stableford a stage to exhibit the envy raised by two means of youthful longevity, one with clearly greater potential for the realization of this dream than the one it is replacing.

Fountains of Youth is set in a more distant future in which the last generation of those enhanced through nanotechnology have died, all the people have been born with the Zaman transformation, and some have even been further genetically modified with four hands instead of two hands and two feet to meet the needs of life as space travelers. Death has seemingly been set at a remote conceptual distance. Yet, there is far more death in this novel than in the previous two. In *Inherit the Earth* there may be one genuine death of a named character, Surinder Nahal, and Stableford has deliberately left the reader unsure even of that one, as part of the creation of doubt about the distinction between reality and virtual reality. In *Architects of Emortality* there are five murders under investigation, plotted by a murderer who is authentically dead by the time they are committed. In *Inherit the Earth* young rebels make authentically violent virtual-reality tapes of street fights, from which they expect to be temporarily in pain, but from which they expect to gain money for increasingly effective upgrades. *Architects of Emortality* focuses on no such comparable phenomenon. In *Fountains of Youth* Stableford introduces Hellward Lucifer Nyxson, who preaches the gospel of the right to die. There are waves of attempted suicides by people seduced by the "pornography of death."

The concept for this book was also first explored in a story, "Mortimer Gray's History of Death" (1996). Mortimer's life work, researching and writing a history of death throughout the ages, is the result of his near-death experience in the "Coral Sea disaster." At that time he and 8-year-old Emily Marchant are the only survivors from one of the shipwrecks caused by an unforeseen eruption from the core of the earth. They become firm friends, though never lovers, corresponding electronically over the years, meeting occasionally. Emily goes to space to make her career. Mortimer, except for one period when he flees to the Moon to escape the attentions of suicide groupies, remains on Earth. His period of dwelling on the Moon gives him a chance to know the genetically engineered space explorers, whose eventual discovery foreshadows the ultimate futility of the experiment in youthful longevity and confronts humankind with fear of death intensified by knowledge that it means the destruction of whole biospheres.

Gray's 364-year life work is completed, in spite of the vicissitudes of his rather accident-prone long life. By an incredible coincidence, Gray is rescued from his potential accidental death beneath the Arctic ice cap by Emily's "multifunctional spaceship, built for deep dives into the atmosphere of Jupiter and the ice-shelled seas of Europa and Titan."

The fourth book in this series, *The Cassandra Complex* is a prequel. Set in the near future of Earth

rather than the far future of the rest of the series, *The Cassandra Complex* carries in its title a literary allusion of unheeded warnings of disasters to come. The original Cassandra from the *Iliad* had the gift of prophecy tainted with the curse that no one would heed her warnings. The "Cassandra" of this novel is a minor character, genetic research scientist Morgan Miller. Rumors about results of his research are the main point of competition and conflict of the whole work. *The Cassandra Complex* is the second murder mystery in this series. The victims, however, are not humans but thousands of laboratory mice, most of them residents in what at first appears to be a long-finished project on overpopulation partly under the supervision of Miller. The principal investigator is forensic scientist Lisa Friemann, and the principal terrorist is Helen Grundy, former wife of Lisa's associate, police inspector Mike Grundy. Lisa, as a former assistant and occasional sexual partner of Miller, is also a target because of what she is believed to know about the results of Miller's genetic research. Puzzled about the possible link between three crimes—the theft of computer and paper files from her apartment, the incineration of the inhabitants of Mouseworld, and the kidnapping of Miller—Lisa not only must use her scientific expertise to search for the criminals but also must reevaluate events from her 40-year friendship with Miller. In *Inherit the Earth* and *Architects of Emortality,* the "Miller effect" refers to the unavoidable senility that overtakes those whose longevity is the result of nanotechnology. The Miller effect of *The Cassandra Complex* observed in mice is that rejuvenating longevity is possible through genetic engineering, but works only in females.

Another carryover from *Inherit the Earth* is the Ahasuerus Foundation, a private group dedicated to research for reliable youthful longevity and also to suspended animation to preserve their founder and other wealthy donors until this goal is finally achieved. Miller's attempts to pass his failed research on to them and another such group misleads radical feminists into believing he has not failed and is trying to sell his work to the highest bidder.

The layers of misdirection in *The Cassandra Complex* and *Architects of Emortality* make these two murder mysteries the most comic of the four novels. "Authentically young" Charlotte and authentically old (at least for her century) Lisa both solve their mysteries. Charlotte, though longing for action, gets little of it beyond rather passively chasing her villain across a continent, through the mountains, across an ocean, then from island to island, only to find that the perpetrator is actually dead. Lisa, whose long career as a forensic scientist has been spent chasing criminals with microscope and crime-scene DNA samples, ultimately finds herself in a showdown in the corridors beneath a dress shop. Branded a traitor by feminist terrorists, Lisa saves them, in spite of themselves, from a mistake that would seriously undermine their cause. Lisa is punished rather than rewarded for her success, forced to undergo an investigation by internal affairs, and fired. Her competence has, however, caught the attention of Megacorp, and Lisa is rewarded for her knowledge, experience, and scientific thinking.

Stableford satirized the "Y2K" hysteria of the 1990s and the popular confusion over when the new millennium actually began, in 2000 or 2001, in short stories written as Francis Amery, the pseudonym he had earlier chosen as a translator of French literature of the 1890s. Published in *Interzone,* "When Molly Met Elvis" (April 1997), "Molly and the Angel" (July 1999), and "Molly and the Men in Black" (September 1999) are parodies of three elements of American popular culture: Elvis Presley, the sentimental television series *Touched by an Angel,* and the parodic science-fiction movie *Men in Black.* Molly is a former prostitute trying to conquer a drug addiction in order to regain custody of the two daughters she has as a result of being raped. Molly seems an unlikely candidate to become the new savior of humankind, but in *Year Zero* (2000) her undauntable maternal instinct drives her into that role. *Year Zero,* published under Stableford's name, blends these earlier stories into a satire of millennialism. The year 2000 is the "year zero" of the title, a year of opportunities to begin again. It is impossible to determine what is real and what is delusion among the people whom Molly meets and the things that happen to her in "year zero." Figments of one delusion go so far as to lecture her on the lack of believability of others. There is even a final confrontation between Molly and the Devil, over the salvation of her teenage daughters, Christine and Angela, whose names have obvious Christian overtones. Her final destiny seems to be to use her unstoppable maternal instinct to re-create and redirect the course of evolution.

Warhammer: The Wine of Dreams (2000), published under Stableford's "Brian Craig" pseudonym, is a fantasy novel centered on the violent coming of age of seventeen- year-old Reinmar Wieland as his formerly peaceful town, Eilhart, and its nearby surrounding vineyards become the site of a battle not so much between good and evil as between wholesome and disgusting. Trained in both the wine trade and in swordplay, Reinmar dreams of adventure away from the familiar. Eilhart becomes the focus of a showdown between the forces of witch hunter Machar

Von Spurzheim and malformed, possibly demonic creatures; eventually the town is saved in spite of the loss of life of most of its citizens. The battle itself, however, seems to have little to do with wine; Stableford concentrates instead on narration of the physical grotesqueness of the creatures attacking the town.

Two themes often used by Stableford are foundations for *Warhammer: The Wine of Dreams.* Not only does the wine bring dreams that in their vividness can compete with the virtual reality in *Inherit the Earth,* but it also grants the partaker a version of youthful immortality as long as more of it can be consumed, even reversing the physical and mental decrepitude brought on by long abstinence. The production of the wine involves a symbiosis in which the human willingly and happily becomes one with the plant. Whereas the transformation of Andris Myrasol in *Chimera's Cradle* is cerebral, the union of human and flower that ultimately results in the wine of dreams is sensual. The theme of youthful immortality is developed through Reinmar's grandfather, Luther; Luther's brother, Albrecht; Albrecht's former mistress, Valeria; and Albrecht's illegitimate son, Wirnt. The first three show effects of extreme old age, especially Luther, who is bedfast and somewhat senile. Reinmar's father, Gottfried, has been so revolted by the older men's addiction that he has taken control of the family business and raised his son with no knowledge of the dark wine. When Reinmar finds the monastery that produces it, steals a vial of the concentrate, brings it back to Eilhart, and tries to conceal it in the wine shop, his extended family, except for his father, are ruined by it, most of them killing each other to gain control of it.

Reinmar also has a romantic crisis appropriate to an inexperienced seventeen-year-old, but that has an unusual twist related to the production of the wine of dreams. He strays from his childhood sweetheart, Marguerite, only to compete with a flower for the love of an exquisitely beautiful Gypsy girl, Marcilla. He finds the source of the dark wine by following Marcilla, who has received a psychic call that draws her to the cavern of the flowers. In this underground setting the flowers dwell and their servant monks attend them, harvesting and distilling their nectar, which they then use in diluted form to create the dark wine. Reinmar sees Marcilla about to be penetrated by the flower and rescues her, believing that he is saving her from a fate worse than death. He destroys that year's harvest of dark wine, except for the vial of concentrate he steals, and brings Marcilla back to Eilhart but never gains her affection. Although his great-uncle Albrecht had once told him "there is no evil in wine, but there is evil in men, and even the finest wine can sometimes draw it out," Reinmar sees the strength of the flower's call to Marcilla, the inevitability of the wine revealing its hidden location to his addicted old grandfather, and the thoroughness with which it leads family members to kill one another. Nevertheless, though he has not yet become an addict, Reinmar chooses to keep and conceal the last of the stolen concentrate.

Warhammer 40,000: Pawns of Chaos (2001), which Stableford also published as Brian Craig, is based on the theme of the long and continuous struggle for dominance between order and chaos; the tale includes several twists. The most sympathetic characters are those on the side of Chaos, especially fifteen-year-old Dathan and his friend Hycilla. The least sympathetic, Orloc Melcarth and Ragan Balberith, are a power-hungry dictator and a fanatical grand inquisitor, whose attempts to displace each other are concealed under the guise of a holy war to purge the planet Sigmatus of heretical, sorcerous mutants. Sigmatus is in an unstable region of the universe, and these mutants are not only the descendants of the first wave of human colonists but also of the so-called Imperium, the second wave of humans marooned on a mission to this world. The troops of the Imperium invade and destroy the peaceful rural village of Odienne, dashing out the brains of one of the children in front of Dathan and Hycilla and preserving for torture only Pater Saltana, the kindly village teacher and wise dreamer. The so-called champions of civilization thus come to seem more morally hideous than the people they claim to be so evil because of the ugly mutations of their outward appearance. The powerful sorceror, Gavalon the Great, whose exterior form has grown the most hideous of all, is a godly worshiper of the Changer of the Ways, a defender of murdered innocents and a hope of refuge and revenge for displaced persons. Gavalon mutilates himself as a form of sacrifice to call to life the daemon Sathorael. Sathorael seems to be a force to preserve the innocent and to punish the greedy, invading fanatics. Within hours of its birth, it rescues Dathan and Hycilla and continues to do so as it metamorphoses into its maturity.

Another twist is revealed through the mental growth of Dathan during the three-day span of the novel, partly triggered by the brutal thoroughness of the invaders, partly by the transforming touch of the daemon, creating a temporary trinity of Sathorael (ultimately a mindless, universal, irresistible force), Hycilla (who represents telepathic emotion), and Dathan (who represents rational reevaluation). In spite of their evil leaders, the discipline of soldiers of the Imperium is ultimately better for survival of the human species than the idiosyncratic freedom of the

forces of Gavalon. The long-term contest is between preservation and destruction of the entire universe. Sathorael is an instrument of the Changer of the Ways, growing into a fully developed "warpstorm" in time to destroy the next wave of ships from the True Imperium. Only Dathan's rational interference as part of the trinity saves three of the twelve ships, which will become the next invaders of Sigmatus, the next persecutors of those humans inhabiting it before their arrival. Through her voice the Changer of the Ways offers to make Dathan a more powerful sorcerer than Gavalon. When Dathan refuses, the Changer of the Ways advises him to travel west in order to save his life. "Even so, when Dathan set out in search of a place to be, he headed eastwards rather than westwards, because he knew now that only a fool would take the word of a god." Dathan's final judgment of the worth of gods is similar to that of Stableford's *Carnival of Destruction:* they are capricious at best, and the universe is a more rational place without them.

Since 1969 Brian M. Stableford's career has fallen into three clearly identifiable periods. Stableford himself has identified many of the works published during his twenties as formula fiction, written to earn a living from publishers such as Ace and DAW, mined and reworked from some manuscript juvenilia. The second decade of his career, corresponding roughly to his thirties, is the period in which he departed temporarily from most of his fictional projects to write the historical and critical works that established his reputation as a major scholar. In the third decade of Stableford's career he returned to fiction as his major focus, meanwhile working in nonfiction, for instance in his award-winning essay "How Should a Science Fiction Story End?" (1995). Sound and competent though it is, his work has not had mass-market appeal. Those who have read him, however, generally agree that Stableford remains one of the most gifted satirists of science fiction.

Interviews:

Jeffrey M. Elliot, "Interview: Brian Stableford," *Starship,* 18 (Summer/Fall 1981): 15–20;

Catie Cary, "Brian Stableford Interviewed," *Vector,* 172 (April/May 1993): 6–10;

Stan Nicholls, "Brian Stableford Cottons On," in *Wordsmiths of Wonder: Fifty Interviews with Writers of the Fantastic,* edited by Nicholls (London: Orbit, 1993), pp. 164–168;

Darrell Schweitzer, "SFC Interview: Brian Stableford," *Science Fiction Chronicle,* 19 (October 1997): 7, 39–40;

Nick Gevers, "Stapledon with Sarcasm: Brian Stableford," *Interzone,* 158 (August 2000): 52–55;

Cheryl Morgan, "Interview: Brian Stableford," *Strange Horizons* (2001).

Bibliography:

Phil Stephensen-Payne, *Brian Stableford, Genetic Revolutionary: A Working Bibliography* (Leeds: Stephensen-Payne, 1997).

References:

Brian W. Aldiss, "Halcyon Drift," in *Survey of Science Fiction Literature,* volume 2, edited by Frank N. Magill (Englewood Cliffs, N.J.: Salem Press, 1979), pp. 936–939;

Charles N. Brown, "Brian Stableford: The Science of Fear," *Locus,* 27 (August 1991): 5, 69;

Casey Fredericks, "The Big Time," in *The Future of Eternity: Mythologies of Science Fiction and Fantasy* (Bloomington: University of Indiana Press, 1982), pp. 65–90;

Colin Greenland, "An Interest in Carpentry," Foundation Forum: Feminism and SF, *Foundation,* 43 (Summer 1988): 76–77;

Chris Hill, "The Loneliness of the Long Distance Biologist: The Early Science Fiction of Brian Stableford, a Retrospective," *Vector,* 211 (May/June 2000): 4–6;

Gwyneth Jones, "The Walrus Is Brian," Foundation Forum: Feminism and SF, *Foundation,* 43 (Summer 1988): 75–76;

Roz Kaveney, "Losing of Paradise: Brian Stableford," *Interzone,* 27 (January/February 1989): 13–17;

David Langford, "Six and a Half Things You Didn't Know about Brian Stableford," Wincon II Souvenir Book (Winchester, U.K.: Wincon II, 1991), pp. 12–14;

Sarah Lefanu, "Engaging the Reader," Foundation Forum: Feminism and SF, *Foundation,* 43 (Summer 1988): 72–74;

David Pringle, "Rats, Humans and Other Minor Vermin: An Assessment of Brian Stableford's Novels," *Foundation,* 15 (January 1979): 19–28;

Pringle, "*Walking Shadow* by Brian Stableford (1979)," in *Science Fiction: The 100 Best Novels,* edited by Pringle (New York: Carroll & Graf, 1985), pp. 195–196;

Gary Westfahl, "Cremators of Science Fiction, 1 & 2: Brian Stableford and John Clute," *Interzone,* 130 (April 1998): 51–53;

Westfahl, "On the True History of Science Fiction," *Foundation,* 47 (Winter 1989–1990): 5–27;

Jenny Wolmark, "There's More to Life Than Crocodile Tears," Foundation Forum: Feminism and SF, *Foundation,* 43 (Summer 1988): 74–75.

Ian Watson

(20 April 1943 –   )

Darren Harris-Fain
Shawnee State University

BOOKS: *Japan: A Cat's Eye View* (Osaka: Bunken, 1969);

The Embedding (London: Gollancz, 1973; New York: Scribners, 1975);

The Jonah Kit (London: Gollancz, 1975; New York: Scribners, 1976);

Orgasmachine, by Watson and Judith Jackson Watson, translated into French by Michel Pétris (Paris: Champ Libre, 1976);

The Martian Inca (London: Gollancz, 1977; New York: Scribners, 1977);

Japan Tomorrow (Osaka: Bunken, 1977);

Alien Embassy (London: Gollancz, 1977; New York: Ace, 1978);

Miracle Visitors (London: Gollancz, 1978; New York: Ace, 1978);

The Very Slow Time Machine (London: Gollancz, 1979; New York: Ace, 1979);

God's World (London: Gollancz, 1979; New York: Carroll & Graf, 1990);

Alan Ayckbourn: Bibliography, Biography, Playography (London: TQ, 1980);

The Gardens of Delight (London: Gollancz, 1980; New York: Pocket Books, 1982);

Conversations with Ayckbourn (London: Macdonald, 1981);

Under Heaven's Bridge, by Watson and Michael Bishop (London: Gollancz, 1981; New York: Ace, 1982);

Deathhunter (London: Gollancz, 1981; New York: St. Martin's Press, 1986);

Sunstroke and Other Stories (London: Gollancz, 1982);

Chekhov's Journey (London: Gollancz, 1983; New York: Carroll & Graf, 1989);

The Book of the River (London: Gollancz, 1984; New York: DAW, 1986);

Converts (London: Panther, 1984; New York: St. Martin's Press, 1985);

The Book of the Stars (London: Gollancz, 1984; New York: DAW, 1986);

The Book of Being (London: Gollancz, 1985; New York: DAW, 1986);

Ian Watson (from James Gunn, The New Encyclopedia of Science Fiction, *1988)*

The Book of Ian Watson (Willimantic, Conn.: Ziesing, 1985);

Slow Birds and Other Stories (London: Gollancz, 1985);

Queenmagic, Kingmagic (London: Gollancz, 1986; New York: St. Martin's Press, 1988);

The Books of the Black Current (Garden City, N.Y.: Doubleday, 1986)—comprises *The Book of the River, The Book of the Stars,* and *The Book of Being;*

Evil Water and Other Stories (London: Gollancz, 1987);

The Power (London: Headline, 1987);

The Fire Worm (London: Gollancz, 1988);

Whores of Babylon (London: Paladin, 1988);

Meat (London: Headline, 1988);

Salvage Rites and Other Stories (London: Gollancz, 1989);

The Flies of Memory (London: Gollancz, 1990; New York: Carroll & Graf, 1991);

Nanoware Time [bound with John Varley's *The Persistence of Vision*] (New York: Tor, 1990);

Warhammer 40,000: Inquisitor (Brighton, West Sussex: Games Workshop Books, 1990);

Stalin's Teardrops (London: Gollancz, 1991);

Lucky's Harvest (London: Gollancz, 1993);

Warhammer 40,000: Space Marine (London: Boxtree, 1993);

Warhammer 40,000: Harlequin (London: Boxtree, 1994);

The Coming of Vertumnus (London: Gollancz, 1994);

The Fallen Moon (London: Gollancz, 1994);

Warhammer 40,000: Chaos Child (London: Boxtree, 1995);

Hard Questions (London: Gollancz, 1996);

Oracle (London: Gollancz, 1997);

The Great Escape (Collinsville, Ill.: Golden Gryphon, 2002).

OTHER: "The Ghosts of Luna," in *New Worlds 7,* edited by Charles Platt and Hilary Bailey (London: Sphere, 1974), pp. 113–118; republished as *New Worlds 6* (New York: Avon, 1975), pp. 132–137;

"EA 5000: Report on the Effects of a Riot Gas," in *Stopwatch: A Collection of International SF Stories,* edited by George Hay (London: New English Library, 1974), pp. 63–79;

"The Forest as Metaphor for Mind: 'The Word for World Is Forest' and 'Vaster Than Empires and More Slow,'" in *Science-Fiction Studies: Selected Articles on Science Fiction 1973–1975,* edited by R. D. Mullen and Darko Suvin (Boston: Gregg Press, 1976), pp. 261–267; republished in *Ursula K. Le Guin,* edited by Harold Bloom (New York: Chelsea House, 1986), pp. 47–56;

"Le Guin's *Lathe of Heaven* and the Role of Dick: The False Reality as Mediator," in *Science-Fiction Studies: Selected Articles on Science Fiction 1973–1975,* edited by Mullen and Suvin (Boston: Gregg Press, 1976), pp. 223–231;

"Immune Dreams," in *Pulsar #1,* edited by Hay (Harmondsworth, U.K.: Penguin, 1978); republished in *Mathenauts: Tales of Mathematical Wonder,* edited by Rudy Rucker (New York: Arbor House, 1987), pp. 112–124;

"Barrington J. Bayley," "Michael Bishop," "David I. Masson," and "John Varley," in *Twentieth-Century Science-Fiction Writers,* edited by Curtis C. Smith (New York: St. Martin's Press, 1981), pp. 39–40, 52–53, 361–362, 552–553;

Pictures at an Exhibition, edited by Watson (Cardiff, South Wales: Greystoke Mobray, 1981; San Bernardino, Cal.: Borgo Press, 1987);

"The Ultimate One-Word First Contact Story," in *Alien Encounters,* edited by Jan Howard Finder (New York: Taplinger, 1982), p. 233;

Changes: Stories of Metamorphosis—An Anthology of Speculative Fiction about Startling Metamorphoses, Both Psychological and Physical, edited by Watson and Michael Bishop (New York: Ace, 1983);

"My Six Favourite Fan Letters," in *The Complete Book of Science Fiction and Fantasy Lists,* edited by Maxim Jakubowski and Malcolm Edwards (St. Albans & London: Granada, 1983), p. 211; republished as *The SF Book of Lists* (New York: Berkley, 1983), p. 211;

Afterlives: An Anthology of Stories about Life after Death, edited by Watson and Pamela Sargent (New York: Vintage, 1986);

"The Author as Torturer," in *Synergy 3,* edited by George Zebrowski (San Diego: Harcourt Brace Jovanovich, 1988), pp. 186–221;

"Evolution" and "Language," in *The New Encyclopedia of Science Fiction,* edited by James Gunn (New York: Viking, 1988), pp. 156–159, 264–267;

"*Who Made Stevie Crye?* by Michael Bishop," in *Horror: 100 Best Books,* edited by Stephen Jones and Kim Newman (London: Xanadu, 1988; New York: Carroll & Graf, 1988), pp. 203–204;

"Dancing on a Tightrope," in *The Work of Ian Watson: An Annotated Bibliography and Guide,* by Douglas A. Mackey (San Bernardino, Cal.: Borgo Press, 1989), pp. 129–134;

"The World Renews Itself: A View on the SF and Fantasy of 1987," in *Nebula Awards 23,* edited by Bishop (San Diego: Harcourt Brace Jovanovich, 1989), pp. 1–21;

"The Alien Beast Within," in *Warhammer 40,000: Deathwing,* edited by Neal Jones and David Pringle (Brighton, West Sussex: Games Workshop Books, 1990), pp. 217–257;

"The Sadim Touch," in *Drabble II: Double Century,* edited by Rob Meades and David Wake (Harold Wood, Essex: Beccon, 1990), p. 69;

"Themes and Variations: A View on the SF and Fantasy of 1988," in *Nebula Awards 24,* edited by Bishop (San Diego: Harcourt Brace Jovanovich, 1990), pp. 1–23;

"The Avalanche: A View on the SF and Fantasy Novels of 1989," in *Nebula Awards 25,* edited by Bishop

(San Diego: Harcourt Brace Jovanovich, 1991), pp. 27–41;

"The Amber Room," in *Tombs,* edited by Edward E. Kramer and Peter Crowther (Clarkston, Ga.: White Wolf, 1995), pp. 25–46;

"Custom-Built Girl," in *Cybersex,* edited by Richard Glyn Jones (New York: Carroll & Graf, 1996), pp. 307–332;

"The Great Escape," in *Dante's Disciples,* edited by Kramer and Crowther (Clarkston, Ga.: White Wolf, 1996), pp. 93–108;

"The Wild Hunt," in *Fantasy Stories,* edited by Mike Ashley (London: Robinson Children's Books, 1996);

"Ahead!" in *The Best of Interzone,* edited by Pringle (London: Voyager, 1997), pp. 198–210;

"The British Scene" and "At the Wrong End of Time: An Appreciation of John Brunner (1934–1995)," in *Nebula Awards 31,* edited by Sargent (San Diego, New York & London: Harcourt Brace, 1997), pp. 16–20, 116–124;

"The China Cottage," in *Destination Unknown,* edited by Crowther (Clarkston, Ga.: White Wolf, 1997), pp. 8–23;

"The British Scene," in *Nebula Awards 32,* edited by Jack Dann (New York, San Diego & London: Harcourt Brace, 1998), pp. 16–20;

"Tulips from Amsterdam," in *The Unexplained: Stories of the Paranormal,* edited by Ric Alexander (London: Orion, 1998), pp. 353–366.

SELECTED PERIODICAL PUBLICATIONS–
UNCOLLECTED: "Three Fables," *Darlite,* 1 (September 1966): 28–30;

"E. M. Forster: Whimsy and Beyond," *Rising Generation,* 115 (1 May 1969): 282–285;

"Elias Canetti: The One and the Many," *Chicago Review,* 20/21 (May 1969): 184–200;

"The Sex Machine," *New Worlds,* 199 (March 1970): 2–4;

"Science Fiction: Form Versus Content," by Watson and Christopher Priest, *Foundation,* 10 (June 1976): 55–65;

"W(h)ither Science Fiction?" *Vector,* 78 (November/ December 1976): 5–12;

"A Rhetoric of Recognition: The Science Fiction of Michael Bishop," *Foundation,* 19 (June 1980): 5–14;

"From Pan in the Home Counties–to Pain on a Far Planet: E. M. Forster, David Lindsay, and How the Voyage to Arcturus Should End," *Foundation,* 43 (Summer 1988): 25–36;

"La Fin de Bon-Bon: A French Science Fiction Story," *Back Brain Recluse,* 11 (September 1988): 24–26;

"The Talk of the Town: The Pictures" *New Yorker* (22 March 1999): 44–46;

"My Adventures with Stanley Kubrick," *Playboy* (August 1999), pp. 82–84, 90, 158–159.

Ian Watson is well known in all fields of fantastic fiction–science fiction, fantasy, and supernatural horror. He is best known, however, as one of the British science-fiction writers who emerged from the New Wave of the late 1960s and early 1970s. While he may not have achieved the prominence of other British figures associated with the New Wave, such as Brian W. Aldiss, J. G. Ballard, and Michael Moorcock, Watson is a writer respected for his highly imaginative narratives that explore the relationship among consciousness, language, and reality.

Watson was born on 20 April 1943 in St. Albans, England, where his father, John William Watson, worked at a radio station during World War II. His mother was Ellen Cowe Watson, née Rowley, and he was the couple's only child. After the war ended in 1945, the family returned to North Shields, near Tynedale in northern England, and his father returned to his job as a postal employee. From ages five to sixteen Watson attended Tynemouth School. During this time he began cultivating two of his interests, writing and gardening, and he read voraciously, everything from science fiction to mainstream literature. A precocious student, he took his graduation examinations two years early and graduated from Tynemouth at age seventeen.

Watson received a scholarship from Balliol College at Oxford University and began studying English literature there in 1960. There he met Judith Jackson, a painter, and when he was only a second-year student and nineteen, the two married on 1 September 1962. In 1963 he graduated from Oxford with a First Class Honours degree in English. He remained at Oxford for further work in English and French literature and continued to write, although he did not produce any work he felt worthy of publication. He received his research degree of B.Litt., similar to an American master's degree, in 1965 upon completion of his thesis, titled "Walter Pater Related to Some Nineteenth Century French Writers: Stendhal, Mérimée, Gautier, Flaubert and Baudelaire."

That year he began teaching literature at University College in Dar es Salaam, Tanzania. During the two years he spent there, he became more politically active, partly in response to the conditions in the African nation, and he wrote critical works on European and African authors. He also submitted some short fantasies to the university literary magazine under the title "Three Fables." In 1967, after a short stay in England, Watson and his wife moved to Japan, where he taught English literature at the Tokyo University of Education, Keio University in Tokyo, and Japan Women's University.

During Watson's three-year stay in Japan he became seriously interested in science fiction again—in part, he says, in response to the adjustment to modern urban life in a major metropolis such as Tokyo. He subscribed to the well-known British science-fiction magazine *New Worlds,* perhaps the chief instrument of the experimental New Wave, and he began writing science fiction himself. His first professional story, "Roof Garden under Saturn," appeared in *New Worlds* in 1969. Suitably enough, the story is set in a Tokyo department store that is an artificial world unto itself. It was republished in *The Book of Ian Watson* (1985). Also in 1969, he published a collection of short pieces titled *Japan: A Cat's Eye View.*

In 1970 Watson and his wife left Japan and returned to Oxford, where he taught classes in science fiction and futurism at Birmingham Polytechnic. He became more politically active, joining the Trotskyist Socialist Labour League, which later became the Workers Revolutionary Party. He was also engaged in ecological issues and Situationist publications. Meanwhile, in addition to his interest in science fiction, he was studying anthropology, structuralism, and linguistics on his own, all of which came together in his first novel, *The Embedding* (1973). In addition, during this time he experimented with LSD, an experience that he claims made him aware of the structure of his perceptions and that also influenced *The Embedding* and other works. Finally, in 1973 the Watsons' daughter, Jessica, was born, their only child.

The Embedding brings together three different stories. The first concerns a linguist named Chris Sole, who is attempting to introduce children to entirely new structures of language. His experiment is related to two key ideas in linguistics: the Sapir-Whorf hypothesis, which maintains that language determines at least in part the way humans conceptualize experience, and Noam Chomsky's theories about the relationship between language and consciousness. According to Chomsky, the ease with which children master complex grammatical systems can be explained by positing that a capacity for language is innate within the human brain; furthermore, he believed, certain structural principles of language must be embedded within human consciousness. Therefore, he believed, all human languages share certain deep structures, despite their many surface differences. Thus, Sole's efforts to "embed" new linguistic structures both draws on Chomsky's theories and attempts to defy them by creating entirely new language systems in the more malleable minds of children.

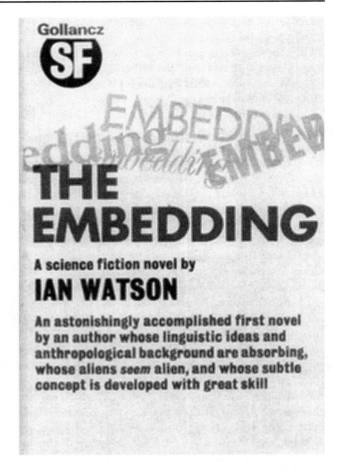

Dust jacket for Watson's 1973 novel, in which human and alien linguists meet to learn how to communicate with one another

The idea behind Sole's experiment is the notion that one's language governs one's sense of reality and that a radically different language would entail a radically different perception of reality.

Meanwhile, Sole's friend Pierre, another linguist, is working with a South American tribe that employs two different languages. One is the everyday tongue, while the other can be accessed only through the use of certain psychotropic drugs. This special language is reserved for the achievement of mystical states of consciousness, since a truly altered state of consciousness can be achieved only through a truly different language.

Both narrative strands of *The Embedding* relate to the third. If it might be possible to embed a radically different linguistic structure in children, and if an Amazonian tribe possesses a distinct second language that leads to a distinctly different perception of reality, then what must the consciousness of aliens be like? A party of aliens ponders this question as they get to know human beings and vice versa. Sole's experiment makes him the logical candidate to achieve communication with the aliens who have landed on Earth, and what they want is simple: to acquire information about human brains and their languages. The aliens, too, are linguists. In exchange, the aliens offer human beings a sampling of their highly advanced technology.

In addition to anthropology, linguistics, and drugs, another influence on *The Embedding,* according to Watson, was the work of the French Surrealist Raymond Roussel. His experiments with taking idiomatic expressions literally and with combining parts of language in original ways helped to shape some of the linguistic material in the novel.

The Embedding was an enormous success in the science-fiction field and brought Watson to the attention of fans and critics who might not have read his short stories in the four years of his professional career that preceded its publication. While it won neither the Hugo nor the Nebula award, it was well received critically. Writing in *Locus,* Michael Bishop called it "the most impressive first SF novel to appear in the seventies," while in the *New Statesman* J. G. Ballard called it "the most remarkable first novel I have read for ten years." It did win the Prix Apollo award for best science-fiction novel, either in French or in French translation, and the Spanish translation won the Premios Zikkurath for best foreign novel in Spanish translation in 1978. In general, *The Embedding* has remained Watson's best-known and most highly acclaimed work, despite a productive and diverse body of work published since that first novel.

In 1974 Watson became a member of the Science Fiction Foundation, a group of writers and academics dedicated to promoting the study of science fiction. The following year he became the features editor of *Foundation,* the journal of the group, to which he contributed several reviews and other pieces. Since that time Watson has published a great amount of critical and historical material on science fiction in addition to his own creative efforts.

In 1975 Watson published his second science-fiction novel, *The Jonah Kit.* Like *The Embedding,* this novel concerns the relationship between language and consciousness. Russian scientists manage to implant within a sperm whale two human minds, of a deceased cosmonaut and a schizophrenic boy—partly to test their linguistic theories, and partly to see what will happen. The Soviets maintain radio contact with the whale, which becomes important when proof for the existence of God, seemingly achieved by an American scientist, is communicated to the whale to pass on to other whales in order to study their reaction. What follows is an exciting, unpredictable plot, combining elements of the thriller with psychological and theological ideas.

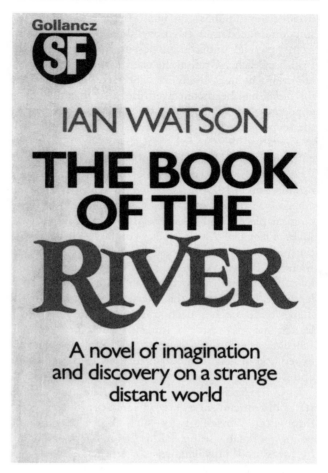

Dust jacket for the first novel in Watson's "Books of the Black Current" trilogy (Richland County Public Library)

The combined successes of *The Embedding* and *The Jonah Kit,* along with a steady stream of short-story sales, encouraged Watson to leave teaching and begin writing full-time in 1976. That year, however, he had more difficulty selling his next novel, a collaboration with his wife, Judith Jackson Watson. They had written the first version, then titled "The Woman Factory," back in 1970. They intended it as a radically feminist text against pornography, but used aspects of pornography in the process. The story tells how Jade, an artificial woman made by the Custom-Built Girl Corporation to be a sex slave, attempts to escape her exploitation. While the authors meant "The Woman Factory" to be an antipornography text, British and American publishers saw the work itself as pornographic, so it was first published in a French translation as *Orgasmachine* in 1976. They continued to revise the novel for English publication, retitling it "The Woman Plant," and it was purchased by Playboy Paperbacks. This publisher, however, was bought by Berkley, who decided not to publish the book. In the late 1980s Watson announced that the novel had been withdrawn from potential publication, despite an offer from the British publisher Grafton; he cited the changed political environment since the more "liberated" days in which the novel had been conceived. But by the late 1990s it appeared that Watson had reconsidered, and part of the revised novel was published as "Custom-Built Girl" in *Cybersex* (1996), edited by Richard Glyn Jones. The entire novel may yet see full publication in English.

Free now to write full-time, Watson became more prolific, and in 1977 he published three books: *The Martian Inca,* a novel; *Japan Tomorrow,* a collection of futurological pieces; and *Alien Embassy,* another novel. *The Martian Inca,* like *The Embedding,* combines the alien with the indigenous, in this case a Martian virus and an Indian in Bolivia. Again the story involves an alteration in consciousness, achieved in this novel not through language but through the effects of the virus. In the man's mind he has been transformed into an Incan leader, and as a result he leads his fellow peasants into rebellion against their oppressors. At the same time, an expedition of American astronauts has landed on Mars and is experiencing similar effects, with different results.

Alien Embassy again involves aliens and altered states of consciousness, but while certain themes recur throughout Watson's work—such as sex, religion, and politics—a notable feature of his fiction is his abundance of ideas and unwillingness to repeat himself. *Alien Embassy* concerns Lila, one of several people selected to search for alien life-forms not through interstellar travel but through psychic explorations aided by tantric yoga. In her astral journeying she encounters the Star Beast, a strange being who seems to be driving some people insane. She also learns that the Star Beast's actions may be part of a plot to keep most of the world insane, although the credibility of this notion is challenged as the story progresses.

In 1978 Watson published his next novel, *Miracle Visitors.* A psychologist named John Deacon studies people's accounts of UFOs, but he is skeptical when he interviews a man named Michael who claims to have been abducted by aliens and to have had sex with them. However, Deacon himself is abducted by aliens—in a Ford Thunderbird, no less. But this vehicle is no ordinary car, as it takes Deacon to the far side of the moon, where he learns about the aliens and their purposes. Moreover, he is introduced into a new state of consciousness, a dream-like "UFO state" that affords him a heightened perception of the nature of reality.

Watson and his family moved from Oxford to the village of Moreton Pinkney in Northamptonshire, sixty miles north of London, in 1979. There he joined the Campaign for Nuclear Disarmament and other groups opposing military installations. Watson also became involved in Labour Party politics at the local level. As secretary of the village hall, he helped to organize social events, and in 1981 he ran for county council, receiving one-third of the vote in a largely conservative area. He ran again, also unsuccessfully, in 1985 and 1989.

In 1979 Watson published his first collection of stories, *The Very Slow Time Machine.* Like *The Embedding,* "On Cooking the First Hero in Spring" deals with matters of anthropology, linguistics, and reality, concerning as it does an alien race, known as the Clayfolk, who possess only a single word in their language but who pass through a succession of different realities. The nature of reality is also the subject of "Programmed Love Story," about a man who calls up a computer-generated version of his former wife in the guise of Imperial Concubine, combining Watson's interests in relationships and in reality versus illusion. In "Our Loves So Truly Meridional" two lovers are divided by the strange force fields that have split their planet into new zones; they attempt to reunite despite the powers that separate them. Separation is not a problem for the two characters in "The Event Horizon"; like the protagonist in *Alien Embassy,* they employ tantric sex as a means of psychically communicating with a powerful alien being, which in this story resides in a black hole. The title story, one of Watson's best, describes how an old man suddenly appears in a laboratory in a machine that appears to be a time machine. As time progresses forward for the scientists who study the man trapped in the machine, time reverses itself for the man within, who grows younger every day. In "A Time-Span to Conjure With" a crew from Earth visits a human colony light-years away and discovers that the humans there have, like the alien race on the planet, developed the ability to see all time—past, present, and future—as simultaneous, like the Tralfamadorians in Kurt Vonnegut's *Slaughterhouse-Five* (1969).

Also in 1979, Watson published another novel, *God's World.* God appears to be contacting several people on Earth, and the messages point them to a site light-years away. A team sets out to investigate, but along the way they are attacked by an insectoid race that reduces their number to six. Pressing on, the six arrive finally at "God's World," where they meet another alien race. While this race is not God, or even gods, they do show the human crew how to achieve a heavenly state of consciousness through dreams. At this point, however, more aliens emerge on the scene, a race of intelligent computers known as the Harxine. Somehow entering the humans' perceptions, they claim that this new heaven-like consciousness is not a mystical state of greater awareness but rather a dangerous illusion. Once again Watson blends disparate elements—space opera, mysticism, and the thriller—into an interesting narrative.

Much of Watson's science fiction up to this time had pushed the borders of fantasy as well, and his next novel blurred the two boundaries considerably. *The Gardens of Delight* (1980), like *God's World,* involves a distant alien world that appears to be a gateway to another level of existence. The world itself was not initially alien, beginning as a human colony, but when a contingent from Earth arrives to see how the colony is faring, they find that the planet has been transformed into something both familiar and astonishingly foreign. Its transformation, in fact, has been modeled on the Flemish artist Hieronymous Bosch's outré triptych *The Garden of Earthly Delights* (1505–1510). Three members of the crew, including the protagonist, psychologist Sean Athlone, explore this transformed world, from its Edenic aspects to its hellish ones, and eventually learn what happened to make the colony planet a reproduction of a bizarre sixteenth-century painting.

This blurring of genre boundaries continued with his next solo novel, *Deathhunter* (1981). The suitably named Jim Todhunter (*Tod* is German for death) works as a guide in a House of Death, a place where people go to die. Because of his profession, he is asked to help a convicted murderer named Nathan Weinberger come to terms with his approaching execution. Weinberger, however, has no intention of dying. Instead he believes that it is possible to capture Death, the personified Grim Reaper of folklore. Weinberger convinces Jim of the feasibility of his plan, and together the two men construct a device, the Thanoscope, meant to entrap Death. Thus fantasy and science fiction come together—the fantasy of a personified Death and the science-fiction technology of the device they build. Still, the story is closer to fantasy, as Jim lives up to his name and becomes a true Deathhunter. It is worth noting that, in this same year, Watson's father passed away.

Also in 1981 Watson collaborated with American fantasy and science-fiction writer Michael Bishop on the novel *Under Heaven's Bridge.* Watson's preoccupations dominate in this story that again combines language, alien contact, and religion; also, the protagonist is of Japanese descent. A linguist named Keiko Takihashi is on a faraway planet teaching the languages of humans to a telepathic race known as the Kybers, so called because of the combination of organic and mechanical elements in their bodies. Their god is a computer-like being, and in their religious rituals they become one with this being. Keiko's lover is fascinated with these rituals and longs to experience this transcendent state, which causes problems—as does the fact that the Kybers' sun is approaching nova. Watson and Bishop

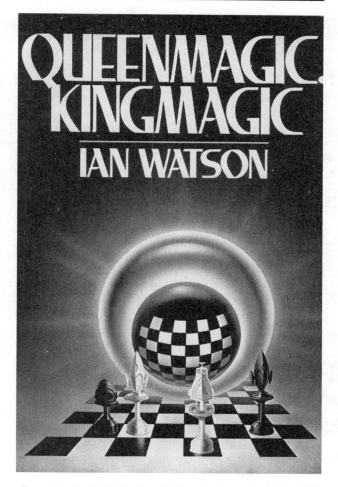

Dust jacket for the U.S. edition of Watson's 1986 novel, set primarily in a fantasy world that resembles a chess set (Richland County Public Library)

combine an exciting plot with original ideas and provoking concepts.

Watson also edited a 1981 short-story collection titled *Pictures at an Exhibition.* The stories, all original to the volume, are, like Modest Mussorgsky's 1874 musical composition of the same title, inspired by works of art and in fact take place within the worlds of the individual paintings. Watson wrote, with Roger Campbell, a linking narrative to connect the different stories, and he also wrote the final piece, "The Mystic Marriage of Salome," in which the head of John the Baptist survives its decapitation.

Sunstroke and Other Stories, Watson's second collection of his own short fiction, appeared in 1982. "The Rooms of Paradise," one of Watson's best and most evocative stories, describes a strange type of afterlife for its protagonist: reborn as an infant, he grows up like a normal human, except that he is alone, his needs tended to by some unknown agency, and each morning he wakes in a different room that is his prison for that day. Another story of entrapment that comes closer to conventional science fiction in the problem it poses for its protagonist is "Insight," in which aliens abduct a man and take him, via a time machine, from 1985 to 3055. Trapped in a single room, he must figure out how to escape. Time travel of another sort appears in "The Milk of Knowledge," in which a forty-one-year-old man suddenly becomes fourteen again, but with all of his adult memories. Given his knowledge of what is to come, he tries to prevent a disaster and thus change the course of history. Alien abduction also appears in "The Call of the Wild: The Dog-Flea Version," in which aliens capture not a human but rather Buck, a flea-circus star. For science-fiction fans one of Watson's more entertaining stories is "The World Science Fiction Convention of 2080." A great disaster has reduced the planet to a level of technology closer to the world of 1880 than to what one might expect from the late twenty-first century, but fandom lives on—even if the attendees have to travel to the Worldcon by means unthinkable to readers of the late twentieth century. Politics and religion are brought together in "A Letter from God," in which God communicates through columns ten miles high in both the United States and the Soviet Union, with a rather obvious message. An outside force is also at work in "The Thousand Cuts," in which humanity in its entirety experiences lapses in consciousness, during which their world has been improved upon.

Watson's next novel, *Chekhov's Journey* (1983), combines the historical with science fiction. The Chekhov of the title is the major Russian author Anton Chekhov, who is the subject of a Soviet motion picture about his journey to the site of a strange disaster. However, the real Chekhov enters the scene when the actor playing him establishes a hypnotic connection between the two men over the years that separate them. This manifestation creates a problem for the actor, who becomes stuck in time. At the same time—if it is possible to use that phrase, given the way the novel plays with temporality—a Russian spaceship is traveling backward through time, heading toward Chekhov and his portrayer.

Also in 1983, Watson edited another anthology, this one in collaboration with Bishop. *Changes: Stories of Metamorphosis* includes, as the fuller subtitle indicates, stories about both psychological and physical transformations, written by British and American authors such as Bishop, Barrington J. Bayley, Ursula K. Le Guin, Thomas M. Disch, Clifford D. Simak, Gene Wolfe, Algis Budrys, R. A. Lafferty, Angela Carter, and Richard Cowper. In addition to his introductory essay, Watson contributed an original story titled "The Day of the Wolf."

Metamorphosis is also one of the themes of *Converts* (1984), expanded from Watson's story "Jean Sandwich, the Sponsor, and I." Like previous novels by Watson, *Converts* unites considerable inventiveness with religious themes. A multimillionaire named Bruno King wishes to use his great wealth to transform himself and a small circle of friends into supermen through genetic experiments. The experiments go somewhat awry, however, creating instead a wild profusion of new creatures. This playing at being God invokes the wrath of a group of fundamentalists known as the God Nuts. Thus *Converts* addresses two concerns central to much science fiction: the question of what it means to be human, especially considered in the context of evolutionary change; and the relationship among society, science, and religion. While the materials are fairly traditional within science fiction, Watson's use of the materials is his own.

In 1984 Watson began a fantasy trilogy titled the Books of the Black Current, which are filled with mythological overtones. *The Book of the River* (1984) introduces the protagonist, Yaleen, whose life changes dramatically when she is pulled into the strange Black Current. The Black Current is not only a river but actually the body of the mysterious Worm, whose powers she masters when she discovers their source by entering the Worm's mouth.

Yaleen's adventures continue in *The Book of the Stars* (1984), beginning with her death at the hands of her enemy, Edrick. The Worm revives her so that she can serve as its spy on Eeden, the world controlled by the mysterious Godmind, the Worm's archenemy. She reappears on Earth as a cherub, whose innocent form belies her goal: to prevent the Godmind from crafting a lens that will destroy all human souls—a matter of grave concern not only to humans but to the Worm, a collector of souls. The novel ends as it began, with Yaleen's death, but once more she is reborn, this time as her own sister, Narya.

The Book of Being (1985) picks up with Yaleen/Narya once more traveling the river. In order to thwart the Godmind's plan to destroy the souls of humans, she encourages everyone she meets in her travels to drink from the Black Current to preserve their lives. She herself dies several more times, successively reincarnated on a series of different worlds. In the end, it seems the Godmind has won and has destroyed the universe, but Yaleen survives and has herself become a god-like force. Life begins again as she creates a new universe.

This fantasy trilogy, one of Watson's more popular works, is noteworthy not only for its mythic plot but also for its depiction of two different societies, one governed by men and the other by women, separated by the Black Current. One element of the Black Current trilogy for which Watson has been praised, in fact, is his depiction of a feminist utopia.

By 1985 Watson, midway through his career, had achieved sufficient prominence in the field to be accorded two honors: he received the Prix Européen de Science Fiction for his work as a novelist, and much of his shorter work, both fiction and nonfiction, was collected in a volume titled *The Book of Ian Watson*. One of the stories reflects upon the genre: in "The Big Buy" aliens go shopping on Earth, and what they want most of all is science fiction. In another story, "The Culling," Earth has achieved peace thanks to an alien entity, but at the price of annual human sacrifice. Watson returned to aliens and linguistics in "The Love Song of Johnny Alienson," in which the aliens who have raised a young human send him back to Earth to take a human bride, with the object of producing children who possess both their own and human linguistic structures. Another story in the volume, "The Real Winston," is a variation on George Orwell's *Nineteen Eighty-Four* (1949). In Watson's tale it is not the Ministry of Truth that is producing lies but some strange force altering the nature of reality, which the State attempts to maintain.

Even more of Watson's short fiction was gathered into his third collection, *Slow Birds and Other Stories* (1985). Many of Watson's best stories concern enigmas of one sort or another, which is also true of "Slow Birds," first published in 1983. The objects of the title are nuclear warheads, which have been displaced through time into a parallel Earth. What exactly is happening, however, is unclear, and two brothers decide to ride the missiles to come to an answer. The story was nominated for both the Hugo and the Nebula. Strange things also happen in "Ghost Lecturer"—the title figure is Lucretius, the first-century B.C. Roman poet and philosopher, author of *De Rerum Natura* (On the Nature of Things), brought back from the dead to give a lecture. Contemporary scientists naturally believe that his metaphysical system has been superceded by modern science, but they find that he may have been more accurate than they supposed when the world starts to resemble the world Lucretius described two millennia ago. "The Bloomsday Revolution" is about another type of afterlife, in which a man and a woman relive their wedding day over and over again until their friends finally suggest that he marry someone else.

In 1986 Watson and American writer Pamela Sargent edited *Afterlives,* a collection of fantasy and science-fiction works about life after death. An assemblage of original stories and poems along with reprints, it includes Watson's story "The Rooms of Paradise," in addition to his and Sargent's introductory essay.

Watson had attended a fantasy conference in Ljubljana, Yugoslavia, in 1984. The visit partially inspired one of the settings of his 1986 novel, *Queenmagic, Kingmagic.* The primary setting, however, is a fantasy world that resembles a chess set, with the kingdoms of Bellogard and Chorny, White and Black, at war. In the midst of this conflict, a white pawn named Pedino and a black pawn named Sara fall in love, and the two manage to escape their rule-bound existence for other worlds, also game environments, each with its own set of rules.

In the early 1980s, inspired by his rural surroundings and continuing his forays outside of science fiction, Watson began writing contemporary horror fiction set in the country. His first published result, *The Power,* appeared in 1987. Like many science-fiction narratives that emerged during the Cold War, it concerns the threat of nuclear warfare. However, Watson chooses not to follow the conventional science-fiction format of apocalypse and survival, even though these figure into the story. Instead, the topic is treated in the context of a contemporary horror novel. The Power of the title is a mysterious being that awakes in a small English village when nuclear war between the United States and the Soviet Union begins. This Power is intent only upon saving itself, but in the process it saves the village as well. Moreover, the Power preserves not only the living but also the dead, whom it revives. However, the Power is hardly a benevolent force, demanding that the living and the resurrected dead worship it. Watson's fourth collection, *Evil Water and Other Stories,* also appeared in 1987.

Watson continued working in the horror vein in *The Fire Worm, Whores of Babylon,* and *Meat,* all of which were published in 1988. In *The Fire Worm* John Cunningham is a psychiatrist who works with patients who believe they are experiencing events from previous lives. Cunningham is also horror writer Jack Cannon, capitalizing on his patients' bizarre tales through his fictional treatments of them. One of these patients, Tony, is of particular interest, claiming that in an earlier life he had been possessed by a great Fire Worm. Jack himself is experiencing possession of a sort, as his authorial persona comes to the fore and leads him into investigating this story for himself, with unexpected consequences.

Whores of Babylon is closer to fantasy or science fiction than horror but still has elements of the latter. The ancient city of Babylon has been re-created in a desert in Arizona, luring Alex Winter and his girlfriend Deborah as tourists. However, they soon find themselves caught up in the life of the city, which has adopted more than mere buildings from its ancient model. Alex becomes a slave and later a lover of a princess named Thessany, while Deborah becomes the bride of King Marduk. It all seems real enough, but Alex comes to doubt the reality of the experience and to search for its cause. In terms of basic plot, the novel has much in common with *The Gardens of Delight* but the setting and story are so different that Watson is hardly repeating himself.

Watson's third novel of 1988, *Meat,* returns to more standard horror fare. A group of animal-rights activists saves a rabbit from becoming a weasel's prey, thus invoking the wrath of a malicious supernatural entity for their meddling. For their pains they are stricken with a variety of punishments, both physical and psychological. Watson's gifts of invention are put to disturbing use as he imagines the many hallucinations and torments with which the group is afflicted.

Salvage Rites and Other Stories (1989) is Watson's fifth collection of short fiction. In "Letters from the Monkey Alphabet" a chimpanzee in a zoo is actually a reincarnated human woman, and using a computer, she informs her keepers of this fact. "Aid from a Vampire" also brings together the mythic with the contemporary, in this case a vampire whose bite actually helps people with AIDS.

The Flies of Memory (1990) again returns to alien visitors and the nature of reality. The flies of the title are the aliens—not flies at all, of course, but strongly resembling them despite their considerable size. Many of Watson's alien visitors not only come in peace but also come with great curiosity, and the alien "flies" are no exception, desiring to "memorize" the places of Earth. When they are attacked by religious fanatics as demonic creatures, however, some of the places the aliens have "memorized" vanish from Earth and reappear on Mars, along with humans who happened to be in the structures at the time, raising intriguing questions once more about the relationship between consciousness and reality.

Watson began exploring a specific type of science fiction, space opera, with the Warhammer 40,000 series, a tie-in connected to a game produced by the British company Games Workshop. In connection with the game, Watson published four volumes in the series, *Inquisitor* (1990), *Space Marine* (1993), *Harlequin* (1994), and *Chaos Child* (1995). Though by their nature these books are probably the most formulaic of Watson's works, Games Workshop has attracted many quality writers for their tie-in books, and the results are better than most such endeavors.

Another science-fiction tradition appeared in Watson's career with the publication of *Nanoware Time* (1990), which was bound with John Varley's *The Persistence of Vision* as a "double novel," like the old Ace doubles of the 1950s and 1960s—two novellas, bound back to back and reversed, each with its own cover. As far as the story itself is concerned, Watson was one of many science-fiction writers of the 1990s to explore the impli-

cations of nanotechnology, the idea of machines that exist and operate at the atomic level. In *Nanoware Time* aliens have given humans microscopic computers that, introduced into the brain, allow humans to develop incredible mental powers.

In 1991 Watson also published his next collection, *Stalin's Teardrops.* One notable story, "The Case of the Glass Slipper," fuses two different sets of characters. The Prince, convinced that his wife, Cinderella, has been replaced with a less-pleasant duplicate, calls in none other than Sherlock Holmes to investigate the matter.

Watson began another short series in 1993 with *Lucky's Harvest,* the first book of the Mana sequence. The series is in part a retelling of the Finnish epic the *Kalevala* in science-fiction terms. Lucky Sariola, an Earth colonist on distant Kaleva, finds a new form of life on an asteroid; this being is unusually responsive to stories. The second volume of the Mana series, *The Fallen Moon,* appeared in 1994, along with Watson's next collection of short fiction, *The Coming of Vertumnus.*

Watson's publications diminished considerably in the late 1990s as his wife became increasingly ill with emphysema. He did, however, publish two novels during this difficult period. *Hard Questions* (1996) concerns an amazing supercomputer that may unlock the secrets of death. Convinced that protagonist Clare Conway knows the secrets behind this device, a cult attempts to secure its incredible powers for themselves. However, these powers are stranger than even they realize. With his conception of the "quantum computer," Watson once again reveals his wild imagination coupled with serious reflections upon the nature of reality.

Oracle (1997) reads like a combination of science fiction and spy novel. A Roman centurion is dislodged from his own time as a result of an experiment conducted by a clandestine spy agency trying to secure intelligence from the future. Meanwhile, the Irish Republican Army is plotting an attack on the queen. While the science-fiction elements are important to the story, the novel has more in common with espionage thrillers.

Another project of the late 1990s involved working with director Stanley Kubrick on a motion picture based on Brian W. Aldiss's 1969 short story "Super-Toys Last All Summer Long." Kubrick's death in 1999 ended their collaboration on the script for the movie they planned to call *AI,* but Watson's script served as the basis for the screenplay by Steven Spielberg, who inherited the project and released the movie in 2001.

Watson devoted his time primarily to caring for his wife until her death in the spring of 2001. He has since returned to writing, preparing another collection of short stories, *The Great Escape* (2002). The title story is a Miltonic tale of the fallen angels in hell preparing for another rebellion, this time not against God but against Satan.

As Orson Scott Card wrote in his review of *Queenmagic, Kingmagic* for *The Magazine of Fantasy & Science Fiction,* "Ian Watson is a writer who never does the same thing twice. Furthermore, he doesn't often do the same thing anybody *else* has done." While these traits have made it difficult to pin Watson down and perhaps have contributed to his relatively low sales compared to some of his contemporaries, Watson's prolific inventiveness and his capacity to integrate serious ideas with entertaining storytelling have marked his long career and established a distinctive position for him within British fantasy and science fiction. His stories are meant to challenge—as he noted in a 1980 interview with Charles Platt, science fiction should present "an alternative-reality paradigm, a different way of conceptualizing reality and the universe."

Interviews:

David Wingrove, "An Interview with Ian Watson," *Vector,* 86 (March/April 1978): 6–11;

Charles Platt, "Ian Watson," in his *Dream Makers: The Uncommon People Who Write Science Fiction* (New York: Berkley, 1980), pp. 235–241;

David Langford, "Ian Watson Interviewed," *Science Fiction Review,* 11 (February 1982): 8–14;

R. Juille, "Etats altérés de conscience: Interview de Ian Watson," *Ovni et Compagnie,* 28 (October–December 1982): 15–18;

Günter Zettl, "Ian Watson interviewt von Günter Zettl," *Heyne Science Fiction Magazine,* no. 8 (1983): 109–119;

Jeffrey M. Elliot, "Gardening Words: An Interview with Ian Watson," *Foundation,* 30 (March 1984): 51–66;

Elisabeth Vonarburg, "Rencontre avec Ian Watson," *Solaris,* 11 (November–December 1985): 17–18.

Bibliography:

Douglas A. Mackey, *The Work of Ian Watson: An Annotated Bibliography and Guide* (San Bernardino, Cal.: Borgo Press, 1989).

References:

Cy Chauvin, "Ian Watson's Miracle Men," in *Critical Encounters II: Writers and Themes in Science Fiction,* edited by Tom Staicar (New York: Ungar, 1982), pp. 44–59;

Gerard Cordesse, "Ian Watson et les limites de la connaissance," *Etudes Anglaises,* 41 (July–September 1988): 335–344;

Walter E. Meyers, *Aliens and Linguists: Language Study and Science Fiction* (Athens: University of Georgia Press, 1980), pp. 185–191;

Timothy J. Reiss, "How Can 'New' Meaning Be Thought? Fictions of Science, Science Fictions," *Canadian Review of Comparative Literature / Revue Canadien de Litterature Comparée,* 12 (March 1985): 88–126;

David Wingrove, "Amazed and Afterwards: Avoiding Neoteny—The SF of Ian Watson," *Vector,* 86 (March–April 1978): 12–21.

Papers:

Some of Ian Watson's manuscripts can be found in the Science Fiction Foundation Collection located at the University of Liverpool.

James White

(7 April 1928 – 23 August 1999)

Darren Harris-Fain
Shawnee State University

BOOKS: *The Secret Visitors* [bound with *Master of Life and Death,* by Robert Silverberg] (New York: Ace, 1957); republished alone (London: Digit, 1961; New York: Ace, 1967);

Hospital Station (New York: Ballantine, 1962; London: Corgi, 1967);

Second Ending [bound with *The Jewels of Aptor,* by Samuel R. Delany] (New York: Ace, 1962);

Star Surgeon (New York: Ballantine, 1963; London: Corgi, 1967);

Deadly Litter (New York: Ballantine, 1964; London: Corgi, 1968);

The Escape Orbit (New York: Ace, 1965); republished as *Open Prison* (London: Four Square Books, 1965; New York: Ace, 1983);

The Watch Below (New York: Ballantine, 1966; London: Whiting & Wheaton, 1966);

All Judgment Fled (London: Rapp & Whiting, 1968; New York: Walker, 1969); republished as *All Judgement Fled* (London: Macdonald, 1987);

The Aliens among Us (New York: Ballantine, 1969; London: Corgi, 1970);

Major Operation (New York: Ballantine, 1971; London: Macdonald/Futura, 1987);

Tomorrow Is Too Far (New York: Ballantine, 1971; London: Joseph, 1971);

Dark Inferno (London: Joseph, 1972); republished as *Lifeboat* (New York: Ballantine, 1972);

The Dream Millennium (London: Joseph, 1974; New York: Ballantine, 1974);

Monsters and Medics (London: Corgi, 1977; expanded edition, New York: Ballantine, 1977);

Ambulance Ship (New York: Ballantine, 1979; expanded edition, London: Corgi, 1980);

Underkill (London: Corgi, 1979);

Futures Past (New York: Ballantine, 1982; London: Macdonald/Futura, 1988; revised edition, London: Orbit, 1988);

Sector General (New York: Ballantine, 1983; London: Macdonald/Futura, 1987);

James White (photograph from the dust jacket for the 1969 edition of The Watch Below, *1966)*

The Interpreters [bound with *A Novacon Garland,* by David Langford] (Birmingham, U.K.: Birmingham Science Fiction Group, 1985);

Star Healer (New York: Ballantine, 1985; London: Macdonald/Futura, 1987);

Code Blue—Emergency! (New York: Ballantine, 1987; London: Macdonald/Futura, 1987);

Federation World (New York: Ballantine, 1988; London: Orbit, 1990);

The Silent Stars Go By (New York: Ballantine, 1991);

The Genocidal Healer (New York: Ballantine, 1991);

The Galactic Gourmet (New York: Tor, 1996);

The White Papers, edited by Mark L. Olson and Bruce Pelz (Framingham, Mass.: NESFA, 1996);

Final Diagnosis (New York: Tor, 1997);

Mind Changer (New York: Tor, 1998);

Double Contact (New York: Tor, 1999);

The First Protector (New York: Tor, 2000).

OTHER: "Crossfire," in *The Best from New Worlds Science Fiction,* edited by John Carnell (London: Boardman, 1955);

"Incident on a Colonising Starship Where All Living Things Are in Suspended Animation . . . ," in *Drabble II: Double Century,* edited by Rob Meades and David Wake (Harold Wood, U.K.: Beccon, 1990), p. 79.

SELECTED PERIODICAL PUBLICATIONS–
UNCOLLECTED: "Starvation Orbit," *New Worlds,* 9 (July 1954);

"Suicide Mission," *New Worlds,* 9 (September 1954);

"The Star Walk," *New Worlds,* 11 (March 1955);

"Pushover Planet," *Nebula Science Fiction,* 14 (November 1955);

"Dark Talisman," *Nebula Science Fiction,* 35 (October 1958);

"Something of Value," *Analog,* 105 (February 1985);

"Type 'Genie' and Run," *Gate,* no. 1 (1989): 53–76;

"Un-Birthday Boy," *Analog,* 116 (February 1996): 70–83.

While conflict is not absent from the science fiction of James White, it is not saturated with the violence that animates much of English-language writing in the genre. Instead, White became well known for fiction centered on healing and set in a great galactic hospital, works that show how beings who seem different from each other can get along. Physical healing and pacifism go hand in hand in White's fiction, which also explores how diverse different lives can be.

James White was born on 7 April 1928 to a Roman Catholic family in Belfast, Northern Ireland. As a young child he spent some time with his parents in Canada, but the family returned to Belfast, where he was educated, first at St. John's Primary School (1935–1941) and then at St. Joseph's Technical Secondary School (1942–1943). He longed to study medicine, which fascinated him, but his circumstances dictated another direction. After graduation, he served as an apprentice at the Ladies' and Gents' Tailoring Company in Belfast (1943–1948), then remained in the garment industry until 1965, first as a salesman

and then, from 1961 to 1965, as a manager. He left this business in 1965 to become a technical clerk with Shorts Aviation in Belfast. He soon transferred to the publicity department, where he remained until he retired in 1984. Though relatively well-received among science-fiction readers, White's fiction was published mostly in magazines and in paperback editions and failed to make enough money for him to write full-time. Thus, for the first thirty years of his literary career, he wrote evenings and weekends after working at a regular job during the day.

White's religious affiliation and residence in Northern Ireland affected the focus of his work. Although he told *Contemporary Authors* that he claimed no political affiliations or sympathies, his science fiction is filled with political situations that resemble the decades of strife between Catholics and Protestants in Northern Ireland. Dealing with the interactions of humans and aliens, humans and other humans, aliens and other aliens, White's science fiction is about how different groups with differing outlooks can live peacefully with each other.

White was introduced to science fiction in 1941, while still in school, when he began reading the influential American magazine *Astounding Science-Fiction.* He was fascinated with the magazine and eventually built a complete collection. He was especially impressed with the science fiction of Robert A. Heinlein and E. E. "Doc" Smith. From Heinlein, White adopted a detailed approach to describing future worlds grounded in the physical sciences while still making the stories character oriented, and from Smith's space operas he developed an interest in far-flung adventures in time and space and the notion that aliens did not have to be the bug-eyed monsters who so often populated pulp magazines.

In his youthful searching for science-fiction magazines—books in the genre were few during the 1940s—White became acquainted with another young fan, Walter A. Willis, with whom he collaborated on two fan magazines, *Slant* (1948–1953) and *Hyphen* (1953–1965). Besides helping to edit the magazines, White provided many of the woodcut illustrations. In addition to the reviews and commentary typical of science-fiction fanzines, *Slant* and *Hyphen* published fiction by professional British writers such as John Brunner and Bob Shaw. During this period of work and fan activity, White married Margaret Sarah Martin on 17 May 1955. They had three children: Patricia Mary, Martin James, and Peter Gerard.

For years White was content to read and write about science fiction, but eventually he thought about writing some of his own. While he remained a faithful reader of *Astounding Science-Fiction,* he began to tire of

*Paperback cover for the 1991 novel for which White created a fictional history of an
alternate Earth governed by an Irish empire (Richland County Public Library)*

the tales of life after nuclear holocausts that dominated
the magazine during the years after World War II. He
was also encouraged by a new British science-fiction
magazine, *New Worlds,* which started in the late 1940s.
Writing did not come easily to him at first, but he kept
trying until *New Worlds* published "Assisted Passage"
in its January 1953 issue. White's fiction often draws
on contemporary issues; in this case White was
inspired by current debates about Australian emigra-
tion. After the appearance of "Assisted Passage,"
White published his stories regularly in *New Worlds*
and occasionally submitted some to the Scottish magazine *Nebula Science Fiction.*

The American magazines were the center of the
English-speaking science-fiction world, and White
aspired to have his stories published there as well.
"The Scavengers" was published in the October
1953 issue of *Astounding Science-Fiction,* but he had less
success with his next submissions, owing in large
part to his interest in aliens as sympathetic characters, which ran counter to the xenophobic attitudes
of John W. Campbell, the editor of *Astounding Science-
Fiction.* In addition, White's early science fiction bore
the flavor of the Golden Age space operas of Smith,
which were popular in the 1930s but already seemed
dated by the 1950s. For example, in "The Scavengers" White wrote:

> The captain had felt [like a knight in shining armor]
> when he was a new boy. . . . Somehow, the feeling
> never quite wore off. It came of belonging to an
> organization dedicated to the job of protecting,
> assisting, and keeping the noses clean generally of
> every race in the galaxy that walked, wriggled, or
> flew and had intelligence. We're just a flock of
> space-going guardian angels, he thought a little cyni-
> cally, all we need are haloes.

While the human paternalism toward alien races in this passage is compatible with Campbell's notions of human superiority, he disliked White's later efforts and rejected them.

While continuing to publish stories in the British magazines, White also began selling to the American paperback market, which had blossomed after World War II. His first book, *The Secret Visitors* (1957), was a novella first serialized as "Tourist Planet" in *New Worlds* (October–December 1956) and then published by Ace in one of its so-called double novels. Thus White's *Secret Visitors* was bound with American writer Robert Silverberg's *Master of Life and Death,* each with its own cover illustration and bound back to back.

The story of *The Secret Visitors* revolves around the discovery that Earth has become a tourist destination for visitors from elsewhere. As the protagonist, Dr. Lockhart, discovers, there is more to their visits than mere pleasure. White combined Cold War tensions with elements of science fiction and the spy thriller to good effect in the novella.

Also in 1957, White began the series of stories and novels for which he is best known. They center around a huge hospital in space, Sector Twelve General Hospital, capable of dealing with every known sentient life form in the universe. Collectively known as the Sector General books, they include *Hospital Station* (1962), *Star Surgeon* (1963), *The Aliens among Us* (1969), *Major Operation* (1971), *Ambulance Ship* (1979), *Futures Past* (1982), *Sector General* (1983), *Star Healer* (1985), *Code Blue–Emergency!* (1987), *The Genocidal Healer* (1991), *The Galactic Gourmet* (1996), *Final Diagnosis* (1997), *Mind Changer* (1998), and *Double Contact* (1999).

After accepting the story "Sector General" for publication in the November 1957 issue, *New Worlds* editor John Carnell encouraged White to submit more stories set at Sector General, and White's setting provided ample room for additional tales. White's hospital consists of nearly four hundred levels and can accommodate all sixty-nine known races of the far-reaching Galactic Federation (drawn extensively from Smith's earlier Lensman books) in all their evolutionary diversity–frigid to torrid climates, atmospheres consisting of different gases or mixtures, and even heavily irradiated environments. In addition, the hospital boasts a staff of more than ten thousand. Such a setting allowed for all kinds of stories, and White exploited the possibilities for decades.

The first collection of Sector General stories, *Hospital Station,* was published by Ballantine Books, a New York paperback firm that became a major publisher of original science fiction by both American and British authors. White built his reputation as a science-fiction writer as much through American markets as through British ones, and his case was hardly unusual among British science-fiction writers during the second half of the twentieth century. In fact, he claimed in interviews, his American publications helped him to secure contracts with British publishers.

While the stories in *Hospital Station* are all set in the same fictional environment, they are not directly related to each other. They include "Medic" (originally published as "O'Mara's Orphan" in *New Worlds,* January 1960), "Sector General," "Visitor at Large" (*New Worlds,* June 1959), and "Out-Patient" (*New Worlds,* June 1960).

White's next book was the short novel *Second Ending* (1962). The general premise is familiar to readers of science fiction: after a worldwide catastrophe, the protagonist finds himself the last person on Earth, but what White did with this science-fiction cliché is intriguing. Finding an army of extremely capable robots at his command, White's protagonist, Ross, employs them to create other humans to help him begin everything again.

Star Surgeon, the second book in the Sector General series, is a novel drawn from two earlier stories, "Field Hospital" (*New Worlds,* January–March 1962) and "Resident Physician" (*New Worlds,* September 1961), and has a greater sense of unity than *Sector Station.* In *Star Surgeon,* Sector General is threatened by aliens who are hostile to its purposes.

Deadly Litter (1964) collects four stories that are not part of White's Sector General series. While the title story (*SF Adventures,* February 1960), "Grapeliner" (*New Worlds,* November 1959), "The Ideal Captain" (*New Worlds,* August 1958) and "The Lights Outside the Windows" (*New Worlds,* February 1957) are competently constructed, they are not as noteworthy as White's hospital stories.

White's novel *Open Prison,* serialized in *New Worlds* (February–April 1964) and first published in book form as *The Escape Orbit* (1965), begins with galactic conflicts typical of space operas, but White's story soon transcends its sources because of his thoughtful treatment of alien races. After an alien race captures a group of humans, it faces the problem of what to do with its prisoners of war, whose atmosphere is considerably different from that of the aliens' world. The aliens' solution is to place the men on a planet with an Earth-like atmosphere, an "open prison" where they are monitored but otherwise left to their own devices. Some of the men resign themselves to their imprisonment and begin farming the land. Others, however, try to evade their captors' observation and plot an escape.

Dust jacket for the penultimate novel in White's best-known series
(Richland County Public Library)

Perhaps White's best-known work outside the Sector General stories is his novel *The Watch Below* (1966), about a merchant ship in World War II and an alien spaceship in search of a planet with an ample water supply. While the aliens are interesting and play an important role in the plot, the real drama involves the human crew, which, after its vessel sinks, manages to survive in a small space filled with trapped air. How they survive and how, decades later, their story combines with that of the alien starship is one of White's best efforts.

The title of White's next novel, *All Judgment Fled* (1968), comes from a passage in William Shakespeare's *Julius Caesar* (1599): "O judgment! thou art fled to brutish beasts, / And men have lost their reason" (III.ii). A crew from Earth is sent to investigate a spaceship that has apparently wandered into the solar system and is twelve million miles past the orbit of Mars. Thinking the ship is unpopulated, they discover on the contrary that it is filled with all kinds of alien races. As in the Sector General books and *The*

Watch Below, a central theme of this novel is the relationships that might emerge among humans and aliens—and, by metaphorical extension, among human beings of various beliefs and nationalities.

The Aliens among Us (1969), White's next collection, includes "Countercharm" (*New Worlds,* November 1960), "To Kill or Cure" (*New Worlds,* April 1957), "Red Alert" (*New Worlds,* January 1956), "Tableau" (*New Worlds,* May 1958), "The Conspirators" (*New Worlds,* June 1954), "The Scavengers" (*Astounding Science-Fiction,* October 1953), and "Occupation: Warrior" (*SF Adventures,* March 1959). As the title of the book suggests, the stories—some of which are set in Sector General—concern interactions between humans and an assorted group of alien beings.

Major Operation, the third volume in the Sector General series, is an example of what scholars call a "fix-up novel." A common phenomenon in the science-fiction field, where writers are often as dependent on magazine sales as on book publications, the fix-up novel is an expansion of an earlier story or stories into a book-length narrative. In this case, White combined his previously published stories "Blood Brother" (*New Writings in SF 14,* 1969), "Invader" (*New Writings in SF 7,* 1967), "Major Operation" (*New Writings in SF 18,* 1971), "Meatball" (*New Writings in SF 16,* 1969), and "Vertigo" (*New Writings in SF 12,* 1968) into a unified narrative about an alien life-form that enters the hospital undetected and begins wreaking havoc.

During this period of White's literary career he was working full-time in the aeronautic industry, an experience that informed his next book, *Tomorrow Is Too Far* (1971), a mystery novel about a security officer for an aerospace company who becomes involved in a dangerous situation with far-reaching implications. Like *The Watch Below,* White's 1972 novel, *Dark Inferno* (published in the United States as *Lifeboat*), is a story of survival, in this instance in escape pods ejected from a starship whose voyage to Ganymede goes wrong.

White's novel *The Dream Millennium* (1974) takes another science-fiction convention, the generation starship, and gives it a thoughtful, original treatment. Given the vast distances that would be involved in interstellar travel, and given a realistic treatment of how fast a starship could travel, any such trip would last centuries, hence the concept of the generation starship. White adhered to many of the conventions of the concept in his novel, but the travelers are placed in a "cold sleep" that will take them through the thousand-year passage. Another innovation is White's use of the ideas of psychologist Carl Gustav Jung, in particular his belief in a collective unconsciousness that is tied to a racial memory.

The travelers, ordinary folk who hope to rebuild a human society far from a corrupt Earth, carry with them the history of the human race. Crew member John Devlin is especially interesting, as in his dreams he relives various stages of human history from its origins as a unicellular organism through its assorted evolutionary and historical stages, concluding with a series of dreams that takes him into the lives of the passengers suspended in cold sleep. The ideas employed in the novel and its structural innovations make *The Dream Millennium* a noteworthy book.

In 1977 White published a collection titled *Monsters and Medics,* which also included an essay titled "Reality in Science Fiction." He returned to Sector General stories with *Ambulance Ship,* a fix-up novel based on the previously unpublished stories "Contagion," "Quarantine," and "Recovery." While many of the previous Sector General stories had focused on the redoubtable Dr. Conway, in *Ambulance Ship* White began to expand his cast to some other important figures in the hospital, in this case Fletcher, the captain of an ambulance ship. The book also includes the essay "The Secret History of Sector General."

Another 1979 novel, *Underkill,* is in many ways similar to *The Dream Millennium* in its critique of humanity's penchant for self-destruction. However, it is much grimmer in tone, both in comparison with *The Dream Millennium* and with the rest of White's work. In *Underkill* the human race, caught up in its ongoing wars with each other, faces the threat of extermination at the hands of an alien race that contemplates severe measures to deal with humanity's problems. Brian Stableford was no doubt correct in calling it a "brutal futuristic satire of life in Belfast."

Futures Past (1982) gathers many of White's early, previously uncollected stories, dating as far back as the 1950s, among them his first published story, "Assisted Passage." He followed this book with his next installment of his most popular series, *Sector General.* This collection is noteworthy for its inclusion of a story about how one of the major characters in the series became involved with the vast space hospital.

The series continued with the novel *Star Healer,* which involves Dr. Conway and other familiar characters from Sector General, but here much of the action takes place not in the hospital but on the world of one of White's interesting alien races. A similar approach is employed with a different story in the next novel in the series, *Code Blue—Emergency!*

Interspecies interactions are also central to White's next novel, *Federation World* (1988), but rather than being set in the worlds of Sector General, the story involves another type of environment altogether: a Dyson sphere. Named after physicist Freeman Dyson, who developed the concept, a Dyson sphere is an enormous shell constructed around a sun, intended to solve overpopulation and energy needs. The sphere in the novel is the domain of a vast Federation of Galactic Sentients, a convocation of many alien races banded together for mutual benefit and cautious about those who would join them.

After the Sector General series and *The Watch Below,* perhaps White's most acclaimed effort is *The Silent Stars Go By* (1991). A detailed treatment of the history of an alternate Earth governed by an Irish empire, the novel is more fully developed than most of White's work and is practically epic in approach. His Hibernian Empire discovers the New World centuries earlier than in recorded history and takes its first step toward fulfilling its aspirations toward the stars in 1492. Less impressive but still interesting is White's next novel in the Sector General series, *The Genocidal Healer* (1991), about a doctor who inadvertently destroys almost an entire civilization while attempting to eradicate a plague and how he tries to come to terms with his errors.

The next book in the Sector General series is the comic novel *The Galactic Gourmet.* Instead of focusing on the heroes of the hospital, it tells the story of how a gourmet chef stumbles into the position of hospital dietitian. The book is a good example of a strong comedic strain in British science fiction, as is David Langford's parody of the series published with White's *The Interpreters* in 1985.

The White Papers (1996) is a tribute volume published in connection with White's appearance as guest of honor at the World Science Fiction Convention in Los Angeles. In addition to collecting ten of his stories, the volume includes some of White's early fan writing as well as some helpful sources on the Sector General series, among them "Notes on the Classification System," about how he grouped his highly diverse alien races, and "The Secret History of Sector General," which offers a time line of the stories in the series.

The next installment in the Sector General stories was White's 1997 novel, *Final Diagnosis.* Like many of the stories and novels in the series, this one poses a problem to be solved, in this case a patient, a human named Hewlitt, who is prone not only to human illnesses but also a host of alien afflictions. Hewlitt and the hospital staff have never seen diseases pass between alien races before—a situation that could obviously be calamitous in Sector General.

Toward the end of the 1990s White, realizing his career was nearing its end, began wrapping up stories in the Sector General series. He did so with

O'Mara, the chief psychologist, in his next novel, *Mind Changer*. White aged his characters over the course of the series, and in this novel O'Mara faces mandatory retirement, rather unhappily. The series concluded with *Double Contact,* in which a doctor establishes first contact with two previously unknown alien races, both hostile, and attempts to establish peaceful relations with them and, more important, between them.

White's health began declining in the 1980s, and he died on 23 August 1999 after suffering a stroke. At the time of his death he was working on another novel, which was published posthumously. *The First Protector* (2000) is a tie-in with the television series *Earth–Final Conflict* (1997–   ), conceived and produced initially by Gene Roddenberry, the creator of *Star Trek*. Rather than dealing with the main characters of the television series, however, the novel expands on an incident mentioned in passing on the show: the visit of a representative of an alien race, the Taelons, to ninth-century Ireland, which White understood well from his research for *The Silent Stars Go By*. Thus, *The First Protector* transcends its nature as a media tie-in.

Even into the 1990s, White's style was often reminiscent of his 1950s pulp-magazine origins, which may have hampered his reception somewhat. He never received a major science-fiction award in the field, though he was nominated for both the Hugo and Nebula on a handful of occasions. He broke out of the paperbacks only a few times, when science fiction briefly became more widely accepted in the late 1960s, and often his books were published on only one side of the Atlantic or the other. In many ways his career illustrates the limits that labels and marketing impose on many midlist science-fiction authors.

Frequently described as a gentle and genial man, James White is fondly remembered by his readers and fans, even to the point of having a detailed website, <http://www.sectorgeneral.com>, devoted to his works and his memory. His name also adorns a short-story award for nonprofessional writers. Thwarted in his desire to practice medicine, White instead indulged his interest in his science fiction, producing some highly entertaining works. These works are almost entirely marked by a prevailing sense of optimism about humanity's future and its ability to live in peace with others. As Mike Resnick, an American writer of a slightly darker temperament, wrote in his introduction to *The White Papers,* "while I may write about *my* universe, I wish I could live in *his*."

Interviews:

Charles N. Brown, "James White," *Locus,* 17 (June 1984);

Brendan Ryder, "Encounter in Bewley's: James White Interviewed," *FTL,* 11 (Winter 1991): 16–17;

Brown, "James White," *Locus,* 30 (March 1993).

Bibliography:

Phil Stephensen-Payne and Gordon Benson, *James White* (Leeds: Galactic Central, 1989).

References:

Gary Louie, "The Classification System" and "The Sector General Timeline," in *The White Papers,* edited by Mark L. Olson and Bruce Pelz (Framingham, Mass.: NESFA, 1996);

Bruce Pelz, "An Introduction to Real Virtuality," in *The White Papers;*

Mike Resnick, Introduction to *The White Papers;*

Brian Stableford, "James White: Understanding the Alien," *New York Review of Science Fiction,* 137 (January 2000): 1, 6–7;

Walt Willis, "James White," in *The White Papers.*

Jeanette Winterson

(27 August 1959 –)

Gayle Irwin
York University

See also the Winterson entry in *DLB 207: British Novelists Since 1960, Third Series.*

BOOKS: *Oranges Are Not the Only Fruit* (London: Pandora, 1985; New York: Atlantic Monthly Press, 1987);
Boating for Beginners (London: Methuen, 1985);
Fit for the Future: The Guide for Women Who Want to Live Well (London: Pandora, 1986);
The Passion (London: Bloomsbury, 1987; New York: Atlantic Monthly Press, 1988);
Sexing the Cherry (London: Bloomsbury, 1989; New York: Atlantic Monthly Press, 1990);
Oranges Are Not the Only Fruit [television script] (London: Pandora, 1990);
Written on the Body (London: Cape, 1992; New York: Knopf, 1993);
Art and Lies: A Piece for Three Voices and a Bawd (London: Cape, 1994; New York: Knopf, 1994);
Great Moments in Aviation; and Oranges Are Not the Only Fruit: Two Filmscripts (London: Vintage, 1994);
Art Objects: Essays on Ecstasy and Effrontery (London: Cape, 1995; New York: Knopf, 1996);
Gut Symmetries (London: Granta, 1997; New York: Knopf, 1997);
The World and Other Places (London: Cape, 1998; New York: Knopf, 1999);
The PowerBook (London: Cape, 2000; New York: Knopf, 2000).

PRODUCED SCRIPTS: *Oranges Are Not the Only Fruit,* television, BBC2, January 1990;
Great Moments in Aviation, television, BBC2, 11 November 1995; released on video as *Shades of Fear,* Miramax, 1997.

OTHER: *Passion Fruit, Romantic Fiction with a Twist,* edited by Winterson (London: Pandora, 1986).

SELECTED PERIODICAL PUBLICATIONS–
UNCOLLECTED:
FICTION
"Only the Best for the Lord," *New Statesman,* 112 (19 December 1986): 46–47.

Jeanette Winterson (photograph © by Jerry Bauer; from the dust jacket for the U.S. edition of The Passion, *1988)*

NONFICTION
"Blooded with Optimism," *Sight and Sound,* 1 (May 1991): 33;
"Outrageous Proportions," *Sight and Sound,* 2 (October 1992): 26–27.

Jeanette Winterson is arguably one of the most talked-about writers of her generation. Her impact on both popular and literary culture in England is owing at least in part to the acclaim awarded to her first book, *Oranges Are Not the Only Fruit* (1985), which garnered a dust-jacket recommendation from Gore Vidal, won the prestigious Whitbread First Novel Award, and was turned into a BBC miniseries. Winterson became an "instant success story," and the intriguing autobiographical glimpses offered in her work served to titillate the press, who sensed a reality-is-stranger-than-fiction formula in Winterson's narrative and duly included stories of her sexual exploits along with reviews and interviews. Since her first novel, Winterson has published books of fiction, several short stories, articles on movies and feminism, a book on female body image and fitness consciousness, and two television scripts (including the television adaptation of *Oranges Are Not the Only Fruit*, 1990). From the start her most significant achievement lay in how she combined a plot full of intriguing, slightly quirky characters with a touch of late-twentieth-century postmodern self-consciousness. With her first four novels, that self-conscious touch took on the genre of the fantastic. From magic realism to parables, from religious iconography come to life to revisionist fairy tales, Winterson's early work flirts with the traditions of Angela Carter, Gabriel García Márquez, Salman Rushdie, and Italo Calvino.

Jeanette Winterson was born on 27 August 1959 and grew up in Lancashire. Her childhood experiences were marked by the trials of living with an adoptive mother driven by religion, and they form the foundation of *Oranges Are Not the Only Fruit*. Some critics have found Winterson coy when it comes to separating the fictive embellishments of her texts from autobiography, but her work seems to highlight how the narratives shaping memory and history are as real as the events themselves. Nevertheless, it is generally known that certain stories from her first novel are taken directly from her life. Winterson was adopted at an early age by John Winterson and Constance Brownrigg, and she spent the first part of her life tied to her new mother's zealous ambition "to do God's work." In training as a missionary, Winterson spent much of her youth honing the skills of rhetoric needed for street-corner proselytizing and attracting converts. When she had a lesbian affair with one of the church converts, however, she was rejected by her church and forced into a macabre exorcism by her mother and the church leader. She left home at age fifteen and worked for a time picking up odd jobs as a makeup assistant in a funeral parlor, an ice-cream vendor, and an orderly in a psychiatric hospital. In 1978 she entered Oxford and received a master's degree in English from St. Catherine's College in 1981. Winterson began writing creatively when an interview for an editing position at Pandora uncovered her gift for storytelling.

In *Oranges Are Not the Only Fruit* the character Jeanette's struggle for autonomy and sexual identity within the repressive fervor of her mother's church is portrayed realistically in the central narrative, but the most striking and poignant passages take place outside the main story, in the Faust-like fantastic character of an orange demon and in a series of fairy tales that interrupt the narrative and complement Jeanette's development as a character and an individual. Jeanette is at once a typical juvenile coming into her own and the quirky product of a fundamentalist fringe group in an English working-class community. Issues surrounding the nature of conversion run throughout the novel, providing the tension that fuses what would otherwise seem like idiosyncratic and superfluous flights into fantasy. The fairy tales (or parables) of sorcerer's apprentices and princesses who become common folk act as a foil for the central plot. They are a graphic illustration of the philosophy that drives people like Jeanette's mentor, Elsie, who believes there is an inner world as well as the physical one, and "If you want to make sense of either, you have to take notice of both."

Throughout the text, Winterson examines the nature of passionate belief. Her mother's drive to rewrite the world according to her gospel is not simply an interpretation of reality, nor is it an essay on faith. Together, her mother and her mother's church exist almost unhindered by the everyday functioning of England in the 1960s; the congregation actually creates a world in the image of their doctrine. It is a world where things make sense. When the young Jeanette is rendered temporarily deaf from an adenoid infection, she is deemed to be in a state of rapture, and when her homosexuality is discovered, the church followers believe she has literally fallen prey to the devil. For Jeanette, raised with the same conviction, these evil forces are not metaphoric, although in her understanding they also are not, strictly speaking, "evil." And so the character of the orange demon is born. Through his wickedly ironic commentary, the "sense" the congregation makes of Jeanette's sexuality is given another interpretive filter, a story with a narrator on a different kind of mission. A trickster figure who personifies transgression, the orange demon is both confidant and sprite, a foil as necessary and as "real" as the character of Jeanette's mother and the religious hierarchy that surrounds her. Each of the fantastic figures in the novel is set up as an alternative voice; they are inspirational, instructive, and at least as reliable as the evangelism that colors her mother's war with the faithless.

Oranges Are Not the Only Fruit is divided into sections named according to the first books of the Bible. In the "Book of Deuteronomy" (the last book of the law), Winterson outlines the play between the fantastic and the real that became a recurring motif in her work:

People like to separate storytelling which is not fact from history which is fact. They do this so that they know what to believe and what not to believe. This is very curious. How is it that no one will believe that the whale swallowed Jonah, when every day Jonah is swallowing the whale? I can see them now, stuffing down the fishiest of tales, and why? Because it is history. Knowing what to believe had its advantages. It built an empire and kept people where they belonged, in the bright realm of the wallet.

Later Winterson muses on how the Romantics managed to escape the dogma of Christianity by inventing their own myths. Only by telling new tales can anyone escape history. Winterson's next three novels are about using the fantastic and the impossible to challenge the flatness that passes for truth in traditional history.

The story of Winterson's life as it unfolds in the pages of literary gossip is neither flat nor entirely believable. The impressive popularity of *Oranges Are Not the Only Fruit* (despite its overtly lesbian theme, its nonlinear experimental narrative, and its irreverent take on family and religious values) provided the young author with an abrupt initiation into the world of literary commodification. Feeling somewhat pressured after her initial success, Winterson published her second novel within a year and almost immediately regretted having done so. She now refers to *Boating for Beginners* (1985) as a "comic book," and the text does have an animator's feel for making fun of the weighty. Like its predecessor, *Boating for Beginners* deals with the intersection between a zeal for biblical certainty and the philosophical wavering of an agnostic society committed to contemporary individualism. But with *Boating for Beginners* the autobiographical framework of *Oranges Are Not the Only Fruit* is replaced by a purely fantastic romp through the past. Winterson's novel is a satiric revision of the Noah story, in the style of Monty Python. The title is actually the title of her character Noah's original best-seller—a book he and his co-author, God, had written for the Hebrew people. The orange demon makes an appearance once more, this time engaging his new heroine, Gloria, in a philosophical debate about Northrop Frye's stages of linguistic communication vis-à-vis personal understanding. The narrative of *Boating for Beginners* is more overtly comic than that of Winterson's first novel, and, as if to underscore the point, the text is periodically invaded by something called Gross Reality, which curbs the fantastic leanings of character and plot only ironically. This world is not the biblical one as readers have come to know it. At the time the cosmic flood is about to unfold, for instance, Gloria's hometown of Ur is fractured by a divisive debate over the use-value of conveniences such as refrigerators. One of the strongest characters in the book is Mrs. Munde, Gloria's mother, and, like Jeanette's mother, she is a fanatical member of a religious organization. This time the cult is led by Noah, a grand patriarch who is skeptical of conve-

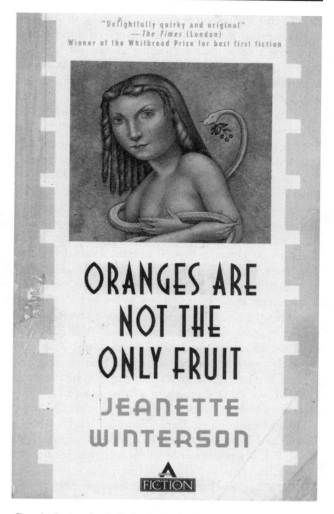

Paperback cover for the U.S. edition of Winterson's 1985 book, which includes an orange demon as a foil character (Richland County Public Library)

nience marketing (hence the obsession with refrigerators and frozen food), but who is perfectly adept at marketing his antimarketing campaign. Embarking upon a project that will capitalize on the growing religion he has created, Noah prepares to take to the road with a movie extravaganza dubbed *Genesis: Or How I Did It*. The script is being written by the famous romance novelist Bunny Mix (a thinly disguised Barbara Cartland, and Noah's mistress to boot). Finally, readers discover that Noah's God is in fact a prodigious mistake that grew out of a mass of fermenting ice cream and its collision with a Black Forest freezer cake.

The parallel between Noah's story of greed and publicity in *Boating for Beginners* and Winterson's own unfolding career is remarkable; clearly this second novel was published in the hope of capitalizing on the author's comic appeal. With sales of *Oranges Are Not the Only Fruit* skyrocketing, Winterson was achieving subculture cult status. She was not unaware of the double-edged irony in the travesty of consumerism in her second novel. Soon after publishing *Boating for Beginners,* she fired her agent and switched publishers. With her next novel she chose to return to a more controlled encounter with the fantastic.

By the time *The Passion* (1987) was published, Winterson's public was ready to write her off as a one-hit wonder. But *The Passion* is a mature, haunting text, and it was well received. Anne Duchêne, in *TLS: The Times Literary Supplement* (26 June 1987), called it "a book of great imaginative audacity and assurance." The novel is set in Europe at the time of the Napoleonic Wars, and it consists of two first-person accounts that form an interlacing double narrative. One account tells the story of Henri, a French peasant enlisted to serve Napoleon Bonaparte; the other story is told by Villanelle, the daughter of a Venetian boatman, born with webbed feet and a canny ability to see herself through the direst of circumstances. *The Passion* abounds with magically real characters and events: Villanelle can walk on water; a defrocked priest has a telescopic eye; an icicle containing a thread of gold never melts; and Villanelle's heart is kept as a memento, still beating, encased in a jar at the back of a lover's closet. *The Passion* offers quiet reminders that some of what one hears may not be wholly truthful. "Trust me," say both Villanelle and Henri from time to time, "I am telling you stories." It is a sentiment Winterson herself has uttered in interviews.

Throughout the development of her career, Winterson has returned to the complexities of trusting tales if not tellers, of the search for "truth" through the process of storytelling. *The Passion,* situated during one of the most spectacular periods in European history, unravels contemporary obsession with witnesses, documentation, and the actual—and as an alternative it offers the timeless magic of the subjective, the imaginative, and the passionate. The novel gained Winterson comparisons to Jorge Luis Borges and Virginia Woolf and was awarded the John Llewellyn Rhys Prize for 1987.

By 1989 Winterson had become an industry. Nicci Gerrard wrote in *The New Statesman and Society* (1989) that Winterson "has a way of fictionalizing herself—making her life into a series of fables and self-consciously fantastical gestures." Gerrard mentioned, for example, that Winterson has bought herself a plot in Highgate Cemetery that she claims to tend "like my second home," and that she had "wanted to buy a coffin where she could keep her foreign editions, until her horrified friends accused her of being macabre." Winterson obviously relishes the attention she receives. Nevertheless, as Gerrard concludes, "behind the stories and gestures, the real self remains hidden." Openly

admitting to spells of antisocial behavior and dysfunctional relationships, Winterson is not shy of the public eye, and she is always in control of the image she projects. "Naked is the best disguise," she quips.

In this atmosphere of celebrity Winterson published her fourth novel, *Sexing the Cherry* (1989), perhaps her most ambitious work to date. Almost picaresque, the novel has a cast of rogues and misfits that includes a monstrous dog-woman bigger than an elephant, a community that literally falls prey to the epidemic of love, toads that sing, dancing princesses, and a boy who has a vision of palm trees and the sea when he looks at the first banana in England. Again weaving together the elements of history and fantasy, Winterson tells the tale of an avenging protofeminist who burns with her own form of justice in an England deeply hypocritical and sharply divided by the Puritan revolution. The backdrop of Charles I's execution, the Great Fire of London, and the "discovery" of the Americas are all so much window dressing when compared to the dog-woman's tale of politics and scandal. Meanwhile, her adopted son, Jordan, has fallen in love with Fortunata, one of the Twelve Dancing Princesses, and he pursues his vision of her to what may actually be the end of the earth. There he finds Fortunata the master of an unusual academy where students learn to dance by being spun around and around until they lose earthly shape and become the purely cosmic products of light and music. *Sexing the Cherry* unfolds to the challenge of postmodernism, Surrealism, and the fantastic. "All times can be inhabited, all places visited," says Jordan:

> In a single day the mind can make a millpond of the oceans. Some people who have never crossed the land they were born on have traveled all over the world. The journey is not linear, it is always back and forth, denying the calendar, the wrinkles and the lines of the body. The self is not contained in any moment or any place, but it is only in the intersection of moment and place that the self might, for a moment, be seen vanishing through a door, which disappears at once.

Winterson received the E. M. Forster Award from the American Academy of Arts and Letters for *Sexing the Cherry* in 1989, and with the added success of the BBC production of *Oranges Are Not the Only Fruit* in 1990, her career as a writer was firmly established. With pop-culture appeal and a reputation as a respected voice for lesbians and feminists in England and the United States, she accepted her fame as her due. The self-appointed Prophet of Hampstead Heath, Winterson combines optimism with self-assurance and responded in the Gerrard interview to speculation about her arrogance by explaining, "I've always thought of arrogance as being pleased with oneself without reason. I have reason to be pleased with myself. . . . Against all the odds I've come from nowhere and been able to make a difference." It is all the more surprising, then, that just one year after the success of *Sexing the Cherry,* her writing project veered sharply.

All the media attention inevitably wore on her; interviews and reviews after 1990 are laced with skepticism. Somewhat overexposed, Winterson assumed a new focus, which could be in part because of criticism of her sexual reputation or perhaps because of the fallout surrounding the death of a close friend. Whatever the reason, her later novels shed her concern with the fantastic and appear committed to the conventions of lesbian confessional realism. In the introduction to her television script for *Oranges Are Not the Only Fruit* (published by Pandora in 1990), Winterson abandons the elements of fantasy as if they were merely a literary device: "The fairy tales and allegorical passages that weave themselves within the main story could be waved goodbye without any pain because their function could be taken over by the camera itself." The BBC miniseries is an essay in comic realism. Similarly, while Winterson's novels *Written on the Body* (1992) and *Art and Lies: A Piece for Three Voices and a Bawd* (1994) still explore the nature of stories and storytelling, they do so without the magic of her earlier work. *Written on the Body* is deliberately and graphically restricted to the physical realm of the possible—so much so that the anatomy of a lover dying of cancer becomes the most potent metaphor behind the narrative quest for meaning.

"The World and Other Places," a short story first published in the periodical *Grand Street* in 1990, best illustrates how Winterson has swung away from the fantastic. As with *Oranges Are Not the Only Fruit,* the story takes its premise from Winterson's life: hearing of her desire to learn how to fly, a fan who was a pilot offered to teach her. "The World and Other Places" follows a young boy who begins his career as a pilot by flying on carpets with his family. Never actually leaving the floor of their living room, the family members take turns constructing stories about cockroach hotels, about the Indians they encounter (who sometimes play the cello), and about barefoot urchins and their scattered alley homes—all worlds they visit on their journeys. These dreams are vivid, colorful, and oddly full of detail. Moreover, they are met when the boy learns how to fly for real, thanks to the generosity of a bomber-jacketed enthusiast. Eventually the boy joins the air force. About seeing and leaving, the self and arrival, "The World and Other Places" explores "the real" in the boy's achievements upon entering adulthood. There is magic in this story, but it is clearly relegated to the world of childhood dreams and the imagination, a zone of nos-

Dust jacket for the U.S. edition of Winterson's 1987 novel, set in Europe during the Napoleonic Wars (Richland County Public Library)

talgia. The parents who participated in the ritual of the flying carpets have been sidelined by the end of the story. Taking on the role of vicarious tourists, they gratefully receive their son's gifts from abroad. The image is poignant. Yet, as his Cessna roars up the neighborhood street used as a runway, and as it pulls into the air, the young man seems resigned; he leaves with the status of hero curling in his wake.

Like the boy who grew up to see the wonders of a world he had previously only imagined, Winterson after *Sexing the Cherry* leaves behind the flights of fancy that characterize a child's faith in the malleability of multiple worlds. By *Art and Lies,* with its poetic flourish and complex narratological dance, the debate over fiction and truth is encompassed in a metaphor of sun, moon, sea, and sand. *Art and Lies,* while formalistically innovative, is by and large confined by the "plausible." Critical reception of this book has been mixed.

Despite its allusions to fairy tales and quantum physics, Winterson's next work of fiction, *Gut Symmetries*

(1997), is neither fantasy nor science fiction. Some of the stories collected in *The World and Other Places* (1998)—such as "Disappearance I" and "Orion"—are in those genres. While *The PowerBook* (2000) is not science fiction, this novel is informed by the possibilities of technology, with its story of the impact of e-mail and the Internet on writers and literature.

Jeanette Winterson has been acclaimed as a writer who "celebrates the power of the imagination" and who "explores alternative interpretations of reality." Michiko Kakutani wrote in *The New York Times* (27 April 1990) that Winterson "possesses the ability to combine the biting satire of Swift with the ethereal magic of García Márquez, the ability to reinvent old myths even as she creates new ones of her own." Before her shift to a stylized realism, her work was hard to categorize, but it consistently incorporated elements of fantasy; *The Passion* is one of the few successful attempts at transporting Latin American magic realism to a European setting. The offhand manner in which she seems to have abandoned the genre with her later novels does little justice to her most important work. Still, Winterson has always been writing from the margins of the canon. A lesbian of working-class background who chose to tackle the sentimentalism of most autobiography by incorporating the "unreal," the "surreal," the "meta-real," and the repoussé, she is widely read for her insight into the issues facing women in the late twentieth century and her ability to weave stories of poetic magic. It remains to be seen whether her reputation in the future will reflect the impact she has had on writing the fantastic.

Interviews:

Nicci Gerrard, "The Prophet," *New Statesman and Society,* 2 (1 September 1989): 12–13;

Carol Anshaw, "Into the Mystic: Jeanette Winterson's Fables of Manners," *Village Voice,* 12 June 1990, pp. 516–517;

Suzzane Scott and Lynn M. Constantine, Interview with Winterson *Belles Lettres: A Review of Books of Women,* 5 (Summer 1990): 24–26;

Mark Marvel, "Jeanette Winterson: Trust Me. I'm Telling You Stories," *Interview XX,* no. 10 (October 1990): 162, 168.

References:

Hilary Hinds, "*Oranges Are Not the Only Fruit:* Reaching Audiences Other Lesbian Texts Cannot Reach," in *New Lesbian Criticism: Literary and Cultural Readings,* edited by Sally Munt (New York: Columbia University Press, 1992), pp. 153–172;

Rebecca O'Rourke, "Fingers in the Fruit Basket: A Feminist Reading of Jeanette Winterson's *Oranges Are Not the Only Fruit,*" in *Feminist Criticism: Theory and Practice,* edited by Susan Sellers (Toronto: University of Toronto Press, 1991);

Susan Rubin Suleiman, "Mothers of the Avant-Garde: A Case of Mistaken Identity?" in *Femmes/Frauen/Women,* edited by Françoise van Rossum-Guyon (Amsterdam: Rodopi, 1990).

Books for Further Reading

Aldiss, Brian W., and David Wingrove. *Trillion Year Spree: The History of Science Fiction*. London: Gollancz, 1986; New York: Atheneum, 1986; revised edition, London: Stratus, 2001.

Ashley, Mike. *Who's Who in Horror and Fantasy Fiction*. London: Elm Tree, 1977; New York: Taplinger, 1978.

Barron, Neil, ed. *Anatomy of Wonder: A Critical Guide to Science Fiction,* fourth edition. New Providence, N.J.: Bowker, 1995.

Barron, ed. *Fantasy and Horror: A Critical and Historical Guide to Literature, Illustration, Film, TV, Radio, and the Internet*. Lanham, Md.: Scarecrow Press, 1999.

Bleiler, Everett F., ed. *Supernatural Fiction Writers: Fantasy and Horror*. 2 volumes. New York: Scribners, 1985.

Bleiler, Richard, ed. *Science Fiction Writers: Critical Studies of the Major Authors from the Early Nineteenth Century to the Present Day,* second edition. New York: Scribner, 1999.

Bloom, Clive, ed. *Creepers: British Horror and Fantasy in the Twentieth Century*. London & Boulder, Colo.: Pluto, 1993.

Boyer, Robert H., and Kenneth J. Zahorski, eds. *Fantasists on Fantasy: A Collection of Critical Reflections*. New York: Avon, 1984.

Cavaliero, Glen. *The Supernatural and English Fiction*. Oxford & New York: Oxford University Press, 1995.

Cawthorn, James, and Michael Moorcock. *Fantasy: The 100 Best Books*. London: Xanadu, 1988; New York: Carroll & Graf, 1988.

Clarke, I. F. *The Pattern of Expectation, 1644–2001*. London: Cape, 1979; New York: Basic Books, 1979.

Clute, John, and John Grant, eds. *The Encyclopedia of Fantasy*. London: Orbit, 1997; New York: St. Martin's Press, 1997.

Clute, and Peter Nicholls, eds. *The Encyclopedia of Science Fiction*. New York: St. Martin's Press, 1993.

Daniels, Les. *Living in Fear: A History of Horror in the Mass Media*. New York: Scribners, 1975.

Greenland, Colin. *The Entropy Exhibition: Michael Moorcock and the British "New Wave" in Science Fiction*. London & Boston: Routledge & Kegan Paul, 1983.

Gunn, James, ed. *The New Encyclopedia of Science Fiction*. New York: Viking, 1988.

Hume, Kathryn. *Fantasy and Mimesis: Responses to Reality in Western Literature*. London: Methuen, 1984.

Irwin, W. R. *The Game of the Impossible: A Rhetoric of Fantasy*. Urbana: University of Illinois Press, 1976.

Jackson, Rosemary. *Fantasy: The Literature of Subversion*. London & New York: Methuen, 1981.

Jones, Stephen, and Kim Newman, eds. *Horror: 100 Best Books.* London: Xanadu, 1988; New York: Carroll & Graf, 1988.

Kroeber, Karl. *Romantic Fantasy and Science Fiction.* New Haven, Conn.: Yale University Press, 1988.

MacRae, Cathi Dunn. *Presenting Young Adult Fantasy Fiction.* New York: Twayne, 1998.

Magill, Frank N., ed. *Survey of Modern Fantasy Literature.* 5 volumes. Englewood Cliffs, N.J.: Salem Press, 1983.

Magill, ed. *Survey of Science Fiction and Fantasy Literature.* 4 volumes. Pasadena, Cal.: Salem Press, 1996.

Magill, ed. *Survey of Science Fiction Literature.* 5 volumes. Englewood Cliffs, N.J.: Salem Press, 1979.

Manlove, C. N. *Christian Fantasy: From 1200 to the Present.* London: Macmillan, 1992; Notre Dame, Ind.: University of Notre Dame Press, 1992.

Manlove. *The Impulse of Fantasy Literature.* Kent, Ohio: Kent State University Press, 1983.

Manlove. *Scottish Fantasy Literature: A Critical Survey.* Edinburgh: Canongate, 1994.

Moorcock, Michael. *Wizardry and Wild Romance: A Study of Epic Fantasy.* London: Gollancz, 1987.

Nicholls, Stan. *Wordsmiths of Wonder: Fifty Interviews with Writers of the Fantastic.* London: Orbit, 1993.

Parrinder, Patrick. *Science Fiction: Its Criticism and Teaching.* London & New York: Methuen, 1980.

Parrinder, ed. *Science Fiction: A Critical Guide.* London & New York: Longman, 1979.

Pringle, David. *Modern Fantasy: The Hundred Best Novels, an English-Language Selection, 1946–1987.* London: Grafton, 1988; New York: Bedrick, 1989.

Pringle, ed., *St. James Guide to Fantasy Writers.* New York: St. James Press, 1996.

Punter, David. *The Literature of Terror: A History of Gothic Fiction from 1765 to the Present Day.* London & New York: Longman, 1980.

Rabkin, Eric S. *The Fantastic in Literature.* Princeton: Princeton University Press, 1976.

Ruddick, Nicholas. *British Science Fiction: A Chronology, 1478–1990.* New York, Westport, Conn. & London: Greenwood Press, 1992.

Ruddick. *Ultimate Island: On the Nature of British Science Fiction.* Westport, Conn. & London: Greenwood Press, 1993.

Sammons, Martha C. *"A Better Country": The Worlds of Religious Fantasy and Science Fiction.* Westport, Conn.: Greenwood Press, 1988.

Schlobin, Roger C. *The Literature of Fantasy: A Comprehensive Annotated Bibliography of Modern Fantasy Fiction.* New York: Garland, 1979.

Scholes, Robert, and Rabkin. *Science Fiction: History, Science, Vision.* New York: Oxford University Press, 1977.

Searles, Baird, Beth Meacham, and Michael Franklin. *A Reader's Guide to Fantasy.* New York: Avon, 1982.

Searles, Martin Last, Meacham, and Franklin. *A Reader's Guide to Science Fiction.* New York: Avon, 1979.

Slusser, George, Gary Westfahl, and Rabkin, eds. *Science Fiction and Market Realities*. Athens: University of Georgia Press, 1996.

Smith, Curtis C., ed. *Twentieth-Century Science-Fiction Writers,* second edition. Chicago: St. James Press, 1986.

Smith, Karen Patricia. *The Fabulous Realm: A Literary-Historical Approach to British Fantasy, 1780–1990*. Metuchen, N.J.: Scarecrow Press, 1993.

Stableford, Brian M. *Algebraic Fantasies and Realistic Romances: More Masters of Science Fiction*. San Bernardino, Cal.: Borgo Press, 1995.

Sullivan, Jack, ed. *The Penguin Encyclopedia of Horror and the Supernatural*. New York: Viking, 1986.

Suvin, Darko. *Metamorphoses of Science Fiction: On the Poetics and History of a Literary Genre*. New Haven, Conn. & London: Yale University Press, 1979.

Thompson, Raymond H. *The Return from Avalon: A Study of the Arthurian Legend in Modern Fiction*. Westport, Conn.: Greenwood Press, 1985.

Tuck, Donald H., ed. *The Encyclopedia of Science Fiction and Fantasy: Through 1968*. 3 volumes. Chicago: Advent, 1974–1982.

Tymn, Marshall B., and Ashley, eds. *Science Fiction, Fantasy, and Weird Fiction Magazines*. Westport, Conn.: Greenwood Press, 1985.

Wagar, W. Warren. *Terminal Visions: The Literature of Last Things*. Bloomington: Indiana University Press, 1982.

Waggoner, Diana. *The Hills of Faraway: A Guide to Fantasy*. New York: Atheneum, 1978.

Winter, Douglas E. *Faces of Fear: Encounters with the Creators of Modern Horror*. New York: Berkley, 1985.

Wolfe, Gary K. *Critical Terms for Science Fiction and Fantasy: A Glossary and Guide to Scholarship*. Westport, Conn.: Greenwood Press, 1986.

Yoke, Carl B., and Donald M. Hassler, eds. *Death and the Serpent: Immortality in Science Fiction and Fantasy*. Westport, Conn.: Greenwood Press, 1985.

Contributors

Bernadette Lynn Bosky . . . . *Yonkers, New York*

Joan Bridgman . . . . *Open University*

Charles Brower . . . . *Columbia, South Carolina*

Frederick M. Burelbach . . . . *State University of New York, College at Brockport*

Edwin F. Casebeer . . . . *Indiana University–Purdue University at Indianapolis*

William J. Collins . . . . *Kutztown, Pennsylvania*

F. Brett Cox . . . . *East Brewton, Alabama*

Gary William Crawford . . . . *Baton Rouge, Louisiana*

Elizabeth S. Davidson . . . . *University of South Carolina, Spartanburg*

D. Douglas Fratz . . . . *Gaithersburg, Maryland*

Robert Galbreath . . . . *University of North Carolina at Greensboro*

Darren Harris-Fain . . . . *Shawnee State University*

John Hollow . . . . *Athens, Ohio*

Earl G. Ingersoll . . . . *State University of New York, College at Brockport*

Gayle Irwin . . . . *York University*

Rob Latham . . . . *University of Iowa*

Gina Macdonald . . . . *Nicholls State University*

Willis E. McNelly . . . . *California State University–Fullerton*

Maureen F. Moran . . . . *Brunel University*

Jefferson M. Peters . . . . *Fukuoka University, Japan*

Deborah Philips . . . . *Brunel University*

Salvatore Proietti . . . . *Università degli Studi di Roma "La Sapienza"*

Amelia A. Rutledge . . . . *George Mason University*

Joe Sanders . . . . *Mentor, Ohio*

W. A. Senior . . . . *Plantation, Florida*

Jeffrey V. Yule . . . . *University of Maine at Fort Kent*

Cumulative Index

Dictionary of Literary Biography, Volumes 1-261
Dictionary of Literary Biography Yearbook, 1980-2001
Dictionary of Literary Biography Documentary Series, Volumes 1-19
Concise Dictionary of American Literary Biography, Volumes 1-7
Concise Dictionary of British Literary Biography, Volumes 1-8
Concise Dictionary of World Literary Biography, Volumes 1-4

Cumulative Index

DLB before number: *Dictionary of Literary Biography,* Volumes 1-261
Y before number: *Dictionary of Literary Biography Yearbook,* 1980-2001
DS before number: *Dictionary of Literary Biography Documentary Series,* Volumes 1-19
CDALB before number: *Concise Dictionary of American Literary Biography,* Volumes 1-7
CDBLB before number: *Concise Dictionary of British Literary Biography,* Volumes 1-8
CDWLB before number: *Concise Dictionary of World Literary Biography,* Volumes 1-4

F

L

N

O

U

V

W

ISBN 0-7876-6005-1

P